LENTON LODGE TO WOLLATON PARK.

L.G.S. del.

THE

# HISTORY

OF THE

# PARISH AND PRIORY

OF

# LENTON,

IN

## THE COUNTY OF NOTTINGHAM.

BY

## JOHN THOMAS GODFREY,

*Fellow of the Royal Historical Society.*

———— — ——

**London:**

BEMROSE & SONS, 23, OLD BAILEY;
AND DERBY.

——

MDCCCLXXXIV.

# PREFACE.

THE legitimate functions of a preface in works of a topographical description appear to be two-fold; the progress of the work should be briefly traced from its inception to its completion, and due acknowledgments made to those persons who have assisted the author in his labours.

Early in the year 1880, materials were collected by the author for a paper on Lenton Priory, to be read at a meeting of a newly-founded society in Nottingham. Before the paper was completed, the society in question, after a brief career, had ceased to exist; but the materials already collected were added to from time to time, with the idea of eventually publishing a short history of the Priory. This has now expanded into a history of the whole Parish.

The task has been one of some magnitude, involving no light amount of labour, and requiring not a little persever-ance. It is no egotism to say that only those engaged in similar pursuits can form a just idea of the time and re-search requisite in collecting and digesting materials for a work of this description. The burden and responsi-bility would have pressed still heavier, but for the kindly assistance of those friends to whom it is my pleasing duty to return my acknowledgments. I am principally indebted to Major A. E. Lawson Lowe, J.P., F.S.A. (whose knowledge of the history of the county of Nottingham is, perhaps, unequalled), for his hearty and friendly co-operation through-out the progress of the work. Not only has Major Lowe communicated from time to time numerous genealogical and historical notes, and rendered other valuable assistance, but he has most kindly permitted me to make unrestricted use of his MS. *History of the Hundred of Broxtow.*

I must also express my obligations to the Rev. J. Charles Cox, author of "The Churches of Derbyshire," for his courteous permission to extract what was applicable to my purpose from his valuable work. I am also indebted to M. Leopold Delisle, Director of the Bibliothèque Nationale, Paris, for furnishing me with interesting extracts from the Clugny MSS. recently deposited in that library; to Sir Henry E. L. Dryden, Bart., M.A., F.S.A., of Canons Ashby, for the loan of his sketches of the tiles found at Lenton Priory, and described on pages 226 and 227; to W. H. St. John Hope, Esq., M.A., F.S.A., for the loan of casts of the seals from which the engravings on pages 231 and 232 have been made; to Edward Joseph Lowe, Esq., D.L., F.R.S., for the valuable meteorological table; and also to Mr. W. Henry Stevenson (Editor of "The Nottingham Borough Records") for several valuable suggestions.

The Rev. George Browne, M.A., Vicar of Lenton, has rendered material assistance by allowing me ready access to the parish registers and other parochial documents in his custody; and the value of the service has been increased by the urbanity and kindness with which it has been rendered. I would also thank the Rev. Percy E. Smith, B.A., Curate of Lenton, for the cordial assistance he has always been ready to afford.

To Mr. James Shipman, of Nottingham, who has contributed a valuable account of the geology of the parish, I beg to return my sincere thanks.  Mr. Shipman's intimate acquaintance with the geology of the neighbourhood of Nottingham has been recognised and appreciated by the officers of H.M. Geological Survey of Great Britain.

I am also indebted to the owner of the *Stretton MSS.* for placing that interesting collection of notes relating to the antiquities of the county at my disposal.  The MSS. had been lost for several years, and only came to light when this work was ready for the press.  They are somewhat mutilated, but contain a mass of valuable information of sufficient interest to justify their future publication.  The MSS., which consist principally of notes on the churches of Nottinghamshire, made at the commencement of this century contain a large number of interesting sketches, fac-similes of three of which appear in my pamphlet on *The Market Crosses of Nottingham.*

With regard to the illustrations, I am indebted to Mr. Frank Johnson, A.R.I.B.A., Mr. Lawrence G. Summers, A.R.I.B.A., and Mr. John A. Stamp, who have kindly contributed the drawings for the photo-lithographic plates; to Mr. Llewellynn Jewitt, F.S.A., who has lent me the woodcuts on pages 11, 227, and 406; and to Messrs. Blackie and Sons for the use of the woodcut on page 166.

I cannot close my list of acknowledgments without a grateful word of thanks to the Librarian of Bromley House Library, Nottingham, and to the Principal Librarian of the Nottingham Free Library, for the facilities afforded me in

consulting the works of reference in their respective libraries.
I would also thank the subscribers to this work for their
financial support.

To conclude. This history of my native place has not
been written with the idea of satisfying any literary ambition.
It pretends to be nothing more than a parochial history, but
if it should be deemed worthy of forming a chapter in a
much-needed history of the County, I shall be amply rewarded for the labour involved in its preparation. "I have
taken this pains, not for the present age, but a future; many
things which were known to our grandsires are lost to us,
and our grandchildren will search in vain for many facts
which to us are most familiar."

JOHN T. GODFREY.

*Radcliffe-on-Trent,*
*Nottingham.*

# CONTENTS.

| SECTION | | PAGE |
|---|---|---|
| I. | GEOGRAPHY, ETYMOLOGY, AND EARLY ANTIQUITIES - - - - - - - | 1 |
| II. | MANORIAL AND EARLY HISTORY - - - | 18 |
| III. | AREA, POPULATION, ETC. - - - - | 44 |
| IV. | THE PRIORY - - - - - - | 53 |
| V. | THE VICARAGE - - - - - - | 235 |
| VI. | THE CHURCHES - - - - - - | 245 |
| VII. | THE PARISH REGISTERS; CHURCHWARDENS' ACCOUNTS; AND PAROCHIAL CHARITY- - | 272 |
| VIII. | HYSON GREEN CHURCH - - - - - | 292 |
| IX. | THE SCHOOLS - - - - - - - | 295 |
| X. | THE NONCONFORMING CONGREGATIONS- - | 298 |
| XI. | THE FAIRS - - - - - - - | 303 |
| XII. | THE INCLOSURES - - - - - - | 316 |
| XIII. | LOCAL GOVERNMENT - - - - - | 334 |
| XIV. | MANUFACTURES - - - - - - | 355 |
| XV. | BESTWOOD PARK - - - - - - | 362 |
| XVI. | THE PEVEREL COURT - - - - - | 386 |
| XVII. | GEOLOGY - - - - - - - | 408 |
| XVIII. | MISCELLANEOUS - - - - - - | 459 |

# LIST OF ILLUSTRATIONS AND
# PEDIGREES.

| | PAGE |
|---|---|
| LENTON LODGE TO WOLLATON PARK | *To face Title.* |
| STONE AXE FROM WOLLATON PARK | 11 |
| ROMAN SWORD FROM HIGHFIELD PARK | 15 |
| ARMS AND PEDIGREE OF PEVEREL OF NOTTINGHAM | 22 |
| ARMS AND PEDIGREE OF GREGORY, OF NOTTINGHAM | *To face* 34 |
| ARMS OF BABINGTON | 38 |
| ARMS OF BURUN, OR BYRON | 102 |
| ROCK HOLES IN NOTTINGHAM PARK | 166 |
| FAC-SIMILE OF PORTION OF MS. OF ST. JOHN'S GOSPEL, CORPUS CHRISTI COLLEGE, CAMBRIDGE | 184 |
| SIGNATURE OF JOHN ILKESTON, PRIOR OF LENTON | 189 |
| ARMS AND PEDIGREE OF LOWE, OF HIGHFIELD HOUSE | *To face* 200 |
| ARMS AND PEDIGREE OF WRIGHT, OF LENTON | ,, 202 |
| ARMS OF ADAMS, OF LENTON | 203 |
| ARMS OF STRETTON, OF LENTON PRIORY | 209 |
| ARMS AND PEDIGREE OF GARLAND, OF LENTON | *To face* 212 |
| PLAN OF SITE OF LENTON PRIORY | ,, 222 |
| MASONRY FROM LENTON PRIORY *(two plates)* | ,, 224 |
| STONE COFFIN FROM LENTON PRIORY | 225 |
| INSCRIPTION ON DISH FROM LENTON PRIORY | 225 |
| ARMS OF MORLEY, OF MORLEY | 227 |
| TILES FOUND AT LENTON PRIORY | *To face* 228 |
| CARVED MASONRY FROM LENTON PRIORY | 228 |
| ANCIENT KEYS FOUND AT LENTON | *To face* 230 |
| ARMS OF LENTON PRIORY | 231 |

PAGE

SEAL OF LENTON PRIORY   ·   ·   ·   ·   ·   ·   ·   ·   ·   ·  231

COUNTERSEAL OF LENTON PRIORY   ·   ·   ·   ·   ·   ·   ·   ·  232

SEAL OF ALAN, SUB-PRIOR OF LENTON   ·   ·   ·   ·   ·   ·   ·  232

ARMS AT WEST END OF OLD CHURCH   ·   ·   ·   ·   ·   ·   ·  247

INCISED SEPULCHRAL SLAB IN OLD CHURCH   ·   ·   ·   ·   ·   ·  256

FONT FROM LENTON PRIORY   ·   ·   ·   ·   ·   ·   ·  *To face*  270

PORTRAIT OF CHARLES, FIRST DUKE OF ST. ALBANS   ·   ·   ·   ·   ·  377

ARMS AND PEDIGREE OF BEAUCLERK, DUKES OF ST. ALBANS   ·   *To face*  378

EMMANUEL CHURCH, BESTWOOD   ·   ·   ·   ·   ·   ·   ,,   382

SEALS OF THE PEVEREL COURT   ·   ·   ·   ·   ·   ·   ·   ·  406

GEOLOGICAL SECTIONS   ·   ·   ·   ·   ·   ·   ·   ·   *To face*  412

INTERGLACIAL ALLUVIUM OF THE TRENT, SPRING CLOSE   ·   ·   ·   ·  447

SECTION OF THE ALLUVIUM OF THE LEEN AT OLD RADFORD   ·   ·   ·  453

SECTION OF THE ALLUVIAL AND DRIFT DEPOSITS OF THE LEEN AT BASFORD  456

# LIST OF SUBSCRIBERS.

His Grace The Duke of St. Albans, Lord Lieutenant of Nottinghamshire (2 copies).

IIis Grace The Duke of Devonshire, K.G., Devonshire House, Piccadilly, London.

The Right Hon. The Lord Middleton, Birdsall House, Yorkshire.

Adams, Miss  · · · · · · ·  The Park, Nottingham.

Bailey, John E., F.S.A.  · · ·  Stretford, Manchester.
Ball, Frederick  · · · · ·  New Lenton, Nottingham.
Bardsley, George ·  · · · ·  Radcliffe-on-Trent, Nottinghamshire.
Bingham, Richard F. ·  · · ·  Old Lenton, Nottingham.
Bloodworth, Charles ·  · · ·  Priory Cottage, Old Lenton.
Bloodworth, Miss  · · · ·  Old Lenton.
Booker, William H., F.R.H.S. ·  ·  Nottingham.
Bradley, Frederick J. ·  · · ·  Beeston, Nottinghamshire.
Bright, Joseph  · · · · ·  The Park, Nottingham.
Brown, Cornelius, F.R.S.L.  · ·  Newark-on-Trent.
Browne, Rev. George, M.A.  · ·  Lenton Vicarage, Nottingham.
Browne, Rev. Henry Joy, M.A. ·  ·  Christ Church Vicarage, Barnet.
Burton, Francis C. ·  · · ·  Corporation Oaks, Nottingham.
Burton, Alderman John  · · ·  New Radford, Nottingham.
Buttrum, George H. ·  · · ·  Cropwell Butler, Nottinghamshire.

Carter, H. H. ·  · · · ·  The Park, Nottingham.
Charlton, Thomas W.  · · ·  Chilwell Hall, near Nottingham.
Chiosso, Antonio M. ·  · · ·  Norfolk Terrace, Bayswater, W.
Christie, Lorenzo  · · · ·  Carholme, Stackhouse, near Settle.
Clark, Thomas ·  · · · ·  Old Lenton, Nottingham.
Clayton, William  · · · ·  Old Lenton, Nottingham.
Cleaver, F. F. ·  · · · ·  Sheriff of Nottingham.
Clements, S. W.  · · · ·  1, Castle Terrace, Nottingham.
Cooper, James ·  · · · ·  Old Lenton.
Cropper, Alderman Henry Smith  ·  The Park, Nottingham.

Daft, Richard - - - - - - Radcliffe-on-Trent, Nottinghamshire.
Dawson, Alfred - - - - - - The Park, Nottingham.
Dennett, Alderman Robert - - - - The Park, Nottingham.
Derry, Joseph - - - - - - Chestnut Cottage, Old Lenton.
Dobson, Samuel H. - - - - - Nottingham.
Dobson, William E., J.P. - - - - The Park, Nottingham.
Dyson, W. Colbeck, F.S.A., Scot. - - Rock House, Batley, Yorkshire.

Ellis, John E., J.P. - - - - - The Park, Nottingham.
Evans, Robert, J.P. - - - - - The Park, Nottingham.

Farmer, Henry - - - - - - Old Lenton.
Fearfield, Joseph - - - - - Stapleford, Nottinghamshire.
Fellows, George, J.P. - - - - Beeston Fields, near Nottingham.
Fletcher, James - - - - - Larkdale Street, Nottingham.
Fletcher, Joseph E. - - - - - Long Eaton Hall, Derbyshire.
Foljambe, Cecil G. S., M.P., F.S.A. - - Care of Messrs. Hatchard, 187, Pic-
                                          cadilly, London, W.
Ford, Alderman William - - - - Mapperley Road, Nottingham.
Froggatt, John - - - - - - Lenton Poplars, Nottingham (5 copies).
Froggatt, Samuel - - - - - Old Lenton, Nottingham (2 copies).

Gell, Samuel H. - - - - - - Clumber Street, Nottingham.
Gerring, Charles - - - - - Melbourne Street, Nottingham.
Gill, John A. - - - - - - Nottingham.
Gordon, Edwin H. - - - - - Bilbie Street, Nottingham.
Gray, Henry - - - - - - 25, Cathedral Yard, Manchester.
Gregory, Mrs. Catherine Sherwin - - Harlaxton Manor, Grantham.

Harwood, Alfred - - - - - - Nottingham.
Hatherly, Henry R., M.R.C.S., Eng. - Arundel Street, Lenton.
Hill, Thomas, J.P. - - - - - The Park, Nottingham.
Hine, George T., F.R.I.B.A. - - - Nottingham.
Hine, Thomas C., F.S.A. - - - Nottingham.

Jennison, Frederick - - - - - Nottingham.
Johnson, Frank, A.R.I.B.A. - - - London.
Johnson, Samuel George - - - - Town Clerk of Nottingham (2 copies).
Johnson, William G. - - - - - Park Hill, Lenton.

Kirkland, William - - - - - Beeston, Nottinghamshire.

Lamb, Richard - - - - - - Nottingham.
Lewis, Chris. J. - - - - - - Forest Road, Nottingham.
Lewis, Frank B. - - - - - - The Park, Nottingham.

Library, Corporation of London - - - Guildhall, London, E.C.
——— Cheetham's - - - Hunt's Bank, Manchester.
——— Free Public - - - - Manchester.
——— Nottingham Subscription - - - Bromley House, Nottingham.
——— Free Public - - - - Nottingham.
——— Mechanics' Institution - - Nottingham.
Lindley, Alderman Leonard - - Ex-Mayor of Nottingham.
Lowe, Major A. E. Lawson, J.P., F.S.A. - Shirenewton Hall, near Chepstow.
Lowe, Colonel Arthur S. H., J.P. - - Gosfield Hall, near Halstead, Essex.
Lowe, Edward Joseph, D.L., J.P., F.R.S. - Shirenewton Hall, near Chepstow.

Maples, Samuel - - - - - - Wolseley House, Nottingham.

Nevill, John B. - - - - - Burns Street, Nottingham.
Newell, James - - - - - Nottingham.

Peat, Edward - - - - - Lenton Sands, Nottingham.
Peat, Edward, jun. - - - - Park Hill, Lenton.
Pegg, H. Carter - - - - Nottingham.
Percy, Edmund, J.P. - - - - Beeston, Nottinghamshire.
Preston, Martin I. - - - - Arundel House, Nottingham.

Renals, John - - - - - The Park, Nottingham.

Sampson, Thomas - - - - New Lenton, Nottingham.
Scattergood, Peter, jun., F.R.H.S. - - Stapleford, Nottinghamshire.
Seely, Lieut. Colonel Charles, M.P. - - Sherwood Lodge, Nottinghamshire.
Shepperson, Thomas - - - - The Park, Nottingham.
Simpson, Henry - - - - Highfield House, Lenton.
Smith, Rev. Percy E., B.A. - - Old Lenton.
Spybey, F. G. - - - - Mapperley Park Drive, Nottingham.
Stamp, John A. - - - - - Nottingham.
Sulley, William - - - - - Balmoral Road, Nottingham.
Summers, L. G., A.R.I.B.A. - - Greenfield House, Radcliffe-on-Trent.

Tate, Clement - - - - - Nottingham (2 copies).
Taylor, A. Claude, M.D. - - - Nottingham.
Tew, William T. - - - - Long Row, Nottingham.
Thorpe, Henry R. - - - - Park Terrace, Nottingham.
Thorpe, John - - - - - Park Road, Lenton.
Tollinton, Joseph - - - - Radford Road, Nottingham.
Toplis, John - - - - - Arthur Street, Nottingham.
Truswell, Walter - - - - Exchange Walk, Nottingham.
Turney, F. N. - - - - - New Basford, Nottingham.
Turney, John, J.P. - - - - Alexandra Park, Nottingham.
Turney, William J., J.P. - - - Park Hill, Stourbridge.
Turpin, Stephen W. - - - - Nottingham.

Walker, William H. -    ·    ·    ·    ·   Lenton Fields, (2 copies).

Windle, William    ·    ·    ·    ·   Low Pavement, Nottingham.

Wright, Colonel C. I. -    ·    ·    ·   Stapleford Hall, near Nottingham.

Wright, Frederick    ·    ·    ·    ·   Lenton Hall, near Nottingham.

Wright, Henry Smith -    ·    ·    ·   Park Hill, Lyndhurst, Hants.

Wright, William    ·    ·    ·    ·   The Park, Nottingham.


York, The Dean and Chapter of -    ·    ·   York.

---

*The impression of this work is limited to 250 copies.*

# THE HISTORY OF
# THE PARISH AND PRIORY OF LENTON.

## SECTION I.

### GEOGRAPHY, ETYMOLOGY, AND EARLY
### ANTIQUITIES.

"Describe the Borough—though our idle tribe
May love description, can we so describe,
That you shall fairly streets and buildings trace,
And all that gives distinction to a place?
This cannot be ; yet moved by your request
A part I paint—let Fancy form the rest."

CRABBE.

HE parish of Lenton is situated in the southern division of the hundred of Broxtow, on the banks of the river Leen, near its confluence with the river Trent.

It is bounded on the north by the parish of Radford, on the east by the parish of Standard Hill and limits of the Castle of Nottingham, and by the town and county of the town of Nottingham ; on the south by the river Trent ; and on the west by the parishes of Beeston and Wollaton.

2

The name of this parish is undoubtedly derived from the river Len or Leen, on which, as previously stated, it is situated. Mr. Flavell Edmunds, in his "Traces of History in the names of Places," derives the name thus, "Len, Lena, Leen, E., land held in fee (Spelman) or farmed out," and as an example he gives "Lenton (Notts.), the town on the farm," but this derivation is as inappropriate as it is improbable, so that it may be passed by without further comment. "Tun," or town, as the word is now generally understood, may appear at first sight a presumptuous title to apply to the handful of huts which made up the Lenton of Saxon days. But, it must be borne in mind that the original meaning of the affix *tun* was no more than a piece of ground surrounded, for purposes of defence, by a hedge, and might comprise but few homesteads. "The English town," remarks one, "was in its beginning simply a piece of the general country, organised and governed precisely in the same manner as the townships around it. Its existence witnessed, indeed, to the need which men felt, in those early times, of mutual help and protection. The *burh* or borough was probably a more defensible place than the common village; it may have had a ditch or mound about it instead of the quick-set hedge or "tun," from which the township took its name."

The river Leen, from whence the parish derives its name, rises in Sherwood Forest, not far from the Robin Hood Hills, between Kirkby-in-Ashfield and Newstead, and in conjunction with several other streamlets, flows on to Newstead Abbey, where, being arrested by an embankment opposite the Abbey, it spreads out into a large and beautiful lake. Wending its way therefrom, through the grounds of Newstead,[1] it is again impounded, and forms the large lower lake, from which, after receiving several accessories, it directs its course to Papplewick; leaving that place a little on the west, it descends southwardly to Bulwell, and collects from the west some important brooks from the higher ground round Linby and Hucknall Torkard, and from the Annesley Hills, as well as some minor ones on the east.

---

(1) "By this *Newstede* rennith *Line* Ryver, that cummeth after to *Lineton*-Abbay, and thens to *Notingham*, and a litle beneth Notingham ynto *Trent*."—Leland's *Itinerary*, vol. i. fo. 110.

Passing through Bulwell it takes a meandering course to Basford, of which place it makes nearly a circuit, and receiving on the east a stream known as the Daybrook, which rises beyond Arnold, and passes through that village and the hamlet of Daybrook, to which it gives its name. Lower down other streams from Nuthall and Hempshill, together with the Whitemoor springs, flow into the Leen from the west. Leaving New Basford to the eastward, the Leen flows on southwardly through Radford, past the great Lodge to Wollaton Park, and on to Old Lenton,[1] which it almost encircles, and then diverges suddenly to the east on its way to Nottingham.

> " Nearing the town, the Leen flows to the east,
> On the left hand, beneath the western sun,
> Climbing with lofty ridge towards the sky
> The rock appears ; its huge mass honey-combed
> By countless caverns, the delightful home
> Of fair chaonian doves." [2]

It should be remarked that the ancient Leen is said to have originally flowed on direct to the south on leaving Lenton, and to have emptied itself into the Trent nearly opposite Wilford Church ; for, in the perambulation of Sherwood Forest, in the sixteenth year of King Henry III., it is stated, "That the boundaries of the Forest came down according to the course of the Leen to Lenton, and from thence *as the same water was wont of old time to run into the water of Trent*," showing that the course of the Leen was diverted long before the reign of Henry III., and there is good reason to believe that the alteration took place when Nottingham Castle was built by the Normans soon after the Conquest, "to which the bringing of the river Leen must have been of great service." An examination of the course of the river, the outlet opposite Wilford Church, and the banks from Lenton to Nottingham, will confirm the statement as to the artificial deviation of the course of the stream beyond Lenton.

---

(1) " There runnith it [the river Leen] by *Linton* or *Lenton*, much frequented and famous in old time for the Abbay there of the *Holy Trinity*, founded by *William Peverell*, the base sonne of King William the Conqueror ; but now all the fame is onely for a Faire there kept."—Camden's *Britain*, trans. by Philemon Holland, 1610, p. 547.

(2) Translation of Latin verses by Huntingdon Plumptre, M.D.

Subsequently to the formation of the Nottingham and Cromford canal, the Leen, from Nottingham Castle, through the town as far as the Cork Hole, has been covered over and made the *cloaca maxima* of Nottingham.[1]   The Leen probably derives its name from the Anglo-Saxon *hlynna*, a brook, or rivulet.

The chief physical feature of the parish is the Leen Valley. This is a somewhat wide but shallow depression with a north and southerly trend, and enters the valley of the Trent between Spring Close on one side and New Lenton on the other.   The Leen itself meanders through a level tract of meadow land, comparatively dry in some parts, but marshy in others, of an average width of nearly 500 yards throughout this parish, though much narrower in places higher up the stream.   The Trent Valley crosses the southern part of the parish in a direction from south-west towards the north-east, while the river Trent itself forms the natural boundary of the parish along its southern side.   A large area in the southern part of the parish thus lies within the valley of the Trent, and is low-lying meadow land drained by natural brooks and streamlets, and by numerous artificial water-courses.   That portion of the northern escarpment or natural boundary of the alluvial plain of the Trent which comes within the parish boundary, is marked by a steep grassy bank or cliff which runs through the middle of Highfield Park and round by Spring Close, where it is broken by the gap through which the Leen enters the valley of the Trent.   The line of escarpment re-appears on the opposite side of the Leen, however, in the low sandstone cliff at the back of the bleach works at New Lenton, and continues on by the " Rock Holes" in Nottingham Park to a more lofty eminence, crowned by Nottingham Castle.   Receding from the banks of the Leen, either to the east or to the west, the ground gradually rises to the most elevated parts of the parish.   The highest point is at Sion Hill, on the Derby Road, which is the extreme eastern limit of the parish.   This is 257 feet above the sea-level,

---

(1) Since the above was written the Leen has been again diverted, and now empties its waters into the canal, passing through a field known as Boot's Close, in Lenton parish, on the western side of the Midland Railway line, and the bed of the river has been filled up from that point to Nottingham Castle.

or about 150 feet above the level of the river Leen near Lenton Station. On the west a gently swelling ridge, picturesquely wooded here and there with plantations or clumps of trees, stretches from the edge of the Trent escarpment in Highfield Park on the south, to Wollaton Hall near the extreme north-west corner of the parish. The charming views of the country for miles round to be obtained from almost any part of this ridge, has caused it to be selected as the sites for such country seats as Lenton Hall, Lenton Firs, Lenton House, and Highfield House. From the grounds of the latter residence a singularly beautiful and extensive view across the valley of the Trent is obtained. To the east, Belvior Castle is plainly visible; more to the south lies Clifton Grove, backed by the Nottinghamshire and Leicestershire Wolds; whilst further southward is Thrumpton Park and Red Hill, with the wooded eminence of Donington Park beyond, and Charnwood Forest forming a bold back-ground; and to the south-west appear Breedon Bulwarks and Church.

The parish, formerly included within the boundaries of the once famous Forest of Sherwood, likewise comprised in earlier days the now extinct villages of Morton and Keighton; and until 1878 the large out-lying tract of land, known as Bestwood Park, was also in the parish of Lenton. Until recent years the modest aspect of the village, with its retired villas and gentlemen's seats, possessed an air of peaceful repose, of which few other places in this busy neighbourhood could boast.

For ecclesiastical purposes the parish is included (as part of the county of Nottingham [1]) in the diocese of Southwell, and in the archdeaconry and rural deanery of Nottingham. For civil purposes it forms part of the borough of Nottingham, and is also included in the Poor Law Union, and County Court District, of Nottingham; but for Parliamentary purposes, it forms part of the Northern Division of the county of Nottingham.

---

(1) Previous to the year 1837 the entire county, with the exception of a portion of two parishes, formed part of the diocese of York, but in that year it was severed from York and united with Lincoln. In February, 1884, the county of Nottingham was severed from the diocese of Lincoln and united to the adjoining county of Derby, to form the new diocese of Southwell.

The high roads from Nottingham to Derby,[1] and from
Nottingham to Birmingham, run through the parish, the latter
road branching off from the former opposite to the second
entrance lodge to Wollaton Park. The Derby Road appears to
have formerly left the line of the present road near to the
"Rose and Crown" Inn, and to have followed the line of the
carriage drive in Wollaton Park as far as the bend (which forms
the corner boundary of Wollaton parish), and along the boundary
of the parishes of Lenton and Wollaton ; near the entrance
lodge to Lenton Hall[2] it crossed the line of the present road and
ran along by the row of old elms in the park belonging to
Lenton Hall, joining the present road near the small pond at
the corner of the park. The course of the road was diverted
when Lord Middleton purchased the land between the old and
present lines of road and enclosed it in his park.

The Cromford and Nottingham canal also crosses the parish,
being joined below Old Lenton by the Beeston canal, commonly
known as "Beeston Cut," and passing out of the parish on the
northern side of the King's Meadows at Nottingham.

The main line of the Midland Railway, from London to
York, divides the villages of Old and New Lenton, the railway
station being on the Derby Road, near to the end of Gregory
Street, formerly the principal street of the parish ; whilst the
Derby, Nottingham, and Lincoln branch intersects another part
of the parish, running along the Trent valley, almost parallel
with the river.

In making a perambulation of the parish, the following
itinerary will be found the most convenient. On quitting Nottingham by the Derby Road, a little beyond Sion Hill, already
spoken of as the highest point of the parish, we come to what
was formerly known as the "Sand Hill," down which the road

---

(1) This road was known as "Derbigate" as early as the year 1301. See "Records
of the Borough of Nottingham," i. 371. In 1335 it is referred to as "regiam viam
quae ducit versus 'Lenton,'" *Ibid.* i. 122.

 In the year 1759 an Act was passed "for repairing and widening the roads from
. . . . Chappel Bar, near the West End of the town of Nottingham, to Saint
Mary's Bridge in the town of Derby, and from the Guide Post in the parish of Lenton
to Sawley Ferry." This Act was amended by four subsequent Acts, passed
20 George III., 39 George III., 59 George III., and 7-8 George IV.

(2) See the Lenton and Radford Inclosure Award, 1768.

runs into the Leen Valley. The "Sand Hill,"[1] or "Lenton
Sands," as it is generally called, derives its name from the deep
sandy nature of the soil in this part, owing to which the Derby
Road was, until a comparative recent period, almost impassable
at certain seasons,[2] and there is little doubt but that for many
years the want of a more convenient means of access between
Lenton and Nottingham materially retarded the increase and
prosperity of the former place. Except for pedestrians, who
have acquired a right to cross Nottingham Park, the Derby
Road forms the only direct communication between Lenton and
Nottingham, but a low-level road, to be named the "Lenton
Boulevard," running directly from the new parish church to the
foot of the Castle Rock at Nottingham, is now in course of
construction. At the top of the Sand Hills, from which a
splendid view of Wollaton Hall and Park is obtained, a place
was reserved under the Inclosure Act of 1768 for holding
Lenton Fair, but this site has long been relinquished, and the
fairs are now held about half-a-mile down the road at the bottom
of the hill, close to the railway station. Passing down the Sand
Hill, having first gardens and a football ground, and then a
considerable tract of arable land on the right, lying between the
Derby Road and the road leading from Nottingham to Ilkeston,
we come first to New Lenton, a thickly populated and thriving,
but most unlovely modern manufacturing district, lying to the
left of the road, and extending on each side of Willoughby
Street as far as Lenton Boulevard, already mentioned. Lower
down the hill, on the same side of the road, and at some distance
from it,[3] stands the new parish Church, and near it the Vicarage
house and National Schools, and close by, but nearer to New
Lenton, a mansion known as Lenton Lodge, the residence of
the Misses Wright. At the bottom of the hill the road crosses

(1) In speaking of the maiden pink, John Ray says, "I find this to be the same pink
which groweth so plentifully by the road side on the sandy hill you ascend going from
Lenton to Nottingham." *Catalogus Plantarum*, 2 ed., 1677. p. 57.

(2) Until the year 1740, the road from Chapel Bar, Nottingham, to the top of the
Sand Hills, was a deep hollow way; at that time Lord Middleton obtained permission from the Corporation of Nottingham to raise the road by casting into it the hills
which lay on both sides. *Blackner's Nottingham*, p. 57.

(3) The Nottinghamshire Agricultural Show was held in the intervening fields in
the years 1880 and 1883.

over the Midland Railway, close by the station, and just beyond
we come to a road crossing the Derby Road, and running almost
parallel with the railway.  To the right, this road, known as
Radford Marsh, leads into the squalid district of Old Radford,
whilst to the left it forms what in modern days has been
dignified, or rather "townified," with the name of "Gregory
Street."  This road, having detached villas on either side, leads
direct into Old Lenton, of which, in fact, it constitutes a part.
Turning down this "street," we come to another road which
turns to the left, and then, branching off, leads on the left hand
past a plain square red brick farm-house, known as the Manor
House, and so past the new Church to New Lenton, and on the
right crosses the Lenton Boulevard, and runs by the southern
end of New Lenton, and across the Park direct into Nottingham.
Just where this road, formerly known as Birch Lane, but now
designated "Sherwin Road," branches off, stands a large square
brick house, built by the late Mr. William Surplice, and beyond
that is Flora Cottage, the residence of Mr. Henry Farmer.
Following Gregory Street, we come to a road leading to the
right past Messrs. Bayley and Company's extensive fellmonger's
establishment, over the Leen and the canal, through Spring
Close, and, leaving the site of Keighton to the left hand, by way
of "Cut-throat Lane" to Beeston.  On the opposite side of
Gregory Street [1] stands the White Hart Inn, and the remains of
the debtors' prison attached to the old Peverel Court, while a
little further on, to the right, is Abbey Street, which, passing a
large steam flour-mill, and the entrance to a modern house,
known as "Lenton Priory," crosses the Leen, and terminates (in
name) at the canal bridge.  The road (which leads to several
outlying farm houses at what is known as Dunkirk) continues
on, however, past a number of recently erected houses, and, near
what are known as the Barn Houses,[2] it runs into an old road

---

(1) The road from the White Hart Inn past the old church to the Leen Bridge was
formerly known as Wilford Road, but in 1878 the Corporation of Nottingham altered
its name, and called the whole length of the road from the Derby Road to the Leen
Bridge, Gregory Street ; the road from the canal bridge near to Lenton Poplars down
to the Trent is still known as Trent Lane.

(2) The Barn Houses originally formed a huge barn, having some initials, now
concealed by colour wash, and the date 1698 in brick work at the gable end.
The barn itself remains intact, but has been divided and converted into dwelling
houses.

which we shall refer to later on. Returning to Gregory Street
we next come to the Old Church, near to which in bygone days
stood the Priory, with its great conventual church and other
buildings. The road, on leaving the village, crosses first the
Leen (by the side of which is an old footway leading direct to
the new Lenton Boulevard), then crosses the canal, and after
passing Lenton Poplars, erected by Mr. William Surplice in
1821, and the railway, and, joining the old road already
mentioned, which will be more fully noticed presently, runs on
to the Trent, the southern boundary of the parish, which it
crosses by an ancient ford, now seldom used. Returning to the
Derby Road, where it passes the end of Gregory Street, and
continuing along it, we cross the Leen by a bridge, built by the
commissioners of the Nottingham and Derby Road in 182—,
previous to which time there was merely a ford here, with a
small wooden bridge for foot passengers. The corn mill on the
right, disfigured by modern *improvements*, occupies the site of
Ingram's Mill, which is several times referred to in ancient
documents relating to the parish. Immediately beyond the mill
is the canal, and beyond the canal bridge, on the right hand,
stands the magnificent archway, forming the principal entrance
to Wollaton Park. This splendid structure, which was erected
at a vast expense by the sixth Lord Middleton, whose arms
appear above the gateway, is in the Elizabethan style of
architecture, some of the details being copied from Wollaton
Hall, and is said to be one of the finest buildings of the kind in
England. Beyond here, the country is reached, the road running
along the side of Wollaton Park wall for more than a mile,
whilst on the opposite side are fields interspersed with fine timber
trees. Leaving the valley of the Leen, and ascending the hill,
we pass on the left what is now a narrow sandy lane, hardly
passable by any but pedestrians. This seems, however, to have
been once a road of some importance, running across what is
now Wollaton Park, past the extinct village of Sutton Passeys,
and into the valley where it is joined by two roads leading
through Old Lenton, and eventually crossed the Trent by the
ancient ford already spoken of. Beyond this old road, near
the top of the hill, stands Lenton Firs, now occupied by Edward

Cope, Esq., and a little beyond that mansion is the entrance lodge to Lenton Hall.

Looking back from this point, a fine view down the valley of the Trent is obtained, whilst nearer at hand Nottingham Castle forms a striking object. Nottingham Park (now entirely built over) is exactly opposite, with Lenton in the foreground, whilst more to the left are the populous manufacturing districts of Radford and New Basford, forming a marked contrast to the quiet rural beauty of the landscape, which stretches for many miles on the right. Further on we come to several large new houses recently built on the outskirts of the park attached to Lenton Hall, and beyond them the high road to Birmingham turns suddenly to the left. Immediately opposite to the Birmingham Road is the castellated lodge to Wollaton Park, commonly known as Beeston Tower, erected by the seventh Lord Middleton. Further on we come to Lenton Abbey, the residence of Mrs. Bayley, which stands embowered in trees at a short distance from the road, on the left hand. The road then runs down another hill,

> "And at the foot thereof a gentle flud
> His silver waves did softly tumble downe,"

and crossing the "gentle flud"—the Tottle Brook—it passes out of the parish. Proceeding along the Birmingham Road and passing a modern residence known as Lenton Eaves, erected a few years ago by Mr. Benjamin Walker, and which is situated just within the angle formed by the two roads, we come to Lenton Fields, on the right, whilst a little further beyond, upon a wooded eminence on the opposite side of the road, stands Lenton House. Beyond, and much nearer to the road, on the right, is Lenton Grove, at present occupied by Francis George Rawson, Esq., and a little further on the road sweeps round to the right on its way to Beeston, and running down a hill crosses the Tottle Brook, and so passes out of the parish. Just at the turn of the road stands the entrance lodge to Highfield House, but the mansion itself being situated upon the higher ground to the left and thickly shrouded in trees, is not seen from this part of the road. Just at the bend of the road it is joined by the foot-road known as "Cut-throat Lane," already mentioned, which, passing between the grounds of Highfield House and Lenton Hall, runs through Spring Close, and, crossing the canal and the Leen, joins Gregory Street in Old Lenton. Continuing our course up Gregory Street, crossing the Derby Road, we enter Radford Marsh, and pass to the left a water corn mill, known as the Prior's Mill. Crossing the railway, we pass the new populous district of Cobden Park on the right, and the great

gas works belonging to the Corporation of Nottingham on the left, and turn up the Ilkeston Road on our way to Nottingham. About two-thirds of the way up this road (which forms the division between the parishes of Lenton and Radford, Lenton lying to the right hand, and Radford to the left) we pass the new Board Schools, and the Lenton—or, as it is erroneously called, the Radford—police station, and ascending the hill we reach the Derby Road near our starting point on Sion Hill.

The early antiquities of this parish are exceedingly meagre.

A fine perforated stone axe was found some years ago on the Sand Hills in Wollaton Park, on the borders of Lenton parish, and is reported to have been the largest of the kind that had been found in Great Britain up to that time.[1]

(1) In 1875, a stone axe of somewhat larger dimensions was found at Canonbie, in Dumfriesshire.

It is formed of a very fine grained, hard, and slightly micaceous grit, and its weight exceeds $7\frac{1}{4}$ lbs. It is somewhat rounded at the hammer end, which appears to have lost some splinters by use, though the broken surface has since been partially reground. The blade is slightly curved longitudinally, and both the outer and inner face have been hollowed from the point as far as the perforation. The sides have each four parallel grooves worked in them, so that they are, as it were, corrugated into five ribs, extending from near the edge to near the centre of the hole. The hollows on the face also show two slight ribs parallel with the sides of the blade, the angles of which are rounded. The shaft hole tapers from each face towards the centre, where it is about $1\frac{1}{8}$ inches in diameter. The grooves seem to have been produced by picking, but have subsequently been made smooth by grinding.[1] This is, so far as we are aware, the sole relic of the stone period that has been found within the parish.

The late Alfred Lowe, Esq., had in his possession several antiquities, chiefly of the Celtic period, which had been found, at various times, in the parish of Lenton, but, so far as we can learn, no particulars of their discovery appear to have been preserved. Amongst these was a good socketted bronze celt of the ordinary type, three small arrow-heads of iron, each measuring about three-and-a-half inches in length, a bronze key, and several bronze ornaments.

It has been stated that Lenton was once a Roman station, and Robert Talbot, "an Oxford student, and Canon of Norwich under Henry VIII., a man well skilled in the antiquities of this island," has maintained that it was the noted *Lindum.* For this opinion he is severely censured by a later writer [2]—" Not far from Nottingham lies Lenton, which Mr. Talbot for some reasons was inclined to believe the ancient *Lindum* of Antoninus. I take it for granted it was the affinity of the two names which first led him to this conjecture, and that drew him to other fancies which might seem in any wise to confirm his

---

(1) Jewitt's *Grave Mounds and their Contents*, p. 111. This axe is now in the possession of Mr. Jewitt, to whom we are indebted for the engraving of it.

(2) Gibson's *Camden*, 1695.

opinion, as that the river which runs through Nottingham into
the Trent, is at this day called Lin, or rather, Lind; but then,
Lenton lying at a pretty distance from it, he is forced to back
it with this groundless imagination, that Lenton might be sometime part of Nottingham; though they be a mile asunder one
from the other.    What he says in defence of Lenton, why
the old town might possibly be there, is very true; *that
it is a thing frequently observed, that famous towns have
degenerated into little villages*, and that, therefore, its present
meanness is no objection against it; but then it can derive
no authority from the river Lin or Lind.   Besides, the obscurity
of a place is really a prejudice to its antiquity, unless the
discovery of camps, coins, bricks, or some such remains,
demonstrate its former eminence.    Nothing that he has said
·in favour of this opinion, taken from distances and such
like, is of force enough to draw it from Lincoln."    From
this it is evident that neither Talbot nor Gibson were well
acquainted with the situation of Lenton, for in Talbot's time
the village was situated on the banks of the Leen, as it is at the
present day.

It is, however, more than doubtful whether the Romans ever
had a station here of any importance, but some traces of Roman
occupation appear, nevertheless, to have been met with.    The
ancient road, locally known as "Coventry Lane," crossed the
Trent near Attenborough, at a spot where, in times of unusual
drought, vestiges of wooden piles, denoting a passage across the
river, may yet be traced.   The line of the road in question
appears to have been northward from the Trent, and may be
supposed to have had a branch road turning off from it near the
bank of the river, taking a more easterly direction; and, after
passing below the villages of Chilwell and Beeston, intersecting
the parish of Lenton.   This supposed branch road has been lost
in places, but an ancient road apparently connecting it with the
passage across the river at Attenborough may be traced on the
Ordnance maps, from point to point, without much difficulty.
On the eastern side of the parish of Beeston the road still exists,
under the name of Hassock Lane.   This lane terminates beyond
Hassock Farm, but the line of the old road may yet be distinctly

traced on across several fields on the Highfield estate. According to some local antiquaries, the road crossed the Leen at a point a little below the site of Lenton Priory, passed across Nottingham Park, and went on from thence northward over Nottingham Forest. This latter statement must, however, be received with some reserve, for the depression, or hollow, where this road is supposed to have entered the Park on the south side, is stated on the other hand to have been formed about the year 1829, when a portion of the rock holes close by, fell in, and the removal of the *debris* having made a convenient approach to the river Leen, the cattle in the Park came there to drink, from which circumstance the hollow became known as the "cow drinks." The next portion of this supposed continuation of the road in question was a cutting on the north side of the Park, which appears to have been made as a ready access to the barracks, which. until recent years stood on the north-west side of the Park. Another supposed remnant of the road was said to be seen on the Forest, running for about a hundred yards in length from the top of what is now Southey Street, in a north-easterly direction towards Mount Hooton road, but even this is of doubtful antiquity. It is therefore probable that a continuous road from the river Leen crossing Nottingham Park to the Forest did not exist until a somewhat recent date. Coventry Lane itself is believed to have been a British trackway, but was probably utilised, as was so often the case, by the Romans. Whether the old road running through the valley in the direction of Lenton was a branch from Coventry Lane constructed by the Romans, must remain a matter of conjecture, as nothing of distinct Roman character in connection with the road itself has been met with; but within a short distance from the line of this road, undeniable evidence of Roman occupation has been found. About fifty years ago, a portion of the foundation of the walls of what would appear to be a *villa urbana* was discovered on the Bath Hill, near Highfield House, but these remains were, unfortunately, never investigated.[1]    Several fragments of tiles

(1) It is somewhat singular that a Roman villa should have been discovered, in the year 1862, under almost similar circumstances, in the neighbourhood of Oxford. A Roman way ran from north to south, about three miles east of Oxford, uniting the

and pottery, found on the spot, together with some small bronze
ornaments, the latter of which are of undoubted Roman origin,
have fortunately been preserved.[1]   It is, however, much to be
regretted that no more satisfactory details as to what was
believed to have been the remains of the villa are obtainable.
In the early part of the present century, it is said, a tessellated
pavement was found in one of the "Keighton meadows," just
beyond the Bath Hill, but definite information as to this
discovery is also wanting.   A small bronze coin, much defaced,
of Constantine the Second (A.D. 340), was dug up in the gardens
at Highfield House six or seven years ago, and in the year 1877
a fine bronze coin of the reign of Tacitus was found on the other
side of the parish, in a garden occupied by Mr. John Place, on
Park Road, New Lenton.

The old inhabitants of Lenton had a tradition, now nearly
forgotten, that a fierce battle was fought between the Britons
and the Romans in the valley to the south-west of Old Lenton,

and that the former were victorious, although they suffered
severe losses.   The skulls of horses as well as human remains

---

two great Roman roads which, starting from the neighbourhood of Tring, diverged,
the one towards the south-west, and the other to the north-west, but united again at
Cirencester, inclosing a large oval space of country between them.   The cross-road
ran over high ground, and is now lost on Headington Hill amongst extensive quarries.
In the neighbourhood of Stow Wood, to the north of Headington, it is very distinct,
but in the neighbourhood of Beckley it is again imperfectly visible, and a portion,
which was formerly considered as part of the main way, appeared to be rather a side
branch of it.   The correctness of this observation was fully proved by the discovery
of a Roman villa at Beckley, about six miles to the north-east of Oxford.   Roman
coins had often been found in the neighbourhood.   The villa was built on the
northern slope of the hill, and must have commanded a very wide expanse of country
to the north and east, of not less than 20 miles.   The villa consisted of four oblong
rooms, the walls of which, when discovered, were scarcely higher than the floor.
The rooms were nearly of equal size, and together they formed a building of a regular
oblong form, about 30 feet long by 20 feet wide, the floors of which were level, and
covered with a tessellated pavement of very rude character.   The tesserae of the
floors are about an inch square.   Numerous fragments of rough Roman pottery have
been found scattered about, and amongst the *debris* a single coin of Constantine, and
several fragments of bone have been discovered.—*The Archæological Journal*, xx. 73.

(1) The articles are now in possession of Edward Joseph Lowe, Esq., F.R.S.   The
most noticeable is a figure of a dolphin, about 2½ inches in length.   There are also
figures of a cock, and of some kind of fish, or serpent, and several which cannot be
so readily identified.

have ocasionally been met with in the Keighton meadows, which appear to confirm the tradition, but, so far as can be ascertained, the only weapon that has been discovered, and of which we give an illustration, is a fine bronze sword,[1] evidently of the Roman period. This was found by some workmen employed in enlarging the lake at Highfield House, about the year 1830, lying near the remains of a human skeleton. The bones of the skeleton quickly perished on being exposed to the atmosphere, and the handle of the sword, which was either bone or wood, and which had been attached to the bronze hilt by four rivets, fell to pieces on being touched. The length of the weapon is about 24 inches, the blade is leaf-shaped and is 19½ inches long, and 1¾ inches in width at the broadest part, whilst the hilt is 4½ inches long. About the same time that this was found, several other articles were also discovered and appropriated by the labourers, one of whom is said to have sold for a trifling sum a small silver cup or vessel,[2] which was quickly melted down and beyond recovery.

We have already remarked that the parish of Lenton comprised the villages of Morton and Keighton. The manor of Morton is supposed to have formed the southern portion of the parish lying between the river Leen and the river Trent, and the village is conjectured to have been situated somewhere near where Dunkirk Farm now stands. The village of Keighton, or Kirkton, appears to have occupied the site between Spring Close and Highfield Park, on the slope of the hill on the south side of the foot road to Beeston, locally known as "Cutthroat"[3] Lane. This place, which formed part of the possessions of Lenton Priory, is not mentioned in the Domesday survey, and apparently had no manorial rights attached to it. The village seems to have fallen into decay as early as the year 1387, when the houses at this place belonging to the Prior of

(1) This is also in the possession of Edward Joseph Lowe, Esq., F.R.S., of Shire-newton Hall, Monmouthshire.

(2) One of the workmen, who subsequently confessed to having been a party to the theft, described it as a silver bell, but it is more likely to have been a bell-shaped cup or vessel.

(3) Properly "Cut-through" Lane, a portion of a small sandstone cliff having been cut through to make way for the road. Recent *improvements* have sadly disfigured this once picturesque spot.

Lenton were stated to be "as much in want of repairs as of tenants." The meadows on the hill side, still known as "The Keightons," present extraordinary and unnatural undulations, the origin of which has been the subject of considerable conjecture. Near to one of these hollows there was, within the memory of man, a subterranean passage hewn out of the sandstone rock, the entrance to which was sheltered by an old thorn bush. There was a tradition amongst the villagers that this passage had originally led to Lenton Priory.[1] The passage, undoubtedly, ran for some considerable distance under the ground, but owing to the dangerous entrance, and the presence of water, it was never thoroughly explored. It was filled up some years ago, and the old thorn bush has since disappeared, but the entrance is still plainly indicated by a visible depression in the bank, and by the difference in the vegetation growing upon the spot.

In excavating for clay on the side of the Bath Hill, at Highfield, a short distance to the eastward of the spot where what is believed to have been the remains of a Roman habitation were found, large quantities of broken pottery were met with about eight years ago. These were all of the earlier mediæval type, and from the fact that most of the pieces were evidently the fragments of utensils which had been distorted, or otherwise damaged, in the process of baking, it seems evident that there must have been a kiln near here, probably belonging to the monks of Lenton, and that these were the damaged articles which had been discarded as worthless.

---

(1) Similar and equally improbable traditions of subterranéan passages in connection with monasteries and castles are to be found in all parts of the country. Of the existence of this particular passage there can be no doubt whatever, but its alleged connection with Lenton Priory must obviously be fallacious.

# SECTION II.

## MANORIAL AND EARLY HISTORY.

HE manorial history of Lenton may be said to commence with the Domesday Book. From this survey, completed in the year 1086, we find that certain lands were in the hands of the king, while the greater portion had been granted to, and formed part of the vast possessions of, William Peverel.

The king's land is thus described :—

S. In Lentone IIII. bov. t'ræ ad gld. Soca in Ernehale. Wasta e'.

Translation :—

Soke. In Lentone (Lenton) four oxgangs of land to be taxed.

Soke in Ernehale (Arnold). It is waste.

The lands held by William Peverel are thus enumerated :—

M. In LENTVNE. hb Vnlof. IIII. bou' t'ræ ad gld. Tra dim' car'. Modo in custodia Willi. Ibi. isd Vlnod ht. I. car'. 7 I. uill' 7 I. bord' h'ntes. I. car'. 7 I. molin' X. solid. 7 X ac' p'ti. 7 acs siluæ min'. T.R.E. ual' X. sol' m° XV.

S. In Lentune. II. car t're ad gld. Soca in Neubold. Tra II. car'. Ibi. IIII. soch' 7 IIII. bord h'nt. II. car' 7 I molin'.

Translation :—

*Manor.* In Lentune (Lenton) Unlof had four oxgangs of land to be taxed. Land to half a plough. It is now in the wardship of William (Peverel). The same Unlof has there one plough and one villane and one bordar having one plough, and one mill of ten shillings, and ten acres of meadow, and ten acres of coppice wood. Value in King Edward's time ten shillings, now fifteen (shillings).

*Soke.* In Lentune (Lenton) two carucates of land to be taxed, soke in Newbold. Land to two ploughs. Four sokemen and four bordars have there two ploughs and one mill.

The origin of William Peverel, the first Norman lord of Lenton, is enveloped in mystery. He is commonly reputed to have been a natural son of Duke William of Normandy, by a daughter of Ingelric, an Anglo-Saxon thane, who was a benefactor, if not the founder, of the collegiate church of St. Martin-le-Grand, in London. This lady's name is doubtful ; by Morant she is called Maud, whilst Leland calls her Ingelrica.[1] It is further stated that Ingelric's daughter, the mistress of the Conqueror, was given in marriage, by Duke William, to one Ranulph Peverel, a Norman knight, who accompanied the Conqueror to England, and that her husband consented that her bastard son should bear the name of Peverel also. The more general account, however, is that the wife of Ranulph Peverel became the mistress of the Conqueror, whose issue by her took the name of her husband's family.[2]

Peverel's connection with the county of Nottingham commences very shortly after the Norman Conquest. In 1068, the newly erected castle of Nottingham was confided to his charge ;[3] and at the time of the compilation of the Domesday survey, he was lord of one hundred and sixty-two manors in England, and possessed in Nottingham alone, forty-eight merchants' or traders' houses, thirteen knights' houses, and eight bondsmen's houses, in addition to ten acres of land granted to him by the king to make a wall round the town,

---

(1) *Collectanea*, i. 55.    (2) Planché, *Conqueror and his Companions*, ii. 265.
(3) *The Conqueror*, etc., ii. 259.

and the churches of St. Mary, St. Peter, and St. Nicholas,[1] all of which he gave, as will be hereafter seen, to Lenton Priory.[2]

The late Mr. Planché, Somerset Herald, remarks that it is a significant fact, "that in all the battles and commotions, of which Normandy was the theatre during the thirty years preceding the Conquest, the name of Peverel, if such a family existed in the duchy, never crops up, even accidentally, in any of the pages of the contemporary chronicles."[3] Such being the case, if the reputed parentage of William Peverel be erroneous, as is now urged by several authorities, how are we to account for the fact that he was endowed by the wary and suspicious Conqueror with such immense possessions, and obtained so responsible and important a trust as the custody of Nottingham Castle, when, if the date of his death in the register of St. James's Priory, Northampton, which he founded,[4] can be relied upon, he could scarcely have then been more than four or five-and-twenty years of age. The story of Peverel's birth is rejected by Mr. Freeman with contempt and indignation, "as the unsupported assertion of a herald;"[5] and Eyton, in his history of Shropshire, discredits the report on the grounds that "it is inconsistent with the general character of Duke William;" and further, because "this alleged liaison with a Saxon lady of rank can have originated in no earlier circumstance than the event of the Duke's visit to the court of Edward the Confessor, in 1051;" whilst "William Peverel must have been born before that period, for he was old enough, in 1068, to be intrusted with one of the most responsible affairs in the kingdom."[6] "To whom," asks Mr. Planché, in reference to the first of these arguments, "shall we refer for the general character of this master of dissimulation, who so thoroughly understood and practised the policy of assuming a virtue if he had it not? To his paid servants and courtly flatterers, Guillaume de Poictiers, his own chaplain, or Guy of Amiens, his wife's almoner, who, if he did write the 'Carmen de Bello,' I consider not worthy to be believed on his oath? These are

---

(1) Domesday Book.

(2) *Mon. Angl.*, v. 113.

(3) *The Conqueror*, etc., ii. 260.

(4) *Mon. Angl.*, vi. 114.

(5) *Norman Conquest*, iii. 656.

(6) Eyton's *Shropshire*, ix. 69.

the only actual contemporaries who could have informed us what was the Duke's general character for morality in Normandy in his own time, and they have not thought it worth while to do so." [1]  Replying to the second objection, Planché very justly observes that it is quite possible "that the Saxon lady of rank might have visited Normandy *before* 1051, a circumstance which would remove the only serious difficulty in the story. [2]  "Mystery" Mr. Eyton admits "there certainly is about the whole subject, and the truth may be buried, very possibly, with some tale of courtly scandal, though not of the precise character pointed out."

"History, it has been said, repeats itself, and the account given by Dugdale of William's liaison with the daughter of Ingelric is curiously similar to that of his father, Robert, with the daughter of Fulbert the furrier......... There is nothing remarkable in such circumstances, except their coincidence with those of Robert and Herleve, nor indeed in that, as they were of common occurrence in Normandy, and tolerated, if not sanctioned, as the custom of the country.  And what if the existence, not only of a wife *more Danico*, but of a son, should have been one of the hitches in the matrimonial arrangements of William and Matilda of Flanders?  Several good reasons might be adduced to show the bearing of the case on the mystery that still enshrouds the singular courtships of the lady, and the unexplained prohibition of the Pope." [3]

Ranulph Peverel, who is also referred to in the Domesday survey as the lord of sixty-four manors, founded the Priory of Hatfield Peverel, in Essex, [4] at the instigation of Ingelrica, his wife, and supposing the story to be true that this lady was the mother of the founder of Lenton Priory, it seems altogether more probable that she became the mistress of Duke William after she had married Ranulph Peverel, for we find that Hammo, or Hammond, the eldest son of this Ranulph Peverel, was settled in England a few years after the Norman invasion, being then one of the chief tenants, or barons, of Roger Montgomeri, Earl

---

(1) *The Conqueror*, etc., ii. 261.          (2) *Ibid.*, ii. 262.

(3) *Ibid*, ii. 265.                          (4) *Mon. Angl.*, iii. 294.

of Shrewsbury. We may venture to conclude that this Hammo
Peverel was the half-brother of William Peverel, of Nottingham,
and besides Hammo, he had probably two other half-brothers,
namely : Payne, or Pagan Peverel, of Bourne, in Cambridgeshire, the founder of Barnwell Priory,[1] in that county, and that
William Peverel who is commonly styled as of Dover. But on
this point genealogists disagree, and it is alleged that there is no
evidence to prove that the Ranulph Peverel, of Domesday, had
any other son than the William Peverel, who was afterwards
called of Essex, or of London, to distinguish him from his contemporaries, William Peverel, of Nottingham, and William
Peverel, of Dover.

### PEDIGREE OF PEVEREL, OF NOTTINGHAM.

ARMS.—(attributed to the family) Vairé or and gules. ∎

William Peverel, of Nottingham ;= Adelina, dau. of.......
founder of Lenton Priory, temp. | said to have died 14
Henry I., died 5 kal. Feb., | kal. Feb., 1119.
1113.

| | | | |
|---|---|---|---|
| William, died 16 kal. May, 1100. | William Peverel, of Notting-= Oddona, ham,[3] heir to his father. dau. of.. Presumed to have died be- ........... fore the year 1149. | Matilda, living in 1130. | Adeliza, mar. to Rich<sup>d.</sup> de Rivieres, lord of Shipbroke, co. Chester. |

Henry, died in his
father's lifetime.

William Peverel, of Nottingham ; living 18 Stephen, 1 Henry
II. ; married Avicia de Lancaster, and, according to doubtful
authority, had a daughter and heiress, Margaret, married to
William, Earl of Ferrers, and had issue.

(1) *Mon. Angl.*, vi. 83.

(2) In Tonge's *Visitation*, circa 1530, the following occurs :—" Peverelles armes ys
golde and azure verrey. And his creste ys a Saresins hed. And his beste ys a lyon
gueules mordrying a dragon with his mouth."—*Harl MS.* 1499., f. 42.

(3) In " Worthies of Nottinghamshire," p. 3., it is stated that this William must
have been very young at the foundation of Lenton Priory, as his brother of the same
name had died in 1100. But it was common in those days for two brothers, living at
the same time, to bear the same Christian name. Innumerable instances of this
might be quoted.

Adelina, his wife (whose parentage has not been ascertained), is mentioned by William Peverel, of Nottingham, in his charter to Lenton Priory, and we find by the same document that he had a son, also named William, and other children who are not named. Two of these children were daughters, Matilda (mentioned in the Pipe Roll, 31 Henry I.), and Adeliza, who, in an Exchequer Roll, is stated to be the wife of Richard de Rivieres. According to the register of the Priory of St. James, Northampton, William Peverel died the fifth kalends of February, in the year 1113, Adelina, his wife, surviving him, according to the same authority, only six years. This, however, does not agree with the fact that, in the fifth year of the reign of King Stephen, "Adelina, mother of William Peverel, of Nottingham," was pardoned by the king eighteen shillings, as appears by the Sheriff's account of the Dane Geld for that year, 1140,[1] unless we are to suppose that the debt incurred by the mother was pardoned to her son, after her death. The register of St. James's, Northampton, also certifies that Sir William, son of the elder William Peverel, died in his father's lifetime, the date of his death being given as the sixteenth of the kalends of May, 1100. It is sufficiently evident that the founder of Lenton Priory had two sons of his own name, one of whom succeeded to his father's possessions. This last named William Peverel was one of the temporal barons who attended King Stephen at the great council held at Oxford in the first year of his reign, and witnessed the laws then ordained and ratified by the King.[2] Two years later (1138) he commanded the Nottinghamshire troops at the battle of the Standard.[3] King Stephen, being afterwards at Nottingham, confirmed to the Prior and Monks of Lenton, at the request of William Peverel, and of Oddona, his wife, and of Henry, their son, the donations of William Peverel (father of this William) and of William himself, who is styled in the charter, "William Peverel, junior."[4] We find from the Pipe Roll (5 Stephen) that in 1140, William Peverel, of Nottingham, gave

---

(1) Thoroton, p. 289.

(2) *Statutes of the Realm,* charter 3 ; Stubbs' *Select Charters,* p. 121.

(3) John of Hexham, p. 119 ; Florence of Worcester, ii., 111.

(4) See the charter, section iv., *post.*

account of the sum of £23 6s. 8d. of the Pleas of the Forest, in Nottinghamshire. In the following year, 1141, was fought the battle of Lincoln, in which King Stephen was taken prisoner, and with him his faithful adherent, William Peverel. The latter appears to have speedily regained his liberty, and contrived, by stratagem, to retake Nottingham Castle, which had been captured on behalf of the Empress Matilda, by William Painel, some time during the previous year.[1] At another time, this second William Peverel, with the consent of *his* heir, William Peverel, the younger, restored to the monks of Lenton the churches of Higham and Raunds, in Northamptonshire, which had been bestowed upon them by William Peverel, his father, at the entreaty of his faithful wife, Adelina, and which, by ill advice he had unjustly detained from the Priory.[2] Thus we have evidence that the before-named son, Henry, had pre-deceased his father, and that a younger son, William, was then heir. This William Peverel, for the health of his soul, and for the repose of the souls of his father and mother, gave to the monks of Garendon, in Leicestershire, all the demesne lands, about thirteen bovates, which they had held of him in Costock. There is no record of the death of the second William Peverel, but it is presumed that it occurred before the year 1149.

Dugdale[3] has made a strange confusion by mixing up the first with the second William Peverel, making the former, who died in 1113, to have been present at the battle of the Standard in 1138, and at the battle of Lincoln in 1141. He mentions only two generations of this family, and his opinion is shared by several eminent genealogists, yet it seems far more probable that Camden is correct in ascribing the following to the grandson, rather than to the son, of the founder of Lenton Priory. In 1152, an agreement was arrived at between Stephen and his opponent, Henry, and in 1154, the death of Stephen gave the throne of England to Henry, who succeeded him as Henry the Second. He was crowned on the 19th of December in the same year, and one of his earliest acts in the following year was to

---

(1) John of Hexham, p. 136, 141.          (2) Thoroton, p. 488.
(3) *Baronage*, i. 436-7.

disinherit William Peverel, upon the charge of his having
conspired with Maud, Countess of Chester, to poison her
husband, Earl Ranulph, surnamed Gernon. The cause of
Peverel's disinheritance is distinctly stated by the *Chronicon
Roffense*, the register of Dunstable, Matthew Paris, Matthew
of Westminster, and Gervase of Canterbury, as being the foul
crime already named.[1] The latter authority adds that Peverel,
either because he feared the rigour of the king, or in expiation
of his crime, left his worldly goods, and caused himself to be
shaven and cowled a monk, and took refuge in a neighbouring
monastery,[2] which was obviously that of Lenton ; in February,
1155, in mortal dread, he secretly escaped and fled away, leaving
all his castles and stores to the mercy of the king.[3] It is,
however, an undisputed fact that King Henry, before he
ascended the throne, most probably in 1152, had given to the
same Ranulph, Earl of Chester, the whole fee of Peverel, only
excepting his manor of Higham, in Northamptonshire, unless
William Peverel could clear himself of his wickedness and
treason.[4] From this there is little doubt that the offence for
which William Peverel was deprived of his lands was the
staunch support that he and his family had afforded to the cause
of King Stephen.[5]

Shortly previous to the forfeiture of his estates, the third
William Peverel appears to have conferred certain privileges
upon the canons of Darley, near Derby, which were confirmed
by Avicia de Lancaster, his wife,[6] between the years 1149 and
1159.[7] From her surname, this lady might be conjectured to
have been a daughter of Roger de Poitou, son of Roger de
Montgomeri, Earl of Shrewsbury, who was sometimes called
Earl of Lancaster, in consequence of the large possessions in
that county which he obtained with his wife. But it is at the
same time possible that she may have been one of the family of
the Barons of Kendal, of whom William de Lancaster was a

---

(1) *The Conqueror*, etc., ii. 71.       (2) Gervase of Canterbury, i. 161.
(3) Gervase of Canterbury, i. 161.       (4) Rymer's *Fœdera*, i. 16.
(5) Blore's *Rutlandshire*, p. 143-4.       (6) *Mon. Ang.*, vi. 361.
(7) *i.e.*, during the episcopacy of Walter (Durdent) of Chester, 1149-1159 (Le Neve,
i. 544).

wealthy and powerful personage in the reigns of Henry the First, Stephen, and Henry the Second.

After Peverel's flight from the kingdom, we hear nothing further of the family; and it is probable that he ended his days in obscurity. The castles and vast possessions constituting the fee of Peverel, which, with the exception of a single manor in Northamptonshire, had been given to the Earl of Chester, reverted to the Crown during the close of the reign of Henry the Second,[1] and were bestowed, in 1174, by that king upon his son, John, Earl of Mortaigne.[2]    On the accession of that prince to the throne, the honour of Peverel became annexed to the Crown, in which it always after.continued.[3]    The famous castle of the Peak, which has caused Peverel's descendants to be known as the "Peverels of the Peak," remained part of the royal demesnes until the close of the reign of Edward the Third, when it was bestowed on John of Gaunt, and the castle thus became absorbed in the Duchy of Lancaster.

William Peverel, the last of his name, is said, according to doubtful authority, to have had a daughter named Margaret, married to an Earl of Ferrers, who, in her right, became heir to a considerable portion of the Peverel estates, or was made so on the disinheritance of her father.    In consequence of this marriage, the Earls of Ferrers are said to have abandoned the ancient arms of their house, and to have assumed those of Peverel.    Deering [4] states that William, Earl of Ferrers, married Margaret, daughter and heiress of William Peverel, and adds that the marriage rites were performed at Canterbury by Archbishop Thomas à Beckett.    He further states that the earl died in 1172, and that the countess died in the same year and month as her husband.    In commenting upon the absence of any mention of this Margaret Peverel in any contemporary document, Mr. Planché proceeds to notice, that although a Plea Roll of the 25th year of the reign of Henry the Third certainly proves that, during the war between the king and his barons, some Earl of Ferrers had assumed a right of heirship to William Peverel, this

---

(1) Gervase of Canterbury, i. 161 ; Robert de Monte, viii. 504.
(2) Benedictus Abbas, i. 78 ; Roger de Hoveden, ii. 69.
(3) See section xvi., *post*.        (4) *Nottinghamia Vetus et Nova*, p. 201.

assumption might be explained upon other grounds than that of a match with the heiress of Peverel.[1] The Oblate Roll of the first year of the reign of King John, states that William, Earl of Ferrers, " gave two thousand marcs for the manors of Higham, Blisworth, and Newbottle, in Northamptonshire, so that the king gave him the park of Higham, which the Lord Henry, his great-grandfather, had given in exchange to the ancestors of William Peverel."[2] " This William, Earl of Ferrers," remarks Mr. Planché, " was the one who unquestionably married Agnes, daughter of Hugh Kivelix, Earl of Chester, and sister and co-heiress of Ranulph Blundeville, the last earl of that line, and consequently he might fairly found his pretensions to the rest of the lands of William Peverel, upon the gift of the whole fee to Ranulph Gernon, his wife's grandfather." Confirmatory evidence of this alleged marriage appears to be altogether wanting.

Such is the substance of all that has been handed down to us of the founder of Lenton Priory, and of his posterity. We have already remarked that the origin of Peverel is enveloped in intrigue and mystery, and in intrigue and mystery we lose sight of his descendants.

Upon the Priory of Lenton, William Peverel bestowed his whole manor of Lenton, excepting four water-mills, together with all his demesne lands in Keighton, Morton, Radford, and elsewhere. The chief manor thus came into the hands of the Prior and Monks of Lenton, and continued in the possession of the confraternity until the final suppression of religious houses in the time of King Henry the Eighth.

The manor of Lenton then, as now, included the whole of the parish of Radford, as is shown by the following perambulation, which is taken from an interesting document from the office of the king's remembrancer in the Exchequer—" Inquisitio tangens divisiones manerii de Lenton per metas et Bundas a manerio de Wilford. Mich. Eliz. ro. 381."[3] The following is a copy of the document :—"Inquisition Indented and taken at the Castle of Nottingham in the County aforesaid the 3rd day

---

(1, 2) *The Conqueror*, etc., i. 70. (3) *Mon. Ang.*, v. 110.

of October in the 17th year of the Reign of our Lady Elizabeth
by the Grace of God of England France and Ireland Queen,
&c., before John Manors [1] Esq[r] Edward Stanhope [2] Esq[r]
Surveyors of all and Singular the Honoiers, Castles, Lordships,
Manors, Lands, Tenements, Possessions and Hereditaments
aforesaid of our Lady the Queen that now is in the County of
Nottingham, and John Bounds, [3] Gent., Commissioners of our
Lady the Queen by Virtue of the Commission of our said Lady
the Queen directed to the said Commissioners and others
Joyned in the Commission upon the Oaths of Henry Stanley
Gent : John Hutchinson Gent : Geo Houghton, John Wylde,
Rich[d] Wylde, W[m] Chamberlayne, Geo Brunt, Gabriel Greves,
Rob[t] Sawell, Rich[d] Newton, Hugh Burrow, Anthony Curteys,
Geo Crossland, Robt Burr, Edm[d] Locke, Rich[d] Heylowe, who
upon their Oaths say, that the Manor of Lenton in the
Commission aforesaid mentioned with Radford reaches to the
several parishes of Lenton Radford and Bilborrow in the
County of Nottingham aforesaid is Divided and separated from
the aforesaid Manor of Wilford in the said Commission also
named by the Limits Meets and Bounds herein aftermentioned
(that is to say) the said Manor of Lenton extends from the
South side of the River Lyne opposite the said Manor of
Wilford in a certain place parcel of the Manor of Lenton called
the Willow Holme part of which place called the Willow
Holme is contiguous and Adjacent to the said Manor of
Wilford and abuts upon a certain Meadow of our Lady the
Queen called King's Meadow in Nottingham in the County
aforesaid towards the North and upon the aforesaid Manor of
Wilford towards the East and is Divided and separated by part
of the said Manor of Wilford called Wilford Meadows the same

---

(1) He was second son of Thomas, first Earl of Rutland, and was subsequently
honoured with knighthood. The story of his elopement with Dorothy Vernon, of
Haddon (now, alas, considered apocryphal), is well known. His grandson
eventually succeeded to the earldom, and was ancestor of the present Duke of
Rutland.

(2) He is doubtless identical with Edward Stanhope, of Grimston, in Yorkshire,
sometime M.P. for that county, who was also afterwards knighted. He was second
son of Sir Michael Stanhope, to whom Shelford Priory was granted by King Henry
the Eighth, and who also held a lease of the site of Lenton Priory for forty years.

(3) Properly Boun, or Bohun.

being contiguous and adjoining by a certain Ancient Ditch which said Ditch begins at the aforesaid Meadow called the King's Meadow Divided and Separated by the said Willow Holme of the aforesaid Meadow called Wilford Meadow towards a certain place Parcel of the aforesaid Manor of Lenton called Lenton Holmes towards the South where a certain Rivulet descends from the Town of Lenton aforesaid and then runs towards the East to the aforesaid place called the Willow Holmes ; Divided and separated by the said Places called Lenton Holmes parcel of the Manor of Lenton aforesaid lying near the aforesaid Meadow called Wilford Meadow parcel of the said Manor of Wilford towards a certain place in Wilford aforesaid called Wilford pastures where beginneth a certain great Ditch with a Quickset Hedge there lately made which said Ditch divides the aforesaid place called Lenton Holmes from the aforesaid place called Wilford pasture towards a certain place in Wilford aforesaid parcel of the said Manor of Wilford called Wilford great Steynour lying at the end of the aforesaid Ditch towards the South and from thence the said place called Lenton Holmes from the South part is Divided and separated by the aforesaid great Steynour near a certain bank towards the West in Length an Hundred and Sixty Feet or thereabout to be repaired and kept up by the Inhabitants of Lenton and afterwards Divided by a Rail between the said Bank and the Trent in Length Sixty Feet or thereabouts likewise to be repaired and maintained by the Inhabitants of Lenton, in the middle of the Rail there should be a Gate for the Inhabitants of Wilford aforesaid for the carriage of Crops growing in the Meadow of Wilford together with passage for their Cattle as there shall be Occasion and the said Rail towards the further part of the said Manor of Lenton towards the West (that is to say) to the West part of a certain place called Prior Wong from thence abutting upon the Meadows of Beeston in the County aforesaid to the West of the said Manor of Lenton, divided and separated from the aforesaid Manor of Wilford by the aforesaid Bank and River Trent to Beeston Stoopes. And afterwards the said Jurors on their Oaths say that the said Manor of Lenton particularly and separately extends to the

place called Beeston Stoopes leaving the Horse Doles towards
a close in the aforesaid Manor of Lenton called [word illegible]
Terry's Close and from thence by the Exterior Hedge of a
certain Close called the Rounds and then following the Hedge
towards [word omitted] called Tuttle berry Gate [1] and from
thence by the Hedge of a certain close within the aforesaid
Manor of Lenton called Broom Close towards ―― Gate and
thus by the Hedge of a certain Field belonging to Francis
Willougbie Knight of Woollaton in the said County of
Nottingham called the Fat Field and so by the Hedge
surrounding a Field called the Sixty Acres to the Gate [called]
Derby Gate and from the said Gate by the Hedge belonging
to our Lady the Queen round one side of the Fields of Lenton
towards a wood called Aspley Wood, half of which is lying and
being in the parish of Bilborrow in the County of Nottingham
aforesaid and so round the said Wood towards a stone called
Franches Stone, which divides the Manor of Lenton aforesaid
from the lands of Anthony Strelley Knight through a parcel of
his Manor of Bilborrow and from the aforesaid Stone towards
a certain Syke [2] between the aforesaid Manor of Lenton and
the Manor of Basford in the said County of Nottingham and
thus following the said Syke to the River Lyne and so
descending by the River Lyne to the Mill called Blackcliff and
from the said Mill to the south end of a close belonging to a
Tenement called Eland Hall and from thence to a Double
Ditch between the said Manor of Lenton and the said Manor
of Basford and then ascending the Top of a Hill called Tohow
and from thence descending by a small Ditch to a certain way
called the Cross way and so descending to a Dale called Swine
Dale so by a way through the middle called the Dale, following
the Metes and Bounds to a stone called Franches Stone of
Nottingham near the Malt Mill and from the said Mill by the
Metes and Bounds of the Town of Nottingham (that is to say)
the Bounder Stoole to the Meadow of our Lady the Queen of

---

(1) The word gate, here and elsewhere, signifies a road. The word with this
signification was formerly in common use throughout the northern parts of England,
and is of Norse origin.

(2) This is an old local word, now nearly obsolete, signifying a small stream of
running water.

Nottingham by the West part of the said Meadow to the River Lyne and over the Water to a Hedge of the Meadow called the King's Meadow where it begins. And Lastly the said Jurors upon their Oaths say that the said Jervas Clifton Knight and his ancestors and all others whose Estates the said Jervas now holds in the said Manor of Wilford of which the Memory of Man is not to the contrary freely and wholly possessed and enjoyed all the water of the River Trent aforesaid contiguous adjacent and running by the Manor of Lenton aforesaid with the course and bed of the same water separately to fish in the same by himself his men and servants Except that all the Inhabitants within the said Manor of Lenton ought to have a passage through the aforesaid Water of the Trent to water and refresh all their cattle from time to time. In witness whereof &c A.D. 1575."

After the dissolution of Lenton Priory, the manor was retained by the Crown until about the commencement of the reign of King Charles the First, when it was granted to the corporation of the City of London. In 1628, the manor of Lenton, together with the ancient fair and all royalties, privileges, rents, and services, thereunto belonging, was granted in fee farm, by letters patent, dated September the 9th, that same year, to Edward Dichfield, salter, John Highlord, skinner, Humphrey Clarke, dyer, and Francis Mosse, scrivener, citizens of London, who were constituted commissioners, and duly authorised and empowered by the Lord Mayor, Aldermen, and Commoners-of the said city, to sell and dispose of such manors, lordships, lands and tenements, as had been granted to them by King Charles the First. Accordingly, by their indenture, dated November the 6th, 1630, the said Edward Dichfield, John Highlord, Humphrey Clarke, and Francis Mosse, sold to William Gregory, gentleman, one of the aldermen of Nottingham, for the sum of £2,500, the manor of Lenton with all due appurtenances, excepting an annual fee-farm rent of £94, which had been reserved by the Crown.[1]

Alderman William Gregory, the purchaser of the manor of

---

(1) Thoroton, p. 219.

Lenton, served as one of the sheriffs of the town of Nottingham in 1618, and was mayor in 1632, and again in 1639. Thoroton says of him that he had by agricultural pursuits " raised a very considerable estate from the lowest beginning " ; [1] yet it seems that he claimed to be descended, through a younger branch, from an ancient family seated at High Hurst, in Lancashire. Sufficient evidence of such descent was not, however, forth-coming at the Visitation of 1662, when armorial bearings were granted to the Nottingham family. The will of " William Gregory, of the town and county of the town of Nottingham, gentleman, one of the aldermen of the said town," which is dated June the 18th, 1650, was proved in London, before the judges for the probate of wills, by his elder son, John Gregory, February the 5th, 1650-1. He devised thereby all those three water corn-mills, with two houses, eight crofts, tofts, closes, or pingles, and eleven acres of land belonging to the same mills, in the parishes of Lenton and Radford, and all his tithe of hay growing within the liberties and territories of Lenton and Radford, to his grandson, George Gregory, eldest son of his son, John Gregory, and to the heirs of his body in tail, and if he should die without lawful issue, he devised the same, in like manner, to his grandsons, Philip Gregory, Francis Gregory, and Edward Gregory, the second, third, and fourth sons of the said John Gregory, in priority of birth successively, and to their heirs, in tail. The whole residue of his lands in the county of Nottingham, and within the town and county of the town of Nottingham, he devised to his elder son, the said John Gregory, and his heirs.

The fee-farm rent of the manor of Lenton, reserved by the Crown, had been granted, by letters patent, dated December the 16th, 1638, to James Stuart, Duke of Lennox and Richmond, and was sold by that nobleman, February the 20th, 1650-1, for £1,460, to the above-named John Gregory, and to George Gregory, his eldest surviving son and heir.[2]

This John Gregory (who, like his father, had espoused the

---

(1) Thoroton, p. 479.　　　　(2) Thoroton, p. 219.

Parliamentary cause in the civil wars [1]) died in January, 1654-5, and by his will, which is dated December the 20th, 1654, and proved at York in the Prerogative Court, he devised his manor of Lenton, with his lands in Lenton and Radford, to his eldest daughter, Elizabeth, until such time as his eldest surviving son, George Gregory, should attain the age of twenty-one years. His widow survived him for more than twenty-five years, and by her will, dated September the 8th, 1681, and proved in the Prerogative Court of York, that same year, she bequeathed to her son, George Gregory, her great silver tankard ; to her daughter, Anne Dand, her diamond ring with six stones ; to her daughter, Winifred Gregory, the diamond ring that her husband had given her; to her daughter, Susanna Gregory, the wife of her son, George Gregory, she bequeathed her amethyst ring ; and there are various small pecuniary legacies.

In 1662, George Gregory, Esquire, the eldest surviving son and heir to the above-named John Gregory, having obtained a patent of armorial bearings, entered his pedigree in the Heralds' Visitation. About a year later, he had permission, by letters patent, dated November 9th, 1663, for another fair to be held within his manor of Lenton, upon the first Wednesday after the feast of Pentecost, and on the six following days. He served as High Sheriff of the county in 1666, and dying in 1684,[2] was buried in St. Mary's Church, Nottingham. His eldest surviving son, George Gregory, Esquire, was High Sheriff for the county in 1694, and for some years represented the borough of Nottingham in the Whig interest. He was also appointed one of the Storekeepers of Ordnance, and was likewise a commissioner "for the sale of rebels' estates," after the futile attempt to restore the Stuart dynasty in 1715. His descendants (who subsequently were seated at Harlaxton Manor, in Lincoln-

---

(1) His name appears, together with James Chadwick, Esquire, Huntingdon Plumptre, M. D., and Alderman John James, as commissioner for collecting the weekly assessment in the town of Nottingham for the payment of the army raised by the Parliament, and to defray other expenses incurred during the civil contentions.

(2) The old mansion in Nottingham, in which this gentleman resided, and which was partly rebuilt by him in 1674, stood on what was then called Swine's Green, near the top of Pelham Street. Messrs. Wrights' Bank now occupies some portion of the site. The mansion is shown in Thoroton's "North East Prospect of Nottingham," and also in an engraving of the "East Prospect of Nottingham," originally drawn by Thomas Sandby, about the year 1750.

4

shire, as may be seen on reference to the accompanying pedigree) continued in possession of the chief manor of Lenton for a considerable number of years.

In 1860, upon the the death of George Gregory, Esquire, the last male heir of this family, the manor devolved upon John Sherwin Sherwin, of Bramcote Hills, Esquire,[1] who was vested as the next in succession under the entail of the will of the late George de Ligne Gregory, Esquire, and who thereupon assumed the name and arms of Gregory, by royal license. John Sherwin Gregory, Esquire, had no issue, and upon his decease, June the 7th, 1869, the manor passed, by devise, to his widow, Mrs. Catherine Sherwin Gregory, who is the present lady of the manor, and one of the chief owners of the soil.

The manor is now reputed to include all such portions of the parishes of Lenton and Radford as did not anciently constitute any part of the demesne lands of Lenton Priory.

The View of the Frank pledge or Great Court Leet, with the Court Leet of the Lady of the Manor, is held on the Tuesday in Easter week. The court roll does not, however, contain many items of interest. The following are taken from the lists of fines :—

April 21, 1747. "Humphrey Hopkins for not scouring his Ditch at Blotoff   -   -   -   -   -   -   6d."
April 4, 1749. "William Dickinson for neglecting to do his Duty as a Juryman along with his ffellows and deserting such his Service   -   -   -   -   -   -   1s."
"Robert Cassells for the like heinous offence   -   1s."

On April 24th in the same year, we find that "Rebecca Garland was admitted as a Freeholder of Lenton at this Court."

Another entry states that Rebecca Garland took the oath of fealty to the Lord of the Manor, April 20th, 1762.

---

(1) There was only a very distant connection between the two families. Reference to the Gregory pedigree will show that Barbara, daughter of George Gregory, of Nottingham, Esq., married George Needham, of Little Wymondley, in the county of Hertford, Esq. The issue of this marriage was three daughters, one of whom became the wife of John Sherwin, Esq., High Sheriff of this county in 1721, who was the maternal great-grandfather of the above-named John Sherwin Sherwin, Esq.

## THE MANOR OF MORTON.

The manor of Morton, which was also within the limits of this parish, seems to have been of superior importance and value to the manor of Lenton at the time when the Domesday survey was taken.

In MORTVNE, hb Boui. I. car' tre 7 dim ad gld. Tra
XII. bou. Ibi Will's h't. I. car' 7 dim' 7 V. soch' de III.
bou huj' tre. 7 XII. vill 7 I. bord' h'ntes. IX. car' 7 dim'.
T. R. E. 7 m° val'. XX. sol'.

[Translation] " In Mortune, Boui had one carucate of land and a half to be taxed. Land to twelve oxen. William has there one plough and a half, and five sokemen who hold three oxgangs of this land, and twelve villanes and one bordar, having nine ploughs and a half. Value in King Edward's time, and now, twenty shillings."

Together with that of Lenton, this manor was bestowed upon the Priory by William Peverel, but it would appear that from an early period it became absorbed in the manor of Lenton, as it yet remains.

It is probable that the manor of Morton extended over the more southern portion of the parish, there being (as already mentioned) some meadows yet known as " The Mortons," lying near the Dunkirk bridge over the canal, midway between the old village of Lenton and the river Trent.

## THE MANOR OF ELMORE.

This was an inferior manor, not referred to in the Domesday survey, and doubtless of more recent origin. There is reason to believe that it was acquired by the Martell family, of Chilwell and Ruddington, and passed, through marriage with the heiress, to Sir William Babington, of Chilwell, Knight.

Sir William Babington was the second of the five sons of Sir John Babington, of East Bridgford, in this county, Knight, (who died 1409) by his wife Benedicta, daughter and heir of Simon

Ward, of Cambridgeshire.[1] The family was descended from
Sir Bernard Babington, lord of Over Babington and Nether
Babington, in the county of Northumberland. Thoroton says,
" I find John Babington resident at Briggeford in the time of
Richard the second, and Henry the fourth."[2] This was the
father of Sir William Babington, who, as already stated, became
lord of the manor of Elmore, in this parish, presumably in right
of his wife. Following the profession of law, he eventually
raised himself thereby to a high position, so that a few details
of his career may not be out of place. He was appointed
Attorney-General, January 16th, 1413, and a year and a half
later became a serjeant-at-law. Babington, and others who were
summoned at the same time, neglected to assume the functions
of serjeants, and there not being a sufficient number to carry on
the business of the courts, a complaint was made to Parliament
in November, 1417. An order was issued forthwith, subjecting
them to severe penalties if they persisted in their neglect ; but,
upon their promise of obedience, they had a respite until the
following Trinity term.[3] Babington was appointed Chief Baron
of the Exchequer, November 4th, 1419, and in the same year
he was joint patron with William Tresham, of the church of
Broughton, in Northamptonshire.[4] He was elevated to the
office of Chief Justice of the Common Pleas, May 5th, 1422, [5]
and resigned that of Coroner of the King's Bench, October
22nd, of the same year. Sir William was created a Knight of
the Bath, either at the coronation of Henry the Sixth, or in the
year 1426.[6] He is mentioned in the Minutes of the Privy
Council on May 18th, 1 Henry VI., and November 4th, 1428.
In 1430, Sir William Babington's name occurs in a deed relating
to the property of his son-in-law, Ralph Leek, of Kirketon,
Esquire.[7] In 11 Henry VI., his name occurs again in a deed
concerning the advowson of the church of South Normanton, in

(1) *Visitation of Notts.* (Harleian Soc., p. 150). Foss, *Judges*, iv. 283.

(2) Thoroton, *History of Nottinghamshire*, p. 151.

(3) Foss, *Judges*, iv. 284 ; *Rot. Parl.*, iv. 107.

(4) Bridge's *Northamptonshire*, ii. 86.

(5) *Cal. Rot. Pat.*, 262, 267, 269 ; 1423, according to Foss, iv., 284.

(6) Harl. MS , 5809, f. 80.            (7) Thoroton, *Nottinghamshire*, p. 129.

this county.[1]   He resigned the Chief Justiceship of the Common
Pleas after thirteen years' service, February 9th, 1436.[2]   On
February 14th, 1436, his name is marked in a list for " c.*li.*" as a
loan for the equipment of an army for France.[3]   On June 25th,
1442, he had a license, with others, to found a chantry for two
chaplains at the altar of St. Catherine, in the church of St.
Peter, at Thurgarton, Notts., to pray for the good estate of King
Henry VI., Sir William Lovell, Knight, and Alice, his wife.
Ralph, Lord Cromwell, of Tattershall, and Margaret, his wife,
Sir William Babington, Knight, and divers of the noble family
of Deincourt, and others, and for the repose of their souls when
they should die.[4]   This license does not seem, however, to have
been fully acted upon, for the foundation of the chantry was not
completed during Sir William Babington's lifetime.   On April
16th, 1455, he was summoned to attend a meeting of the Privy
Council for·May 21st;[5]   and on May 14th, his name is included
with those of four other persons (the Prior of Lenton being one)
as a commissioner for raising money in Nottinghamshire for the
siege of Calais.[6]   Sir William Babington had married Margaret,
daughter and heir of Sir Peter Martell, of Chilwell, Knight.[7]
She died February 2nd, 1442, and was buried in Flawforth
Church.   By his will, dated October 3rd, 1454, and proved in
the Prerogative Court of York, Sir William Babington desires
thereby to be buried in the church of the Holy Trinity, at
Lenton (*Monasterii de Lentona*), in the chapel of St. Mary, " *de
novo ibidem constructa;*"[8] and gave eighteen pounds of wax to
be made into fifty candles to burn round his tomb; and to every
priest present at his funeral and obituary masses he gave the
sum of eighteenpence ; whilst to the Priory of Lenton he gave
forty marcs, or two sets of vestments, namely : two chasubles,

(1) Privy Council Proc., iv., 289, 327.        (2) Foss, *Judges,* iv., 285.

(3) Privy Council Proc., iv., 289, 327.        (4) Thoroton, *Nottinghamshire,* p. 305.

(5) Privy Council Proc., vi., 341.        (6) Ibid, vi., 243.

(7) The mansion at Chilwell, occupied by the Martells, and subsequently by Sir
William Babington and his descendants, stood on the site where Chilwell Hall, the
residence of Thomas Broughton Charlton, Esq., now stands.   When Thoroton wrote
his " Antiquities of Nottinghamshire," a part of the original mansion seems to have
still been in existence, and he mentions some stained glass in one of the windows
representing the arms of *Babington,* impaling *Martell.*

(8) *Testamenta Eboracensia* (Surtees Soc.), ii., 5.

with as many tunicles, and three copes, with albs, stoles, and maniples. He also made bequests to the Grey Friars, and to White Friars, in Nottingham, and to the churches of St. Peter, Nottingham ; Beeston, Attenborough, and Rolleston. By the double inquisition, *post mortem*, 33 Henry VI. (1455), Sir William Babington died seized of various manors and lands in Bedfordshire, Salop, Nottinghamshire, and Derbyshire.[1] The latter inquisition refers to a chantry in Flawforth Church, in this county, the foundation of which was contemplated by Sir William Babington and his wife's relatives, and towards which his wife contributed 600 marcs, but the foundation was actually completed by his son William,[2] who endowed the same with lands in various parishes, including forty acres of arable, and sixteen acres of meadow land in Lenton, presumably part of the manor of Elmore. The foundation was completed some time previous to the year 1460. Sir William Babington

having lived to the age of ninety-nine years in "godly life and conversation," his son, William Babington, Esquire, was found by inquisition to be his son and heir. The arms of Babington were—*Argent*, ten torteaux, over all a label of three points, *azure*.

No other reference to the manor of Elmore has been met with, nor is it known what portion of the parish was included within its limits.

In 1276, Hugh Croft held, *int. al.*, two mills in Radford and Lenton by the service of carrying a falcon at the summons of the king, and Richard Grey held them under him.[3]

In 1290, there was a suit between John de Grym and Geoffrey de Gresley, concerning eight messuages and other property in Lenton and elsewhere.[4]

---

(1) *Inq. p.m.*, iv., 163, 298.   (2) Proc. in Chancery, i., 101.   Thoroton, p. 66.
(3) *Rot. Hund.*, ii., 314.   (4) *Ab placitor*, p. 231.

In 1335, William de Wynthorpe, clerk, held certain lands in Lenton for the Prior and Convent of Newstead [1]

In 1354, William Beston, rector of Cotgrave, held lands, etc., in Lenton,[2] with which he partly endowed the chantry of St. Catherine in Beeston Church, as will be more fully detailed hereafter.

In the Records of the Borough of Nottingham are several documents referring to lands in Lenton.

In the reign of King Edward the Second, Robert, son of Geoffrey de Lenton,[3] granted to John de Henovere, burgess of Nottingham, two selions of arable land lying upon "Blacclivegate,"[4] between which lies the land of William, son of William the Parson, which lands lie "*in territorio de Lenton.*" William de Lenton was a witness to this deed.[5]

On June 25th, 1301, Roger, son of William de Lenton, granted to Hugh de Wolaton, of Nottingham, half an acre of arable land in the fields of Lenton and Radford, lying in the Longebothem, between the road which is called "Caketherngate" on the east, and the land of Henry de Wolaton on the west, and abutting upon the king's highway which is called "Derbigate" towards the south, and upon the land of William Kaytsank towards the north. Robert, son of Geoffrey de Lenton, was one of the witnesses to this grant.[6]

On March 2nd, 1334, John, son of John de Henovere, of Nottingham, granted the same two selions to Henry de Cesterfield, of Nottingham.[7]

On April 16th, 1316, Alice, who was the wife of Augustin de Athillewell, [Chillewelle ?] of Nottingham, in her pure widow-

---

(1) *Cal. Inq. p.m.*                (2) *Inq. p.m.*, ii., 190.

(3) Of the many persons who have borne the surname of *Lenton*, we may mention :—
*Simon de Lenton*, Bailiff of Nottingham, 1327—8.
*John de Lenton*, vicar of Ashbourne, Derbyshire, 1333 to 1349, when he resigned.
*William de Lenton*, sacrist of Lichfield Cathedral, and immediate predecessor of Roger le Mareschall, who held the same office in 1346.
*John de Lenton*, vicar of St. Michael's, Derby, from 1487 to his death in 1491.
*Thomas Lenton* occurs as Abbot of Pipewell in 1535.

(4) The mill of Blackcliff is often referred to amongst the possessions of Lenton Priory. This land evidently adjoined the road leading to the mill.

(5) *Records of the Borough of Nottingham*, i., 365.

(6) Ibid, i., 370.                (7) Ibid, i., 396.

hood, released to William de Mekesburgh, her right in one acre and a half of arable land in the field of Lenton.[1]

John, son of Ralph de Wollaton, of Nottingham, July 29th, 1369, granted to William de Crescy, vicar of the church of Greasley, and to Roger, parson of the church of Nuthall, all his lands and tenements, rents, services, etc., in the towns of Nottingham, Lenton, and Radford, which formerly belonged to William de Amyas, of Nottingham, and which descended to him after the death of the said William, excepting the annual rent from divers tenements assigned to the chantry founded by the said William.[2]

On October 23rd, 1370, the above named William de Crescy, and Roger, granted the said lands, etc., to John Wolaton, of Watnowe, son of Ralph de Wolaton, of Nottingham, and to Margery, his wife.[3]

" In the 22nd Henry VI. a fine was levied between John Cokefield, Esquire, and Margaret his wife, querent, and Richard Bingham and William Foljambe, defendants, of the manor of Nuthall and Basford, with lands in Radford and Lenton, and the advowson of Nuthall, the right of John and Margaret his wife. By an inquisition 4th Edw. IV., it is found that Margaret, wife of John Cokefield, was seized of the manor of Nuthall, etc., as before, and that John Cokefield died without issue, and that Margaret was sister to Sir Thomas Foljambe, Knight, and that Thomas Foljambe, son and heir of Thomas Foljambe, is her heir, and is four years old." [4]

The above-named Margaret Cokefield was the daughter of . . . Foljambe, and widow of Ralph Monboucher, Esquire. She afterwards married John Cokefield, of Nuthall, Esquire, who died in 1453, and by whom she had no issue. By her will, dated at Wollaton, 15 kal. July, 1462, and in which she describes herself as " Ego domina Margareta Cokefeld," she desires to be buried in the chapel of the Blessed Mary, in the church of St. Patrick, at Nuthall, near to John Cokefield, her late husband.

---

(1) *Records of Borough of Nottingham*, i., 379.

(2) Ibid, i., 408.　　　(3) Ibid, i., 408.

(4) *Notices of Family of Foljambe*, by Nathaniel Johnston, M.D., 1701. Gough MSS., Bodl. Lib.

She bequeathed to the confraternity of the Holy Trinity of Nottingham (this appears to have been Lenton Priory), "a chest overlaid and bound with iron, for her own soul and the souls of her benefactors." [1] On the death of John Cokefield, the husband of Dame Margaret, the representation of the ancient family of Cokefield, or Cockfield, had centred in the issue of Agnes Cokefield, who married John Taylboys, of Stallingborough, in Lincolnshire, by whom she had a son, John, whose only daughter and heiress, Margaret, married John Ayscough, Esquire. Dame. Margaret Cockfield, when she made her will, must have been well stricken in years. She was probably residing with her relatives, the Willoughbys, at Wollaton, and the bequest of the remainder of her substance to her cousin, Richard Willoughby, was no doubt an acknowledgment of the kindness and attention of his family.

The following account of an aggravated assault committed at Lenton, taken from the proceedings in the Borough Court of Nottingham, August 16th, 1437, is sufficiently interesting to be given in full :—

"John Gilbert and Joan his wife in their own proper persons complain of John Malefield, of Nottingham, wright, of a plea of trespass against the peace of our Lord the present King. And whereupon they say that the aforesaid John Malefield, at the feast of the Holy Trinity, in the 15th year of the reign of King Henry the Sixth, here at Nottingham, with force and arms, to wit, with a club and dagger, lay in ambush and made an assault upon the aforesaid Joan, wife of the aforesaid John Gilbert ; and beat, wounded and evilly treated her, so that her life was despaired of, and other injuries did to her, to the grievous damage of the aforesaid John Gilbert and Joan his wife, and against the peace of our Lord the King aforesaid : whereby they say that they are injured and have damage to the value of 100s. ; and therefore they bring suit. And the aforesaid John Malefield comes in his own proper person, and as to the coming with force and arms, etc., and whatsoever there is that is against the peace of our Lord the King aforesaid, and all the rest of the trespass aforesaid supposed to have been committed, he says that he is thereof in nowise guilty ; and as to the remainder of the trespass aforesaid, the same John Malefield says that the aforesaid John Gilbert and Joan his wife ought not to have an action against him, because he says that the aforesaid Joan together

---

with one Margery her daughter with abusive and quarrelsome
words, at Lenton without the liberty of the town of Nottingham,
in the house of one Robert Daniel, made an assault upon him,
John Malefield, and called him 'false thief' (*falstheff*), and
continued the same assault thence to the place where the trespass
aforesaid is supposed to have been committed, and the aforesaid
Joan, taking the said John Malefield by the neck, threw him on
the ground; and the damage that the same Joan had and
received was of her own proper assault: all and singular of
which the same John Malefield is ready to verify as the Court,
etc.: wherefore he does not think that any wrong can be assigned
against his person; and he prays judgment, if the aforesaid
plaintiffs ought to maintain their aforesaid action against him.
And the aforesaid John Gilbert and Joan his wife say that they
ought not to be excluded from their aforesaid action for
anything before-alleged, because they say, that the damage that
the same Joan had was of the wrong and assault of the said
John Malefield, and not of the assault of the said Joan; and
this they seek to verify by the country, etc. To which the same
John Malefield, protesting that he does not acknowledge any of
the things before-alleged by the aforesaid John Gilbert and Joan,
says as he has above pleaded, and that the damage that she
had was of the assault and wrong of the aforesaid Joan: all and
singular of which in manner and form aforesaid before-alleged
and pleaded he is ready to verify; wherefore he prays judgment,
and that the aforesaid John Gilbert and Joan he precluded from
their aforesaid action, etc.—Judgment is respited until the
coming of the Recorder on account of the diversity of the
plea."

The inhabitants of Lenton at this period do not appear in a
very favourable light. The following extract is from the list of
fines in the Borough Court of Nottingham for the year 1467-8. [2]

"Surety for the fine of John Daubes, of Lenton, for regrating
of corn in common market before the striking of the bell
assigned for this purpose, by surety: William Thornes."

In the Borough Records of Nottingham [3] there is a quaint
contract for building a house, dated July 20th, 1479, and made
between William Hurst, of Nottingham, of the one part, and
Pers Hydes and Roger Hydes, of Lenton, of the other part, the
builders. The amount of the contract was six pounds, and the
penalty for failing to complete the work within a specified time

(1) *Records of Borough of Nottingham*, ii. 162.

(2) Ibid, ii. 275.            (3) Ibid, ii. 389.

was ten pounds. William Hurst subsequently sued Roger Hydes for breach of contract.

William Willoughby, Esq., of Normanton-on-Soar, by his will, dated October 3rd, 1587, left to his son Gilbert, and his heirs and assigns, all his lands in Nottingham, Lenton, and Radford, on the fulfilment of certain specified conditions. From the slight distinction in their armorial bearings, these Willoughbys were presumably a branch of the ancient house of Willoughby, of Wollaton, though their precise descent does not seem to be recorded. Thomas Willoughby, the first of this branch of whom we have evidence, was a wealthy alderman of Nottingham, living in the time of King Henry the Eighth.

The Edges, of Strelley, were also landowners in this parish, though their estate here seems to have been but small. Walter Edge, of Nottingham, Attorney-at-law, the first of this family who was connected with the neighbourhood, died in 1660, and by his will, dated on the 7th of April in that year, he devised all his lands in Nottingham, Southwell, Upton, and Lenton, to his eldest son, Ralph. This Ralph Edge, who subsequently acquired the Strelley estates, died without issue, September the 4th, 1684. He is described upon his tomb-stone in Strelley Church as "an eminent Attorney-at-law, who was some time Town Clerk, upwards of twenty years Alderman, and thrice Mayor of the Corporation of Nottingham, and Justice of the Peace for this County." From "a rentall of the estate late of Ralph Edge, Esq^r, dec^d, as the same is lett in the yeare of our Lord, 1691," it appears that all he had possessed in Lenton was a cottage and a cow gate, then in the tenancy of one Abraham Adams. Richard Edge, Esq., subsequently occurs as a freeholder in Lenton, and Ralph Edge, Esq., at a somewhat later period.

Exclusive of that portion of the parish which anciently formed the Priory demesne, and of which full particulars will be given hereafter, the principal landowners at the present time are, the lady of the manor, Mrs. Catherine Sherwin Gregory, Henry Abel Smith, Esq., of Wilford, and the Right Hon. Lord Middleton.

# SECTION III.

## AREA, POPULATION, &c.

REVIOUS to the year 1877, the parish of Lenton consisted of Old and New Lenton, Bestwood Park, and part of the ecclesiastical district of Hyson Green, the area of the parish being then about 6,327 acres, made up as follows :—

|  | A. | R. | P. |
|---|---|---|---|
| Old and New Lenton (about) - | 2,326 | 0 | 32 |
| Portion of Wollaton Park - - | 112 | 0 | 15 |
| Bestwood Park - - - - | 3,711 | 3 | 21 |
| Part of Hyson Green - - | 176 | 3 | 12 |
| Total | 6,327 | 0 | 0 |

When the parish of Lenton was annexed to the Borough of Nottingham by Act of Parliament in 1877, Bestwood Park was detached from the parish, and the area was consequently reduced to 2,615 acres.

By an order of the Local Government Board, dated December 11th, 1880, and issued under "The Divided Parishes and Poor Law Amendment Act, 1876," and "The Poor Law Act, 1879," the portions of the parish of Radford hereafter described ceased to be parts of that parish, and were amalgamated with the parish of *Lenton*, the order taking effect on the eighteenth day of March, 1881.

(1.) The isolated and detached part of the parish of Radford, known as the Bleach Works, Park Road, Lenton, which is locally included in the parish of Lenton, and containing 1a. 0r. 22p., or thereabouts.

(2) The isolated and detached part of the parish of Radford known as the Mill, Marsh Road, also locally included in the parish of Lenton, and containing 1a. 1r. 8p., or thereabouts.

(3.) The ·nearly isolated and detached part of the parish of Radford lying to the south of an imaginary line running along the middle of the Ilkeston Road, Nottingham, known as part of Wollaton Park, Canal and Wharf, and adjoining the parish of Lenton.

(4.) That part of the parish of Radford lying to the south of an imaginary line running along the middle of the Ilkeston Road aforesaid, known as Cobden Park (including the Gas Works), and adjoining the said parish of Lenton.

(5.) That part of the parish of Radford lying to the south of the imaginary line aforesaid, known as Sion Hill, and adjoining the said parish of Lenton.

By another order of the Local Government Board, dated December 11th, 1880, it was ordered that on and after March 18th, 1881, the following isolated and detached parts of the parish of Lenton should cease to be parts of that parish, and be amalgamated with the parish of *Radford*.

(1.) All that portion of Hyson Green which previously formed part of the parish of Lenton, containing 176a. 3r. 12p., or thereabouts.

(2.) That isolated, irregular shaped portion of the parish of Lenton, situated between Ilkeston Road and Bilborough Road, and between Radford Station and the canal.

The effect of these orders was an improvement in the boundary of Lenton Parish, at the cost of a curtailment of its area, which is now estimated at 2,080 acres.

## POPULATION.

|  | Inhabited Houses. | Total Population. |
|---|---|---|
| 1801 |  | 893 |
| 1811 |  | 1197 |
| 1821 | . | 1240 |
| 1831 | 631[1] | 3077[2] |
| 1841[3] |  | 3436 |
| 1851 | 1089 | 4527 |
| 1861 | 1274 | 5828 |
| 1871 |  | 6315 |
| 1881 | 1887 | 9246[4] |

In the Subsidy Roll for the year 1666,[5] taken in pursuance of
" An Act for raising Moneys by a Poll, and otherwise towards
the maintenance of the present war, made in the xviijth yeare
of the Reigne of our Soveraigne Lord King Charles the second,"
we find the following entry :—

" Francis Revell and John Greene subcollectors
of Lenton for the sum of -　-　-　-　11l.　12s.　od."

The total amount raised in the hundred of
Broxtow being　-　-　-　-　-　£420　13s.　10d.

" The Names of the ffreholders y[t] Poll'd at the County-Court
held at Nottingham, the 18th & 19th of August, 1698, for
Electing Members to serve in Parliament for the County of
Nottingham.

*Lenton.*

John Tompson
Thomas Oldham
Thomas Lister
Henry Bernard
William Rudsby [6]

---

(1) No less than 400 had been built since 1821.
(2) Exclusive of 10 prisoners in the Peverel Prison.
(3) In 1844 there were 764 houses, and 4,467 inhabitants.
(4) 4,344 being males, and 4,902 females.
(5) Subsidy Roll, $\frac{180}{332}$　　(6) Harl. MS., 6,846, f. 325.

At the election in April, 1722, for two members of Parliament for the county of Nottingham, the following residents in Lenton polled in respect of freeholds situated elsewhere :—

Thomas Allicock for a freehold at Lambley.
William Asson    „    „    Basford.
Thomas Lester    „    „    Bramcote.
Richard Norris    „    „    Greaves Lane.

The following persons held freeholds in Lenton, but resided elsewhere :—

Edward Attenborough, of Beeston.
George Gregory, Esq., of Nottingham.
Thomas Hunt, of Nottingham.
Henry Porter, gent., of Nottingham.

The assessment, or levy, of the parish made in the year 1743, upon the basis of a valuation made eleven years previously, and which contains a complete list of all the ratepayers at that period, is still in existence. It commences, "An Assessm$^t$ or Levy Upon all Men's Lands w$^{th}$ in y$^e$ Parish and Libertys of Lenton made y$^e$ 1$^{st}$ of June 1743 according to Every Man's Rent after y$^e$ Rate of 1$^d$ one penny in y$^e$ pound according to a Rentall Upon Every Man's Estate w$^{th}$ in y$^e$ P$^{sh}$ and Liberty afores$^d$ taken on y$^e$ 29$^{th}$ of June 1732." The total amount of a rate at one penny in the pound amounted to £7 4 4¾.

In the Poor Rate book for the year 1825, the parish is divided into districts as follows :—Hill Side ; Town Street; Leen Gate ; Abbey ; Trent Side and Dunkirk ; High Fields ; Mr. Milnes' Property ; Mr. Surplice's Property ; Gardens near the Park ; Nottingham Tenants; Beeston ; Radford ; Lord Middleton ; Bestwood Park ; Ison Green (Lenton Row, Union Row, and Lumley Place); and Middleton Place.

The following table will show the extraordinary increase in the rateable value of the parish within the last hundred and forty years :—

| £ | | | | £ | | |
|---|---|---|---|---|---|---|
| 1743 | - | - | 1,722. | 1840 | - | - | 9,869. |
| 1782 | - | - | 1,748. | 1845 | - | - | 11,882. |
| 1793 | - | - | 1,760. | 1849 | - | - | 16,500. |
| 1805 | - | - | 2,603. | 1876-7 | - | - | 26,318. |
| 1814 | - | - | 3,301. | 1879 | - | - | 29,870. |
| 1825 | - | - | 6,869. | 1881 | - | - | 31,803. |
| 1837 | - | - | 8,380. | 1883 | - | - | 35,105. |

In olden times parochial perambulations were important institutions.

> " That ev'ry man might keep his owne possessions,
> Our father's used, in reverent Processions
> (With zealous prayers, and with praiseful cheere),
> To walke their parish-limits once a year ;
> And well knowne marks (which sacrilegious hands
> Now cut or breake) so bord'red out their lands,
> That ev'ry one distinctly knewe his owne ;
> And many brawles, now rife, were then unknowne."
> Wither's *Emblems*, fol. 1635, p. 161.

The following are all the dates we have been able to collect from the various parish books of the occasions on which the parish of Lenton has been perambulated by its officials.

*Bestwood Park*—May 5, 1719 ; May 13, 1724 ; May 14, 1729 ; May 21, 1734 ; May 31, 1739 ; May 24, 1759 ; May 11, 1802 ; May 20, 1019 ; May 1, 1856 ; May 29, 1862. *Wollaton Park*—May 28, 1728 ; May 26, 1731 ; May 31, 1764 ; June 2, 1859. Other portions of the parish were perambulated in 1787, 1799, May 13, 1847 ; May 17, 1855.

Probably the most notable perambulation in the parish of Lenton was the one made May 1, 1856, of the detached portion of the parish known as Bestwood Park. The following account of the proceedings on that occasion illustrates the public spirit of Lenton at that period.

Thursday last being May Day (1856). was a great day in the parish of Lenton, and that too in a part little accustomed to have the welkin roused with the *vox populi*. It appears, however, that for three years past the parish officers of this spirited village and extensive parish, have been engaged in completing a perambulation of their boundaries, and in placing boundary stones, scribes, and paint marks. The two preceding years having been devoted to the perambulation of the home bounds of the parish, and of those within Wollaton Park, the present and concluding perambulation was directed towards the famous region of Bestwood Park—once a Royal demesne stocked with deer, and environed by a buck leap of 14 feet all round (to which, it will be seen, the parishioners of Lenton lay especial claim), and distant about five miles from Lenton, in the direction of Mansfield. There has not been a parochial perambulation of the boundaries for the space of 37 or 38 years, although a private perambulation, at the instance of the late Duke of St. Albans, was carried through 15 years ago, in 1841 ; Mr. Thomas Godfrey, of Lenton, being the only person present at the perambulation of Thursday last who had taken a part in it.

Almost by cock crow in the morning the parishioners of Lenton were astir, and the note of preparation resounded through the village—for it was known that the new and spirited churchwarden, Mr. Shaw, would have such a display as to render himself and the occasion illustrious; and it was felt that in the instance of Bestwood Park, where a small portion of the buck leap of 14 feet has been enclosed and planted by the agents of the Duke, the parish of Lenton were embarking on important claims of a business nature. So that, along with the May Day festivities, the more serious details of valuable interests were felt to be at stake.

The office bearers, parishioners of Lenton, and others, having assembled for Morning Service in the parish church at half-past 7 a.m., the prayers and psalms, with the appropriate lessons for the day, were read by the Rev. Mr. Hopkins, the curate of Lenton.

The following hymn for the occasion was composed by William Selby, a parishioner :—

> Lift up your hearts, lift up your voice,
> And in the Lord your God rejoice ;
> His love has been for ages past,
> Oh may it still for ever last !
>
> We go this morning to possess,
> Be with us, and our labours bless :
> Oh guide and guard us with Thy might,—
> Teach us to do the thing that's right !
>
> And whilst our ancient rights we claim,
> We praise and bless Thy holy name ;
> Our labours crown with great success,
> And fill our hearts with holiness.

On the conclusion of Morning Service, the following order of procession was formed in Church Street, and moved off amidst the cheers of a large throng of persons assembled :—

5 .

Mr. Thomas Godfrey, on horseback, with the map.
Two pioneers, mounted.
Two trumpeters, on grey horses.
Mr. Shaw, churchwarden, and 30 gentlemen on horseback,
two and two.
Mr. Shaw's carriage, containing Mr. J. Froggatt, jun., Mr. R.
Browne, Lenton Vicarage, and Mr. S. Froggatt, Lenton Poplars.
Carriage containing the Parish Officers.
Carriages containing the parishioners.

At half-past eight the procession left the church, and after
perambulating the streets of the village amidst admiring crowds,
betwixt 9 and 10 a.m., excited the greatest astonishment whilst
passing down the Derby Road and through the Market Place of
Nottingham, turning up Clumber Street into the line of the
Mansfield Road. Mr. Shaw, who rode from end to end of the
line as it moved rapidly along, attracted throughout much
attention. Having been joined at Sherwood Rise by a number
of the parishioners from Hyson Green, the procession advanced to
" The Old Spot " Inn, on the Mansfield Road, which is situated
not far from the verge of Bestwood Park. Without stopping,
however, they entered the avenue leading to Bestwood Hall, the
residence of George Rawson, Esq., where they were joined by
nearly the whole of the tenantry of His Grace the Duke of St.
Albans, who had assembled to take part in the perambulation.
Having deployed within the avenue, the procession returned to
near its commencement ; and having dismounted, formed into
working order for the perambulation.

At 10 a.m., Mr. Godfrey having assembled around him those
present, to the number of betwixt 100 and 200, intimated that
they had come thither on business, by way of elucidating which
he read the following memorandum :—

" I am directed by the Parish Officers of Lenton to announce
to you that we are assembled here to-day for the purpose of
perambulating and marking the boundary of Bestwood Park,
and we do claim possession of said park as a part and parcel of
the parish of Lenton ; and we this day take possession of the
park accordingly. It may be interesting to our young parishioners to tell them that Bestwood Park contains 3,711 acres,
3 roods, 21 perches of land, and is the property of His Grace the
Duke of St. Albans. The connection of Bestwood Park with
the parish of Lenton is of very early date according to history ;
for we find that King Henry I., during a visit to Nottingham,
granted to the Monastery of Lenton, which was founded in
1105 by William Peverel, two loads of dead wood and heath
daily from Bestwood Park ; which grant it is said constitutes the
foundation of the parochial connection between Lenton and
Bestwood Park. In 1356 the park was inclosed with paling, and
was well stocked with red deer ; and in 1362 King Edward III.

resided here, and dated two letters patent at his park at
Bestwood. About 1676 a large portion for the park was ploughed
up, and there was scarcely wood or venison left. About this
time it was the residence of the celebrated Nell Gwynne, a
mistress of King Charles II., and it has been in the possession
of her descendants, the Dukes of St. Albans, ever since. I
must also tell you that we are come here upon business, and
request order and attention to the business of the day. We
will now proceed and claim 14 feet of the deer leap where it is
not enclosed, and remember that we shall walk on the boundary
of the park, and that all the land to the right hand is in the
parish of Lenton. The usual custom of cutting out the soil and
throwing it over the fence will be observed where the deer leap
is not enclosed."

Mr. Godfrey then proposed "three cheers for Lenton," which
having been raised, business proceeded—the spadesman having
first taken out a spadeful of earth and thrown it over the 14 feet
into a strip of plantation in the park, and a Bestwood boy being
caught and inverted in the cross, with that wholesome ceremonial
of discipline, doubtless invented and exercised by the monks of
old in walking their marches, or by some other ancient teachers
of mankind, as the best mode of lending the rising generation a
smarting recollection of the facts, and thus transmitting them to
*posterity*.

(Here follow particulars of the route of the perambulating
party.)

Being now on the opposite side of Bestwood Park from where
the perambulation had started, Mr. Godfrey, the clerk, again
read over the statement and claim already given—betwixt 100
and 200 persons being again present. After which the whole
company united in singing the doxology, "Praise God from
whom all blessings flow." At the request of Mr. Godfrey, three
cheers were also given for "The Duke of St. Albans," and the
perambulation was resumed.

(Further details of the boundary.)

At last they emerged once more upon the Mansfield Road,
not far from Mr. John Lamin's hospitable farm-house, where the
leaders of the expedition entered with the master of the house,
and were regaled with refreshments. On resuming procedure,
the mounted escort, headed by Mr. Churchwarden Shaw, were
espied at a distance, cantering up to the scene of operations, over
which they kept guard as far as the road at this part admitted.
And here it must be related that it having come to the turn of
the poet laureate of the expedition, William Selby, like all the
other great men of the day, to be inverted for the good of the
parish, he being called upon, gave the assembled perambulators

a specimen of his powers by improvising the following roundelay, standing in the cross :—

> " Near forty years have rolled away
> Since Lenton people here did stray
>      To place there " P " and " L ; "
> Near this spot I well remember
> It was in May and *not November*—
>      The rain in torrents fell.
> Our parson was a hearty fellow,
> And Mr. Nutt held an umbrella
>      Whilst he the prayers did say.
> We now return to trace the Park,
> And place again our bound'ry mark."

(Here follow further particulars of the perambulation until the party returned to the starting point, when) Mr. Godfrey, in conclusion, thanked them for their assistance in carrying it out; and ended by requesting "three cheers for the Queen." Not only were these heartily given, but preceded by the singing of the Royal Anthem, and extended at its close to " three times three." Three cheers were then given " to the health, happiness, and prosperity of the tenants in the park ;" three more " for the Parish Officers and the perambulation ;" and then being marshalled anew in procession, the company, preceded by two trumpeters, retraced their steps.[1]

---

(1) Condensed from the *Nottinghamshire Guardian*, of May 8th, 1856.

# SECTION IV.

## THE PRIORY.

**T**HE Priory of Lenton was one of the multitude of monastic foundations which arose in this country shortly after the Norman Conquest.

The Anglo-Normans were essentially a building people. Architecture was their passion, and castles and abbeys, built, as William of Malmesbury states, in a style that was unknown before, rose wherever they settled. It is most difficult in the present day to realise the immense amount of energy that was thus expended during the century that succeeded the advent of the Conqueror. When we consider the long series of great architectural works belonging to this period in every part of England, and survey the massive grandeur of all their structural features, and the immense solidity of the masonry, and bear in mind the comparatively feeble mechanical resources of those days, we cannot but feel astonished at the indomitable energy and apparently inexhaustible resources such buildings imply, while a feeling of admiration is awakened by the religious zeal which prompted the devotion of the best of the founder's labour, and treasure, and skill, to the honour and glory of God, and the service of His Church.

Henry I., on his accession to the English throne, in the place of his elder brother, Robert, Duke of Normandy, whose crown he had usurped, seeing that it would be to his advantage to conciliate his subjects, granted them various privileges and immunities, and made great concessions to the Church, promising "that at the death of any bishop, or abbot, he would never seize the revenues of the See or Abbey during the vacancy, but would leave the whole to be reaped by the successor ; and that he would never let to farm any ecclesiastical benefice, nor dispose of it for money." The king was especially anxious to gain the confidence of the clergy, because he proposed to marry Matilda, the daughter of Malcolm III., of Scotland, and niece to Edgar Atheling, but, as she had been brought up in a convent, under the charge of her aunt, Christina, abbess of Wilton, or, as some say, of Rumsey, in Hampshire (sister of Edgar Atheling), the legitimacy of the act became a matter of doubt. This difficulty the Church alone could overcome. The unanimous decision of a council of bishops, abbots, and monks, was that Matilda had never taken the vows of a nun, and was therefore free to dispose of herself. The concessions to the Church which have been referred to, together with other circumstances, tending to give confidence to the clergy, caused religious houses to spring up with such rapidity, that, during the thirty-five years of Henry's reign, no fewer than one hundred and fifty were established, the Clugniac Priory of Lenton being amongst the number.

Before, however, detailing the foundation of the monastery, it may be advisable to give some particulars of the Clugniac order, to which the Priory of Lenton belonged.

This order was a reformed congregation, following the Benedictine rule, as finally revised by Odo, of Clugny, about the year 912. The parent house was at Clugny, in Burgundy, the first priory of this order in England being founded at Lewes, in 1077. The churches were noted for their magnificence, and were denounced by St. Bernard in his "Apology" (1127), on account of their enormous height, excessive breadth, empty space, and sumptuous ornament. All the churches of this order in England are now in ruins, Wenlock alone possessing indications of its former glory. Lewes, Castleacre, Bromholm, and Thetford, retain some of the minor conventual buildings. The chief peculiarity of the Clugniac churches in France was a large ante-church, or galilee, for penitents ; but in this country this characteristic of the

normal ground plan is only to be found at Lewes.  In England,
the churches were very irregular in plan, and built chiefly in populous places.   According to strict rule, the first churches, like those
of the Cistercians, were dedicated to St. Mary, and were to be
devoid of organs, pictures, and superfluous carving, painted
crosses of wood only being allowed.   This rule appears to have
been honoured more in its breach than in its observance, for we
find that, from an early period, the churches were richly and
beautifully adorned, and the ceremonial specially elaborate;
William of Malmesbury describing the Clugniacs as "rich in
this world, and of shining piety towards God."   The dress of
the order was a black frock, a pelisse, a hood of lamb's wool,
red hose, a white woollen tunic, and black scapular ; in choir,
copes of linen, and in cloister and refectory, a white pall.   They
occasionally wore a pelisse, a frock, and a cowl of scarlet cloth,
to show their readiness to shed their blood for the sake of Christ.
They had three or four courses at dinner ; electuaries, spiced and
perfumed, and delicate cooking were used.   This general luxu-
riousness led to the great revulsion which ended in the establishment of the Cistercian reform.

"They every day sung two solemn masses, at each of which a
monk of one of the choirs offered two hosts......If any one would
celebrate mass on Holy Thursday, before solemn mass was sung,
he made no use of light, because the new fire was not yet blessed.
The preparation they used for making the bread which was to
serve for the sacrifice of the altar is worthy to be observed.
They first chose the wheat, grain by grain, and washed it very
carefully.   Being put into a bag appointed only for that use, a
servant, known to be a just man, carried it to the mill, washed
the grindstones, covered them with curtains above and below,
and, having put on himself an alb, covered his face with a veil,
nothing but his eyes appearing.   The same precaution was used
with the meal.   It was not boulted till it had been well washed ;
and the warden of the church, if he were either priest or deacon,
finished the rest, being assisted by two other religious men, who
were in the same orders, and by a lay brother particularly
appointed for that business.   These four monks, when Matins
were ended, washed their faces and hands: the three first of

them did put on albs ; one of them washed the meal with pure
clean water, and the other two baked the host in the iron
moulds ; so great was the veneration and respect the monks of
Cluni paid to the Holy Eucharist."

Mabillon, in the "Annales Ordinis S. Benedicti," has printed
from a MS. in the Vatican Library a most interesting description
of the buildings of a Clugniac Monastery at the beginning of
the eleventh century, c. 1007, as described by the monk
Johannes, and transmitted for imitation by the Abbot Hugh to
the Abbey of St. Mary, Farfa, in the States of the Church in
Italy.

The Church of St. Peter and Paul, Clugny, was in Burgundy.
Le Noir gives the ground plan in "L'Architecture Monastique,"
II. 43, reproduced in Walcott's "Church and Conventual Arrangement," and exhibiting the characteristic galilee.  Expilly states
the dimensions to have been 600 ft. by 120 ft.; the main transept
200 ft., and the choir transept 120 ft.  With this Fargeau may
be compared, measuring 200 metres by 40 metres (the nave
being 31 metres high, and the aisles 18 metres in height), and
containing 60 pillars.   Gregory of Tours (Hist. c. xiv.) thus
describes one of the earliest French churches :—

" It is in length 155 ft., in breadth 60 ft.; it is in height to the
vaulting (camera) 45 ft.; it contains 32 windows in the presbytery
(altarium), and 20 in the apse (capsum) ; 41 pillars ; in the whole
building 52 windows, 120 pillars, 8 doors (3 in the presbytery, 5
in the apse).  The church is 150 ft. long, 60 ft. broad ; is 50 ft.
high in the apse to the vaulting, and has 42 windows, 70 pillars,
and 8 doors."

The Clugniac Abbey is thus described by the monk John :—
" The church should be 140 ft. long and 43 ft. in height, and 160
windows.  The galilee, or nave, as we say, must be 65 ft. long ;
there should be two towers in the front, with a court beneath
where the layfolk should stand in order not to impede the
procession ; 280 ft. must intervene between the south and north
gates."

By the rules of the order, "the part of the new Minster on
the left side behind the left choir (i.e., the aisle) shall not be open
to clerks and layfolk, except on Sundays and great feasts, from

tierce to the end of High Mass, except to pilgrims who wish to
approach the high altar or matin altar for the sake of devotion,
or to make an offering." The retro choir was reserved for the
monks' private devotions, and the matin altar was dedicated to
St. Mary. (*Stat. Clun.*, liii., 1039.)

" The sacristy should be 58 ft. long, with a tower erected at
the upper end (caput). The Lady Chapel (oratorium) must be
45 ft. long and 20 ft. broad, with walls 24 ft. high. The length
of the dormitory must be 160 ft. by 34 ft. in breadth, and have
97 glass windows, as high as a man can reach with the tips of
his fingers, the width being 2 ft. 6 in., and the height of the walls
23 ft." By the rules of the order, the chapter-house must be
" 45 ft. long and 34 ft. broad, with 4 windows to the east, 3 to
the north, and on the west 12 balks (balcares), with two pillars
in each." These probably enclosed a vestibule. " The parlour
(auditorium) must be 30 ft. long, and the chamber 90 ft. long.
The calefactory[1] should be 25 ft. broad and of equal height; and
from the church door to the calefactory door there should be
75 ft. The refectory should be 95 ft. long, and 25 ft. broad, and
the height of the walls 23 ft., with 8 windows upon each side
5 ft. high and 3 ft. in breadth. The regular kitchen should
measure 30 ft. by 25 ft. The lay kitchen must have the same
dimensions. The length of the cellarage should be 70 ft. by
60 ft. The cell of the Almonry should be 60 ft. long, corresponding to the width of the cellarage, and 10 ft. wide. The
infirm should have 6 cells. The first cell must be 27 ft. wide by
23 ft. long, with 8 beds, and as many cells in the porch along
the outer wall of the cell. The fence (claustrum) of each cell
should be 12 ft. wide. The second, third, and fourth cells should
have the same dimensions. The fifth should be smaller, for the
assembly of the infirm to wash their feet on Saturday, or for
brethren who are hot to change their habit. In the sixth cell
the servants should wash the dishes and furniture."

By the rule XIX., in the Clugniac Infirmary, which contains
five separate chambers (habitacula) under one roof, the ancient
order of silence and conversation should be preserved in the

---

(1) A chamber provided with a fireplace or stove, used as a withdrawing room by
the monks.

central portion allotted to the brethren and in the upper portion
on the south, and so in the cell of the novices, the adjoining
cloister, the offices, all the workshops, sacristies, cemeteries,
cemetery cloister, and the slype leading to the upper houses
which adjoin the great church. (*Statuta Clugniac,* 1031.)

" Outside of the Refectory there should be twelve crypts and
tubs ready, where the brethren may take their baths at proper
times."

Shaving was arranged by the chamberlain, who kept the
razors in an aumbrey (scrinio) at the entrance of the dormitory.
The monks sat in two lines in the ante-bays of the cloister (in
cancellis claustri) and next the wall (l. iii., c. xvi.) ; those who
came late were shaved in the calefactory, like the infirm.

There was a general bath before Christmas and Easter (l. iii.,
c. xvii. Migne, tom. 149.)

" Adjoining this site should be the novices' cell, formed like a
quadrangle ; the first division for meditation, the second a
refectory, the third a dormitory, and the fourth a gong.

" Between the aforesaid crypts and the novices' cell should be
another chamber (cella) for goldsmiths, setters, and glass-workers,
125 ft. long by 25 ft. broad ; in length reaching to the bakery,
which should be 90 ft. broad and 70 ft. long, with a tower built
at the head of it."

A curious custom of the Norman founders was that of putting
hair of the head and beard into the wax of seals. The author
of the " History of St. Augustine's Abbey," says the hairs of the
first Earl Warrenne's head remained in the seal in his day
(p. 118., Monast. Anglic., v. 12.) ; and so the Earl of Lincoln,
who endowed Castleacre, a cell of Lewes, says :—" In evidence
whereof I have bitten the seal with my teeth ; Muriel, my wife,
witness, the marks still being visible." The second Earl
Warrenne and his brother Ralph had the hairs of their heads
cut off with a knife before the altar by Henry, Bishop of
Winchester, in token of seizin." (*Monast. Anglic.,* v. 15.)

" Near the galilee or nave of the church should be built the
palace, 135 ft. long and 30 ft. wide, to receive guests who came
on horseback to the monastery. On one side of the house there
must be forty beds with straw pillows, for men only, and on the

other side thirty beds for countesses and other respectable
women. In the middle of the palace, tables should be fixed
like those in the refectory, to accommodate both men and
women. At great feasts the house should be adorned with
curtains, palls, and bankers along the seats. In front of it
should be another house, 45 ft. long and 30 ft. broad, reaching
lengthways to the sacristy in it ; the tailors and cobblers should
perform the commands of the chamberlain. Between this house
and the sacristy, and the church and galilee, must be the
cemetery for the laity."

The following extracts from the rules will throw light on some
of the arrangements :—

A guest was required to pay his devotions at the Holy Cross,
the high altar of the choir, St. John's, in the right arm (dextro
membro, *i.e.*, north transept), and the Lady altar. Udalrici Cons.
Cluniac, lib. III., C. xxii. (Migne 149, p. 764). The claustral
prior, after compline, stood at the church door to see that the
brethren bowed to the altar, and the priest who sprinkled them ;
he then went his rounds to see that the almonry, regular kitchen,
and refectory, were locked, and inspect the infirmary, dormitory,
and gong, and in winter between nocturns and matins visited the
beds and all the altars. (C. vi.) The circators or rounds were to
keep up a frequent patrol of the cloisters. (C. vii.) Novices
slept in their part of the dormitory and in the gong, " sedes eis
in medio duobus circulis ligneis sunt prænotatæ in quibus eis
venientibus nullus audeat ut sedet." They received the habit in
the sacristy. (C. viii.) They entered the church at the east end
(plagam) and the brethren came in at the west ; in cloister they
sat each on a trunk ; in church they had cross forms or footstools ;
and sometimes sat on the ground. They sat next the wall in
cloister, and their masters in the carols (cancellis claustri) (Ibid.).
There was an aumbry for books in the cloister. (C. ix.) The
chamberlain had his office or camera for clothing. (C. xi.) The
tabula was beaten at the cloister door to announce that a monk
was dying. (C. xvii.)

The Clugniacs differed from Cistercians in the following
divergencies of rule. (Petr. Ven., Epist. lib. VI., 17.)

1. They did not acknowledge the diocesan's authority.

2. They did not prostrate at the reception of guests.

3. They did not kneel or prostrate at the hours.

4. They admitted novices to monkhood before the end of a year of probation.

5. They re-admitted fugitive monks, even after three offences, although not in a dying condition.

6. They did not wash their guests' feet.

7. Abbots did not dine with guests.

8. They did not salute or bless their guests.

9. They had more than two general messes in the day.

10. They did no manual labour.

11. They did not uncover or bow to each other in passing.

Guests were allowed to visit the almonry, cellarage, kitchen, refectory, novices' cells, dormitory, and infirmary, in silence. They might go into the church to pray at the rood, at the high altar, at St. Mary's altar, or St. John's in the north arm; if they arrived late they were not allowed to sit with the abbot at high table. (Cons. Clun. l. iii., c. xxii.)

The gates were locked after compline, and opened at daylight. (Ibid.)

From the south gate to the north gate, along the west side, should be built a house 280 ft. long by 25 ft. broad, as stables for horses, and above it a solar for servants and guests of inferior degree.

By the rule, the prison should have a descent by a ladder, a door not visible, and no window. Here is a description of Croyland by the pseudo Ingulphus, whose history is debateable, but which no doubt correctly depicts the monastic arrangements of a Benedictine monastery in a manner as minute and rare as the statement of the dimensions of Clugny. "The granary contained above, all manner of grain, and in the lower part, farm vessels; over the stables of the abbot and guests were the servants' rooms. The whole west side of the abbot's court was enclosed by the stable, granary, and bake-house, facing the town; on the south was the guest house with two large chambers; on the east were the jailer's and converts' hall, which, with the abbot's hall, kitchen chamber, and chapel, closed the monks' cloister eastwards; on the north side of the abbey was the great gate, with the poor men's hostel on the east."

Wenlock, Bromholm, Castleacre, and Thetford do not offer a parallel to Clugny as described by the monk Johannes, so close as Lewes.

Having thus described the chief characteristics of the order of Clugny, we may turn to the foundation of this particular monastery.

Lenton Priory was founded by William Peverel in honour of the Holy Trinity,[1] and for the love of divine worship and the common remedy of the souls of his lord, King William, and of his wife, Queen Matilda, and of their son, King William, and of all their and his ancestors, also for the health of his present lord, King Henry, and Queen Matilda, his wife, of William, their son, and Matilda, their daughter, for the state of his kingdom, and for the health of his own soul, and of Adelina, his wife, and his son William, and all his own children, and gave it to God, and to the Church of Clugny, and to Pontius the Abbot there, and his successors, yet so that it should be free, on the payment of a marc of silver annually

---

(1) Roger Wendover, in his "Flowers of the Histories," written about the year 1235, in mentioning the death of Leofric, Earl of Mercia, under year 1057, gives the legend of the Earl wagering his Countess Godiva to make an undress ride through the market of Coventry, and thereby to free the town of Coventry from a certain service due to the earl, which was burdensome to it; and concludes the account thus:—"Moreover the said earl, under the influence of his countess, nobly enriched with lands, buildings, and various ornaments, the churches of Worcester, St. Mary of Stowe, and St. Wereburg of Chester, together with the monasteries of Evesham, Wenlock, and Lenton." This statement concerning the beneficence of Leofric to the Church seems to be an abridgment of Florence of Worcester's account in his Chronicle of chronicles, written previously to A.D. 1118; but he has Leonense, and not Lentona. The same may be said of other early writers, among whom we have Bromton, who has "Leonese juxta Herefordiam." It appears to be certain that Florence intended Leominster (Leonis Monasterium), which is said to have taken its name from the fact of the Mercian king, Merwald, having founded it on the spot, where, in a vision, he had seen a lion. It has, however, been suggested that the name comes from the Welsh *Lhan Lieni, i.e.*, church for nuns. It may be noted that in Domesday it is styled Leofminstre, which, perhaps, is a shortening of Leofric's-minster. It appears as though Wendover supposed the name Leonense to have some etymological connection with the Leen; but one would think that this of itself could not be sufficient to cause him to conclude that Lenton monastery was intended, especially when we bear in mind that he was likely to know some little about that monastery, historically and locally, as he was not altogether a stranger in this district, being for a time prior of Belvoir. His mistake, however, is unaccountable if it was then believed that there was no monastery at Lenton before Peverel's; but, on the other hand, not difficult to account for if traditions were then current of an earlier monastery, which was supposed to have had its origin in the rocks by the Leen, the rock chapel of St. Mary being a remnant of it.

as an acknowledgment. Peverel endowed this monastery with the town of Lenton and its appurtenances, except four mills, of which he held two in his own demesne, his wife, Adelina, the third, and Herbert, his knight, the fourth, the rest of the mills, seven in number, being given to the monks. He likewise gave to the Priory the towns of Radford, Morton, and Keighton, with all their appurtenances, and whatsoever he had in Newthorpe and Papplewick, in wood, plain, etc. Also Courteenhall in Northamptonshire, with the wood and all thereto belonging, except the fee of one knight, and the land of Thurstin Mantell, likewise two parts of the tithes of his demesne, of all things which could be tithed, viz., in Blisworth, in Northamptonshire, with a villain, who held a virgate, to gather the tithes, in Duston, also in Northamptonshire, in Newbold, Tideswell, Bradwell, Bakewell, Hucklow, Ashford, Wormhill, and Hulme, in Derbyshire, two parts also of the tithes of his demesne pastures in the Peak, namely, in Shalcross, Fernilee, Darnall, Quatford, Buxton, Shirebrook, Staden, Cowdale, Croxall, Callow, Dunningestede, Chelmorton, and Sterndale; the whole tithe of colts and fillies, where he should have a stud (*haracium*), or any one else, in his demesne pastures; the whole tithe of his lead, and of his venison or hunting, as well in skins as flesh, and the whole tithe of his fishery at Nottingham. He gave also, with the consent of King Henry the First, the church of St. Mary in the English borough of Nottingham, with its land, tithes, and appurtenances; the church of St. Peter, and the church of St. Nicholas, likewise in Nottingham; the churches of Radford, Linby, and Langar, in Nottinghamshire, with land, tithes, and other appurtenances, and a villain holding a virgate of land; the church of Foston in Leicestershire, with a virgate of land; the churches of Harlestone, Courteenhall, Irchester, and Rushden, in Northamptonshire, with a villain in the latter vill holding a virgate of land. He likewise granted to the monastery whatsoever his homagers, or feodaries, should bestow on it for the benefit of their souls. Of these, the first was Avenel, who gave two parts of the tithes in his demesnes in Haddon, Meadow-place, and Monyash. Safred gave the same in

Empingham and Basford, and Robert FitzPain the same in Basford. Robert de Heriz gave the same in Ashbourne and Oxcroft ; Geoffrey and William in Arnesby, in Leicestershire ; Norman de Montfautrel, in Haselbeech, Northamptonshire, in Chilwell, and in Harpole ; Roger Brito, in Walton and Knowle, in Derbyshire ; Jocelin, in Wathenoch ; Ralph Malaherbe, in Asply ; Serlo Blundus, in Thorpe-in-the-Glebe ; Herbert, in Gonalston ; Helgot, in Husbands Bosworth, and in Cotes, in Leicestershire; Robert de Paveley, in Houghton, in Northamptonshire; Walter Flammoynth, in Haversham, Bucks. ; Hugh, son of Richard, in Claydon, Buckinghamshire ; Norman de St. Patric, in Desborough and Blakesley,[1] in Northamptonshire, and in Rowland, in Derbyshire ; Geoffrey de Heriz, in Stapleford ; Aldelmus, in Langley ; and Robert, the son of Warner, in Toton ; Robert de Moretain also, and his heirs, gave a yearly rent of ten shillings for ever.

The witnesses to this charter were Gerard, Archbishop of York, Robert, Bishop of Lincoln, Robert, Earl of Medlent, Simon, Earl of Northampton, Hugh, Sheriff of Leicestershire, Robert de Chauz, Hugo de Burun, Odo de Boneia, Avenel de Haddon, Robert de Heriz, and others.

The exact year when Peverel granted his charter is not known, but it must have been between the year 1103, when Matilda, daughter of King Henry I., who is mentioned in the charter, was born, and the year 1108, when Gerard, Archbishop of York, one of the witnesses, died. We are thus enabled to bring the date of the foundation of the monastery within five years.

## CHARTER OF WILLIAM PEVEREL.[2]

" Notum sit omnibus fidelibus sanctæ ecclesiæ Dei clericis et laicis Francis et Anglis qui modo sunt, et qui venturi sunt, quod ego Willielmus Peverellus pro divini cultus amore et communi remedio animarum dominorum meorum Willielmi regis, et uxoris ejus Matildis reginæ, et filii eorum Willielmi regis, et omnium

---

(1) This grant, as far as it relates to this place, was probably resisted or withdrawn by the successor of the grantee, as there was no reserved pension to the priory out of the church of Blakesley. Baker's *Northamptonshire*, ii., 28.

(2) This is taken from an Inspeximus charter of King Edward the Second, where the foundation charter is recited, apparently *verbatim*.

parentum suorum, et meorum, necnon et pro salute domini mei Henrici regis, et uxoris ejus Matild. reginæ, et filii eorum Willielmi, et filiæ eorum Matildis, pro statu quoque regni sui, necnon et pro salute animæ meæ, et uxoris meæ Adelinæ, et filii mei Willielmi, et omnium liberorum meorum, pia devotione et devota largitione offero Deo et ecclesiæ Cluniacensi et Poncio abbati, ejusque successoribus imperpetuum substituendis, monasterium quod in honore sanctæ Trinitatis in Lentona constitui, jure perpetuo, sub prioratu, ac dispositione ipsius Cluniacæ institutionis justè liberèque instituendum, et possidendum cum universis quæ in hac carta subscribuntur; ita tamen ut ipsum monasterium erga Cluniacum sit liberum et quietum pro una marca argenti de recognitione per annum. Beneficia igitur et possessiones quas ego ipsi monasterio sanctæ Trinitatis et monachis Cluniacensibus ibidem Deo serventibus dono et presenti carta confirmo, ista sunt nominatim; villam Lentonæ cum omnibus pertinentiis suis, exceptis quatuor molendinis quorum teneo duo in meo dominio et Adelina uxor mea tertium, et Herbertus miles meus quartum; cætera molendina monachorum sunt, et propriè septem. Similiter Radeford, Morthonam, Kichthonam, cum omnibus pertinentiis earum. Et quicquid habeo in Newtorp, et Papelvich, in bosco et in plano et in omnibus aliis rebus. Item Blacowella in Pecco cum omnibus pertinentiis suis. Item Corthahala in Hantesyra cum bosco suo et omnibus aliis pertinentiis suis, excepto feodo unius militis et terra Turstini Mantelli.

Item duas partes omnium decimationum de dominiis meis, de omnibus rebus quæ decimari possunt; videlicet de Blideesworda cum quodam rustico virgatam terræ tenente ad colligendas decimas. In Dostona similiter, in Neuboda similiter, in Tindeswella similiter, in Bradewella similiter, in Badecowella similiter, in Hoccalawa similiter, in Esseford similiter, in Wrmevill similiter, in Momar similiter, in Hulma similiter. Item duas partes decimationum dominicarum pasturarum mearum in Pecco quarum nomina sunt hæc. Sachalcros, Ferneleia, Dernehala, Quatford, Buchestanes, Sirebroch, Stafdona, Cudala, Crochil, Chaldelawa, Dunninggestede, Chelmordona, Stauredala. Item totam decimam pullorum et pullarum ubicumque haracium habuero in Pecco, vel aliquis alius super dominicas pasturas meas. Item totam decimam plumbi mei et venationis meæ, tam in coriis quam in carnibus et totam decimam piscium piscariæ meæ de Notingham. Item, concedente domino meo rege Henrico, dono eis ecclesiam sanctæ Mariæ de Burgo Anglico, de Notingham, cum terris et decimis, et omnibus aliis pertinentiis suis, ecclesiam sancti Petri cum omnibus pertinentiis suis, ecclesiam sancti Nicholai cum omnibus pertinentiis suis, ecclesiam de Radeford cum omnibus pertinentiis suis, ecclesiam de Lindebeia cum omnibus pertinentiis. Ecclesiam de Langara cum terris et decimis et omnibus pertinentiis suis; et cum uno villano virgatam terræ tenente. Ecclesiam de Fotestona cum una virgata terræ et decima et aliis omnibus pertinentiis suis. Ecclesiam de Herlestona cum omnibus pertinentiis suis, ecclesiam de Corthahala cum omnibus pertinentiis, ecclesiam de Irencestria cum terris et decimis et omnibus aliis pertinentiis suis, ecclesiam de Rissendena cum una virgata terræ et decima tota et omnibus aliis pertinentiis suis, et unum villanum in eadem villa virgatam terræ tenentem. Hæc omnia præfato monasterio dono et confirmo in liberam et perpetuam elemo-sinam et ab omni servicio et seculari exactione quieta ; ego enim et hæredes mei adquietabimus ea imperpetuum, et erga regem et erga omnes homines. Præterea concedo ipsi monasterio quicquid homines mei eidem contulerunt pro remedio animarum suarum, videlicet duas partes omnium decimarum dominicorum suorum de omnibus rebus quæ decimari possunt ; horum primus est, Avenellus qui hoc contulit de dominiis suis in Haddona et in Methdweploth et Mamar, Safredus in Empingaha et in Baseford, et Robertus filius Pagani in eadem villa similiter, Robertus de Hertz in Hesburna, et in Ossecropht similiter, Godefridus et Willielmus in Ernesbeia similiter, Normannus de Montfaltrel in Asebech, et in Chilwella et in Horpol, similiter Rogerius Britto in Walenthona, et in Kalahala similiter, Gocelinus in Wathenoch et Radulphus Malaherba in Aspeleia et Serlo Blundus in Tortp, et Erbertus in Gonolvestona, similiter, Helgotus in Baresworda, et in Cotis, Robertus de Pavelliaco in Hoctona, Walterus Flammeth in Hauresham, Hugo filius Ricardi in Claindona, Normannus de sancto Patricio in Deresburch, et in Blacol Wesleia, et in Raalund, Gaufridus Heriz in Stapelford, Adelelmus in Langueleia, et Robertus filius Warnerii in Thonethona, similiter Robertus de Moretuein, et hæredes sui decem solidos vel decem solidatas per singulos annos imper-petuum. Hujus donationis et scripti testes sunt Girardus archiepisc. Eboracensis, Robertus episc. Lincoln, Robertus comes de Medlent, Simon comes de Nordhamthona, Hugo vicecomes Leicestriæ, Robertus de Chauz, Hugo de Burun, Oddo de Boneia, Avenellus de Haddona, et omnes alii homines mei prædicti." [1]

The founder's charter was confirmed by King Henry the First, whose charter is as follows :—

" In the name of the Holy and Undivided Trinity, be it known to the pious devotion of the faithful of the holy church, that I Henry, King of England, for the love of Divine worship, and the remedy of my soul, etc., and also for the health and safety of my son William, and of my daughter Matilda, etc., at the strenuous and earnest request that this should be done, of

---

(1) *Mon. Ang.*, v. 110.

William Peverel founder of the same church, with his wife
Adelaide, and his son William, grant the church of the Holy
Trinity, which is in Lenton, to the government and religion of
the Clugniac monks who serve God in the same place, to be held
in perpetual right under the Prior and at the disposition of the
Clugniac institutions, and to be henceforth possessed undistur-
bedly and inviolably and free from litigation, together with all
things which have been attached to the same church by the said
William Peverel of Nottingham, that is, ten carucates of land
with very many tithes, and the manor of Courteenhall, except
the fee of one knight, which Walter the son of Winemerus holds,
and the land of Turstin Mantell, But in recognition, the aforesaid
William and his successors shall each pay one marc of silver
annually of their own to the aforesaid church of Clugny.
✠ The sign of King Henry. ✠ The sign of Queen Matilda.
✠ The sign of William Peverel of Nottingham. ✠ The sign
of Adelina his wife. ✠ The sign of Earl Ro., and of other
good witnesses." [1]

Before proceeding further, it will be convenient to trace the
history of some of the more important donations which the
Priory received from the founder.

Omitting his grant of the whole town of Lenton and the lands
in Radford, Morton, and Keighton, all of which formed the Priory
demense, and which must frequently be referred to, we come first
to the donation by William Peverel of all that he had in
Newthorpe and Papplewick, in wood and in plain, and in all
other things. By a charter which will be noticed later on, King
Henry the Second gave to the Priory eighty acres of assarts [2] in
Courteenhall, Northamptonshire, and the mill of Blackcliff in
exchange for the land belonging to Lenton Priory at Papplewick,
which he then gave to his newly-founded Priory at Newstead. [3]
In 1535 the Priory derived from rents in Newthorpe £7 2s. 4d.
per annum.

The whole lordship, or manor, of Courteenhall, in Northamptonshire, with the exception of a knight's fee and the lands held

---

(1) *Mon. Ang.*, v. 113.

(2) "Verely when that the pleasant woods of the forest or thick bushie places meet for
the secret feeding of the wilde beasts be cut downe and plucked up by the rootes, and
the same ground made a plaine and turned into arable land, then by the law of the
forest is properly said to be an *assart* of the forest, or land assarted."—*Manwood.*

(3) Thoroton, p. 260.

by one Thurstin Mantell, was likewise bestowed upon the Priory by the founder.

In the 24th year of Edward I., the prior of Lenton was found by inquisition to hold the township of *Corteenhall* of the King *in capite*, but by what service is not mentioned : and in the 9th year of Edward II., the said prior was certified to be Lord of the Manor. In the 3rd year of Edward III. he was summoned by a writ of *quo warranto* to show cause why he claimed to have view of frank-pledge with other privileges in his manor of Courteenhall, and pleaded prescription.

In the 28th year of Henry VIII., Nicholas Heyth, prior of Lenton, being attainted of high treason, the manor was seized into the King's hands. (Esc. anno 36 Hen. VIII., n. 270.)

The advowson of the rectory was given with the manor to Lenton Priory by William Peverel. In 1254, 38 Hen. III., as also in 1291, the rectory was valued at nine marcs. In 1535 it was rated at £13 8s. 1d., out of which was deducted for synodals and procurations, 10s. 7d., besides a yearly pension of 6s. 8d. to the Prior of Lenton.[1]

Peverel also gave to the priory two parts of the tithes of all things which could be tithed, with a villain, holding a virgate of land in Blisworth, in Northamptonshire. In 1254, as also in 1291, the rectory of Blisworth was valued at ten marcs, exclusive of the portion of the prior of Lenton, which was rated at 16s. In 1535 it was rated at £20 14s. 4d., out of which was deducted 10s. 7d. for procurations and synodals.[2]

The priory had, also, of the gift of William Peverel the founder, two parts of the tithe of his demense in *Duston*, in Northamptonshire, of whatever was titheable ; which Philip, prior of Lenton, quitclaimed to the abbot of St. James, Northampton, for a yearly pension of 20s., reserving to himself one virgate of land with its tithes. In the taxations of 1254 and 1291, the priory of Lenton had 6s. yearly rent here. By the inquisition taken in the thirtieth year of Henry the Eighth, on the attainder of Nicholas Heyth, late prior of Lenton, he was found to have held (*int. al.*) an annual pension of 20s. out of

---

(1) Bridge's *Northamptonshire*, i. 352.
(2) Bridge's *Northamptonshire*, i. 337.

Duston church, and a close and three virgates of land worth 22s. yearly. The rectory of Duston was valued in the taxations of 1254 (38 Hen. 3) and 1291 (20 Edw. I.) at 11 marks (£7 6s. 8d.) per ann., deducting a yearly pension of 20s. to the Prior of Lenton, and in the minister's accompts at the dissolution, the farm of the rectory, then on lease to ————— Langtree, was £5 per ann, and amongst the reprises was the annual pension to the Prior of Lenton.[1]

William Peverel, as we have seen, gave to the Priory of Lenton two parts of the tithes of all things that could be tithed in his lordships of Newbold, Tideswell, Bradwell, Bakewell, Hucklow, Ashford, Wormhill, Monyash, and Hulme ; also two parts of the tithes of the pastures pertaining to his lordships in the Peak, including those at Shalcross, Fernilee, Darnall, Quatford, Buxton, Shirebrook, Staden, Cowdale, Croxall, Callow, Dunningstede, Chelmorton, and Sterndale ; also the whole tithe of colts and fillies in the Peak, wherever he had a stud of horses, and the whole tithes of hunting, and of lead, in the same district. When the great estates of the Peverels were confiscated in the reign of Henry II., they were given by the king to his second son, John, Earl of Mortaigne. Richard had no sooner ascended the throne than his brother John began to play the part of a conspirator. Hugo de Nonant, Bishop of Coventry and Lichfield, a man of large estates and considerable influence, but in disposition thoroughly secular and turbulent, was one of his readiest and ablest allies in the midland counties. But when his attachment to John, and his consequent opposition to the king appeared to show a decline, the earl bought his further support by the gift of the churches of Bakewell, Hope, [2] and Tideswell, with all their appurtenances. On John's accession to the throne, he confirmed the gift of the Peak churches to the bishopric during the episcopate of Geoffrey Muschamp; but his successors, William Cornhill (1215-1224) and Alexander

---

(1) Baker, *Northamptonshire*, i., 142.

(2) "King John, while he was Earle of Moriton, to his grant of ye Church of Hope, in Derbyshire, made unto ye canons of Lichfield, affixed his gold ring wth a Turkye stone in it, to ye silke string whereunto ye seale was putt wth this expression—Non solum sigilii mei Impressione, sed proprii annuli appositione roboravi." *Harl. MS.* No. 4,630.

Stavenby (1224-1240), transferred these rights to the Dean and
Chapter of Lichfield.  Immediately on the completion of this
transfer, litigation seems to have commenced between the Priory
and the Dean and Chapter, which continued, with certain intervals of peace, for fully three hundred years.  During that period
there were no less than five several appeals to the Court of
Rome ; and we have evidence that the monastic revenues were
seriously taxed to defray the expenses of these protracted suits.
The matter at issue between Lenton and Lichfield was always
of the same character, viz. : (1), the extent of the lordships of
William Peverel, (2), whether he had the right of bestowing
tithes of land not under cultivation during his lifetime, and (3),
how far the charters of the Earl of Mortaigne overrode those
of William Peverel, whose descendants had suffered sequestration.

In the year 1248, the dispute assumed a serious aspect, but
the first time that matters came to a decided head was in the
years 1250-1, when the monks of Lenton by force of arms
seized on certain tithes of wool and lambs in the parish of
Tideswell.  " The same Prior and Convent (Lenton) despoiled
the same Dean and Chapter (Lichfield) in the same parish,
(Tideswell) in the summer and autumn of the year of grace,
1251, by continuing the first spoiling in the aforesaid places, and
by, in a great measure, exceeding that spoiling by seizing with
force of arms, and by carrying off both their greater and lesser
tithes—namely, in the town of Tideswell, and in the places of
Wormhill, Tunstead, Greatrakes, Meadow, in the summer four-
score and three lambs, which-are valued at 58s., and one sack
and a half of wool, which are valued at 12 marcs—and of the
sheep, the special property of the church, having broken the
doors of the sheepfolds placed at the bottom of the church
itself, they violently robbed them of 14 lambs, and 18 lambs
they trampled under the feet of the horses, and some they slew
with swords, and some they pierced with lances, and caused
them to be carried over to the cells of their satellites as if they
were hares : by savagely beating the ministers of the church,
and by seriously wounding some as above; and the door having
been violently broken in the church itself, their satellites seized

part of the wool, shedding blood in the church, and in the churchyard, and the estimate of the said lambs and wool is 2½ marcs. Also they despoiled the same in the same year, and in the same place, of a certain portion of the hay to the value of 20s , and of 25 geese, which are valued at 4s. 2d. Thus far in the summer. Also in the autumn of the same year, they despoiled the same in the same places of 1,060 thraves[1] of sheaves of oats, and upwards. Also in a certain culture of Richard Daniel, which is called Mill Field, of 28 thraves, of which he formerly received nothing, and the aforesaid thraves are valued at 15 marcs."

The scandal had now assumed such large proportions that Bishop Wcseham saw that in an appeal to Rome lay the only hope of reducing the quarrel, and himself recommended the adoption of this course. Pope Innocent IV. appointed, in the first instance, the Prior of Launde to act as his commissioner, but the Prior transferred his powers to the Master of the Schools at Lincoln; on the failure of this commission the Pope transferred the hearing of the case to the Abbots of Burton and Rocester, and the Prior of Kenilworth, but they, too, failed to effect a reconciliation. The Archdeacon of St. Albans was next appointed by the Roman Court, and, though he obtained full evidence on oath, he was not able to put an end to the quarrel.

In the year 1252, an agreement was made between the Priory of Lenton and the Chapter of Lichfield, in order to settle certain alleged encroachments made by the Priory upon the privileges granted to the Chapter by King John, who had bestowed on them the churches of Bakewell, Hope, and Tideswell. The grant of the king had been held to over-ride, in certain particulars, the charter of William Peverel, but this view of the matter had not been agreed to by the Priory. The Dean and Chapter claimed £60 as damages, and 40 marks for expenses, and the quarrel was ultimately referred to Rome. Pope Innocent IV., after the failure of three commissions, appointed a fourth commission, consisting of Brother Walter,

---

(1) A thrave was twenty-four sheaves. The word is still in common use in some districts in the West of England.

warden of the Friars Minor, of Leicester, and Adam, Arch-
deacon of Chester, there being a third judge, the Prior of the
Black Preachers, of London, legally excused on good ground.
The case was heard in the Church of St. Mary, at Leicester,
when Master Walter appeared on behalf of the Chapter, and
Master Alan, the sub-prior, on the part of Lenton Priory. It
was then agreed that the Priory of Lenton should pay to the
Sacristan, at Lichfield, 100 marcs as a fine; that all the greater
and lesser tithes of Tideswell were to belong to the Dean and
Chapter, excepting two-thirds of the tithes of lead on the
demesnes of William Peverel, two-thirds of the tithe of the mill
of Richard Daniel, and two-thirds of the tithe of the stables,
and of hunting ; that the Dean and Chapter of Lichfield should
pay 14 marcs out of the tithes of Bakewell and Hope to the
Priory of Lenton ; and that two-thirds of the great tithes only
should go to the Priory in other parts, and of pastures and
places then cultivated at Bakewell, Ashford, Nether Haddon,
and Chapel-en-le-Frith.[1]

This decision secured peace in the Peak between the rival
religious bodies for twenty or thirty years, when the strife broke
out again almost as fiercely as ever.

A considerable number of documents relating to this almost
unending litigation exist among the Lichfield muniments. The
following particulars refer to nine of the earlier of these records.

The *first* is the undated Confirmation Charter of Bishop
Stavenby of the Peak churches to the Chapter of Lichfield.
It is written on a slip of parchment only eight inches by four,
and the ink is as black and legible as when first penned.
The *second* is the formal abrogation, dated at St. Albans,
February 25th, 1251, by the Archdeacon of St. Albans, of
the powers entrusted to him by the Holy See. He recites
the appointment by the Roman Court of the Prior of
Launde, of the Abbots of Burton and Rocester, and the
Prior of Kenilworth, and of himself and others to act as
commissioners, and finally declares that he found it impossible
to terminate the quarrel, owing to the astuteness and con-
tumacy of the Prior and Convent of Lenton. The document

---

(1) *Harl. MS.,* 4799.

is in excellent preservation, and is an admirable specimen of
the caligraphy of those days. The *third* document is a
beautifully written narrow roll, three feet long, giving full
particulars as to the estimated value of the tithes received
by the Priory of Lenton, in the different townships of Bakewell,
Hope, and Tideswell; together with an account of the violent
seizure of the sheep in Tideswell Church, and of the damage
done. It is a transcript of two Inquisitions taken on oath in 1251,
with additional remarks, and intended for the use of the proctors
engaged in the cause. The *fourth* is a similar sized document
to the third, but is in bad condition, and contains one of
the Inquisitions in the second document. The *fifth* contains
the depositions, unfortunately incomplete, taken before the
Papal Commissioners at Tideswell, "on Friday next after
the Epiphany of the Lord, continued on the Wednesday next
following," in the year 1252, in proof of the parochiality of
the church of Tideswell, which the Chapter of Lichfield contended was no longer to be regarded as a mere chapelry of
Hope. The *sixth* is a deed from Henry de Lexington, Dean
of Lincoln, lessee under the Dean and Chapter of Lichfield,
of the church of Bakewell, by which he covenants to pay
fourteen marcs to the Priory of Lenton, in accordance with
the decision of the Papal Commissioners. Dated at Lincoln,
February 16th, 1252. The *seventh* is the formal decision of
the Warden of the Friars Minor of Leicester, and Adam de
Stanford, Archdeacon of Chester, as Papal Commissioners,
given at St. Mary's, Leicester, on the Sunday next after the
feast of the Purification of the Blessed Virgin, 1252. The
document is in good preservation, and remarkably well written.
This copy of their judgment, to be preserved by the Chapter,
has appended to it, in addition to the seals of the Commissioners, the seal of Lenton Priory, and also the seal of
Alan, the sub-prior of Lenton, who had appeared on behalf
of the convent before the commission. The *eighth* document
is a small undated Indenture between the Priory and the
Chapter, relative to the tithes of the three Peak churches,
apparently drawn up as an additional security for the carrying
out of the Papal judgment. The *ninth* is also an undated

Indenture, but apparently of about this period, or rather later, between the Priory of Lenton and the Chapter of Lichfield, relative to a compromise touching the tithes of five hundred acres of newly cleared lands at Fairfield.[1]

At the Pleas, held at Derby in the year 1241, the Prior of Lenton, and the Dean and Chapter of Lichfield, had to show cause why the king should not present to Chapel-en-le-Frith, then vacant. It appears that in the year 1225, the foresters and keepers of the deer became so numerous that they bought a piece of the king's land, held by William de Ferrers (grandson of Robert de Ferrers, first Earl of Derby), and erected a chapel, which was called the Chapel in the Forest. The lands of William Peverel having been acquired by William de Ferrers, and confirmed by him to Lenton Priory, it naturally followed that the advowson of this chapel, with the tithes of the new parish surrounding it, should be claimed by the prior, but this claim was disputed both by the king and the Dean and Chapter of Lichfield. On the present occasion the Prior of Lenton claimed two parts of the greater tithes, and all the small tithes belonging to the chapel, on the ground that William Peverel had granted the tithes of all his land, which had been inherited by William de Ferrers, to the Priory. The Dean and Chapter of Lichfield claimed a portion of the tithes, because the new chapel was situated, they asserted, within the parish of Hope, the church of which belonged to them. On the other hand, Adam de Eston, on behalf of the king, contended that William de Ferrers had taken possession of Peverel's lands during the war between the late king and the barons, that no royal warrant had been obtained either by Ferrers or the Chapter as to the chapel, and that the lands on which it was built were waste and uncultivated when Peverel made his grant to to Priory.

It was decided that if either the Prior, or Dean and Chapter produced any charter or confirmation from the king, it should not be set aside.[2]

---

(1) These nine documents are printed, for the first time, in full in the *Journal of the Derbyshire Archæological and Natural History Society*, v. 133-164.

(2) Abbrev. Placit. 25 Hen. III., rot. 25.

The Prior of Lenton subsequently established his claim to the greater portion of the tithes, but the advowson was held by the Dean and Chapter of Lichfield.

A few years later the great tithes of Chapel-en-le-Frith, according to the Chapter registers of Lichfield, were valued at twenty marcs, and the small tithes at ten marcs ; two-thirds of which sum was appropriated by Lenton Priory, and the remainder by the Chapter of Lichfield.

The appropriation of the tithes of Chapel-en-le-Frith by the Priory of Lenton does not appear to have been quietly acquiesced in by the inhabitants, for in the year 1318, an Inquisition was held at Fairfield, when upwards of forty foresters, verderers, keepers, and freemen affirmed upon oath that the chapel of Chapel-en-le-Frith had been built by the inhabitants on the king's land in Henry's reign, and that the rights of baptism and burial had been conferred upon it by Bishop Alexander (Stavenby, of Coventry and Lichfield, consecrated 1224, died 1238), so that it was then a parish church. They also declared that the Prior and Convent of Lenton, and the Dean and Chapter of Lichfield held the church to their own use, and that they (the foresters) were ignorant as to whether they (the prior, etc.) had a true title to the advowson and appropriation, or not.[1]

It would appear by the above that in the year 1318, Chapel-en-le-Frith was a place of considerable size, as it is spoken of as a "villa," and the parish is said to contain many hamlets, "plures hamaletti." The land belonging to the Ferrers family was confiscated by the king, Henry III., owing to the frequent rebellions of William de Ferrers, and his son Robert. This Robert, being in rebellion in the year 1266, was defeated by Henry, son of the King of the Romans. He fled for refuge to the church, where he concealed himself, but he was betrayed by a woman and taken prisoner. He was deprived of his earldom, and his estates were confiscated to the king, amongst which the parish of Chapel-en-le-Frith was included. In 1372,

---

(1) *Inq. ad quod damnum*, 11 Edw. II., No. 97. Cox, *Churches of Derbyshire*, ii., 140.

the Chapel in the Frith was granted to John, Duke of Lancaster.

In the reign of Henry VIII., the Priory of Lenton derived £6 per annum from it, as tithes.

In the year 1323, a dispute arose between the Priory of Lenton and the Dean and Chapter of Lichfield, as to the tithes of Fairfield, two-thirds of which were claimed by Lenton Priory. The dispute was referred to the decision of Pope John XXII., who appointed the prior of Charley (acting for the abbot of Gerendon) to hear the case as his commissioner. According to a document dated July, 1324, the prior of Lenton was cited to appear before the prior of Charley, in the church of St. Margaret, at Leicester, "on the fourth legal day next after the day of St. Kenelim next ensuing." On the 10th of the following month, the commissioner gave his decision in favour of the Chapter of Lichfield, and in the following September, the Archdeacon of Stafford issued a mandate to the vicars of Bakewell, Hope, and Tideswell, informing them of the decision, and ordering them to observe it.[1]

We have already briefly stated that Peverel gave two parts of his tithes in Bakewell to Lenton Priory on its foundation, and that John, Earl of Mortaigne, granted the church of Bakewell to the Dean and Chapter of Lichfield.

According to an Inquisition *ad quod damnum* held at Fairfield, on the Monday next before the feast of St. Luke the Evangelist, 1318, "King John was the true patron of the churches of Bakewell, Tideswell, and Hope, with the chapels annexed to the said churches, which churches are appropriated to the Dean and Chapter of Lichfield, and the Prior and Convent of Lenton, of which advowsons and appropriations the said Dean and Chapter of Lichfield, and Prior and Convent of Lenton, say that they hold the charters of the said king."

At the same time that John confirmed (3 Ric. I.) his grant of the church of Bakewell to Lichfield, he bestowed the manor of Bakewell on Ralph Gernon. The manor remained in this family till 1383, when Sir John Gernon died seized of it, and

---

(1) Cox, *Churches of Derbyshire*, ii., 270.

it passed through one of his daughters and co-heiresses, in turn, to the families of Botetourt, Swinburne, Helion, Tyrell, and Wentworth, when it was at length sold, in the year 1502, to Sir Henry Vernon.[1]

The following is a copy of a manuscript in the Wolley collection, and relates to the tithe of the lead ore in the Peak of Derbyshire.

"In the bundle of the Quo Warranto in the Tally Office at Westminster is a Quo Warranto brought against Gernoon then owner of the mann'r of Bakewell to show by what right hee claimed a market and faires there, gallowes, stockes, pillory, a free warren and severall other things, to which there is a plea and judgm't on that plea for Gernoon about the fourth year Edwardi tertii. (Only for part of the liberties) William Peverell by his deed without date but seemeth to be made in Henry the firsts reigne did grant to the prior and co'vent of Lenton in free alms (that monastery being founded by him) int. al. Two parts of all tithes of his lordships and of his demesne pastures in the Peake, naming them particularly, &c., *Item totam decimam pullorum et pullarum ubicunque haracium habuero in Pecco, vel aliquis alius super dominicas pasturas meas. Item totam decimam plumbi mei et venationis meæ, tam coriis quam in carnibus.* And hee did further hereby grant and confirm unto the same monastery whatsoever his men had granted unto it vid'z, *Duas partes omnium decimarum dominicorum suorum, et omnibus rebus quæ decimari possunt, horum primus est, Avenellus qui hoc contulit de dominiis suis in Haddona et in Methweploth,* &c. This appeareth by the records in the tower of London in Rotul Cartarum de anno decimo r's Edvdi soc'di And also de anno 30° r's Edvi 3 tii no° 7°. The miners have by custom used to digg and get lead ore in the s'd lordships & demesne pastures wch were Pev'ells in the Peake & have converted the same to their own uses paying lott & cope to the lords of the fees thereof etc and have paid the tithe or tenth dish of their said lead ore there gotten as followeth (vizd) two third parts thereof to the s'd prior and co'vent of Lenton & those who have had their estate therein & one third part thereof to the Dean and Chapter of Litchfield & those who have had their estate therein. And when the s'd miners have neglected or refused to pay the s'd tithe, customary duty, or tenth dish of lead ore, the s'd proprietors thereof have obtained decrees for the same against the miners within the parishes of Bakewall Tidswell, & Hope in the Peake. But never any miners did get lead ore by any custom within the *manor of Haddon,* nor was there ever any tithe dish or customary

---

(1) Cox, *Churches of Derbyshire*, ii., 16.

duty of lead ore paid by the owners of the said manor for the
lead ore they have gotten therein (though great quantities have
been gotten in several ages) but the owners of the same manor
have converted all the lead ore there gotten from time to time
to their own uses without setting out any tithe or tenth part for
those that have the right of the prior & convent of Lenton and
dean and chapter of Litchfield." Then follows in Mr. Wolley's
handwriting: "5 Feb. 94. Copied the above from an old parchment writing lent me by Mr. Wm Wilson, of Alfreton."[1]

According to an inquisition taken in the year 1272, the
following tithes were due to Lenton Priory:—Bakewell, £3 3s. 4d.;
Ashford, £6; Hulme, £5 8s.; Nether Haddon, £3 8s. 8d.;
Monyash, £1 11s. 8d.; Blackwell, £2 13s. 4d.; Chelmorton, etc.,
£27 6s. 8d.; Bradwell, 15s. 4d.; Hucklow, 4s.; Fairfield, £8 6s. 8d.
Shalcross and Fernilee, 11s.; Tideswell, £1 6s. 8d.; Chapel-en-le-
Frith, £20 6s.; and other dues in Bakewell, Hope, Tideswell, and
Greenlow, amounted to £8.

The Taxation Roll of Pope Nicholas (1291) estimates the
annual income of the Priory from the parish of Bakewell "cum
membris," at £66 13s. 4d., in addition to £5 6s. 8d. from the
church of Glossop.

According to an inquisition of Edward I., the Priory held the
"decima venacionis" of the whole of the Peak district. (Inq.
post mort., 3 Edw. I., No. 37.) A survey of Alien Priories,
taken 3 Richard II., only assigns £4 of the tithes of the parish
of "Capella del Frythe" to Lenton.

On the Tideswell side of the valley known as Monk's Dale, it
appears that the monks of Lenton had a grange where they
probably collected or received the portion of the tithes of the
district given to them by William Peverel. The outline of the
foundations of a chapel attached to the grange is still visible,
the only remains, however, being the carved stones of the low
septum, or stone screen, dividing the chancel from the nave.
They are of 14th century work, and correspond exactly with
those still occupying a similar position in the church of
Chelmorton.[2]

---

(1) Add. MS., 6681. Plut: clxxxiii. D.

(2) Amongst the notes of Francis Bassano, who visited Chelmorton Chapel in 1709,
is one to the effect that "in ye south wall is a little raised tomb, and on ye covering

Reverting to the gift by Peverel to Lenton Priory of two parts of the tithes of his demesne pastures in Chelmorton, the right of which to the Priory was not disputed by the Dean and Chapter of Lichfield, it appears that Archbishop Peckham, in his visitation in 1280, taking this into consideration, treated the case of the chapel of Chelmorton on different terms to the remainder of the chapelries, and ordained that two-thirds of the expense of providing books and ornaments (except the missal and chalice) should be provided by the monks, and only one-third by the Dean and Chapter. The Chapter, however, was to provide the minister, and pay him the yearly stipend of five marcs, as the prior had never held the appointment of minister.[1] According to the *Valor Ecclesiasticus*, Lenton Priory paid thirty shillings annually to the minister at Chelmorton Chapel, Richard Dowkyn being the minister, and the Dean and Chapter of Lichfield received a pension of four shillings from the same chapelry.

We next come to the important donation of the three parish churches of Nottingham, which William Peverel, with the consent of his lord, King Henry the First, bestowed upon the Priory. These were the church of St. Mary, described in the foundation charter as being within the English borough, and the churches of St. Peter and St. Nicholas, both described as being in the French borough, of Nottingham. According to the Taxation of Pope Nicholas, the income derived by the Priory from St. Mary's church was £40. In 1340, the ninth of the sheaf was valued at £10 13s. 4d., sixty acres belonging to St. Leonard's Hospital were uncultivated, and the chapel of St. Michael (which belonged to St. Mary's, and valued at £9 6s. 8d.) was destroyed with the suburbs of the town; the tithe of corn and hay amounted to £2, and the oblations, mortuaries, altarage,

---

stone is a Pastorall Staff." The remains of this tomb have now vanished, but the pastoral staff undoubtedly indicates the burial place of an abbot or prior.

The Rev. J. C. Cox remarks that "it is reasonable to conjecture that here was interred a former prior of Lenton. From the fact of the tomb being in the wall it was probably to the memory of one who had given largely to the building or re-building of the chapel. Lenton Priory drew so large a share of their emoluments from the Peak district, and especially from this chapelry, that we can well understand one of their priors contributing extensively, if not exclusively, to the erection or restoration of Chelmorton Chapel, and requesting that his bones might on that account here find a resting place." Cox, *Churches of Derbyshire*, ii., 85.

(1) Cox, *Churches of Derbyshire*, ii. 80.

etc., to £23.  In 1535 the vicarage was valued in house and
glebe at £1 10s., tithes of bread and beer, £1 6s. 8d., tithes of
wool and lambs, £4, tithe of pigs, chickens, etc., £1, tithes of
fruit, 1s. 8d., and Easter tithes, £3 ; making a clear annual value
of £10 4s. 9d.  The tithes received by the Priory at this time
amounted to £18, and the oblations to £9.

In 1291 the Priory received from St. Peter's church,
Nottingham, a pension of 16s.  In 1340 the ninth of the fleece
and lambs was valued at 2s. 6d., because it had not the sheaf ;
the oblations, altarage, etc., amounted to £6 0s. 2d.  In 1535 the
Rectory was valued at £8 7s. 6d., the pension payable to the
Priory being 16s.

From St. Nicholas's church, Nottingham, Lenton Priory
received in 1291, a pension of 15s.  In 1340 the ninth of the
fleece and lambs was valued at 5s., and the altarage, etc., at
£3 6s. 8d. ; there was no sheaf, because a great part of the
parish was occupied by the brethren of Mount Carmel, who had
acquired divers tenements in the parish.  In 1535 the Rectory
was valued at £3 6s. 8d., exclusive of 10s. payable as pension
to the prior of Lenton.

Peverel also gave to the Priory the church at Radford, from
which, in 1291, the Prior derived an income of £6 13s. 4d.  In
1535 a similar sum was payable to the Priory, as tithes.

The advowson of Linby church was likewise given to
Lenton Priory by its founder.  By a later charter, which
may be referred to here, William Peverel (the younger) granted
to God and the Church of the Holy Trinity, at Lenton, and his
brethren there serving God, the town of Linby, and whatsoever
he held in it, viz., lands tilled and untilled, in wood and in
plain, in meadows and in pastures, with the church of the
same town, and the mill of *Blaccliff,* for the treasures which
his mother bestowed on that church, and which he, compelled by very great necessity, had taken himself ; and for
all other excesses, in which he, by the instinct of the enemy
against that church, imprudently had exceeded, contrary to
the command of his father, and the bargain which he made
with him, and with his mother.[1]

(1) Thoroton, p. 258.

In 1292, Lenton Priory had a pension of 6s. 8d. per annum. In 1340, the ninth of the fleece was valued at £3 13s. 2d., thirty-four acres of land at 15s. 4d., and oblations, etc., at 15s. 6d. In 1535, the Rectory of Linby was valued in house, two bovates of land, and tithes, at £4 9s. 8d., the amount payable therefrom to the Priory being 6s. 8d.

In addition to his gift to the Priory of two parts of the tithe of his demesne lands in Langar, with a villain, holding a virgate of land, to collect the same, which William Peverel conferred by his foundation charter, he also gave the monks the church of Langar. The prior and monks of Lenton do not seem, however, to have attained the advowson, for in the year 1131, Pagan Tibtot held the manor and church of Langar, as of the Honour of Peverel.[1]  In 1316, Thomas Atte Brigg, for the chantry of Langar, held rents.[2]  In 1379, Margaret, wife of Robert Tibtot, held the manor and advowson.[3]  In 1535, the Rectory was valued, exclusive of the portions of Lenton and Thurgarton Priories, at £10 7s. 10d., the portion of Lenton Priory being £12. Other charters relating to Langar, in connection with the monastery, will subsequently be noticed.

The church of Foston, in Leicestershire, with a virgate of land, formed part of the benefaction of William Peverel to the Priory.

In the Matriculus of 1220, *Foston* is described to be under the patronage of the Prior of Lenton; the rector, William de Hinglesham, having been instituted by Hugh, *bonæ memoriæ*. late bishop of Lincoln; and paying to the monks of Lenton 10s. *nomine pensionis ab antiquo*. In the Taxation of 1291, Foston was charged, inclusive of the prior's pension, at 15 marcs.

In 1534, the procurations were 7s. 6¾d.; the rectory was taxed at — marcs; and paid 2s. for Peterpence. The prior of Lenton was then the patron, and had a pension of 10s. from this church. In 1534-5, the procurations and synodals were 11s. 0¾d.; and the rectory was worth £14 13s. 4d.[4]

(1) *Inq. ad quod dam.*, p. 231.     (2) *Inq. a. q. d.* p. 251.

(3) *Inq. post mort.* iii. 23.     (4) Nichol's *Leicestershire*, iv. 172.

The church of *Harleston*, with its appurtenances, was also granted to Lenton Priory by Peverel, in his foundation charter. In 1279 (7 Edw. I.) the advowson was claimed by William de Ferrers (as representative of Peverel), Hugh de Staunton, and Clemencia, his wife ; but, upon an assize of *Darrein Presentment*, was adjudged to be the right of the convent. The practice of deciding legal claims by the sword, and of having champions for that purpose, was common in England in the 12th century. One of the latest instances on record, and perhaps the only one where a church was the object of contention, occurred in 3 Edw. III. (1329), between Thomas, son of Hugh de Staunton, plaintiff, and the Prior of Lenton, defendant. The plaintiff, in support of his claim to this advowson, alleged that in the time of Hen. III., his ancestor, William de Staunton, being seized of it in fee, presented one William de Grendon, who was admitted and instituted to the rectory ; whilst the Prior of Lenton rested his pretensions on the grant of William Peverel. Both parties agreed to submit the decision of their cause to single combat, and William Fitz-Thomas was appointed champion for the former, and William Fitz-John for the latter. Dugdale introduces a circumstantial detail of the proceedings on this occasion, by remarking that it is the most exact narrative which he had ever seen of " the formalities in arming of the combatants and other particular circumstances preparatory to this kind of Tryal." The combat did not, however, actually take place, for after the champions had been sworn at the bar, according to ancient custom, and were ready to advance, the parties obtained a licence of agreement, whereby Staunton released and quit claimed all right in the advowson for himself and his heirs to the prior and his successors for ever.

In 1254, 38 Hen. III., the rectory of Harleston, deducting 40s. for a pension to the Prior of Lenton, and 10s. the portion of the Prior of St. Andrew's, was valued at sixteen marcs.[1] In 1535 the Priory derived, as a pension from Harleston, 2l. a year.

---

(1) Baker, i. 171 ; Bridge, i. 514.

7

The church of *Irchester*, with the tithes belonging to it, were likewise given to Lenton Priory by Peverel. But in the 53rd year of Hen. III., the prior and convent released the church, with all their right to a yearly pension issuing from the profits of the same, to Margaret de Ferrers, Countess of Derby,[1] who then levied a fine of it to the use of herself and her heirs. (Fin. Com. North, anno 53 Henry III.)[2] The special inducements which led the confraternity to divest themselves of this property, which had been granted to them by the founder of their house, does not appear.

The church of *Rushden*, in Northamptonshire, with the tithes and appurtenances belonging to it, and one virgate of land, together with the villain holding the same, was given to the Priory by William Peverel. In 1254 the profits of the rectory of Rushden were rated at ten marcs. In 1535 it was let to farm to Richard Throgmorton at 13*l.* 6s. 8d., out of which was deducted 10s. 7d. in procurations and synodals. The income derived from Rushden at this time by Lenton Priory was 12*l.* a year in tithes, and 4s. as pension. The advowson fell to the Crown on the suppression of the Priory.[3]

We now come to the donations of his subinfeudatories, which William Peverel granted and confirmed to the monastery in the foundation charter. These have all been already enumerated, but there are several of which it will be necessary to give some further details.

At the time when Peverel endowed the Priory with two thirds of the tithes of divers lordships in the Peak, Haddon, Monyash, and Meadow Place were held by William de Avenel, and were specially included in the charter. Although this share of the tithes of Meadow Place belonged to Lenton, it is somewhat remarkable that the land itself, in conjunction with the adjacent hamlet of Conksbery and its water mill, together with twenty acres of land in Over Haddon, were given by William de Avenel to the Abbey of Leicester.[4]  His

---

(1) William de Ferrers, Earl of Derby, d. March 24, 1253-4 (38 Hen. III.), leaving a widow, Margaret, dau. and coheir of Roger de Quincy, Earl of Winchester.
(2) Bridge's *Northamptonshire*, ii. 180.    (3) Ibid, ii., 192.
(4) Cox, *Churches of Derbyshire*, ii. 344.

son, William de Avenel, was likewise a benefactor to the Priory of Lenton, to which monastery he granted an annual income of five shillings out of his mill at Rowsley, by a charter, of which the following is a translation:

"Know present and future that I William de Avenel of Haddon have granted to God and to the Church of the Holy Trinity of Lenton, and to the monks there serving ·God, five shillings out of my mill of Rowsley, to be paid to them yearly on the feast of Saint Mark, or the next day following, which is to be paid to them yearly from my treasury to provide a light in the cloister upon the tomb of my ancestors, my grandfather, my father, and, my mother, and for the safety of my soul, and of my wife, and if the returns of that mill be deficient the five shillings shall be paid to them from some other of my mills, and shall be in perpetual alms. These being witnesses, Master Selone, the miller, Gilbert, chaplain of Nottingham Castle."[1]

This grant was confirmed by Simon de Basset and Richard de Vernon, who had married Elizabeth and Avicia, the two daughters and co-heiresses of William de Avenel.

"Know present, etc., that I Richard de Vernon and Simon de Basset, and our heirs, have granted to the Church of the Holy Trinity of Lenton and to the monks, etc., five shillings from the mill of Rowsley, which William Avenel for the health of himself and of his parents, gave and conceded in perpetual alms, as his charter testifies. The witnesses to this confirmation are Matthew priest of Bakewell, Reginald chaplain of Haddon, and others.[2]

Richard de Vernon, one of the grantors of the foregoing charter, obtained a grant of lands in Tideswell from John, Earl of Mortaigne, in the year 1192, and held the office of Custos of the county of Lancaster. He was buried at Lenton Priory. By his wife, Avicia, he left a son, William (also buried at Lenton Priory), who married Margery, daughter of Robert de Stockport, and was succeeded by his son, Richard.

Safred, or Sasfrid, whose gift of two parts of the tithes of his demesne lands in Basford and in Empingham, in Rutland-shire, was confirmed by his lord, William Peverel, in his foundation charter of Lenton Priory, was one of Peverel's principal feudatory tenants, holding under him the manors of Catesby, in Northamptonshire, Great Ashby, in Leicestershire,

---

(1, 2) Add. MS. 6666, f. 239.

Empingham, in Rutlandshire, and Basford, in this county.
His posterity eventually adopted the local surname of De
Esseby, or Ashby, but his immediate descendants seem to
have varied their names with their residence, and were almost
indifferently styled De Esseby, De Basford, or De Catesby.
Philip, the son of this Safred, was also a benefactor to the
Priory of Lenton, as will be seen hereafter.

Another similar donation, confirmed in the foundation
charter, was that of Robert Fitz Pain (the son of Pagan),
who gave two parts of the tithes of his demesne lands in
Basford, but nothing beyond this fact seems known of him.

Robert de Heriz, who gave two parts of the tithes of his
demesne lands in Ashbourn and Oxcroft, in Derbyshire, is
usually believed to have been identical with that Robert
who is recorded in the Domesday survey as holding lands
under William Peverel, in Tibshelf and South Wingfield, in
that county, but may, perhaps, have been his son. Besides this
donation, which is duly confirmed in the foundation charter, this
same Robert de Heriz afterwards bestowed upon the Prior and
monks of Lenton his mill at Wissendon, in Derbyshire. He
appears to have had two sons, namely, William and Ivo, the
latter of whom confirmed his father's gift of the mill at Wissendon, and gave an annual rent of ten shillings to the monastery.
Ivo de Heriz married Emme, the elder of the two daughters
and coheiresses of Herbert, the Knight of William Peverel, for
whom one of the mills in Lenton was specially reserved in the
foundation charter, and who was himself a benefactor to the
Priory. William de Heriz, lord of Widmerpool and Gonalston,
the eldest son of this Ivo de Heriz, was also a benefactor, as
will be seen hereafter.

The next gift confirmed by the founder in his charter was
that of Godfrey and William, who gave two parts of the tithes
of their demesne lands in Arnesby, in Leicestershire. According
to Nichols,[1] the historian of that county, the monks of Lenton
received *ab antiquo* the tithes from the demesne lands of James
de Mara and Geoffrey le Despenser, and from one virgate of

---

(1) Nichols' *History of Leicestershire*, Vol. iv., p. 13.

land of the fee of Hugh de Alneo, but whether these were derived from the donation of the above-named Geoffrey and William cannot now be determined.

The foundation charter further confirmed the donation by Norman de Montfaltrel of two parts of the tithes of his demesne lands in Chilwell, and in Haslebeech and Harpole, in Northamptonshire. The donor, however, subsequently resumed a portion of his grant, and transferred the tithes of Harpole to the Abbey of St. Albans.[1]  This Norman de Montfaltrel was the father of one Adeline, who gave certain lands in Harpole to St. James's Abbey, near Northampton (another of Peverel's foundations), and her son, Sir Robert de Saucei, or de Salceto, was Sheriff of Northamptonshire in the year 1161.

Passing by the donations of Roger Britto and Jocelin, and of Ralph de Malaherbe and Serlo Blundus, the two latter of whom gave respectively two parts of the tithes of their demesne lands in Aspley, and in Thorpe-in-the-Glebe, we come to that of Herbert, the Knight of William Peverel, who gave two parts of the tithes of his demesne lands in Gonalston. This Herbert, who has previously been alluded to, subsequently gave to the Priory a marc of silver yearly to be paid out of his mill on the river Leen, situated between *Blaccliffe* and the village of Radford. Herbert had no male issue, and dying some time about the year 1138, his lands were divided between his two daughters and coheiresses. Emme, the elder of these, inherited her father's possessions in Gonalston, and in Killamarsh, in Derbyshire, and married Ivo de Heriz; whilst Ivicia, the younger daughter, had her father's lands in Bilborough, and in Mollington, in Northamptonshire, and was married to one of the Fitz Aman family, by whom she had two sons.

Helgotus gave two parts of the tithe of Bosworth and Cotes, in Leicestershire; Robert de Pavelliaco gave the same in Houghton, in Northamptonshire; and Walter Flammeth gave the same in Haversham, in Buckinghamshire, as did Hugh, the son of Richard, in Little Claydon, in that county. All of which gifts were duly confirmed in the foundation charter.

---

(1) Baker's *History and Antiquities of Northamptonshire*, Vol. i., p. 178.

Norman de St. Patric, who, following the example of Peverel's other feudatory tenants, gave to the Priory two parts of the tithes of his demesne lands in Desborough and Blakesley, in Northamptonshire, and in Rowland, in Derbyshire, was the son of Geoffrey de St. Patric, who had held Desborough under Peverel, and doubtless the progenitor of those St. Patrics who subsequently held a part of Nuthall under the Honour of Peverel. The church of Nuthall was given to this monastery by Sir Geoffrey de St. Patricio, or St. Patric, one of this family, as will be seen hereafter.

Geoffrey de Heriz, whose gift of two parts of the tithes of his demesne lands in Stapleford was confirmed in the foundation charter, was very probably a son of that Robert named in the Domesday survey as holding lands in Stapleford under William Peverel, and he might reasonably be identified with that Robert de Heriz, who held lands under William Peverel, in Tibshelf and South Wingfield, in Derbyshire, were it not for the fact that he is usually assumed to have been identical with that Robert who was living at the time when the Priory was founded, and who, as already shown, was himself one of those whose gifts of two parts of the tithes of their demesne lands were confirmed in the foundation charter by their feudal lord. The relationship between this Geoffrey de Heriz and Robert de Heriz, the ancestor of the De Heriz family, lords of Widmerpool and Gonalston, is, therefore, doubtful.[1] With reference to this donation, we find that nearly two centuries later—in the year 1259, the Prior and Convent of Lenton passed both the great and small tithes which they had in the parish of Stapleford to the Prior and Convent of Newstead, in Sherwood, in consideration of an annual rent of five marcs, but, if the canons of Newstead were found to be losers by the transaction, or, if from any cause they should be excluded from the church of Stapleford, then the agreement was to be null and void. Richard de Sutton, canon of Southwell, John, his brother,

---

(1) If, however, as elsewhere suggested (see p. 84), the Robert named in the Domesday survey as holding lands in Tibshelf and South Wingfield, may have been the father of that Robert de Heriz whose name appears in the foundation charter of Lenton Priory, there is no difficulty in the matter, for he and the above-named Geoffrey de Heriz would probably in that case be brothers.

Rector of Lexington (now called Laxton), William Bishop, Rector of St. Nicholas, Nottingham, and others, were witnesses to this agreement.[1]

The two next gifts confirmed by the founder in his charter were those of Adelmus and Robert, the son of Warner, who gave respectively two parts of the tithes of their demesne lands in Kirk Langley, in Derbyshire, and in Toton. The latter was the son of that Warner who is named in the Domesday survey as holding lands in Toton under William Peverel.

The last gift confirmed by the founder is that of Robert de Moretein, who, in lieu of a portion of the tithes of his demesne, gave to the Monastery an annual rent of ten shillings for ever. This Robert de Moretein held Wollaton, together with a part of Cossal, under William Peverel, and was ancestor of a family which remained seated at Wollaton until the earlier part of the fourteenth century, when their lands were acquired, partly through marriage, and partly by purchase, by the Willoughby family.

We have thus traced the extensive spiritual and temporal possessions which the Prior and Monks of Lenton derived from their founder and his tenants, and next come to those donations which were subsequently granted to the confraternity.

Philip, son of Safrid, and Maud, his wife, by the consent of William Peverel, gave to the Monks of Lenton, in honour of the high and undivided Trinity, twenty-four acres of their demesne, viz., a little essart at *Broculstow* [Broxtow], and a tilled place (or wong) called *Trucchere Welle*, and another called *Thorniwang*, another *Copperodes*, besides two bovates which William, son of Gilbert, held, and two which Alfer had in Basford.

Robert,[2] son of the said Philip, confirmed the four bovates of the villanage of Basford, and the twenty-four acres of demesne which his father gave, and likewise confirmed to the church of Lenton all the land in Awsworth of his fee, with a meadow

---

(1) Thoroton, p. 212.

(2) Either this Robert, or his father, was the founder of a nunnery at Catesby, in Northamptonshire.—Baker's *History and Antiquities of Northamptonshire*, Vol. I., pp. 276, 277.

called *Brademedoe;* he likewise released to the same church a meadow, which he once sued the Monks for, namely, "the upper Island which the water of Lene did anciently compass."

William Peverel the younger, with his wife, Odonna, and his son Henry, obtained from King Stephen the following charter in favour of Lenton Priory :—

"Notum sit fidelium sanctæ Dei ecclesiæ piæ devotioni quod ego *Stephanus* rex Anglorum, pro divini cultus amore, et animæ meæ remedio, et uxoris meæ reginæ, et patris mei et matris meæ, et antecessorum meorum, et pro salute filiorum meorum, regiæ excellentiæ autentica largitione concedo ecclesiam S. Trinitatis quæ est in Lentonâ, ac religioni monachorum Cluniacensium ibidem Deo servientium, Willielmo Peverello juniori, cum uxore suâ Oddonâ, et filio suo Henrico id fieri obnixe augitante, plurimumque deprecante, jure perpetuo sub prioratu ac dispositione Cluniacæ institutionis inconcussè et inviolabiter, ac prorsus omni remotâ calumpniâ possidendam, cum universis quæ a patre ipsius Willielmo Peverello, et ab eodem Willielmo, et ab aliis benefactoribus eidem ecclesiæ collata sunt ; id est Radeford et Mortone," etc. (*Ex Registro Prioratus de Lenton in com. Nott. penes S. Roper ar. anno* 1670, *p.* 14*b.*)

Shortly after the foundation of the Priory, we find that Odo de Boneia, one of the witnesses of the foundation charter (who appears to have had considerable possessions at Bunny and elsewhere in that part of the county, which he held of the fee of Ralph Fitz Hubert), gave to the Prior and Convent of Lenton the church of Barton-in-Fabis, and one of the medieties of the church of Attenborough, with their lands, tithes, and other appurtenances, together with such lands in Chilwell as were held by Reginald, his tenant, and two parts of the tithes of his demesne lands in Bunny and Bradmore. This gift was confirmed, at a subsequent period, by one Edward and Aeliz his wife, whose charter was witnessed by Ralph Barre, Ranulph de Insula, Hugh de Boney, and Ralph, his son, Ernald, and others.[1]

Ralph de Bellofago gave to God and to the church of Lenton for the souls of his parents, and his lord King Henry I., two bovates of land, and a short wong, and one acre of meadow in the *Ker,* with Duran his man, who then held that tenor in the

----

(1) Thoroton, p. 43.

territory of Gunthorpe. To his deed were witnesses Remigius, Prior of Shelford, Richard the Canon, Thomas de Bellofago, William de Bellofago, Robert de Burton, William Bret, Gervase de Ludham, Hugh, son of Simon, and many others. He gave likewise to the Monks of Lenton the tithe of his mill at Gunthorpe, situate upon the river Trent, and four shillings yearly, payable out of the profits of his passage (or ford) across the river at Gunthorpe.[1]

Hornius, the reputed ancestor of the Martell family, gave the whole tithe of his demesne lands in Ruddington to the newly-founded Monastery at Lenton, "he offering his gift, and laying his knife upon the altar of the Priory church, Margery, his wife, William, his son, and Duran, the deacon of Flawford, being present and praising the act."[2]

Robert, son of Ralph (de Hickling), for the love of God, and of his lord William Peverel, gave two bovates of land in Crophill-Bishop, to the Priory of Lenton, where he, the said Robert, himself, and Dame Adelina, his wife, and William his son, offered the gift with their own hands upon the altar of the Holy Trinity in the conventual church.[3]

Robert de Bellomont, Earl of Mellent, in Normandy, and Earl of Leicester, early in the reign of Henry I., gave the church of Wigston, in Leicestershire, with the tithes of all his demesne in that lordship, to Lenton Priory. This nobleman was the son of Roger de Bellomont, lord of Pont Andomar, by Adeliza, his wife, sister and heiress of Hugh, Earl of Mellent, and was possessed of vast estates both in this country and in Normandy. He was created Earl of Leicester by King Henry the First, in 1107, and was the founder of the collegiate church at Leicester. His death occurred on the fifth of June, 1118, at the Abbey of Preux, in Normandy, where his remains were interred. He

---

(1) Thoroton, p. 288.

(2) Thoroton, p. 65. It was formerly the custom, when the property given was immovable, to place some symbol upon the altar. In the case of land, a turf or twig was laid upon the altar. Sometimes a knife was offered as a symbol, and very frequently, either that it might be preserved from being stolen, or perhaps, also, that it might be remembered, the knife was bent before the witnesses, and in some cases it seems to have been broken.

(3) Thoroton, p. 95.

was succeeded in his English earldom by his second son,
Robert de Bellomont, surnamed le Bossu, by whom these gifts
were confirmed about the year 1140; from him the lordship of
Wigston descended to Roger de Quincy, Earl of Winchester,
in right of his mother, Margaret, one of the daughters and
coheirs of Robert Fitz Parnell, Earl of Leicester.

### Charter of Robert Bellomont.

"Notum sit omnibus Dei fidelibus, quod ego Robertus comes
de Mellent concedo ecclesiam de Wichingestonâ pro animâ meâ
& dominorum atque antecessorum meorum, nove ecclesie Sancte
Trinitatis de Nottingham, cum omnibus supradicte ecclesie per-
tinentibus. Testibus: Comitissa, & Ricardo Pincernâ, Gilberto
capellano, Gaufrido Medico, Albedo-ido Accipitre. [*Reg. Lenton,
penes Sam. Roper, de Heanor,* 1677, fol. 126).

### Confirmation Charter of Robert Bossu.

"Notum sit omnibus Dei fidelibus, quod ego Robertus comes
Legrecestrie concedo ecclesiam de Wichingestonâ, sicut pater
meus eam concesserat, pro animâ meâ & antecessorum meorum,
ecclesie Sancte Trinitatis de Nottingham, cum tribus virgatis
terre eedem adjacentibus, & cum tribus toftis & croftis. Testibus, Ernaldo de Bosco, &c."

The right of the Prior of Lenton having after this been
called in question, it was thus confirmed about the year 1210,
by Saher de Quincy, Earl of Winchester.

"Omnibus Christi fidelibus has literas inspecturis, Saherus de
Quincey, comes de Wintonie, salutem in Domino. Noverit
universitas vestra quod ego, per fidedeq.nam & diligentem
inquisitionem tam clericalem quam laicalem, certificationem
quod jus patronatûs ecclesie de Wykingeston pertineat ad prioratum de Lenton, unanimi assensu & voluntate Margarete comitisse
uxoris mei & Roberti de Quinci heredis mei, renunciavi jus
patronatûs ecclesie predicte, quod aliquando ad me & heredes
meas debere pertinere vendicavi, & pro me & meorum predicte
prioratui in perpetuum quietam clamavi. Hiis testibus; Roberto
de Quinci, Patricio, Willielmo de Trumpetonâ, Everardo de
Trumpetonâ, Willielmo de Oappewell, Briteno, & multis aliis."

In the Matriculus of 1220, Wikingeston is described to be
under the patronage of the Prior of Lenton, the rector A
having been instituted by Hugh, Bishop of Lincoln, and paying

to the monks of that Priory 40s. as an ancient pension, and 40s. more *nomine* procurationis de novo; and the Monks of St. Ebrulf had then 3s. for two parts of the demesne lands of the Monks of Leicester, who had demised the same to the rector at an annual rent of two marcs.

In the Taxation of Pope Nicholas IV., 1291, "Ecclesia de Wykingston, præter XLVIII. marcas & dimidiam," paid a pension of 100s. to the Prior of Lenton. Wigston was therefore valued at 56 marcs, or £37 6s. 8d.

On August the 19th, 1316, King Edward II. confirmed to the Priory of Lenton, *inter alia* "concessionem quam Robertus comes de Mellent fecit predicte ecclesie Sancte Trinitatis de ecclesia de Winchengestone, cum omnibus pertinentiis suis; & concessionem quam Robertus quondam comes Legrecestrie fecit predicte ecclesie Sancte Trinitatis de predictâ ecclesiâ de Winchengestoniâ, & de tribus virgatis terre ei adjacentibus cum tribus toftis & croftis cum pertenentiis suis."[1]

In 1324, the Monks of Lenton obtained a confirmation grant from King Edward III. for the church of Wickingston.[2]

In 1344, the procurations were 7s. 6¾d.; the vicarage was taxed at 56 marcs, and paid 4s. for Peter-pence. The then patron was the Prior of Lenton, who had a pension from it of 100s.

No further mention of Wigston is to be found till 1506, when the endowment of the vicarage from the appropriation was settled at 13 marcs and a half (£9).

The value of the vicarage in 1534 is stated to be, *in decimis majoribus & minoribus, cum manso et aliis proficuis, communibus annis, 9l. 8s. 9d.*

According to the register of Croxton Abbey, in Leicestershire, William the Conqueror bestowed a complete knight's fee (containing twelve ploughlands) in Nether Broughton, Leicestershire, upon Albert Bussell, or Buissell, by the service of paying ten shillings annually as castle-guard, and performing suit of court to the Honour of Leicester. This Albert Bussell granted to the Prior and Convent of Lenton six bovates of land in

---

(1) Cart., 10 Ed. II., No. 50.     (2) Pat. 7 Ed. III., p. 1, m. 18.

Nether Broughton, at an annual rent of thirty shillings, payable by the monks or their tenants at the feast of St. John the Baptist.[1]

At a later date, Richard Bussell, a member of the same family, gave to the Monks of Lenton the church of Nether Broughton, with all its appurtenances and liberties, and a certain chapel which belonged to it, and fifteen acres of land in the same place, for maintaining the services of the said chapel.

" Sciant omnes fideles presentes & futuri, quod ego Ricus Bussellus dedi in eleemosinam finalitèr, pro meâ & omnium antecessorum meorum animabus, sex bovatas terre, de meo dominio de Brochtonâ, priori Humfro & conventui Sce Trinitatis de Lentonâ ; superaddeus unum toftum, ad fratribus meis carissimis unam mansuram faciendam &c. in remissionem peccatorum meorum & omnium parentum meorum ; quod sigilli impressione corroboravi, & per unum cultellum quem super majus altare posui, coram priore & conventu, & Robto filio Drogonis, & Gilbto Malecunei, & Petro de Baseford, & Robto de Scâ Mariâ, and Robto Tornatore, & Rico Coco ; & postea ad Brochtonam, coram istis Alberto & Gawford, fratribus meis hoc donum laudantibus ; Warino presbytero de aliâ Brochtonâ ; & Willo de Cranillâ, Goiâ Turulfo, ac Werno Clerico Alwin." (This deed is of the time of Henry I. from the Lenton Register, fol. 110, formerly belonging to S. Roper.)

" Notum sit tam presentibus quam futuris, quod ego Ricus Buissellus dedi Deo & monasterio Sce Trinitatis de Lenton ecclesiam de Brochtonâ, cum capellâ que est in eâdem villâ, cum gardino quod est subtùs eam versùs meridiem ; & medietatem curtis mee, &c. Testes sunt horum, Adam capellanus, Robtus Malebisse, Assur de Nottingham ; Ausketillus, frater ejus ; Waltus Forcard, Swanus, & Adam, armigeri ejusdem Rici ; Edwardus de Lenton, Gaufridus Molendarius." (Ex Libro de Lenton penes S. Roper.)

" Sciant presentes & futuri, quod ego Adam, filius Elie, amore Dei & penitentiâ ductus, recognovi & reddidi priori & monachis de Lenton' totam terram meam de Brochton', quam carta Rici Bussell dat eis & testatur eos habuisse infra villam & extra, tali conditione quod ipsi eam monachi concesserunt, ad tenendum de eis totâ vitâ meâ, pro quinque solidis annuatim persolvendis ; & post decessum meum reddam illis totam terram illam, liberam & solutam de me & heredibus meis, excepto servitio forinseco, quod persolvent heredibus meis, si Brochtonam tenuerunt ; &, ad confirmationem hujus rei, faciam eos habere cartam albi

---

(1) Nichols' *History and Antiquities of Leicestershire*, ii., 109.

Alberti Bussel ad confirmandam donationem fratris sui super
easdem terras. Testes sunt, Willus de Heriz, Willus de Villers,
Robtus filius Radi, Adam de Moretein. Et ego Adam, cum
eâdam terrâ, reddo meipsum, sive in vitâ, sive in morte, ad
monachatum recipiendum." (Roper MS.)

It appears, however, that Henry le Faukener and his wife,
Honora, had previously given to their son, Ralph, the advowson
of the church of Broughton, with the chapel belonging to it,
and also fifteen acres of land for the service of the said chapel,
together with twelve bovates of land.

This Ralph, succeeding to the inheritance on the death of
his father and mother, held the same during his life ; and was
succeeded by his son and heir, Peter de la More, who is
mentioned in the Testa de Nevill, about 1230, as holding a
knight's fee under the Honour of Leicester.   Peter enfeoffed
Walter, the Cook (Walterum cocum), of Dalby, in three virgates
of land at Broughton, and four tofts, on a rent of 54s. ; and
afterwards demised to the *Abbot and Convent of Croxton*
the entire lordship, on performing the accustomed annual
services.

This donation of Peter de la More was before 1241 ; for in
that year the Abbot of Croxton exhibited his complaint against
the Prior of Lenton, for his not paying to the Abbot of Croxton
the rent of 12d., for twelve bovates of land belonging to Lenton,
and lying at Brotton.

To confirm the title of the Abbot and Convent to their
property at Broughton, we find them afterwards petitioning the
king ; who, by a writ, dated at Westminster, Feb. 6, 1256, and
by a second from St. Albans, March 8, directs the sheriff of
Leicester to convene the proper officers of the pleas of the
crown, and the bailiff of the Honour of Lancaster ; and then
to discover, by the oaths of a jury, the true value of the
premises, and by what tenures they were held.  And on this
inquisition it was returned, that the lands and tenements which
Peter de la More had given to the Abbot and Convent owed
no suit to the county court, nor to that of any hundred ;
but to the court of the Honour of Lancaster it was of the
annual value of half a marc ; and the view of Frankpledge

from the Abbot's tenants and servants was worth 2s. ; and that
no other services or outgoings were then due to the king,
except the 10s. payable *ad wardam castri Lancastrie.*

The King thereupon confirmed the gift, which included
" dominicum, homag', wardas, relevia, & escheat'." ; and it is
particularly observed in the deed, that the Prior of Lenton
was answerable to the Abbot of Croxton for the payment of
the castle-guard of Lancaster, and had fifteen pence a year
to pay for 12 bovates of land, which had then been in arrear
for two years.

After this, however, the Abbot and Convent were entangled
in several successive suits of law concerning their property at
Broughton, which may be best explained by transcribing portions of the proceedings :

" Sciendum quod villa de Brocton respondet pro quatuor
franciplegiis, quorum tres sunt in feodo abbatis de Croxton, &
unus de feodo prioris de Lenton, qui faciunt sectam predicte
curie bis in anno, vid', ad magnam curiam post festum Sci
Michaelis, & ad magnam curiam post Pasch'.

" Idem vero prior de Lenton tenet in villâ de Brocton, in
comitatu Leic', in valle de Beuver, xii. bovatas terre & vii. toft',
que reddunt xv. den' ad wardam Lanc' ad Nativitatem Sci
Johannis Bapt', & omnia forinsec' servitia tanto tenemento
pertinentia in eâdem villâ.  Item respondet pro tanto tenemento
predictâ villatâ ad omnia provenientia dicte ville pertinentia.
Et sciendum quod Rog' de Normanton, prior de Lenton, fecit
omnia servitia prenominata abbati Galfrido de Croxton.     Et
prior Damascenus de Lenton, predecessor dicti Rog', fecit eadem
servicia predicto Galfr' abbati tempore suo.  Que quidem servitia
forins' dictus Rogerus prior subtraxit post festum Sci Michaelis
anno Dni M.CC.XL. primo, & annum servitium xvd. debitum
abbati & conventui de Croxton, & sepius solutum, pro duodecim
bovat' terre."

" Omnibus xpi fidelib' presens script' vis' vel audit', Henr'
Marescall salutem in Domino.   Noverit universitas vra me
concessisse, obligâsse, & fide mediâ presenti scpto confirmâsse
dno Galf' n'c abbati de Croxton, quod nunquam aliqd bellum
cont' predictum abbatem vel successores suos quoscunque
manucapiam pro dno Rogero priore de Lenton, vel successor'
suis quibuscunque, de terrâ in villâ de Brocton, super quâ motum
est placitum inter partes superius nominat'.  Et ad majorem
hujus rei secur' robur & firmitatem presenti scripto sigillum
meum apposui.  Hiis test'.  Dat'."

In 1268, the abbot and Convent of Croxton were again involved in a lawsuit on account of their possessions at Broughton, on the termination of which the property of the Priory of Lenton was thus defined :—

" Et de feodo Petri de la More viii. carucatas terre ; de quibus prior de Lenton habet unam carucatam & dimidiam ; & abbas de Croxton habet unam carucatam, pro duobus solidis reddend' ad festum Sci Martini pro omni servitio. Et dominus Petrus de la More & villani sui habent quinque carucatas terre & i. virg', & Walterus filius Henrici Falcanare unam virgatam.

" Item prior de Lenton habet in villâ de Brocton donationem ecclesie, & duas bovatas terre liberas, pertinent' ad dictam ecclesiam ; & habet dictus prior duodecim bovatas, que reddunt annuatim septem solidos & forinsecum servitium. Et sciendum quod tota terra dicti prioris in Brocton est de dono Alberti Bussel,[1] & donatio ecclesie."

In the 5th year of Henry III., the Prior of Lenton occurs as patron of the church of Broughton. The then parson was John de Bradley, instituted by Hugh de Welles, Bishop of Lincoln. The said John de Bradley paid the Prior a pension of 30s., the original amount having been 10s. In 1344, the procurations were 7s. 6d., the rectory was taxed at 20 marcs, and paid 2s. for Peter-pence. The Prior of Lenton had also from it a pension of 30s. In a subsequent taxation, Broughton is rated at 17 marcs, and 10s., and the Prior of Lenton's pension was 30s. In 1534-5, the procurations and synodals were 11s., the Prior's pension 30s., and the value of the rectory £13 13s. 4d.

Soon after the foundation of the Monastery, Richard de Barneston gave two bovates of land in Colston Basset, together with the villein who held them. This gift was confirmed to the Monks of Lenton by his son, Gervase de Barneston, who likewise with the consent of Margaret, his faithful wife, and of Richard, his son and heir, bestowed upon the Priory two bovates of land in Wiverton, with the man who held them. In 1179, this last-named Richard de Barneston came before John Cumin, Alan de Furneus, Hugh de Raherst, and William de Bending, the king's itinerant justices, who were then at

---

(1) Croxt Reg., p. 3.

Nottingham, and confirmed his father's donation to the Priory
of Lenton, in the presence of Robert de Davidville, Serlo de
Grendon, William Fitz-Ranulph, Samson de Strelley, Gervase
de Wiverton, and very many others.[1]

Odo, the son of John, for the repose of the soul of his son,
John, and Matthew, son and heir of the said Odo, for the
repose of the soul of his said brother, together gave to the
Priory of Lenton all that land in Normanton-on-Soar, which
had been held by Herbert, the father of John (and presumably
grandfather of this Odo), being in all about sixteen acres, lying
on both sides of the way at the west end of the village, and then
held, at an annual rent of four shillings, by Ogga and Junger.
There was a subsequent reference to this land in the Monastic
Register, for, in 1247, Thomas de Arches, in consideration of the
sum of one hundred shillings paid him by the Prior, released, by
fine, all his claim to the same.[2]

Robert de Gresle (who appears to have derived his descent
from a common progenitor with the noble house of Basset) gave
one bovate of his demesne in Cotgrave to the Priory of Lenton;
Ralph, then rector of that mediety of the church of Cotgrave
which was in the patronage of this Robert de Gresle, being a
witness to his gift.[3]

Andrew de Cortingstoc (conjectured by Thoroton to have
been the son of that William who held certain lands in Costock
under Ralph de Burun at the time of the Domesday survey)
gave two bovates of land to the Priory of Lenton. His son
Robert confirmed this gift, and gave his churches of Cortingstoc
and Rempstone to the said Priory, with a great curse upon his
heirs, if any of them should annul his gift; which was confirmed
by Roger de Burun, his lord, and likewise by Roger, the said
Robert's own son. Upwards of a century later, William de
Corthingstock, the son of Philip Corthingstock, gave a certain
toft in Costock to the Prior and Convent of Lenton for two
shillings of yearly rent, which he and his ancestors were wont
to pay them for two bovates of land here, together with the

(1) Thoroton, p. 81.          (2) Ibid, p. 5.
(3) Ibid, p. 83.

advowsons of the churches of Corthingstock [Costock] and
Rempstone, which they held of them.[1]

According to the registers of Felley Priory, it appears that a
part of an open hay, or wood, called Fulwood, was bestowed
upon the Monks of Lenton, at an early period, by Robert, the
son of John de Newthorpe. Henry de Grey (the youngest son
of Sir Henry de Grey, Lord of Codnor, and Dame Isolda, his
wife), for the repose of the souls of his parents, and of the souls
of his ancestors, and of all the faithful departed, subsequently
released to the Prior and Convent of Lenton all claim and right
of common pasture in Fulwood, either belonging to the Castle
of Codnor, or to the town of Eastwood, or to any of his villeins.
His charter was witnessed by his eldest brother, Sir Richard de
Grey, and by Sir Henry de Perpount, Sir Gervase de Clifton,
Sir Geoffrey de Stapleford, and others.[2]    In 1286, Ranulph
Paskayle, of Eastwood, for himself, his heirs, freeholders, and
villeins, released to the Priory all claim and right of common
pasture in the same place; Robert de Kynmarley, William de
Bellew, Robert de Watenhowe, John Passeys, and Robert
Frauncis, being witnesses to his charter. About the same time,
William Pascayl, of Eastwood, likewise released his right of
common in Fulwood to the monastery; as did William, son of
Godfrey de Estwait, Thomas, son of William de la Rode, and
others. Whereupon the Prior of Lenton enclosed Fulwood, and
appropriated it to the exclusive use of his monastery.[3]    This
proceeding was resented by Adam de Markham, then rector of
Eastwood, who, in 1290, instituted a suit against the Prior and
Monks of Lenton, alleging that they had unjustly deprived him
of his right of common in about one hundred and fifty acres of
pasture in Fulwood. The Prior pleaded that Fulwood was an
extra-parochial place, and gained the suit.[4]    But there was,
however, another trial concerning the same matter, wherein the
Prior pleaded that Fulwood was in Newthorpe, in the parish of
Greasley, and this having been proved to the satisfaction of the
jury, the rector of Eastwood was again defeated.[5]    There is a

---

(1) Thoroton, pp. 28, 29.    (2) Ibid, p. 237.    (3) Ibid, p. 237.
(4) *Abbreviatio Placitorum*, p. 224.    (5) *Ibid.*

8

small extra-parochial district, known as Fulwood, not far from
Sutton-in-Ashfield, which was formerly included in the perambulations of Sherwood Forest, being described as the "coppice-
wood of our lord the king called ffulwood ;" but this could hardly
have been the place enclosed by the Prior of Lenton. On the
other hand, there is no place called Fulwood to be found in the
neighbourhood of Eastwood or Newthorpe.

Ralph de Insula, and Matilda Malebisse, his wife, gave to the
Priory the church of Tollerton, which gift was confirmed, in the
reign of King Henry the Second, by their grandson, Richard
Barri,[1] Lord of Tollerton, with the consent of Beatrice, his wife.
And, about the same time, Serlo de Torlavistune gave his
moiety of the same church to Lenton Priory, at the request, and
with the consent of William de Olive, then parson of it. The
charter of Serlo Torlavistune was witnessed by Adelina, his
wife, and by the above-named Beatrice, the wife of Richard
Barri.[2]

In 1195, the Prior of Lenton recovered the advowson of the
church of Tollerton from Ralph Barre,[3] the son of that Richard
Barri who had confirmed the original grant of the church to the
Monastery.

Ralph, son of Richard, the Knight of Bradmere, gave and
granted to Robert de Glamorgan, who was the Pope's sub-
deacon and rector of Bunney, the homages, rents, and services
of John, the son of Thomas, the chaplain of Plumptre, and his
heirs, and of William, his own son and heir, and of very many
others who held of him in Bradmore; all which, with divers
other lands, rents, and services, were given by the said Robert
to God and the blessed Virgin, and Roger, the Prior of Lenton,
and the monks there serving God, for the souls of his ancestors
and his successors, chiefly of Philip de Glamorgan, his father,
and Amabile, his mother ; and that the said Prior and Convent

---

(1) He was ancestor of the Barry family, of Tollerton, which became extinct in
the male line in the latter half of the sixteenth century. The heiress of the Barry
family married into the Pendock family, whose heiress carried the Manor of Tollerton, by marriage, to the Neales. The present representative is Robert Otter-Barry,
Esq., who recently sold the Manor of Tollerton, which had been held for so long a
period by his ancestors.

(2) Thoroton, p. 84.          (3) *Abbreviatio Placitorum*, 99.

should pay him and his successors at Boney, yearly, on Easter Day, a penny for all services, yet so that they should, of their charity, celebrate his obit, and the obits of the said Sir Philip, his father, and the Lady Amabil, his mother, of Britan de Fressenville, and Willimina, his wife, every year.[1]

Robert, son of Ralph, and all his heirs, gave to God and the church of the Holy Trinity, at Lenton, two bovates of land in Sutton Passeys.  One of them was that which Erchin held with a toft, divided into three parts ; the other was half a bovate, which Matthew held, but he filled it up and made a whole one of it out of his demesne.  This gift was offered by Robert, before God and His saints, upon the altar of the Holy Trinity, in the conventual church at Lenton, for the health of the soul of his most dear wife, Adelina, that her memory might be celebrated every year. The witnesses to this donation were Richard, Abbot of Leicester ;[2] Robert Avenell, Roger, the son of Adelina ; Peter de Sandiacre, Jofrid Bochart, Gubert de Nottingham, Herbert, son of Gladwin ; Ralph, son of Lewin ; Hugh de Sutton, Helric de Sutton, Grunquetel, Anselinus de Radclive, Everard de Lenton, and Gervase, his son, and many others.

Robert de Passeys subsequently gave to God and the building of the church of the Holy Trinity, at Lenton, for the health of his soul, and of Alice, his wife, and William, his father, and Adelina, his former wife, fifteen acres of his demesne in Sutton.

William de Passeys, son of Robert de Passeys, confirmed the fifteen acres of the gift of his father, and gave four acres himself.[4]

The family of Passeys held Sutton by petty sergeancy of finding a horse and sack for the army of Wales (Testa de Nevill).[5]

---

(1) Thoroton, p. 49.

(2) Richard was elected Abbot of Leicester in 1144.

(3) Thoroton, p. 220.        (4) Ibid.

(5) The village of Sutton Passeys existed in the reign of Queen Elizabeth, for it is entered in a Subsidy Roll of the year 1558.  In Thoroton's time, however, it was "totally decayed," and the site lost in Wollaton Park.  It is probable that it had disappeared many years before this time.

The Prior of Lenton held sixteen acres of this sergeancy, and paid the king 3s. per annum. William Passeys afterwards came and warranted that land to the Prior, and held the rest of the sergeancy, then valued at 100s.[1]

In 1144, Hugo de Burun, and Hugo called Meschines, his son and heir, gave to God and the monastery of Lenton, the church of Ossington, in this county, and that of Horsley, in Derbyshire, and half the church of Cotgrave, which one Nicholas then held. This was done with great solemnity in the chapter-house of the Convent, many witnesses being present, and among the rest his younger son, Roger, who much approved of the gift his father was making to God.[2]

This Hugo de Burun, whose seat at this time was Horistan Castle, in Horsley Park, Derbyshire, afterwards gave, with the consent of his sons, Hugh and Roger, to Lenton Priory, Turchetill, his man, of Cotgrave, with his children and lands, and all things he held of him ; and all the land which Walter, son of Jocelin, held of him in the said town, and the land of Swinecliff and Greendale, which were of his demesne.

In 1147, he also gave whatsoever he had in the town of Cotgrave, except the knights, which he kept in his own hand, for the service of the king, and for his son and heir. To this were witnesses of his own men—Robert, son of Andrew, of Costock ; Robert de Rosello ; Robert, son of Serlo ; Albert the Knight, who was his steward, and described as of Kilburne ; Hugo de Busli, his chamberlain, and several others.[3]

He also gave the Monks three bovates of his demesne lands in Cotgrave, in exchange for three bovates which they had in Ossington ; and he likewise gave them as much meadow as appertained to these three bovates in Cotgrave, and also

---

(1) Thoroton, p. 220.        (2) Ibid, p. 355.

(3) A fine was levied, 2 John, whereby the Prior of Lenton released to Robert de Burun, grandson of Hugo de Burun, two carucates of land in Cotgrave, in exchange for three bovates and a half Geldehomor.—*Thoroton*, p. 82.

six acres of meadow land on the Wolds, for which the Monks
gave him a war-horse, valued at ten marcs of silver.[1]

This gift was confirmed by an undated charter of King
Stephen, as follows :—

"Stephen, king of England, to the Archbishop of York,
and to the justiciers and sheriffs and barons and ministers and
to all his faithful French and English, of Nottinghamshire,
greeting. Know ye that I have confirmed and granted that
gift which Hugo de Burun made to the church of the Holy
Trinity of Lenton and to the Cluniac monks there serving God
of his whole land which he had in Cotgrave, except the service
of four knights as the said Hugo gave and by his charter
confirmed to them. Wherefore I will and firmly enjoin that they
well and in peace shall hold the same honourably and freely
and quietly as Hugo ever better and more freely held it and as
they hold his other gifts—Witness, Richard de Canvill, R. de
Curci, Baldwin son of Gilbert, W. Peverel, and W. de Albini,
at Lincoln." [2]

Hugo de Burun, considering out of the reasoning given
him of God, the life of this sliding age to be short and
troublesome, and that he that giveth to the poor of Christ,
lendeth to God, on the day when the Lady Albreda, his wife,
was buried, for her soul, his own, and the souls of his sons
and daughters, and all his ancestors, by the consent of his
sons, Hugh and Roger, gave to the church of the Holy
Trinity, at Lenton, his land of Almeton, which gift he and
his beloved sons laid on the greater altar, in the presence
of Humphrey the Prior, and the convent of brethren.[3]

Roger de Burun flourished in the reign of Henry II. His
wife, Nichola, was, after his death, married by the Earl of
Chester to Anketina de Brikesard, without the consent of
the king, and was, therefore, diseised of divers, if not all her
lands, for some of which she compounded about the second
year of King John.

Roger de Burun recited all those parcels given to Lenton
by his father, and many others; two bovates of the land of
Hugh Rosel; thirteen acres given for the soul of Albrea,

---

(1) Thoroton, p. 82.        (2) *Mon. Angl.*, v. 112.
(3) Thoroton, p. 373.

his own mother, and twenty acres above Cotgrave Wood, etc. To his deed Gervase de Clifton was a witness.[1]

The arms of the ancient family of Burun or Byron, are, *Argent*, three bendlets enhanced *gules*.

Radulphus de Burun, temp. Will. I.[2] = .....

Hugo de Burun = Albreda

Hugo Meschines, fil et hær, Monachus, sine prole.

Roger de Burun, 12 H. 2, Bar. de Horistan Castro — Nichola fil. Roeland de Verdun, postea nupta Anketina de Brikesard.

Hugo de Burun, the elder brother of the last-named Roger de Burun, gave his body to God and the church of the Holy Trinity, at Lenton, and there took the habit and religion of the Cluniac Monks, that God might avert the scourge of his wrath from him, due for the very great multitude of his sins ; and for the soul of his lord, King Richard the First, his ancestors and heirs, and likewise for his own, gave and granted to God, the said church of Lenton, and the monks there serving God, the whole town of Ossington, with all its appendages. It appears, however, that he had previously given the same to the hospitallers of St. John of Jerusalem, which occasioned suits among the religious, especially for the advowson of the church. Walter Smallet by his deed inrolled 5 John, for the souls of King John, the Queen, Roger de Burun, his father, mother, and their ancestors, confirmed the town of Ossington to the hospitallers, retaining nothing but the prayers of the

---

(1) Thoroton, p. 82.

(2) These Buruns were the ancestors of Lord Byron, the poet, who writes in the following strain about Ralph or Radulphus de Burun, the grantee of William I. :—

"I can't complain, whose ancestors are there,
Ernius, Radulphus, eight-and-forty manors
(If that my memory doth not greatly err)
Were their reward for following Billy's banners ;
And though I can't help thinking 'twas scarce fair
To strip the Saxons of their *hydes*, like tanners,
Yet, as they founded churches with the produce,
You'll deem, no doubt, they put it to a good use."

*Don Juan*, c. x., s. xxxvi.

house of that hospital. The Prior of Lenton, 9 John, produced
the gift of Hugh de Burun and confirmation of Roger, as it is
before mentioned. The Prior of the hospital of St. John
pleaded that they had seisin of the town of Ossington, where
the church was situate, of the gift of Roger de Burun, who gave
them that town, and produced his charter testifying the same,
and also another charter, which especially spoke concerning the
church. The Prior of Lenton's attorney did not wish to state
his case to the jury before he had consulted with his client, and,
therefore, the case was postponed until fifteen days after Easter,
at which time, the jury found that Roger de Burun presented
the last parson, who died, to the church of Ossington, and,
therefore, held that the brethren of the hospital should have the
seisin, and the Prior of Lenton be in mercy.[1] Yet not very
long before, Roger, Archbishop of York, admitted and instituted
Geoffrey, the clerk, parson of this church, upon the presentation
of the Prior and monastery of Lenton, and gave to the Priory
two shillings a year, as a pension out of the benefice.[2]

The dispute appears to have been finally settled in 1209, for,
on the Monday after the feast of St. Andrew in that year,
there was a fine levied at Leicester, between Peter, Prior of
Lenton, and Robert, the treasurer of the Prior of the Hospital
of St. John of Jerusalem, whereby the Prior of Lenton released
to the hospitallers all claim to the church of Ossington, in
consideration of which the hospitallers transferred to the Prior
and monks of Lenton the right of advowson to that mediety
of the church of Hunsworth, in Yorkshire, which they had
held.[3]

The church of Horsley was erected by the Buruns, who gave,
as we have seen (p. 100), the advowson to Lenton Priory. In
1291, according to the Taxation Roll of Pope Nicholas IV., the
church was valued at £26 13s. 4d. per annum. In 1304, the
vicar was instituted on the presentation of the Prior of Lenton.

The annual value of the vicarage is estimated at £7 5s. 5d. in
the *Valor Ecclesiasticus.*

---

(1) Abb. plac., p. 60.        (2) Thoroton, p. 355.
(3) Ibid.

In 1304, as appears from the Lichfield registers and the returns of the First Fruits Office, one William le Malinere held the vicarage of Horsley. His successor was Herbert Poucher, who was instituted in 1309, and he was succeeded, in 1313, by Henry Pouger, who resigned his benefice two years later, and was succeeded by his brother, Herbert Pouger, who resigned the vicarage of Horsley, on being presented to the rectory of St. Nicholas, Nottingham, in 1317. On the death of the next vicar, Henry de Halum, in 1317, Roger de la Place de Ambaston became vicar, and on his resignation in 1342, Robert de Rodyngton was presented to the vicarage by the king, who then held the Priory of Lenton (as an alien monastery). On the death of the last-named vicar, in 1349, Richard de Broydeston was presented to the benefice by the king, and a few years later (though the precise date does not seem to be recorded), the Prior and Convent of Lenton presented Richard de Grey, who in 1363 exchanged livings with William de Bromley, vicar of Sawley, by the mutual consent of their respective patrons. On the resignation of the next vicar, John Gylot, in 1418, Thomas Stacey became vicar. He resigned in 1442, and was succeeded by John Vycare, upon whose death, in 1457, Richard Ellys was presented to the vicarage. He resigned in 1464, and was succeeded by John Byngeley, who died in 1468. His successor, Henry Kent, died in 1486, and was succeeded by Nicholas Wodishawe, who died in 1500. Upon the death of the last-named vicar, Thomas Mayson was presented to the benefice, and he was succeeded by Thomas Browne, who was the last vicar of Horsley presented by the Prior and Convent of Lenton.[1]

Gilbert, the son of Eustace de Broculstowe, gave to the church of the Holy Trinity at Lenton, and the monks there serving God, one toft lying in Broxtow, on the eastern side of the church.[2]

About the same time, John de Laci, Baron of Haulton, and Constable of Chester, gave to God and the Church of the Holy Trinity at Lenton, and his brethren, the monks there serving

---

(1) Cox's *Churches of Derbyshire*, iv. 243.
(2) Thoroton, p. 232.

God, any first draught of sperlenes (smelts or gudgeons) next after the draught of his steward, in his fishing of Chilwele ; and whatsoever in the said draught God should bestow on the said brethren, as salmon or lamprey, or any other kind of fish, he gave them freely.  The witnesses to this charter were Henry Biset, and Albreda de Lisures, his wife (sister of John de Laci), and Geoffrey, the said Constable's son ; Samson de Strelley, Geoffrey, Hugh, and Philip, his sons ; Roger de Weston, and many others.  At another time, he gave to the monks a draught in the river of *Berse*, called *Sandewarpe*, so that the fish should be for the monks' own use, and not let to farm ; and in the same charter he gave the third draught in the fishing of Chilwell, together with an acre of his demesne to enclose, to make a dwelling for their servants to look after their fishing.  In consideration of these gifts, the monks were to make an anniversary for his father and mother during his life, and afterwards for himself.  To this charter were witnesses (after some clergy) Roger de Laci, his son and heir, Ralph de Furneis, Sampson de Strelley, Richard and Geoffrey, younger sons of the donor, and many others.[1]

John de Laci was the grandson of Eustace Fitz-John, the builder of the castle at Castle Donnington, in Leicestershire, who had married for his second wife, Agnes, daughter and co-heiress of William Fitz Nigel, Baron of Halton and Constable of Chester, and had succeeded to those dignities in right of his wife.  His son, Richard Fitz-Eustace, had married Albreda de Lisures, half-sister and heiress of Robert de Laci, lord of Pontefract ; and after his death in 1193, she seized his barony, whereupon her eldest son, John (the benefactor to Lenton Priory), assumed the surname and arms of De Laci.  John de Laci married Alice, daughter of Geoffrey de Mandeville, the founder of Walden Abbey, in Essex, by whom he had five sons. The eldest of these, Roger de Laci, was surnamed "Helle" from his fierce disposition.  Richard, the third son, whose name also occurs amongst the witnesses of the second charter granted by his father to Lenton Priory, died of leprosy, and was buried in the chapter house of Norton Abbey, in Cheshire.  This same

---

(1) Thoroton, p. 206.

John de Laci was also a benefactor to Garendon Abbey, in Leicestershire, and in 1178 he founded a Cistercian Abbey at Stanlaw, in Cheshire, not far from his castle of Halton, but the situation which he had chosen was low and unhealthy, and the monastery was almost inaccessible at spring-tides, so that it was afterwards removed to Whalley, in Lancashire. He also took part in the Crusades, and died at Tyre, when on a pilgrimage to the Holy Land, in 1190.

Four charters were granted to the Priory by King Henry the Second.

The first one is as follows :—

Henry, King of England, etc., greeting. I command that all things which men can assert to be the property of the Prior of Lenton may be free from tax and toll, and every custom ; and I forbid any one to disturb them or to do them any injury or insult upon forfeiture of ten pounds. Witness, Warine, son of Gerald the Chamberlain, Robert of Dunstanville, and Master Alvered. At Brockenhurst.[1]

The second charter, also undated,[2] confers a fair of eight days, with other important privileges, and runs thus :—

Henry, King of England, etc. Know ye that I have granted, and by this my charter have confirmed, to the Monks of Lenton, a fair of eight days at the feast of St. Martin, with full tolls of all things from which toll may be taken, excepting on those purchases which are made for food or clothing, which upon this quittance I have given and confirmed. Wherefore, I will, etc. I also enjoin that neither the Sheriff nor the Castellan of Nottingham shall molest the said monks in the slaughter of oxen, nor in anything else to which they have been accustomed ; but shall buy in such market as others coming to the fair from long distances. I also command that the said monks, and their goods, chattels, and tenants, shall be free and quit from all secular service and charges. And if any one shall claim against the aforesaid house any part of their possessions, or shall harass it in any way, or wish to go to law with it, I command that they shall not reply to any matter, nor enter into negotiation that anyone shall cause them to plead, except before me or my chief justice. Witness, Roger, Archbishop of York, Gilbert, Bishop of London, William, Bishop of

---

(1) *Mon. Ang.*, v , 112, No. 3. This charter is undated, but Mr. Eyton (*Court, Household, &c., of Henry II.*, p. 34.) ascribes to it the date of *circa* Feb., or March, 1158.

(2) Mr. Eyton gives the probable date of this charter as October 6-20, 1164.

Norwich, Richard de Humet, and William, son of John.  At Northampton.[1]

The third charter of King Henry II., likewise undated,[2] is as follows :—

Henry, by the grace of God, King of England, Duke of Normandy and Aquitaine, and Count of Anjou, To the Archbishops, etc.  Know ye that I have granted and given, and by this present charter have confirmed, to the Church of the Holy Trinity of Lenton, and the Monks there serving God, in free and perpetual alms, eighty acres of land and assarts in Curtenhall, and the mill of Blaccliff, in exchange for the land of Papplewick, which I have given in free and perpetual alms to the Canons of Newstead in Sherwood, which I have there founded.  Wherefore I will, etc.  Witness J. Bishop of Norwich, G. son of the king,[4] Rand. de Glanville, Hugh de Creissi, Geoffrey de Perche, Robert de Stuteville, William fitz Ralph, Ralph fitz Stephen, Chamberlain.  At Nottingham.[5]

The cell of KERSALL, in Lancashire, was likewise granted to Lenton Priory by King Henry the Second, some time previous to 1184, in which year Bartholomew, Bishop of Exeter, the witness to the charter, died.

" Henry, by the grace of God, King of England, etc.  To R. son of Bern. and to all his servants and foresters between the Ribble and the Mersey, greeting.  Know ye that I have given and conceded and by this my charter have confirmed to the monks of Lenton, for the health of myself and my heirs, and for the souls of King Henry and my grandfather, and my ancestors, the hermitage of Kershall, with all its appurtenances, in free, pure, and perpetual alms.  Wherefore I will, etc.  Witness Bartholomew, Bishop of Exeter.  At Porchester." [6]

King John confirmed the foregoing grant by his charter dated April 6th in the first year of his reign.[7]

The Cole MSS.[8] in the British Museum contain the copy of an original deed, designating Ralph de Gernon, Earl of Chester (who died in 1156), as the real founder of Kersall.  Cole says, " My worthy and much respected friend, Dr. Farmer,

---

(1) *Mon. Ang.*, v. 112.

(2) To this charter Mr. Eyton gives the date Christmas, 1176.

(3) Courteenhall, Northamptonshire.

(4) Geoffrey, Bishop-elect of Lincoln.        (5) Harl MS. 6748, f. 11.

(6) *Mon. Ang.*, v. 112.        (7) *Ibid.*        (8) Add. MS. 5860, p. 188.

communicated the following papers to me in 1780. The first
is a very ancient deed, about Henry the Second's reign, on a
piece of parchment of six inches deep, and four broad, which,
being used as a lining to the cover of an old book, has
suffered a trifle by being worm-eaten." The other papers were
letters. The following is a copy of the deed.

"R. Consul Cestriæ episcopo Cestriæ, archid. et omnibus
ordinatis Dei, et constab. Cestr. dapif. B . . . . justiciariis, vice
comitibus, ministris, et ballivis, et omnibus hominibus suis,
clericis et laicis, Francis, et Anglis, salutem. Sciatis me concessisse et dedisse Deo et Sanctæ Mariæ et monachis Sanctæ
Trinitatis de Lenton in elemosinam Kereshalam, locum ad
servicium Dei edificandum, et pasturam, et ad se dilatandum
de essartis, et piscariis, et de rebus illis omnibus quibuscunque
se dilatari et aisiari poterint. Quare volo et firmiter præcipio
quod prædicti monachi bene et honorifice prædictam elemosinam
solam et quietam et liberam de omni seculari servicio habeant,
ne aliquis meorum super timorem Dei. et meum amorem temere
perturbet. T. Mathild. comitissa Cestriæ, et Kadwaladr. rege
Waliarum, et Willielmo filio Alani, et Symone Corbet, et
Roberto Napifero, Ric. Pincerna, et Henr. Pultrell, et Willielmo
capellano apud Cestr."

Commenting upon this document, Cole remarks that :—

"Ranulph Gernon, Earl of Chester, married Matilda, daughter
of Robert, Earl of Gloucester, natural son of King Henry I, and
died 1156."

And adds :—

"The Bp of Lichfield was comonly stiled Bp. of Chester...
'B . . . Dapif' is probably the same among the Witnesses
where he is called Rob. Napif' thro' Inadvertency ; for the B
of the first Letter of the Word, (the other Letters being eaten
by Worms) is as plain as Rob below, and N instead of D.
It is curious for the signature of Cadwallader, King of Wales,
[to come] after the Countess."

In the *Valor Ecclesiasticus* the annual value of the cell was
returned at 9l. 6s. 8d., less 1l. paid to Sir John Byron,
seneschall there.

During the reign of King Henry the Second, Simon Fitz
Simon, a younger son of Simon de Kyme,[1] Lord of Kyme,

---

(1) Simon de Kyme, the founder of Bullington Priory, in Lincolnshire, in 1136,

in the parts of Kesteven, in Lincolnshire, gave to the Priory a marc of silver, to be paid annually out of the rents of a certain mill upon the river Leen, called *Bobursmilne* [Bobbers Mill], in order that the Monks might pray for the repose of the soul of Walter de Kyme, his brother.[1]

Hugh de Lambcote, and William, his son and heir, put into the hands of Ralph de Weldebof a certain rent of twelve pence yearly, from the mill of Awsworth, to be paid to the Prior and Convent of Lenton, by the said Hugh and his heirs at Pentecost; which appeased the strife betwixt the said Prior and himself concerning that mill. At a subsequent period, Peter, Prior of Lenton, and the Convent of that place, restored and confirmed to Adam, son of Robert de Aldesworth, the whole land of Awsworth, which Robert, his father, and his ancestors had held, paying to the Priory a marc yearly at the feast of St. Martin. This was in the time of Henry II., or Richard I.[2]

About the close of the reign of King Henry the Second, Herbert de Brampcote confirmed to the Holy Trinity and the Monks of Lenton, the gift that Azor, son of Ulsac, made of two carucates of the fee of Arnold, which the said Herbert held in Bramcote, leaving to his heirs the curse of Almighty God, and his own, if they should ever attempt to go against his grant. Hugh de Nevill confirmed to the said Priory eight bovates of land in Bramcote, and four in Sutton, of his soc of Arnold, concerning which there had formerly been some controversy in the King's court, reserving 12s. yearly rent to himself and his heirs. To this deed were witnesses H. de Burgo, the King's justice, William Briwer, Stephen de Seagrave, Raph de Nevill, Philip Marc, William Rufus, Robert de Harlestone, Walter de Estwayt, John de Leke, Helyus Briton, and Gervas de Arnale.[3] The following entry in the Close Rolls has reference to this gift :—

"Mand' est Ph' Marc q'd h're fac' s'n' dil'one Priore t Con-

---

married Rose, daughter of Robert, the steward to Gilbert de Gaunt. His younger son, Simon Fitz Simon, otherwise de Kyme, held considerable possessions in Northamptonshire, Yorkshire, and Lincolnshire, and had his chief seat at Brikesworth, in the first-named county. He married Isabella, sole daughter and heiress of Thomas de Cuckney, lord of Cuckney, and founder of Welbeck Abbey, by whom he had three daughters and co-heiresses.

(1) Thoroton, p. 231.        (2) Ibid, p. 244.        (3) Ibid, p. 209.

ventui Lenton' plenar' saisina' de t'ra de Bramcot' cū p'tin' suis
qᵃm Hug' de Nevill' de d'no Rege tenuit.  T. Reg. apud Corf',
viij. die Jul."  [Rot. Lit. Claus. 18 John. m. 7.]

Ralph, son of Hugh de Redinges, otherwise styled de
Watenhow, gave to the Priory of Lenton a bovate of land
in Watnall, which Toly had held, and afterwards Geoffrey Stoyle,
and which, during his life, he held himself, paying to the Monastery
sixteenpence a year, but after his death the Priory might dispose of it as of their other lands ; and he granted common to their
tenant, as the rest of the men of Watnall had in all places.  This
land he gave to the Monks to make an anniversary for his father,
and left a bitter curse for his heirs, if any of them should
attempt to go against, or hinder, his gift.  The Monks demised
it to Robert, son of Roger de Watenhow, for his life ; and after
that, when Sir Simon de Hadon was sheriff, in the time of
Henry the Third, to Sir Robert de Lathom, during his life,
for a noble yearly ; and afterwards in 1277 (5 Edw. I.) to
Robert, son of Robert de Watenhowe, for the same rent,
during his life.[1]

Hugh, son of Hugh de Somervile, of Keyworth, gave to
God and the church of Lenton, one bovate of land in Key-
worth, which Azor then held.  The witnesses to his charter
were his brothers Richard and Gervase, Robert Andegavansis,
Gervase, the son of Gervase de Clifton, Stephen, the priest of
Wilford, and Elias, his son, and Geoffrey de Lutterell.[2]

Beatrix de Whatton, widow of Robert de Whatton,[3] gave
to the Priory of Lenton, by the consent of William de Heriz,
and of Adelina, his wife, her sole daughter and heiress, two
bovates in Newthorpe, reserving to herself a yearly rent of
two shillings out of the same.[4]

William de Heriz (son of Ivo de Heriz, and grandson of
that Robert de Heriz who is named in the foundation-charter),

---

(1) Thoroton, p. 242.          (2) Ibid, p. 42.

(3) Robert de Whatton, lord of Whatton-in-the-Vale, in this county, was the son
of William de Whatton, a benefactor to the Priory of Blythe, whose father is said
to have been a younger son of Gautier de Tirel, seigneur de Poix, in Picardy, and
to have come over to England with William the Conqueror.  This Robert de
Whatton died without male issue, but the descendants of his younger brother,
Walter, long continued in this county.

(4) Thoroton, p. 238.

by the consent of his wife, Adelina (daughter and heiress of
Robert de Whatton, lord of Whatton, and Beatrix, his wife), and
of Robert de Heriz, his brother, gave Arnald, his man, of Wid-
merpole [Widmerpool], with his whole land, viz., four bovates,
and all customs and services thereunto belonging, and his mill at
Widmerpool, and wood out of his woods at Huccanel [Hucknall
Torkard], to make and mend it for ever ; and half his mill at
Gonolveston [Gonalston], and the like power in his woods there ;
and divers other things, to God and the Church of Lenton, upon
the great altar, whereon this gift was offered by himself and his
wife, in the presence of very many witnesses. Robert de Heriz,
and William, his uncle, Simon, son of Richard, and Herbert, his
brother, William Pietas, and Roger, his brother, Robert, the
Sheriff, and William, his brother, Robert, Raph, and William,
his son, Henry, the clerk of the Sheriff, and Henry of Huccanel,
Henry Medicus (the Leech), Roger de Burthon, Peter Palmer,
Reginald de Aslacton, Walter de Whatton, and Richard, his
son, Ambrose, and John, Plungun, and Fulc, servants of Sir
Ulf de Widmarpole, and Gilbert, the Parson, and many others
there named.[1]

This William de Heriz died without issue before the year
1180, when Robert de Heriz, his younger brother, gave account
for one hundred pounds for having the lands that had been held
by William ; and, at the same time, Adelina, the widow of
William de Heriz, was found to owe one hundred marcs, for
obtaining the king's permission not to marry again, save at her
own pleasure. Reginald de Aslacton (probably descended
from Uluric, or Walchelin) was a witness, as was also Roger
de Burton, to a charter of the Lady Adelina de Whatton, who
thereby, with the consent of William de Heriz, her husband,
gave to the Priory of Lenton her two men, or tenants, Hugh
and Henry, with the three bovates of land they held in Aslacton,
which gift she and her husband offered on the high altar of the
Holy Trinity, at Lenton.[2] Robert de Heriz gave to the canons

---

(1) Thoroton, p. 40.

(2) Thoroton, p. 137. Adelina, the wife of William de Heriz, survived her
husband, and gave the church of Whatton to the Abbey of Welbeck for the repose
of the souls of Robert de Whatton, and Beatrice, his wife, her father and mother,
and of William de Heriz, her husband. She subsequently married Adam de
Newmarch, to whom she carried the manor of Whatton in frank marriage.

of Darley, in Derbyshire, his right of advowson to the church
of South Wingfield, in that county, in pure and perpetual alms ;
and he subsequently confirmed the gifts that his elder brother
had bestowed upon the Prior and Monks of Lenton, and he
himself gave the brethren his whole portion of corn growing
upon his land at Widmerpool, and desired that his body should
be christianly buried in the Priory Church at Lenton.   The
liberality and devotion to the Church displayed by this pious
family is remarkable.   Ivo de Heriz, the son and successor of
the last-named Robert, is believed to have built the church of
Tibshelf, in Derbyshire, of which place he was lord, about the
close of the twelfth century, and gave that church to the Priory
of Brewood, in Staffordshire.   His son, Sir John de Heriz, was
a benefactor to the Priory of Felley, and founded a chantry
chapel in the parish of South Wingfield, and he was father
of another John de Heriz, the last male heir of the family, who
was probably the founder of the Hospital of Brodbuske,[1] near
Gonalston.   He died before the year 1329.

Gilbert de Meringes[2] granted to Ralph Murdac (High Sheriff
of the counties of Nottingham and Derby, 30 Henry II.) six
acres of meadow in Meering, in that called *Esteng*, which Roger
de Caisneta held of him for two shillings per annum, as the
said Ralph Murdac was to do, who thereupon gave it away to
the Priory of Lenton, for the health of his own soul, and of
Alexander de Cheney, or Cheinais ; and together with it, for
the more abundant firmness and security of the said gift, he
gave the writing which he had from the said Gilbert de
Meringes, for which, after his death, the monks were to make
a perpetual anniversary, as for one of their advocates, or
principal benefactors.[3]

Sir Geoffrey de St. Patric, lord of Nuthall (who was,
undoubtedly, a descendant of Norman de St. Patric, the

---

(1) According to Dodsworth, this hospital was founded in 1326, by John, the
son of John de Heriz. Tanner calls the founder William de Heriz, but this is, in
all probability, an error.

(2) The descendants of this Gilbert de Meringes continued resident at Meering, in
this county, down to the sixteenth century.  Junior branches settled at Collingham,
Hucknall Torkard, and elsewhere in the county, but this ancient family is now
believed to be extinct in the male line.

(3) Thoroton, p. 118.

subfeudatory of William Peverel, whose gifts to the monastery were confirmed by the founder in his charter), gave the advowson of the church of Nuthall to the Prior and Convent of Lenton. The gift was duly confirmed by Roger, Archbishop of York, and subsequently by Pope Lucius III.,[1] but it did not pass unchallenged, and the advowson appears to have eventually reverted to the donor's family. In the year 1200, William de St. Patric paid one marc to the king for licence to have a jury of twelve free and lawful men of the neighbourhood of Nuthall, who should be examined upon oath, as to whether Geoffrey de St. Patric gave the church of Nuthall to Lenton Priory, and made his charter thereof when he was of sound mind, or whether the charter was executed upon his death-bed, under undue influence.[2]    At the same time " the Prior and monks of Lenton exhibited a charter which testified that Geoffrey de St. Patric, grandfather of William de St. Patric, gave his advowson of the church of Nuthall, confirmed by Roger, Archbishop of York."[3]

Michael, the son of Richard de Rutington, gave to the Priory of Lenton four bovates of land in Ruddington, which had formerly been held by Fulco, brother of the said Richard, and, since his death, by his son William. This gift was afterwards confirmed to the Priory by Richard, the son of Michael de Rutington, whose sons, William and Ralph, likewise yielded all claim to the same in the presence of the monastery. William de Rutington (one of the last-named) confirmed the gift of four acres of land in Ruddington, which had been bestowed upon the Priory by Geoffrey de Malquinci, his uncle. And at another time, Richard de Rutington, son of this same William, being at Lenton fair in 1234, confirmed certain gifts which Richard, his grandfather, had made to the monastery, and gave to the monks a certain meadow called *Godwinsholme*, which lay near to the water-mill at Clifton.[4]

---

(1) Thoroton, p. 244.
(2) Madox, Hist. of Excheq , i. 436.
(3) Abb. Plac., 1 John, rot. 3, in dorso.
(4) Thoroton, pp. 65, 66.

9

Geoffrey Torkard,[1] with the consent of Maud his wife, and Henry his son, for the health of his soul, and of his ancestors and successors, and for the soul of Alexander de Cheney, gave to God and the church of the Holy Trinity at Lenton, and the monks there serving God, one cart to be continually wandering about, to gather up his dead wood of Hucknall : the witnesses were Ralph Murdac,[2] Ralph de Cheines, Hugh his brother, Philip de Beaumes, Hugh de Lichelade, Gilbert, the chaplain of the Castle ;[3] Alan, Robert, and Gregory, clerks ; Silvester, Geoffrey Torkard, of Chilwell, William de Davidville, Henry Torkard his own son, and others.[4]

Ralph Rosell, son of Hugh Rosell, confirmed to the monks of Rufford his whole land at Almpton, viz., twelve bovates, reserving six shillings to himself and his heirs at Midsummer, and six shillings to the Prior of Lenton, at the feast of St. Martin, in winter ; but there was a fine levied in the King's Court at Doncaster, the Wednesday after the feast of Saint Margaret, in the fourth year of King John, between Peter, Prior of Lenton, and Ernis, abbot of Rufford, who called Ralph Rosell to warrant the twelve bovates in Almpton, for which he and his heirs were to have but four shillings per annum, and the Prior of Lenton six shillings, who had also thirty-five marcs of silver of the abbot for the bargain. The same Ralph afterwards released the four shillings rent, and so the greater part of the township came into the possession of Rufford Abbey.[5]

Towards the close of the twelfth century, Adam de Cokefield [6] gave to Lenton Priory eight shillings yearly rent to be paid by

---

(1) Hucknall Torkard acquires its distinctive affix from this ancient family, whose mansion was at that place, closely adjacent to the parish church. Its site might readily be traced not many years ago.

(2) He was Sheriff of Notts. and Derbyshire from 27 Henry II. to 1 Richard I., Constable of Nottingham Castle, and a Justice Itinerant.

(3) Gilbert, the Chaplain of Nottingham Castle, appears as a witness to several charters relating to the Priory of Lenton.

(4) Thoroton, p, 256.          (5) Ibid, p. 373.

(6) Adam de Cokefield, or Cockfield, lord of one of the chief manors in Nuthall, was the representative of a family derived from Roger de Vere, a younger son of the baronical house of Oxford, who held the lordships of Cockfield in Suffolk, under the Abbots of Bury immediately after the Conquest, from which place his descendants derived their surname. His wife, Agatha, to whom he was married in the seventh year of King John, appears to have been the heiress of the De Nuthall family, and to have survived her husband.

the miller out of his mill of Nuthall, and if the mill should fall
or be removed, or anything else happen that the rent could not
be had, he promised to make it good out of some other land in
the county.[1]

After the death of Adam de Cokefield, his widow, "Agatha
de Cokefield, Lady of Nuthall, gave her mill of Nuthall, situate
on the rivulet between the town and Hendeshill [Hempshill],
to the Priory of Lenton, out of which those monks were wont
to receive 8s. yearly rent (granted by Adam de Cokefield), and,
together with the said mill, the suit of all Nuthall, except
her own house, so that men of Nuthall should always grind
according to their due and ancient custom.    She likewise
granted, that if any of the men of Nuthall (except those who
were free when she conferred that charter) should be intercepted grinding at another mill when he might grind at that,
it should be lawful for the miller, or any person else deputed
by the said monks, to arrest him, and the sack with the corn
was to be the monks'; but the man so intercepted, for his
forfeit, was to be in the mercy of her and her heirs." [2]

Her elder son, Sir Robert de Cockfield, married Alice,
daughter and coheiress of Geoffrey de Constable, lord of Melton
Constable, in Norfolk, and acquired the other manor in Nuthall
which had been held by the family of St. Patric.[3]   The
descendants of this Sir Robert de Cockfield remained seated
at Nuthall until about the middle of the fifteenth century.

---

(1) Thoroton, p. 245.

(2) Thoroton, p. 246.  Both windmills and watermills appear to have been used
from a very early period, and as no mill could be established without a licence
from the Crown, they were very valuable property.  In many cases they appear to
have been attached to the manor, and to have been transferred along with it, thus
frequently becoming the property of monastic bodies ; they were also frequently
granted to monasteries.  In the Patent Rolls frequent instances occur of licences
to establish mills, or to transfer them with the manor to which they belonged.
Mills were so frequently the property of the monks to whom they had been granted,
that in the 14th century this monopoly was felt to be a serious inconvenience, and
handmills were brought into use for domestic purposes.  (*Rebelliones Villanorum
temporibus Ricardi Secundi—Cotton MS. in Brit. Mus. Claud. E. iv.*)  Their
introduction, however, met with serious opposition from the monks, and violent
quarrels arose between the people and the heads of various monasteries.  During the
popular insurrections which occured in this country, the insurgents did not forget to
stipulate for the privilege of using handmills.    At St. Albans it is recorded that
in 1327, Queen Isabella was way-laid on her journey by the townspeople, who
protested against their compulsory use of the abbey mills.

(3) See ante p. 86.

Thoroton states that "John, Earl Morton, was at Nuthall when he granted to the Prior of Lenton the heath about the wood of Bestwood, and about his other woods in Notts. and Derbyshire. Witness Roger de Silan and Ralph Murdac." [1]

Matthew, the son of Matthew de Hathersage (presumably the last male heir of his family, and the father of Matilda, the wife of Sir Walter de Gonshill, of Hoveringham, and Cecilia, the wife of Nigel de Langford), gave to the Priory of Lenton his manors of Holme and Dunston, in Derbyshire, with all that appertained to the same.

About the same time, Ralph, son of William de Toueton, gave to the church of the Holy Trinity, at Lenton, and the monks there serving God, all his rents in Kimberley, viz., half-a-mark of silver yearly. To this deed were witnesses the Abbot of Darley, Sampson de Strelley, Warnet de Beheleg, Richard de Roissalt, Robert, son of Fitz-William, Henry, Richard de Hartill, Hugh, son of Sampson, William, his brother, Ralph, son of Hugh de Watenhow, Matthew, his brother, Gilbert de Broculstow, and others. [2]

Eustachius de Moreton, Lord of Wollaton, confirmed the alms which Robert de Moreton, his grandfather, and Adam, his father, gave to God and the church of the Holy Trinity at Lenton, and the Clugniac monks there serving God, namely, sixteen shillings a year out of that which Gerard de Algar-thorpe held of him and his ancestors, namely, ten shillings at Pentecost, or within the Octave, and six shillings within the Octave of Saint Martin. This gift was confirmed by Adam de Moreton, brother of the said Eustachius. [3]

King John granted to Lenton Priory the following charters, in the first year of his reign :—

"John, by the grace of God, King of England, etc. Know ye that we have granted and by the present charter have confirmed to the church of the Holy Trinity of Lenton, and to the monks there serving God, in free and perpetual alms, eighty acres of land of the essarts of Curtehall, and the mill of Blackcliff in exchange for the lands of Papplewick, which

---

(1) *Antiquities of Notts.*, p. 244.
(2) Thoroton, p. 243.          (3) Ibid., p. 234.

King Henry, our father, gave in free and perpetual alms, to the canons of Newstead, in Sherwood, which he founded there. Wherefore we will, etc.   We have also granted, and by this our charter have confirmed, to the same monks of Lenton for the health of ourself, and our heirs, and for the souls of King Henry, our great grandfather, and King Henry, our father, and our ancestors, our hermitage of Kershall with all its appendages, in pure, free, and perpetual alms.   Wherefore we will, and firmly enjoin, that our said monks, freely, and quietly, and honourably, shall hold the said hermitage in peace as Hugo de Burun, monk of theirs, freely and quietly held it   We have also granted, and by this our charter have confirmed, to the same monks a fair of eight days, at the feast of Saint Martin, with full tolls of all things from which it is possible to take toll, except those purchases which are appointed for the table or for their clothing, which upon this acquittance we have given and confirmed.   Given by the hand of Simon, archdeacon of Wells, and John de Gray, at Worcester, the sixth day of April, in the first year of our reign." [1]

"John, by the grace of God, King of England, etc.  Know ye that we have granted and by this present charter have confirmed to God and to the monks of the convent of Lenton, the churches of Maperteshal [Meppershall, in Bedfordshire,] and Falmersham [Felmersham, in Bedfordshire,] with all their appurtenances, which are of our sergeancy, in pure and perpetual alms, as Robert, son of William, gave and confirmed to them by his charter.   And moreover we have confirmed and ratified to them in perpetual alms, whatever they have of the gift of their patrons or other faithful, whether of buying or selling, as their charters and writings testify.   We have granted all these things in perpetual alms, for the souls of King Henry, our great grandfather, and of King Henry, our father, and of our ancestors, and for the health of ourself and of all our faithful, as the charter of King Henry, our father, reasonably testifies.   We have also granted to them that they shall have free entry and exit, every day, without the hindrance of our foresters, in our forest of Berkswud [Bestwood], with a cart to take dead wood, and with two carts for heather, of which they shall freely take as much as shall suffice for their own proper use.   Given by the hand of Simon, archdeacon of Wells, and John de Gray, archdeacon of Gloucester, at Guildford, the 22nd day of April in the first year of our reign." [2]

The church of Felmersham appears to have been a subject

---

(1) *Mon. Angl.*, v. 112.  A copy of this charter is preserved amongst the Clugny MSS., in the Bibliothèque Nationale, Paris.

(2) *Mon. Ang.*, v. 112, No. 8.

of contest at a very early date :—" In the assize for the last
presentation to the church of Felmersham which Gilbert de
Malperteshal claimed against the Prior and Monks of Lenton,
the Attorney of the Prior said that it was not vacant, because
the Prior and Convent are the " parson," and he produced the
charter of Robert, father of the said Gilbert, in which he is
stated to have given to the church of the Holy Trinity of
Lenton the advowson of the church of Felmersham, and whatever he lawfully held in the same church, and exhibits the
charter of the lord King John, confirming to the church of
Lenton, the church of Felmersham, with all its appurtenances,
etc., as the charter of King Henry, his father, reasonably
testifies, etc." [1]

King Edward III., on July 25th, 1342, granted the advowson
of Felmersham, with the chapel of Pavenham [2] attached, to the
warden and scholars of King's Hall, Cambridge, now absorbed
in Trinity College. [3]

In the year 1207, King John issued the following mandate
to Brien de Insula :—

" The King to Brien de Insula, etc. We command you that
the Prior and Monks of Lenton be permitted to have their
easement without waste (of property) and injury to the tenants
(*exilio*) of the wood in their woods in your Bailiwick, through
the view of yourself and your foresters. Witness myself at
Nottingham, 16 day of August." [4]

In the year 1212, the King issued another mandate to Brien
de Insula, commanding him to supply to the Prior and Monks
of Lenton dead wood from the hay or wood of Willoughby,
" for the sustentation of their house of Lenton." [5]

By the third charter, dated December 2nd, 1212, King John
granted to Lenton Priory the tenth of all the game taken in
the counties of Nottingham and Derby.

Know ye, that we from the fear of God and for the safety
of our soul, and of the souls of our ancestors, have given,

---

(1) Abb. Plac., p. 51.
(2) Pabham according to Palgrave's *Rotuli Curiæ Regis*, i. 46.
(3) *Memorials of Cambridge.*
(4) Rot. Lit. Claus., i., 90.          (5) Ibid, i. 120.

granted, and confirmed by this our charter, to God and the Church of the Holy Trinity of Lenton, and to Peter the Prior and his successors, and likewise to the monks who serve and will serve God there, the tenth part of the game taken in the counties of Nottingham and Derby ; that is to say, of stags, hinds, bucks, does, hogs, and hares, to be held for ever as· free, pure and pepetual alms.   Wherefore, we will, etc.   Given by the hand of Master Richard de Marisco, Archdeacon of Northumberland, at Westminster, the second day of December, in the fourteenth year of our reign.[1]

Two years later (1214), the king commanded the sheriff of Lincolnshire to give to P. Prior of Lenton full seisin of all the lands and tenements within his bailiwick belonging to the Priory, saving only the king's escheats.   A similar mandate was issued to the sheriff of Yorkshire.[2]

On the 17th October, 1214, the king commanded Philip Marc, sheriff of the counties of Nottingham and Derby, to permit the bailiff of the Abbey of Clugny to have the custody of the Priory of Lenton, peacefully and without molestation, until the king should command otherwise.[3]

Nichols[4] states that, in his time the Segrave Chartulary contained three deeds relating to Lenton Priory, namely—a grant by the Prior and Convent of Lenton to Katherine, widow of Arnald of Twyford, in the county of Leicester, of a carucate of land at Welby, in the same county, on the annual payment of ten shillings ; a transfer of the same carucate from Edo, son of the said Arnald, to Gilbert de Segrave ; and a (confirmatory) grant of the same, from Peter, then Prior of Lenton, and his convent, to Gilbert de Segrave.[5]   The Priory appears to have received an annual rent of 13s. 4d. from this land in 1387.

The Prior and convent of Lenton, having remitted to Gerard de Rodes the custom of tithing his corn at Langar, after it was brought into the barn, and, out of their liberality, agreed to take it in the field, his successor, Ralph de Rodes, did, in

(1) *Mon. Ang.* v. 112, No. 9.        (2) Rot. Lit., Claus. i., 207.

(3) Ibid i., 173.        (4) History of Leicestershire, ii., 284.

(5) Gilbert de Segrave, Lord of Segrave, in Leicestershire (whence he assumed his surname) held the fourth part of a knight's fee there in 1166.   He was living in 1198, when he gave 400 marcs to King Richard the First in support of his wars.

the third year of King Henry the Third, make his acknowledgment thereof, and engage himself, that if the Prior and convent should have any loss by so doing, they should enjoy their old custom again by tithing at the barn ; and this he did in full chapter before W. de Rotherham, Archdeacon of Nottingham, to whose jurisdiction and constraint, if he should fail, he submitted himself, without appeal, by a sealed instrument, as the custom then ordinarily was in such cases.

The Prior and Convent likewise granted to this same Sir Ralph de Rodes, lord of Langar and Barnston, and his Lady Berta, permission to have a chapel within their court at Langar, provided the chaplain should be presented to the parson of Langar, and swear not to hinder the mother church, and to be liable to be suspended by the patron if he did ; and that the lord and lady should come and hear divine service at the church on all the festivals, except there was manifest cause of hindrance ; but they were to have no bell in the said chapel.[1]

King Henry the Third, in the year 1220, commanded the sheriff of Nottinghamshire to permit the Prior and monks of Lenton to have two waggons (*carros*) or three carts wandering every day in the Hay of Boscwod [Bestwood] to collect dead wood or heather for their own use as fuel.[2] This injunction was repeated in 1221[3] and 1224.[4] The privilege was, no doubt, so highly valued by the monks that they took the precaution, from time to time, to have it confirmed.

Walter Grey, Archbishop of York, on the twelfth of the kalends of March, in the eighth year of his Pontificate, being then at Lenton, admitted Ralph, the clerk, on the presentation of the Prior and convent of Lenton, to be the perpetual vicar of Radford, which vicarage he made to consist of the whole altarage of that church, and four bovates of land belonging to the said altarage, with the tithes thereto belonging, and likewise the tithe of two mills, and all the toft lying between the toft of that church and the river Leen, but the vicar was

(1) Thoroton, p. 103.
(2) Rot. Lit., Claus. i. 421.
(3) Ibid, i. 452.                    (4) Ibid, i. 595.

to sustain the burdens of the bishop and archdeacon, that is synodals and procurations.[1]

On the 10th of March, 1223, the King commanded the venditors of fallen wood in the county of Nottingham that they should give, as a donation from the king, to R[oger], Prior of Lenton, ten loads of the fallen wood of the lord King in his Hay of Bestwood [Bescwud] for the reparation of the church and house of Lenton.[2]

In 1224, the Prior of Lenton (Roger) was sent by King Henry the Third to France, together with the Master of the Temple and the Chancellor of London, to make a truce with King Louis the Eighth. It is a singular mark of royal confidence that the Prior of Lenton should have been selected for such an important mission.

The following is a translation of the letter of credence with with which they were entrusted :—

" To his lord, when it shall please him, Louis, by the grace of God, the illustrious King of the French, Henry, by the same grace, etc., greeting and esteem.

"We send to you our well-beloved in Christ, Alan Martel, Master of the Knights of the Temple in England, and the Prior of Lenton, and Master H——, Chancellor of London, to whom you will give credence upon those things which they shall say to you in our behalf, as to proroguing the truce between you and us for four years from Easter in the year of grace 1224. Understanding that we shall hold firm and acceptable whatever they shall thereupon do on our behalf.

"Witness myself, at the New Temple, London, 28th day of April, in the eighth year [of our reign]. Before the Lord Archbishop of Canterbury, Hubert de Burgh, justiciary, and J[oceline], Bishop of Bath, and [Richard] Bishop of Salisbury."

Similar letters were made, in which was placed, "to whom you will give credence, or to two of them, if all be not able to attend to this "[3]

---

(1) Thoroton, p. 219, from Lenton Register.

(2) Rot. Lit., Claus. 7 Hen. III., m. 15.

(3) Pat. 8 Hen. III. m. 3. d. ; Rymer's *Fœdera*, i. 270.

The expenses of the Prior of Lenton on this occasion amounted to ten marcs.[1]

Philip Marc (who was sheriff of the counties of Nottingham and Derby in the latter part of the reign of King John, and seven or eight years of the beginning of the reign of King Henry the Third) and Anne, his wife, having purchased certain lands at Keyworth, of the fee of Hugh de Bellomont, gave nine bovates thereof to the Priory of Lenton, where he desired that his body might be honourably entombed. After the death of Philip Marc, Sabina, the widow of the said Hugh de Bellomont, [2] in consideration of the sum of four shillings, and a quarter of rye, in her very great need released her dower in three bovates and a half of the nine bovates given by Philip Marc to the Priory, and swore on the Holy Gospels that she would never go against her release, nor in any way else disturb the Prior and his brethren in their quiet possession of the said land.[3]

In the year 1234, R., Prior of Lenton, and the convent of the same, confirmed to Robert, son of Ingleram, of Nottingham, and his heirs, all their land and meadow belonging to it, with toft and croft, all which belonged to the church of Saint Stephen, of Sneinton, he paying them thirteen shillings yearly. They also granted, released, and confirmed to this Robert Ingram, knight, for his counsel and service, had, and to be had, during his life 21s. 6d. issuing to them out of his lands in Sneinton and Nottingham.[4]

Robert Ingram had a son Laurence, who in 1265 paid half a marc for having a writ *ad terminum*. He appears to have been in rebellion with the barons, for about this time the lands of Laurence Ingleram, of Sneinton, were given to Simon de Arden, a "varlet" of Prince Edward. Robert had probably died before this date, or his son would not have been in possession of his

---

(1) Rot. Lit. Claus. i. 597.

(2) Hugh de Bellomont (youngest son of Robert de Bellomont, Earl of Leicester, already referred to as a benefactor to this monastery) obtained the Earldom of Bedford from King Stephen. Dugdale records of him that "being a person remiss and negligent himself, he fell from the dignity of an earl to the state of a knight ; and in the end to miserable poverty." The sad straits to which his widow was reduced may be seen from the transaction which is recorded above.

(3) Thoroton, p. 42.        (4) Ibid, p. 277.

lands. The Ingram family appear to have been the original owners of the water mill at Lenton.[1] In all ancient writings it is called "Ingrams," and was afterwards the property of Sir Geoffrey Bakepuz, who with his wife Amicia, demised it, during their lives, to the Prior and convent of Lenton, for twenty shillings a year, upon condition that the people of their house and family, of Wollaton, should be allowed to grind there for the toll of the "twentieth grain," "which suit Hugh de Weloghby, lord of Wollaton, also granted for his life to Sir Geoffrey [de Rochero] the Prior, and the convent, in the eighth year of the reign of King Henry the Fourth, to their said mill upon the same terms."[2]

On Nov[r] 30th, in the year 1234, Walter Grey, Archbishop of York, issued a set of rules to the hospital of St. John the Baptist, Nottingham, the portions of which relating to Lenton Priory are here given :—

"To all the faithful in Christ inspecting these letters, Walter, by the Grace of God, Archbishop of York, Primate of England, greeting in the Lord. We would have it come to the notice of you all that we, as well by the authority of the Pope which we exercise in this district, as by ordinary, with the consent of the rectors and patrons of S. Mary at Nottingham, by the prompting of charity, have granted to the brethren of the Hospital of Saint John of Nottingham that they may have a chapel and chaplain to minister divine service to them and to their guests, saving the church of Saint Mary, in whose parish the hospital is situated, indemnified as to the receipt of all revenue howsoever accruing by reason of the celebration of divine service in the same hospital. So that whosoever shall be chaplain for the time being, either religious or secular, shall take upon himself, over the saintly relics, a sworn obligation to the Prior and Convent of Lenton[3] (conventui de Lenton juratoriam cautionem inspectis sacro-sanctis præstabit), that he will in nowise defraud the said church [of S. Mary] of any temporal due, and will not receive money for singing annual, trienniel, or septenniel, or anniversary, or anything of this description of that parish. . . .

---

(1) This mill occupied the site of the one still standing near the great lodge to Wollaton Park, where the high road from Nottingham to Derby crosses the river Leen. In later days it came into the hands of the Nix family.

(2) Thoroton, p. 223, from Lenton Register.

(3) It will be remembered that the church of St. Mary, Nottingham, had been given to the Priory by the founder, and the rectory had, sometime previous to the period referred to above, been appropriated to the monastery.

The same brethren for themselves and their successors, have renounced petitioning against this ordination. In everlasting memory whereof we have caused our seal together with the seal of the Prior and Convent of Lenton, and the Vicar of S. Mary's, to be appended to this writing remaining in the possession of the master and brethren of the Hospital. Dated at Laneham, on the day of the feast of Saint Andrew, in the 1234th year of the Incarnation of the Lord." [1]

The brethren of the hospital paid one marc of silver yearly to the Prior of Lenton, viz., half a marc within the octave of the Invention of the Holy Cross, and half a marc within the octave of St. Martin.

About this time, Robert, son of Robert de Kynmerley, and Roger, Prior of Lenton, agreed that a division should be made between the woods of the Prior and the wood of the said Robert in Newthorpe. Robert le Vavasour, of Chyppeley [Shipley, in Derbyshire], was to fence the Prior's wood, which lay next to a certain holme in Newthorpe, which Roger, Prior of Lenton, gave to him and his heirs, from any loss or damage it should sustain from his millers, or people coming to his mill, or else permit the Prior to fence it in close. [2]

In the 25th year of King Henry III., the Prior of Lenton was summoned to show why he did not permit his Lord the King to present a suitable "parson" to the chapel of Frich, etc. [Chapel-en-le-Frith]. [3]

In January, 1240, a law suit of forty years' duration in the court of King's Bench, between Sir Henry de Grey, of Codnor, in Derbyshire, and the Prior and Convent of Lenton, concerning the patronage of one mediety of Attenborough Church, was terminated by Sir Richard de Grey, son of the said Sir Henry, on succeeding to his father's estates. The whole case was submitted to the decision of the Archbishop of York (Walter de Grey,[4] 1215—1255), "who, to make peace, *and avoid the effusion of blood*, ordained that the Prior and his successors should have tithes to the value of forty shillings

---

(1) Appendix to part I. of Grey's Register, p. 168.

(2) Thoroton, p. 238.        (3) Abb. Plac., p. 112.

(4) The fact that the Prior of Lenton should have submitted to the arbitration of the Archbishop, who was the younger brother of his opponent, is remarkable, and shows the extraordinary character for probity which that prelate must have enjoyed.

yearly, in the name of a simple benefice in that moiety to which the chapel of Bramcote was attached, and of which Robert Stamford was then Rector, and that the right of patronage of the other moiety should remain with the said Sir Richard de Grey and his heirs. The Prior was to pay a pound of frankincense every year at Attenborough feast." [1] The advowson of Attenborough Church was subsequently granted (11 Edw. III.) by John de Grey, of Codnor, to the monks of Felley, and their successors. [2]

In the year 1241, Richard de Beauchamp, lord of Beeston, gave two bovates of land in Beeston, which Jordan, the son of Yvo, then held, together with the said Jordan and all his *sequela*, [3] to the Priory of Lenton. [4]

In 1249 the Prior of Lenton had permission, dated at Westminster, March 15th, to dig stone in the coppice of Nottingham within the enclosure of Sherwood Forest, for the fabric of his church. [5]

The Prior obtained a similar permission from the King, dated at Westminster, May 12th, in the following year. [6]

In 1253, the king granted permission, dated at Portsmouth, July 24th, to the Prior of Lenton, to take seven score cartloads of stone in the king's quarry within Nottingham Wood for works at Lenton. [7]

In the reign of King Henry the Third, Robert Bluet gave to the Priory a certain mill at Thorp-in-Glebis, in order that masses might be celebrated by the monks of this house for the health of his own soul, and for the souls of his brother, Hugh Bluet, who was at that time the Prior of Lenton, and of another brother, named Ralph. [8]

In 1258, Sampson, son of Alan de Leke, lord of Staunton Harold, in Leicestershire (whose name appears amongst the

---

(1) Thoroton, p. 205.        (2) Ibid., p. 206.

(3) *Sequela*, the goods, chattels, etc., of a villein which were at the disposal of his lord. The expression also includes the offspring of the villein.

(4) Thoroton, p. 210.

(5) Rot. Lit. Claus. 33 Hen. III., m. 12.

(6) Ibid. 34 Hen. III., m. 12.        (7) Ibid. 37 Hen. III., m. 5.

(8) Thoroton, p. 38.

benefactors of the Cistercian Abbey of Garendon, in that
County), released to the Prior and monks of Lenton for four
marcs of silver, four bovates of land in Keyworth, which he
had recovered in the previous year in a suit before the
King's itinerant Justiciers at Nottingham.[1]

The following report of the visitation of Lenton Priory, in
the year 1262, by the visitors of Clugny Abbey, gives some
interesting details of the manner in which the temporal and
spiritual affairs of the monastery were conducted, together
with the number of monks and lay brethren, and the debt of
the Priory.

"1262. Also we enquired at Lenton through brother Alfred,
of Lenton, sub-cellarer, and of Richard, the almoner of the same
place, from which it was evident to us that the state of the
house in spiritual matters is good; the service of God is there
performed agreeably as it has hitherto been accustomed to be
performed. There are twenty-two monks and two lay brethren
there. Concerning the circumstances of the house, we inquired
the truth from the Prior and two of the said monks, from
which it appeared to us that the house was honourably indebted even to the value of a thousand pounds of the money
of the realm."[2]

In the same year an exchange was made between Roger
the Prior, and the Convent of Lenton, and John Barre,[3] of
Tollerton; the Prior gave all his lands in Keyworth of the fee
of Sir Thomas Fitz-Williams, of Plumptre, for all the lands of
the said John Barre, in Bradmore. Sir Philip de Colwick [of
Nether Colwick), and Sir John de Vilers (of Kinoulton], were
witnesses to the exchange.[4]

In December, 1264, certain bishops, barons, and a great
number of abbots and priors (including the Prior of Lenton)

---

(1) Thoroton, p. 42.

(2) Clugny MS., Bibliothèque Nationale, Paris.

(3) This John Barre, who succeeded his elder brother William, and died about the
year 1283, was the representative of an ancient family long seated at Tollerton, in this
county. According to Thoroton's pedigree, he was fourth in descent from that
Richard Barri, by whom the grant of the church of Tollerton made to the monastery
by Ralph de Insula and Matilda Malebisse, his wife, was confirmed to the Priory in
the time of King Henry the Second. (See p. 98.)

(4) Thoroton, p. 49.

together with two knights from each shire, and two burgesses from each borough, were called together by the following mandate, to consult with Simon de Montford, who, "in all but name a king," having defeated the royal army at Lewes, held King Henry a prisoner at the time this summons was issued.

" Henry, by the grace of God, King of England, Lord of Ireland and Duke of Aquitaine, to the Prior of Lenton, greeting. Forasmuch as after serious contests and disturbances which had long been taking place in our realm, our dearest first-born son, Edward, was given up and detained as a hostage in order to secure and confirm peace in our realm, and now (blessed be God) that the aforesaid disturbance is quieted, it behoves us to take measures for making secure provision for the liberation of the same, and for confirming and completing full security and tranquillity of peace, the honour of God and the benefit of our whole realm, and about certain other affairs of our realm which we are unwilling to despatch without your advice, and that of our other prelates and magnates :  We command you, desiring you by that fidelity and love in which you are bound to us, to postpone every pressing matter and lay aside all other affairs, and be with us at London on the Octave of Saint Hilary next to come, to discuss with us and the aforesaid prelates and magnates whom we have caused to be summoned to the same place, and to give your advice :   And this, as you love us and our honour and yours, and the common tranquillity of our realm, by no means omit.  Witness the King at Woodstock, the twenty-fourth day of December." [1]

A great lawsuit was ended in 1266, between Roger, Prior of Lenton, and Tortus, son of Adam Wolf, Knight, canon of Anaquin, rector of the church of St. George, Barton in Fabis, " upon the Prior paying 300 marcs, wanting 12, and taking his parsonage to farm five years, for 32 marcs per annum, of good, new, and lawful sterling money, 13s. 4d. to the marc."  The dispute arose in consequence of the Prior presenting Thomas Raley, whom the plaintiff had been nine years getting out with his apostolical letters. [2]

In the following year (1267), the Prior and Convent of Lenton

---

(1) Rymer's *Fœdera* i., 802; Dugdale's *Perfect coppy of all Summons of the Nobility to the great Councils and Parliament from 49 Hen. III*; Ashmolean MS. 816, p. 36.
(2) Thoroton, p. 51.

granted permission to Robert de Rempston [1] to have a chantry chapel at Rempston manor, on condition that he did not admit the parishioners to divine service to the prejudice of the mother church, and that his chaplain should swear fealty to the rector. [2]

In the third year of King Edward the First, Robert, son of Robert de Costinton, sought against Peter de Esswayt, two messuages and two bovates of land at Barton-on-Trent, and against the Prior of Lenton, one bovate in the same place.[3]

In the same year (1275), complaint was made that King Henry the Third had made a certain weir beyond the water of Trent, which flooded the meadows of the King below the Castle of Nottingham, and the meadows of the Prior of Lenton. [4]

Shortly before this time, William de Latimer, escheator of the King, seized the Priory of Lenton when it was vacant, and placed there a certain doorkeeper, who stood there for the fourth part of a year. [5]

In 1275, the Priory of Lenton was certified to hold, in Cotgrave, a fee of the honour of Byron. [6] The Priory also held, about this time, two bovates of land in Willoughby-on-the-Wolds, of the gift of Sir Richard de Willoughby.[7]

In the year 1276, the Prior of Lenton held two bovates of land at Hal, in Lincolnshire, of Gilbert de Gaunt, valued at two marcs per annum.[8] The same land was held by the Prior in the year 1330.[9] In the same year (1276), the Prior of Lenton held half a fee in Cotgrave of the Honour of Byron, of the gift of Hugh Byron.[10]

In the following year, Thomas Malet, son and heir of Alan Malet, released all actions against the Prior and Convent of

---

(1) Robert de Rempston was the representative of an ancient family deriving their surname from the manor of Rempston, in this county, which continued in their possession down to about the middle of the fifteenth century.

(2) Thoroton, p. 30.

(3) Rawlinson collection, Bodl. Lib., No. 116, f. 4.

(4) *Rot. Hund.*, ii., 314. (5) *Ibid* ii., 317. (6) *Ibid*.

(7) *Ibid.* ii., 319. He was the son of Richard Bugge (son of Ralph Bugge, of Nottingham) who was styled de Willoughby, from his estate at Willoughby-on-the-Wolds, where he resided. This Sir Richard de Willoughby was the father of another Sir Richard, a Justice of Common Pleas, who settled at Wollaton, which ultimately became the chief seat of the family.

(8) Hundred Rolls, i. 244. (9) Ibid. i, 316. (10) Ibid. ii. 313.

Lenton, and their bailiffs, for the waste made in his estate at Cotgrave, while it was in their custody. Amongst the witnesses to the agreement were Henry de Tibtot, constable of Nottingham Castle, Walter de Stircley, sheriff of the counties of Nottingham and Derby, Richard de Jorz, of Burton, Gervase de Wilford, etc.[1]

When the Priory was visited in the year 1276, the number of monks and lay-brethren had increased, but the visitors discovered that they were in the habit of infringing the rules of the order in the particulars detailed in the following report :—

" 1276.  On Friday next before the Feast of St. Peter in Cathedra,[2] we visited at Lenton. There are twenty-seven monks and four lay-brethren. The house owes a thousand and four score marcs, nothing at usury. As to saddle-backs, shoes with latchets, eating of flesh, reading in the infirmary, and staying (up) after compline, we ordered as at Montacute.[3]  We found, also, that the lay-brethren wore cloth of russet ; we ordered that in future they should wear gowns blacker than usual. We corrected what ought to be corrected."[4]

In 1278, Robert, son of William Gyon, of Bramcote, gave to the Prior and Monks of Lenton an annual rent of four shillings, which Hugh de Stapleford, clerk, then paid him for four bovates of land in Sutton Passeys, with homage, ward, relief, and all other appurtenances. Sir Robert de Stretley, Sir Geoffrey de Dethec, Sir Ralph de Arnale, John de Cortlingstock, Henry de Watenhow, John de Passeys, and William Torkard were amongst the witnesses to his charter.[5]

In the following year the visitors from Clugny Abbey were again at Lenton, and were able to report a better state of things than existed in 1276 ; the Prior at that date having apparently resigned in the meantime.

---

(1) Thoroton, p. 82.

(2) Friday, February 21, 1276, the feast of St. Peter in Cathedra being on the 22nd of that month.

(3) " De postela, sotularibus corrigiatis, esu carnium, de lectione in infirmaria et de mora post completorium, precepimus sicut apud Montem Acutem."

(4) Clugny MSS., Bibliothèque Nationale, Paris.

(5) Thoroton, p. 220.

"1279. On Thursday after the feast of St. Augustine[1] we were at Lenton, where there are twenty-five monks, as is customary. They live regularly and honestly, and perform the divine offices well. The Prior is an influential person, of honest life and far-reaching fame; he came to the house indebted in nine hundred and thirty-five marcs, and in forty sacks of wool, and a sack is worth fifteen marcs. He has paid thirty-two sacks, and still owes eight. On the other hand, he is indebted in a thousand and thirty marcs; the reason is because of the great dispute he has, and had, with the Chapter of Lichfield,[2] who are rich men, powerful, and of the council of the King, concerning a certain tithe worth two hundred and fifty marcs of annual rent; and now the Prior has expended for that suit, one hundred and sixty marcs; and he believes that it will be necessary to go to court for the said reason. Also, when he came to the house, he did not find a sufficiency of temporal goods. Also, he gives to his predecessor, every year, forty marcs, of which he is in great need. Also, that a certain manor of his is indebted to the value of forty shillings, which debt Prior Roger made." [3]

King Edward the First, in the year 1283, granted a charter sanctioning the exchange of the advowson of the church of Horsley, in the diocese of Lichfield, for the advowson of the church of Felmersham, in the diocese of Lincoln.[4]

In the year 1284, a jury declared upon oath at Nottingham, "that William, son of Nicholas de Cantilupe, was born in the Abbey of Lenton ('*in Abbatia de Lenton*'), and was baptized in the church of the said Abbey, that is to say, on Palm Sunday, twenty-one years ago; and they briefly declare that the said William, son of Nicholas, was of full age on the said Palm Sunday last past." [5]

---

(1) Thursday, June 1st, 1279.
(2) See pp. 68-73 ante, for the particulars of this dispute.
(3) Clugny MSS., Bibliothèque Nationale, Paris.
(4) *Cal. Rot. Chart.*, p. 112.
(5) *Calendarium Genealogicum*, i. 139.
Nicholas de Cantelupe, who married Eustachia, dau. and heiress of Ralph, son of Hugh Fitz Ralph, was the fourth son of William de Cantelupe, Baron Cantelupe by tenure, and Seneschal to King John, and was the father of William de Cantelupe, who

In 1288, the Official of York gave definitive sentence that the two parts of the great tithes of Elias de Bradmere, Ralph de Freschville, lord of Bunny, the Lady Maud Torkard, Agnes de Staynton, Richard, son of Felice, Maud Holfin, William Smith, of Bunny, Amice Poyne, of Bradmere, and William, son of Ralph, of the same place, within the parish of Bunny, belonged to William Heccredibire, rector of Bunny, and not to the Prior and Convent of Lenton.[1]

In the year 1289, Thomas de Normanville, escheator beyond the Trent, was commanded to "take into the hand of the King all the lands and tenements belonging to the Priory of Lenton, vacant through the resignation of brother Reginald de Jora, until lately Prior of the same."[2]

In the year 1289, Pope Nicholas IV. addressed the following bull to the King on behalf of Peter de Siviriaco, Prior of Lenton, who appears to have been deprived of his office, by one of the monks, Ranandus, being put into his place.

" Nicholas, Bishop, servant of the servants of God, to his well-beloved son in Christ, Edward the illustrious King of England, greeting and apostolic benediction.

Some while ago we thought it proper, by our letters, to bring under the notice of the King, how our beloved sons, Brother Peter de Siviriaco of Lenton, of the Order of Cluniacs, in the Diocese of York, and some other Priors of Priories, Monks of the Monastery of Cluny.

Carefully taking note that some statutes which G. IX. Pope, our predecessor, of blessed memory, published on the reformation of the said order, and which he, in virtue of obedience,

---

must obviously have been identical with that William, who was, as above stated, baptized in Lenton Priory on Palm Sunday, 1263. In 1303, the said William was found by the jury to hold the manor of Greasley after the death of Sir William de Roos, Knight, who held the same for his life, "by the courtesy of England," he being the second husband of the above named Eustachia, heiress of the said manor. In 1294, William de Cantelupe took part in the expedition into Gascony, and a few years later he joined in the invasion of Scotland. In 1299, he was raised to the peerage as Baron Cantelupe, by writ of summons, dated December 29th, 1299. He was succeded at his death in 1308, by his son William, who made proof of his age in 1313, probably on attaining his majority. This William died not long after, and was never summoned to Parliament as a baron. His younger brother, Nicholas, Lord Cantelupe, had license to castellate his mansion at Greasley in 1340, and three years later he founded Beauvale Priory.

This branch of the Cantelupe family bore for arms. *Gules*, a fesse *vair*, between three leopards' heads reversed, jessant de-lys *or*. The elder branch of the family, who had the barony of Abergavenny, bore the same arms, omitting the fesse.

(1) Thoroton, p. 46.    (2) Ab. Rot. Orig., I. 65.

commanded to be strictly and inviolably observed, were not in the least attended to in the Order,

Therefore, on this account, and for certain other reasons, they have appealed to the Apostolic See,

And lest ———— Abbot of the said Monastery, after this their appeal, depriving them of their access to the Roman Court, should make any new attack upon them, or upon any one of them, or their adherents, or those who wish to adhere to them, or attempt any attack, either by citation, warning, or excommunication, suspension and sentence of interdict, or should proceed to remove or despoil them of their said Priories and houses, by themselves or by others, by whatever authority, have in their own name, and of those who wish to support them in this contention, for the second time appealed to the said See against the above-mentioned Abbot, and even applied for the prosecution of the above-named persons coming in person to the same See,

Which attempts having been carried into effect, as the Abbot has before stated, as also the Surveyors of the General Chapter have unjustly deprived these Priors of their Priories and administration, contrary to law, brother Ranandus, monk of the above mentioned monastery, having been instituted *de facto*, though not *de jure*, into the Priory of Lenton, receiving whom (on the presentation of the Abbot) as Prior of the above mentioned Priory, of which you are said to be the patron, you have caused him to be put in possession of the Priory, and its goods and rights.

We, therefore, looking to the peace and prosperity of the Monastery, and of the persons living therein, and considering attentively that as brother Peter before stated, as well as the other above-mentioned Priors, have been unjustly despoiled of their Priories and have suffered loss of that which should have been of emolument to them, have, justice demanding it, by the assent of the Proctors of the above Abbot, restored to him the above named Priory of [Lenton], removal from or spoliation in this manner notwithstanding ;

Earnestly praying your Royal Highness and entreating you devoutly to unite with the Apostolic See to cause to be restored to the same brother Peter, Prior, full possession of the above-mentioned Priory of Lenton, and of its rights and goods, all obstacles being removed, and to keep him in possession thereof by the aid of your Royal favours.

If you will kindly and liberally carry this out, reward from God, and the abundance of our high praises will be bestowed upon you.

Moreover, you will know that it has lately come to our knowledge that the above named Abbot, whilst the said Priors were still in the Roman Court, has paid the debt of nature, and that the unanimous election of another, so it is said, has been held in the above named Monastery, and it is reported that the Elect is about to come shortly to the Court, humbly to ask for the confirmation of his election,

On account of which it behoves the said Prior, along with the above mentioned Priors, to remain at the Apostolic See until the Elect one arrives, in order that the good estate of the Monastery may be the more advantageously and efficaciously, with God's help, provided for :

As therefore the above mentioned Prior, on account of this hindrance, cannot personally return to England, to take actual possession of his, the said Priory, we have thought well to ask and entreat your Royal Highness, out of reverence for us and of the Apostolic See, to cause the corporal possession of the above named Priory, and all its goods and rights to be assigned to —————— Proctor of the said Prior, in his name, and for him, all contrary customs notwithstanding.

Thus faithfully yielding to our requests and effectually fulfilling that which we seek, so in like manner we will worthily praise the promptitude of your royal devotion, which we hope will, in this matter, be an easy task.

If, however, any one in the same Priory of Lenton shall say that he has any rights, we are prepared to do him full justice, after we shall have investigated his cause.

Given at Rome, at St. Mary Major, the third of the Ides of December, in the second year of our Pontificate."

(Under the hempen thread.)[1]

According to the Taxation of Pope Nicholas the Fourth, made in 1291,[2] the annual income of the Priory was derived as follows :—*Spiritualities*, Lincoln diocese, £15 19s. 4d. ; Coventry and Lichfield diocese, £66 13s. 4d. ; York diocese, £108 12s. 10d. Total of spiritualities £191 5s. 6d. *Temporalities*, Lincoln diocese, £37 3s. 10½d. ; Salisbury diocese, 13s 4d. ; Coventry and Lichfield diocese, £17 6s. ; York diocese, £92 12s. 6d. Total of temporalities, £147 15s. 8½d. Total valuation of Priory, £339 1s. 2½d.[3]

In 1294, John, son of Thomas the Leech (*medicus*), of Newthorpe, released all actions and demands to William, Prior of Lenton, who was his guardian during his minority.[4]

---

(1) Rymer's *Fœdera*, ii., 453.

(2) Pope Nicholas IV., to whom the first-fruits and tenths of all benefices belonged, granted the tenths, in 1288, to King Edward I. for six years, towards defraying the expenses of a Crusade ; and in order that their full value might be collected, the King caused a valuation roll to be drawn up under the direction of John, Bishop of Winchester, and Oliver, Bishop of Lincoln. This taxation, completed in 1291, held good for the purpose of the taxation of benefices until the new survey of 27 Henry VIII. was made.

(3) *Mon. Ang.*, v. 109.          (4) Thoroton, p. 238.

In the year 1297, the Prior of Lenton was returned by the sheriffs of the counties of Northampton, Nottingham, and Derby, as holding lands or rents to the amount of twenty pounds yearly value, and upwards, either in capite or otherwise, and as such was summoned under the general writ to perform military service in parts beyond the sea. The muster to be at London on Sunday next after the octave of St. John the Baptist, 25 Edw. I.[1]

In the same year the Priory was taxed at £6 13s. 4d., on the occasion of the King going into Gascony.[2]

In the British Museum there are copies of the account of Robert Bozun of the issues of the Priory of Lenton, from the Sunday next after the feast of St. Margaret in the 25th year of the reign of King Edward the Third (July 21st, 1297) to the feast of St. Michael next following;[3] also from the feast of St. Michael in the 25th year of King Edward the Third, ending at the same feast in the following year.[4]

In the 30th year of King Edward I., John le Paumer or Palmer,[5] and his wife Alice (sister and heir of Hugh de Stapleford, son of Robert de Stapleford, of Nottingham), obtained a license to endow two chaplaincies in the chapel of St. Mary on Hethbeth Bridge, Nottingham, with £6 13s. 5d. of annual income.[6] Thoroton states that the Palmers gave this rent "to a certain chaplain to celebrate Divine Offices for their souls, etc., in the chapel of St. Mary on Hethebethe Brigg, where there is an arch, yet known by the name of Chappell Arch."[7] From this, and other documents, it appears that the Trent Bridge at Nottingham was anciently known as Heyghbeythbrugg, Hethbethe, or Heybeth Bridge. This name has, however, long fallen into desuetude. The sixth arch of the old bridge (from the Nottingham side) was formerly known as the Chapel Arch, and some remains of the chapel were found here when the bridge was repaired in 1826.

---

(1) Parl. and Mil. Writs, i. 702.        (2) Testa de Nevill, p. 22.

(3) Add. MSS., 6164, f. 514.        (4) Ibid, f. 517.

(5) Mayor of Nottingham, 1302, 1306, and 1311.

(6) Inq. p.m., 30 Edw. I., No. 102.

(7) Antiquities of Notts., p. 492.    The chapel is mentioned in the *Valor Ecclesiasticus* as being the property of Lenton Priory.

We find that King Edward I. was at Lenton in April, 1302, and on the 10th day of that month addressed a letter, dated at Lenton, to Henry, King of Spain, on the proposed marriage of Prince Edward of England, with Isabella, Infanta of Spain.[1]

In the following year the King was again at Lenton. On the 9th of April, 1303, he addressed a letter, dated at Lenton, to the Count of Namur, in which he refers the count to the bearer for the King's reply to his letter.[2] On the following day (April 10th, 1303) the King addressed a letter, also dated at Lenton, to the councillors of Bruges and other communes in Flanders, in which he refers them to the bearer of the letter for his answer to their letters.[3]

In the year 1307, King Edward II. was at Lenton Priory. On September 29th, in that year, Walter de Jorz, archbishop of Armagh, renounced, " in Camera Regis in prioratu de Lenton," all claim to the bulls of his appointment which were prejudicial to the King's power. The witnesses to this renunciation were, the King, the Patriarch of Jerusalem, J., Bishop of Chichester, Henry de Lacy, Earl of Lincoln, V., Earl of Hereford,[4] Thomas Plantagenet, Earl of Lancaster, Hugh le Despenser, W. Inge J. de Benested, clerico, Brother J. de Lenham (? Lenton), W. de Melton, A. de Osgoteby, and R. de Bardelby.[5]

The Prior of Lenton at this time must have been an important and wealthy personage, not only to be honoured by such guests, but to possess the means of entertaining so distinguished an assemblage.

On the following day (Sept. 30) the King addressed a letter, dated at Lenton, to John de Britannia, Earl of Richmond, the King's lieutenant in Scotland, directing him to proceed to Galloway to suppress the rebellion of Robert de Brus.[6]

By a statute, known as the " Statute of Carlisle," passed in the year 1307, the King prohibited all abbots, priors, or other religious persons of whatsoever condition, from thenceforth

---

(1) Rymer's *Fœdera*, ii. 900.          (2) Ibid., ii. 922.

(3) Ibid.

(4) Humphrey de Bohun was then Earl of Hereford.

(5) Rymer's *Fœdera*, iii. 13.          (6) Ibid., iii. 14.

sending any money under any name or pretence whatsoever as a payment to their superiors beyond the sea.

"Alien superiors having set divers unwonted and heavy payments and impositions on the monasteries in subjection to them in England, the King can no longer suffer such losses and injuries to be winked at, and provides a sufficient remedy, etc."

In the year 1310, the Prior of Lenton impleaded William de Shaldeford, chaplain, and many others, for taking forty lambs of the value of forty shillings, at Langar, for tithes.[1]

In the year 1316, the Prior of Lenton was certified, pursuant to writs tested at Clipston, March 5th, as lord of the manor of Lenton, in the county of Nottingham, and of the manor of Courteenhall, in Northamptonshire. He was likewise certified to be the joint lord of the manors of Cotgrave, Owthorpe, Crophill Bishop, Kinoulton, and Newthorpe, in Nottinghamshire.[2]

The *inspeximus* charter of King Edward the Second, dated at York, August 19th, 1316, after reciting and confirming Peverel's foundation charter, a charter of Stephen, four of Henry II., and three of John, concludes with an enumeration of various grants by other persons. These are—the church of Wigston, with its appurtenances, by Robert, Earl of Medlent; the tithe of assarts in the forest of High Peak, by William de Ferrers, Earl of Derby; of the churches of Ossington and Horsley, by Hugh de Burun and his son, Hugh Meschines, with a moiety of the church of Cotgrave; of the church of Broughton, a chapel and certain lands in that town, by Richard Bussell; the manors of Holme and Dunston, by Matthew de Hathersage; and a moiety of the church of Attenborough, the land of Reginald, in Chilwell, the church of Barton (in Fabis), and two parts of the tithe of his demesne in Bunny and Bradmore, by Odo de Boneia.[3]

The Prior of Lenton was, by a writ tested at Gloucester, February 16th, 1322, requested by the King to raise as many men-at-arms and horse and foot soldiers as he could, to march

(1) *Ab. Placitor*, p. 312.     (1) Parliamentary Writs, iv. 1092.

(3) Mon. Angl., v. 112.

against the rebels or adherents of the Earl of Lancaster, " who
are destroying our people, and besieging with an armed force
our castle of Tickhill;" the muster to take place at Coventry,
on the first Sunday in Lent (Feb. 28). On the 16th of the
following month, the battle of Boroughbridge put an end to
this rebellion, and on the 23rd March, the Earl of Lancaster
with a number of his adherents were executed.

Rex, Priori de Lentonia salutem.

Quia Scoti, inimici & Rebelles nostri, qui tempore Domini
E. quondam R. Angliæ, Patris nostri (contra quem in Rebellionem
proruperunt) & nostro postmodum, infra Regnum nostrum,
Homicidia, deprædationes, incendia, & alia Dampna innumera
multipliciter perpetrarunt. Finitâ Treugâ, inter nos & ipsos
nuper initâ, dictum Regnum nostrum in magna multitudine
ingressi, in eodem consimilia facinora perpetrantes, Ætati, vel
Sexui, seu loco, sacro vel Religioso, non parcentes. Ac quidam
Magnates de Regno nostro, nobis Subditi, a jamdiu, nobis
Inobientes & Rebelles, se in magna multitudine ad partes Boriales
transtulerunt, populum nostrum destruentes, ac Castrum nostrum
de Tykhull Armatâ potentiâ Obsedentes. Per quod ordinavimus
& esse proponimus, Domino concedente, apud Coventre, primâ
Dominicâ Quadragesimæ, proximo futurâ, cum equis & Armis,
quanto decentius & potentius poterimus, ad proficiscendum
exinde contra dictos Inimicos, Inobedientes & Rebelles nostros,
ad eorum malitiam & proterviam, cum Dei adjutorio refrænandas ;
Nos, de vestra fidelitate ad plenum confidentes, sperantes etiam
quod, in tanto & tam arduo Negotio, nos, & Statum, ac sal-
vationem Regni nostri prædicti specialiter tangente, manum
porrigere velitis adjutricem, Vobis, in fide & dilectione, quibus
nobis tenemini, firmiter injungentes, mandamus ; vos etiam
specialiter requirimus & rogamus, quantinus de Hominibus ad
Arma, Equitibus & Peditibus, quanto decentius poteritis, con-
sideratâ diligenter qualitate Negotii prædicti, nos juvetis ; & eosdem Homines, Armis competentibus bene munitos, habeatis ad
nos, ad diem & locum prædictos, ad proficiscendum exinde
nobiscum in Obsequium nostrum supradictum ; vel de alio subsidio competenti nos, ad eosdem diem & locum, ita curialiter
respiciatis & gratanter, quod, vestro mediante subsidio, negotia
nostra prædicta, ad nostrum & vestrum honorem & commodum,
& Populi Regni notris tranquilitatem & quietem perpetuam,
feliciter valeant expediri, & quod vobis exinde in futurum artius
teneamur. Et, si forsitan, ad eosdem diem & locum, obstante
aliquo impedimento, quod absit, præmissa facere non possitis,
tunc ea postea ita festinanter compleatis, quod ex hoc perpendere
possimus qualem affectionem ad nostram expeditionem optatam
geritis & habeatis ; pensantes intime quod, in prædicto negotio
status totius Regni nostri, tam Ecclesiæ, quam Populi, versatur.

Et de eo, quod inde facere volueritis, nos, sine dilatione aliquâ, reddatis per vestras Litteras certiores.

Teste Rege apud Gloucestriam, decimo sexto die Febuarii.

Per ipsum Regem.[1]

King Edward the Third, on his accesion to the throne, by an instrument dated at Westminster, February 4th 1327, restored to the Prior of Lenton, and sixty-four other alien Priories, their lands in England, seized by his late father on account of the war in Aquitain. [2]

In the same year, Geoffrey, Prior of Lenton, being troubled by the Court of Rome, "to the great destruction of his house of Lenton," for not obeying a Papal mandate to put Cardinal Pouget in possession of the church at Radcliffe-on-Soar, prays the King, for the love of God, to forward letters excusatory to the Pope.

A n're Seign'r le Rey monstre son petyt Chapelyn si ly plest Frere Geffrey Prior de Lenten', qe coment jadys la venyst Comaundeme't de p' n're Piere la Pape, q'il meyst le Cardinal Pouget en possession de l'Eglise de Radeclyve sus Sore. Et le dit Prior sousyt, q'il n'osa faire le dist Comaundemet, partant q'il fust defendu p Bref le Rey de sa Chauncelerye, tant que le play de l'Avoyeson de la dist Eglise qe pendist entre le Conte de Lancastre & le Prior de Norton fust trie. Pur lagle chose le dist Prior est mult malemetz tretez & demenez a la Court de Rome, a la g'nt destrucion de sa meson de Lenton. Prye le dist Prior a n're Seign'r le Rey pur l'amour de Dieux, q'il ly pleyse prier affectuosement a n're dist Piere le Pape p' ses L'res, q'il pur l'amour de ly voile aver le dist Prior pour escuse a ceste fethe, & aver regard al defense qe fait ly fust p' Real Poer. Et q'il ly pleyse charger les messageres qe irront la, q'ils voillent escuser le dist Prior en le maner sus dite, & psenter les Lres nre dist Seignr le Rey a la Pape.

*Responsio.* Il semble au Conf' q le Roi li deit aider, mes jadumeins devant le Roi.[3]

The King, acceding to the Prior's request, addressed the following letter, dated at Nottingham, May 15th, 1327, to the Pope :—

Papæ Rex devota pedum oscula beatorum.

Religiosi Viri et nobis in Christo dilecti, Fratris Galfridi,

---

(1) Rymer's *Fœdera*, iii. 927.    (2) Ibid., iv. 246.

(3) Rolls of Parliament, ii. 393.

Prioris de Lenton, ordinis Cluniacensis. Quietem et commoda affectantes, ea pro ipso vestræ clementiæ devotâ intentione suggerrimus, et, pro salubri appositione remedii, sedulis insistimus Precibus et votivis, per quæ ipsius tranquilitatem conspicimus inquietari, et spiritualis Profectûs devotionem impediri.

Dudum siquidem, Pater Sancte, ut didicimus, in quodam Negotio Provisorio, Ecclesiam de Radeclive, super Sore, Eborum Diocesi, contingente, per executores ejusdem Negotii, eidem Priori injunctam erat, ut Procuratorem, Venerabilis Patris, Domini B Tituli Sancti Marcellini, Presbyteri Cardinalis, in Possessionem dictæ Ecclesiæ induceret, virtute Provisionis, seu Gratiæ, eidem Cardinali a Sede Apostolicâ indè factæ.

Quod quidem Mandatum idem Prior, pro eo quod, super Advocatione dictæ Ecclesiæ, inter, bonæ memoriæ, Thomam, tunc Comitem Lancastriæ, et Priorem de Nortonia, in Curiâ, Magnifici Principio, Domini E nuper Regis Angliæ, Patris nostri, Lis mota fuit, et inhibitum ei, ex parte dicti Patris nostri, nè, pendente hujusmodi Lite, aliquam Personam induceret in Ecclesiam supradictam, necnon, ob metum ; præfati Comitis, exequi non audebat :

Et quamquam idem Comes, postmodum Patronatum dictæ Ecclesiæ, contra præfatum Priorem de Norton, judicialiter evicisset, sicque dicta Provisio ad præfatam Ecclesiam, utpote de Laico Patronatu existentem, se nullatenus extendebat, idem nichilominus Prior de Lenton, ad respondendum præfato Cardinali de contemptu, extitit personaliter ad Sedem Apostolicam evocatus :

Et, pro eo quod non comparuit, juxta vocationem illam (transitu maris, per dictum Patrem nostrum, ei tunc, certis de causis, penitus prohibito) idem Prior metuit Processus aliquos, contra ipsum, in eâdem Curiâ factos esse ; sicque jam, per longa tempora, eo timore, abstinuit a Divinis.

Verùm quia, per inspectionem Judicii, in Lite prædictâ redditi, nobis constat evidenter quod prefatus Comes evicit Patronatum dictæ ecclesiæ, et quod præfatus Prior de Norton nichil juris habuit in eadem.

Beatitudini vestræ sinceris affectibus supplicamus quatinùs præfato Priori de Lenton, qui, pro petendâ Statûs sui Reformatione, ad vestræ Sanctitatis præsentiam personaliter se divertit, benignum dignemini præbere Auditum, eique, præmissorum contemplatione, Sinum Paternæ pietatis, in suis justis Postulationibus, benignitate solitâ aperire.

Conservet etc.

Dat apud Notingham decimo quinto die Maii.[1]

The King also, at the same time, addressed the following letter, on the same subject, to the Cardinal of St. Susanna.

---

(1) Rymer's *Fœdera*, iv. 289.

Venerabili in Christo Patri, Domino P. Dei gratiâ, Tituli
Sanctæ Susannæ Presbitero Cardinali, Amico suo carissimo,
Edwardus, Dei gratiâ &c et Dux Aquitaniæ, Salutem, et sinceræ
dilectionis affectum.

Referente nobis, dilecto nobis in Christo, Fratre Galfrido,
Priore de Lenton, Ordinis Cluniacensis, didicimus qualiter in
quodam Negotio Provisorio, Ecclesiam de Radeclive, super Sore,
Eborum Diocesi, contingente, per Executores ejusdem Negotii,
eidem Priori injunctum erat, ut Procuratorem, Venerabilis Patris,
Domini B tituli Sancti Marcellini, Presbyteri Cardinalis in Possessionem dictæ Ecclesiæ in duceret, *&c prout supra usque hæc*
*verba ; viz.*

Patenitatem vestram affectuosis Precibus requirimus et rogamus, quatinùs præfato Priori de Lenton. Qui pro petendâ
Statûs sui Reformatione, ad Sedem Apostolicam personaliter
se divertit, in prosecutione negotiorum suorum, assistere velitis,
nostri contemplatione rogaminis, Consiliis et Auxiliis oportunis ;
eademque Nogotia penes dictum Dominum Summum Pontificem
(Cui pro eisdem scribimus) modis, quibus meliùs expedire vide-
ritis, efficaciter promovere.

Dat apud Notingham decimo quinto die Maii.

In the year 1329, a dispute arose between the Abbot of
Vale Royal (Cheshire), and the Prior of Lenton, in consequence
of the latter selling the tithes of beasts pasturing in Edale.
The Abbot entreated Queen Isabella, at that time lady of the
Castle and Honour of the High Peak, that she would give
instructions to her Bailiff of the High Peak, to liberate to the
Abbot the tithes of the wild beasts and domestic animals
pastured in Edale, for the benefit of the church of Castleton,
of which the Abbot was Rector. The Queen accordingly
instructed Ralph de Spaynynge, her Bailiff, to make an
inquisition on oath, as to the ancient rights and privileges
of the Abbot and the church of Castleton. The result was
that the claim of the Abbot was confirmed to him.[1]

The following translation of the *Placita de quo warranto*
relating to Lenton, held at Nottingham before W. de Herle,
and his associate, justices-itinerant, on Monday next after the
feast of St. Martin, 1329, is of very great interest, as showing
the rights and privileges enjoyed by the Priory at that
time.

---

(1) Harl. MSS., 2064, fo. 251.

The Prior of Lenton was summoned to answer to his lord the King, by what warrant he claimed to have a yearly fair, lasting eight days, at Lenton, to be held at the feast of Saint Martin, with all things belonging to the said fair; and to have in his said manor of Lenton, infangthef and outfangthef with a gallows, and a view of frankpledge there of all his tenants of Lenton, Radford, Keketon, and Newthorp, twice a year, with all pertaining to a view of frankpledge, also pillory, tumbrell, and thew; and to have at the same manor of Lenton wayf; and to have at his manor at Cotgrave, a view of frankpledge twice a year, of all his tenants of Cotgrave, with all pertaining to a view of frankpledge. And how it was that at the time of a certain vacancy of the Priory of Lenton—whether it was by death, by resignation, or by any other cause—no eschator or other, our servant came to the said Piory of Lenton, nor entered, nor received any of the profits thereof, except indeed that the sheriff of Nottingham, or the constable of the Castle of Nottingham, at that time, whichever the first of them had been required thereto by the sub-prior and convent of the said Priory, had placed one of his servants at the gate of the said Priory, there to remain for the safety of the property of the Priory, lest it should be squandered, but who, immediately on the fealty of the new Prior to the King being taken, ought to withdraw without receiving anything except his sustenance in food, during the time of the said vacancy. And why he and his monks should be exempt from fair and market dues, of whatever sort they may be, on crossing bridges [and] at seaports; from toll, from dane-geld, and from all monies and aids to the wapentake, and hundred, shire, trithing, and tenemental aid, from murder [money], scutage, assise, and summons, and hidage and ward, from frank-pledge and all pleas and fines, processes and forfeiture, from decisions and customs, and from every land service and secular exaction.

And the Prior came by John de Shirwood, his atttorney. And whereas he is summoned to answer, &c., by what warrant he claims to have a fair at Lenton for eight days, &c., he says, that the late lord Henry the second after the conquest, King of England, by his charter granted and confirmed to the Monks of Lenton a fair of eight days at the feast of St. Martin with full toll of all things from which toll may be taken, excepting those purchases which were appointed for the table or for their dress which upon this quittance he gave and confirmed, willing and firmly enjoining that no one should sell or buy in Nottingham within the eight days during which the fair lasted, and that all persons coming and going to the fair should be free of all claims; also enjoining that the Sheriff or the Castellan of Nottingham should not vex the said Monks in the slaughter of cattle, nor in anything else as they have been accustomed, but should buy in such fair like others who come to the market

from a distance. And he produces the said charter of the said
·King Henry, &c., which testifies this, &c. And whereas he is
summoned to answer by what warrant he claims infangenthef
and outfangenthef with gallows at his manor of Lenton, &c., and
likewise why he and his Monks should be exempt in fairs and
markets of whatever sort, &c , from toll &c. on all the articles in
the same quittance above contained those articles being excepted,
and from all pleas and fines and processes and forfeitures and
decisions,—he says, that the lord King John late King of
England, progenitor of the present King, by his charter granted
and confirmed to God and the convent of monks of Lenton,
infangthef and outfangenethef and soc and sac and tol and
theam ; and that these monks hold all their tenements free and
quit of toll, danegeld, and all monies and aids, and [free] of
wapentake, hundred, trithing, shire and tenemental [charges],
and of murder and scutage and other quittances above named,
except all pleas, &c., as is above said. And he produces the
charter of the said John, late King, &c., which testifies to this,
the date of which is at Guildford the 22nd day of April in the
first year of his reign. And as to the having quittance from all
pleas, fines, processes, and forfeitures and decisions he claims
nothing at present. And as to the view of frank-pledge at his
manor of Lenton of all his tenants of Lenton and other towns
above named twice a year, with all pertaining to a view, pillory,
&c. ; and to have weyf at the said manor of Lenton ; and to
have view of frankpledge of all his tenants of Cotgrave at his
manor of Cotgrave, &c., as is above contained in the said writ,
&c.,—for the view of frankpledge he says that he and all his
predecessors from time whereof no memory exists have had
view of frankpledge at his manor of Lenton of all his tenants of
Lenton, Radford, Keketon, and Newthorpe, and likewise at his
manor of Cotgrave, of all his tenants who were residents, twice
a year, together with all pertaining to a frank-pledge, &c.
Likewise he and all his predecessors had weyf at his said manor
of Lenton from time immemorial. And by these warrants he
claims the said liberties.—And whereas in the time of a certain
vacancy of the Priory of Lenton no Escheator nor other servant
of the King came to the said priory nor received the profits
thereof, except that the sheriff of Nottingham or the constable of
the Castle of Nottingham at that time, whichever the first of
them had been required by the sub-prior and convent of the said
Priory, had placed one of his servants at the gate of the said
priory, there to remain for the safety of the property of the priory
lest it should be squandered, but who immediately on the fealty of
the new Prior to the King being taken, ought to withdraw without
receiving anything excepting his sustenance in food during the
time of the said vacancy, he says that the lord the King that
now is assigned his beloved and faithful John de Annesley,
Richard de Willoughby, and John del Ker to inquire in the

presence of the Sheriff of Nottingham and the Constable of Nottingham, or their lieutenants [locum tenentes] more fully into the articles contained in the same declaration. And by the inquisition taken by the said John, Richard, and John in the presence of the Sheriff of Nottingham, and the lieutenant of the Constable of the said Castle, returned into the Chancery of the lord the King, it was found that the Sheriff or the Constable aforesaid, whichever might first come to the said Priory in time of vacancy on the request of the said sub-prior and convent, was accustomed to place one of his servants at the gate of the said Priory for the safety of the goods of the said Priory, &c., who, immediately on fealty to [the King's] progenitors being taken [by a new Prior] withdrew without receiving anything more than his sustenance, &c., as above is declared : And that the King's progenitors had received no profits from the said priory in time of vacancy. Which inquisition in all its articles so returned, the King warranted by his charter, willing and granting for himself and his heirs that no Escheator or other servant of the King whatever in time of vacancy of the said Priory should enter on either temporalities or anything else belonging to the said Priory, or should meddle with the said priory or its temporalities in any way whatsoever, saving that the Sheriff of the County or the Constable of the Castle for the time being on the requisition of the sub-prior and convent of the said place and their successors may place one of his servants at the gate of the said Priory for the safety of the goods of the said Priory who shall remain there during the vacancy, and when the fealty of the new Prior has been taken shall go away without receiving anything except his sustenance, as above is said. And he now produces the said charter of the said King, which testifies the premisses in form above said, dated at Nottingham the 8th day of November in the 1st year of his reign.

And William de Dene, who follows on behalf of the King says, that though the said Prior claims the view of frank-pledge at his manor of Cotgrave, with all pertaining to the said view, etc., the said Prior has not in the said manor a pillory nor a tumbrell, by which delinquents of any kind in the said view ought to be punished in his cause, etc.

And the Prior says that he admits that he has neither pillory nor tumbrell, yet he and all his predecessors from time immemorial had a view of frank pledge in the said manor as above is said.

And William who follows, &c., asks judgment for the king, because as the said Prior recognizes expressly enough that he does not possess there the kind of judicial powers [judicialia] which are required at a view of frank-pledge, the said liberty will be lost, &c. He asks also that it shall be inquired on behalf of the king how he and his predecessors have exercised the other liberties which he claims above, &c. Therefore it is inquired for the king.

Twelve jurors say upon oath, that the said Prior and all his predecessors have had the said fair at Lenton for eight days, in form as is above declared, from the time when the fair was granted to the predecessors of the Prior by King Henry the Second after the Conquest, without interruption. And the fair has been well used. And likewise that he and his predecessors have used and have had infangthef and outfangthef with gallows at his manor of Lenton, and those liberties have been well exercised from the time they were granted. And likewise that he and his monks were and are accustomed to be exempt in any fairs and markets whatever, on crossing bridges, at sea-ports, from toll and other liabilities above written, except those which he disclaims above. They say also that he has a view of frank-pledge at Lenton of all his tenants at Lenton, Radeford, Keketon, and Neuthorp, twice a year, of those who were resident, together with all belonging to that view, pillory and tumbrell and thewe and weyf at the manor of Lenton, and likewise at his manor of Cotgrave, a view of frankpledge of all his tenants of Cotgrave twice a year, together with all pertaining to that view, excepting pillory and tumbrell and thewe there. And likewise at his manor of Cotgrave, a view of frankpledge of all his tenants of Cotgrave twice a year, together with all pertaining to that view, excepting pillory and tumbrell and thewe there. And that he and all his predecessors from time immemorial have had those said views pertaining to the said manors of Lenton and Cotgrave, and those views have been exercised thus, namely, in the amercing of all those who transgress by breaking the assize of bread and ale, and other articles of the said views, whatsoever they may have transgressed, and never by inflicting corporal punishment on any kind of delinquents. And they say that the present Prior was Prior at the time when the said inquisition was taken before the said John de Annesley, Richard, and John, as to how the said Priory ought to be kept in the time of vacancy. And they say that the said Priory has never been vacant since.

And William who follows, &c., says, that none of these liberties were claimed in the last Itinerary before J. de Vall and his colleagues the justices last travelling in the time of King Edward, grandfather of the present King. Therefore the said View shall be seized into the King's hands. Afterwards came the said Prior and paid a fine of forty shillings to our lord the King in order to have back his liberties by the hand of John de Skeryngton and John de Shirwood of the same county. There-fore he regains his liberty, &c., saving the right of the King, &c. And he is told that he should exercise them as he ought, &c., and as to all other liberties the said Prior at present [has them] *sine die*, saving the King's right, &c.[1]

---

(1) *Placita de quo Warranto*, p. 643.

The pleas relating to the rights of the Prior of Lenton in the manor of Courteenhall, in Northamptonshire, were held at Northampton, on the Monday next after the Feast of All Saints, 1329, before Geoffrey le Scrop and his associate justices itinerary.[1]

The pleas as to the rights of the Prior in the manor of Blackwell, in the High Peak of Derbyshire, were held before W. de Herle and his associate justices itinerant in the counties of Nottingham and Derby, on the Monday next after the Feast of the Apostles Peter and Paul, 1330.[2]

From an early period, the Priory had acquired the advowson of Beeston, and in the year 1330, the rectory of that parish was appropriated by Lenton Priory, and the church became a chapel, subject to the mother Church of Lenton. This appropriation was effected by the aid of Popes Alexander III. and Lucius III., whose letters were produced in support of the claim "against the parishioners and poor vicar." Two commissioners, John de la Launde, rector of Arnold, and William de Hundon, rector of Barmburgh, in Yorkshire, were appointed to determine the dispute as to repair of the chancel by the parishioners, and the payment of twenty-two shillings yearly by the vicar to Lenton Priory.[3]

The monastery retained the advowson and appropriate tithes of Beeston[4] down to the dissolution, and the arms of the Priory

---

(1) *Placita de quo warranto*, p. 576.          (2) *Ibid.*, p. 137.
(3) Thoroton, p. 211.

(4) William de Willesthorpe was instituted to this benefice, October the 12th, 1327, on the presentation of the Prior and Convent of Lenton, but during the latter half of the fourteenth century the advowson was retained by the Crown, owing to the restrictions then placed upon alien monasteries. Towards the close of that century the Prior and Convent were permitted to resume their right, and Richard Mason was instituted on their presentation. On his decease, the Prior and Convent presented Henry Searle, who was instituted March the 21st, 1401. Five years later they presented Thomas Marchall, who was instituted January the 30th, 1405. On his resignation they presented John Thimelby, who was instituted January the 26th, 1420. He resigned three years later, and John Gynger was instituted September the 17th, 1423. Thomas Smyth, who occurs as the next Vicar, was doubtless presented by the Prior and Convent, and on his resignation they presented John Katull, who was instituted April the 7th, 1431. John Meyson was instituted January the 28th, 1451, on the same presentation, as was also his successor, John Emott, on whose death the Prior and Convent presented Nicholas Bubwith, who was instituted August the 13th, 1455. On his resignation they presented William Taylor, who was instituted March the 18th, 1456. He was succeeded by Richard Ellesley, on whose resignation, the Prior and Convent presented Nicholas Blackwell, who was instituted March the 28th, 1465. Richard Burton, instituted March the 18th, 1500, on the death of

I I

were carved at the eastern end of the nave of Beeston church when that part of the fabric was rebuilt in the year 1844.

According to John Capgrave,[1] Lenton Priory appears to have been the meeting place of the captors of Roger Mortimer at Nottingham Castle, in the year 1330. "In the IIII. yere was a Parlement at Notyngham; where Roger Mortimere was take be nyte in the qween chamber behinde a corteyn. It is seid comounly that there is a weye fro the hous of Lenton onto the castel of Notyngham, under the ground; and this wey cam thei in that took him, of whech the principales were too Ufforthis. The queen was logged in the castelle, and this Mortimere next hire, and the Kyng forth in the court. The keyes were in the keping of Mortimere. So these knytes, whan they were com into the castelle, thei cleped up the Kynge, and told him who Mortimere had ymaged his deth, that he myte be Kyng: thei told him eke who he mysused his moder the queen, and then thei broke up the dore, and fond him behinde the curteyn, as we saide, and sent him to London, and there was he ded."

Lenton Priory would appear to have been an exceptionally favourable rendezvous for this expedition, as the range of cells and passages in the face of the rock along the banks of the river Leen would effectually screen from observation a party of knights advancing from Lenton Priory in the direction of the Castle. Capgrave, who flourished 1393-1464, states that in his day, it was a *common report* that the party advanced on the castle in this manner, although other and more recent writers assert that the residence of Sir William Eland, at Algarthorpe, in the parish of Basford, was the chosen starting place.

On February 12th, 1333, the King addressed the following letter, dated at Pontefract, to the Prior of Lenton, refusing to accept his excuse in the matter of the subsidy on the marriage of the King's sister, Eleanor.

---

Nicholas Blackwell, was also presented by the Prior and Convent, as was Christopher Twistfeld, who was instituted July 10th, 1510, on the resignation of Richard Burton. He was succeeded by William Garforde, who was instituted August the 4th, 1528. He was the last Vicar presented by the Prior and Convent. On his death, ten years later, William Mottram was presented, August the 3rd, 1538, by King Henry VIII.—*From Torre's MSS., Archdeaconry of Nottingham*, p. 668.

(1) *Chronicle of England*, p. 200.

Rex dilecto sibi in Christo, Priori de Lenton, salutem.   Vos nuper, per litteras nostras, meminimus nos rogâsse, ut in Subventionem Magnorum Sumptuum, quos pro Maritagio Alianoræ, Sororis nostræ carrissimæ, Nobili Viro, comiti de Gerb, fecimus, tale subsidium nobis faceritis, ut vestris desideriis, exinde deberemus fieri merito promptiores, significantes vobis quod hujusmodi Subsidium, quod in tanto necessitatis, Articulo faceritis, non deberet vobis, seu aliis, aliquod præjudicium facere, seu in Consequentiam trahi in futurum.   Ac Vos Nobis, per vestras litteias, quasdam Excusationes rescripsistis, quas insufficientes penitus reputamus, Quamobrem vos iterato rogamus quod, habitâ consideratione ad dictas preces notras, hujusmodi Excusa-tionibus cessantibus, tale nobis Subsidium, ob causam præmissam, sicuti et alii Prælati, et Religiosi, Regni nostri, gradenter, juxta Facultates suas fecisse dinoscuntur, facere studeatis, quod vestram exinde erga Nos Benevolentiam experiri erga vos ex hâc causâ provocari minime debeamus.   Et quid inde duxeritis faciendum, nobis per litteras, et Latorem præsentium, rescribatis.   Teste Rege apud Pontemfractum duodecimo die Februarii.[1]

On October 16th, 1336, by a letter or instrument dated at Lenton, Nicholin de Flisco, cardinal of Genoa, agreed to accept the sum of eight thousand marcs, assigned by the King as redress for the losses of Yvan Luccan.[2]   The said Nicholin, on the 30th October following, came into the King's Chancery at York, and acknowledged his act and deed.

In the eighteenth year of Edward III. (1344), the Commons protested against strangers being enabled to enjoy ecclesiastical dignities in England, "and showed divers inconveniences ensuing thereby," such as the decay of national prosperity, and the export of money to nourish the King's enemies.  The Pope having granted to two cardinals divers livings within the realms of the annual value of 10,000 marcs, the Commons required the King and nobles to find some remedy for this oppression, or to help them to expel the power of the Pope.  Consequently, in the twentieth year of this reign, it was ordered " That all foreign monks do quit this realm by Michaelmas, and that their livings be disposed of to young English scholars, for that many of such aliens as be advanced to livings, were in their own country but shoemakers, tailors, or chamberlains to cardinals, therefore

---

(1) Rymer's *Fœdera*, iv. 546.  Similar letters were addressed to the heads of over 140 other priories, etc.

(2) Rymer's *Fœdera*, iv. 712.

they should depart, and their livings be disposed to poor English scholars."

The result of this ordinance was that Lenton Priory, being
the only monastery in the county of Nottingham subject to
foreign jurisdiction, was placed under sequestration, from which
it was not relieved until the sixteenth year of Richard II., when
the monks obtained the privileges of denizenship. From that
time Lenton seems to have no longer acknowledged the Abbey
of Clugny as the mother-house, and although the ecclesiastics
who presided over this monastery never attained any higher
dignity than that of Prior, it is worthy of remark that the
monastery itself was not unfrequently styled an Abbey. Several
examples of this will be quoted.

In 1348, William Hut, of Cotgrave, recovered seisin from the
Priory of a corrody.[1]

In 1351, William de Ferrours released to the Prior of Lenton
all his right and claim in the lands and tenements of Ralph de
Newthorp, and all his goods which were in his own house, where
the said Ralph dwelt.[2]

In the fourteenth century, private persons often founded a
perpetual light to burn before the high altar, in token that the
Church was ever watching. In the year 1354, we find that Sir
John de St. Andrew,[3] of Gotham, gave eight shillings of rent
derived from a messuage, and a virgate of land at Newthorpe,
to maintain a light in the conventual church of Lenton, "as he
should order it." [4]

In the same year (1334), Richard Samon, of Nottingham, and
John de Eyton, chaplain, gave a marc for the confirmation of a
certain writing of the Priory granting them a corrody in the
Priory.[5]

The following interesting pleas in the Borough Court of
Nottingham, in April, 1355, relating to the repairing of a Pyx
belonging to Lenton Priory, give some idea of the splendour

---

(1) *Ab. Rot. Orig.*, ii. 199.          (2) Thoroton, p. 238.

(3) This was the representative of another ancient Nottinghamshire family, of
whom a long pedigree is given by Thoroton. He appears to have died about the
year 1360.

(4) Thoroton, p. 238.          (5) *Ab. Rot. Orig.*, ii. 256.

and value of the sacred vessels pertaining to the conventual church :—

Peter, Prior of Lenton, complainant, by his attorney, appeared against Walter le Goldsmith, defendant, on a plea of agreement; and he complains that, whereas the same Peter, on Monday next before the Feast of the Purification of the Blessed Virgin Mary, in the twenty-ninth year of the reign of the present King,[1] at Nottingham, in the house of the same Walter, by one Dawnestes, his fellow-monk, agreed with the said Walter to repair a vessel of crystal to carry the body of our Lord Jesus Christ, with pure silver and gold, the same Walter broke the agreement thereupon made between them, in these three particulars : in not making the said vessel of pure silver, nor well and suitably gilding it, and in soldering the aforesaid vessel with tin, whereas he should have soldered it with silver, to the serious damage of the said Prior of 100 shillings, wherefore he enters suit. And the aforesaid Walter comes, and says that he has broken no agreement hereupon made between them, as the said Prior has set forth against him, but that he repaired well and suitably the aforesaid vessel, and this he will verify by a good inquest; and the aforesaid Prior likewise. Therefore it is ordered that a good inquest be summoned against the next Court between the parties aforesaid.

Peter, Prior of Lenton, complainant, appeared against Walter le Goldsmith, defendant, on a plea of debt ; and he makes plaint that he unjustly withholds from him a noble and a halfpenny of gold, and unjustly because, whereas the same Peter, the Prior, on Monday next before the Feast of the Purification of the Blessed Virgin Mary, in the twenty-ninth year of the reign of the present King, at Nottingham, by his servant, delivered to the same Walter two nobles of gold, to gild a vessel of crystal with, to carry the body of our Lord Jesus Christ, which vessel he gilded with a halfpenny ; the same Prior, by his aforesaid servant, came and sought the aforesaid noble and halfpenny ; the same Walter would not pay them, but withheld them, and withholds them up to this time, unjustly, to the damage of the same Prior of a hundred shillings, wherefore he enters suit. And the aforesaid Walter comes, and says that he owes him nothing, nor withholds anything, nor delivered anything, as the same has set forth against him, and this he will verify by a good inquest ; and the aforesaid Prior likewise. Therefore it is ordered that a good inquest be summoned against the next [Court] between the aforesaid parties.

Walter le Goldsmith, complainant, appeared against Peter, Prior of Lenton, on a plea of debt ; and he makes plaint that he unjustly withholds 36s. in silver, and unjustly because,

---

[1] Monday, Jan. 26, 1354-5.

whereas the same Prior, on Monday next before the Feast of the Purification of the Blessed Virgin Mary, in the twenty-ninth year of the reign of the present King, at Nottingham, by one Dawestes, his fellow-monk, acknowledged himself to be bound to the said Walter in the aforesaid 36s. for the repairing of a certain vessel of crystal, to carry the body of our Lord Jesus Christ, to be paid to the same on Monday in the first week of Lent then next following, on which day the same Prior, although frequently requested, paid him nothing, but withheld the aforesaid money, and withholds up to this time, unjustly, to the serious damage of the said Walter of 100s., wherefore he enters suit.   And the aforesaid Prior comes, by his attorney, and says that he owes him nothing as he has set forth against him, and this he will verify by a good inquest ; and the aforesaid Walter likewise.   Therefore, it is commanded that a good inquest be summoned against the next Court between the aforesaid parties.[1]

In 1355, William de Beckford, or de Beeston, sometime vicar of Beeston, but then rector of Cotgrave, founded a chantry, dedicated to St. Catherine, in the south aisle of Beeston church, for his own soul, and the souls of John, his father, and Felice, his mother, and of his brothers and sisters, and of Alice de Langton.   He appointed John de Beeston (probably his brother) the first priest, to whom, and to his successors, he gave a messuage and two pieces of land in Beeston, lately held by Matilda Rotour, also a messuage in Beeston, which was Hugh Manisterson's, together with the reversion of two bovates of land adjoining, held by Margaret Hereward for the term of her life. Likewise, a messuage and piece of land, which were John de Strelleyes, of Nottingham, and the reversion of a piece of meadow, called Doddesholme,[2] near Lenton, and twelve-pence yearly rent.   He also gave to the said John de Beeston, two messuages and 34 acres of arable land in Lenton, which he had of John de Tumby, of Nottingham.   The foundation of this chantry was completed on the festival of St. Peter ad Vincula (Aug. 1st), 1355, and confirmed by John Thoresby, Archbishop of York, by an instrument dated at his manor, near Westminster, May 19th, 1356.[3]

---

(1) *Records of the Borough of Nottingham*, i. 161.

(2) This seems to form a part of what is now the Highfield estate, and is just below the lake.

(3) Thoroton, p. 210.

" All his gold and his goods hath he given
    To holy church, for the love of heaven ;
`    And hath founded a chantry with stipend and dole,
    That priests and that bedesmen may pray for his soul."

In the year 1361, the King restored to the Prior of Lenton all his lands, tenements, fees and advowsons, goods and chattels, lately in the hands of the King, by reason of the war between England and France. The letters patent were dated at Westminster, February 16th, 1361.[1]

Ten years later, 1371, the custody of three messuages and 164 acres of land at Kersall was committed to Lenton Priory.[2]

From several Extents of the Priory possessions, taken in the third year of Richard the Second, its spiritual and temporal revenues in Leicestershire amounted to £8 10s. ; in Nottinghamshire to £227 11s. 10d., and in Derbyshire to £68 19s. 10d., making a total of £305 1s. 8d.[3]

According to the following valuation, made in 1387, the total revenues of the Priory then amounted to £300 14s. 4d.

" Inquisition taken on Wednesday in the fourth week of Lent in the tenth year of the reign of King Richard the second after the conquest of England in the presence of Thomas of Derby and John Elyngham, sergeants of the lord King at Arms, at Lenton, in the county of Nottingham of divers articles and circumstances affecting the lord King and of all other things appertaining to the Crown, upon the oath of Robert Fitz-Robert, William de Thorp, Richard Wright, Adam Brokestowe, and others, jurors, who say upon their oaths that the site of the manor of Lenton is worth in herbage and pasturage £4 a year beyond outgoings. And they say that there are belonging to the same priory three carucates of arable land of the demesne land, and each carucate is worth 20s. a year beyond the outgoings. And they say that there are three other carucates of land in the said priory, each carucate of which is worth 10s. a year and no more, because they lie uncultivated and neglected. And there are in the demesne meadows four score acres of meadow, of which each acre is worth 2s. 6d. a year. And they say there is there a spinny wood worth 13s. 4d. annually beyond outgoings. And they say that the fair which belongs to the said priory held about the feast of All Saints and Saint Martin in the winter, is

---

(1) Rymer's *Fœdera*, vi. 311.    (2) Ab. Rot. Orig., ii. 314.
(3) Add. MSS., 6164, ff. 365, 391.

worth £35 a year beyond outgoings. And they say that there are belonging to the same priory certain lands and tenements in the hands of divers tenants, some free men, and others natives, in Lenton, Kyrkton, Radford, and Newthorpe, and these are worth £40 4s. 4d. a year. And the perquisites of the [manorial] Court are worth 60s. 8d. a year. And they say that a water mill belongs to the said priory, and is worth 77s. 6d. a year. And they say that the third part of another water mill belongs to the said Priory and is worth 10s. a year beyond outgoings. And they say that a place called 'le Roche' belongs to the said Priory and is valued at 71s. 8d. a year beyond outgoings. And they say that there belongs to the said priory £15 15s. 2d. of fixed rents in the hands of divers tenants in the following towns, namely in Bradmore, Cotgrave, Crophill Bishop, Keyworth, Colston Basset, and Wiverton. And also 13s. 4d. at Stanton on the Wolds in the county of Nottingham. And they say that there belongs to the said priory the tithe of corn of the rectories of Lenton, Radford, Kyrkton, and Sutton, which is worth £20 a year. And they say that there belongs to the said priory the rectory of the church of Saint Mary of Nottingham with all tithes and profits of corn, fleeces, lambs, and of all titheable things arising from the said church, and valued at four score marcs. And they say that the rectory of the church of Beeston with a certain pension which belongs to the said church is worth £20 14s. annually, beyond outgoings. And they say that a certain tithe of two parts of the church of Langar, namely of corn, fleeces, lambs, and all other titheable things belonging to the said rectory is worth £22 a year, beyond outgoings. And they say that a certain portion of the tithe of the rectory of the church of Ruddington belonging to the said priory, is worth 100s. a year beyond outgoings. And a certain other portion of the tithes in 'Thorp in the Clottes' belongs to the same priory, and is worth 13s. 4d. a year beyond outgoings. And a certain portion of the tithes in Bunny belongs to the same priory which is worth 46s. 8d. a year. And a certain portion of the rectory of the church of Cotgrave which is worth 13s. 4d. a year belongs to the said priory. And they say that the following pensions belong to the said priory, namely, of the rectory of the church of Cotgrave 12s., of the rectory of Rempstone 20d., of the rectory of the church of Costock 2s., of the rectory of Barton 5s., of the rectory of Saint Peter in Nottingham 16s., of the rectory of the church of Saint Nicholas in Nottingham 10s., of the rectory of the church of Linby 6s. 8d., of the rectory of the church of Stapleford 66s. 8d. And they say that there belongs to the said priory a certain portion of the tithes in Attenborough, and worth 106s. 8d. a year beyond outgoings. And they say that there belongs to the said priory fixed rents in Basford amounting to 20s. And they say that a certain portion of the tithe of corn in Basford and Catesby is worth 13s. 4d. And they say that there belongs to the said priory a certain pension of Nether Broughton which is worth 20s. a year.   And they say that there belongs to the said priory certain fixed rents in Nether Broughton, of the proceeds of which they are ignorant.   And they say that there belongs to the said priory 13s. 4d. of fixed rents in Welby. And they say that the custom of the fisheries, which belong to the said priory are worth every year 13s. 1d.   And they say that a certain pension of the rectory of Wigston belongs to the said priory, and is worth 100s. a year.   And the said jury being asked if any waste was made in any houses belonging to the said priory, or not, say upon oath that there were five cottages belonging to the said priory in Kyrkton, as much in want of repairs as of tenants, which in the time of the present Prior, who holds the same in fee-farm, fell into ruins to the detriment of the lord the King and of the said priory, to the amount of ten marcs. And they say that within the said priory every house and building is maintained and repaired, without any waste, and require no repairs.   And they say that the manor of Blackwell belongs to the said priory of Lenton, and there are in the said manor two carucates of arable land with appurtenances, which are worth 40s. a year in all things, except outgoings.   And they say that there belongs to the said manor 30s. of fixed rents. And they say that there belong to the said priory 52s. 8d. of annual rents derived from divers tenements, namely in Ashford, Tideswell, Wormhill, Staunton, and Nether Haddon in the county of Derby.   And they say that there belongs to the said priory a chief messuage, with all its appurtenances in Dunston in the said county, which is worth £8 a year in all things except outgoings.   And they say that there belongs to the said priory the rectory of the church of Bacwell [Bakewell], which is in the proper use of the said priory, in the said county, and is worth £54 13s. a year.   And the rectory of the church of Horsley in the said county, which is worth £16 13s. 4d. a year.   And they say that the prior of the said priory has a certain parcel of arable land with all its appurtenances in Derby in the said county which is worth 26s. 8d. a year beyond outgoings.   The said jurors of the articles required in the said letters patent say upon their oath that they know of nothing further to present.   In testimony of which thing they have placed their seals alternately to this inquisition.   Total valuation £300 13s. 4d." [1]

King Richard the Second, by letters patent, bearing date at Nottingham, July 8th, in the 16th year of his reign (1392), granted a licence to John Plumptre,[2] of Nottingham, to found

(2) John de Plumptre belonged to an ancient Nottingham family, whose surname was doubtless derived from the neighbouring village of Plumtree.   This John, who at one time represented the borough of Nottingham in Parliament, died in 1415, and was buried in St. Peter's Church.   The descendants of his brother, Henry de Plumptre, continued in Nottingham for several centuries, but eventually removed to Fredville, in Kent, the present seat of the family.

and endow within the said town an hospital, or house of God,
of two chaplains, one of whom should be the Master, or
Guardian (magister sive custos) of the said hospital, and of
thirteen widows bent by old age, and depressed by poverty
(senio contractis et paupertate depressis), in a certain messuage
of the said John Plumptre, with the appurtenances, in Nottingham, and to give the said messuage, and ten other messuages,
and two tofts, with the appurtenances in Nottingham to the
said Master and Warden, and his successors, namely, one
messuage for the habitation of the said chaplains and widows,
and the rest for their sustentation, to pray for the good estate
of the said John Plumptre, and Emma, his wife, during their
respective lives, and for their souls afterwards.[1]

By an Instrument of Foundation, bearing date July 12th,
1400, and confirmed by Richard, Archbishop of York, July 22nd,
in the same year (as appears from an official extract from the
Archbishop's Register), the said John Plumptre, after stating that
he had, for the honour of God, and of the Annunciation of the
Blessed Virgin, built an hospital at the end of the bridges of
Nottingham for the support of thirteen poor women, ordained
that there should be within the chapel which he had built within
the said hospital a perpetual chantry of two chaplains, who
should celebrate Divine Service at the altar of the Annunciation of the Blessed Virgin, for the welfare of the king, and
of the founder and his wife, while living, and for their souls
after their deaths; and for the welfare of the whole county
of Nottingham, and for the souls of all faithful deceased
persons; and particularly those who should at their deaths
have given any goods and chattels to the said hospital, and
to the support of the widows dwelling therein; one of which
chaplains should be, and should be called, the Master and
Guardian, and the other the Secondary Chaplain. The founder
reserved to himself during his life the presentation of the
chaplains to the said chantry, and directed that after his death
the presentation should belong to the Prior and Convent
of Lenton.[2] And he assigned to each of the said chaplains

---

(1) Thoroton, p. 494.

(2) Post obitum vero meum, volo quod ad Priorem et Conventum de Lenton,
quicunq.; pro tempore fuerint, pertineat Presentatio ejusdem in perpetuum).

and their successors for their stipend and support, 100s. yearly. The Instrument contains various other directions relating to the chantry and hospital, and the Master and Chaplain; and the founder thereby reserved to himself a power during his life of interpreting, altering, adding to, or abstracting from, the ordinances thereby made.

John Plumptre made a second Instrument of Foundation, bearing date the Monday after the feast of the Conception of the Blessed Virgin, in the year 1415, and confirmed by the Archbishop of York, February 5th following (as also appears from an extract from the Archbishop's Register).

This Instrument in its general tenor is the same as the former, but differs from it in some respects, and particularly in stating that the hospital built by him was for the support of seven poor women, and in directing that the stipend of the Master should be 6*l.*, and that of the Chaplain should be 5*l.*

We learn from a manuscript history of this hospital, which is stated to have been compiled by one of the Plumptre family, that at the time of the dissolution of the chantry, in the reign of Edward 6th, no widows were maintained in the hospital, and that the lands were then wholly used for the benefit of the Master;[1] that previously to 1645, each of the widows, then seven in number, received only one penny a day; that in that year their allowances were increased to 2s. 10d. each per month, with the addition of sixpence each on New Year's-day; and that in 1650 (in which year the hospital was rebuilt by Huntingdon Plumptre, the then Master), the widows' monthly allowance was raised to 5s. each.

Under the statutes for the dissolution of chantries, etc., this hospital, and the lands belonging to it, became vested in the Crown, and from the reign of Queen Elizabeth to the present time, the office of Master of the hospital has been from time to time granted by letters patent to persons for life, being, with very few exceptions, of the founder's name and family.[2]

A monk of Lenton, named William Repyngdon, having in the year 1396 obtained Papal Bulls and Letters Apostolic to

---

(1) Thoroton, p. 494.
(2) Report of Charity Commission, 421-2.

hold certain offices in the Priory of Lenton, "to the manifest peril" of the King's hereditary rights and authority over the Priory, the King issued by letters patent the following warrant for his apprehension.

"The King to his well beloved Sheriff of Nottingham and Derby, John de Plumptree Mayor of the Town of Nottingham, John de Croweshawe, Richard Wylford, Thomas de Columbelle of Burton, and William de Deryngton, sendeth greeting.

Insomuch as it has come to our knowledge that a monk, brother William de Repyngdon, has sought beyond our realm of England and of the Roman Curia, without our licence, divers Papal Bulls and Letters Apostolic to certain offices in the priory of Lenton, Although from its foundation by our ancestors all patronage thereat has appertained to the Kings of England and to ourselves he has sought to exercise for his life certain offices without our assent or will. He has done these things within our realm to our contempt and prejudice, and without our order and to the manifest peril of both our Crown and our hereditary rights as also to the perpetual destruction of our authority over the Priory, unless we bring to bear on this thing an opportune remedy. Now therefore we for our security and wishing to take care of our command of the Priory have assigned to you this duty, that conjunctively and separately, when or wherever you may find the said William, whether within or without your liberties, to seize and take him together with the said bulls and apostolic letters; you shall immediately bring him before us and our council in our Chancellery for trial and punishment according as our council shall deem fitting on this part.

And further we command you, and all of you, that around the premisses you shall diligently search and examine according to aforesaid forms.

And we also give to all and singular the sheriffs, mayors, bailiffs, ministers, constables and others our faithful subjects within and without their liberties, orders to aid and to council you as far as may be necessary for you and each of you strictly carrying out our orders in and according to the tenor of these presents.

Witness the King at Scroby on the 11th day of August.[1]

Geoffrey de Rochero occurs as Prior of Lenton in the Minutes of the Privy Council, January, 1403. These proceedings respecting the Alien Priories, appear to have arisen from the resolution of the King and the Peers, on the petition of the Commons, in the Parliament which met at Westminster,

---

(1) Pat. 19 Ric. II., p. 1., m. 21 d.

on the 30th September, 1402, that all Alien Priories, excepting conventual Priories, with their lands, tenements, rents, advowsons, etc., should be resumed into the King's hands.[1]

By his will dated Thursday next after the feast of St. Hilary, 1413, John Tannesley, of Nottingham, bequeathèd "to the Prior and Convent [of Lenton], for tithes forgotten in the collection, ten pounds (?) and to the Convent of the same place, twenty shillings."[2]

The Priory appears to have owned a piece of land in Stoney Street, Nottingham, in the year 1416. In that year, John Wysow, parson of the church of Hickling, and Henry Gamelston, chaplain, granted by charter to John Tannesley, of Nottingham, and Alice his wife, *int. al.*, a chief messuage, "situate in the Stonstrete, on the western side of the same street, and extends from a vacant piece of ground belonging to the Prior and Convent of Lenton, on the south to a tenement belonging to St. Mary's, where John del Ile, corviser, dwells, on the north."[3]

In 1421, Thomas Elmham, Prior of Lenton, and that Convent, demised to Hugh Willoughby, and Richard, Nicholas, and Thomas, his sons, their lands, which lay within the precinct of Radford, between the enclosure called *Stokkinge*, on the south, and the field of Broxtow, on the north ; and which abutted on the enclosure of John de Brokstowe, on the west, and on the east on the highway leading from Broxtow to Radford, during all and any of their lives, paying two shillings per annum, at the feast of the Invention of the Cross, and Saint Martin in Winter ; but every day the rent should remain unpaid after the said time, it was to be doubled ; the Prior retaining the right of free passage over the land with carriages, the same as enjoyed by the said Hugh and his sons.[4]

There is little doubt but that the condition as to rent would ensure prompt payment.

Thomas Elmham, Prior of Lenton, in 1422, granted a lease of Lenton Mill to John Botre, for ten years at £3 per annum.[5]

---

(1) *Proc. Priv. Coun.* i., 191-5.     (2) *Nottingham Borough Records,* ii. 91.
(3) *Nottingham Borough Records,* ii. 111.
(4) Thoroton, p. 219.     (5) Thoroton, p. 223.

A *quare impedit* was recovered in 1428 by Guy Fairfax and William Akworth, plaintiffs, against John Elmham, Prior of Lenton, and Thomas Smith, clerk, of the advowson of the church of Langar.[1]

By his will dated January 6, 1431-2, William Barston, of Nottingham, chaplain, bequeathed "to the Prior and Monastery of Lenton four marcs, and to the Convent of the same place thirteen shillings and four pence."[2]

In the Borough Court of Nottingham, on April 25th, 1436, John Elman, Prior of Lenton, and John Dyghton, a fellow monk of the same place, by John Ode, their attorney, complained of Robert Selby, of Nottingham, carpenter, of a plea of debt of 2s. 8d. It was alleged that Selby, on Sunday, May 8th, 1435, at Nottingham, bought from Dyghton "a cowl of black worsted," "paying there to the same John Dyghton at the feast of the Nativity of St. John the Baptist then next to come, and he has not yet paid, but hitherto has refused to pay him, and still does refuse, whereby they say that they are injured, etc, to the value of 12d.: wherefore they bring suit, etc."[3]

Another action was brought by John Elman, and his fellow monk, Gilbert, against Selby, for a table and pair of trestles that he had given to Gilbert, but which he refused to deliver."[4]

In the same Court, on September 13th in the same year, John Elman, Prior of Lenton, and John Manchester, of Nottingham, complained of Thomas Ironmonger of a plea of debt of 5s. 11¾d. for tithes of hay, etc., and who had made several defaults, etc. The said Thomas put himself in mercy for license to agree.[5]

Sir Hugh Willoughby, of Wollaton, knight, by his will dated September 15th, 1443, bequeathed to Alice Willoughby, his daughter "till her mariage, besyde a some of mony that is comprehendid in my will, that I will that my feffes fulfill to the behove of her mariage, first, xij spones of silver marked with R and P, also a square salar of silver single, sometyme Phelipp Repyngdon, *also a maser, sometyme Thomas Elveham, Priour of Lenton*, etc."[6]

---

(1) Thoroton, p. 105.        (2) *Nottingham Borough Records,* ii. 125.

(3) *Nottingham Borough Records,* ii. 153.        (4) Ibid.        (5) Ibid. ii. 155.

(6) Test. Ebor. ii. 132.  Sir Hugh Willoughby died November the 15th, 1448, and his body was interred, according to the directions contained in his will, "before the altar of our Lady" in the church of Willoughby-on-the-Wolds.

William West, a monk of Lenton, was presented by King Henry VI. to the Priorate of the Benedictine Monastery of Blyth, and admitted August 3rd, 1451. He resigned his office, and was succeeded by Robert Bubwith, a monk of Blyth, who was admitted December 14th, 1458. [1]

King Henry the Sixth, May 14th, 1455, appointed commissioners in various parts of the country to raise money for the defence of Calais. The commissioners for the county of Nottingham were, the Prior of Lenton, Sir Thomas Chaworth, of Wiverton, Sir William Babington, of Chilwell, Robert Clifton, of Clifton, and Richard Willoughby, of Wollaton. [2]

John, Prior of Lenton, was licensed by the archbishop, Nov. 7th, 1456, to marry Gervase, son of the above-named Robert Clifton, Esq., and Alice, widow of Richard Thurland, of Nottingham, in the private chapel of Thomas Neville, Esq., at Rolleston. [3]

In the year 1464, the then Lord Chamberlain was at Lenton, most probably a guest at the Priory. According to the accounts of the chamberlains of Nottingham, [4] the corporation made a present to the distinguished visitor :—

*" Presauntes to dyvers Lordes.*

"Item for iij. galons of reede wyne gif[fen unto my L]orde Chamberleyn, [5] on Estenmasse-day, [6] when he came to Lenton . . . . [ijs]."

In the same year, Robert Babington, of Lower Kiddington and Asterley, co. Oxon, Esquire, fourth son of Sir William Babington, Knight, previously mentioned under Elmore Manor, hereditary keeper of the Royal Palace at Westminster, and first warden of the Fleet prison, died at Lower Kiddington, and was buried at Lenton Priory, near his father's tomb. [7]

---

(1) Raine's " History and Antiquities of the Parish of Blyth," p. 51.

(2) Privy Council Proc., vi. 243.

(3) Test. Ebor. iii. 184. This Alice, who had previously been married to Richard Thurland, of Nottingham, was a daughter of the above-named Thomas Neville, and was the first wife of Gervase Clifton, who was subsequently knighted, and was receiver-general of the counties of Nottingham and Derby, and High Sheriff in 1472, 1478, and 1483.

(4) *Records of Borough of Nottingham*, ii. 378.

(5) William, Lord Hastings.        (6) Easter-day, April 1st, 1464.

(7) *The Topographer and Genealogist*, i. 266.

On August 29th, 1466, license was granted to the Prior of
Lenton and to William Gull, S.T.P. Rector of St. Peter's,
Nottingham, to marry John, son of John Delves, Esquire, of
Donington, in the diocese of Coventry and Lichfield, and
Elizabeth, daughter of William Babington, Esq., of Atten-
borough, in the chapel of the manor house of Chilwell,[1] after
the publication of banns.[2]

Richard Willoughby, of Wollaton, Esq., by his will, dated
September 15th, 1469, bequeathed twenty shillings to the Prior
and Convent of Lenton.[3]

By his will, dated January 16th, 1470, Thomas Thurland,
of Nottingham, burgess, desires to be buried in St. Mary's
church, Nottingham, and bequeathes " To the Priour of Lenton,
parson of the same chirche, for my tithes and offerynges
forgetten, xls. To the convent of the same place to prey for
my soule, xxs."[4]

In the year 1483, in the borough court of Nottingham, John
Alestre, keeper of the free chapel of the Castle of Nottingham,
complained of Richard, Prior of Lenton, of a plea of debt of
11s. 8d. The plaintiff stated that on October 20th, 1482, he
did, at Nottingham, demise and at ferm let to the Prior his part
of the tithe, to wit, the moiety of the tithe of corn of the mills
of the castle, at the yearly rent of 13s. 4d. After several
adjournments, on Monday next before the Conversion of St.
Paul, the Prior, by Walter Bowes, his attorney, said he ought
not to appear before any secular judges, because King Henry III.,
by his charter, made May 21st, in the thirty-ninth year of his
reign, granted to God and the Convent of the Holy Trinity
at Lenton (here the record ends abruptly).[5]

On the feast of St. Clement, 1484, a covenant was entered
into between Henry Kent, vicar of Horsley (Derbyshire), with
the consent of Richard Dene, Prior of Lenton, and Lawrence

---

(1) See page 37.

(2) Reg. Geo. Neville, Abp. of York, i. 536.

(3) *Test. Ebor.*, iii. 171. He was the eldest son of Sir Hugh Willoughby (see
p. 157) by his first wife.

(4) Ibid., iii. 184.

(5) *Nottingham Borough Records*, ii. 337.

Lowe, of Denby, in Derbyshire,[1] to have a priest to say mass
daily in the chapel of Denby. The vicar acknowledged that
his predecessors had, from time immemorial, provided and paid
a resident priest at Denby, and an undertaking was now given
that this should be done in the future. No resident priest,
however, being provided, Lawrence Lowe had engaged Sir
Christopher Bury from the previous Michaelmas day to say
the divine service daily, for one year, for the stipend of seven
marcs. Providing that the vicar now paid these seven marcs,
and continued to do so yearly, to the said Sir Christopher Bury,
or some other suitable priest, the present agreement was to
be void ; but, if not, the vicar bound himself to pay a fine of
£40 to the said Lawrence Lowe.[2]

Noveritis universi per presentes me Henricum Kent vicariam
ecclesiæ parochialis de Horseley in Com Derb teneri et firmiter
obligavi Laurentio Lowe in quadragint' lib' legalis mo'eta
Angliæ solvend' eidem Laurent suo certo attornato hered' vel
executorib' suis in festo natalis d'ni proxime futuro post datum
presencium. Ad quem quidem solut . . . fideliter faciend'
obligo me heredes et executores meæ p presentes. In cujus rei
test' sigillum meum apposui, et quod sigillum meum quam
pluribus est incognitum, ergo sigulla venerabilium virorum
clericorum prepositorum domus sanctæ Trinitatis de Lenton
Oliveri Blackwall clericus officialis Notinhamiæ et Johis Mayewe
clericus presentibus apponi proponerem. Datum in festo
Sancti Clementi Papæ anno post regni regis Ricardi tertii post con-
questum secundo. Et nos predict' clericus prepositi domus scæ
Trinitatis de Lenton Oliverus Blackwall clericus officialis
Notinghamiæ et Johes Mayewe clericus ad instanciam et
specialem rogationem dich' Henrici Kent et admanus et evi-
dentias fidei et testimonii omnium et singulorum commissorum
adhibenda sigilla sua present' apposuimus die et anno supra-
dictis.[3]

In another hand—

"The condition of y[s] obligation is such, y[t] whereas y[e] within
named Laurence Lowe hath claymed for him and his tenants of

---

(1) This Lawrence Lowe was descended from a Cheshire family, and had acquired
estates in Derbyshire through marriage, which continued for nearly three centuries
with his descendants in the male line. He was a sergeant-at-law, and held the office
of Recorder of Nottingham.

(2) Add. MSS., 6666, f. 208.

(3) Ex. vet. copia penes Godf. Meynell, Arm., Add. MSS., 6666, fo. 207.

12

Denby, in y$^e$ county of Derby, to have a priest founden yearly, daily and continually by y$^e$ within bounden vicar in y$^e$ chapell of Denby aforesaid, in y$^e$ parish of Horseley, for evermore, there being and doing service & administering y$^e$ sanct$^s$ of Holy Church, y$^e$ w$^{ch}$ priest hath been founden there in y$^e$ manner & form aforesaid, & at all times keeping residence in Denby aforesaid, & founden by y$^e$ said vicar & his predecessors both aforetime of mind & since, as it was said and alleged by y$^e$ said Laurence, and proved by notable proofs, y$^e$ w$^{ch}$ c$^d$ not be denied by y$^e$ said vicar, but openly confessed y$^e$ same. If y$^e$ said Henry, vicar of Horseley, from henceforth & at all times hereafter during his life natural, keep and find daily and yearly at y$^e$ said chappel of Denby, a good and convenable priest in y$^e$ manner & form aforesaid and continually keeping residence in Denby aforesaid, And whereas y$^e$ s$^d$ Laurence in the *Defance* (Qu. Defiance) of y$^e$ s$^d$ vicar, hath hired constantly S$^r$ Christopher Bury, priest, from y$^e$ feast of S$^t$ Mich. y$^e$ A. Angel last past, afore y$^e$ date of these presents, for y$^e$ space of a whole year thence next following, for seven marks, to say divine service in y$^e$ s$^d$ chappel, if y$^e$ s$^d$ vicar content & pay to y$^e$ s$^d$ S$^r$ Christopher ye s$^d$ seven marks in form following, that is to say, 23$^s$ 4$^d$ at y$^e$ feast of y$^e$ nativity of o$^r$ Lord now next ensuing, & 23$^s$ 4$^d$ at y$^e$ feast of y$^e$ annuntiation of o$^r$ lady S$^t$ Mary y$^n$ next following, & 23$^s$ 4$^d$ at y$^e$ feast of y$^e$ nativity of S$^t$ Jo$^n$ bapt. y$^n$ next ensuing & 23$^s$ 4$^d$ at y$^e$ feast of S$^t$ Mich$^l$ y$^e$ A.A. y$^n$ next ensuing, & so forth yearly at y$^e$ s$^d$ feasts, at every feast 23$^s$ 4$^d$ as long as y$^e$ s$^d$ Laurence & y$^e$ s$^d$ S$^r$ Christopher or any such other priest singing can agree, And if y$^e$ s$^d$ vicar stand to perform y$^e$ ordinance, doom & award of y$^e$ Rev$^d$ Father in God Rich$^d$ Prior of the house of y$^e$ Holy Trinity of Lenton, Oliver Blackwall &c. of & concerning all manner of tythes w$^{ch}$ y$^e$ s$^d$ vicar claims to have in Denby afores$^d$ & y$^e$ s$^d$ ordinance &c. for his part well & truly keep & perform so y$^t$ y$^e$ s$^d$ ordinance &c. of him & y$^e$ premisses be made & given afore y$^e$ feast of S$^t$ Mich$^l$ now next ensuing, & to y$^e$ s$^d$ Laurence & vicar deliver'd in writing under y$^e$ seals of y$^e$ s$^d$ arbitrators afore y$^e$ s$^d$ feast &c. y$^t$ y$^n$ y$^o$ obligation to be void, or else stand yet in strength and virtue." [1]

On the southern side of Nottingham Park there are the remains of a very singular chapel and a range of cells, formerly appendant to Lenton Priory, excavated out of the face of a semi-circular sweep of sandstone rock, which crops out on the bank of the Leen. The river formerly wound round the other half of the circle,[2] leaving, between the rock and the river, a

---

(1) Add. MSS., 6666, fo. 208.

(2) The course of the Leen from New Lenton to Nottingham Castle was filled up in 1883-4, the water being diverted into the canal.

space of greensward, upon which the cells open. The whole place is now enclosed, and forms part of a private garden. In former days this hermitage was just within the verge of the park of the royal Castle of Nottingham; it was doubtless screened by the trees of the park, and its inmates might pace to and fro on their secluded grass-plot, fenced in by the rock on the one hand, and the river on the other, secure from every intruding foot, and yet in full view of the walls and towers of the castle, with the royal banner waving from its keep; and catch a glimpse of the populous borough; and see the parties of knights and ladies prance over the level meadows which stretched out to the neighbouring Trent like a green carpet, embroidered in spring and autumn by the purple crocus which formerly grew wild there in myriads, and still exists, though in sadly diminished numbers. Stukeley gives a view and ground-plan of these curious cells. He is of opinion that they are of British origin, and describes them as "a ledge of perpendicular rock hewn out into a church, houses, chambers, dove-houses, &c. The church is like those in the rocks at Bethlehem and other places in the Holy Land: the altar is natural rock, and there has been painting upon the wall; a steeple, I suppose, where a bell hung, and regular pillars. The river here, winding about, makes a fortification to it; for it comes to both ends of the cliff, leaving a plain before the middle. The way to it was by gates cut out of the rock, and with an oblique entrance for more safety."[1]

Throsby states that in his time these excavations were generally known as the *Papist Holes*, the Parliamentarian forces having, during the preceding century, destroyed part of them "as being relics of popery." He describes them as having the "appearance of a ruin of magnitude, destitute of design: they neither afford the mind an idea of grandeur, nor simplicity."[2]

Laird, who visited the caves about the year 1812, says that they had even then suffered considerably since Stukeley's time. The outer part had fallen down in several places, evidently from

---

(1) *Itinerarium Curiosum*, 2 ed., 1776, i., 53.
(2) Throsby's edition of Thoroton, ii. 5.

the effects of damp and frost; but the church and altar, and
even some vestiges of ancient paintings might be clearly traced.
He adds that some of the pillars had carved capitals, the form
of the Gothic arch being well imitated in the living rock. But
no care was taken to preserve these remarkable excavations,
which at that time seem to have been the nocturnal resort of
the destitute and depraved.[1]

Again, Blackner[2] has "little doubt" but "that these caves
were originally hewn and set apart as places of worship for the
ancient Britons."

More recent writers[3] have advanced an opinion that the
excavations are of Roman origin, and have been used as a
*sepulchrum commune* and *columbarium*, the larger of the two
caves having been the *bustum*, or place of incineration, and the
smaller one, at a higher level, the *columbarium*, containing from
150 to 160 *ollaria*, or cells, for the reception of the urns containing the ashes of the dead.

It is stated as an argument in favour of this theory, that the
smoke flue of the *bustum* still remains, and that the small
recess, styled the *columbarium*, has been formed at some distance
from the ground in order that the inurned ashes of the dead,
supposed to have been deposited therein, might "be more secure
and less likely to be disturbed by marauders or thoughtless
people." It is more probable, however, assuming the smoke
flue to be an ancient one, that it has been used as the flue of
the kitchen, which would necessarily form part of the monastic
establishment located in this rock. The small cave has undoubtedly been the dove-cote attached to the monastic cell.
This form of dove-cote is by no means uncommon. We have
scriptural proof that it is the habit of the dove to "dwell in the
rock," and make "her nest in the sides of the hole's mouth."
That this excavation was spoken of as a dove-cote as far back
as the year 1687 is evident from the following reference to the
"Douecoate Close in Nottingham Parke":—

---

(1) *Beauties of England and Wales*, vol. 12, part I., pp. 115, 116.
(2) *History of Nottingham*, p. 36.
(3) *Old Nottinghamshire*, pp. 118, 119.

October y⁰ 12th, 1687.

Receiued then by mee Edward Lord Viscount Latimer
Keeper & L^d Warden of his Ma^ties Forrest of Sherwood & Parke
of Fulwood of Darcy Molyneux Esq^r High Sheriffe of y^e County
of Nottingham the Sume of Nine pounds of Lawfull English
Money For one yeares Wages Due to his Ma^ties Nine Keepers
w^thin his Ma^ties said Forrest of Sherwood in y^e said County of
Nottingham Ending at y^e Feast of St. Michiall y^e Archangell
last past. Alowed out of the Rents of Tenn pounds and Tenn
shrillings charged Uppon George Earle of Rutland for the Fee
Farme Rent of a Certain Close Called y^e Douecoate Close in
Nottingham Parke & all those Medowes Called y^e Kings
Medowes near y^e Towne of Nottingham aforesaid J Say
Receiued the Said Summe.

P mee.[1]

For many years the caves were resorted to by the boys from
the neighbouring town and villages as a play place. Millhouse,
the artisan poet of Nottingham, in the following sonnet, refers
to his visits to the rock in his boyhood.

> " Thou mouldering relic of forgotten time !
>     Well I remember how in youth I came
>     And grav'd yon rude initials of my name,
> Unwistful then, that I, in manhood's prime,
>     Should be an anxious candidate for fame :—
> Long hast thou borne the onsets of the storm,
>     Like speechless horror frowning in dismay ;
> But age thy latest vestige shall deform,
>     And waste thy moss-grown chronicles away ;
> Yet, let not avarice hasten on thy fall,
>     But leave thy destiny to Nature's power ;
>     So may the stripling shelter from the shower,
> And ponder o'er the records on thy wall,
>     Or mount thy top to seize the hanging flower."

The gnawing tooth of time has effected a considerable change
in the appearance of the caves since Stukeley's day, the west
end having fallen down about fifty years ago. At the present
they consist of a cave (which was considerably altered and

---

(1) The original, unsigned, is in the possession of Mr. M. I. Preston, of Nottingham, to whom we are indebted for the above copy.

enlarged several years ago to form a skittle alley), the dove-
cote—also known as the "doctor's shop," and two or three small
caves.

Many engravings of these rock holes exist. The engraving
by Samuel Buck is well known, and being the earliest representation of these excavations which we have met with, it
possesses especial interest. Less than half of what is shown
in this engraving exists at the present day. In addition to the
view given in Stukeley's work and in the local histories by
Deering, and Blackner, and in Throsby's edition of Thoroton,
two views, from sketches made in the year 1788 by the Rev. J.

Swete, were published in the "Antiquarian and Topographical
Cabinet."

Carter also figures them in his "Ancient Architecture," pl. 12,
and gives details of a Norman shaft and arch in the chapel.
He thus describes them :—" These excavations evince rather
a regular plan for a monastic building, for we meet with a
chapel and various apartments, the latter both on the first and
second stories, with a staircase, chimneys, etc. ; they are, however, deprived of their original fronts, as well as some of their
groins or ceilings."

In a patent-roll of King Edward the First, mention is made

of a house of Carmelite friars at Lenton. There is every reason to believe, both from the peculiarity of the situation and other circumstances, that these excavations owed their origin to the Carmelite friars, who established themselves here prior to the close of the thirteenth century ; and as no later reference to the Friary has been found than the one which is quoted above, it seems probable that the monks of Lenton in some way acquired the place from the Carmelites, though all record of the transaction appears to have been lost.[1]

This place is most probably identical with the cell said to have been *under* the Castle of Nottingham in the reign of Henry the Third.[2]

According to an inspeximus and confirmation, dated December 5th, 1485, of letters patent, dated Westminster, June the 20th, 14 Edw. IV., granting to the Prior and Convent of the Holy Trinity, in Lenton, near Nottingham, of the order of Clugny, within the diocese of York, £10 sterling a year out of the fee-farm of the town of Arnoll, during the life of Leonard Say, son of Sir John Say, Knt., or until the said Prior and convent shall come into possession of a chapel with other premises, we learn that by letters patent, dated Aug. the 10th, 11 Edw. IV., the free chapel within the castle of Tickhill, parcel of the duchy of Lancaster, had been granted by the King to the above-mentioned Leonard Say for life. By subsequent letters patent, the King granted that whenever the same chapel should be void by the death of Leonard Say, the Prior and Convent should have the·same and the custody thereof, with all things pertaining thereto ; to hold in pure alms for ever, in compensation for a certain chapel of St. Mary, called "le Roche," and all the lands and tenements within the pale thereof belonging to the said Prior and Convent, and also for two closes, called le Roche closes, "on the south side of the water of Leene," lying opposite to the chapel, and two small parcels of meadow adjoining to the same closes, granted to the King by

---

(1) Deering, p. 190.

(2) " In stipendiis duorum monachorum ministrantium in capella S. Mariæ de Rupe subtus castrum de Nottingham, vi*l.* i*s.* viii*d.*"—*Collect. Dodsworth. e mag. rot. pipæ,* 29 *Hen.* 3.

the Prior and convent; and also for release and remission from three cartloads of wood per diem "in Beskwode, within the forest of Shirwode," which the Prior and Convent had received on behalf of the expenses of the monastery. It is added that Leonard Say lives on, and the said Prior and Convent consequently do not obtain possession of the said chapel.[1]

The following extract from the Act of Resumption, of the first year of the reign of Henry the Seventh, 1485, elucidates the foregoing :—

"Provided alway, that this Acte of Parliament, nor noon other Acte, be prejudiciall nor hurtfull to the Priour of Lenton, within our Shire of Notyngham, nor to his Successors, for any Graunte or Grauntes, L're Patent or L'res Patent made to the said Priour, or to any of his Predecessours, by Kyng Edward the IIIIth, or for any Graunte made of oure free Chapell within our Castell of Tykhill, parcell of our Duchie of Lancastre, within oure said Shire of York, made by the said Kyng to any of the Predecessours of the said Prioure, or for the Advowson of the said Chapell of Tykhill, within oure said Countie, or for any Confirmation of the same made by Richard the Third Kyng of England, late in dede and not of right, to the said Priour or any of his Predessours, or for any confirmation made by us to the said Priour, and to the Convent of the same, or where the said Kyng Edward the IIIIth, by his L'res Patents beryng date the Xth day of August, the XIth yere of his Reigne, graunted the said fre Chapell of Tykhill, to oon Leonard Say, to have and to hold to hym for terme of his Lyf; and afterwards by his L'res Patents beryng date the XIIIth day of June, in the XIIII. yere of his Reigne, graunted the said fre Chapell, to oon Thomas, then Priour of the Hous and Monastery of the Holy Trinite of Lenton aforesaid, besydes Notyngham, of the Ordre of Clune, and of the Diocese of the Shire of Yorke, and to the Covent of the same and their Successours, that whensoever the said free Chapell be voide, by the Deth of the said Lenard, or any otherwise, that then the said Prioure and Covent shall have the said free Chapell, with all things perteyning therto, to theym and to their Successours for ever: all their said Grauntes made to the said Priour, or to any of his Successors, to stond in force and effect in oure Lawes: this Act of Resumption, or any other Acte made unto the contrarie, notwithstanding."[2]

A second inspeximus, made October 27th, 1486, at the

---

(1) *Materials for History of Henry VII.*, i. 196.
(2) *Rolls of Parliament*, vi. 346.

instance of Richard Dene, then Prior of Lenton, states that on June 2nd, 1475, an indenture was made "between Edward the Fourth and Thomas, Prior of the Monastery of the Holy Trinity at Lenton, near Notyngham, of the Cluniac order (York dioc.), and the Convent there, which witnesseth that the said Convent had, by their writing, dated 4 June last past, granted to the King and Gervase Clifton, Esq., for ever, the chapel of St. Mary, called the Roche, and the lands and tenements within the new Park there, two closes, called the Rock closes, to the south of the water of Leene, opposite to the said chapel, and two small parcels of meadow, adjoining the said closes, together with their rights of three cart loads of wood a day in Beskewood, in the forest of Shirwod ; further, that in recompence for the premises a grant in perpetual frankalmoign had, 14th June (14 Ed. IV.), been made to the said Convent of the custody of the free chapel in the castle Tykhyll (parcel of the Duchy of Lancaster) in reversion on the death of Leonard Say, son of John Say, Knt. ; and further, the said Convent agrees to provide a monk to say mass in the chapel of St. Mary of Roche for the good estate, &c., of the King, Elizabeth, the queen consort, and Edward, prince of Wales, duke of Cornwall, and earl of Chester, and to celebrate the anniversaries of the King's father, Richard, late duke of York, and of the said King ; also for ever, at their own expense, to oversee and take care of a small boat on the Leene water, and a garden near the said chapel, called 'Le Roche,' within the pale of the said park."

One of the Harleian manuscripts has the following entry :— " The prioure and convent of Lentone have £ 10 of the fee farm of Arnoll during the life of Leonard Say."[1] In the fifth year of Henry the Seventh, by writ of Privy Seal, the sum of forty pounds was paid " To the Prior of the Monastery of St. Trinity of Lenton." In the year 1504, the royal free chapel, or collegiate church of Tickhill, which had for some time belonged to Lenton Priory, was transferred to the Abbey of St. Peter, Westminster.[2]

On the 8th of February, 1488, the King granted a license to Sir John Babington, Knight, and Ralph Savage, to found a

---

(1) Harl. MSS., 433, f. 104.    (2) *Mon. Ang.*, v. 109.

perpetual chantry of one secular priest, to be called "the chauntrie of blessed Marie Virgyn in the chirch of Seynt Elyn of Northwynfeld" (North Wingfield, in Derbyshire). The priest was to be allowed an annuity of eight marcs "of the Monasterie or Priorie of the Holy Trinite of Lenton, in our countie of Notyngham. The priest was to pray for the good estate of the King, his fully dere wyffe, Elizabeth, Queene of England, and his best beloved first-begotten son, Arthur, Prynce of Wales and Earl of Cornwalle, and of us the aforesayd John Babyngton, and Rauf Savage, and also of John Savage, Knight, Thomas Revell, serjeaunt-of-lawe, Thomas Babyngton, of Dethyck, John Savage, of Huknall, Thomas Orston, and Edmond Savage, preeste, whiles we lif and liffen, and for the soules of the aforesaid when we shall pass oute of this worlde, and also for the soules of Arnold Savage, Esqwyer, Agnes Leversage, and Helyn Orston, and all our ancestors."

The licence concludes with the following injunction ·—" That these ordinances be not forgotten they shall on ye feast of St. George, afore ye beginning of high mass, and on Wednesday in Whisson weke, be read openly in mother tongue by ye priest of ye chantry in ye parish church or churchyard."[1]

The chantry house, adjoining the north-east corner of the churchyard, has been for many years used as an ale-house, and is known by the sign of the " Blue Bell Inn."

Robert Calverley, of Calverley, in the county of Chester, Esquire, by his will, dated February 15th, 1498, bequeathed the sum of three shillings and fourpence to the *Abbot*[2] of Lenton " to say *Messe* and *Derige*."[3]

The advowson of Arksey Church, near Doncaster, in York-shire, which had continued appendant to the manor until the beginning of the sixteenth century, was granted to Lenton Priory on the attainder of Sir John Windham, Knight, in 1502. In an Act, passed in 1513, by which the attainder was reversed,

---

(1) Add. MSS. 5152, a copy of which is amongst the Nottingham Corporation Records.

(2) This seems to show that the monastery must then have been not unfrequently denominated an abbey.

(3) Test. Ebor., iv. 157.

the rights of the monks of Lenton were protected.[1] An appropriation quickly followed, and a vicarage was ordained. The tithe of corn and hay was reserved to the Monastery.[2]

Henry Lee was instituted vicar of Arksey, June 22nd, 1504, on the presentation of the Prior and Convent of Lenton. On his death, John Knolles was instituted October 26th, 1507. He died, and was succeeded by William Wildbore, March 6th, 1532, also presented by the Prior and Convent of Lenton.

In the year 1504, the vicarage of Middlewich, in the county of Chester,[3] was appropriated to the Priory of Lenton.

In 1522, the Prior and Convent of Lenton demised the advowson to Sir Henry Willoughby, of Middleton, in the county of Warwick, and of Wollaton, in this county, who, in the following year granted the same by lease, of which the following is an abstract, to Sir Henry Brereton, of Brereton, in the County of Chester.

"To All crysten peple to whom this p'sent wrytyng shall come, Syr Henry Willoughby of Myddylton in the Countie of Warr. Knyght sendith gretyng. Whereas Thomas Prior of the monastre of the holy Trinitie of Lenton in the Countie of Notyngh'm and the Convent of the same by their dede indentyd under their Convent Seale beryng date the xxj$^{st}$ day of Aprill in the xiij$^{th}$ yere of the reigne of our sov'aygn' lord Kyng Henry the viij$^{th}$ have demised graunted and to ferme lett unto the seid S$^r$ Henry Willoughby their p'sonage of y$^e$ p'yshe Churche of Medulwyche w$^t$yn the Countie of Chester w$^t$ alman'

---

(1) Sir John Windham was engaged in the conspiracy of Edmund de la Pole, Earl of Suffolk, and being convicted of high treason, was beheaded on Tower-hill, May 6th, 1502. His son, Sir Thomas Windham, was attainted at the same time, but the attainder was reversed by Act of Parliament, 1513.

(2) Hunter's *South Yorkshire*, i. 327.

(3) "This Church was appropr.[iated] to [the] Monastery of Lenton in Notting$^{ah}$ an [no] 1504, 19 H. 7, and [the] Mon.[astery] obliged to pay to [the] B.[ishop] of Cov.[entry] and Litch.[field] 13$^s$ 4$^d$ [to the] D.[ean] and Chap.[ter] of Litch.[field] 3$^s$ 4$^d$ [to the] Archd.[eacon] of Chester 20$^s$. *Reg. R. R. e Reg. [of the] D.[ean] and Chap.[ter of] Cov.[entry] and Lich.* fol. 76. *Lib. Tho. Godfull. cler. Cap.* This Pens.[ion] in [the] Cat.[alogue of] B.[ishop] Bridg.[man] is set down 13$^s$ 4d, *Reg.* p. 202, owned by L$^d$ Brereton an.[no] 1627, but not paid. Vicar presented, an.[no] 1505, by [the] Prior and Conv.[ent] of Lenton. *Inst.* [*itution*] *B.*[ook] 1., p. 1. An[no] 1579, by Q.[ueen] Eliz. B. 2. p. 2. Improp$^{rs}$ severall persons, Mr. Low, who bought y$^e$ greatest part of y$^e$ Tyths, presented once; but upon a Dispute w$^{th}$ L$^d$ Brereton, whose Grandf.[ather] sold y$^e$ Tyths, it appeared y$^t$ y$^e$ advows[on] of y$^e$ Vic.[arage] was not granted away, for L$^d$ Brereton's Present.[ation] an.[no] 1719, held good."—*Bishop Gastrell's Notitia Cestriensis, Camden Soc.*, i. 247.

of tithes oblac'ons mortuaries glebe lands and all other emoluments and p'fetts to the seid p'sonage in eny wyse app'teynyng
or by ryght belongyng To have & to hold the seid p'sonage
and other the p'misses with their appurtenances to the seid
S$^r$ Henry his executors or assignes ffrom the fest of seynt Marke
the ev'ngelist next ensuyng the date of the seid lees unto th'ende
and t'rme of vij. yeres then next followyng fully to be complett
and endet. Yeldyng and payeng therfore yerely to the seid
Priory and Convent and to their successours att the seid
monastre of Lenton xxx$^{tij}$ li of lawfull money of England att
ij t'mes of the yere. . . . Also the seid S$^r$ Henry coven'ntyth
& —tyth by thise p'sents ffor hym his executors & assignes to
pay yerely duryng the seid t'me to the Vicar of y$^e$ p'sshe Church
of Medellwyche ffor the tyme beyng & to his successours Vicars
of the seid Church xijli. xiijs. iiijd. lawfull money of England
on the hie aultar of the said Churche before xij. of the Clock
of eny of the t'mes ffeasts or dayes hereaft'r ffolowyng. . . Know
ye that I the seid S$^r$ Henry Willoughby by thise p'sents do
dymyse gyff & ffully g'nt to S$^r$ Will'm Brereton of Brereton
in the Countie of Chester, Knyght, his exectitors & assigns all
my right title int'est cleyme & t'me which I the seid S$^r$ Henry
have in the seid p'sonage and other the p'mysses. . . . (Dated
17th June, 14 Henry VIII.)[1]

In 1535, Lenton Priory derived £30 per annum from Middlewich for tithes and other profits.

It appears that after the dissolution of the Priory, the impropriate rectory was vested in the Crown, from whence, about
1579, it passed to the Breretons, of Brereton, by whom some
portions of the tithes were sold to several persons ; but the
vicarage was reserved.

In 1663, William, Lord Brereton, sold the advowson,
together with the greater part of the tithes, to Mr.
Robert Lowe,[2] of Newton Hall, which is now vested in his
descendants in the female line. A few years previously a
portion of the tithes had been held by Henry Ireton, of Attenborough, the Parliamentary General, this portion being described
in the conveyance as " heretofore......... in the occupac'on of

---

(1) From the original in the possession of Major A. E. Lawson Lowe.

(2) Elder brother of Mr. John Lowe, the direct ancestor of Alderman Joseph Lowe,
of Nottingham, who purchased a part of the manor of the Priory demesne, and built
Highfield House, in this Parish. (See the pedigree of that family.) The Lowes thus
appear to have been connected with the Priory lands longer than any other family
except the Gregorys.

Henry Ireton, in the County of Chester, Esquire, late deceased."
Francis, Lord Brereton, presented in 1719, on the recommenda-
tion of Bishop Gastrell, but the representatives of the Lowe
family regularly from that time. In a letter to Dr. Stratford,
dated Christ Church, Oxford, October 21st, 1719, the Bishop
says, "I have this morning instituted one Everard to the rectory
of Brereton, who tells me that there were some motions made
at the Assizes with relation to Middlewich. Let me know what
they were." Concerning an augmentation to the vicarage of
Middlewich of twenty pounds per annum, see the case of Sir
Lister Holte, et al. Appellants, and Robert Lowe, Esq., respondent, heard and determined in favour of the respondent by
the House of Lords, April 26th, 1736.[1]

In the first year of the reign of Henry the Eighth, John
Mauntell, Esq., died siezed *int. al.* of a wood, in Rode, in the
county of Northampton, called Shortwood, which he held of
the Prior of Lenton by fealty, and the annual presentment of a
red rose. He was succeeded by his son, Sir William Mauntell,
who died in the twenty-first year of Henry the Eighth, leaving
the wood called Shortwood, which he held of the Prior of
Lenton, to his son, John Mauntell, Esq. In the thirty-third
year of the same reign, this John Mauntell was tried and condemned for a murder committed in Sussex,[2] and his lands
being forfeited, that portion of them lying in Rode was annexed
the same year by Act of Parliament to the Honour of Grafton.
The wood which he held of the Prior of Lenton was, in the first
year of Queen Elizabeth, granted to Henry Carey, Lord
Hunsdon.[3]

On the sixth of June, 1511, by writ of Privy Seal, "a corrody
in the Monastery of Lenton" was granted to "Robert Penne,
gentleman, of the Chapel Royal."

The payment of one shilling per annum as quit rent, or fee
farm, was formerly made by the Guild of St. George, in the
church of St. Peter, Nottingham, to the Prior and Convent of
Lenton, for a tenement in Houndsgate, Nottingham. The first

---

(1) *Ducarel's Rep.*     (2) Stow's Annals, p. 582.
(3) Bridge's *Northamptonshire*, i. 320.

mention of this payment in the Guild Book is in the account
for the year ending with the Feast of the Conversion of St.
Paul, in the fourth year of King Henry VIII. " Et de xijd sol
priori de lenton de lib'o reddit hoc a'o. Et de iiijd resol vicebz
de cons reddit." (And of 12d. paid to the Prior of Lenton for
quit rent this year. And of 4d. paid to the sheriffs for the same
rent). The next year's account shows that the 12d. was paid to
the Prior for a tenement in *Hundgate*, and the 4d. to the sheriffs
of Nottingham for another tenement in *Lystergate*. During the
next twenty-five years the payment of 12d. is frequently given
in connection with the 4d. paid to the sheriffs, appearing for the
last time in the account ending January 25th, 1539, thus—" Et
de 12d solut p' feod' firme nup' debit p'or de Lento' Et de 4d
solut vic ville Not' p' feod' firme." The next year the payment
was diverted from Lenton, for the sixteenpence was then paid
to the Lord the King, and the sheriffs of the town of Nottingham, and in the following year the same sum was paid to the
sheriffs of Nottingham. In later years the amount is merely
entered as " p' feod' firma," no mention being made as to whom
it was paid.

The following extracts from Dame Agnes Mellers'[1] foundation
deed of the Nottingham Free School, dated 22nd Nov., 1513,
show that, under certain circumstances, she gave great authority
in its government to the Prior and Convent of Lenton.

" To all Christian people, to whose knowledge this present
writing triplicate indented shall come to be seen or read, Agnes
Mellers, widow and vowess, sendeth greeting, in him that is the
root of Jesse produced to the salvation of all people." * * * *
" And here if it should fortune the said mayor, aldermen, and
common council to be negligent and forgetful in finding and
choosing of the schoolmaster and usher forty days next after
such time as it shall fortune him to be amoved or deceased,
keeping and doing the obiit yearly in manner and form
expressed in such like time ; or the lands and tenements, or
hereditaments, and other possessions, or the yearly rent of them,

---

(1) Widow of Richard Mellers, of Nottingham, the noted bellfounder, an alderman,
and Mayor of Nottingham in 1499 and 1506. Dame Agnes's will was proved in the
year 1514.

into other uses than finding of the said free school be convert, then I will, ordain, and establish that the Prior and Convent of the Monastery of the Holy Trinity, of Lenton, for the time being, and their successors shall have as a forfeiture the rule, guiding, and oversight of the said lands, tenements, or hereditaments, schoolmaster, &c., with all other things to the premises in any wise appertaining to the intent above expressed, in as ample and large wise as the mayor and burgesses have, or should have had the same, by this my present constitution and ordinance."[1]

In the year 1522, the Prior of Lenton contributed the sum of £133 6s. 8d. towards "the loan," an annual grant to be made by the spirituality for the King's personal expenses in France for the recovery of the crown of the same.

The taxation of Pope Nicholas IV., made in 1291, held good, and all taxes from benefices were regulated by it, until a new survey, known as the *Valor Ecclesiasticus*, was completed in the 27th year of King Henry the Eighth. From this document the following particulars of the income of Lenton Priory, at that date, are derived :— [2]

### John, Prior.[3]

|  | £ | s. | d. |
|---|---|---|---|
| *Cheshire.*—Tithes and other profits : Middlewich ... | 30 | 0 | 0 |
| *Derbyshire.*—Tithes and other profits : Horsley, £6 13s. 4d. ; tithes of lead ore in the High Peak, £6 13s. 4d. ... ... ... ... ... | 13 | 6 | 8 |
| Portions : Ashford, £1 3s. 6d. ; Bradwell, 10s. ; Blackwell, Hope, and Chapel-en-le-Frith, £6 ; Blackwell Mill, 4s. 5½d. ; Buxton, £1 11s. 8d. ; Chapel-en-le-Frith, £8 ; Chelmorton, £3 ; Cowdale, Sterndale, and Staden, £2 ; Fairfield, Cowlow, Wolow, and Pigter, £2 13s. 4d. ; Glossop (from Basingwork Priory) £10 13s. 4d. ; Holmesfield, 13s. 4d. ; Meadow-place (from Leicester Abbey), 3s. ; Monyash and Flagge, 16s. 8d. ... ... ... ... ... ... | 37 | 9 | 3½ |

---

(1) Deering, *Nottinghamia Vetus et Nova*, p. 156.

(2) *Valor Ecclesiasticus*, v. 147.

(3) This was John Annesley.

£ s. d.

Rents, etc.: Ashford, 8s.; Bradwell, 15s.; Black-
well, £8 7s.; Denby, £1; Holme, Dunston,
Birley, and Whitwell, £8; Tideswell, 11s.;
Trokehill, £1 2s. ...     ...     ...     ...     ... 20 3 0

*Lancashire.*—Profits belonging to Kersall Cell,
£9 6s. 8d., less the fee of Sir John Byron, £1 ...  8 6 8

*Leicestershire.*—Tithes, oblations, etc.   Wigston,
£33 0s. 2d., less the payments to the Vicar, to the
Bishop, and Dean and Chapter of Lincoln, to
the Archdeacon of Leicester, to the poor of
the parish (to pray for the soul of Henry VII.,
King of England), to the Abbot and Convent
of Leicester, to the Dean and Canons of Leicester, and to the Bishop of Lincoln, and the
Archdeacon of Nottingham, for synodals and
procurations, leaving the clear annual sum of ... 19 6 8
Portion: Husbands Bosworth ...     ...     ...  0 10 0
Pensions: Nether Broughton, £1 10s.; Foston,
10s.; Prestwold (by the Prioress of Bolington),
4s. ...     ...     ...     ...     ...     ...  2 4 0
Rents, etc.: Broughton ...     ...     ...     ...  1 13 8

*Northamptonshire.*—Portions: Duston (by St. James's
Priory, Northampton), £1; Rushden, £12    ... 13 0 0
Pensions: Courtenall, 6s. 8d.; Harleston, £2;
Floore, 3s. 6d.; Rushden, 4s.    ...     ...  2 14 2
Rents: Courtenhall, £28; Dunston, 16s.; New-
bottle, 6s. 8d.     ...     ...     ...     ... 29 2 8

*Nottinghamshire.*—Tithes of corn and hay: Beeston,
£8; Lenton, £6 13s. 4d.; St. Mary's, Nottingham, £18; Radford, £6 13s. 4d; oblations at
St. Mary's, Nottingham, £9     ...     ...     ... 48 6 8
Portions: from Beauvale Priory, for tithes in
Greasley, 6s. 8d.; Catesby Priory, for tithes in
Basford, £1 13s. 4d.; tithes in Cotgrave, 8s. 6d.;
Felley Priory, for tithes in Attenborough,
£6 13s. 4d.; Langar, £12; Newstead Priory, for
tithes in Stapleford, £3 6s. 8d.; portion of tithes
in Ruddington, £3; Sutton, £2; Thorpe-in-
the-Glebe, 8s.; Ulverscroft Priory, for Bunny,
£2 6s. 8d. ...     ...     ...     ...     ...     ... 32 3 2
Pensions: Barton-in-Fabis, 5s.; Basford, 4s.;
Costock, 2s.; Cotgrave, 14s.; Lenton, £1 6s. 8d.;
Linby, 6s. 8d.; Nottingham, St. Nicholas's, 10s.;
St. Peter's, 16s.; St. John's Hospital, 13s. 4d.;
Hospital of St. Mary at the end of the bridge
of the town of Nottingham, 6s. 8d.; Remp-
stone, 2s. ...     ...     ...     ...     ...     ...  5 6 4

£ s. d.

Demesne lands, rents, mills, fair, etc.: Lenton,
£54 10s.; Newthorpe, £6 9s.; Nottingham,
£1 17s. 2d.; Radford, £15 17s. 6d. ... ... 78 13 8
Rents: Awsworth, 13s. 4d.; Almeton, 6s.; Barton-in-Fabis, 6s.; Bradmore, £3 3s.; Costock,
6d.; Cotgrave, £8 18s. 3d.; Cropwell Butler, 4s.;
Keyworth, £1 8s. 2d.; Mansfield, 13s. 4d.;
Normanton, 18s. 8d.; Rempstone, 4s.; Watnall,
9s. ... ... ... ... ... ... ... 17 4 3
*Yorkshire.*—Tithes of corn and hay (Arksey) ... 28 0 0
                                               ————————
                                               £387 10 10½

## PAYMENTS.

£ s. d. £ s. d.

To the Warden of Clifton College, in the
county of Nottingham, to pray for
the souls of William Booth, formerly
Archbishop of York, and Sir Gervase Clifton, £10; to Thomas Bate,
chantry-priest in York Cathedral, to
pray for the souls of Thomas Rotherham, formerly Archbishop of York,
and Henry Carnebull, priest,
£6 13s. 4d.; to Thomas Pylley, chantry
priest in Rotherham Church, to pray
for the same souls, £6 13s. 4d.;[1] to
John Wilson, chantry-priest in the
church of North Wingfield, to pray
for Ralph Savage, £5 6s. 8d.; to
Richard Dowkyn, curate of Chelmorton, £1 10s.; to the prior of
St. James's cell, Derby, from lands
in Dunston, 10s. ... ... ... 30 13 4

Alms: To five needy men, named William
Brewer, Charles Howson, John More,
Roger Wilson, and Thomas Revell,
to pray for the souls of William
Peverel and Adelina, his wife, of
Henry the First, King of England,
and Matilda, his Queen, and his heirs,

---

(1) In an undated return of the annual income of " The chauntrye of ij prestes at
th'altar of Jhesus & Our Lady in the Parysshe Churche of Rotherham," this entry
occurs :—" Firste, a yerely Rent commyng furthe of the lands & possessyons of
the late Monasterye of Lenton payd by thandes of the Kynges maiestie recevor
vj^{li} xiij^s iiij^d."—*Certificates of Colleges*, No. 67., P.R.O.

|  | £ s. d. | £ s. d. |
|---|---|---|

in daily meat and drink, with lodging and firing, and one penny each per week, £14 1s. 8d. per annum, and £2 13s. 4d. distributed in money to the poor on the anniversary of William Peverel, and of Adelina, his wife, namely, the 20th of January and the 28th of the same month .. 16 15 0

Fees: To Sir John Willoughby, Knight,[1] seneschall of the Priory, £2 per annum; Roland Collingwood, general receiver of all the lordships, manors, lands, and tenements of the Priory, £1 6s. 8d. per annum, and Henry Statham, auditor, an annual fee of £1 ...  ...  ...  ...  ...  4 6 8

[2]£51 15 0 57 15 0

Clear annual value ...  ... £329 15 10½

Shortly before the dissolution of the Priory, "Nycholas [Heyth] Prior of Lenton," addressed a letter, dated "·Lenton Abbey,[3] 12 April," to "Mr. Henege, grome of the stoole to the King's Grace," stating that Dan[4] Hamlet Pencriche, one of the brethren, who last year laid an unjust accusation against the Prior before the Council, has fled from his religion, as he did

---

(1) Sir John Willoughby, of Wollaton, Knight, was the son of Sir Henry Willoughby, of the same place, Knight, by his first wife, Margaret, daughter of Sir Robert Markham, of Cotham, Knight.   Sir John married Anne, one of the sisters and coheiresses of Sir Edward Grey, Viscount Lisle, and died without issue.

(2) It should be noted that there is a difference of £6 between the amount of payments deducted from the gross income to give the clear value of £329 15s. 10½d., and the amount of the payments when added together.   From this we may assume that an amount of £6 has been omitted from the latter.

(3) We have here proof that at this time the Monastery was styled an Abbey by the monks themselves.

(4) *Dan* appears to have been a title generally assigned to a monk.   It is an abbreviated form of the Latin *dominus*, and appears also in French *dan*, Spanish *don*, and Portuguese *dom*.   The O. Fr. form *dans* was introduced into English in the fourteenth century.   In the *Catholicon Anglicum*, an English-Latin word book of the year 1483, we find "*a Dan, sicut monachi vocantur.*"   In the Monk's Prologue, the host, asking him his name, says :—

"Whether shall I call you my lord *dan* Johan,
Or *dan* Thomas, or elles *dan* Albon ?"

See an account of the word in "Leaves from a Word-hunter's Note-book," A. S. Palmer, p. 130.

twice before, by the instigation of certain men of Nottingham, " who love not this poor house." He has taken goods belonging to the house, which the said men have received. The Prior asks Hennege's favour, and for his credence for the bearer.[1]

The last mention made of the Prior of Lenton, previous to the proceedings relative to the dissolution of the Priory, is contained in the following note :—" Sir James Foljambe, of Walton, in Derbyshire, by his first wife, Alice, daughter and coheir of Thomas Fitzwilliam, of Aldwarke (who was slain at Flodden Field, 5 Henry VIII.), had, among other children, twin sons, George and James  George, the elder of the twins, was born at Walton, on Friday, about midnight, 21 June, 1538. James was born about two o'clock on Saturday morning. His godfathers were the Prior of Lenton, and Sir John Dunham, Knight, and his godmother, Helena, relict of Roger Foljambe, Esq."[2]

## THE PRIORS OF LENTON.

*Humphrey* occurs temp. Henry I.,[3] and about 1144 (10 Stephen).
*Philip.*[4]
*Alexander* was one of the witnesses to the charter, by which
    John, Earl of Mortaigne, confirmed the charter of his father,
    King Henry II., to the burgesses of Nottingham, c. 1189.[5]
*Peter*[6] occurs October, 1200,[7] 1203,[8] 1209,[9] 1212,[10] and 1214.
*Robert de Lexington*, Prior of Lenton, was the son of Richard
    de Lexington, who " brought up his sons so fortunately,
    that Robert, who was a clergyman, canon of Southwell,
    became a great judge and baron ; while John, the eldest
    brother, was Lord Keeper, and Henry, the youngest, became
    Bishop of Lincoln." Lexington does not appear to have

---

(1) *State Papers, Henry VIII.*, v. 440.
(2) *Notices of Family of Foljambe*, Gough MSS., Bod. Lib.
(3) Nicholl's *Leicestershire*, ii. 419.    (4) Baker, *Northamptonshire*, i. 142.
(5) *Nottingham Borough Records*, i. 9.
(6) Transcripts of Fines, P.R.O., p. 1558.
(7) See Thoroton, p. 244, and Nicholl's *Leicestershire*, ii. 284.
(8) Thoroton, p. 373.    (9) Ibid., p. 355.    (10) Cart. 14 John, n. 32., Dec. 2.

filled any higher ecclesiastical office than that of canon, although he was once elected Bishop of Lichfield, but declined the honour.[1] In the 10th year of King John, he acted, however, as custos of the Archbishopric of York during its vacancy. He appears to have added military service to his other duties, and to have received various proofs of the royal confidence and favour. In the eighth year of Henry III., he was custodian of the castles of the Peak and Bolsover, in Derbyshire, and later on was governor of Oxford Castle. There is a letter from him to Hubert de Burgh, detailing the progress of William, Earl of Albemarle, through Nottingham, with his own preparations to oppose him, and stating his intention to proceed himself into Northumberland.[2] He was appointed, when Prior of Lenton, one of the King's Justices Itinerant, February 5th, 1219, and held a judicial appointment until the 27th year of Henry III., being mentioned in July, 1234. as the oldest judge on the bench. In 1240, he was placed at the head of the justices sent by the King into the northern counties, to extort money under the guise of redressing grievances. [3] Having, in the discharge of his official duties at Lincoln, in common with his brother justices, heard capital causes on Sunday, and having punished the Dean, when he censured them, Lexington received a letter of rebuke from Grosseteste, Bishop of Lincoln.[4] The subsequent entries of his acting in his judicial capacity do not extend beyond Hilary term, 1243 (27 Henry III.), in all of which he is placed at the head of his associates. He then probably retired, and must have been far advanced in age.[5] Lexington died on the 4th of the calends of June, 1250, his death being thus recorded by Matthew Paris:—" On the 29th May, in this year, died Robert de Lexington, who had long continued in the office of Justiciary, and had acquired a distinguished name and ample possessions. A few years before his death, however, he was struck with palsy, and

(1) *Annals of Dunstable*, iii. 149.      (2) 4th Report Pub. Rec. App., ii. 157.
(3) *Matthew Paris*, iv. 34.      (4) *Roberti Grosseteste Epistolæ*, p. 266.
(5) Foss' Judges, ii. 385.

gave up the aforesaid office ; so that, like the Apostle St. Matthew, he was summoned from the receipt of custom to a better life, and employing himself in bountiful almsgiving and devout prayers, he laudably terminated his enfeebled life."[1]

*Roger*[2] occurs 10th March, 1223,[3] and was one of the witnesses to an agreement dated Nov. 17, 1225, between the Burgesses of Nottingham and the Burgesses of Retford.[4]

*Damascenus, or Dalmasius,* was succeeded by

*Roger de Normanton,*[5] who was made Prior in 1233[6] and occurs in 1234[7] and 1241.

*H——* Prior of Lenton, occurs in an instrument dated 1251. [8] This Prior is obviously identical with Hugh Bluet, who is described as Prior of Lenton in a charter of his brother, Robert Bluet, in the time of Henry the Third. (See p. 125)

*Roger Norman,* formerly Prior of Montacute, was appointed Prior of Lenton, Sep. 16th, 1259,[9] and occurs in the years 1262 and 1266.[10]

*Matthew,* formerly Almoner of Lewes Priory, received the temporalities of Lenton from the King, March 14th, 1269.[11]

*Reginald de Jora* was probably the next Prior ; he is mentioned in 1289 as having lately resigned the Priorate, but this event may have taken place a few years before.[12]

*Peter de Siviriaco,* or *Siriniaco,* received the King's letters of protection, Dec. 1st, 1281,[13] and is mentioned in a bull of Pope Nicholas IV., dated Dec. 11th, 1289.

*William* had the King's letters of protection, Aug. 30th., 1290.[14] Occurs 1294 and 1296.[15]

---

(1) *Matthew Paris,* v. 138.

(2) See Rymer's *Fœdera,* i. 270.        (3) Rot. Lit. Claus., 7 Hen. III., m. 15.

(4) *Nottingham Borough Records,* i. 20.

(5) Nicholl's *Leicestershire,* ii. 110.        (6) Pat. 18 Hen. III. m. 11., dorso.

(7) Thoroton, p. 277.        (8) *Cart. Harl. Antiq.,* 84 F. 35.

(9) Pat. 44 Hen. III. m. 3. Sept. 16.        (10) Thoroton, p. 51.

(11) Pat. 54 Hen. III., Mar. 14.

(12) *Ab. Rot. Orig.,* i. 65.  "Mand' est Thome de Normanville esc' ultra Trentam q'd cap' in man' R. omnes terr' & ten' ad prioratum de Lenton p'tin' vacant' p' resign' f'ris Reginald' de Jora nup' P'or' ibidem donec, &c."  *Anno R. E. fil' R.H.,* xvii.

(13) Pat. 10 Ed. I., Dec 1.        (14) Pat. 19 Edw. I.        (15) *Ab. Placitor,* p. 292.

*Stephen* occurs in 1312.[1]

*Reginald* occurs in 1313.[2]  He resigned.

*Geoffrey* was the next Prior.  The temporalities were restored to him, March 7th, 1315.[3]

*William de Pinnebury* occurs in 1324.[4]

*Geoffrey* occurs May 15th, 1327.[5]

*Astorgius*, or *Antorgius*, occurs March 22nd, 1336,[6] and in 1346.[7]

*Peter de Abbeville* occurs April, 1355.[8]

*Geoffrey de Rochero* occurs in 1403[9] and 1407.

*Richard Stafford.*  Prior.

*Thomas of Elmham*—sometimes called *Ellingham*[10]—was a monk of St. Augustine's monastery, Canterbury, where he held the office of treasurer in 1407, the year in which he had been arrested at the suit of Henry Somerset, for an alleged excess of vigour in discharging the duties of his office.  In 1414, he ceased to be a Benedictine monk, and, following in the steps of others, panting for a higher measure of monastic austerity, joined the Clugniac order, and was appointed Prior of Lenton, the temporalities of which appointment were made over to him on the 11th June, 1414 (2 Henry V.).  Subsequently to his instalment as the Prior of Lenton, Elmham was, in 1416, appointed vicar-general to Raymund, Abbot of Clugny, for the kingdoms of England and Scotland.

Ten years later (in 1426) he received a fresh promotion

---

(1) Reg. Greenfield, Abp. York, p. 2.

(2) Pat. 7 Edw. II.                    (3) Pat. 9 Edw. II., p. 2.

(4) Plac. 17 Edw. II., Term Hil.

(5) *Rolls of Parliament*, ii. 373; Rymer's *Fœdera*, iv. 289.

(6) Pat. 10 Edw. III.                  (7) Ab. Rot. Orig., ii. 191.

(8) *Nottingham Borough Records*, i. 160.

(9) Proc. Priv. Coun., i. 191-5.  In vol. v., p. 146, of the *Mon. Angl.*, it is stated that Geoffrey de Rocherio became Prior of Thetford, in Norfolk, on the deposition of James in 1355.  He occurs also as Prior of Thetford in 1369.  He commenced the history of the monastery, printed in the *Monasticon*, vol. v., p. 157, but, according to the same authority, died before its completion.  It is more likely, however, that he resigned the priorate of Thetford for that of Lenton, where he probably died about the year 1410.

(10) The following account of this Prior is principally derived from the valuable prefaces to the "Historia Monasterii St. Augustini Cantuariensis," and "Memorials of Henry the Fifth," published by direction of the Master of the Rolls, and from Hearne's "Thomæ de Elmham vita et gesta Henrici quinti Anglorum regis," published in 1727.

to the office of commissary-general in spirituals and temporals[1] for all vacant benefices belonging to the Clugniac order in England, Scotland, and Ireland. In the same year he voluntarily resigned the Priorate of Lenton,[2] in favour of John Elmham, presumably a relative of his own, who was then collated to the vacant office on the nomination of Thomas Nelond, Prior of Lewes. The latest glimpse that we obtain of Thomas of Elmham's private history is in a metrical piece, where he invokes the friendly criticism of the "glorious doctor, Mr. John Somersethe,"[3] with whom he stood, as it appears, on very intimate terms. This John Somerset was the celebrated tutor and physician of King Henry VI.; but although elected as a fellow of Pembroke Hall, Cambridge, as early as 1410, his reputation was not established till considerably later, perhaps not till 1440, soon after which date he was appointed, as chancellor of the exchequer, and a man of eminent learning, to assist in drawing up a code of statutes for the original foundation of King's College, Cambridge.

Elmham was the author of several historical works of considerable importance. The principal of these, "A History of the Monastery of St. Augustine, Canterbury," forming one of the series of "Chronicles and Memorials," was published in 1858.[4] In this work, which contains numerous references

---

(1) Hearne's *Preface*, xxii.                     (2) Ibid.

(3) Harl. MSS. 864, sec. 2. The next section of the same MSS. contains a "Laus M. Johannis Somerset Metrice," by the same hand.

(4) The following, which is related by Camden, probably refers to one of the two monks of this name, who successively held the office of Prior of Lenton :—

"Dan Elingham, a monke of Lenton, of Saint Benedict's order, comming to the White-Friers in Nottingham, found there John Baptist painted in a White-Friers weede, whereat maruelling, he coled out these rymes vpon the wall neere to the picture :—

'Christa Baptista, vestis non te decet ista,
Qui te vestiuit fratrem, maledictus abiuit.
Nunquam Messias frater fuerat, nec Helias,
Non stat plebs læta, dum sit pro fratre phropheta.
Si fratrem Jonam fingis, Geezi tibi ponam :
Ac Jebusæum, ne jungas his Helizæum.'

"But a White-Frier there answered Elingham, with these following, in the person of John Baptist :—

'Elingham mentiris, metris fatuis quoq. miris
Atq. ea quæ nescis, sic astruis ut ea quæ scis,
Nam Deus est testis, decet hæc me candida vestris,
Plusquam te vestris pulla, sive nigra cuculla,
Sum Carmelita merito, sed tu Geezita,
Ac frater fictus Benedicti, non benedictus.'"

*Remaines Concerning Britain*, 6th edit., 1657, p. 307.

to Norfolk, the author manifests his deep antipathy to the Lollards. "Everything most vile, most murderous, and most sacrilegious, which he finds in the earlier annals of his country, rises up before him as a dark precursor of the modern heretics, who dared to say that temporal riches ought never to have been bestowed upon the monasteries and ministers of holy church."[1] The history contains a coloured drawing of the high altar of the Abbey Church of St. Augustine's, and the ledge above it, whereon were deposited certain books which are minutely described. Other books are also mentioned as being preserved in the sacristy, but all these have now disappeared with the exception of the Book of the Gospels (Textus Evangeliorum) which was presented by Archbishop Parker to the library of Corpus Christi College, Cambridge. The writing in this book, of which we have here reproduced (one half size of original) the first three verses of St. John's Gospel, is judged by the best palæographers to be of Pope Gregory's date, and it is extremely interesting to know that this is one of the books sent by Gregory to Augustine, in 601, and from which, in all probability, he read out aloud in that church which he had "recovered" from the Romans, in presence of King Ethelbert, whom he had converted to the faith of Christ. That this MS. once belonged to St. Augustine's Monastery, there is the clearest evidence : on one of the pages is copied a charter of a gift of land to that monastery in the ninth century, and on another page one of a grant in the tenth century, and the writing of these charters appears contemporary with their date. So that,

INPRINCIPIOERAT
UERBUM
ETUERBUMERAT
APUDDMETDS
ERATUERBUM
HOCERATINPRIN
CIPIOAPUDDM
OMNIAPERIPSU
FACTASUNT
ETSINEIPSOFACTU
ESTNIHIL
QUODFACTUMEST
INIPSOUITAERAT

---

(1) " Historia Monasterii St. Augustini Cantuariensis," edited by C. Hardwick, M.A., Preface, p. xx.

although some monk put the book to a *quasi* secular use
by copying a charter on one of the blank leaves, this Book
of the Gospels was clearly a book of importance in the
monastery as early as the ninth century.   There is ample
evidence that the History of St. Augustine's Monastery
was written by Elmham, for besides the numerous references
to Norfolk, which lead to the conclusion that the writer was
a native of that county,[1] we have, in a metrical account of
the foundation of St. Augustine's, the following lines in
honour of St. Pancras:—

> " Marcida dum tellus patet, hanc tu germine justi
> Ornas Augustini ; flos datur inde novellus.
> Nunc juvenes puerique, senes, laudes date lenes ;
> Almiphonis jubilate tonis, per rura colonis."

On turning to the acrostic verses of the author on his own
name, we again meet with lines very nearly approaching to
those just quoted.   They occur in a profane *Te Deum*[2] in
honour of the Blessed Virgin :—

> " Marcida jam tullus patet, hinc tu germine sacro
> Ornes theothocos flore virente novo.
> Nuncia sacra tibi, quæ contulit angelus angli,
> Almiphonis resonent perpetuanda tonis."

The manuscript of this history is in the possession of
the Master and Fellows of Trinity Hall, Cambridge, and
was presented to them by Robert Hare, the Cambridge
archæologist, who died Nov. 2, 1611.   A modern copy is
preserved in the Harleian Collection, No. 686.   The editor
of this volume is of opinion that " in the work before us,
where the matter is original, and not entirely or in substance
borrowed from more elegant writers, no one will dispute the
miserable want of skill in composition, or defend the
author's turgid epithets and his declamatory diction."
Elmham was also the author of a prose Life of Henry V.,

---

(1) There is a village known as North Elmham, near East Dereham, in Norfolk,
of which Prior Elmham may have been a native, or perhaps the descendant of a
family taking their name from that place.   In the adjoining county of Suffolk there
are no less than six villages called Elmham.

(2) Cotton MSS., Vesp. D. XIII. ; Julius, E. iv. 3.

published, in 1727, by Thomas Hearne,[1] a work which, though written in a verbose and inflated style, is of considerable historical value. "The style of this work is so extremely inflated as occasionally to suffocate the sense,[2] and according to Archdeacon Wilkins (preface to Bishop Tanner's "*Bibliotheca Britanno-Hibernica*," pp. xliii. xlv.), the better known work of Titus Livius Forojuliensis is little more than a compilation from Elmham's prose history— "with this merit, however, that the Thrasonic and turgidly poetic style of the original is changed for one of greater severity, and more befitting the historian." A copy of this work is preserved in the Cottonian Collection (Julius, E. iv.).

The third work, *attributed* to Elmham, entitled "Versus Rythmici de Henrico Quinto," also forms one of the series of the "Chronicles and Memorials," and was published in 1858, being edited by Mr. Charles Augustus Cole. In line 139, there is evident proof that the writer was an ecclesiastic and a member of the royal household, for he here speaks of himself as reading, or rather intoning, mass in the King's presence. Again, in line 208, he identifies himself with the monks of Westminster Abbey. "As to any further or clearer information beyond this, or even inference, relative to his personal history, it seems impossible to arrive at it, either by indication or conjecture.[3] A description of the person of the King is given in lines 69-88. His head is described as being of a spherical form, with thick, smooth, brown hair, a face becomingly oblong, with a straight nose. His complexion is florid, his eyes bright, large, and of an auburn tinge, dovelike when unmoved, and fierce as those of a lion when in anger. His teeth are even, and white as snow, his ears graceful and small, his chin divided, his neck fair and of a becoming thickness throughout, his cheeks of a rosy hue in part, and partly of a delicate whiteness, his

---

(1) "Thomæ de Elmham, vita & gesta Henrici quinti Anglorum regis. E codicibus MSS., vetustis descripsit, & primus luci publicæ dedit Tho. Hearnius. Oxonii E. Theatro Sheldoniano. MDCCXXVII."

(2) "Monument. Britan," Genl. Int., p. 29.

(3) Preface, p. xxviii.

lips of vermilion tint, his limbs well-formed, and the bones and sinews of his frame firmly knit together. We are also informed that Henry, notwithstanding his attention to his religious duties (his weekly practice of confession being deemed worthy of special remark), the calls of the cares of state, his study of the art of war, the pursuits of hunting, falconry, and archery, could often find time for the study of books. " Vivat Rex talis," exclaims the loyal writer. By way of comparison, we give Hall's delineation of the person of the King, although it differs in one or two particulars. " He was of stature more than the comen sort, of- body lene, well mebred [membered] and stro[n]gly made, a face beautiful, somewhat long-necked, black heered, stout of stomake, eloquent of tong, in marcial affaires a very doctor, and of all chivalry the very paragone" (*Hall's Chronicles*, p. 113, edition 1809). The Lollards, who are mentioned in a disparaging tone in line 136, are again introduced in lines 151-168 in reference to their criminal designs against the Romish Church. The manuscript of this work, written in the hand of the earlier half of the fifteenth century, is contained in six vellum leaves, paged 173 to 178 inclusive, in a small quarto volume among the Cottonian Manuscripts (Cleopatra, B. i.). The present *History*, as the writer seems inclined to call it, appears to have been written by Elmham as an afterthought, and by way of supplement to his prose history, to which work distinct allusion is made. Notwithstanding the character of the composition, its grammar is considered to be quite on a par with that of similar writings of the same age.

The fourth work which we have to notice, and one of which Elmham was undoubtedly the author, is the "Liber Metricus," printed in the same volume as the "Versus Rythmici." Thomas Hearne, in his preface to Elmham's prose History (p. xxviii.), speaks in but disparaging terms of this work; his reason, however, for thus expressing himself, there are grounds for believing, is mainly based upon the fact that the writer's meaning was too obscure for him to take the trouble to comprehend it. The intense antipathy of the writer to the Lollards, expressed in his other works, here again manifests itself. The uncomplimentary terms in which he speaks of John Oldcastle are remarkable for their vehemence ; and he even looks upon that bold reformer as of sufficient importance to be identified with the "great dragon" of the 12th chapter of Revelation, ver. 4, whose "tail drew the third part of the stars of heaven,"—"That satellite of hell, I mean, the Heresiarch of Arch-Lollard, John Oldcastle, whose stench is noted to have ascended most horribly to the nostrils of the Catholics, even like that of a dunghill." Line 104 is also deserving of remark, as implying that Oldcastle was indebted to demoniacal agency for his escape from the Tower. Elmham has taken particular care to let the reader know he is the author, by inserting his name, "Thomas Elmham," as an acrostic, at the commencement of the metrical narrative. The work ends with the fifth year of Henry's reign. Seven MS. copies of the "Liber Metricus" are accessible to the English reader, two being preserved in the Bodleian Library, Oxford, and five in the British Musuem. The text in the present volume is printed from Julius, E. iv., collated with Vespatian, D. XIII., and the Harleian MSS., No. 861. The Julius MS. consists of 24 leaves, written on both sides, in the court-hand in vogue in the reign of Henry VI., and is a fine specimen of penmanship. It commences at folio 89 of the volume, the manuscript immediately preceding it being a copy of Elmham's prose History.

The verses,[1] written as a *Te Deum* in honour of the Blessed Virgin, and forming an acrostic on the name of the writer, "Thomas Elmham, Monachus," are, at the conclusion of Vesp. D. XIII., written in the same hand as the rest of the manuscript. For a second copy of this *Te Deum*, see Cotton MSS., Julius E, iv. 3, where the hymn is said to be "ad laudem Dei Genetricis Mariæ, propter gloriosam expeditionem regis Henrici quinti, et pro succursu regis

---

(1) Hearne, p. 375.

Angliæ, dolis suæ, quæ cunctas hæreses cum hæresiarcha
Johanne Old-Castel, suis precis intereunt."

*John Elmham.* His appointment received the royal assent,
February 18th, 1426.[1]   He resigned in 1450.

*John Middylburgh* received the royal assent, October 18th,
1450.[2]

*Thomas Wollore* was appointed by the King, July 5th, 1458.[3]
Edward IV., in the first year of his reign, confirmed the
Priorate to him for life.[4]   Occurs in 1476.[5]

*Richard Dene* appointed Prior, February 21st, 1481,[6]  occurs
2 Henry VII.,[8] also in 1492[9] and 1495.[10]

*John Ilkeston* occurs as Prior in 1500[11] and 1501.[12]  On
December 3rd, 1508, he is referred to as John Hilston.[13]
The signature of this Prior is attached to an undated

exemplification, written in an early 16th century hand,
of Sir Avery de Sulney's allowance of the right of the
Burgesses of Nottingham to pasture in Basford, and of
Sir Robert de Cockfield's release of the acknowledgment
paid for the same.   The document is thus attested,
"Thes be the trewe copyes of ij. dedis undre saille
whiche we have seyn, as dothe apere here above writyn.
By me, John' Prior of Lenton.   By me, Johnn' Willughby,
Kt."[14]

---

(1) Pat. 5 Hen. VI., p. 1.        (2) Pat. 29 Hen. VI., p. 1.

(3) Pat. 37 Hen. VI., p. 2.

(4) Pat. 1 Edw. IV., p. 1.        (5) Tanner *Notitia Monastica*, app.

(6) Pat. 21 Edw. IV., p. 1.

(8) Add. MSS., 6666, f. 208.        (9) *Testamenta Vetusta*, ii. 414.

(10) *Records of the Nottingham Corporation*, MS. No. 1375, p. 115.

(11) *Records of the Nottingham Corporation*, MS. No. 1380, p. 31.

(12) Tanner *Notitia Monastica*, appendix.

(13) *Records of the Nottingham Corporation*, MS. No. 1382, p. 24.

(14) *Records of the Borough of Nottingham*, i. 407.   Through the courtesy of the
Town Clerk of Nottingham, we are enabled to give a fac-simile of the autograph
of this Prior.

*Thomas Guyllam*, or *Gillame*, succeeded to the Priorate in 1509,[1] being sued on September 7th in that year in the Borough Court of Nottingham, for goods ordered by his predecessor, Hilston.[2]  He occurs also in the year 1522.[3]

*Thomas Notyngham*, alias *Hobson*, succeeded to the Priorate March 2nd, 1525, on the death of Thomas Guyllam.

*John Annesley* was appointed Prior Jan. 17th, 1531, on the resignation of Thomas Notyngham, *alias* Hobson.

*Nicholas Heth*, or *Heythe*—the last Prior.

The events which led to the suppression of Lenton Priory may be briefly stated.  Early in the year 1534, Parliament prohibited every kind of appeal, and every kind of payment, to the Pope, and confirmed the King's title of supreme head of the English Church, and vested in him alone the right of appointing to all bishoprics, and of deciding in all ecclesiastical causes.  Thus the tie which for so many centuries had united England with Rome was completely severed.  In November of the same year, the firstfruits and tenths were annexed to the Crown for ever, and a new oath of supremacy was introduced.  In the following year, some of the clergy refused either to take the oath, or to proclaim in their churches and chapels that the Pope was Antichrist.  The system adopted with regard to them was simple and expeditious ; they were condemned for high treason, and hanged.  Shortly afterwards, the King, acting on the advice of Cromwell, appointed commissioners to visit the monasteries or other religious houses in England, and "to search into the lives and manners of religious persons."  They were also commanded to make all the monks and nuns renounce the authority of the Pope, and to take the oath of supremacy.  In 1536 a formidable insurrection in favour of the monks broke out at Louth, in Lincolnshire, which was quickly followed by the still more formidable rising in Yorkshire, known as the " Pilgrimage of Grace."  The King, enraged

---

(1) He resigned the Priorate of Lenton for the Abbey of Pipewell, in Northampton-shire.  In 1535, Thomas Gyllam, *alias* Lenton, and thirteen monks, surrendered the Abbey of Pipewell to the Crown.  Bridge's *Northamptonshire*, i. 333.

(2) *Records of the Nottingham Corporation*, MS. No. 1382, p. 108.

(3) See p. 171.

at this new rebellion, wrote to the Duke of Norfolk to execute a large number of the insurgents in every town and village, and "forasmuch as all these troubles have ensued by the solicitation and traitorous conspiracies of the monks and canons of these parts, we desire you at such places as they have conspired or kept their houses with force since the appointment at Doncaster, you shall, without pity or circumstance, cause all the monks and canons that be in anywise faulty, to be tied up without further delay or ceremony, to the terrible example of others."[1] The Duke of Norfolk obeyed this order and hanged seventy-four persons, including the abbots of Kirkstead, Barlings, Fountains, Jervaulx, Rievaulx, the Prior of Bridlington, Lord Hussey, Lord Darcy, Aske, and others. The Prior of Lenton most probably suffered the same fate, there being a tradition that he was hanged above the gateway of his Priory. The *inquisitio post mortem* of the possessions of Nicholas Heth, late Prior of the house or monastery of the Holy Trinity of Lenton, attainted, was taken at Nottingham, September 3rd, 1538, before Francis Merynge, Esquire, Escheator of the counties of Nottingham and Derby, the whole of the possessions of the Priory being confiscated to the King.

One important fact should be made clear. The dissolution of the monasteries had, historically, no connection with the Reformation. The religious confraternities, with some exceptions, had acknowledged the royal supremacy. The dissolution of the lesser houses was accomplished by Act 27 Henry VIII. c. 20; the dissolution of the greater houses took place in May, 1539, by Act 31 Henry VIII. c. 13. By Statute 31 Henry VIII. c. 14, in June of the same year, the Statute of the Six Articles was passed, confirming the doctrine of the mass and celibacy of the clergy.[2] It was not until ten years later that the

---

(1) In the same letter the King says : "We desire and pray you to have good respect to the conservation of the lands and goods of all such as shall be now attainted, that we may have them in safety, to be given, if we shall be so disposed, to such persons as have truly serve[l] us ; for we be informed that there were amongst them divers freeholders and rich men, whose lands and goods well looked into will reward others well, that, with their truths, have deserved the same."

(2) *Parl. Hist.*, i. 587.

reconstruction of the devotional offices took effect. The
Reformers, therefore, had no share in the reign of terror and
cupidity, or its destructive consequences. [1]

Although the monasteries were, in many respects, perfectly
indefensible, yet they are entitled to higher praise than the
qualified approbation frequently accorded to them. Their
position is the more striking by the strong contrast they
presented to the outer world. In days of lawless violence and
rapine, they afforded the only sanctuary for the oppressed,
the timid, and the weak. When all around breathed of war,
and studied its arts alone, they fostered the more enduring
arts of peace. And when the world was immersed in ignorance
and barbarity, learning and science found their only asylum
within the friendly walls of the monastery. But, at the same
time, they contained within themselves the seeds of dissolution.
Their wealth was the provocative of their ruin. Unchecked
by external supervision, the monks in many instances became
indolent and self-engrossed ; and, making due allowance for
exaggeration, grossly vicious, yet, "it appears to be the testimony of history, that the monks and clergy, whether good
or bad in themselves, were, in all times and places, better than
other people."

" Monachism itself, so rich and fruitful once, is now all rotted
into peat ; lies sleek and buried,—and a most feeble bog-grass
of Dilettantism all the crop we reap from it! That was
frightful waste ; perhaps among the saddest our England ever
saw. Why will men destroy noble forests, even when in part
a nuisance, in such reckless manner ; turning loose four-footed
cattle and Henry-the-Eighths into them! The fifth part of our
English soil lay consecrated to ' spiritual uses,' better or worse ;
solemnly set apart to foster spiritual growth and culture of the
soul, by the methods then known ; and now—it too, like the
four-fifths, fosters what? Gentle shepherd, tell me what?" [2]

The site of Lenton Priory and that portion of the parishes

---

(1) Walcott, *English Minsters*, ii. 52.
(2) Carlyle, *Past and Present*.

of Lenton and Radford which formed the demesne of the monastery appear to have constituted a distinct manor, and yet continue separate from the manor of Lenton.

In 1539, King Henry the Eighth granted a lease of the site of the Priory, with certain lands in "Carleholme, Lenton, and Radforde," for forty years, at an annual rent of £38 13s. od., to Sir Michael Stanhope, Knight, who had previously obtained a grant of the site of the dissolved Priory of Shelford, in this county.

In 1563, the reversion of the site and demesne of Lenton Priory was granted to Sir John Harrington, Knight, and to John Harrington, his son and heir, and Isabel his wife, for the term of their lives.

In 1604, the site and demesne of Lenton Priory was granted in fee farm to Sir Michael Hicks, Knight, and his heirs. Sir Michael was descended from a Gloucestershire family, and was the son of Robert Hicks, a wealthy citizen and mercer of London, and elder brother of Sir Baptist Hicks, who was raised to the peerage as Viscount Campden in 1629. He was a barrister-at-law, and became secretary to the eminent statesman, William, Lord Burghley, Lord High Treasurer of England, to whose influence he mainly owed his advancement, and who "stood god-father to his eldest son, and named him William, after his own name." [1]   Sir Michael Hicks purchased the manor of Ruckholt, in the parish of Leyton, in Essex, which he made his principal residence, and he likewise acquired by purchase Beverston Castle, in Gloucestershire, afterwards the chief seat of the family.   He died at Ruckholt Hall, August 5th, 1612, aged 69.   Dame Elizabeth Hicks, his widow, died in February, 1634, and was interred near her husband, in the chancel at Leyton.   His son and successor, Sir William Hicks,[2] was created a Baronet, July 21st, 1619, shortly after attaining his majority, and was subsequently appointed Lieutenant of the Forest of Waltham.   He was married at Drayton, in Middlesex, September

(1) Morant's *Hist. of Essex*, vol. i., p. 24.

(2) Thoroton, usually so accurate, is in error in stating that the site of Lenton Priory was granted to this Sir William Hicks, in 1604. The "Calendar of State Papers" shows clearly that the grant was to his father, Sir Michael Hicks, and his heirs. In 1604, Sir William Hicks could only have been about seven years of age.

14

the 8th, 1625, to Margaret, eldest daughter of William, Lord
Paget, of Beaudesert ; and by this lady (who was buried in
Henry the Seventh's chapel in Westminster Abbey, September
the 10th, 1652) he had several children.   His eldest son, Sir
William Hicks, the younger, received the honour of knight-
hood from King Charles the Second, upon one occasion when
His Majesty was entertained at Ruckholt after he had been
hunting in Epping Forest.   This second Sir William Hicks,
married Marthagnes, eldest daughter and co-heiress of Sir
Henry Coningsby, of North Mimms, in the County of Hertford,
Knight, by whom he had a family of thirteen children.   Sir
William Hicks, the elder, died October 15th, 1680, in the
eighty-fourth year of his age, and was buried in the chancel
at Leyton.[1]   He had suffered severely from his devotion to
the royal cause during the civil wars, and he and his son had
been compelled to alienate a considerable portion of their
estates.   He died in possession of the site and demesne of
Lenton Priory, but, four years after his decease, the property
passed, by purchase, to the Winford family.

   In 1684, Thomas Winford, Esq., second Prothonotary of the
Court of Common Pleas, together with Richard, Lord Gorges,
Peter Barwick, M.D., Robert Winford, and William Winford,
Gentlemen (who were the trustees of the marriage-settlement
of the said Thomas Winford and Sarah, his wife, daughter
and sole heiress of Michael Pearce, of Drury Lane, in the city
of Westminster, apothecary), purchased from Sir William
Hicks, of Ruckholts, in the County of Essex, Knight and
Baronet, and Dame Marthagnes, his wife, the manor of the
Priory demesne, with the site, circuit, and precinct of the
dissolved Priory of Lenton, and two messuages, three cottages,
two tofts, one water-mill, four hundred acres of arable land,
two hundred acres of meadow, one hundred acres of pasture,
and two hundred acres of furze and heath, with all due

---

(1) The two large and stately monuments in Low Leyton Church, with the effigies
of this Sir William Hicks, and his father and grand-father, which formerly stood in
the chancel, on either side of the altar, have been displaced in a recent so-called
"restoration" of the fabric, and, to the disgrace of all concerned, have been consigned
to an obscure position beneath the tower, at the west end of the church.  The
questionable taste displayed in the monuments of that period can afford no apology for
such unpardonable interference with the memorials of the dead.

appurtenances, in the parishes of Lenton and Radford. The amount of the purchase-money was £9,650.

Thomas Winford, Esq. (who was the son of Sir John Winford, a gallant and devoted royalist who attended King Charles the Second at the battle of Worcester) was created a Baronet, July the 3rd, 1702, with limitation to the heirs of his elder brother, Henry Winford, of Glasshampton, in the county of Worcester, Esquire, who had married Mercie, one of the sisters and co-heiressess of Sir Thomas Cookes, of Norgrove, in the same county, Baronet, by whom he had a son, Thomas Cookes Winford. Sir Thomas Winford, the first Baronet, died without issue, September the 22nd, 1702, less than three months after the creation of the title, and was succeeded by his nephew, above-named, who was twice married. His first wife was Beata, youngest daughter of Sir Henry Parker, of Honington, in the county of Warwickshire, Knight, and after her decease he married Elizabeth, daughter of the Rev. Thomas Wilmot, Vicar of Bromsgrove, in Worcestershire, but he had no issue by either of these ladies. Sir Thomas Cookes Winford, Bart., died January the 19th, 1743-4, and upon his death the baronetcy became extinct. His widow, Dame Elizabeth Winford, to whom the manor of the demesne of Lenton Priory and other property had passed by devise, died shortly after her husband, having bequeathed the same to her niece, Elizabeth Wilmot, who became the wife of Edward Milward, M.D. Their only daughter and heiress, Miss Elizabeth Milward, of Newman Street, in the parish of Mary-le-bone, in the county of Middlesex, first mortgaged her estates in the parishes of Lenton and Radford, and eventually sold the same for £36,000, to Thomas Pares, the younger, of the town of Leicester, and Thomas Paget,[1] of Scraptoft, in the county of Leicester, Gentlemen.

The estate was then described in the following schedule as " All that manor and lordship and site, circuit and precinct of the late dissolved Priory of Lenton, and those several closes, or grounds enclosed, situate, lying and being in the parishes of Lenton and Radford " purchased by Thomas Pares, the younger, and Thomas Paget, Gentlemen.

---

(1) These gentlemen were in partnership as bankers in the town of Leicester.

| | | | |
|---|---|---|---|
| Church-yard close (where the Priory stood) ... | 4 | 1 | 26 |
| South part of the Mill, or Great Pond, Yard ... | 0 | 3 | 14 |
| North part of the Mill Close (called about the year 1684, the Abbey Orchard, and since intersected by the Nottingham canal) ... ... | 0 | 3 | 15 |
| Five Acre Meadow (in two parts) ... ... ... | 6 | 2 | 0 |
| Messuage and Croft (being the North part of the Mill, or Great Pond, Yard) ... ... ... | 0 | 3 | 14 |
| Water-mill (formerly a Corn-mill, heretofore a Paper-mill, afterwards a Thimble-mill, and since a Leather-mill) on the river Leen | | | |
| Messuage and Croft, called Little Pond Yard ... | 0 | 1 | 25 |
| Water-mill. | | | |
| Close, heretofore divided and known as the South part of the Mill Close (formerly the Abbey Orchard) and David's Close ... ... ... | 2 | 2 | 33 |
| Nether Farnworth Close ... ... ... ... | 4 | 3 | 20 |
| East Farnworth Close ... ... ... ... | 6 | 2 | 26 |
| West Farnworth Close ... ... ... ... | 6 | 1 | 34 |
| South Farnworth Close ... ... ... ... | 4 | 1 | 3 |
| Nether Wheat Croft... ... ... ... .. | 14 | 2 | 9 |
| Leggett, or Leggett Wong ... ... ... ... | 11 | 3 | 4 |
| Prior's Meadow ... ... ... ... ... | 5 | 0 | 7 |
| Barn Close ... ... ... ... ... ... | 19 | 3 | 12 |
| Rye Close (in two parts) ... ... ... ... | 22 | 1 | 11 |
| Great Littling Meadow ... ... ... ... | 11 | 3 | 39 |
| South Littling, or Jervas's, Meadow ... ... | 6 | 1 | 6 |
| The Littling Meadow, or Littling Hook ... ... | 2 | 3 | 39 |
| South West part of Cow Close ... ... ... | 11 | 2 | 10 |
| South Alder Plantation ... ... ... ... | 0 | 3 | 27 |
| South East part of Cow Close ... .. ... | 10 | 3 | 1 |
| Small part of Cow Close with cottage ... ... | 0 | 1 | 20 |
| The Rounds, or Barley's Close ... ... ... | 8 | 13 | 0 |
| Lane Close (which in 1684 formed the more southern part of "The Greens") ... ... | 3 | 2 | 0 |
| North Gorsie Close ... ... ... ... ... | 13 | 0 | 22 |
| South Gorsie Close ... ... ... ... ... | 10 | 1 | 17 |
| Nether Littling ... ... ... ... ... | 3 | 0 | 7 |
| Middle Littling ... ... ... ... ... | 8 | 0 | 9 |
| Great Littling ... ... ... ... ... | 8 | 3 | 10 |
| North Cow Close ... ... ... ... ... | 7 | 3 | 7 |
| Second part of Cow Close ... ... ... ... | 15 | 0 | 23 |
| Northern Alder Plantation ... ... ... ... | 0 | 3 | 26 |
| West Round Close (in two parts) ... ... ... | 6 | 2 | 26 |
| Middle Round Close (in two parts) ... ... | 6 | 3 | 33 |
| East Round Close ... ... ... ... ... | 5 | 3 | 23 |
| Parcels of land occupied by the Nottingham Canal Company and by the Trent Navigation Company, with an old cottage and a garden attached ... ... ... ... ... ... | 0 | 0 | 36 |

| | | | |
|---|---|---|---|
| Old cottage and garden ... ... ... ... | 0 | 0 | 6 |
| Old cottage and garden ... ... ... ... | 0 | 0 | 3 |
| Farm-house, with Far Fan Broom Close ... ... | 9 | 0 | 12 |
| Near Fan Broom Close ... ... ... | 10 | 0 | 22 |
| Middle Broom Close (with stack-yard) ... ... | 12 | 2 | 0 |
| Near Broom, or Home Close, with farm-yard, gardens, buildings, &c. ... ... ... ... | 6 | 2 | 33 |
| Broom Close ... ... ... ... ... ... | 4 | 1 | 0 |
| Long, or Broom Meadow ... ... ... ... | 8 | 0 | 22 |
| Second Broom Close ... ... ... ... | 8 | 1 | 4 |
| Home Abbey Field ... ... ... ... ... | 11 | 1 | 9 |
| Second Abbey Field... ... ... ... ... | 12 | 1 | 18 |
| Farm, with yard and buildings ... ... ... | 1 | 1 | 11 |
| Oxhouse Close and Dog, or Day-house Close ... | 4 | 2 | 25 |
| Pingle, or Duck Meadow ... ... ... ... | 0 | 0 | 33 |
| Lane Close (formerly the Northern part of "The Greens") ... ... ... ... ... | 2 | 4 | 34 |
| Broom Meadow ... ... ... ... ... | 10 | 0 | 13 |
| Calf Close (called in 1684, Greeson's Close) ... | 4 | 2 | 28 |
| Dove-house Close ... ... ... ... ... | 10 | 3 | 11 |
| Salter Close, and Great Trin's or Terne's Close .. | 2 | 3 | 24 |
| Little Trin's, or Terne's Close ... ... ... | 1 | 0 | 0 |
| Trin's, or Terne's Close ... ... ... ... | 1 | 1 | 10 |
| Abbey Field (next Turnpike Close) or Little Abbey Field ... ... ... ... ... | 13 | 0 | 11 |
| Abbey, or Sandy Field (in two parts) ... ... | 22 | 2 | 20 |
| Lodge Field (next to the Derby Road) ... ... | 17 | 2 | 0 |
| Sand Hill and Sand Hill Field ... ... ... | 19 | 2 | 22 |
| Pitt Field (in two parts) ... ... ... ... | 11 | 0 | 0 |
| The Six Acres ... ... ... ... ... | 6 | 2 | 17 |
| Third Abbey Field ... ... ... ... ... | 17 | 2 | 12 |
| Rushy Meadow ... ... ... ... ... | 4 | 1 | 24 |
| Little Rushy Close (called in 1684, the Doe Park) | 1 | 2 | 3 |
| Turnpike Close, or Little Abbey Field ... ... | 6 | 3 | 24 |
| The Fourteen Acres (called in 1684, the High Hill Close) ... ... ... ... ... ... | 14 | 3 | 3 |
| The Fourteen Acres (called in 1684, the Lower Hill Close) ... ... ... ... ... | 14 | 0 | 29 |
| Lower Highfield, or Barn Ground ... ... ... | 7 | 0 | 22 |
| Home Field ... ... ... ... ... .. | 8 | 2 | 23 |
| South Highfield (called in 1684, the Lower Highfield Park) ... ... ... ... | 7 | 2 | 31 |
| North Highfield (called in 1684, the Lower Highfield Park, and then united with the South Highfield, the Lower Highfield, the Home Field, and probably several others) ... ... | 7 | 3 | 25 |
| North High Close ... ... ... ... ... | 4 | 2 | 29 |
| South High Close ... ... ... ... ... | 4 | 2 | 0 |
| Duck, or Gutt Meadow ... ... ... ... | 3 | 3 | 11 |

| | | | |
|---|---|---|---|
| The two Highfield Closes ... ... ... ... | 13 | 1 | 15 |
| Highfield Meadow (also forming, with the two Highfield Closes, another part of the High-field Park) ... .. ... ... ... | 3 | 0 | 2 |
| Turnpike, or Gutt Close ... ... ... ... | 7 | 2 | 0 |
| Seven Acres Meadow .. ... ... .. | 7 | 2 | 1 |
| Coal-house Close, adjoining the Bridge (called in 1684, Carleholme) ... ... ... ... | 2 | 0 | 0 |

Amounting in all to  620   0   13

And likewise "all manner of tithes, tenths, oblations, obventions, fruits and profits of every sort, &c., arising from any part of the said manor, lordship, site, circuit and precinct aforesaid."

Almost immediately after this purchase, a portion of the property lying on the southern side of the parish of Lenton was resold to Joseph Lowe, Esq., an Alderman of Nottingham, who had previously held the tenancy of some part of the same ; and other portions were afterwards purchased by John Wright, Esq., and by Matthew Needham, Esq., Thomas Wright Watson, Esq., Francis Evans, Esq., and William Stretton, Esq. These gentlemen thus seem to have become joint lords of the manor of the Priory demesne, in proportion of their several purchases, as is usual in such cases, but it does not appear that any manorial rights have been claimed in respect of this manor for many years past.

That portion of the manor of the Priory demesne, situated at the southern extremity of the parish of Lenton, nearest to Beeston, and which had been purchased by Joseph Lowe, Esquire, was known as the High-field, and here, upon a considerable elevation, overlooking the valley of the Trent and commanding an extensive and varied prospect, embracing parts of the adjoining counties of Lincoln, Leicester, and Derby, he built a plain substantial mansion, called Highfield House. The natural beauty of the situation was greatly enhanced by the number of trees which he planted, and the delightfully sylvan aspect yet retained in this part of the parish is mainly due to Mr. Lowe, and to those who subsequently followed his

example.[1]  Another feature in the Highfield estate is the
artificial lake (so well-known to skaters), which was afterwards
formed at the foot of the eminence upon which the house had
been built.  Joseph Lowe, Esquire (who was for more than
thirty years an Alderman of Nottingham, and served as Sheriff
in 1763, and filled the office of Mayor in 1787, 1797, and 1807),
died at Highfield in 1810, leaving an only son, Joseph Hurst
Lowe, Esquire, who made some additions to the property by
the purchase of adjoining lands from the Gregory family and
others.  He was father of the late Alfred Lowe, Esquire, who
was in possession of the estate for nearly forty years, and who,
throughout that period, continued to take an active part in the
affairs of the neighbourhood.[2]  "A lover of the Arts and
Sciences," so says the memoir of this gentleman in the
Transactions of the Meteorological Society, of which he was
one of the original members, "he mainly contributed to the
establishment of Amateur Musical Societies in Nottingham.
He was a nice discriminator of paintings, and his collection at
Highfield House was much esteemed by connoisseurs.[3]  Mr.
Lowe inherited considerable landed property from his ancestors.
His estate in every part displays the refined taste which he
possessed and exercised in bringing it to its present state of
beauty and perfection. . . . . Mr. Lowe was a member
of the Meteorological Society from its commencement, and
kept regular observations for many years, continuing them to
the 31st of July, 1856 (only ten days before his death).  He
also took much delight in astronomy, and built an observatory.
He was a Justice of the Peace for the county of Nottingham,
the duties connected with which demanded a great portion of
his time ; and was also appointed a Justice of the Peace for

(1) It is said that whilst the plantations were young, serious damage was done to
the trees by the mischievous youths of the neighbourhood, and that in the hopes of
saving the trees and of sparing his friends and neighbours the annoyance caused them
by this wanton mischief, the Reverend Thomas Bigsby, then Vicar of Beeston,
preached a sermon in Beeston church specially upon the subject.  With what effect
we know not !

(2) Amongst other things, he was one of the founders of the Nottingham Mechanics'
Institute, and his portrait, by Gilbert, which formerly adorned the great hall, was
unfortunately destroyed when the building was burnt down in 1867.

(3) This collection was removed from Highfield House in 1880, and is now at
Shirenewton Hall, in Monmouthshire.

the town of Nottingham, but he never acted in the latter
capacity. Had his powers of body been equal to his mind,
his usefulness would have been more extended and appreciated ;
his general kindness and benevolence won the esteem and
regard of all who had the pleasure of his acquaintance. He
died on the 10th of August, 1856, from disease of the heart."
Under his will, the Highfield estate devolved upon his son,
Edward Joseph Lowe, Esquire. This gentleman, who is known
to the world by his scientific works, was born at Highfield
House, November the 11th, 1825. As early as the year 1840,
he commenced that valuable series of daily meteorological
observations, which have been continued to the present day.
In 1846, he published "A Treatise on Atmospheric Phenomena."
About 1848, he assisted the late Professor Baden Powell in the
meteor observations for the British Association, and was the
first to point out the convergence of meteors to a point in the
heavens. "Prognostications of the Weather," a small work by
him, appeared in 1849. In 1850, he became a member of the
Meteorological Society,[1] of which he was one of the founders.
In 1853, he wrote two valuable local works, entitled "The
Climate of Nottinghamshire," and "The Conchology of Nottinghamshire." In the same year he likewise assisted the late
Professor Edward Forbes, in the compilation of his work on
"British Mollusca," and issued the first parts of the well-known
"Natural History of British and Exotic Ferns." His next
work, on "British Grasses," appeared in 1858, and he subsequently wrote two other botanical works on "Beautiful-leaved
Plants," and "New and Rare Ferns," in 1861 and 1862. His
last work is entitled the "Chronology of the Seasons." In
1860, he was one of those who accompanied the Government
expedition to Spain for the purpose of observing the solar
eclipse, and was placed in charge of the meteorological departments in the Santander district. He was also one of the first
to send daily telegrams to the Government Meteorological
Office, originally established under the care of the late Admiral
Fitzroy. In 1868, he was president of the Nottingham

---

(1) This society subsequently obtained a Royal Charter, and in the year 1883 it
became the Royal Meteorological Society.

*; family papers, &c.*

ARMS.—The ancient near Middlewich ; but this branch bear—*Argent*, on a hand engrained *gules*, the chain reflexed over the back.

Literary and Philosophical Society; and he was also for many years a vice-president of the Nottingham Mechanics' Institute, in which office he succeeded his father. Besides being the author of the works enumerated, Mr. Lowe has contributed papers on divers subjects to various learned societies, and to the British Association, and has for many years delivered occasional lectures on various scientific subjects. He was the inventor of the dry powder tests for the ozone observations used in the scientific balloon ascents. He was also the discoverer of an entirely new and distinct species of British worm, the *Megascolex Rigida (Baird)*. He has likewise devoted much time and attention to botany and horticulture, and has been the raiser of many abnormal British ferns; and was the first who was able to successfully hybridise two distinct species of British ferns, namely, *Polystichum angulare*, and *Polystichum aculeatum*. Mr. Lowe has been for many years a Justice of the Peace and Deputy-Lieutenant for Nottinghamshire, and is also a Justice of the Peace for Monmouthshire. He is a Fellow of the Royal, the Royal Astronomical, the Geological, the Linnæan, the Zoological, the Royal Horticultural, and the Royal Meteorological Societies.[1]

In 1882, the estate was purchased from Mr. Lowe by the present owner, Mr. Henry Simpson, of Nottingham, lace manufacturer.

John Wright, Esquire, by whom another portion of the Priory demesne was purchased, as already stated, likewise erected upon his estate a large mansion, formerly called Lenton House, but now known as Lenton Hall. This gentleman, who was descended from a family which had been resident in the adjacent town of Nottingham since about the conclusion of the civil wars (as is shown by the accompanying pedigree), was the head of the well-known banking establishment in Nottingham, originally commenced by his grandfather, Ichabod Wright, Esquire, in 1761, and was likewise the principal proprietor of the Butterley Ironworks, one of the most extensive concerns in this part of the kingdom. John Wright, Esquire, died at Lenton in 1840, in the eighty-second year of his age, and his eldest son having

---

(1) From "Men of the Time," with additions.

died about twelve years previously, leaving no male issue, the estate devolved upon his second son, Francis Wright, Esquire, who gave the site for the new parish church of Lenton, and served as High Sheriff for this county in 1842. He subsequently removed to Osmaston Manor, near Ashbourne, in Derbyshire, where he had erected a magnificent mansion at vast expense. He sold Lenton Hall with a portion of the estate to Digby, seventh Lord Middleton, but the remainder of the property was inherited at his death, in 1873, by his eldest son, John Wright, Esquire, who assumed the surname of Osmaston in 1876, in lieu of his patronymic. This last-named gentleman has recently disposed of the whole of his property in the parish of Lenton to various purchasers. After the purchase of Lenton Hall by Lord Middleton that mansion was occupied by tenants for more than twenty years. His lordship died unmarried in 1856, and his cousin and successor, Henry, eighth Lord Middleton, sold Lenton Hall and the surrounding lands in 1868, to Henry Smith Wright, Esquire, who resided here for several years, and eventually sold the Hall to his younger brother, Frederick Wright, Esquire, the present owner of the property. A portion of the park surrounding the mansion has been leased in detached lots, and is now being built over.

A smaller portion of the Priory demesne, lying to the west of Highfield, was purchased by Matthew Needham, of Wilford, Esquire,[1] who built thereon the mansion which is now called Lenton House. He died in 1840, and was succeeded by his eldest son, William Needham, Esquire, a Deputy-Lieutenant for this county, and Justice of the Peace for the counties of Nottingham, Derby, and Monmouth, by whom one part of this property (upon which another residence, known as Lenton Fields, had been built) was sold to the late Henry Hadden, Esquire, whilst Lenton House and the remainder of the property was sold shortly afterwards to the late William Paget, of Sutton Bonnington, Esquire, and now belongs to his eldest son, William Byerley Paget, of South Fields, in the county of Leicester, Esquire.

---

(1) He was the only surviving son of Matthew Needham, a surgeon and apothecary, of Nottingham, by Sarah, his second wife, daughter and sole heiress of William Lee, of Wilford, Gentleman.

ARMS.—(Granted in 18… chevron *argent*, three spears' heads *gules*, in chief two unicorns' head…ds, one and two, also *gules*.

CREST.—(Granted in 1…

MOTTO.—" Ad rem."

…… ; survived her husband ; died …; buried at Stowmarket.

her husband,    Other issue.
1.

…    Other issue.

Lenton Fields was sold by Henry Hadden, Esquire, to James Holwell Lee, Esquire, a magistrate for the borough of Nottingham, and from him the property is leased by the present occupier, Mr. William Heape Walker, lace manufacturer.

The mansion, known as Lenton Grove, was erected upon another portion of the Priory demesne, purchased by Francis Evans, Esquire,[1] an eminent attorney-at-law, who for some years held the office of Prothonotary of the Court of the Honour of Peverel. This gentleman died in 1815, and, having no male issue, the property ultimately devolved upon his eldest daughter and coheiress, Miss Anne Elizabeth Evans, and is now vested in her representatives. It is a somewhat remarkable fact that, with this exception, no part of the Priory demesne continues in the possession of the descendants of those gentlemen who purchased the various portions when the manor of the Priory demesne was divided in the latter part of the last century.

The portion purchased by Thomas Wright Watson, Esquire, lay on the north-east side of the Lenton Hall estate, and upon it was built the mansion called Lenton Firs. This property was purchased by Henry, sixth Lord Middleton, and the house was for many years occupied by tenants. Henry, eighth Lord Middleton, sold Lenton Firs to Thomas Adams, Esquire, a Justice of the Peace for the county of Nottingham, and also for the borough, who resided here until his decease in 1873. This gentleman, who was a native of Sible Hedingham, in Essex, and an extensive lace manufacturer in Nottingham, obtained a grant of these armorial bearings : *Vert*, a cross parted and fretty between two mullets in the first and fourth, and as many cinquefoils in the second and third quarters,

(1) Through his mother this gentleman was one of the representatives of a branch of the old Nottinghamshire family of Hacker. His father, Robert Evans, an attorney-at-law, residing at Thurland Hall, in Nottingham, had married Dorothy, daughter and sole heiress of the Rev. Henry Francis, by Dorothy, his wife, one of the daughters and coheiresses of John Hacker, of Trowell, Gent., who died in 1735, and was the last male heir of that branch of the family.

*or*. Crest—A talbot passant *sable*, semeé of cinquefoils *or*, supporting with the dexter foot a mullet of the last. His widow occupied the mansion for upwards of a year, and upon her death the property passed to her second son, John Adams, Esquire, who subsequently sold it to William Lambert, Esquire, an Alderman of Nottingham.

This mansion was at one time occupied by the late John Storer, Esquire, M.D., F.R.S., the first president (1816-1819) of the Nottingham Subscription Library, where a full-length portrait of this gentleman, by Barber, of Nottingham, may be seen on the staircase.[1]  Lenton Firs is now occupied by Edward Cope, Esquire.

William Stretton, Esquire, who purchased that portion of the demesne close, by the site of the Priory, built thereon a mansion, which he designated "The Priory," and which seems to occupy pretty nearly the site of the Prior's lodgings. Mr. Stretton was the eldest son of Mr. Samuel Stretton, who removed from Longdon, in Staffordshire,[2] to Lenton, early in the year 1750 (being married at Lenton, July 14th, 1754, to Elizabeth Wombwell, the daughter of a wealthy yeoman resident in this parish), and subsequently resided at Standard Hill, Nottingham, where he carried on the business of an architect and builder. His son, Mr. William Stretton, also practised for several years as an architect in Nottingham, and was engaged in the erection of many of the public and private buildings in that town, amongst which were the Borough Gaol and St. James's Church. Mr. Stretton, in conjunction with his father, built the Barracks in Nottingham Park, occupying four acres; they were finished by contract in sixteen weeks. The grand stand on the race-course was built by the Messrs. Stretton, Mr. John Carr, of York, being the architect. Mr. William Stretton also built Lord Middleton's Park Gateway in 1790;

---

(1) At the first meeting held at Thurland Hall, Nottingham, March 4th, 1816, to promote this library, John Wright, Esquire, of Lenton Hall, occupied the chair, Dr. Storer taking the most active part in its formation.

(2) "The Strettons resided for centuries at Longdon, in Staffordshire, where my grandfather (and father) was born to good property, which the former dissipated, and obliged the latter to leave Longdon, from whence he came into Notts., 1750."— *Stretton MSS.*, No. 31, f. 41.

improved, or in part built, Mr. William Gregory Williams' house at Rempstone in 1792; and built the Riding School, near the Castle, in 1798. The first stone of the seven arch bridge on the Flood Road, Nottingham, was laid by Mr. Stretton, September 15th, 1796, and the bridge was completed by him in the following year. Mr. Stretton also built the first boat (the "Nottingham Castle," 67 feet in length, and carrying 70 tons) on the Nottingham Canal, in 1796. The first cargo of slates from Lord Penrhyn's quarries at Llandegai, in Carnarvonshire, were brought to Nottingham, in 1790, by Mr. Stretton, and were the first introduced into this part of the country.[1] Mr. Stretton also restored St. Mary's and St. Peter's churches, Nottingham, and his own parish church at Lenton.

Mr. Stretton had a taste in articles of *vertu*, of which, at the time of his death, he possessed an extensive museum, at all times open to the inspection of persons of a kindred taste. For several years previous to his decease, his leisure time had been principally employed in the collection of materials (many of which are still extant) for a work on the History and Antiquities of Nottinghamshire. A collection of old documents known as the *Stretton MSS.*, with two or three drawings, are preserved in the Free Public Library, Nottingham. This gentleman made a series of excavations, which will be hereafter alluded to, on the site of Lenton Priory, with the view of ascertaining its ground plan, but the notes which, doubtless, were made at the time, are, unfortunately, not to be found amongst Mr. Stretton's papers. During his residence at Lenton, Mr. Stretton took an active interest in all public matters, and filled the several parish offices in an efficient manner. Mr. Stretton left Lenton Priory, and went to reside on Standard Hill, Nottingham, June 25th, 1814,[2] and was residing there in August, 1817, in which month he visited Paris and Rouen, going by Dover and Calais, and returning by Dieppe and Brighton.[3] He appears to have returned to Lenton Priory, where he died on the 12th of

---

(1) *Stretton MSS.*, No. 32, f. 21.
(2) *Stretton MSS.*, No. 29, f. 5.          (3) *Ibid*, No. 34.

March, 1828, in the 73rd year of his age, and was interred in the churchyard at Lenton. His death is thus announced in a local newspaper :—" On Wednesday, the 12th inst., in the 73rd year of his age, after a long and painful affliction, sustained with true Christian fortitude and resignation, William Stretton, Esq., of Lenton Priory. Words would but faintly convey the deep grief which his irreparable loss has occasioned to those who knew his worth. In him antiquarians have lost a fund of general and useful knowledge, and the poor a warm and benevolent friend."[1] By his wife, Susanna, the daughter of Mr. William Lynham, of Eakring, in this county, he left, with other issue, two sons, each of whom attained much distinction in the army.

Lieutenant-Colonel Sempronius Stretton, eldest son of Mr. William Stretton, was born at Nottingham on the 15th May, 1781. He entered the army at an early age, commencing his military career in the Nottinghamshire Militia,[2] which he joined at Dumfries, in April, 1800. In the following November, he entered the 6th Regiment of Foot as an ensign, joining the depôt of that regiment at Chatham. In the following April, he was promoted to a lieutenancy in the 49th Regiment, and, shortly afterward, sailed with it to Quebec. In this regiment, Lieutenant Stretton served under Colonel Brock, who generally selected him to act as his aide-de-camp in his visits to the upper country to distribute presents, or meet the Indian Chiefs in council. Having been promoted to a company in the 40th Regiment, he returned to England, and was employed for some time on the recruiting service. In 1812, Captain Stretton sailed for Lisbon, where he met his only brother, then an ensign in the 68th Light Infantry, and the two brothers proceeded to join the army under Lord Wellington. Captain Stretton's first engagement with the enemy was at the battle of Vittoria, June 21st, 1813. The regiment afterwards took an active part in the investment of Pampeluna, and the numerous brilliant actions during the passage of the Pyrenees ;

---

(1) *Nottingham Journal*, March 15th, 1828.

(2) This regiment, afterwards so well known as the Royal Sherwood Foresters, is now disguised under the title of the 4th Battalion of the Derbyshire Regiment.

and on July 28th, 1813, Captain Stretton received the thanks
of Lord Wellington, conveyed to him through H.R.H. the
Prince of Orange, for the gallant defence made by the 40th,
under his command, supported by two Portuguese regiments,
in defending the key of the position on the heights before
Pampeluna, against an overwhelming force of the enemy.  For
this service Captain Stretton was awarded the gold medal, and
received the brevet rank of major.  He was present in the
numerous actions with the enemy, which terminated in the
battle of Toulouse, and the abdication of Napoleon.  When
the army was withdrawn from France, he accompanied the
40th in the expedition to New Orleans, in 1814, and narrowly
escaped with his life when shipwrecked, with part of his corps,
in the *Baring* transport, in Bantry Bay, on the 10th October ;
on which occasion all the baggage was lost, and many soldiers
drowned.  Having returned to Cork, Major Stretton again
sailed, in the *Wellington* transport, and arrived in the Mississippi
on January 9th, 1815.  The disastrous results of that unfortunate
expedition are too well known to require recapitulation here.
The troops returned to Portsmouth ; and the 40th, with other
regiments, proceeded to Flanders, and joined the army assembled
near Brussels, in time to share in the memorable victory of
Waterloo.  On the arrival of the allies in Paris, Lord Wellington, in acknowledgment of Major Stretton's services, appointed
him commandant of the 5th Arondissement of that city, which
post he held for a considerable time.  He also obtained the
brevet rank of lieutenant-colonel.  When the British troops
were withdrawn from France, Lieutenant-Colonel Stretton, with
his regiment, was quartered successively both in Scotland and
Ireland.  On the corps being ordered for service in New South
Wales, he retired on half-pay, and passed several years in
travelling on the Continent, returning occasionally to his
residence at Lenton.  His military services obtained for him
the rank of colonel, and the companionship of the Order of
the Bath.  He received the gold medal, as before stated, for
the battle of the Pyrenees, and the silver medal for Waterloo,
but died before the Peninsular medal was granted.  Colonel
Stretton had the good fortune to escape being wounded in the

various actions in which he was engaged,[1] but he had one of his epaulettes shot away in the Pyrenees, and his charger was wounded at Toulouse ; he had also a horse killed at Waterloo. For many years, Colonel Stretton was a much-honoured guest at the annual banquet given by the Duke of Wellington on the anniversary of the battle of Waterloo, and a portrait of him is to be found in Salter's celebrated painting of that scene. Colonel Stretton was an able draughtsman, and during his services in Canada, and travels on the Continent, made many valuable contributions to his father's extensive museum. He was twice married ; first, in 1821, to the Honourable Catherine Jane Massey, daughter of General the Right Hon. Nathaniel William, second Lord Clarina, who died shortly after marriage. He married, secondly, the Honourable Anne Handcock, daughter of the second Viscount Castlemaine, but had no issue by either of these ladies. Colonel Stretton died at Croydon, February 6th, 1842, in the 62nd year of his age, and was buried in Bromley churchyard, in Kent, where a plain monument marks his last resting place.[2]

Lieutenant-Colonel Severus William Lynham Stretton, who is still living, was the second son of Mr. William Stretton. Evincing an early desire for the profession of arms, a commission was obtained for him in the Nottinghamshire Militia, which he joined at Plymouth, in 1810, and accompanied the regiment to Ireland. In 1812 he obtained an ensigncy in the 68th Light Infantry, and joined the regiment in Portugal. Having been severely wounded at the battle of Vittoria, by two musket balls, lodged in the body, he was removed, in a very precarious state, to England ; prior to this, one of the balls was extracted, but the other, at different periods, has been a source of great trouble and pain, relieved only by severe surgical operations. The excellent nursing and skilful medical treatment he received, whilst at his father's house at Lenton, restored him so far that in the course of twelve months afterwards he was enabled to rejoin his regiment, then stationed in Ireland. He accompanied

---

(1) The verse adapted from the 140th Psalm, engraved upon his cenotaph in the old churchyard at Lenton (vide post), was evidently chosen in allusion to this.

(2) Bailey's *Annals of Nottinghamshire*, iv. 431.

the same regiment to Canada in 1818, and in 1825 was promoted to an unattached company; shortly after which he exchanged
to the 64th regiment, and joined it at Gibraltar. He succeeded
to the lieutenant-colonelcy and command of this regiment in
1842, having accompanied it to the West Indies and Novia
Scotia, from whence he returned with it in 1843. Lieutenant-
Colonel Stretton, in 1848, exchanged to his brother's old
regiment, the 40th, of which he retained the command until
June, 1852. He was subsequently lieutenant-colonel of the
Hampshire Militia. He was awarded the Peninsular medal,
and he is also in receipt of a government pension for wounds.
He inherited the Lenton property from his brother, but never
resided there. In October, 1851, Lieutenant-Colonel Stretton
married the Honourable Catherine Adela de Courcy, youngest
daughter of the 28th Lord Kingsale.[1]

The arms used by this family are—
*Argent*, a bend engrailed *sable*, plain
cotised *gules*.

"The Priory" is now occupied by the
Sisters of Nazareth, as a house of refuge
for the aged, sick, and infantine poor
of the neighbourhood, without reference
to sex or creed.

Another portion of the Priory demesne, lying near to the
western extremity of the parish, and which appears to have
been sold off at an earlier period, was purchased from Henry,
eighth Lord Middleton, by the late Mr. Thomas Bayley, the
proprietor of the extensive fellmongery establishment at Lenton.
This part has been known for at least two centuries as "the
Abbey fields," and there was an old house here, which has been
conjectured to have been originally the grange, or farmstead of
the monastery. Some part of this old house still remains
incorporated with the mansion known as Lenton Abbey, which
was built towards the close of the last century by Thomas
Green, Esquire. The thickness of the walls in the old part
sufficiently attest the antiquity of the work. Lenton Abbey
is now the property of Mrs. Bayley.

---

(1) Bailey, *Annals of Nottinghamshire*, iv. 433.

Previous to the division of the manor in the last century, small portions of the Priory demesne seem to have been granted to various persons by the Crown from time to time. Several of these were ultimately purchased by the Nix family, who thus obtained a moderate estate in this parish.

By an indenture, dated August the 17th, 1613, a certain cottage in Lenton was conveyed to Leonard Nix, of the town of Nottingham, merchant, by John Kilborne, of Lenton, baker, which cottage had been granted by King James the First, by letters patent, dated February the 7th, 1606, to Roger Howtone, of Lenton, for the term of forty years, and had been conveyed by him to William Stephenson, of Lenton, weaver, who had reconveyed the same to the said John Kilborne. By another indenture, dated May the 18th, 1614, Richard Willoughby, of Lenton, Gentleman, and James Wolffe, of the town of Nottingham, skinner, together conveyed to John Atkinson, of the town of Nottingham, Gentleman, and to George Ryley, of the same town, chandler, for the proper use of Susanna Burbage, of Lenton, widow, and of the said Leonard Nix, a cottage with a garden and one rood of meadow in Lenton, which had been granted and let to farm by Queen Elizabeth, by letters patent, dated July 24th, 1601, to Thomas Cooper, late of Porkington, in the county of Salop, Gentleman, and Philip Hanmer, and Thomas Hanmer, both of Radford, Gentlemen, who had sold the same, August the 20th, 1610, to Gervase Annesley, of Ruddington, Esquire, and William Gregory,[1] of the town of Nottingham, Gentleman, from whom the cottage and lands had been purchased, January the 6th, 1611, by the said Richard Willoughby and James Wolffe. By another indenture, dated April the 6th, 1615, Francis Small, of Newark-upon-Trent, Gentleman, conveyed to the said Leonard Nix a certain messuage with a garden and one close, containing about an acre; two oxgangs of arable land, and six acres of meadow in Lenton, the whole of which had been granted by King James the First,

---

[1]—This gentleman, who was Town Clerk, and represented the borough of Nottingham in several Parliaments, must not be confounded with Alderman William Gregory, who purchased the manor of Lenton in 1630, nor were the two families in any way related. The above-named William Gregory died in 1616. Thoroton says he was "related to those of that name now seated at Barneby-on-Dun, in Yorkshire."

by letters patent, dated at Westminster, February the 8th, 1612, to John Eldred and William Whitmore, of the city of London, Esquires, for threescore years, at an annual rent of twenty-four shillings, and which had been sold by them, June the 10th, that same year, to Thomas Gonnyson, of Radford, Gentleman, from whom the same had been purchased by the said Francis Small. By another indenture, dated April the 30th, 1615, George Kirke, of Lenton, conveyed to the said Leonard Nix a cottage in Lenton, which had been granted by King James the First, by letters patent, dated May the 11th, 1610, to the said John Eldred and William Whitmore, Esquires, for threescore years, and had been sold by them on the day following to Francis Matthew, of Lenton, yeoman, who conveyed the same, October the 10th, that same year, to the said George Kirke. By another indenture, dated May the 24th, 1617, William Rodes, the son and heir of Robert Rodes,[1] of Lenton, conveyed to the said Leonard Nix, on the death of his father, another cottage, with a garden and one acre of meadow in Lenton, which had been granted by King James the First, by letters patent, dated February the 7th, 1606, to Roger Howtone, of Lenton, for the term of forty years, and which he had sold to the said Robert Rodes. By another indenture, dated June the 27th, 1617, John Brodbent, of Stapleford, Gentleman, conveyed to the said Leonard Nix another cottage, with a garden and croft and one acre and a half of meadow in Lenton, which had been granted by King James the First, by letters patent, dated March the 14th, 1611, to the said John Eldred and William Whitmore, Esquires, for threescore years, and by them conveyed, February the 1st, 1612, to the said John Brodbent.

Leonard Nix, by whom all these small portions of the Priory demesne were thus acquired, was Sheriff of Nottingham in 1591, and Mayor in 1617, 1624, and 1631. By his indenture, dated January the 1st, 1633, he conveyed all his lands and tenements in Lenton, as above recited, to William Nix, of Nottingham,

---

(1) From the procceedings in Chancery in the reign of Queen Elizabeth, it appears that there was a suit between Robert Rodes and John Seywell and Margaret his wife, whereby the first-named claimed a certain messuage and land in Lenton, held for a term of years by John Rodes, father of the plaintiff, and by him devised to the said plaintiff, and to the defendant, Margaret Seywell, who seems to have been the widow of the said John Rodes.

merchant, and Richard Hardmeat, of the same town, skinner, for the sum of £200.

This William Nix,[1] who was doubtless of the same family, though his precise relationship with Leonard Nix has not been seen, was also an Alderman of Nottingham ; he was Sheriff in 1619, and Mayor in 1636, 1643, 1644, and 1649.   He was son of Robert Nix, of Wilford, and was married at Barton-in-Fabis, February the 4th, 1615-16, to Mrs. Millicent Sacheverell, by whom he had several daughters, and an only son, Robert,[2] who left no male issue.   Alderman William Nix died in September, 1650, and was buried in St. Peter's Church, Nottingham.   Upon his decease, the whole of his property in this parish, including freehold lands which he had purchased, passed under settlement to his eldest daughter, Tabitha, who had married Thomas Charlton, of Chilwell, Esquire, High Sheriff of this county in 1667.   Their grandson, Thomas Charlton, Esquire, who died unmarried in 1703, barred the entail of a portion of the family estates, and re-settled them upon his half-brother, and the heirs of his body, with remainder, in default of issue, to his four sisters and their heirs.   His half-brother, Nicholas Charlton, Esquire, who was the last male representative of the elder branch of the Charltons of Chilwell Hall, died unmarried in 1748, when the Lenton property passed to Miss Rebecca Garland and her sister, Lucy, the wife of George Brentnall, of the town of Derby, Gentleman. These ladies were the only surviving daughters of John Garland, of Lenton, Gentleman, by Lucy, his wife, one of the four sisters of the above-named Thomas Charlton, of Chilwell, Esquire. This John Garland, who had inherited a small estate in this parish from his father, had died in 1721, and the elder daughter, Rebecca (whose benefaction to the poor of Lenton will be elsewhere referred to), having died unmarried in 1769, the whole

---

(1) Alderman William Nix resided in an old mansion in Bridlesmith Gate, Nottingham, on the site subsequently occupied by the Post Office. This mansion afterwards belonged to the Charlton family.

(2) Sarah, only daughter and heiress of the above named Robert Nix, was married in 1676 to Thomas Grimsditch, of Grimsditch Hall, in the county of Chester, Esquire, but it does not appear that either this lady or her husband possessed any interest in the parish of Lenton.

# Pedigree of Garland, of Lenton.

*(From Major Lawson Lowe's MS. Collections.)*

ARMS.[1]—Paly of six *or* and *gules*, a chief per pale of the second and *azure*, in the dexter chief a demi-lion rampant issuant, and in the sinister chief a garland, both of the first.

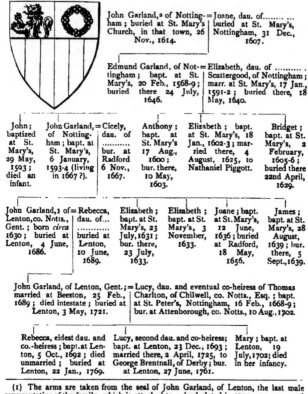

| | |
|---|---|
| John Garland,[2] of Nottingham; buried at St. Mary's Church, in that town, 26 Nov., 1614. | = Joane, dau. of......... ... buried at St. Mary's, Nottingham, 31 Dec., 1607. |

| | |
|---|---|
| Edmund Garland, of Nottingham; bapt. at St. Mary's, 20 Feb., 1568-9; buried there 24 July, 1646. | = Elizabeth, dau. of .......... Scattergood, of Nottingham; marr. at St. Mary's, 17 Jan., 1591-2; buried there, 18 May, 1640. |

| John; baptized at St. Mary's, 29 May, 1593; died an infant. | John Garland, of Nottingham; bapt. at St. Mary's, 6 January, 1593-4 (living in 1667 ?). | = Cicely, dau. of .......... bur. at Radford 6 Nov., 1667. | Anthony; bapt. at St. Mary's 17 Aug., 1600; bur. there, 10 May, 1603. | Elizabeth; bapt. at St. Mary's, 18 Jan., 1602-3; married there, 4 August, 1625, to Nathaniel Piggott. | Bridget; bapt. at St. Mary's, 2 February, 1605-6; buried there 22nd April, 1629. |
|---|---|---|---|---|---|

| John Garland,[3] of Lenton, co. Notts., Gent.; born *circa* 1630; buried at Lenton, 4 June, 1686. | = Rebecca, dau. of... .......... buried at Lenton, 10 June, 1689. | Elizabeth; bapt. at St. Mary's, 23 July,1631; bur. there, 23 July, 1633. | Elizabeth; bapt. at St. Mary's, 3 November, 1633. | Joane; bapt. 12 June, 1636; buried at Radford 18 May, 1656. | James; bapt. at St. Mary's, 28 June, 1639; bur. there, 5 Sept.,1639. |
|---|---|---|---|---|---|

| | |
|---|---|
| John Garland, of Lenton, Gent.; married at Beeston, 25 Feb., 1689; died intestate; buried at Lenton, 3 May, 1721. | = Lucy, dau. and eventual co-heiress of Thomas Charlton, of Chilwell, co. Notts., Esq.; bapt. at St Peter's, Nottingham, 16 Feb., 1668-9; bur. at Attenborough, co. Notts., 10 Aug.,1702. |

| Rebecca, eldest dau. and co.-heiress; bapt. at Lenton, 5 Oct., 1692; died unmarried; buried at Lenton, 22 Jan., 1769. | Lucy, second dau. and co-heiress; bapt. at Lenton, 23 Dec., 1693; married there, 2 April, 1725, to George Brentnall, of Derby; bur. at Lenton, 27 June, 1761. | Mary; bapt. at Lenton, 19 July,1702; died in her infancy. |
|---|---|---|

(1) The arms are taken from the seal of John Garland, of Lenton, the last male representative of the family, which is attached to a deed, dated in 1702, now preserved amongst the documents at Chilwell Hall.

(2) He was very probably a son of Anthony Garland, Sheriff of Nottingham in 1530, though evidence of this is wanting. In 1594, the will of William Towle, of Nottingham, was proved in the Prerogative Court of York by Francis Wynfield and John Garland, his executors.

(3) There is reason to believe that this John Garland may have been twice married, for the registers of St. Peter's, Nottingham, record the burial of " Alice, wife of John Garland, of Nottingham Castle, Gentᵐ.," September the 13th, 1658. If so, this must have been his first wife, and she must have died within a year or two after her marriage, and assumably without issue. That John Garland should be described as "of Nottingham Castle" is a little remarkable. It is possible that after the garrison had been disbanded, part of the Castle was converted into one or more dwelling houses; or John Garland may have held some appointment in connection with the Castle during the Commonwealth.

property passed to the Brentnall family. Thomas Brentnall, of Spondon, in the county of Derby, Gentleman, sold his estate in Lenton to a Derby attorney, named Upton, for an annuity ; and about the year 1800 the entire estate was sold off in detached lots. The Right Honourable Lord Middleton and John Wright, Esquire, were the principal purchasers, and it is stated that sixteen acres of land purchased at this time by the latter, were re-sold in the year 1815 at a rate of £1,000 per acre, at least ten times the amount which had been given for it only about fifteen years previously.[1] The village of New Lenton now occupies the whole of this. The old house where the Garland family resided seems to have been used in the earlier part of the present century as the village poor-house.

Many grants of portions of the possessions of the Priory in other places were made at intervals during the century succeeding its dissolution :—

On the 3rd of February, in the 30th year of Henry VIII. the site of Kersall cell was (int. al.) leased to John Wood for 21 years, at £11 6s. 8d. per annum.[2]

On the 24th of July, in the 32nd year of the same reign, the site of the cell was granted to Baldwin Willoughby, Esquire,[3] and was sold by him to Ralph Kenion, of Gorton, who, on the 10th of September, in the 2nd year of Edward VI., conveyed two parts of the cell, manor, and demesne lands to Richard Siddall, of Withington, and James Chetham, of Crumpsall, gent., for £248.[4]

The cell finally passed to the Byroms, though not without some litigation,[5] and was for many years the residence of Miss

---

(1) Bailey's *Annals of Nottinghamshire*, p. 555.

(2) *Mon. Ang.*, v. 115.

(3) Baldwin Willoughby, who was presumably the second son of Baldwin Willoughby, of Grendon, in Northamptonshire, was a naval commander, and in 1522 kept the seas between Cambre and the Channel Islands.

(4) *Notitia Cestriensis* (Chetham Soc.), vol. ii., pt. i., p. 69.

(5) John Byrom, the poet-stenographer, of Manchester, resided at Kersall Cell for several years. He was the younger son of Mr. Edward Byrom, of Kersall Cell, and Hydes Cross, Manchester (descended from Ralph Byrom, of Salford, 15—), and was baptized February 29th, 1691-2. He was sent to Merchant Taylors' School, London, and was admitted thence to Trinity College, Cambridge, July 6th, 1708. He took his B.A. degree in 1711, and proceeded M.A. in 1715, having been elected a fellow of his college in the previous year. After studying physic at Montpellier, he married, February 14th, 1720-1, his cousin, Elizabeth (daughter of Joseph Byrom, of

Atherton, a descendant of that family. Coffins and bones have been found on the site.[1] Considerable alterations have been made in the residence from time to time, but there are still the remains of the old chapel, and of the black and white house. A portion of the wall exposed to view is of wattle and daub. In an upper room are some antique mouldings of the arms of the Byroms, *Argent*, a chevron between three hedge-hogs, *sable*. The house, which is now occupied as a ladies' school, is furnished throughout in accordance with its ancient character.

The Corporation of Nottingham having petitioned the King (Henry VIII.) to grant them the advowson of the church of Barton-in-Fabis, a commission of inquiry was appointed, the result being that the King, February 19th, 1542, granted the advowson to the Archbishop of York, with whom it still remains, the rectory being charged with an annual pension of five shillings to the King.[2] This payment appears to have been subsequently transferred, for, at the present time "five shillings per annum is paid out of the Rectory as a fee farm rent to the Duke of Leeds."[3]

The same King "in consideration of the good, true, faithful, and acceptable services of his beloved and faithful servant Francis Leek, Knight, to him before these times in many ways performed," granted to the same Sir Francis, March 23, 1544, certain lands at Holme, Dunston, Whitwell, and Ledwort, in the High Peak, lately belonging to Lenton Priory.

The manor of Newthorpe, with divers lands there, lately

---

Byrom Hall, Esq.), and commenced to give instructions in the system of shorthand-writing which bears his name. He was elected a Fellow of the Royal Society in 1723. On the death, in 1740, of his elder brother, Edward, he succeeded to the family estate of Kersall. Byrom was the author of the well-known hymn, "Christians, Awake," and was "generally admired for his entertaining productions and un-common flow of genius ; nor was he less esteemed on account of his humanity, extensive benevolence, and universal charity." "This great and good man " died, September 26th, 1763, aged 72 years, and was buried in the Byrom Chapel in the Collegiate Church, now the Cathedral, of Manchester. His eldest daughter, Elizabeth, who died unmarried at Kersall Cell, December 2nd, 1801, was the author of the Journal of the visit of the Pretender to Manchester in 1745. *Vide* "The Private Journal and Literary Remains of John Byrom," forming vols. xxxii., xxxiv., xl., and xliv., of the publications of the Chetham Society, and "The Palatine Note Book," ii., 96.

(1) Aitken's *Manchester*, 1795, p. 209.

(2) Harl. MSS., 6969, p. 39.        (3) Terrier of Barton-in-Fabis.

belonging to Lenton Priory, was granted, July 13, 1545, to John and George Mylle.[1]

King Edward the Sixth, July 13, 1547, granted the Rectory of Rushden, in Northamptonshire, to the Master and College of the Virgin Mary and All Saints at Fotheringay, in that county.[2]

The advowson of the church of Linby was granted, August 6, 1548, to Robert Strelley, Esquire, and Frideswide, his wife.[3]

In 1552 the advowson of the church of Harleston was granted to Edward Lord Clinton and Saye, in exchange for manors and lands conveyed to the Crown, and in compensation for former grants which were rendered void by having been previously granted to other persons.[4]

King Philip and Queen Mary, May 31, 1557, granted to Thomas White, and Agnes, his wife, and the heirs of the former, the manor of Cotgrave, with its appurtenances.[5]

The reversion of the herbage and pannage of Aspley Wood, in the parish of Radford, parcel of the manor of Lenton, demised to Edward Southworth, gentleman, for 21 years, was granted (*int. al.*) August 6th, 1564. to Richard Pype, of London, leather-seller, and Francis Boyer, of the same place, grocer.[6]

Queen Elizabeth, January 29 1574. granted to John Dudley and John Aiscough, the tithes in the parish of Langar, in the tenure of Sir John Chaworth, of Wiverton, Knight, at £12 per annum.[7]

In 1575, a messuage in Bradmore, lately part of the Priory possessions, was granted by royal letters patent to Roger Manners.[8]

On February 27th, in the same year, the Queen granted to Anthony Rotsey, and William Fisher, a messuage and seven bovates of land, another messuage with a croft, and a toft and half a bovate, in Keyworth, in the occupation of John Sewell and others.[9]

---

(1) Thoroton, p. 238.        (2) Ibid., p 35.        (3) Ibid., p. 259.

(4) Bridge's *Northamptonshire*, I., 514.

(5) Thoroton, p. 83.        (6) Ibid., p. 219.

(7) Thoroton, p. 105.        (8) Ibid., p. 49.        (9) Ibid., p. 42.

The same Queen also granted, March 15, 1577, to Richard Ouseley, Esquire, Clerk of the Privy Seal, the manor of Courtenhall, in the county of Northampton, at the yearly rent of £30; with the reversion after Margaret, John, and Richard Clarke, of two tenements with land thereto belonging, at the yearly rent of £2 5s. 4d.; also three tenements with land at the yearly rent of £2 5s. 6d.; with hedgebote, firebote, plough-bote, and carbote; also the office of bailiff and rent-collector of lands of the late monastery of Lenton, in reversion after Richard Conyers, for twenty-one years, commencing 1611, at an annual fee of forty shillings.[1]

In 1587, the rectory and tithes of Foston, in Leicestershire, were demised by Queen Elizabeth, for twenty-one years, to Thomas Ryale, at the annual rent of thirteen shillings and four-pence.[2]

The same Queen, on June 17th, 1599, granted to Henry Pierrepont, all the tithes of corn in Nottingham and Sneinton formerly belonging to Lenton Priory, and then valued at £20 a year.[3]

King James the First, by letters patent dated at Westminster, June 2, 1614, granted to Sir Edward Palmer, Knight, and Benjamin Harris, gent., their heirs and assigns, *int. al.*, the Manor of Radford, with all its appurtenances.

The documentary history of the Priory buildings is of the most fragmentary description, only two contemporary references to the conventual buildings having been met with. Thoroton[4] quotes a charter of Robert de Passeys, already referred to, by which he gave fifteen acres of his demesne lands in Sutton Passeys to the Prior and Convent towards the building of the church of the Holy Trinity of Lenton. This charter is undated, but it must have been about the earlier part of the reign of Henry the Second. The other reference is of much later date. Sir William Babington, of Chilwell, whose will is dated October 3rd, 1454, desires to be buried in the Priory Church of Lenton, within the Chapel of St. Mary, then newly built. From the

---

(1) *State Papers, Domestic*, 1566-1579, p. 510.

(2) Nichol's *Leicestershire*, iv. 172.          (3) Thoroton, p. 277.

(4) Thoroton's *Antiquities of Nottinghamshire*, p. 220.

first, it is evident that the erection of the church had not been completed in the time of Henry the Second. It seems probable that Peverel would erect a range of buildings for the monks, and a portion—most likely the choir—of the conventual church. It was the custom in all the orders first to build an oratory of the church, upon such a plan that the cloister and surrounding buildings could conveniently be added thereto. Further endowments would furnish the means for, as more monks would necessitate, additional accommodation ; the church would, therefore, be further enlarged, and a corresponding extension made of the conventual buildings. The recent discovery of a quantity of carved stones belonging to the Perpendicular period, show that this was evidently the case at Lenton.

Immediately on the dissolution of the monasteries, they were in most instances, partially, if not completely, demolished. The grantee of Repton, in Derbyshire, in a single Sunday pulled down that noble church ;[1] and the method adopted, and the time occupied in demolishing the conventual church of Lewes, the principal monastery of the Clugniac Order in England, are detailed in a contemporary letter of the year 1537.[2] The King's Commissioners appear to have issued general instructions for the destruction of such conventual buildings as could not be converted into farm buildings.[3] This general destruction was taken advantage of by the populace, who appropriated whatever materials they could lay their hands on, the result being that in many instances the grantees of monastic buildings placed persons in charge to sell the ready-worked stones to the best advantage. This probably would be the case at Lenton, for the absence of building stone in the neighbourhood, and the

---

(1) *Mon. Ang.* vi. 429.

(2) " Letters relating to the Suppression of the Monasteries," Camden Soc , p. 180.

(3) John Freeman, writing to the Lord Privy Seal about the razing of the abb. ys in Lincolnshire, says :—" The King's Commission commandeth me to pull down to the grounde all the walls of the Churches, stepulls, cloysters, fraterys, dorters, chapter howsys, with all other howys, saveyng them that be necessary for a farmer," the charge of doing this, he continues, would be so great that he thinks it would be best to take down the bells and lead and pull down the roofs and battlements and stairs, and " lete the wallis stande, and charge som with them 'as a quarre of ston to make salys of as they that hath nede will fetche." Sir Henry Ellis' *Original Letters*, 3rd series, vol. iii., p. 269.

exceedingly scanty remains, warrant the supposition that it was utilized as a stone quarry.

We have no evidence of the demolition of the conventual buildings prior to 1551, when Sir Richard Sackville wrote to the porter of the King's Castle of Nottingham, on the 11th of May, directing him to deliver the lead in his custody at Nottingham Castle to William Hever, servant to the Earl of Wiltshire, Lord High Treasurer, to be removed to London for the King's use. On the 13th of the same month, the Earl of Wiltshire and the Earl of Rutland addressed letters to John Pottes, porter of Nottingham Castle, to the same effect. From a curious letter, dated March 5th, 1555, and written by William Bolles, of Osberton, the Receiver General of the County of Nottingham, to Thomas Mildmay, Esquire, we find that the lead in question came from Lenton Priory. It appears that there were 198 fodders of lead[1] removed from Lenton to Nottingham Castle, of which only 160 fodders had been delivered by Pottes to Hever. The conversation between Bolles and Pottes as to the deficiency in the quantity of lead removed to London, is detailed in the following quaint letter[2] :—

Right worshipfull S$^r$ I have sins [     ] byn att Nottingham Castell and have declared to John Pottes porter their that ther was lefte of the leade of the late attaynted monastery of lenton c$^{xx}$iiij xviij fodres, whereof ther was delyv'd to W. Hever but clx fodres And so there shuld yet & now remayne xxxviij fodres. who made answer he delyverd all that ther was And that ther is none remaynyng Then I demanded of hym how moche he delyv'd he said he coulde not tell noweghther what waight nor yet how many p'cels and it was not waide. To whom I said so ye myght delyv'r cc fodres and he or they who receyved it myght (if they wold) say the receyved but one hundrith fodres And this not w$^t$standyng I cowde have none other answer than I had before. Then I demanded of hym the sight of the l'rs of my Lord Tresaurer my L of Ruthland and M$^r$ Chauncellors. he made answer he had now found theym & shewed theym to me Whereof I toke the true copies w$^{ch}$ I have sent unto you herynclosed And wheras I persayved in the said M$^r$ Chauncellors l're one clause (amonge others) $^w_w$ That his l're togither w$^h$ a book of the contents & just waight of the same Lead. so by hym

---

(1) A fodder of lead varies, according to local custom, from 19½ to 22½ cwt.

(2) This curious correspondence is now preserved in the Public Record Office.

to be delyv'd should be his sufficient warrant & discharge for
the delyvry of the same.   I red the same clause to hym ij or iij
tymes.   And demanded of hym if he had folowed his conyss'on
& made suche a book, he answered no.   Then s$^d$ I y$^e$ have done
amysse and not folowed your comysson And therfor chargeabill
still for the Lead as M$^r$ Chauncellors l're to you porportith, who
then said hever red not that clawse to hym To whom I answerd
I thought not so unwise but that he wold have had bothe others
to have red his l'rs (than hym who brought theim) and also have
had advise and councell how to have delyverd the said Lead
(beyng so great a charge) after such sort as myght & shuld have
byn a sufficient discharge for hym Then he heryng me say so
although he is a witty man he dissymulated a great symplenes
sayeinge he cowde not rede nor [        ] no skill of such maters
And had never sene so moche lead before And he had done the
best he cowde (to his knowledge & [        ] skill) and had delyv'd
all accordyng to his l'rs And S$^r$ this is all I can do at this p'nt
And therfor referre the mater to your better wisdome Untill I
know ferther your pleasure w$^h$ att all tymes I shal be glad
t'accomplisshe to my power And thus rest att your comandment.

Written the xxiiij$^{th}$ day of March, 1555. Anno ij$^o$ & iij$^o$ Re$^s$ &
Re$^m$ ph : & Mar : w$^t$ the hand

of yours ever to comand

W. BOLLES.

S$^r$ I m'vell that hever wold not se it waied for his owne discharge before he receyved it and had it away.   In my openyon
(if they had all thought well) it shuld nowghther have byn
delyvred nor yet receyved w'out waight.   S$^r$ Although I write
you playnlie my fantesy towchyng all the parties yet I trust
y$^e$ will not shew this wherby I myght have disspleasure for my
good will and travelle

To the right w$^r$shipfull M$^r$<br>
Thomas Myldmay Esquier<br>
at his hows in St. thomas<br>
Appostell's parisshe      in<br>
hast<br>
in London.

The copie of my L Tresaurers l're.

To my frend the porter of the Castell of Notingh'm and all
other charged with the keeping of the Kyng's said Castell,
and w$^h$ the Lead w'yn the same.

I comende me hertily to you And for that the Kynges lead
lyeing in the Castell of Notyngh'm is appoynted to be brought
to the tower of London for the Kynges use I have sent you
this brynger Will'm Hever. w$^t$ my Lord of Rutlands l'rs and
M$^r$ Chauncellers l'rs and this my l're to you for your helpe to

be shewed to Will'm Hever about the doyng thereof hertily praying you in the behalf of the Kyngs ma^tie to aide and assiste hym abowte the carriage thereof to the waterside And he shall pay the charge and do all thyngs nessessary w^h your aides for cariage and all other thyngs nessessary for tne same whereof I pray you se he lakke not. Thus fare you well. Written the xiij day of May 1551.

W. WILTESS.

The copie of my Lord of Ruthlandshire's l're.

To my s'vant John Potes, porter of the Castell of Notyngham.

I comende me to you And for asmoche as the Kynges highnes pleasure is that all the lead of the Kynges ma^ties Remaynyng at Notyngh'm shalbe taken from thens And [removed?] to sondry places to his owne use Theis are to will you Imediately upon the rec'pt hereof To delyv^r unto the brynger herof All the King's ma^ties Lead remayning at Notyngh'm And this my l're shalbe your sufficient discharge for the delyvry of the same. Thus fare you well. Written att my hous halywell the xiiij day of May 1551.

Y^r M^r th'erll of<br>RUTHLAND.

The copie of S^r Ric Sakvell his l're

To the Porter of the Kynge's Castell of Notyngham & all other charged w^h the lead ther

After right hartie comendac'ons And forasmuche as the Kyngs pleasure w^h thadvise of his graces most honorable Councell is that all suche Lead of his highness Remaynyng in your costody at Notyngh'm shalbe delyv'd unto the right honourabell & my veray good Lord therlle of Wiltess high Tresaurer of England to be collected and [redused?] to such place as the said Lord Tresaurer shall thynk mete to appoynt to the kynges high^ss use. Theis be to require you Imediately upon the Rec'pt herof To delyver unto Will'm Hever s'vant to the said Lord Tresaurer all suche Lead of the Kynges ma^ties remayning in your Custody at Notyngham to be collected and [redused?] to london to the Kyngs highness use Acordyng to the said Lord Tresaurers appoyntment w^w And theis my l're togither w^h a book of the contents & just waight of the same Lead so by you to theym ther delyv'r'd shalbe your sufficient warrant & discharge for the delyvry of the same. Thus fare you well. Written the xj of May 1551.

Y^r lovyng frend<br>Ric Sakvile.

The ruthless demolition of monastic buildings that prevailed under the sway of the nominees of Queen Elizabeth, caused

Her Majesty, in a royal proclamation of 1560, to forbid any further instances of "churches and places spoiled, broken, and ruinated, to the offence of all noble and gentle hearts." This injunction doubtless came too late to save the stately conventual church at Lenton.

Some considerable portion of the conventual buildings probably remained in the year 1573, when the Assizes were held at Lenton, probably on account of gaol fever, or some other pestilence being prevalent in the neighbouring town of Nottingham. The only record of this circumstance are certain entries in the accounts of the chamberlains of Nottingham.

> Given to Justices in Eyre, at the Assize held at *Lenton,*
> 2 gallons of Wine, and 1 lb. of Sugar 5s. 8d.

It was probably owing to the accommodation for the courts to be obtained in some portion of the conventual buildings, which led to Lenton being selected as the place for holding the Assizes, in preference to some of the neighbouring villages.

We find from the parish register of Lenton, that in 1601 some portion of the monastic buildings remained, for on November 26th of that year, Thomas, son of Andrew Bradforde was baptized, "qui quidem Thās natus erat in monasterio, in domo Thsā Birche," but Thoroton, writing in the year 1677, states that at that time "there was only one square steeple left of the Monastery, which, not long since, fell down, and the Stones of it were imployed to make a Causey through the Town."[1]

The Priory gate-house was, however, in existence for more than a century after Dr. Thoroton's time, and stood across the Wilford Road, near the end of Abbey Street, and was in existence at the commencement of the present century, part of it being occupied for parochial purposes up to the time of its demolition.[2] The Peverel Court was held in the room over the archway for a short time after the removal of the Court to Lenton, towards the end of the last century.

---

(1) Thoroton, p. 219.

(2) The following entry occurs in the overseer's accounts for the year 1791. " Paid Glazr for repairs Windows at Abbey Gate house—6s. 9d."

In making some excavations on the Priory site, the late
Mr. William Stretton "not only dug out seven very fine
specimens of the ancient pillars, to the height of a few feet
above their bases," but was also "enabled nearly to trace out
the ground plan of the whole."[1]  At the corner of Priory Street
and Old Church Street, in a garden which is now the property
of the Rev. Kirke Swann, M.A., of Forest Hill, Warsop,
the bases of two of these pillars, which are fine specimens of
Norman work, are to be seen *in situ*.  One of these bases has
a portion of the pillar still standing on it to a height of three
feet.  These bases are five feet in diameter and five feet apart,
and exhibit the base mouldings entire.  Mr. Swann informs
us that when his father purchased the garden,[2] there were
bases of four pillars remaining, of equal size, and at equal
distances apart, forming a square.  Two of these have now
disappeared, except some portion of the foundations, which
have been found in digging at the spots pointed out by Mr.
Swann.  The positions of these are indicated by the letters
B and C on the accompanying plan.  These pillars must have
formed part of the great calefactorium.

On the south side of the old churchyard, some massive
fragments of masonry, from which the external ashlar casing
has been removed, remain, which are supposed to have formed
part of the wall of the north transept of the great conventual
church.

Between the conventual church and the river Leen stood the
Prior's lodge, beyond which, stretching towards the south, were
the Prior's orchards.  Some portion of the foundations of the
Lodge were found when the modern "Priory" was erected by
the late Mr. William Stretton.

It may be here mentioned that a local tradition exists to the
effect that the ancient porch attached to the south aisle of St.

---

(1) "Beauties of England and Wales," vol. 12, part i., p. 181.  It is a matter of
regret that these interesting details are not to be found amongst Mr. Stretton's MSS.,
which contain several sketches of masonry found on the site of the Priory.

(2) This property was purchased by the late Kirke Swann, Esq., father of the
present owner, who, in conjunction with the late Mr. William Stretton, took much
interest in local antiquities, and purchased the garden referred to, solely that he might
be able to preserve from destruction the last relics of the great Priory of Lenton.

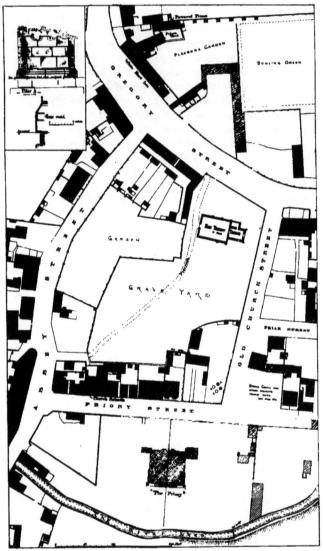

PLAN OF PRIORY SITE.

LG.S., del

Mary's Church, at Nottingham, originally belonged to Lenton Priory, from whence it was removed, on the dissolution of the monastery, to the position it now occupies.

Although the remains *in situ* of the Priory are so scanty, there are architectural remains scattered over the parish sufficient to indicate the character and size of the monastic buildings. The more interesting specimens of masonry are to be found in the grounds of what is now called the "Priory," and consist principally of Norman work. Several large stones, consisting of the responds of large pillars, in the possession of various residents, appear to have formed portions of buildings of great size.

The following extract from a local newspaper gives some interesting particulars of the relics discovered on the site of the Priory about thirty years ago.

"In the course of laying down pipes in the streets of Old Lenton for the supply of water, several discoveries of considerable interest have been brought to light by Mr. John Froggatt, of Lenton Poplars,[1] and others taking an interest in archæology, in the vicinity of the once extensive and magnificent Priory of Lenton. The recent excavations in Old Church Street, and along the main street of Old Lenton, as well as along Abbey Street, including within these bounds an area of several acres of ground, have, however, revealed the great extent of the Priory grounds, and shown by the exhumation of the bones of men and animals, of the carved and moulded architectural stones of the former ecclesiastical buildings, such as the volutes of pillars and the mullions of windows, as well as occasionally a rare old coin, that all traces of the monks are not yet absolutely extinct. In the course of digging in Old Church Street, a small, but extremely rare old coin of Queen Mary, which the possessor presumes to mean Mary, Queen of Scots, was picked up. It is very small, rude, and not intrinsically valuable, being composed of silver alloy. Shortly before, a curious iron key was also found, much corroded, with an oval ring at the head, and highly ornamented and intricate in the wards. A fragment of mediæval pottery, a rude red clay crock, or portion of a patera, were also turned up. A profusion of bones of men and horses, unaccompanied, however, by any other relics, were disinterred about the same period in Old Church Street—"heaped and pent, rider and horse"—as if they had been slain in battle, and had been

---

(1) Mr. Froggatt made numerous memoranda of the various objects found in making these excavations, but the book in which they were recorded was unfortunately destroyed in the great flood of October, 1875.

hurriedly buried on the spot. In Abbey Street, another
description of bones, evidently those of oxen, were turned up,
and human skulls, &c., have been found in abundance all along
the line of excavation. Undoubtedly the most remarkable ossi-
fications which the ground has yielded were the bones in a
tremendous stone coffin found several years ago, and transmitted
by Mr. Froggatt to Dr. Hood, of London. These gigantic bones
were dug up whilst enclosing a garden at the extremity of Old
Church Street, on the left of the way. The spot had previously
been an open field, the property of Mr. Kirke Swann. The
stone coffin measured internally the enormous size of nearly
eight feet, and the bones found within it corresponded in dimensions. Those entire consisted of two thigh bones, two tibiæ or
leg bones, and an under-jaw, with the whole of the teeth in a
state of wonderful preservation. During the recent excavations
in Abbey Street, many carved stones and fragments of window
mullions, beautifully carved and moulded, were also turned up;
a whole cart-load of the stones having been drawn to Hyson
Green to build a wall, and others used in repairing the roads, &c.
One of the workmen also found here, in a bent condition, a
splendid specimen of the English Rose noble of Edward III.
(1344) in pure gold, which, on being cleaned and straightened,
presents as bright and beautiful an appearance as the day it was
coined. In addition to the above, a remarkable antique stirrup
iron was likewise turned up some time ago within the monastic
precincts. It greatly resembles in form and ponderosity a door
scraper, but appears to be of tempered iron or steel, and
strikingly illustrates the picture in which similar stirrup irons are
represented from the Bayeux Tapestries of the Conquest, or the
Field of the Cloth of Gold, *temp*. Henry VIII., with strength
enough to resist the blow of a weapon, and capacity sufficient to
repose the long pointed iron shoe of the knight in armour."

From the fact that numerous human remains were found
about this time in excavating the vacant piece of ground at
the south end of Old Church Street, it may reasonably be
inferred that this was the site of the monastic cemetery—

> " And questionless here in this open court
> Which now lies naked to the injuries
> Of stormy weather, some men lie interred—
> Loved the Church so well, and gave so largely to't,
> They thought it would have canopied their bones
> Till domesday."
>
> Webster, *Duchess of Malfi*, v. 3.

The supposition that this was the conventual burial ground
appears to be supported by the discovery of several stone

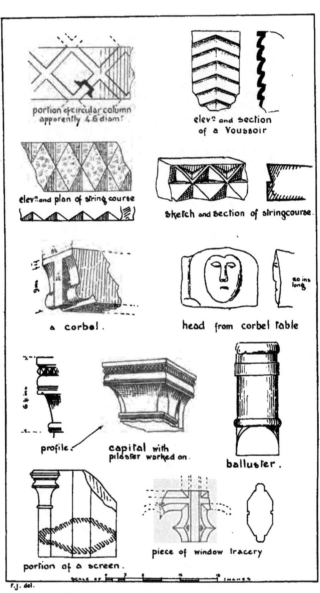

portion of circular column
apparently 4.6 diam?

elev? and section
of a Voussoir

elev? and plan of string course

sketch and section of stringcourse.

a corbel.

head from corbel table

profile.

capital with
pilaster worked on.

balluster.

portion of a screen.

piece of window tracery

F.J. del.

MASONRY - LENTON PRIORY.

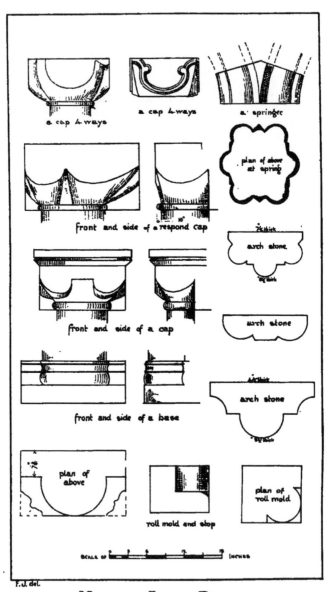

a cap 4 ways     a cap 4 ways     a springer

plan of above
at spring

front and side of a respond cap

arch stone

arch stone

front and side of a cap

arch stone

front and side of a base

plan of
above

roll mold and stop

plan of
roll mold

SCALE OF        INCHES

F.J. del.

MASONRY — LENTON PRIORY

coffins in the grounds of the "Priory" as well as on this site.
A drawing of one of these coffins, made by Mr. Stretton, is in
existence.  The accompanying sketch is a copy of the same—

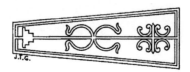

The recent diversion of the river Leen into the canal near
New Lenton, has led to the discovery of numerous pieces of
worked masonry, including a small Norman capital, in the
wall forming the right bank of the river, and further investigation would probably prove that this wall is principally, if not
entirely, built of stones from the Priory, several worked stones
being noticeable in the face of the wall near to the present
"Priory" house.

A most interesting discovery has recently been made in
taking down part of the walls of the old parish church previous
to its restoration.  It was then found that the stones of which
the walls had been built were pieces of worked masonry, placed
with their flat sides out, to form the face of the wall, the interior
being filled up with mortar and rubble.  These stones appear
to have formed some part of the interior of the Priory Church,
the chiselling being as clean and sharp as it was the day when
it was done.  They are principally of the Perpendicular period,
and probably formed part of the stone stalls in the choir or
chapter-house.

In the "Gentleman's Magazine" for the year 1786,[1] is an
engraving (here reproduced) of an inscription round the centre

## DER:TNFRID G EHWART

of a large circular dish of brass, apparently once gilt.  The
dish, which was found at Lenton, was about sixteen inches in
diameter, and had an embossment in the middle, the inscription

---

(1) *Gentleman's Magazine*, vol. 56, p. 220.

16

being, with slight variation, four times repeated.  The writer
of the note was of opinion that it had "been used in the
administration of the Sacrament, perhaps in the monastery of
Lenton, in which parish, tradition says, it has remained upwards
of a century."  This curious dish has unfortunately disappeared
from the neighbourhood, and all endeavours to ascertain what
became of it have proved futile.

In the "Gentleman's Magazine" for the year 1797,[1] is an
engraving of a curious copper plate, which weighed upwards
of seven ounces.  This plate bears on the obverse a finely-
executed representation of the Crucifixion of our Saviour, and
on the reverse several figures which do not appear to have
been completed.  It was discovered on the site of the Priory
upwards of a century ago, and is "supposed to have been left
there by Cardinal Wolsey, on his way to Leicester Abbey,
where he closed his ambitious and disquiet life."  Laird states
that "it was found adhering to a wooden crucifix above the
transverse piece."[2]  It appears, however, to have been originally
a pax or *osculatorium*.[3]  The plate was at one time in Greene's
Museum, at Lichfield,[4] but its present location is unknown.

About the year 1848, the late Colonel Stretton gave to Sir
Henry Dryden, Baronet, of Canons Ashby, Northamptonshire, a
large earthenware jug, fourteen encaustic tiles, and a small
piece of carved masonry, found on the site of Lenton Priory.[5]

The jug, which is $12\frac{1}{2}$ inches in height, is of coarse earthenware, glazed with a green glaze, which has partly shelled off,
and is now without a spout.

The tiles, which are considerably damaged, are, with the
exception of Nos. 2, 12, 13, and 14, about five inches square,
and of various thicknesses.  Six of the tiles are heraldic in

---

(1) *Gentleman's Magazine*, vol. 67, p. 281.

(2) *Beauties of England and Wales*, xii. 180.

(3) For an interesting note on the pax and its use, see North's *Chronicle of the Church of St. Martin, Leicester*, p. 68.

(4) A manuscript catalogue of this once noted museum is now in the possession of Mr. William Greene, of Lichfield, who informs us that it contains no mention of the plate.

(5) These articles were presented by Sir Henry Dryden to the Corporation of Nottingham, in the year 1881.

character, and do not appear to be in any way connected with
Lenton Priory.

Major Lowe remarks that "in many instances there can be
no doubt that where armorial tiles were used, the appropriate-
ness of the arms was often completely ignored, and therefore
the arms of personages are found upon tiles in buildings with
which they had no connection whatever. This practice is very
remarkable, as prevailing at an age when heraldry was deemed
of so much importance." One of the tiles (No. 1) found at
Lenton illustrates, in a striking manner, the peculiar practice
referred to. This tile exhibits
the arms of Morley, lords of the
manor of Morley, in Derbyshire,
which were assumed by the
Stathums of Morley after their
alliance with the heiress of that
family. It was probably made
for Morley Church, where it
may be seen in the north aisle,
for in three of the angles the
space above the shield is filled
by the figure of a bell, and there

is evidence that John Stathum, Esquire (who died November
6th, 1454), gave a bell to Morley Church,[1] hence the appro-
priateness of the device upon a tile used there, but there could
be no such signification in a tile used at Lenton, unless we are
to assume that the same benefactor gave a bell, or bells, to the
Priory, of which there is no evidence whatever. The arms of
Morley are—*argent*, a lion rampant *sable*, crowned *or*. A
similar tile was found within the abbey church at Dale, during
the excavations made by the Derbyshire Archæological Society
in 1878-9. The tile (No. 2) bearing the inscription " Mentem
sanctam, spontaneum honorem Deo, et patrie liberacionem,"
occurs also at Great Malvern, and at the abbey church,
Shrewsbury. The legend (rendered "The holy mind, honour
freely rendered to God, and liberty to the country ") was used
as a charm "for fyre," being found on the great bell given to

---

[1] Cox, *Churches of Derbyshire*, iv. 330.

Kenilworth church by Prior Thomas Kedermynstre, who was
elected to the priorate in 1402. The tile is engraved full size
in Nicholl's "Examples of Decorative Tiles," 1845.

No. 3 is an heraldic shield bearing two chevrons within a
bordure. No. 4 is evidently intended to represent the arms of
the royal Duchy of Lancaster, viz., England, differenced with a
label of three points *azure*, each point charged with as many
fleurs-de-lys *or*. No. 5 exhibits the royal arms of *France
(ancient) and England quarterly*, and is consequently of an
earlier date than the year 1405-6, when *three fleurs-de-lys* were
substituted for a field *seme*, in the arms of France. It will be
noticed that on this tile the device is reversed, which is probably
accounted for by the artificer cutting the block with the device
the right way on, which, on being impressed on the wet clay,
would have the effect of reversing the pattern. No. 6 may
possibly be intended to represent the arms of the town of
Derby, but the device is, in this instance, and probably for the
same reason, shown reversed. No. 7 is presumably intended
as a portrait of King Edward the Third. No. 8 exhibits a

single fleur-de-lys. Nos. 9, 10,
and 11 have merely ornamental
patterns. The three small tiles,
Nos. 12, 13, and 14, have
respectively the letters F, Q,
and a small bird.

The piece of carved masonry
bears two crossed keys and a
sword, and may represent the
arms of the See of Exeter,[1] but
more probably, the sword and
keys are not, strictly speaking,
heraldic, but rather emblematic

of SS. Peter and Paul.

The following extract from a local newspaper[2] probably refers

---

(1) George Neville, Bishop of Exeter and Lord Chancellor, afterwards Archbishop
of York, visited Nottingham several times in the year 1464. It is possible that he
may have sojourned at, and been a benefactor to, Lenton Priory on one of these
occasions, and for this reason the arms of the See of Exeter may have been carved in
some part of the Priory buildings to commemorate the event.

(2) *Nottingham Journal*, March 30, 1782.

...Tiles found at Lenton Priory...

Scale of [ | | | | | | | ] inches

L.S.S. del.

to the discovery in the church-yard of some tiles similar in character to those just described :—

"A few days ago, as the Sexton of the Parish of Lenton, in this Neighbourhood, was digging a Grave, he discovered a foundation which seemed to produce some very good Stone ; whereupon the overseers ordered him to take it up, in doing which, he discovered a Pavement of Roman Bricks quite perfect, upon which were a Variety of Coats of Arms, etc., curiously inlaid and glazed. It seems, from its Form and Situation, that this was the Floor of a Bath belonging to the Antient Priory of Lenton......"

Mr. Stretton relates that "in digging the foundation for a new Methodist Meeting House at the north end of George Street (late Gregory's Paddock), Nottingham, in May, 1816, at about five or six feet from the surface, was found an immense quantity of broken monastic paving tiles, evidently the refuse of a manufactory of those articles, as none of them had ever been in use, but were such as had been injured or broken in the process of burning, and consequently not useful ; there appeared to be about a cart load of them,......................wherefore it may fairly be conjectured that this was the market for those curious tiles with which the chapels and oratories of our Churches, and the floors of our religious houses were paved.[1]" "On digging the foundations for a house near the centre of this late Paddock under the Writer's [Mr. Stretton's] superintendence for Mr. Thos. Elliott, in the month of February 1817, a complete kiln was discovered, in which these tiles were evidently burnt, in and about which a large quantity of them were found.[2]

"On digging other foundations for a set of maltrooms, subsequently to the discovery of the above mentioned kiln, in March, 1818, another kiln and large quantities of imperfect and unfinished tiles were discovered, which to a demonstration proves the manufactory to have been on this piece of ground, and which was within the walls of the Town.[3]"

"In digging the foundations for Saint Paul's Church,

---

(1) *Stretton MSS.*, No. 30, f. 24.     (2) Ibid, No. 31, f. 31.
(3) *Stretton MSS.*, No. 31, f. 32.

Nottingham, in July, 1821, two distinct kilns for burning these monastic tiles were found, very complete, three or four feet under ground, with numerous fragments of this and other ancient pottery ; and also very considerable excavations, extending nearly under the whole of the Church, consisting of habitations and places for religious worship.[1]

"In the manufactory of these tiles the following process must have been pursued—the Tiles composed of fine strong red clay (for which the neighbourhood is famous), were, after having been taken from the mould, impressed with various shields, figures, and devices, from stamps (most probably cut in wood), which impression, not more than the tenth of an inch deep, was filled in with a white clay, and afterwards glazed in the burning." "This manufactory," remarks Mr. Stretton, "was in all probability carried on here till the dissolution of religious houses, and it appears that not only this county, but the neighbouring ones, were supplied from it, as numerous devices from the *same* stamps are to be found in the churches and remains of religious houses of the neighbouring counties of Leicestershire, Derbyshire, etc, as well as of this. The writer made near 100 drawings of the different shields and devices impressed upon tiles found in the floors of the oratories and other appartments of the Priory of Cluniac Monks at Lenton, near Nottingham (upon the site of which he built a mansion), in digging the foundations for which, these,[2] as well as some stone coffins and other relics, were discovered."[3]

Several ancient keys have at various times been found on the site of the Priory and elsewhere in the parish of Lenton. The eight keys[4] shown in the accompanying drawing are, with the exception of Nos. 6 and 8, much corroded. Nos. 4, 6, 7 and 8 have barrels, the remainder have pikes, the pike on No. 2 having originally been much longer. The

---

(1) *Stretton MSS.*, No. 30, f. 24.

(2) "Some thousands" in number. *Stretton MSS.* No. 30, f. 24.

(3) *Stretton MSS.*, No. 31, f. 24.

(4) Nos. 1 to 6 are now in the possession of Edward Joseph Lowe, Esq., F.R.S., of Shirenewton Hall, Monmouthshire, and were acquired by his father, the late Alfred Lowe, Esq., of Highfield House ; Nos. 7 and 8 belong to Mr. F. G. Spybey, Long Row, Nottingham.

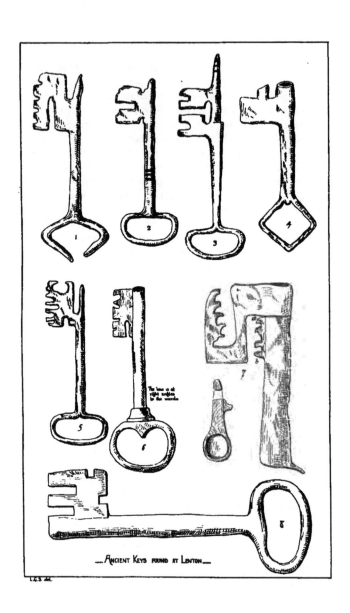

The bore is at right angles to the wards

ANCIENT KEYS FOUND AT LENTON

shaft of No. 3 is flattened at the back. No. 7 is a very curious old key, much corroded. It is made of iron, but appears to have been plated with thin brass, which would effectually conceal all the defects in construction. The bow is broken off, but both it and the wards have been fixed on the barrel. A straight crack extends the whole length of the barrel, beneath the wards, and into it are fixed the wards, or teeth, *ab*. No. 8 is a more modern key, of hammered iron.

The arms of Lenton Priory are described in Tong's Visitation of the Northern Counties in 1530, as follows— "The Armes of the House ys golde and azure quarterly, over all a playn crosse sable, borderid golde."[1] They are now usually blazoned—Quarterly, *or* and *azure*, over all a cross calvary *sable*, fimbriated of the first ; and are thus represented in Tong's Visitation. No earlier example of the arms has been found.

An imperfect impression of the seal of Lenton Priory is appended to the Harleian Charter, 44, F. 19. It is of a pointed oval form, in red wax, and represents our Saviour seated apparently upon a rainbow, the feet being upon an orb, to represent the world, holding in the left hand a closed book, the right hand being raised in benediction. The inscription, which is partly obliterated, runs thus—[SIG]ILLVM CONVENTVS SANC[TI TRINITATIS DE L]EN-TO[NA]. On the reverse is

---

[1] *Harl. MSS.*, 1499, f. 42.

a small counter-seal, also oval, with the half figure of a monk, bearing in his right hand a sceptre terminating in a fleur-de-lis, inscribed—✠ SIGNVM PETRI P[RIOR]IS DE LENTONA.

An impression of what is apparently the same seal of Lenton Priory is appended to a deed amongst the muniments at Lichfield Cathedral, dated in the year 1252 (see page 72). This is *vesica* shaped, 2½ inches long, and 1¾ inches broad. The upper part of the seal is wanting, but in the centre is a similar representation of our Saviour to that on the seal previously described. The inscription is—[SIGILLVM CONVE]NTVS S[ANCTI] TRINITATIS DE LEN[TONA].

The counterseal, engraved real size, is a pointed oval, and appears to have consisted of an oval intaglio, set in a metal mount,[1] round which is inscribed—✠ GRACIA · DEI · SVM · ID · QOD · SVM.

The seal of Alan, sub-prior of Lenton, also broken, is appended to the same document. It is circular in shape, 1¼ inches in diameter, and bears in the centre two lions combattant, surrounded by the inscription— 'SALANI SVB PRIOR' [DE LEN]TO'.

Tanner notices three Registers of Lenton Priory, the first which he describes as "Registrum penes Sam. Roper de Heanore in com. Derb. arm., 1677," appears to have been that which was used by Dr. Thoroton, in compiling his "Antiquities of Nottinghamshire," and which is so frequently quoted in that work.

(1) The practice of using heathen gems, surrounded by Christian legends, as seals, was not uncommon amongst the ecclesiastics of the twelvth and thirteenth centuries. The seal of Roger de Pont l'Evepue, Archbishop of York, 1154-1181, consisted of a gem bearing three heads, Jupiter, Apollo, and Saturn, conjoined, surrounded by the inscription ✠ CAPVT · NOSTRV' TRINITAS · EST. Two of the seals of Walter Gifford, Archbishop of York, 1266-1279, consist of an intaglio, bearing the conjugated portraits of M. Antoninus, the philosopher, and his master, Plato, surrounded in each case by a different inscription. That Archbishop Gifford considered the gem a valuable possession may justly be inferred from his having it set a second time when he changed his seal.

The second is described as "Registrum quondam penes dom. Franc. Willoughby." Whether either of these two registers is yet extant has not been ascertained ; but it is not improbable that the latter may still exist amongst the muniments at Wollaton Hall.

The third is thus described by Tanner. "Registrum in bibl. Cotton. Otho B. xiv." The Cottonian manuscript Otho, B. xiv. here mentioned, disappeared in the disastrous fire at the Cotton Libary, Westminster, in 1731. The following is the description which is given of it in Smith's Catalogue of the Library. "Chartularium prioratus de Lenton in agro Nottinghamiensi a Gulielmo Peverello fundati, cum syllabo maneriorum, advocationum ecclesiarum, portionum garbarum et fœni, pensionum, terrarum, et reddituum, ad ejusdem priorem et conventum spectantium." It was a folio volume, containing 184 leaves of vellum, exclusive of six leaves at the beginning, and three leaves at the end, which contained an index. The present manuscript marked Otho, B. xiv., in the Cottonian Collection at the British Museum, is not the same which was placed under that number previous to the fire.[1]

### SAINT ANTHONY'S HOSPITAL.

Within the courtyard of the Priory there was a hospital " for the free and charitable sustentation of such as should be troubled with St. Anthony's fire." Here

> " strangely visited people,
> All swoln and ulcerous, pitiful to the eye,
> The mere despair of surgery,"

received that surgical treatment for which many of the monasteries were famous.

The following extracts from Thoroton give all the information we are able to obtain respecting this hospital.

"Mr. Gervase de Somerville gave to the Hospital of St. Anthony, within the Court or Church Yard of Lenton, seven bovates of land at Bradmore, for the free and charitable sustentation of such as should be troubled with St. Anthony's fire.

---

(1) *Mon. Ang.*, v. 119.

Raph de Freschvile confirmed the said seven bovates, and added the service of the eighth, which they had of the gift of the said Mr. Gervase de Somerville, with common of pasture, as well as turbary of Boney, belonging to Bradmore. Sir Geoffrey de Boney, and Sarah, his wife, confirmed the same seven bovates."

"Archer, son of William, son of Froue de Boney, or Bradmere, gave three roods of medow in Boney to God and the hospital of St. Anthony, at Lenton, in pure alms." [1]

There is a tradition that, after the suppression of the monastery, the chapel of this hospital was converted into the parish church. The situation of the old church would exactly correspond with that of the hospital, but the church appears to have been rebuilt after the dissolution out of the materials supplied by the demolished conventual buildings. It is very probable, however, that the church may have been erected upon the foundations of the chapel of this hospital.

---

(1) Thoroton, p. 46.

# SECTION V.

--- —

## THE VICARAGE.

. . —

**F**ROM the foundation of the church[1] until the final suppression of religious houses, and the consequent confiscation of their possessions, this benefice remained in the hands of the Prior and Monks of Lenton, but upon the dissolution of the monastery the advowson was seized, and is yet retained by the Crown.

Before the close of the thirteenth century, the rectory had been appropriated to Lenton Priory, and subsequent to the dissolution of that house the impropriate rectory was held for upwards of eighty years by the Crown, but was granted by King Charles the First, together with the manor, to the Corporation of London, and ultimately passed to the Gregory family by purchase. The impropriate tithes remained appendant to the manor until the year 1768, when they were commuted for an allotment of seventy-three acres of land. In 1796, when the Forest lands were enclosed, a further allotment was made, comprising twenty-two acres, one rood, and four perches. The tithe-allotments now belong to the lady of the manor, Mrs. Catherine Sherwin Gregory.

---

(1) The question as to whether there was anciently a distinct parish church or whether the parishioners were permitted to resort to some part of the Priory church set apart for that purpose, is elsewhere discussed.

In 1292, when an inquisition was made by order of Pope Nicholas the Fourth, with a view to the payment of the tenths of ecclesiastical benefices to King Edward the First for six years, being a grant to him from the Pope in aid of an expedition to the Holy Land, it was found that the annual value of the church of Lenton (which had been appropriated to the Priory) was £13 6s. 8d., the vicar receiving an annual pension of £4 13s. 4d.

A more detailed account of the sources from which the emoluments of this benefice were derived during the first half of the fourteenth century is furnished by the Nonæ Roll. This was a subsidy of the ninth of corn, lambs, and wool, in every parish, granted by the Parliament to King Edward the Third in 1341, as an aid in his wars with France. At an inquisition taken at Nottingham on the Tuesday after the feast of St. Gregory, in that year, before the venditors and assessors of the subsidy of a ninth of corn, fleeces, and lambs, and of a ninth of chattles in cities and boroughs, and of a fifteenth of all foreigners and of dwellers in forests and wastes, lately granted to the King in the county of Nottingham, John de Brokilstowe, Geoffrey de Brunnesley, William de Selston, Henry de Wynkeburn, Roger de Lenton, Robert de Beskewod,[1] John de Mauncestre, William de Worthington, William de Warde, John de Henowre of Sutton, John Gervis, and Thomas de Langeton, declared upon oath, amongst other things, that the ninth of corn, lambs, and wool throughout the parish of Lenton, was of the annual value of eighteen marcs, six shillings and eightpence; that thirty-one acres of land belonging to the endowment of the church were estimated to be worth three marcs, four shillings and fourpence per annum; that the tithe of hay was worth eleven shillings per annum; and that oblations, mortuaries, and other small tithes, amounted to four marcs, three shillings and eightpence, throughout the year; and the church was accordingly rated at twenty-seven marcs.

In 1534, in the ecclesiastical survey made upon the dissolution of religious houses, in pursuance of an Act of Parliament,

---

(1) The above seems to be the only instance on record of this as a local surname.

Richard Matthew, then Vicar of Lenton, is recorded to have had a house with one acre of glebe land, and was entitled to the tithes of lambs and fleeces, pigs, fowls and eggs, flax and hemp, and certain other things, including daily meals in the kitchen of the Priory, and fodder for one horse, provided by the Prior, which, together with oblations and all other ecclesiastical dues, amounted in all to £10 11s. 1d. per annum; but out of this the Vicar had to pay an annual pension of £1 8s. 8d. to the Prior of Lenton, so that his clear yearly stipend, at that period, was £9 2s. 4d.[1]

In 1559, the Commissioners who made a Visitation of the Province of York, reported of the parishioners of Lenton that "they have neither vicar nor curate."

At the official survey taken previous to the suppression of chantries, the church of Lenton was found to possess a certain piece of arable land, estimated to be of the annual value of three shillings, which had been given for the perpetual maintenance of a lamp and other lights within the church.[2]

During the Usurpation, at an inquisition[3] taken at the Shire Hall, in Nottingham, on the 14th of August, 1650, before John Hutchinson, Gervase Pigot, Robert Raynes, Nicholas Charlton, and Clement Spelman, Esquires, and John Martyn, Gentleman, by virtue of a commission from the Keepers of the Liberty of England, by authority of Parliament, under the Great Seal of England, to them and others directed, Thomas Newton, Nathan Newton, Nicholas Strey, Jeffery Brock, and John Langford, Gentlemen, George Brough, Humphrey Neede, Thomas Cumminge, Thomas Smyth, Lancelot Everingham, and Thomas Brightman, good and lawful men of the county of Nottingham, declared upon oath, amongst other things, that the impropriate rectory of Lenton was then of the annual value of forty-six pounds, which William Gregory, Alderman of Nottingham, received for his own use. The Vicarage was then worth only seven pounds per annum, and was held by

---

(1) *Valor Ecclesiasticus.*
(2) Certificates of Chantries, Roll 37.
(3) MS. Survey in Lambeth Library.

Robert Ollerenshawe, who was declared to be "a preaching minister," but "a drunkard and of an ill conversation."[1]

In 1676, from a return made by John Francis, then Curate of Lenton, of the number of persons residing within the parish of an age to communicate, together with the number of Papists and other nonconformists, it appears that there were then 160 communicants, and not a single Papist or nonconformist in the parish.[2]

In 1759, a terrier, enumerating the emoluments of the benefice, was exhibited to the then diocesan, His Grace the Archbishop of York. The following is a copy of the same :—

"A True Terrier of all the Glebe Lands, Portions of Tithes, and other Rights belonging to the Vicarage and Parish Church of Lenton in the County of Nottingham and Diocese of York, and now in the use and possession of Mr. George Wayte, Curate there, or his Tenants, taken made and renewed according to the old evidences and knowledge of the antient Inhabitants, this twenty ninth day of August in the year of our Lord, 1759, and exhibited in the Primary Visitation of the Most Reverend Father in God, John, Lord Archbishop of York, holden at Nottingham on the first day of September, 1759. First, one small Close called the Vicarage Yard ; Also one half acre of arable land in the Beck Field lying on a Furlong called Long Hill : Commons belonging to the said Vicarage ; Three Cow Gates ; One Horse Gate and fifteen Sheep Gates ; Also to the Vicar is paid yearly by the Auditor of the King's Chief Rents a Pension of five pounds, eleven shillings and eleven pence ; Also all Tythes within the said parish of Lenton are paid to the Vicar in their proper kind and there are no Customs in the Parish, but only three half pence for every new-milched Cow, and one penny for every Stropper, instead of Tythe milk ; Four pence for every Foal ; and Seven Shillings yearly to the Vicar, and One Shilling to the Clerk, for the Tythe of a large parcel of land called Beskwood Park ; Also

---

(1) It is more than probable that Robert Ollerenshawe earned the bad character given him by the Commissioners by his adherence to his King, and it is by no means unlikely that his "ill conversation" was directed against the Roundheads, then in power.

(2) Tanner MSS. 150, f. 129. Bodleian Library, Oxford.

to the Vicar belong the Tythes of Wool, Lambs, Eggs, Geese, Ducks, Chickens, Pigeons if sold, Pigs, Gardens and Orchards, Turnips and Potatoes, Easter Offerings, Surplice Fees and Mortuaries, and all other Tythes and Ecclesiastical Duties except the Tythes of Corn and Hay both from Grass and Seeds."

Witness, GEO. WAYTE, Curate.[1]

JOHN CHAMBERLIN, WILLIAM NORRIS, } Church Wardens.

GEO. WOMBWELL, JOHN FRITH, THOMAS TOWNSEND, JONATHAN TOWNSEND, } Inhabitants.

The living is now worth about £380 per annum, inclusive of a good vicarage-house, built in 1842 upon a site given by the late Francis Wright, Esquire. At the enclosure of this parish in 1768, the vicarial tithes were commuted for an allotment of twenty-two acres, one rood and five perches of land. A further allotment of one acre, two roods and thirty-four perches was made when the Forest lands were enclosed ; and the Vicar has one acre, two roods and thirty-one perches of glebe. There are likewise about seventeen acres of land at Belchford, near Horncastle, in Lincolnshire, purchased with a sum of money allotted for the augmentation of this benefice by the Governors of Queen Anne's Bounty. The benefice has been further augmented by a grant of £80 per annum from the Ecclesiastical Commissioners. There is an annual pension from the Crown to the Vicars of Lenton of £5 11s. 11d. ; whilst the Vicar has to pay a rent-charge of £1 1s. 6d. yearly to the Commissioners of Woods and Forests " for the use of Her Majesty." Bestwood Park formerly paid a modus of seven shillings yearly to the Vicar of Lenton, and one shilling to the parish clerk, in lieu of tithes. But since the year 1874,

---

(1) As will be elsewhere remarked, there seems to have been no presentation to the vicarage of Lenton at one time for a considerable period. Several of the vicars of the adjoining parish of Radford were permitted to hold the benefice—*in commendam*, and the Rev. George Wayte, who signs the above as " Curate," was one of these.

when Bestwood Park was formed into a separate benefice by the Ecclesiastical Commissioners, this payment has been transferred to the incumbents of Bestwood. Easter Offerings were formerly received by the Vicars of Lenton, and are still legally due to them ; but owing to the difficulty of collecting the same, and the odium attending it, these offerings have been discontinued by the present Vicar.

## THE VICARS OF LENTON.

*Robert Anger*, presbyter.    Patron, the Prior of Birstall (?) Instituted 8 Nov., 1274.

*John de Berde*, presbyter.    Patrons, the Prior and Convent of Lenton.    Instituted 2 Aug., 1300, and held the vicarage until his death.

*Adam de Graneby*, cap.    Patrons, the Prior and Convent of Lenton.    Instituted 4 Feb., 1331, and held the vicarage until his death.

*Robert de Radeford*, cap.    Patron, King Edward III.    Instituted 6 Sept., 1349.

*John Blakeman*, resigned for the rectory of Bulwell.

*Michael de Lyndeby*, pbr.    Patron, King Edward III.    Inisttuted 19 October, 1358.

*Robert de Thornton*, resigned for the rectory of Cortlingstock. He was probably buried at Lenton.[1]

*Henry Broksop*, pbr.    Patrons, the Prior and Convent of Lenton. Instituted 24 Oct., 1410, and held the living until his death.

*William Clyfton*, pbr.    Patrons, the Prior and Convent of Lenton.    Instituted 30 July, 1425, and resigned the living the year following for the rectory of Wilford.    Probably a younger son of the ancient family of Clifton, of Clifton.

*John Peeke*, pbr.    Patrons, the Prior and Convent of Lenton. Instituted 10 October, 1426, and held the living until his death.    By his will, dated July the 22nd, 1442, and proved in the Prerogative Court of York, October the 11th, that same year, he commends his soul to God Almighty, St.

---

(1) See the will of John Peeke, Vicar of Lenton, who died in 1442.

Mary, and All Saints, and desires that his body should be
buried in the churchyard at Lenton, near to the grave of
Robert de Thornton. To the church of Lenton he devised
the sum of three shillings and fourpence.

*William Fyndern, B.D.* Patrons, the Prior and Convent of
Lenton. Instituted 6 October, 1442.

*William Odo,* pbr. Resigned, and was succeeded by

*John Mayewe,* pbr. Patrons, the Prior and Convent of Lenton.
Instituted 16 Oct., 1459, and held the living till his death.
Died intestate before 6 Oct., 1496, when administration
was taken of his estate.

*John Milnes,* pbr. Patrons, the Prior and Convent of Lenton.
Instituted 14 Oct., 1496, and held the living till his death.
By his will, dated December the 15th, 1514, and proved
in the Prerogative Court of York, January the 25th, 1514-15,
he commends his soul to God Almighty, St. Mary, and
All Saints, and desires that his body should be buried in
the church of the Holy Trinity at Lenton.

*Robert Burton,* pbr. Patrons, the Prior and Convent of Lenton.
Instituted 3 June, 1515, and held the living until his death.
By his will, dated March the 12th, 1516, and proved in
the Prerogative Court of York, May the 7th, 1516, Sir
Robert Burton, pbr., Vicar of Lenton, desires that his body
should be buried in the parish church of Lenton,[1] on the
south side of the high altar.

*Alexander Penhill,* pbr. Patrons, the Prior and Convent of
Lenton. Instituted 25 March, 1517, and resigned in 1527.

*Robert Mathew,* diac. Patrons, the Prior and Convent of
Lenton. Instituted 26 Feb, 1527, and resigned in 1543.

*Robert Mayburn.* Patron, King Henry VIII. Instituted 5
March, 1543. He resigned.

*Thomas West,* clericus. Patrons, King Philip and Queen Mary.
Instituted 18 Jan., 1556. He must have vacated the
benefice within about three years.

---

(1) This may possibly refer to that portion of the Priory church that was used for
parochial purposes. Otherwise we have here a special reference to a distinct parish
church prior to the Reformation.

17

*Thomas Askewe*, cler.    Patron, Queen Elizabeth.    Instituted
    26 Oct., 1571, and held the living until his death.
*John Fisher*, cler.    Patron, Queen Elizabeth.    Instituted 13
    July, 1572, and held the living until his death.    He was
    probably buried at Lenton, but a page containing the
    burials from 1589 to the earlier part of 1593, has, unfor-
    tunately, been cut out of the parish registers.
*John Wood*, cler.    Patron, Queen Elizabeth.    He was instituted
    July the 12th, 1592, and held the living until his decease.
    The parish registers record the burial of his wife, July the
    28th, 1595, and his own burial, September the 10th, 1623.
    Various entries relative to his descendants are to be found
    in the registers of Lenton and Radford.
*Robert Ollerenshawe, M.A.*    Patron, King James I.    He was
    instituted, September the 28th, 1623, and retained his
    benefice for at least twenty-seven years.    Judging from
    the bad character he received from the Parliamentary
    Commissioners in 1650 (see page 238), he must have been a
    Royalist, and was probably ejected.
*John Webster*, is described as "minister" in the parish registers
    in 1659.    He was evidently the Puritan divine put
    into the benefice after Cromwell's usurpation.
*William Parker*, described as "Vicar" in 1660, was likewise a
    Puritan.    From the Minute Book of the Nottingham
    Classis it appears that "Mr. William Parker, preacher of the
    Word at Lenton," was examined and approved April 4th,
    1660, and on the 4th of the following month he was
    ordained, after the manner of the Presbyterians, Mr. Boole
    (the Puritan incumbent of Clifton), propounding the
    questions and praying, and he, together with six other
    ministers, subsequently officiating at the imposition of
    hands, the ceremony taking place in St. Mary's Church,
    Nottingham.    William Parker must ultimately have con-
    formed and received episcopal ordination, for he held this
    benefice, together with the vicarage of Radford, for some
    years after the Act of Uniformity had come into operation.
    His name is but once mentioned in the Lenton registers,
    but those of Radford record the baptisms of two sons of

William Parker, Clerk, and Dorothy his wife. One of them was baptized in 1670, and the other in 1674. The date of William Parker's decease has not been ascertained, nor is it known up to what date he held this benefice.[1]

*William Rudsby.* This clergyman's name first occurs in the Lenton registers in 1693, when he styles himself "Vicar." There is, however, reason to believe that although he was fully instituted into the vicarage of Radford, he was merely permitted to hold this benefice *in commendam,* and was never, strictly speaking, Vicar of Lenton, though he enjoyed all the rights and privileges as such for many years. He was married at St. Peter's, Nottingham, to Mary Scattergood, widow, May the 2nd, 1728, but appears to have had no issue. He died, July the 25th, 1731, aged 68 years, and was buried at Radford. The stone which marks the spot where he was interred within the church is now concealed beneath the pews.

*John Swaile* succeeded the last-named clergyman in the vicarage of Radford, to which benefice he was instituted August the 6th, 1731, and appears to have held that of Lenton in like manner as his predecessor, no formal institution to this benefice being recorded. He was like-wise Master of the Nottingham Free School and Curate of Sneinton, at which place he was buried, December the 17th, 1731. The registers of St. Mary's, Nottingham, record the baptism of his son, Cleasby, in 1730, and of a posthumous daughter, Mary, in 1732.

*George Wayte, M.A.* This clergyman was a native of Repton, in Derbyshire, where he was educated at the Free Grammar School, and subsequently graduated at Oxford. In 1732, shortly after taking priest's orders, he was presented by the Crown to the vicarage of Radford, holding the vicarage of Lenton *in commendam,* never being fully instituted into that benefice. In 1732, he was also appointed Usher of the Nottingham Free School, a post which he held until

---

(1) In 1676, in a return of the number of persons of an age to communicate, etc (which has been referred to elsewhere), William Parker described himself as Curate of Radford, but John Francis, who was also Curate of Bramcote and Stapleford, then describes himself as Curate of Lenton.

1747. On Trinity Sunday, 1782, Mr. Wayte preached a sermon at Radford in the morning, and at Lenton in the afternoon, telling his hearers that he had preached that sermon in the same churches on Trinity Sunday fifty years ago. He was then seventy-five years of age, and died on the 7th of June following. His remains were interred at Radford.

*William Pickering, B.D.*, was presented to the vicarage of Radford on the death of George Wayte, and he, too, held that of Lenton *in commendam* for upwards of twenty years.

*Edward Cresswell, M.A.* Patron, King George the Third. He was presented by the Crown to the vicarages of Lenton and Radford, and was duly instituted into both benefices, May the 3rd, 1803, being the first actual Vicar of Lenton for upwards of a century, the living having been held *in commendam* throughout that period, as already stated. He died April the 11th, 1840, and was buried at Radford, where there is a mural monument to his memory.

*George Browne, M.A.*, of Trinity College, Dublin. Patron, Her present Majesty. Instituted in July, 1840. This much-esteemed gentleman, who has held the living for upwards of forty-four years, was Curate-in-charge of Lenton at the time of his presentation. He is the fifth son of the late Right Honourable Denis Browne, M.P., younger brother of the first Marquess of Sligo.

# SECTION VI.

## THE CHURCHES.

### THE OLD CHURCH.

**A**LTHOUGH there is no mention of a church being at Lenton at the time of the Domesday Survey, such omission must not be taken in itself as proof of the non-existence of a church at that period ; but the foundation charter of Lenton Priory is also silent on the same subject, and no specific reference to the parish church is to be found previous to the dissolution, although the benefice is mentioned as early as the year 1292 in the Ecclesiastical Taxation of Pope Nicholas the Fourth. It is therefore probable that, previous to the dissolution of Lenton Priory, some portion of the conventual church was set apart for the use of the parishioners. Many of the greater monasteries had churches standing in their closes, or a collateral church. These churches, which were distinct from the conventual church, were at first regarded as mere chapelries, served by a chaplain at an altar, which was considered as being included within the conventual church, as if it stood under the same roof, which was actually the case in some churches. Although the fact yet remains to be proved, we may probably infer that a portion of the conventual church of Lenton was used by the parish, its altar being served by the Vicar, who, in a limited sense, would be independent of the monks. Such an arrangement, though not uncommon in some other Orders, is, however, seldom to be found in the Clugniac monasteries[1] In the year 1200, the canons of Westminster forbade a monk to be placed alone in a parish church, and required him to keep within his cloister. In 1268, the Papal legate imposed a restriction upon the appropriation of churches to any priory or other monastery, and made an order that all religious, exempt and not exempt, Cistercians and others, who held such churches, should present a resident vicar for institution by the diocesan, providing him with a sufficient portion out of the endowment, and a house with a garderobe and chimney after the French fashion. Usually, the dependent vicar received a "robe of clerical suit," and, as at Lenton, daily rations when near a convent.[2] There is a tradition to the effect that after the dissolution of the Priory, the chapel, or some other portion of the Hospital of St. Anthony, which formerly stood in the courtyard of the Priory, was converted into the parish church. It is somewhat remarkable that, with the exception of the following certificate of church goods taken in the year 1552, no particulars relative to the church in the sixteenth or seventeenth centuries have been met with, neither are there any notes of old monuments or stained glass.

The certificate of Church Goods belonging to the parish of Lenton, is dated September 5th, 6 Edward VI. [1552], and is as follows :

"ffyrst. one sanctus bell.

it. ij vestments of whyte ffustyan.

it. one vestment of dornyxe.[3]

it. one albe.

it. one chalyse w$^{th}$ a patene of sylv$^{r}$.

---

(1) In a correspondence with Major Lawson Lowe upon this subject, Mr. Mackenzie Walcott, one of the greatest authorities on conventual arrangements, says that in all probability the laity were permitted to make use of the nave of the conventual church in the Clugniac Priories of Castle-acre and Bromholme, in Norfolk, and Mendham, in Suffolk.

(2) Walcott, *English Minsters*, ii. 30.

(3) Coarse damask, made at Doornix, or Tournay.

it. one cowpe of red sey.[1]

it. ij belles, the one callyd a hande bell and the other a sacryng bell."

The certificate is signed by

ROBERT GAYBONE—Vicar.

JOHN LECEST[R] } p'shioners.
ANTHONY WESTON

JOHN BOWSER } Ch. wardens.
AVERY WALKER

The existing fabric, which is now (April, 1884) undergoing restoration, is of comparatively little interest in itself, and consists merely of a nave, measuring externally about 42 feet by 36 feet, and a chancel measuring about 28 feet by 18 feet, having on the northern side a small brick vestry of modern construction. There was a good Perpendicular window of two lights built into the west wall on the south side of the doorway, and above the doorway itself is an old stone, upon which are carved two shields, the one charged with three crowns, and the

other with as many fleurs-de-lys.[2]  On the north side of the same doorway is a small window also of two lights.  The other windows in the church (all of which are now removed) exhibited the ordinary round-headed lights and plain chamfered mullions of the later Tudor period.  Of these there were three windows on the north side of the nave, each having three lights, while on the south side there were six windows of two lights each.

(1) Silk and wool mixed.

(2) Several writers have erroneously assigned the latter of these two coats to the family of Hicks, who bore—a fesse wavy between three fleurs-de-lys.  The arms are, however, of considerably earlier date than the period when the Hicks family first became connected with the parish.  It is impossible to identify them with any degree of certainty.

In addition to these there was a three-light window of similar character on the south side of the east end of the nave. Judging from the character of the masonry discovered in pulling down a portion of the walls, it is evident that the church was built of worked masonry from the Priory shortly after its dissolution, probably upon the foundations of the chapel of the Hospital of St. Anthony. Previous to the partial demolition of the church in 1843, there was a wooden belfry at the west end of the nave. This belfry, or "steeple," as it is called in the parish books, was newly boarded over in 1725, and again in 1764, and contained a bell bearing the inscription—

WILLIEM WARD AND
TOMAS SERENE OF LENTON
1591 [1]

A new bell was placed therein in 1829.[2] The church had an open timber roof until the year 1775, when it was ceiled. On a key of the plastering over the entrance to the sacrarium was—EH.IB.1775.,[3] and in front of the old oak Communion Table were the letters—(HG.TH.CW.)[4]

At a meeting of the inhabitants of Lenton, held October 18th, 1805, it was unanimously resolved that the church was inadequate to the accommodation of the parish, and was so damp as to render it dangerous to the health of the inhabitants assembling there for public worship. It was determined, therefore, to take steps to raise the floor and the walls of the church sufficiently high to admit of the erection of a gallery at some future time, if necessary, to cover the roof with slates, and to entirely repew the church. Several committee meetings were held to consider the reports of Mr. Stretton and Mr. Staveley, but at a general meeting of the inhabitants, held January 8th, 1806, it was resolved that a new church for the parish was *not*

---

(1) *Stretton MSS.*, No. 27, f. 61. William Ward is probably identical with the person of that name who was buried at Lenton, October 26th, 1595.

(2) The old bell is said to have been broken in a vain attempt to knock a wedding peal out of it by means of sledge hammers. The bell that replaced it in 1829 is now at Hyson Green Church.

(3) Edward Hollingworth and John Bradshaw were churchwardens in 1775.

(4) *Stretton MSS.*, No. 27, f. 61.

then necessary.   At a meeting held February 19th, 1807, it
was resolved to repew and repair the church, the new pews to
be wholly allotted by the Ordinary.   During the same year,
therefore, the floor of the church was raised and laid dry, a
vestry erected, the church repewed, and a stove for warming
introduced.   The cost of these works was £574.

In 1811, the churchyard walls were rebuilt, and iron gates
fixed therein to make the churchyard entire, and in the following year trees were planted round the churchyard.[1]

The condition of the church and churchyard at this period
are described in detail in the following observations of Archdeacon Eyre.

"On Thursday, the 27th of June, 1811, the Revd. John Eyre,
of Babworth, Archdeacon, visited the Church of Lenton, and
made the following remarks and observations.

"That the Roof, Walls, (and especially the lower part of them,)
and the Steeple, are in a ruinous and bad state—that, at all
events, it is necessary that the Roof be taken off and renewed ;
that a new Steeple be made ; that the Walls be well repaired
and pointed, especially towards the Basement, which ought to
be particularly examined and underpinned with good sound
Materials.

"That, as to the interior of the Church, he gives the
Parishioners credit for having done all in their power to render
it neat, clean, & comfortable, but is sorry to find that there is a
great want of accomodation, and that many absent themselves
from Church for want of it ; and as a considerable Expence will
necessarily be incurred by the above Reparation, he very strongly
recommends the taking down and rebuilding the Church, if the
Parish could accomplish it, and by raising the Walls sufficiently
high, upon the same Foundations, to erect a spacious Loft,
whereby all those who are now destitute might be accomodated
with Seats—this might be done, he thinks, without any material
injury to the present Pews.

"He was glad to find a disposition in the Parishioners to keep
the Church Yard entire, and was pleased with the improvements
that were taking place for that purpose ; but was sorry to find
that large Cattle are pastured therein, as the Graves and Stones
were thereby trodden down and injured ; Sheep he recommends
to be permitted to graze, but no larger Animals.

"The old Wall adjoining the Ruin on the East side of the

_____

(1) *Vide* Churchwardens' Accounts, *post.*

Church Yard ought to be rebuilt; and Mr. Gregory should be requested to repair his Fences next the Church Yard.

"The Parish Registers, he observed, ought to be particularly attended to, the Entries therein should be correctly and regularly made, that it was the Business of the Churchwardens to see that this was done; and for this purpose they should attend in the Vestry every Sunday a little before Service time, and after such correction and examination, they should sign every Page. The Ages of the deceased should always be entered as well as any other necessary information for the identifying the Persons meant to be recorded therein. That a new Terrier should be made of all the property of the Church, whether of the Vicar, or that vested in the Churchwardens, as of the Vestments, Furniture, Books, Communion Plate, Registers, Fees, &c., &c., (in which it is to be observed that the Clerk's Fee for every Funeral should be two shillings and sixpence, &c.) and that a Copy of it should be entered in the Parish Register, and called over and given in church to every succeeding Churchwarden, on entering upon his Office.

"The Awards, Maps and Registers, should be kept in the Parish Chest, as well as all other Papers and Documents belonging to the Parish.

"A Table of Donations, if any, to the Church or Poor, should be written and fixed in some public part of the Church.

"The above Statement accurately records all the remarks and observations which I made during my Visitation of the Church of Lenton, and I most strenuously recommend it to the Parish to carry them into execution, in a manner suitable to its respectability & Spirit.

"Their Obedt. Servant
"JOHN EYRE, Archd<sup>n</sup>."

The foregoing report was apparently drawn up by Mr. Stretton shortly after the Archdeacon's Visitation, and forwarded to him for his approval. This the Archdeacon readily granted in a letter of which the following is a copy, and in which he complimented Mr. Stretton on his skill as an architect, and expressed a hope that the Church might be rebuilt during that gentleman's term of office as churchwarden.

"Sir,

"Just upon the point of setting out to London, I have received your letter, inclosing an account of my observations on the Church at Lenton, most accurately and excellently drawn up: so much so that I have no occasion to delay my answer in order to reconsider them. I am in great hopes the Parish will accede to the proposal of rebuilding the Church during your Wardenship, as I am convinced it will be well done, and the antient style of architecture appropriate to those buildings preserved. I shall be at Southwell the two following months and shall be happy to see you at the Residence if anything brings you that way. In great haste,

" I am, Sir, Your most obedt. servant,

" Babworth, Aug. 27, 1811.                        " JOHN EYRE.

" WILLIAM STRETTON, Esq<sup>re</sup>,
    " Lenton Priory, Nottingham."

At a vestry meeting of the parishioners, held March 10th, 1829, it was resolved to provide a new bell for the church, and to make such repairs or alterations to the belfry as might be required, the total cost of such work not to exceed the sum of fifty-eight pounds.

At a vestry meeting, held April 1st, 1841, it was resolved to erect a wall of Bulwell stone on the boundaries of the churchyard and Old Church Street (then called Churchill Close), also between the churchyard and the garden plot belonging to Mr. Kirke Swann, and to levy a rate of twopence-halfpenny in the pound to cover the expense of building such . walls.

The church being totally inadequate to meet the requirements of the parish, a new church was erected midway between Old and New Lenton in 1842, and in the following year a faculty (of which the following is a copy) was obtained to take down the old church, except the chancel and vestry.

GEORGE WILKINS, Clerk, Doctor in Divinity, Archdeacon of the Archdeaconry of Nottingham lawfully constituted To our well beloved in Christ the Reverend George Browne, Clerk, the Vicar, and Francis Wright and Joseph Bell, the Churchwardens of Lenton in the County of Nottingham and within our said Archdeaconry, Greeting ; Whereas on your Petition We issued our Citation calling upon all and singular the Inhabitants of the Parish of Lenton aforesaid and all others who have or pretend to have any right title or interest in or unto the Old Parish Church of Lenton aforesaid or to any pew or pews therein, or to any grave, tombstone or monument in or about any part thereof to appear before us or our lawful Surrogate or other competent Judge in the Court held this day in the Parish Church of Saint Peter in the Town of Nottingham (and by adjournment at our Registry Office in the same Parish) to show

just and lawful cause if they had or knew any why a Faculty or
License should not be granted to you the said Reverend George
Browne, Francis Wright and Joseph Bell, for the purposes
therein mentioned And Whereas no person having appeared at
the said Court and time and place mentioned in the said Citation, We, therefore do, by every power and authority in us
vested Grant to you by these presents our Faculty or License
to take down the said Old Church (save the Chancel and Vestry)
and to make use of, or sell the old materials, and apply the
proceeds in or towards the erection of a Chapel of Ease at Ison
Green in the said Parish of Lenton (now being built)—you the
Vicar and Churchwardens taking care to have the west end of
the said chancel and vestry properly built up, and the same put
into good repair and condition in order that Burial Service may
be performed therein, and also that any mural monument or
tablet on the walls of the said ancient Church be removed and
duly placed upon the Walls of the new Parish Church (recently
erected in the said Parish and to which all Parochial rights
privileges and emoluments have been legally transferred) but in
or upon such part as you may deem most suitable.  Given at
the Town of Nottingham under the Seal of our Office this ninth
day of October in the year of our Lord one thousand eight
hundred and forty three.
    (The seal of the Archdeaconry
        of Nottingham)
                        CHAS. GEO: BALGUY,
                                    Registrar.

    At a vestry meeting, held March 25th, 1844, it was resolved
" That the churchwardens be directed to get the chancel of the
old church put into proper repair and enclosed, and that shutters
be put to the outer windows to make it a fit and proper place
for any purposes relating to the parish, or other business."

    A few years later—in 1857—the Lenton Burial Board ordered
the boundary wall of the churchyard to be repaired, and requested all persons having relatives or friends interred in the
closed ground[1] should fix some mark to determine the site
before January 1st, 1858. After that date the Board ordered
that the ground should be levelled and planted, that the old
church door be removed, and a new common gate put up
instead, that ivy be planted against the old church walls, inside
and outside, that the elder trees be taken down, and the church
gates be cleaned and painted.

---

(1) Burials in the churchyard were discontinued April 1st, 1857, by order of the
Privy Council.

All that now remains of the old church are the chancel and vestry, and the roofless walls of the nave, until lately luxuriously mantled with ivy. The architectural features, such as they are, have already been described. Divine service was, until recently, held in the chancel, which was fitted up with plain wooden benches, the old clerk's desk, placed under the east window, doing duty for reading-desk and pulpit. The old reading-desk and pulpit are now in the church at Hyson Green, and the font is in the new church. For several years the altar-rails served the purpose of a fence to the River Leen at the end of Friar Street. On the west wall is a board (removed from the west end of the church), on which are painted the royal arms of the time of King Charles the Second, with the initials C. R. (altered to G. R.), and the date 1722, the latter having probably been added when the arms were renovated.[1]

The church is now in course of restoration, the memorial stone having been laid by the Lady of the Manor of Lenton. The stone bears the following inscription, "To the Glory of God this stone was laid by Mrs. J. Sherwin Gregory, and consecrated by Christopher, Bishop of Lincoln, November 22nd, 1883." It is proposed to leave standing as much of the old walls as possible, and to work new windows to replace the present decayed ones. In the west wall of the nave there will be a three-light traceried window, and a single light at the west end of each aisle. Nave arcades will be built, and surmounted by a clerestory, with two single-light windows in each

---

(1) In an old edition of Burn's "Ecclesiastical Law" (1824, vol. i., p. 374), speaking of Ornaments of the Church beyond those ordered in the Prayer-Book and in the Canons, the writer says :—

"Besides what hath been observed, in particular there are many other articles for which no provision is made by any special law, and therefore must be referred to the general power of the Churchwardens, with the consent of the major part of the Parishioners, as aforesaid, and under the direction of the Ordinary ; such as the erecting galleries, adding new bells . . . organs, clock, chimes, *King's arms*, . . . and such like."

It would appear that the practice is not dependent on any law. It was a custom which crept in during the sixteenth century, but it is not easy to assign a date for their first appearance. During the Usurpation, the royal arms were removed from the churches, and replaced by that curious heraldic composition which had been adopted as the arms of the Commonwealth. These latter were, of course, destroyed at the Restoration, and the royal arms again set up. Those at Lenton date from that period, and with the exception of those in St. Nicholas's Church, Nottingham, they are, so far as we are aware, the only example of the royal arms of that date remaining in Nottinghamshire.

bay. There will be a bell turret at the west end of the nave.
The church is designed to accommodate about 250 persons,
and the estimated cost of the restoration is £1,800.

> "Now shall the Sanctuary
> And the House of the most High be newly built ;
> The ancient honours due unto the Church
> Buried within the ruined Monasteries,
> Shall lift their stately heads, and rise again
> To astonish the destroyers' wondering eyes.
> Zeal shall be decked with gold ; Religion,
> Not like a Virgin robbed of all her pomp,
> But bravely shining in her gems of state,
> Like a fair bride be offered to the Lord."
>
> Webster, *Fam. Hist.*, ed. Dyce, 173.

The only monument in the chancel is a plain tablet of white
marble, on the north wall, which is thus inscribed :—

Sacred
to the memory of
George Stretton,
late of Nottingham,
died December VII<sup>th</sup>, MDCCCXXXIII, aged LXII years.
Also one son and one daughter.
George Burbage Stretton,
died March VI<sup>th</sup>, MDCCCXVII, aged XVII years.
Elizabeth Stretton
died July VI<sup>th</sup>, MDCCCXXVIII, aged XXVI years.

There were formerly several floor-stones in the chancel to
various members of the Garland[1] family, but these were
probably removed when the church was repaved in 1807.

On the south wall of the now roofless nave, near to the west
end, is a large oval tablet, thus inscribed :—

In Memory of
George   Blanchard
the Son of

----

(1) See the pedigree of this family, p. 212.

John and Ann Blanchard [1]
who departed this life
the 18th day of July, 1805,
Aged 8 years and 6 months.

The inscriptions on the slabs in the floor of the nave are
as follows :—

Here Lieth the Body of
RICHARD NORRIS
who Departed this Life
Octr 10th, 1726.

Here Lieth the Body of
ELIZABETH ye Wife of
RICHd NORRIS, who Departed
this Life. April 20, 1731.

Here lieth the Body of Ann
Chamberlain, Daughter of John and
Martha Chamberlain, who Departed
this Life Febry 5th, 1748
Aged 26 years.

MARTHA CHAMBERLAIN, 1753.

JOHN CHAMBERLAIN, 1766.

William Norris died March 10th, 1788, aged 75 years.

John, Son of
Thos. Needham, Gent.
and Elizabeth his Wife
of Sandbeach, in Cheshire
died April...............
Aged 3 years &......months.

(1) An inscription upon a floor-stone beneath adds that the above-named John
Blanchard was Veterinary Surgeon in the Third, or King's Own Regiment of Light
Dragoons. The regiment was at that time quartered at the barracks in Nottingham
Park. The Park was then extra-parochial, but by ancient custom those who died
within the limits of the Park or Standard Hill were interred at Lenton. Numerous
entries of the burials of soldiers who died at the barracks are to be found in the
parish registers.

The only sepulchral memorial, dating from mediæval times, is a portion of a broken slab bearing the shaft of an incised cross, having a chalice on one side and a (clasped?) book on the other. These emblems denote that it originally indicated the grave of an ecclesiastic—possibly one of the Vicars of Lenton.

Laird,[1] who wrote in 1813, before the church was dismantled, and who seems to have derived much of his information relative to this place from Mr. William Stretton, mentions an ancient monumental stone, near the reading-desk, on which a cross and chalice are carved, with the date 1333. This was perhaps the same slab as the one just mentioned, although there is no indication of any inscription on the part that remains.

Another slab has upon it the initials and date:—

J. G. 1721.

This slab marked the grave of Mr. John Garland,[2] who died in that year, and has probably been moved out of the chancel.

In the churchyard, near the west end of the church, is this inscription upon a large tomb, surrounded by iron railings:—

In Memory of Mary, the daughter of
Tho$^s$ Wright Watson and Elizabeth his wife
who died 30$^{th}$ Sept$^r$ 1801, aged 5 years.
Also Tho$^s$ Wright Watson,
who died 20$^{th}$ April, 1802, aged 44 years.
Likewise Henry the son of
Tho$^s$ Wright Watson and Elizabeth his wife
who died 8$^{th}$ May, 1802, aged 17 years.

---

(1) "Beauties of England and Wales," vol. 12, part i., p. 180.
(2) *Stretton MSS.*, No. 32, f. 18.

A plain flat stone adjoining this monument, and likewise
enclosed within iron railings, records that James Watson, of
Nottingham, Gent., died January 25th, 1808, aged 82 years.

Upon a plain slate tablet affixed to the churchyard wall :—

Herbert

Son of

Alexander & Sarah Foxcroft

Died 6ᵗʰ October 1817

Aged 15 months.

Upon a stone monument near to the one last-named, is
this inscription :—

"Sacred to the memory of Anne, the wife of Thos. Brown
Milnes, who departed this life on the 12th of August, 1816, in
the 27th year of her age. Also to Elizabeth, their daughter,
who died June 22nd, 1816, aged 4 years and 6 months. Blessed
are the dead which die in the Lord."

The family vault of the Wrights, of Lenton Hall, stands
near the gateway at the south western corner of the churchyard, and two plates upon the railings, each surmounted by
the Crest of the family, state that " This vault was erected by
John Wright, Esq., A.D. 1823." A slab on the vault records
the burials of John Wright, Esq., of Lenton Hall, who died
April 21st, 1840, aged 81 ; Elizabeth, his wife, eldest daughter
of Francis Beresford, Esq., of Ashbourne, who died December
18th, 1833, aged 74 ; John Wright, their eldest son, who died
at Naples, January 24th, 1828, aged 25 ; Annie, wife of
Richard Perrin, Esq., who died at Lenton Hall in 1838 ; and
Frances, eldest daughter of John Wright, Esq., who died
January 10th, 1873, aged 77.

Close to, is a large monument in the form of a sarcophagus,
bearing the following inscriptions on slabs of black marble :—

"Sacred to the memory of William Stretton, Esq., late of
Lenton Priory, who departed this life March 12, 1828, aged
72 years."

"Here lieth entombed, Susanna, wife of William Stretton,
a pattern of piety and virtue, who, having borne the rod of
affliction near twenty years with almost unexampled fortitude,

18

resigned her soul to God who gave it Dec. 7, 1815, aged 58 years;' leaving to the world this momento : 'Tho' afflicted, not forsaken. Reader ! if thou hast never yet considered the state of thy immortal soul, or that but briefly, go home and examine thyself, the present moment to thee is invaluable. But if thou be a true follower of Jesus Christ, lift up thy heart with praise and thanksgiving to thy Blessed Lord and Saviour, and pray Him to keep thee in the true faith. For what shall it profit a man if he gain the whole world and lose his own soul, or what shall a man give in exchange for his soul ? "

"In memory of Colonel Sempronius Stretton, C.B., late of the 40th Regiment, who died at Croydon, February 6, 1842, aged 59 years, and was buried at Bromley, in Kent. His distinguished services in the Peninsula, and at the memorable battle of Waterloo, were rewarded with several honorary decorations, and he was also made a Companion of the Most Honourable Order of the Bath. O God, my Lord, the strength of my salvation, thou has covered my head in the day of battle. Glory be to thee, O Lord."

" In memory of Thomas Naylor, of Standard Hill, who died November 5, 1818, aged 48 years. Also, Stella, his wife, who died at Lenton, September 18, 1863, aged 82 years. She was a tender and loving mother, and beloved most by those who knew her best. He, which raised up the Lord Jesus, shall raise up us also by Jesus."

" Sacred to the memory of Agnes Stella, youngest daughter of the late Thomas and Stella Naylor, of Standard Hill, Nottingham, who departed this life in the year of our Lord, 1866, in the 49th year of her age."

Near to is a plain headstone inscribed :—

" In memory of Ellen Maria, second daughter of the Reverend Herbert Napleton Beaver, Vicar of Gringley, Nottinghamshire. Born November 13th 1843. Died November 18th 1851."

Another plain headstone adjoining is inscribed :—

" Severus, son of W. & S. Stretton, Born Nov! 7th 1783. Died Dec! 19th 1785.

" When y* Arch Angel's Trump shall sound,
And Souls to Bodies join,
What Crowds will wish their Lives below,
Had been as short as Thine."

Other memorials adjoining record the burials of the following
members of the Stretton family :—Elizabeth, wife of Samuel
Stretton, died February 22nd, 1802, aged 70 years ; Samuel
Stretton, died May 11th, 1811, aged 80; Ann, daughter of
Samuel and Elizabeth Stretton, and relict of Samuel Pinkney,
of Dublin, died April 11th, 1820, aged 63 years. Also, Samuel
Bilby, son of George and Mary Stretton, died March 4th, 1805,
aged — months; George Burbage Stretton, died March 6th,
1817, aged 17 years ; Elizabeth Stretton, died July 6th, 1828,
aged 26 years ; and George Stretton, died December 7th, 1833,
aged 62 years.

Placed against the south wall of the churchyard is a square
monument, inscribed :—

Sacred to the memory of
John Wright Killingley, Gent.,
who departed this life XXIV. May, MDCCCXXIX,
Aged LXVIII. years.
. Also, of Elizabeth, his wife,
Who departed this life XI. January, MDCCCXLV.,
Aged LXXXII. years.

Near to, upon a large stone slab, inclosed by iron railings :—
" Sacred to the Memory of William Huthwaite, Gent?, who
died Oct! 17th 1824, aged 61 years. Also of three of his
Children who died in their Infancy and were buried here. And
of Lucy, a Daughter, who died November 24th 1817, aged 21
years, and was buried at St. Mary's Church, Whitechapel, in
London. Also Lucy, Wife of the above William Huthwaite,
who died October the 12th, 1852, in the 81st year of her age.
Also William Francis, Son of the above Will™ and Lucy
Huthwaite, who died October the 3rd 1834, Aged 34 years,
and was buried at St. Matthews Church at Brixton in Surrey."

A small slate headstone is inscribed :—

" In Memory of Francis Gill who departed this life February
25th 1823, Aged 53 years."

Upon two plain headstones :—

" Here Lieth yᵉ Body of Sarah the Wife of James Feild, who departed this Life the 26ᵗʰ Octoʳ 1746, aged 46. Also the Body of Jane Dealtry, her Mother, who departed this Life yᵉ 26ᵗʰ Janʳʸ 1731-2, Aged 68."

" Here lyeth the Body of Joseph Feild the Son of James and Sarah Feild, who departed this Life the 9ᵗʰ day of April 1726, Aged 8 months. Also the Body of James Feild who Departed this Life the 24 Day of January, 1749-50, aged (27 ?) Years."

Near to is a small headstone, inscribed —

HERE
LYeth The BodY
of Ralf LOUet W
hO deParted ThiS
Life The 24 of OCtO
1722

Opposite to the Wright's family vault is a headstone, inscribed :—

" Sacred to the Memory of John Aspin, late Rough Rider in the Royal Regiment of Horse Guards, who after serving his King & Country faithfully seven years & eight months fell a Victim to the King of Terrour on the 10th Day of December 1800, in the 29th year of his age.

> " No Routes nor Riots now molest,
> Safe in this hallowed Ground,
> I'll wait 'till Christ shall call the blest,
> By the last Trumpet's sound."

Upon another headstone :—

" Sacred to the Memory of William Pattin, Cornet in the late 23ʳᵈ Light Dragˢ, Aged 32 years; who departed this Life the 22ⁿᵈ of April, 1804 : was born in the 7ᵗʰ Dragoon Guards where he remained until he was 29 years of age."

Upon another headstone :—

"In Memory of Anthony Alexander, Infant Son of Ant<sup>y</sup> Alex<sup>r</sup> O'Reilly, Esq<sup>re</sup> of the Fourth, or Royal Irish Dragoon Guards, and Ann his wife. He died May the 10<sup>th</sup> 1810 Aged 14 months.

Upon a plain headstone, near the last :—

"Sacred to the Memory of Lucy Abigail Rich Scales, the Daughter of William Scales, Serg<sup>t</sup> Major of the 9<sup>th</sup> L<sup>t</sup> D<sup>n</sup>, and Emma his Wife. She departed this life Feb<sup>y</sup> 1<sup>st</sup> 1816. Aged 18 months."

Upon a large square tomb on the south-east side of the churchyard, is this inscription :—

Within this Tomb are deposited the Remains of
JOHN CHAMBERLAIN, who died the 18<sup>th</sup> April, 1810,
Aged 85 Years. Also ELIZABETH his Wife
who died the 7<sup>th</sup> January, 1810, Aged 80 Years.

In another part of the churchyard is the vault of the Needham family, formerly of Lenton House, on the covering stones of which "M.N. 1822." is deeply incised. Above are two plain slate slabs ; one stating that Matthew Needham died August 1st, 1840, aged 41 ; that Mary, his wife, died August 26th, 1837, aged 68 ; and that Caroline, his daughter, died March 15th, 1850, aged 44 ; and the other, that Henry Enfield died July 23rd, 1869, aged 66, and Eleanor Sara, his wife, died June 1st, 1880, aged 67.

Immediately adjoining, is a plain monument, bearing the following epitaph, written by the Rev. John Kenrick, M.A., of York, in memory of the Rev. Henry Turner, a Unitarian Minister, of Nottingham, who died January 31st, 1822, aged 29 years :—[1]

(1) For an obituary article on this minister, see "The Monthly Repository," vol. xvii., p. 121.

H. S. E.
Henricus Turner. V.D.M.
Ecclesiæ Nottinghamiensıs
Unum Deum Patrem, Mediatore Christo, colentium
Per quinquennium fere, alter e Pastoribus.
Quo, morte, ipsi non immaturâ, abrepto,
Filium, conjugem, amicum
Pietate, sanctitate, ingenio, præstantem.
Consuetudine, et sermonibus jucundissimum
Sui desiderant,
Ecclesia vero se vitæ duce ac magistro
Ad omnem honestatem
Non præceptis magis quam exemplo incitante
Orbatum esse testatur.
Obiit Prid. Kal. Febr. A.D. M.DCCC.XXII,
Ætat. XXIX.

A short distance from this is a headstone bearing a singular
inscription in memory of Eliza Place, who died February 11th,
1835, aged 31 years. Close to is a large monument bearing
the following inscription in memory of Francis Evans, Esq.,
of Lenton Grove:—

M. S.
Francisci Evans Armig<sup>ri</sup>.
Obiit die quarto Octobris A.D. MDCCCXV,
ætatis LX.
Vir, Pater, Maritus,
Pietate Ingenio Moribus,
Vere præstans.
Quem eruditum fuisse Lector
Testatur Doctorum consensus ;
Quem et dilectum,
Uxoris eheu, et trium Filiarum,
Necnon amicorum lacrymæ ;
Virtutum denique
in Bonorum omnium desiderio
Comprobationem videas !!

In the middle of the churchyard, on the west side of the footpath, is a stone monument having on one side a slate slab bearing an inscription, but as the tomb has sunk into the ground only the following portion of the inscription is visible.

"To the Memory of M<sup>r</sup> James Thain who died April the 7th 1771, Aged 70 years."

Near to is a small headstone inscribed :—

RICHARD
DAWSON
BVRIED THE
30 OF DECEM
1683

A very small stone bears the date 1677, but no further inscription. This is the earliest date in the churchyard. There is, however, another stone, probably older, inscribed :—

E. H.
GRIEVE NOT AT ALL THE LORD
DOTH CALL

Another old stone is inscribed :—

JEREMIAH
ROADES WAS
BVRIED THE 10
OF IVLY 1678.

The erection of tombstones in churchyards was not a common practice prior to about the middle of the seventeenth century.[1]

---

[1] See *Notes and Queries* (3rd series, vi., *passim*) for many interesting particulars on this point.

## THE NEW CHURCH.

The New Church, dedicated to the Holy Trinity,[1] stands midway between Old and New Lenton. The first stone was laid June 11th, 1841, by Francis Wright, Esq., of Lenton Hall, who contributed £3,000 towards its cost, besides giving the land for the site, and the church was consecrated by the Bishop of Lincoln, October 6th, 1842. It is a large stone building, with high pitched slated roofs, and consists of a nave with clerestory, north and south aisles, chancel, vestry, organ chamber, north porch, and lofty square pinnacled tower. The style of architecture is the Early English, but the general effect of the building is far from pleasing, the high narrow clerestory placed upon its disproportionate side aisles giving it a distorted appearance. " It is not impossible that the prejudice in favour of building the tower at the west end, coupled with the rule not to build one narrower than the clerestory, and with the fact that the funds were not sufficient to make the tower larger than it is, was the cause of the pinched up proportion of the clerestory, while an idea of future side galleries was the cause of the heavy looking side aisles being combined with the said lank clerestory. If so, Mr. Stephens [the architect of the church] deserves more credit and less blame than most spectators will award to him." A clock was placed in the tower in 1844 ; it is now illuminated, and, in connection with the bells, plays the Cambridge chimes at the hours and quarters. Previous to the year 1856, the tower contained only one bell, but in that year five additional bells, cast by Messrs. Taylor & Co., of Loughborough, were placed

---

(1) This was the dedication of the Priory. It has already been remarked that previous to the dissolution of the monastery there does not seem to have been a parish church, properly so-called, though some portion of the conventual church was doubtless appropriated to the use of the parishioners. The village feast, or wakes, was formerly held on Trinity Sunday, but at a meeting of the inhabitants, convened for the purpose of taking into consideration the propriety of altering the annual feast from Trinity Sunday to Whit-Sunday, held in the parish church on April 15th, 1805, it was " resolved unanimously as the opinion of this meeting that it is desirable that the annual feast, which has hitherto been held in Trinity week, shall be kept in Whitsun-week for the future ; and also that an advertisement declaratory of this resolution be twice inserted in the 'Nottingham Journal,' and that the lord of the manor, the minister of the parish, and the churchwardens and overseers be requested to sign this advertisement." This alteration was duly carried out, and the feast is still nominally observed at Whitsuntide.

therein, through the liberality of Mr. John Shaw, churchwarden.
The bells are in the key of A, and, although somewhat deficient
in weight, are very musical in tone.

The bells are thus inscribed :—

> First (or treble)—" Lord have mercy upon us."
> Second—" Christ have mercy upon us."
> Third—" Lord have mercy upon us."
> Fourth—" O Lord save the Queen."
> Fifth—" Thomas Mears, Founder, London, 1842."
> Sixth (or tenor)—" Hallelujah."

In addition to these inscriptions, each of the bells, with the
exception of the fifth (the old bell), has upon it :

> " George Browne, Vicar.
> Thomas Hopkins, Curate.
> Thomas Adams, Lace Merchant,  } Churchwardens.
> John Shaw, Tanner and Fellmonger,
> 18   V. (Crown) R.   56."

For several years after the erection of the church, the east
end of the chancel, which was partitioned off from the remainder
of the church, was used for the purposes of a vestry, but in 1862
the partition was removed, and a vestry erected on the south
side of the chancel.  This alteration brought to view the reredos,
erected in 1858, at a cost of £43.  It is executed in Ancaster
stone, the Agnus Dei being carved in the centre, and bears the
Lord's Prayer, Decalogue, and Apostles' Creed, upon panels of
Hill's patent consolidated glass.  The organ chamber was
erected on the north side of the chancel in 1870.

The church contains three stained glass windows.  The east
window of three lights, and containing conventional floral
devices in brilliant colours, with the text, " For as the earth
bringeth forth her bud, and as the garden causeth the things that
are sown in it to spring forth, so the Lord will cause righteous-
ness and peace to spring forth before all the nations," has the
following inscription :—" Erected by his sons, friends, and
tenants in memory of Francis Wright, Esq^rs., the founder of this

Church.—Born Dec. 21, 1806. Died Feb. 24. 1873." The second window, to the memory of Thomas Adams, Esq., is in the south aisle. It is of two lights, each divided into two compartments, and represents the Pharisee and Publican in the Temple, with the text, "God be merciful to me a sinner;" the just steward, with the text, "Well done good and faithful servant;" the return of the prodigal son, with the text, "Bring forth the best robe, and put it on him;" and the good Samaritan, with the text, "Go and do thou likewise." At the foot of the window is the inscription, "To the memory of Thomas Adams, Esq. J.P., of Lenton Firs, Born Feb. 5, 1807. Died May 16, 1873. Erected as a testimony of the high esteem of his friends and neighbours." Painted on the wall above the window is the Crest (somewhat inaccurately represented) granted to the late Mr. Adams. A small window at the east end of the south aisle is also to the memory of the same gentleman. It represents in the upper portion a woman instructing her child in the Scriptures; in the lower portion is an open book, on the pages of which is written, "All flesh is as grass, all the glory of man is as the flowers of grass." The window bears these inscriptions, "From a child thou hast known the Holy Scriptures," and "In memory of Thos Adams Esqʳᵉ J.P. 1873."

The memorial tablets in the church, six in number, are all of white marble.

On the north wall of the chancel, near the east end, is a large tablet bearing the Crest of the Wright family and the following inscription :—

*Crest.*—A unicorn's head *argent*, erased *gules*, armed and maned *or*, charged on the neck with three spear heads, one and two, of the second.

In affectionate memory of JOHN WRIGHT, of Lenton Hall,
Esquire,
Who died April 21ˢᵗ 1840, aged 81 years.

And of ELIZABETH, his wife, eldest daughter of FRANCIS
BERESFORD, Esquire,
of Ashbourne, who died Decʳ 18ᵗʰ 1833, aged 74 years.

Also of JOHN, their eldest son, who died at Naples, Jan$^y$ 24$^{th}$
1828, aged 35 years.

Also of ANNIE, wife of RICHARD PERRIN Esq$^{re}$ and niece
of the above,
Who died at Lenton Hall in 1838 and was interred in the
same vault in the old churchyard.

" Come now, let us reason together, saith the LORD,
Though your sins be as scarlet, they shall be white as snow ;
Though they be red like crimson, they shall be as wool."

ISAIAH i. 18.

Upon another tablet on the south wall of the chancel:—

Sacred
To the memory of
JOSEPH FENTON
who died March 22, 1853,
aged 67 years.
And of ANN, his wife,
who died December 14, 1853,
aged 60 years.

" Enter not into judgement with thy
servant, O Lord, for in thy sight shall
no man living be justified."

Near to the last are two tablets, thus inscribed :—

In
affectionate remembrance of
ELIZABETH ANNE,
the beloved wife of the
REV$^D$ GEORGE BROWNE,
Vicar of this Parish,
She fell asleep Dec$^r$ 8$^{th}$ 1870,
aged 63 years

" Looking for that blessed hope and the glorious
appearing of the great GOD and our Saviour
Jesus Christ."
" Her children arise up and call her blessed."

Also to the memory of
WILLIAM JOHN,
who died May 31ˢᵗ 1858, aged 2 years,
EDWARD,
who died May 18ᵗʰ 1842, aged 12 years,
JAMES PETER,
died January 14ᵗʰ 1844, aged 6 months, and
DENIS GEORGE,
Died February 19ᵗʰ 1848, aged 19 years.
The beloved children of
REVᴰ GEORGE & ELIZABETH ANNE BROWNE.
"I will pour my Spirit upon thy seed,
and my blessing upon thine offspring."
Isaiah, 44. 3.

On another tablet near, is :—
In loving memory of
FRANCIS BROWNE B.A.
Late Vicar of Christ Church, Enfield,
And some time Curate of this Parish.
Born October 7ᵗʰ 1844.
Fell asleep in Jesus Aug 8ᵗʰ 1879,
" He walked with God and was not,
For God took him."
" To be with Christ which is far better."

In the south aisle is a tablet, surmounted with a Crest and
Motto, thus inscribed:—

*Crest.*—A talbot passant *sable*, semée of cinquefoils *or*,
resting the dexter paw upon a mullet of the last.

*Motto. Animo Fideque*

To the memory of their beloved Father
THOMAS ADAMS
of Lenton Firs,
J.P. for the Borough and County of Nottingham,
This tablet is erected by his grateful children.
He was born 5ᵗʰ Febᵞ 1807,.
Fell asleep in Jesus May 16ᵗʰ 1873,
And was buried in the Church Cemetery.
" He was a faithful man and feared God above many."
Heb : 7. 2.
" By the grace of God I am what I am." 1 Cor. 15. 10.

Also in memory of their beloved mother,
LUCY ADAMS,
Born Aug<sup>st</sup> 28<sup>th</sup> 1807, died Aug<sup>st</sup> 28<sup>th</sup> 1874.

" Safe in the arms of Jesus."
" The righteous shall be in everlasting remembrance."
Psalm 112, 6.

A large gallery, capable of seating 214 persons, extends,
across the west end of the nave. Beneath this gallery stands
the font, which undoubtedly belonged to Lenton Priory, and
was probably placed in the old parish church at the dissolution
of the Priory. For several years it stood in the garden
of the late Mr. Stretton, to whom it had been presented
by the then churchwardens, but it was restored to the parish
church on the erection of the new fabric in 1842, by Lieut.-
Colonel Stretton, at the request of the present Vicar.
When first placed in the new church, it stood on four
pedestals near the chancel, but was afterwards removed to
its present position, and placed on a plain stone slab. This
font, one of the finest and most perfect examples of
Norman work remaining in this county, is of a square form,
measuring 34 inches by 30 inches, and is 30 inches high. The
sculptures upon its sides are both curious and interesting, and
have evidently been coloured. At one end is a very curious
representation of the Crucifixion, the figure of the Saviour
occupying the centre, extended upon a large cross with foliated
ends. On the right is a soldier piercing His side with a spear,
and on either side are the two thieves upon smaller crosses.
From the mouth of one issues a small figure, representing his
soul, flying upwards, and from the mouth of the other issues a
similar figure falling into the extended jaws of a huge monster,
the head of which only is seen. Above this group are figures
of angels represented in the act of swinging censers. At the
opposite end of the font is a large cross of ornamental foliage.
One side is divided into a double row of recesses, each of which
is occupied by the figure of an angel or cherub, excepting the
central one of the lower row, of larger size than the others
which contains a group considered to represent Christ's descent

from the cross. A fair engraving of this side is given in Paley's "Baptismal Fonts." The other side is in four divisions. Mr. M. H. Bloxam, the veteran archæologist, is of opinion that the first may represent Christ before Pilate, the second appears to be the Resurrection, the third is the three Marys going to the sepulchre, and the fourth represents the church built over the sepulchre. The bowl measures 30 inches by 26 inches, and is 18 inches deep. It is of quatrefoil form, and appears to have been intended for the practice of immersion. The top is ornamented with eight fleur-de-lys, and there is evidence of the former existence of hinges. The font is placed in an inconvenient position for inspection, and although it possesses a water drain, it has not, until recently, been used for the purpose for which it was intended, the rite of Holy Baptism having been performed by means of water contained in a basin placed *inside* the font.

The communion plate is of the same date as the church.

At the west end of the nave is a board, removed from the old church, recording the following charitable bequest—

"1781.[1] Mrs. Reb: Garland left to the Vicar and Church-wardens of Lenton, for the time being, Ten Pounds, the Interest to be given in Bread on St. Thomas's Day, to such poor Persons as do not receive Parochial Relief"

Another board has inscribed upon it—

"This Church was built in the year 1842, by which means Six Hundred and Eighty four additional sittings were obtained; and in consequence of a Grant from the Incorporated Society for promoting the Enlargement, Building, and Repairing of Churches and Chapels, Four Hundred and Forty of that number are hereby declared to be Free and Unappropriated. The provision of Church-room in the Parish previously to the building of this Church being to the extent of Two Hundred and seventy six Sittings, Seventy of which number were Free.

A Plan, showing the number and situation of the Free Seats is fixed up in the Vestry Room.

GEORGE BROWNE, Vicar.

FRANCIS WRIGHT,  } Churchwardens"
SAMUEL KEETLEY, }

---

(1) Why this date is given we are unable to explain. Reference to the Garland pedigree (see p. 212) shows that Rebecca Garland died in 1769, and was buried in the old parish church of Lenton on the 22nd of January in that year.

—East Elevation—

—North Elevation—

—West Elevation—

Plan of
top of Font

—Scale of [⊢⊢⊢⊢⊢⊢⊢⊢⊢⊢] Inches—

Font from Lenton Priory

The churchyard, enlarged in 1859, contains a few monuments worthy of notice. In a corner near the tower is one in memory of John Shaw, formerly churchwarden of Lenton, who died October 26th, 1864, aged 59 years, and of Margaret, his wife, who died April 11th, 1869, aged 63 years. Other monuments are to the memory of William Weatherall, who died April 24th, 1873, aged 29 years ; George Stanton, who died July 11th, 1882, aged 80, and Hannah, his wife, who died April 20th, 1882, aged 80 ; John Froggatt, of Lenton Poplars, who died April 28th, 1861, aged 71, and Sarah, his wife, who died November 14th, 1879, aged 90 ; John Godfrey, who died December 25th, 1860, aged 73 years, and Jane, his wife, who died April 29th, 1883, aged 96 years ; William Kirk, who died August 13th, 1866, aged 59 ; and Thomas Wood, of Dunkirk, who died November 23rd, 1879, aged 45 years. There is also a plain granite slab near the end of the chancel in memory of Alice Josephine Smith Wright, and Caroline Henrietta Smith Wright, infant children of Henry Smith Wright, Esq., of Lenton Hall ; the former died May 25th, 1871, and the latter died February 24th, 1873.

By an order of the Privy Council, dated March 20th, 1857, it was directed that from and after the first of April following, burials should be discontinued in Lenton New Church, and in the burial ground adjoining within three yards of the church, "with the exception of now existing vaults and walled graves, which can be opened without disturbing soil that has been already buried in, and in which each coffin shall be embedded in a layer of powdered charcoal, four inches thick, and be separately entombed in an airtight manner," and, that "with the exception of vaults and family graves, only one body be buried in a grave, and, that with the same exception, no grave be re-opened."

# SECTION VII.

## THE PARISH REGISTERS; CHURCHWARDENS'
## ACCOUNTS; AND PAROCHIAL CHARITY.

" Untwist the linkèd bouts of pedigree,
And on a point where Garter's self might err,
Quote—fearless quote—the Parish Register."

HE Parish Registers[1] date back to the year 1540,
and the entries of baptisms, marriages, and burials,
from that year down to 1748, with certain exceptions, are contained in four volumes of parchment. These registers are, with two exceptions (those of
Ordsall and Askham), the oldest in the county of Nottingham,
but it is somewhat remarkable that only the marriages and
burials date from 1540, no baptisms being recorded prior to
1598.[2] The first volume is in good preservation, and is

(1) Extracts from these registers were first published in " The Reliquary" (Vol.
XIII., p. 11.) by Major A. E. Lawson Lowe, F.S.A., to whom we are indebted
for the numerous annotations that follow.

(2) The original mandate for keeping registers of baptisms, marriages, and burials
in each parish was issued in 1536, but seems to have been only partially carried into
effect, for parish registers that date back beyond 1550 are comparatively uncommon.
The mandate was repeated in more rigorous terms on the accession of Queen Elizabeth, hence the number of registers which date from about that period. In 1597, it
was ordained that parchment books should be provided in every parish, and all the
names from the older books (which had been kept on paper) should be therein
transcribed. The Lenton registers, so far as the marriages and burials are concerned,
appear to have been copied, as directed, in 1598, but the baptisms, for some unknown
reason, were not copied in like manner, and consequently they only date from that
year.

evidently a copy of the original paper register.  Nearly all the entries are in Latin, and the writing being neat, may be read without much difficulty.   The book consists of thirty-eight leaves, 13½ inches long by 5¼ inches wide, and is without covers. The first page commences—"A Register of all wedings as they are founde In the oulde Register Booke since the year 1540, etc.," and the marriages are continued to the end of the year 1652, except that the leaves containing the marriages from February, 1589, to December, 1612, and from October, 1644, to December, 1647, are missing.  The burials then follow from February, 1541, to September, 1647, but a leaf containing the entries of burials from 1589 to the earlier part of 1593 has been abstracted from the registers, and the volume concludes with the baptisms which commence in 1598, and continue until September, 1651, except that the leaves containing the baptisms from March 25th, 1626, to July, 1629, and from September, 1651, to December, 1655, are lost.   At the bottom of the last page of this volume is written :—  "Gulielmus Rudsby, Vicarius, natus Anno Domi 1663, sexto die mensis martij, cui dedit Oxonium māmas Wintonia cunas."

The second volume consists of fifteen leaves, 13½ inches by 6 inches, with a front parchment cover.  It is badly written, and is in many places quite illegible.   It commences—"A true and p'fect Register of all that are borne within the parish of Lenton, begun in yᵉ yeare 1655," and the baptisms are continued to March 25th, 1678.   The marriages commence in March, 1655, and continue until the end of 1678, and the burials follow from 1653 to the end of 1678.

The third volume consists of fifteen leaves, 12 inches by 6¼ inches, and back parchment cover.   It is in very indifferent condition, and the entries are carelessly written.   It commences with the baptisms from 1679 to 1706, then follow the marriages from March 25th, 1680, to the end of 1707, and after these are the burials from 1679 to 1707.   The burials for 1692, 1693, and 1694, are written on the inside of the back cover.

The fourth volume is of larger size, and written with much greater care.  It consists of 49 leaves, 15¼ inches by 7 inches,

19

·and is bound in parchment covers. This volume contains the baptisms from 1706 to 1784, the marriages from 1708 to the end of 1753, and the burials from 1707 to 1784. The words " Insp^d W. Lister" are written in the margins of the entries of baptisms and burials between September 12th and October 11th, 1784, indicating that the register had been inspected between those dates.

The following are the entries in the first four volumes which appear most worthy of note :—

### VOLUME I.

1540.  John Warton and Joan Matthew, married 26 February.
1541.  Thomas Ducket, buried 8 February.
—  John Warton, buried 14 September.
1548.  Robert Ward and Isabella Mirrian, married 22 January.
1568.  Robert Taylor and Katherine Birche, married 20 January.
1573.  Richard Norwood and Agnes Robinson, married 17 May.
1577.  " Radulphus Lees nupt est 17 die April." (No mention of the wife).
—  " Mulier quædam pauper sepulta est 22 die Maij."
1578.  " Puer quidam pastor sepultus est 13 die Aprilis."
       Isabella, daughter of Richard Lecester, buried 28 June.
       Anne Lecester, mother of James Lecester, Gent.,¹ buried 18 July.
1580.  Jane, wife of James Lecester, Gent., buried 19 November.
1582.  Cicilia Cost, the wife of the herdsman (*bubulci*), buried 8 August.
—  Luke, son of John Lecester, buried 13 December.
1584.  John, son of John Lecester, buried 14 July.
1585.  Cassandra Wood, buried 11 January.
1586.  William Gregory and Elizabeth Dolphin, married 17 April.
—  William Warde and Anne Matthew, married 16 May.
1587.  William Chamberlaine and Elizabeth Chalens, married 24 April.
       Margaret, daughter of James Lecester, buried 12 July.
       Thomas fforster,² minister, and Jane Digbye, married 24 December.
       Peter Toule and Catherine Toule, married 29 January.
1588.  Alice Mirian, buried 25 May.

---

(1) No particulars as to this family have been seen. Some of the Lecesters were resident in the parish of Lenton as late as about the middle of the last century, but, apparently, in somewhat reduced circumstances, for they do not seem to have then ranked amongst the gentry.

(2) Thomas Forster, here described as " minister," was possibly stipendiary curate of Lenton, but was never incumbent of the living. As may be seen from the list of vicars (p. 242), John Fisher was presented to the benefice in 1572, which he held until his decease in 1592.

1588. William Bushellᵗ and Aloisia Matthew, married 25 July.

George, son of James Lecester, Gent., buried 20 December.

1589. James Charnocke, Gent., and Anna Faile, married 4 February.

1594. William Dolphin, yeoman, buried 4 October.

— Humphrey, son of James Lecester, buried 13 January.

1595. Meriella (Muriel ?) wife of John Wood, clerk,² buried 12 June.

William Warde, buried 26 October.

Henry Lecester, Gent., buried 11 February.

Humphrey Gilbert, yeoman, buried 24 March.

1596. William Bushell,³ yeoman, buried 15 June.

1597. Samuel Byllay, a youth, buried 21 May.

"Tho: Graisley porcarius sepultus est 26 die Augusti."

William Lovelas, Gent., buried 2 September.

Robert Walker, miller, buried 21 October.

Helen, wife of Ralph Mirian,⁴ buried 3 February.

1598. Francis, son of John Pearson, baptized 17 April.

1599. "Richardᵛ Gatneby, Eboracensis," buried 10 July.

— Margaret, daughter of William Gregorye, baptized 19 August.

1600. William, son of Christopher Mirrian, buried 30 January.

1601. Bathshuah, daughter of William Foster, Gent., baptized 3 April.

"A soldier, formerly of Lincolnshire, whose name is unknown to us," buried 25 October.

"Jana Pillinge peregrina sepulta est 20ᵐᵒ die Martij."

"Tha's filius Andreæ Bradforde, bapt est 26ᵗᵒ die Nove'brix qui quidem Tha's natus erat in monasterio in domo Th'sa. Birche."

1602. "Fraciscus filia Joh'is Leeminges bap. apud Radford 11ᵐᵒ die Maij." [inserted.]

Frances daughter of William Cliffe,⁶ minister, baptized 29 August.

James Lecester, a youth, son of James Lecester, Gent., buried 27 December.

Elizabeth, daughter of John Brouley, Gent., buried 3 Feb.

---

(1) See his burial in 1596, and hers in 1606.

(2) Meriella Wood was wife of John Wood, vicar of Lenton, who had been presented to the living about two years previously. See his burial in 1623.

(3) The will of William Bussell, of Lenton, in the county of Nottingham, gentleman, dated May the 22nd, 1596, was proved in the Prerogative Court of York, October the 7th, that same year. He desires thereby that his body may be interred within the parish church of Lenton.

(4) The Herald's Visitations record that Richard Willoughby, of Grendon, in Warwickshire (the representative of a younger branch of the Willoughbys of Wollaton), married Elizabeth, daughter of Ralph Mirian, of Lenton, assumably identical with the above. (Harl. MSS., 1400-1555.) Several entries relative to members of the Mirian, or Merrian, family are to be found in the earlier portion of the Lenton registers.

(5) This entry has been obviously interpolated, probably by Robert Ollerenshawe, vicar of Lenton, to whom this Frances Leemeinge was married in 1629. See that year.

(6) "William Cliffe, minister," has not been identified.

1603.   "Johēs filius Johēs Byshopp ut asseritur ex Helena Fenton genitus bapt
        est 15to die Octobris." [1]

1604.   Richard Toone, Gent., buried 21 October.

1605.   Catherine, wife of Peter Toule, buried 6 April.

1606.   Aloicia, wife of William Bushell, Gent., buried 17 July.

—       John Lecester, Gent., buried 12 September.

1607.   William Foster, Gent., buried 29 March.

1608.   Thomas Smedley, miller, buried 16 Jan.

1609.   Elizabeth, daughter of Ralph Bunington, Esquire,[2] buried 10 October.

1612.   Mary, dau. of Sir Thomas Cave, Knight,[3] buried 15 August.

—       Bridgett, dau. of Richard Willoughby, Gent,[4] bapt. 24 October.

1613.   John, son of Thomas Wood, Gent.,[5] bapt. 20 September (born 17 Sep-
        tember).

—       Edward, son of Edward Leicester, baptized 25 March.

—       Anne, daughter of James Lecester, Gent., buried 29 November.

1615.   John Brown, painter, buried 18 July.

        Mary, wife of James Lecester, Gent., buried 15 September.

—       James Lecester, Gent., buried 12 November.

        Roger Ayskough and Mary Ouldfeeld, married 31 Jan.

1616.   Frances, daughter of Thomas Wood, Gent., baptized 22 September
        (born 11 September).

—       Mary, daughter of Edward Lecester, baptized 2 February.

1617.   Sarah, wife of William Forster, Gent., buried 7 July.

1618.   "Anthonius Harison[6] custos de Nott: parke sepultus est 9no die Junij."

—       Elizabeth, daughter of Thomas Wood, Gent., baptized 10 July (born
        3 July).

1619.   "Anna filia Guilielmi Ward agricolæ bapt. est 17mo die Octobris."

        Robert Cowlishaw and Mary Leemeinge, married 25 November.

---

(1) A not unusual form of registration of baptisms of illegitimate children.

(2) There was an armigerous family of the name of Bunington or Bonington seated
at Barrowcote, in Derbyshire,·at this period.   The Visitation of Derbyshire, made in
1662, shows that William Bonington, of Barrowcote, had a younger son, Ralph,
contemporary with the above, who was married and had issue.

(3) Sir Thomas Cave, the father of the child whose burial is recorded above, was
of Stanford, in Leicestershire, and was the eldest son of Roger Cave, Esq., of that
place.   His grandson was created a baronet in 1641.   It is somewhat difficult to
understand how a child of Sir Thomas Cave's came to be buried at Lenton.

(4) Bridget Willoughby was the youngest daughter of Richard Willoughby, of
Grendon, in Warwickshire, by Elizabeth his wife, daughter of Ralph Mirian, of
Lenton.

(5) Thomas Wood, the father of the child whose baptism is here recorded, was
the son of John Wood, vicar of Lenton.   He married Elizabeth, eldest daughter of
Richard Willoughby, of Grendon, by whom he had several children.   The baptisms
of four of his daughters are recorded in the Lenton registers, in 1616, 1618, 1619-20,
and 1621.   The burial of Thomas Wood, gentleman, appears in the Radford registers
in 1639.

(6) Nottingham Park was well stocked with deer until about the year 1750; after
then the Park was let to the people of Nottingham for their cattle to graze in.   The
custom of interring at Lenton the remains of those who died within the limits of
Nottingham Park or Standard Hill has already been remarked upon.   (See p. 255).

1619.	Elizabeth daughter of Andrew Naile, of London, bapt. 2 Jan.
	Dorothy, daughter of Thomas Wood, bapt. 16 Feb.
1620.	Bryan Bylay, Esquire, buried 4 March.
1621.	Brigetta, daughter of Thomas Wood, Gent., baptized 9 November (born 7 November).
1622.	Humphrey, son of Philip Hanmer, Gent.,[1] baptized 15 Aug.
1623.	John Wood, clerk,[2] buried 10 September.
—	" Advena qui claudus erat sepult 17to die Novem."
1625.	"Anna filia Gulielm. Wright (paup ignotus) bapta 2do die Junij."
—	William Warde and Barbara Empingham, married 2 July.
1626.	Sarah, daughter of Edward Leycester, buried 6 August.
1627.	John Cowleyshawe, buried 3 Sept.
1628.	Joane, wife of Edward Lecester, buried 10 December.
—	Edward Lecester buried 29 December.
1629.	"Robertus Ollerenshawe,[3] et Francisca Leemeinge nupti fuerint 25to die Junij."
—	Mary, wife of John Leycester, Gent., deceased, bur. 19 Dec.
1631.	William, son of John Mundie, Esquire,[4] baptized 28 Feb.
1633.	George Revill, Gent., buried 9 June.
1635.	William Elsam and Elinora Leemeinge, married 24 Nov.
	William Broadband and Elizabeth Wood, married 9 February.
1636.	Christiana, daughter of Peter Towle, baptized 25 Sept.
1637.	Joan Time, Gentlewoman, buried 29 January.

(1) Philip Hanmer, gent., above-named, appears to have resided at Radford. He was the elder of the two surviving sons of Humphrey Hanmer, Esq., of Radford, by Winifred his wife. That lady had been previously married to Edward Southworth, Esq., of Radford, who by his will, dated June the 25th, 1573, and proved in the Prerogative Court of York, May the 25th, 1574, devised all his lands in the parishes of Lenton and Radford, with the exception of one close in Lenton, called Willowholme, to his wife, for her life, together with the house at Radford in which he dwelt. She afterwards married Humphrey Hanmer, Esq., as already stated, whom she likewise survived. Her will, which is dated October the 31st, 1604, and was proved in the Prerogative Court of York, January the 17th, 1605-6, names her stepdaughter, Ann Southworth, her own daughters, Ellinor, Cicely, Winifred, Grace, and Mary Hanmer, and her sons, Philip and Thomas Hanmer, the latter of whom were placed under the care of Sir William Hanmer, of the county of Flint, knight. The Hanmers, of Hanmer, in that county, are one of the oldest families in North Wales, and have recently been raised to the peerage.

(2) John Wood is remarkable as being the only incumbent of this parish who has been interred at Lenton during a period of nearly three centuries and a half. He was likewise vicar of the adjoining parish of Radford.

(3) Robert Ollerenshawe, who succeeded John Wood in the vicarage of Lenton, was probably a member of the old Derbyshire family of that name, formerly seated at Ollerenshawe, in the parish of Chapel-en-le-Frith. Frances Leemeinge, his wife, was a daughter of John Leemeinge, of Radford. See her baptism in 1602, presumably interpolated in the Lenton registers by her husband.

(4) William Mundie, or Mundy, whose baptism, curiously enough, appears to have taken place at Lenton, was the second son of John Mundy, Esq., of Markeaton, in Derbyshire, and eventually succeeded to the family estates, his elder brother, Francis, having died without issue in 1657. William Mundy, Esq., died in 1682, and was buried in the chancel at Allestree, in Derbyshire. The slab which marks his grave still exists, though the inscription is all but illegible. The family appears to have had no connection whatever with this place.

1638.  George, son of Robert Terwet, Esquire, buried 23 February.

1639.  George Johnson and Joane Sherwin, married 17 January.

1640.  Joan, wife of Edward Copley, Esquire,¹ buried 31 July.

1641.  Ralph Copley, Esquire,¹ buried 23 June.

1643.  " Advena quidam cuius nomen nobis fuerat incognita et apud Beskwood
         parke macecratus fuerat sepultus erat 17mo die mensis Maij."

         Henry, son of John Bishopp, baptized 27 August.

         William Lecester and Elizabeth Chadwick, mar.————.

1646.  Thomas, son of William Leicester, baptized 23 August.

1649.  Henry Flower and Hellina Preston, married 21 April.

1650.  ————, son of William Leicester, baptized 26 October.

1651.  Edward Smith and Thomasine Beacock, mar. 27 Nov.


## VOLUME II.

In 1653, during the Usurpation, an Act was passed by the Barebones Parliament requiring the incumbents of parishes to give up their register books to laymen, who were to be called "Parish Registers." These new officials were to be chosen in every parish by the inhabitant householders on or before the 22nd of September, 1653, and as soon as he had been sworn and approved by the magistrates, his appointment was duly entered in the register-book. The second volume of the Lenton registers contains the following memorandum of this appointment:

iiijth ffebruary, 1653.

Bee it remembred that Edmund York, Clerk, came before us and being chosen by the Inhabitants of Lenton for their p'ish, and wee conseivinge him a fitt p'son for that Imploym' doe allow and approve of him to bee p'ish Register thereof and have given the oath as so directed by Acte of Parliam'..

Witnes our hands

P. SPELMAN.

THO. CHARLTON.

———————————————————————————

(1) The ancient Yorkshire family of this name, seated at Sprotborough, near Doncaster, became connected with this county about the time of King Henry the Eighth, through marriage with the heiress of a branch of the Fitz-William family, by which they acquired the manor of Plumtree, near Nottingham, and other estates. The registers of St. Mary's, Nottingham, record the burials of several members of the Copley family, assumably belonging to a younger branch of the Copleys of Sprotborough ; as also are those who are named above.

1653. Francis Matthew, of Radford, buried 21 February.
1654. James Merriam, buried 23 March.
1655. Mr. Robert West,[1] buried 14 May.
    Elizabeth, wife of Robert Cowleyshaw, buried 25 June.
    Ellen, wife of John Bishopp, buried 15 December.
1656. Isabelle Cowleyshawe, buried 23 July.
1658. Robert Willoughby,[2] buried 25 January.
1659. Francis Lester, buried 30 May.
    Isaac Cowleyshawe, buried 10 January.
1663. Elizabeth Wood, buried 10 April.
1665. John Wood, buried 6 January.
1669. Dorothy Wood, buried 23 Dec.
    Francis Singlehurst, of Attenborough, and Sarah Humfrey, of Lenton,
        married 18 January.
    Christopher Noble, of Cropwell-Butler, and Elizabeth Flower,[3] of
        Langar, married by license, 22 January.
    Henry Farnworth, of Selston, Gent., and Mary Fletcher, of the same
        place, Spinster, married "with a Lysance," 29 January.
1670. John Smith and Mary Greaves, both of St. Peter's parish, Nottingham,
        married by license, 30 January.
    Elizabeth Webster, buried 18 February.
1671. Catherine, daughter of Richard Godfrey, buried 13 January.
—  John Benton, of Askham, and Catherine Hall, of Mansfield, married
        by license, 13 March.
1677. William Wright and Alice Shipman, of Radcliffe-on-Trent, married by
        license 8 June.
1678. "Vicesimo ye son of Rosomon tounsend, baptized november ye 16."

---

(1) Mr. Robert West was the son of William West, of Rotherham, in Yorkshire,
and grandson of Thomas West, of Beeston, in this county, who was the youngest of
the three sons of John West, of Aughton, in Yorkshire.  A pedigree of the Wests,
of Aughton, may be found in Hunter's " South Yorkshire " (vol. ii., p. 173), but it is
wanting in various particulars, and is perhaps not altogether correct.  Robert West,
whose burial is thus recorded in the Lenton registers, was presumably buried at
Lenton, but the fact is certainly open to question, for his burial is likewise recorded
in the registers of the neighbouring parish of Beeston, where a branch of this family
was seated.  The Wests of Beeston derived their descent through Gilbert West, half-
brother of this same Robert West.  Armorial bearings were granted to the Wests of
Rotherham in 1634.

(2) Robert Willoughby was the third son of Richard Willoughby, of Grendon, in
Warwickshire, by Elizabeth his wife, daughter of Ralph Mirian, of Lenton.  He
appears to have died unmarried.  The Grendon branch were descended from the
Willoughbys of Wollaton, through Baldwin Willoughby (a younger son of Sir Hugh
Willoughby, knight, who died in 1488), whose wife was the sole heiress of John
Mortimer, of Grendon.

(3) The registers of Langar contain very many entries relative to the Flower family,
for some time resident in that parish.  Henry Flower, Esq., of Langar, entered his
pedigree in the Heralds' Visitation of 1614, but his line was extinct at this period,
and Elizabeth Flower must have belonged to a junior branch of the family.  She is
probably identical with Elizabeth, the daughter of George Flower, and Judith, his
wife, who was baptized at Langar, March the 27th, 1653.

## VOL. III.

1679.  Isabelle, wife of Barnaby Wartnaby,[1] buried 17 Apiil.

1680.  Mary Lenton, the child of a wanderer, buried 26 Nov.

1682.  "A peew sett up in the Alley, under the Reading-pew, with the consent of the Minister and the Churchwardens, for the use of Thomas Peninton and his fameley."

1686.  Mr. John Garland,[2] buried 4 June.

1689.  Rebeckah, wife of John Garland, buried 10 June.

Hannah, daughter of Mr. Philip Brownlo,[3] buried 28 June.

"John Godfrey yᵉ son of Richard Godfrey buryed August yᵉ 9th "

1690.  Isabelle, daughter of Thomas Otter, baptized in August.

Philip, son of Mr. Philip Brownlow, buried 11 Sept.

"Richard Cleaton[4] and Sarah Drewry married February 18."

1691.  Hannah, daughter of Mr. Rowland Sutborrowe, buried 7 January.

1692.  Mr. Rowland Suttbere buried 7 February.

—     Rebecca, danghter of John Garland, baptized 5 October.

1693.  Hanah Mariah, dau. of Roland Suttborowe, baptized 5 April.

Lucia, daughter of John Garland, baptized 23 December.

1696.  John Baggshaw, of Stanley, in the county of Derby, and Mary Burton, married [date illegible].

Richard Norris[5] and Elizabeth Parker, married 31 December.

---

(1) Barnaby Wartnaby was a wealthy iron-worker of Nottingham, and served as Sheriff of that town in 1652.  In 1665 he built and endowed almshouses at the corner of Pilcher Gate, Nottingham, for three poor aged widows and as many widowers.  He was twice married, the above-named Isabelle being his second wife. The registers of St. Mary's, Nottingham, record the marriage, by civil contract, of Barnaby Wartnaby and Isabel Hearson, in 1657.  By his will, dated October the 30th, 1672, Barnaby Wartnaby desires that his body may be " buried in the parish church of St. Mary in the said town of Nottingham under a stone where my late wife Ellen Wartnaby was buried, being at the end of the seat where I, the said Barnaby Wartnaby, used to sit in the said church." Amongst the various legacies named in the will is one to his second wife's sister, Alice Goodwin, widow, "dwelling at Lenton, in the county of Nottingham," and it might be conjectured that Isabel Wartnaby was residing with her, at the time of her decease.

(2) See the pedigree of this family (p. 212).

(3) This Mr. Philip Brownlow has not been identified.  The name occurs occasionally in the Nottingham registers throughout the latter half of the sixteenth century, and in 1551 one John Brownlow was Sheriff of Nottingham, and Mayor in 1567,1568, 1582, and 1589.

(4) The family of Cleaton (properly Clayton), of Codnor Breach, was one of long standing in the county of Derby.  The last male representative was Richard Clayton, of Codnor Breach, upon whose decease the estates at Codnor, Waingroves, and Loscoe, which had been held by his ancestors since about the year 1600, were divided amongst his daughters and co-heiresses.  One of the ladies married Robert Strelley, Esq., of Oakerthorpe, in Derbyshire, and died in 1833, leaving issue. Sarah Drewry (properly Drury) was a member of a family for many years resident in the town of Nottingham, several of whom have filled the highest offices in the Corporation.  This family is now represented, in the female line, by William Drury Lowe, Esq., of Locko Park.

(5) See their monumental slabs in the old church.

1696. William Chamberlin, of Keyworth, and Mary Browne, of Bramcote, married 2 January.

1700. "A child of Mr. Clarke's dyed here att Lenton, ffebruary." [1]

1702. Mary, daughter of John Garland, baptized 19 July.

1703. "Sarah, ye wife of George Smith, died August ye 29, and was buried in St. Petter's Church, in Nottingham, August ye 31, ye last day.

1705. Charles Clay, of Mansfield, and Mary Hutchinson, of St. Peter's, Nottingham, married 12 September.

Matthew Markland, gent., and Elizabeth Flower, spinster, both of the parish of St. Peter, Nottingham, married by license 18 December

John Fletcher, of Heanor, co. Derby, and Mary Gadsby, of Bramcote, widow, married 12 February.

## VOLUME IV.

1706. Margaret, dau. of Sam. Collishaw and Mary his wife, baptised July 22. (1st entry in book.)

1708. Richard Stevens, of Leicester, gent., and Mrs. Sarah Sulley, of Nottingham, spinster, married 7 Oct.

1710. Vicesimus, son of Vicesimus and Mary Townsend, baptised Feb. 4.

1713. William Neep, clerk, and Anne Gee, of Plumtree,[2] married by license, May 20.

1716. "May the 30 ffrancis son of francis needham and of Isabell his wife were born neer two of the clock in the morning and Baptized June the 24."

1717. Thomas Lester, of Lenton, and Hannah Buck, of Bramcote, widow, married May 26.

1718. "Jan: 16 Tho: orston of gedling widower and Elizabeth Burdin of Shelford widdow were married at Lenton by will Rudsby vic:[3] there by virtue of a License granted by mr Tymothy fenton Surrogate and mr of arts."

1721. John Garland, gentleman, buried May 3.

1722. James, son of James Feild, gent., and Sarah, his wife, baptised 17 June.

— Thomas Smith, of Sawley, in the county of Derby, gent., and Mary Wombwell, of Lenton, spinster, married by license, 14 February.

---

(1) The following entry in the registers of St. Nicholas's, Nottingham, obviously has reference to the above : " William, son of Mr. Peter Claik and Miliscent his wife, buried February the 8th, 1700-1."

(2) The bride was presumably a daughter of the Rev. John Gee, rector of Plumtree, who died this same year, and was buried within the altar-rails in Plumtree Church.

(3) The Rev. William Rudsby is here described as vicar, though, as already stated, it is doubtful if he was ever fully instituted into the benefice. The Rev. Timothy Fenton, surrogate, was rector of St. Peter's, Nottingham, and previously vicar of Arnold.

1723. Anne, dau. of James Feild, gent., and Sarah, his wife, bapt. 1 March.

1724. "Ignotus [erasure] baptized," April 22.

1725. David, son of James and Christian Thaine, buried March 6.

—    George Brentnall, of the parish of St. Mary, Nottingham, and Lucia Garland, of Lenton, married by license, April 2.

1726. Joseph, son of James and Sarah Feild, buried 10 April.

1729. James Feild, buried Jan. 26.

1730. Elizabeth, dau. of James and Sarah Feild, baptised 10 June.

1731. Isabel Thane, spinster, buried Feb. 4.

—    "Tho. thane, intered" Mar. 17.

1732. Mary Feild, an infant, buried 31 Oct., 1732.

1733. William Smart, parish clerk, buried Mar. 17.

—    Vicesimus Townshend and Mary Hooley, both of Lenton, married by license, Sep. 15.

1734. Samuel, son of Samuel and Johanna Keetley, baptised July 28.

—    Samuel, son of Samuel and Johanna Keetley, buried Nov. 29.

1735. Mary, daughter of James and Sarah Feild, bapt. 16 September.

George, son of Samuel and Johanna Keetley, baptised Oct. 19.

Vicesimus, son of Vicesimus and Mary Townsend, baptised Feb. 15.

1736. William, son of Mr. James Thaine, buried July 6.

John, son of Samuel and Johanna Keetley, bap. Jan. 2.

George,       do.        do.        buried Feb. 13.

1737. Gervase, son of Thomas and Mary Roughton, bap. May 1.

—    James, son of James and Sarah Feild, bap. July 5.

1738. John, son of Humphrey and Sarah Hopkins, bap. Nov. 14.

John Town, clerk, of St. Peter's parish, Nottingham, and Anne Broughton, of St. Mary's parish, Nottingham, married by license, Dec. 26.[1]

1739. Joseph, son of Samuel and Johanna Keetley, bap. Apl. 1.

"Mr. Lemuel Gladwyn of Tupton in the Parish of North Wingfield, in the County of Derby, and Mrs. Sarah Dobb of Teversal, in the County of Nottingham," married April 25.

Vicesimus Townshend, buried June 17.

1740. Samuel, son of Samuel and Johanna Keetley, bap. Feb. 15.

—    do.        do.        do.        buried Feb. 25.

1741. Mary, dau. of Mr. James Feild, buried 27 Oct.

—    Henry Brown, sen., carpenter, and Elizabeth, his wife, buried Jan. 14.

1742. William, son of Samuel and Johanna Keetley, bap. May 2.

—    John, son of Humphrey and Sarah Hopkins, bap. May 2.

1744. James, son of Samuel and Johanna Keetley, bap. Apl. 22.

1746. William Walker, of Wollesthorpe, co. Lincoln, and Elizabeth Thaine, of Lenton, married by license, May 1.

—    Elizabeth, dau. of Sam. and Joh. Keetley, bap. June 1.

---

(1) The Rev. John Towne, above-named, became rector of Shirland, in Derbyshire; Anne Broughton was the eldest daughter of Peter Broughton, Esq., of Lowdham, at which place she was baptised on the 22nd of June, 1718. She survived her husband, and subsequently married the Rev. William Wheeler, vicar of Chesterfield.

1746. "A Stranger his name unknown" buried Aug. 14.
"Sarah, wife of Mr. James Feild," buried Oct. 31.

1747. "John — a Vagrant from Canterbury," buried Dec. 6.

— Samuel, son of Sam. and Joh. Keetley, bap. Mar. 13.

1748. Ann, daughter of Mr. John Chamberlain, buried February 8.

1750. Anne, dau. of Sam. and Joh. Keetley, bap. May 13.

1751. Thomas, son of Sam. and Joh. Keetley, bap. Sep. 2.

1752. "A Stranger found dead in the King's Meadow supposed to be Thomas
Meller, of Nottingham, Labourer," buried Aug. 20.

— Truth Hall, widow, buried Dec. 16.

1753. Martha, wife of Mr. John Chamberlain, buried August 23.

1754. Mr. Walter Johnson, of the parish of St. Martin, Friday Street, London,
and Mrs. Margaret Thaine, of Lenton, married by license, Jan. 3.

Matthew, son of Samuel and Johanna Keetley, bap. Sep. 17.

Matthew Feild, founder, buried Dec. 18.

1755. William, son of Samuel and Elizabeth Stretton, baptised April 20.

1757. Ann, dau. of Samuel and Elizabeth Stretton, baptised April 24.

Ann, dau. of Sam. and Johanna Keetley, bap. April 24.

John, son of Charles Townley, Esq.,[1] Clarencieux King of Arms, and
Mary, his wife, baptised July 17.

Vicesimus, son of Jonathan and Mary Townsend, baptised Aug. 21.

1758. Mr. James Feild, founder, buried May 14.

1759. Elizabeth, dau. of Sam. and Joh. Keetley, baptised June 3.

— Elizabeth, dau. of Samuel and Elizabeth Stretton, baptised June 3

1760. Mary, do. do. do. do. Jan. 20.

1761. Lucy, wife of Mr. George Brentnall, of Derby, buried June 27.

— Samuel, son of Samuel and Eliz. Stretton, bap. Aug. 23.

1762. Christian, wife of Mr. James Thaine, of Wollesthorpe, buried Aug. 7.

1763. Sarah, dau. of Samuel and Elizabeth Stretton, baptised July 3.

1765. Mercy Feild, widow, buried Feb. 13.

1766. Mr. John Chamberlin, husbandman, buried October 29.

1767. Vicesimus, son of Vicesimus Townshend, jun., and Elizabeth, his wife,
baptised July 12.

1768. "John Allworthy, Menial Servant," buried Sep. 16.

1769. "Mrs. Rebecca Garland, Spinster," buried Jan. 22.

1770. Samuel Keetley, blacksmith, buried April 6.

---

(1) Charles Townley, Esq., the father of the child whose baptism is here recorded,
was of Long Whatton, in Leicestershire. His father had married Sarah, daughter
and co-heiress of William Wilde, of Long Whatton, gent., and had thus acquired an
estate in that parish. Charles Townley was for many years a member of the Heralds'
College. In 1735 he was appointed York Herald ; in 1751, Norroy King of Arms ;
in 1755, Clarencieux King of Arms ; and in 1761 he received the honour of knighthood at the coronation of King George the Third. Sir Charles was appointed
Garter King of Arms in 1773, but he only held that high office about a year, dying
at Islington, June the 7th, 1774. His remains were interred in a vault belonging to
his family, beneath the north porch in the church of St. Dunstan in the East, in
London. Mary, his wife, who is also named above, was the younger of the two
daughters and co-heiresses of George Eastwood, Esq., of Thornhill, in the county of
York.

1771. James Thaine, of Wollesthorpe, co. Lincoln, gent., buried April 9.
— Grace Freeman, widow, buried April 19.
1772. Johanna Keetley, buried Dec. 3.
1777. Thomas-George, son of Thomas and Mary Richmond, baptised Sep. 21.
1778.    do.    do.    do.    do.    buried Mar. 30.
1781. Vicesimus Townshend, buried Feb. 11.
1782. Thomas Bacon, who had been parish clerk forty-five years, buried Aug. 27.
— "Rebecca Daughter of Thomas Wright and Elizabeth his wife [baptised] N.B. this Infant was the first that the Revd. Mr. Pickering Baptiz'd at Lenton, and on the first Day he came to do Duty at the Church."
1784. James Thain, of Denton, co. Lincoln, gent., formerly of Lenton, buried May 17.

The greatest number of baptisms recorded in these registers occur in the years 1762 and 1780, when there were 27 in each year, and the smallest number occur in the years 1673 and 1682, there being 4 in each of those years. The greatest number of marriages occurs in the year 1652 when there were 37. There were no marriages recorded in the years 1553, 1564, 1656, 1657, and 1659, and only one marriage in each of the years 1544, 1551, 1552, 1554, 1555, 1557, 1559, 1560, 1561, 1569, 1570, 1579, 1612, 1663, 1735, 1742, 1747, and 1752. The greatest number of burials, 46, occurs in the year 1727. There were no burials recorded in the year 1725.

The following entries in the later registers are of interest:—

1754. Samuel Stretton and Elizabeth Wombwell, married 14 July.[1]
— James Feild and Mercy Ault, married 24 Dec.
1787. Margaret, wife of the late Adjutant Shaw, buried 18 June.
1788. William Norris, Gent., buried 15 March.
1801. Robert Lord,[2] dissenting minister, buried 20 December.
1802. Elizabeth, wife of Samuel Stretton, of Nottingham, buried 25 February.
1803. Thomas Naylor, of Mansfield, and Stella Stretton, of Lenton, married November 10.
1811. Samuel Stretton, of Nottingham, Gent., died 11 May, buried 16 May, aged 79 years.

---

(1) Mr. Samuel Stretton was an architect and builder, living at Standard Hill, Nottingham ; Elizabeth Wombwell, to whom he was married as above, was the daughter of an opulent yeoman resident in this parish. Their eldest son, William, whose baptism is recorded in 1755, was the gentleman whose antiquarian researches have already been alluded to in these pages.

(2) Robert Lord was for some years minister of the old Presbyterian meeting-house at Knutsford, in Cheshire.

Sarah, wife of James Green, Esq., of Lenton Abbey, buried 23 November, aged 60 years.

1817.   Jester Annis, buried April 16, aged 19 months.

1828.   William Stretton, of Lenton, buried March 18, aged 72.

1829.   John Chamberlain, buried January 19, aged 76.
        John Wright Killingley, buried June 5, aged 68.

1842.   Edward Browne, buried May 23, aged 12.  "Son of the Revd. G. Browne, Vicar of Lenton.  Interred first in Mr. Wright's vault in Old Church Yard, and removed from that to Porch Vault in New Church, Novr. 4th, 1842."

1842.   George Townsend, buried November 4, aged 12.  "This was the first interment in new yard."

1847.   John Maples, buried May 14, aged 78.

1848.   Denis George Browne, buried February 22nd, aged 18.  "Eldest son of the Rev. G. Browne, Vicar of Lenton."

## CHURCHWARDENS' ACCOUNTS.

The following entry, remarkable if only for its orthography, occurs in one of the parish books ;—

"June ye 9 1720 the ACounts of Robard Lasey and John Nags Church wardings seen and aLoud by us In Habetants of Lenton and wee find the towne his indebted to him two shillings Eight-pence halfe penny to be paid by the next Churchwardings wee a Low of three a Counts and sine them once for all."

The accounts do not contain any entries of more than ordinary interest; the following are the principal :—

|  |  | £ | s. | d. |
|---|---|---|---|---|
| 1783. | When I was Chose Churchwarden | | 3 | 6 |
| | To four Briefs at 6d. each | | 2 | 0 |
| | Keeping the Book and Serving the Office | | 19 | 0 |
| | Expenses at giving up the Accounts | | 3 | 6 |
| | This Book for the parish | | 1 | 4 |
| 1784-5. | To seven Briefs | | 5 | 6 |
| 1785-6. | To myself and Mr. Keetley at the Court of Correction | | 7 | 0 |
| 1786-7. | To a new Belrope | | 1 | 6 |
| | To going to Red Hill to meet the Justices to give an account of the Legacies belonging the poor and also the Saturday after at the White Lion Nottingham | | 4 | 6 |
| | To 2 Briefs for Loss by Fire 2s. each and 3 more that was to be gathered from house to house | | 7 | 0 |
| 1787. | Mending the Church Key | | 1 | 0 |
| | a new Almanack | | | 7 |
| | " Charges aboute the Pramblelation." | 10 | 0 | 11 |

|  |  | £ | s. | d. |
|---|---|---|---|---|
| 1789. | Paid for a new Tankard lid |  | 1 | o |
| 1790. | pade at the Cort of Correction |  | 7 | 2 |
|  | Ditto for My trobel that day |  | 5 | o |
|  | pade for anew belrope |  | 1 | 5½ |
|  | pade for tow botels of wine |  | 3 | 2 |
| 1791. | Paid for the Bassoone Mending |  | 12 | o |
| 1792. | Paid for Breefts |  | 4 | 6 |
|  | Paid James for Shufling the abbe gates |  |  | 6 |
|  | Paid for anue spaid for the Church |  | 4 | o |
|  | Paid one the Touns account for sum vagarants by the order of Mr Wright |  | 5 | o |
| 1793. | Paid for Wine at Wissen tide |  | 4 | o |
|  | To makeing the Sismint [assessment] |  | 2 | o |
| 1794. | Paid for Eight Hundred of Coles for to Dry the Church |  | 4 | 8 |
|  | To Our Trobill Drying the Writings that was damaged by the flood |  | 5 | o |
|  | Paid for thra Locks for the Chiste |  | 5 | o |
| 1798. | pade at Cortofckrection for two deners |  | 10 | o |
| 1799. | (Perambulation expenses) | 12 | 1 | 5 |
| 1802. | (Perambulation expenses, including two pig's chaps) | 20 | 4 | 4 |
|  | for goind to allestre for the Tarrias |  | 7 | o |
| 1810. | Jos. Folks a Bill for 2 Clarinets |  | 5 5 | o |
|  | Humphry Hopkin for a Bassoon |  | 5 5 | o |
|  | Geo. Hudson for Board and Painting |  | 16 | 10 |
|  | Geo. Hudson's Bill for Chest | 10 | o | o |
|  | J. Trueman "for Pulpit dress-making" |  | 14 | 6 |
| 1812. | 20 Trees &c. for the Church Yard |  | 16 | o |
| 1815. | James Lee for four Chesnut-trees |  | 5 | 6 |
|  | (In February, 1821, the Church was robbed, and several items in the accounts relate thereto.) |  |  |  |
| 1826. | Distressed Seaman |  | 5 | o |
| 1829. | Thomas Wade on acct of New Bell and alterations in the Church | 30 | o | o |
| 1831. | Paid Topley for Assisting to take some Riotous Boys |  | 1 | o |
|  | Joseph Core, A Bill for Hanging Bell A New Wheel & other Work |  | 4 o | 6 |

The total amount of the church rates levied during the twenty-four years, 1783 to 1807, was £872 18 10, the amount raised during the year 1806-7 being £471 18 10.

## CHURCHWARDENS.

1552. John Bowser ; Avery Walker.

The following Churchwardens occur during the incumbency of

the Rev. John Wood (1592-1623), but the years when they served
the office cannot now be determined :—

> Peter Toule ; Jo. Warde.
> John Allen ; George Leeson.
> Roger Hooton ; Thomas Birche.[1]
> William Hill ; Andrew Webster.
> John Kilborne ; Thomas Eller.
> Francis M———— ; William Graisley.

| | |
|---|---|
| 1678. | Gregory Aston ; Thomas Kelladine. |
| 1704. | Joseph Kirk ; William Simpson. |
| 1705. | Thomas Allcock ; Henry Browne. |
| 1709. | Joseph Lacy ; George Dickinson. |
| 1715. | Christopher Wrest ; Francis Roberts. |
| 1718. | John Roberts ; Robert Lacey. |
| 1719. | Robert Lacey ; John Knaggs. |
| 1720. | Thomas Allcock ; William Wombawl. |
| 1721. | William Wombawl ; John Chamberlain. |
| 1722. | John Chamberlain ; John Mosley. |
| 1723. | John Mosley ; John Western. |
| 1724. | John Western ; Arthur Beardsley. |
| 1725. | Arthur Beardsley ; John Swinscow. |
| 1726. | Richard Beesley ; William Marshall. |
| 1727. | William Marshall ; Richard Beesley. |
| 1728. | John Swinscow ; James Field. |
| 1729. | James Field ; Thomas Wheatley. |
| 1730. | Thomas Wheatley ; William Spencer. |
| 1731. | William Spencer ; Thomas Firth. |
| 1732. | Thomas Frith ; Thomas Newham. |
| 1733. | Thomas Newham ; John Chamberlain. |
| 1734. | John Chamberlain ; William Norris. |
| 1735. | William Norris ; Thomas Roughton. |
| 1736. | Thomas Roughton ; John Clarke. |
| 1737. | John Clarke ; James Field. |
| 1738. | James Feild, Humphrey Hopkins. |
| 1739. | Humphrey Hopkins ; William Burton. |
| 1740. | William Burton ; Robert Castle. |
| 1741. | Robert Castle ; William Dickinson, junr. |
| 1742. | William Dickinson, junr. ; Samuel Keatley. |
| 1743. | Samuel Keatley ; Benjamin Ault. |
| 1744. | Benjamin Ault ; William Shipman. |
| 1745. | William Shipman ; Joseph Roberts. |
| 1746. | Joseph Roberts ; John Chamberlain. |
| 1747. | John Chamberlain ; John Chapman. |

---

(1) Mentioned in the parish register as residing in part of the old monastery
buildings in 1601.

1748.  John Chapman ; William Norris.
1749.  William Norris ; Thomas Roughton.
1750.  Thomas Roughton ; John Clarke.
1751.  John Clarke ; James Feild.
1752.  James Feild ; Humphrey Hopkin.
1753.  Humphrey Hopkin ; Edwd. Hollingworth.
1754.  Edward Hollingworth ; John Bradshaw.
1755.  John Bradshaw ; Samuel Keatley.
1756.  Samuel Keatley ; Joseph Roberts.
1757.  Joseph Roberts ; John Chamberlin.
1758.  John Chamberlin ; William Norris.
1759.  William Norris ; Matthew Welch.
1760.  Matthew Welch ; Ralph Porter.
1761.  Ralph Porter ; Thomas Roughton.
1762.  Thomas Roughton ; Edward Hollingworth.
1763.  Edward Hollingworth ; John Bradshaw.
1764.  John Bradshaw ; John Kettleby.
1765.  John Kettleby ; Samuel Keetley.
1766.  Samuel Keetley ; Joseph Roberts.
1767.  Joseph Roberts ; William Hopkin.
1768.  William Hopkin ; John Chamberlin.
1769.  John Chamberlin ; William Norris.
1770.  William Norris ; Matthew Welch.
1771.  Matthew Welch ; John Hopkin.
1772.  John Hopkin ; Thomas Roughton.
1773.  Thomas Roughton ; William Shaw.
1774.  William Shaw ; Edwd. Hollingworth.
1775.  Edwd. Hollingworth ; John Bradshaw.
1776.  John Bradshaw ; John Keetley.
1777.  Thos. Stevenson ; John Keetley.
1778.  John Keetley ; Thomas Roughton.
1779.  Thos. Roughton ; John Chamberlin.
1780.  John Chamberlin ; Gervase Boot.
1781.  Gervase Boot ; Thomas Roughton.
1782.  Thomas Roughton ; John Hopkins.
1783.  John Hopkins ; Thomas Roughton.
1784.  John Bradshaw ; Thomas Stevenson.
1785.  John Stevenson ; John Keetley.
1786.  John Keetley ; John Shaw.
1787.  John Shaw ; Thomas Roughton.
1788.  Thomas Roughton ; John Chamberlin.
1789.  John Chamberlin ; Gervas Boot.
1790.  Gervas Boot ; John Hopkins.
1791.  Thomas Roughton ; Elias Roberts.
1792.  Elias Roberts ; Thomas Roughton.
1793.  Edward Hollingworth.
1794.  Thomas Roughton ; Edwd. Hollingworth.

1795. John Shaw ; William Wigley.
1796. William Wigley; Thomas Stevenson.
1797. Thomas Stevenson ; Gervas Boot.
1798. ¹Gervas Boot ; Mr. Chamberlin.
1799. Mr. Chamberlin ; Gervas Boot.
1800. T. Roughton ; J. Shaw.
1801. J. Rowton ; R. Nutt.
1802. R. Nutt ; J. W. Killingley.
1803. R. Nutt ; J. W. Killingley.
1804. J. W. Killingley ; M. Needham.
1805. Matthew Needham ; William Surplice.
1806. William Surplice ; Francis Evans.
1807. Francis Evans ; William Surplice.
1808. John Wilkinson ; James Green.
1809. James Green ; John Wright, Esq.
1810. John Wright, Esq. ; William Stretton.
1811. William Stretton ; John Burton.
1812. John Burton ; Edward Hallam.
1813. Richard Chamberlin ; Edward Hallam.
1814. Richard Chamberlin ; John Wilkinson.
1815. James Nutt ; John Shaw.
1816. James Nutt ; John Shaw.
1817. James Nutt ; Samuel Keetley.
1818. Thomas Brown Milnes ; William Weston.
1819. T. B. Milnes ; W. Weston.
1820. John Burton ; William Weston.
1821. William Weston ; John Burton.
1822.      Do.      ;      do.
1823.      Do.      ;      do.
1824.      Do.      ; James Nutt.
1825.      Do.      ;      do.
1826.      Do.      ; Samuel Keetley.
1827. Samuel Keetley ; James Nutt.
1828.      Do.      ; John Maples.
1829.      Do.      ; James Nutt.
1830.      Do.      ; Thomas Kirk.
1831.      Do.      ; William Yeomans.

(1) Mr. Boot and Mr. Chamberlain likewise filled the office of overseers for this same year. "At a Vestry-meeting held this 31st day of August, 1798, in the Parish Church of Lenton, pursuant to a notice for making a rate for the relief of the poor of the said parish ; It appeareth that the Church and Poor rates of this Parish are assessed with much inequality, Resolved that the Churchwardens and Overseers are instructed to obtain a proper Valuation of the Parish in order to make an equal Rate, and they are requested for that purpose to take the advice and assistance of Mr. John Bayley, or if he shall refuse or not be able to attend, some other competent Surveyor." This resolution was signed by W. Gill (on behalf of the Vicar) ; J. Stubbins (on behalf of George de Ligne Gregory, Esqre.) ; T. Paget ; Samuel Smith ; Francis Evans ; Joseph Lowe ; Thos. Pares, junr. ; William Wigley ; and James White.

20

| 1832. | Samuel Keetley ; John Maples. |
| 1833. | Do. ; do. |
| 1834. | Do. ; do. |
| 1835. | Do. ; do. |
| 1836. | Samuel Keetley. (only).¹ |
| 1837. | Do. ; John Herbert. |
| 1838. | Do. ; John Froggatt. |
| 1839. | Do. ; Francis Wright. |
| 1840. | Do. ; do. |
| 1841. | Do. ; do. |
| 1842. | Do. ; do. |
| 1843. | Joseph Bell ; do.₂ |
| 1844. | Samuel Keetley ; do. |
| 1845. | Do. ; William Parsons. |
| 1846. | Samuel Keetley ; Thomas Hall. |
| 1847. | George Langford ; Thomas Wood. |
| 1848. | Do. ; do.₃ |

\* \* \* \* \* \*

| 1871. | Thomas Adams ; John Thomas Giles. |
| 1872. | Do. ; do. |
| 1873. | Thomas Adams⁴ } do. |
| | Henry Smith Wright } |
| 1874. | John Thomas Giles ; Henry Smith Wright. |
| 1875. | Do. ; do. |
| 1876. | Do. ; John Benjamin Nevill. |
| 1877. | Do. ; do. |
| 1878. | Do. ; Edward Peat. |
| 1879. | Do. ; do. |
| 1880. | Do. ; do. |
| 1881. | Do. ; do. |
| 1882. | Frederick Wright ; John Thomas Giles. |
| 1883. | Do. ; James Harvey. |
| 1884. | Do. ; do. |

(1) This is the only instance in which only one churchwarden seems to have been appointed instead of two, as customary in this parish. We are unable to explain the circumstances under which this took place.

(2) This election was a contested one, the candidates being Mr. Hill and Mr. F. Wright. After a poll of two days the latter was elected by a majority of 105 votes.

(3) Owing to the inaccessibility of the later vestry books we are unable to continue this list between the years 1848 and 1871.

(4) Mr. Adams, who had for many years taken the most active interest in all church matters connected with the parish of Lenton, died on the 16th of May, 1873.

## GARLAND'S CHARITY.

This is the only charity belonging to the parish of Lenton. Miss Rebecca Garland, an inhabitant and landowner in Lenton, who died in January, 1769, bequeathed to the poor of Lenton the sum of £10, to be disposed of in such manner as the Vicar and Churchwardens should think well. At the west end of the nave of the Church is a board bearing an inscription relative to this bequest (see p. 270), but which is incorrect in almost every particular.[1] The following extract from Miss Garland's Will, with the remarks of the Rev. George Wayte thereon, may be accepted as correct.

"I give to the Poor of the Parish of Lenton aforesaid Ten Pounds to be paid by my Executrix within Six Months after my Decease into the Hands of the Minister & Churchwardens of the said Parish of Lenton for the Time being to be by them disposed of unto and amongst or for the Benefit of the said Poor of Lenton in such Manner as to them shall seem most meet."

N.B. Notwithstanding the manner of Expression in the foregoing Clause of MRS. GARLAND'S Will it was her mind and Desire (Frequently declared to me by Word of Mouth during her Life Time) that the said Summ of Ten Pounds should be placed out at Interest & that the Interest or Produce should be Distributed Annually by the Minister & Churchwardens amongst the Poor of the said Parish and generally amongst such Poor as did not receive weekly Pay as to them should seem most meet & the more effectually to comply with her earnest Desire I have ever since her Decease kept the said Ten Pounds in my hands & every Year on St. Thomas Day together with the Churchwardens have Distributed Ten Shillings (The legal Interest of the said Ten Pounds) according to her Intent & desire in the foregoing Clause & propose to continue to do so as long as I shall Continue Minester of the Parish of Lenton as Witness my Hand

GEO: WAYTE.

This Memorandum was made & Signed the 14th Day of June 1781 in the presence of

JOHN SINGLEHURST.

---

(1) In the 21st report of the Charity Commissioners (p. 431) the inscription on the board is taken as evidence of the date of this bequest. At the time of the Commissioner's enquiry the £10 was in the hands of Mr. James Nutt, who paid 10s. a year to the churchwardens for its use. As Mr. Nutt wished to pay in the principal, the Commissioners suggested that it should be invested in the Savings Bank. A memorandum in the Churchwarden's Account Book states that the principal was repaid Dec. 19, 1828, and deposited in the Savings Bank, Dec. 22 following. The money is now lodged in the Nottingham Joint Stock Bank.

# SECTION VIII.

## HYSON GREEN CHURCH.

**T**HE Consolidated Chapelry of Hyson Green, formed in 1843, contains 269a. or. 38p.—176a. 3r. 12p. being then in Lenton parish, and 92a. 1r. 26p. in Radford parish. The whole district is now comprised in the parish of Radford.[1]

The Church, originally built as a chapel-of-ease, and dedicated to St. Paul, is situate on the glebe land awarded to the vicar of Lenton in 1799. It is built of stone, in the Early English style of architecture, and consists of nave with central aisle, semi-octagonal apse, and a tower on the south side of nave. There is a small vestry on the north side of the nave, corresponding with the tower. The internal arrangements of the church are of the simplest character. At the west end is a gallery, containing the organ, and beneath the gallery, opposite the west door, the font is placed. Over the chancel arch is inscribed, "O come let us worship and bow down ; let us kneel before the Lord our Maker;" and the text, " Glory to God in the highest, and on earth peace, good will towards men," surrounds the chancel. On the south side of the chancel a small white marble tablet, to the memory of the father of the

---

(1) See p. 45, *ante*.

first incumbent of the chapel, is affixed, bearing the following inscription :—

Sacred to the memory of
Rich<sup>d</sup> Blakeney, Esq<sup>r</sup>. First Lieut<sup>t</sup>. Royal Marines,
Father of the respected Incumbent of this Church.
During the late European War, he served his country
with acknowledged merit.
As a father he was the most affectionate,
as a husband the best,
and as a Christian, of the deepest piety to God.
He died XXVI Sept<sup>r</sup>. MDCCCXLVIII, aged LX years,
And his remains repose near this spot in the chancel
Where he worshipped and which he loved.
"So he bringeth them unto their desired haven."—PSALM cvii. v. xxx.
A Token of affection from a few sincere Friends.

The Creed, the Lord's Prayer, and the Ten Commandments,
painted on boards, are also affixed in the chancel.    There
are no stained glass windows in the church.    The tower
contains one·small bell, removed from old Lenton Church when
it was partially dismantled in 1844.  The inscription upon the
bell is as follows :—

J. NUTT AND S. KEETLEY, LENTON.

SAMUEL ASTON, NOTTINGHAM.  1829.

The church, capable of seating about 500 persons, and cost-
ing £1,911, was built by public subscription, aided by grants,
from the designs of Mr. Stevens, architect, of Derby.    The
first stone was laid July 17, 1843, and the building was consecrated by the Bishop of Lincoln, April 18th, 1844.    The
silver communion service was presented by the late Rev. Robert
Simpson, vicar of Basford.    A small burial-ground, in which
numerous interments have been made, surrounds the church.
The principal tombstone is to the memory of James Fisher,
who died January 7th, 1877, aged 70, and Emily Fisher, who
died June 21st, 1861, aged 15.    Near this tomb is a headstone to
the memory of Samuel Ragg, the blind organist of the church,
who died June 25th, 1852, aged 17 years.    At a meeting of
the Privy Council, held March 20th, 1857, it was ordered that
from and after the first of April following, burials should be
discontinued in the Episcopal Chapel of Hyson Green, and

in the burial-ground of the same chapel within three yards of the chapel.

The living, which is a vicarage of the yearly value of £206, formerly in the patronage of the Crown, is now vested in trustees. The Rev. Richard Paul Blakeney, B.A.,[1] formerly curate of Lenton, was the first incumbent ; and on his resignation, in 1852, the Rev. David Carver, B.A., of Caius College, Cambridge, the present incumbent, was appointed by the then Lord Chancellor, the late Lord St. Leonards.

The Vicarage House, a substantial stone structure, situate a short distance from the church, was erected in 1857, from the designs of Mr. S. S. Teulon, of London, architect.

---

(1) The Rev. R. P. Blakeney, D.D., is now vicar of Bridlington, Yorkshire.

# SECTION IX.

## THE SCHOOLS.

THE National School, with master's and mistress's residences, built of brick, with stone facings, situate in Church Street, opposite to the church, was erected in 1841, at a cost, of £2,305, the site having been given by Francis Wright, Esq. In 1855, Dr. Langford, her Majesty's Inspector of Schools, having strongly recommended the enlargement of the school, in consequence of the greatly increased attendance in the boys' school, the building was extended by two-thirds of its original size by the erection of a new and spacious room. Alterations were at the same time effected in the offices and drainage ; boundary walls surrounding the whole premises were erected, and new furniture and fittings provided. The total cost of these alterations was £510, towards which the Committee of Council on Education made a grant of £170. There is accommodation for 180 boys and 120 girls, and the average attendance is large.

The Infant School, accommodating 200 children, was erected in 1851, at the expense of the Misses Wright, of Lenton Lodge.

In 1871, a temporary school, conducted upon purely unsectarian principles, was opened in an unoccupied factory at New Lenton. During the first week 194 children were enrolled upon the school registers, and at the end of three years the number of children on the books was 438, the average attendance being 307. The committee of management, finding the temporary rooms did not afford the required accommodation, took active steps to erect a permanent school. This desire of the promoters was greatly facilitated by the previous action of the Lenton School Board, which had, in October, 1872, passed a resolution to the effect that, as certain gentlemen had promised to build, by voluntary subscriptions, a school to be conducted on unsectarian principles, the Board, considering the offer a noble and honourable one, which would not interfere with the rates, were willing to further the project. After several efforts, a site was obtained, and the building commenced, the memorial stones being laid November 8th, 1873, by Mr. Anthony John Mundella, M.P., and Mr. Benjamin Walker. The schools were publicly opened by the Mayor of Nottingham, June 29th, 1874. The building, situate at the corner of School Street and Sherwin Road, comprises three large, lofty, and well lighted rooms, for boys, girls, and infants respectively. Immediately connected with each is a spacious class-room, so arranged as to be capable of easy division into two good-sized apartments with separate entrances. Accommodation is thus provided for 400 children, in the proportion of 150 boys, 120 girls, and 130 infants. A good play-ground is attached to each division. The whole of the buildings are arranged to form one group, but the several portions are practically distinct, each having its own approach and entrance door, as well as a separate communication with the play-ground. The style adopted for the building is Lombardo-Venetian-Gothic, the materials employed on the exterior being red brick, with Ancaster and Hollington stone. Staffordshire blue bricks are used in some of the dressings to the doors and windows, and moulded bricks are also introduced into the cornices. The principal external feature, however, is the bell tower, 80 feet high, which forms a prominent object from whatever point the building may be approached. The schools are now under the control of the Nottingham School Board.

The Board School on the Ilkeston Road was erected in the year 1883, on a site adjoining the Lenton Police Station, purchased by the Nottingham School Board from the Trustees of the late John Sherwin Gregory, Esq. The building is two storeys high, and provides accommodation for 240 boys, 240 girls, and 320 infants. Extensive play-grounds and a residence for the caretaker are also provided. The materials used in the structure, which is in the Queen Anne style, are red bricks, with red terra cotta dressings, the roof being covered with red tiles. The official opening of the school took place November 5th, 1883.

The schools attached to Hyson Green Church, conducted on the National School system, are substantial stone buildings, situate on the Lenton glebe. The boys' school was erected in 1845, and the girls' and infants' school in 1860. Accommodation is provided for 500 children, in the following proportions :—150 boys, 170 girls, and 180 infants. The schools are supported by voluntary subscriptions, aided by Government grants.

# SECTION X.

## THE NONCONFORMING CONGREGATIONS.

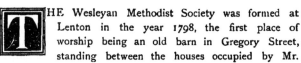HE Wesleyan Methodist Society was formed at Lenton in the year 1798, the first place of worship being an old barn in Gregory Street, standing between the houses occupied by Mr. Roughton and Mr. Wilkinson. In June, 1803, there were 31 members. On the demolition of the barn, the society removed to a room in Bog Row (now Knight's Yard), and continued there until the Chapel in Priory Street was built. This chapel, consisting of one room, with a small vestry in the rear, was opened February 7th, 1826. The Society appears to have increased rapidly in the number of its members, for we learn that in March, 1827, "Lenton, which has long been a desert, is fresh and green: the society is more than doubled." A branch society was formed, and a chapel erected, at New Lenton, in 1830. In September, 1847, there were 50 members at Old Lenton, and 127 members at New Lenton. The chapel at Old Lenton was sold to the Primitive Methodists in 1853, the old Society having migrated to New Lenton. The chapel in Willoughby Street is a plain brick building, consisting of a large room having a gallery all round and a vestry at the back. This building being much too small to accommodate the increased number of worshippers, a site for a new chapel in Church Street was purchased, and the memorial stones laid, September 28th, 1882. The new chapel, built in the Byzantine style of

architecture, contains, in the basement storey, a commodious schoolroom, two classrooms, and kitchen. The building contains a minister's vestry, and a small gallery at one end for the school children, or choir. The materials employed externally are bricks, with white stone dressings to the window and door openings, and ornamental terra cotta work introduced in the principal front. A flight of steps approaches the central entrance door from Church Street. The chapel, which accommodates about 500 worshippers, was opened May 17, 1883. There are now 90 members.

About the year 1852 a small number of members of the Primitive Methodist body met in a room at the west end of Chain Row, Old Lenton. In 1853, they purchased the chapel in Priory Street, previously occupied by the Wesleyan Methodists, and on April 17th, of that year, commenced to hold their services there. This chapel being insufficient to meet the requirements of the society, a new chapel was erected in Abbey Street, the memorial stones being laid November 27, 1882. The chapel is built in the Gothic style of architecture, and, with the end gallery, provides sitting accommodation for 450 persons. On the left of the principal front is a square tower, with lead lights and tinted glass, which adds considerably to the appearance of the structure. At the back are schools designed to accommodate 150 children, having a classroom and infants' room, with minister's vestry in the rear. The total cost, including the site, was about £1,900. The chapel was opened July 5th, 1883. The old chapel has been purchased for a Sunday School in connection with the old Church, and was opened for that purpose November 22nd, 1883.

The Methodist New Connexion Society at Hyson Green was formed in 1826, chiefly through the instrumentality of Mr. Anderson, who kept a day school in the village. A society-class was formed, which met in Pleasant Row, and a Sunday School was commenced about the same time, in a room in Forest Row. The village, which in 1800 had one house only, was at this time rapidly increasing in population. The rooms being too small, Lenton Street chapel was built in 1828, the opening service being held August 5th in that year. In

1882 the society numbered 30 members, but at the present time there are over 100 members, 200 Sunday School scholars, and 20 teachers. A disused burial ground adjoins the chapel. The Trustees are now erecting in Archer Street, at a cost of about £2,500, a new chapel to seat 600 persons, with school and classroom accommodation. The memorial stones of the new building were laid July 19, 1883.

For several years previous to the year 1851, the General Baptist cause flourished in Lenton, part of the members being identified with the General Baptist Chapel, Broad Street, Nottingham, and part with the Chapel in Stoney Street, Nottingham. These two sections seceded from their respective chapels, and formed themselves into a separate branch of New Connexional Baptists, August 17th, 1851. They then numbered 51 persons. On April 13th, 1852. at the General Baptist Conference held at Beeston, the Lenton Chapel was placed on the list of General Baptist Chapels for the district. The members of the denomination were then the owners of a chapel in Park Street, New Lenton, where the newly-formed body continued to meet, until the increase in the number of members rendered the erection of a new chapel necessary. In July, 1853, a plot of land was purchased in Church Street, and negotiations for the building commenced. The Chapel in Church Street, erected in 1856, in the Italian style of architecture, of red brick, with cement dressings, contains 484 sittings, and has a schoolroom underneath. The old chapel was sold to the Reformed Methodists. The number of members in 1882 was returned as 130, also 3 local preachers. In connection with the Chapel is a Sunday School. The chapel is duly licensed for Public Worship, and for the solemnization of marriages.

Twenty-five years ago the chapel in Park Street, New Lenton, now known as the Methodist Free Church, was purchased from the Baptists. The sect at that time numbered only 20 members, but subsequently it was found necessary to make certain improvements and alterations in the chapel to meet existing requirements. The "church" at the present time numbers 50 members, and in the Sunday-school there

are 21 teachers and 156 scholars.   The building being in an
unsuitable locality, and presenting anything but an attractive
appearance, efforts are now being made to purchase land on
which to erect a new chapel.

The Park Hill Congregational Chapel, erected by the
Congregational body formerly worshipping in St. James's
Street, Nottingham, consists of a nave and side aisles, divided
by stone arcades, supported on Anston Moor stone columns
with moulded bases and carved capitals.   The pulpit, which
is of the platform type, occupies a spacious recess at the north
end of the nave, the recess having in front a moulded stone
arch, supported by stone columns with carved caps and
moulded bases.   Over the nave arcades is a lofty clerestory,
the nature of the site requiring that the chapel shall be
principally lighted from above.   The nave roof is arched
and boarded, and has main timbers of ornamental design
carried on stone corbels and shafts.   A rose window occupies
the space over the arch at the north end of the nave.   The
windows are all traceried, and filled with cathedral-tinted
glass.   One of the windows at the south end is filled with
coloured glass, and has the inscription, " To the glory of God
and in memory of John Ward."   On the east wall are four
marble tablets, removed from the old chapel in St. James's
Street.   They commemorate (1) the Rev. John Wild, pastor
of that chapel from July, 1832, to May, 1868, born Jan. 25,
1801, died Jan. 7, 1871 ; (2) Mary, wife of the Rev. John
Wild, died Feb. 8, 1861, aged 62; (3) Alderman William
Wilson, deacon, died Oct. 26, 1833, aged 64 ; (4) Mary, wife
of Mr. John Harrison, deacon ; she was for nearly 40 years a
member of the chapel, " having been one of four persons who
constituted this church at its formation in 1824 " ; died at
Southport, October 12, 1863, aged 69.   The style of architecture
is Middle Pointed, the materials used being red Loughborough
bricks, with dressings of Mansfield and Ancaster stone, the
walls internally being finished in trowelled stucco.   Externally,
the principal feature is the front to the Derby road.   It consists
of a central gable, rising to a height of seventy feet above
the road, and contains the principal entrance.   Over the

entrance doorway are two-light traceried windows, over which
again the gable is relieved by stone panelling and tracery.
The gable is flanked on each side by a turret, that on the east
side being surmounted by a gabled pinnacle, panelled and
traceried, terminating in a cross. In the rear of the chapel is
a lecture-hall, to seat 150 persons, and two commodious classrooms or vestries ; but these are only of a temporary character,
the building being designed with a view to enlargement at a
future date. The chapel is designed to seat 500 persons on
the ground floor, and about 100 in the end gallery. The
memorial stone was laid June 15th, 1882, by Mr. Arnold
Morley, M.P. for Nottingham, and the chapel was opened
April 11th, 1883.

# SECTION XI.

## THE FAIRS.

**F**AIRS held under the shadow of the convent gates, with their attendant pastime and mirth, enriched taverner and tradespeople by the influx of merchants, visitors, and customers from all parts. " Besides the men who came for serious business, there would be a mob of pleasure-seekers also. The crowds of people of all ranks and classes from every part of the country, with the consequent variety of costume in material, fashion, and colour— the knight's helm and coat of mail, or embroidered *jupon* and plumed bonnet, the lady's furred gown and jewels, the merchant's sober suit of cloth, the minstrel's gay costume, and the jester's motley, the monk's robe and cowl, and the peasant's smock frock, continually in motion up and down the streets of the temporary canvas town, the music of the minstrels, the cries of the traders, the loud talk and laughter of the crowd—must have made up a picturesque scene full of animation." [1] Provisions, furniture, and clothing were usually purchased by the country people at the fairs held in their respective neighbourhoods, which were frequently the only means of social intercourse enjoyed by the people. Occasional scraps of news were obtained from travellers, and something of state affairs was learned from the strolling minstrel, who was often welcomed as much

---

(1) Cutt's *Characters of the Middle Ages*, p. 506.

for his gossip as for his song, but the annual re-union of the
country people took place at the fairs. The inhabitants then
made merry with fresh arrivals of welcome guests, and the
cellarer took the first choice of all wares exhibited on the stalls
in the fair conceded by charter to the convent.

It has been stated[1] that previous to the year 1163, a fair of
eight days, commencing on the feast of St. Martin in every year,
was granted to Lenton Priory by King Henry the Second. This
grant, which conferred on the monks many privileges to the
exclusion of the town of Nottingham, was confirmed April 6th,
1200, by a charter of King John.[2]

In the 26th or 27th year of King Edward I., the Chancellor
and Barons of the Exchequer enjoined the Sheriff of Nottingham and Derby (then present in the Court) to cause, by himself
and his Bailiffs, the King's Peace to be kept at the Lenton Fair,
which was then near at hand, so that the Peace might not be
broken through the neglect of him or his Bailiffs.[3]

The restrictions imposed on the inhabitants of Nottingham
during the continuance of Lenton fair, and the possible preference of traders to bring their goods to Lenton fair rather than
to the two fairs held annually at Nottingham,[4] resulted in a contention, about the year 1300, between the Prior of Lenton and
the Mayor of Nottingham as to their respective rights and
privileges. This dispute was settled by the following agreement

---

(1) See p. 106.

(2) See p. 117. This grant was again confirmed by the Inspeximus Charter of
King Edward II., 29 Aug., 1316.

(3) "Notingham. Præceptum factum Vicecomiti Notingamiæ pro Pace servanda.
Memorandum quod die S. Leonardi Abbatis, præsente hic Radulpho de Schirlegh
Vicecomite Notingamiæ & Derbiæ, Injunctum est eidem Vicecomiti per Cancellarium
& Barones de Scaccario Regis, quod per se & Ballivos suos, custodiri faciat Pacem
Domini Regis in Nundinis de Lenton quæ erunt ad instans festum S. Martini ; Ita
quod Pax Domini Regis pro negligencia sua & suorum Ballivorum non lædatur ibidem ;
maxime pro eo quod Prioratus Loci prædicti de Lenton in manu Domini Regis esse
dinoscitur, eo quod Prior ejusdem Alienigena est et de Potestate Regis Franciæ.
*Mich. Communia*, 26 & 27, *E. I., Rot.* 5. *b.*"
Madox "History of the Exchequer," vol. ii, p. 106.

(4) King Edward I., by charter given at Lincoln, February 12, 1283, granted to the
burgesses of Nottingham, in addition to their fair of eight days at the feast of St.
Matthew the Apostle, a second fair of fifteen days at the feast of Saint Edmund the
King and Martyr, "unless this fair shall be to the damage of neighbouring fairs."
(Rot. Chart., 12 Ed. I., No. 51.) The latter fair was exchanged by charter of King
Richard II., dated March 19, 1377, on the petition of the Mayor and burgesses, for
a fair of five days at St. Peter in Cathedra. (Nottingham Borough Records, i. 194.)

from which it will be seen that the Prior and Convent of Lenton got the best of the bargain. From this agreement we also learn that the term of the fair had been increased from eight to twelve days by charter of King Henry III.

"Let all the faithful of Christ seeing or hearing the present writing know that, whereas contention had arisen between the Prior and Convent of Lenton, on the one part, and the Mayor and Burgesses of Nottingham, on the other, in regard to the fair of Lenton, in certain liberties pertaining to that fair, the said contention between them is at length, through the mediation of discreet men, amicably settled in this wise : to wit, that the said Prior and Convent, by the unanimous assent and common counsel of their Chapter, have released and quit-claimed to the Mayor and Burgesses of Nottingham, and their heirs, four days of the increment of their fair of Lenton, which the Lord Henry King of England, son of King John, granted to them, and by his charter confirmed : so that the said Prior and Convent, and their successors, shall not hold the fair except for eight days fully complete, and the fair shall begin on the eve of Saint Martin, and shall endure from the morning of the same day until the end of the eighth day. They have also granted in good faith, for them and their successors, that neither they, nor their successors, shall hereafter make any petition towards the Lord King, nor towards any other man, to obtain any days, beyond the eight days, for the augmentation of their fair, to the damage and detriment of the Mayor and Burgesses of Nottingham, or of their heirs. Moreover the aforesaid Prior and Convent have granted, for them and their successors, to the said Mayor and Burgesses of Nottingham, that cloth merchants, apothecaries, pilchers, and mercers of the community of the town, who wish to hire booths in the fair of Lenton, shall give for each booth covered with the covering of the Prior, or of their own proper covering, 12d., for as long as the fair lasts, and each of them, according to his condition, shall have a booth amongst the other stranger merchants, to wit, the best amongst the best, and the middle class amongst the middle class, the smaller amongst the smaller, excepting those selling ' Blacks ' and accustomed cloths, and each of them shall give 8d. for a booth covered with their own proper covering, or not covered. And all others who may desire to hire booths shall give for every booth 8d., excepting those selling iron, and each of them who may desire to hire a booth and occupy land, shall give for the booth 4d., and if he do not occupy land, each of them shall give 2d. : so that tanners and shoemakers who do not occupy land, shall be quit of covered and uncovered stalls, and from all action pertaining to stallage. And be it known that each booth shall be of the measure of 8 feet in length, and 8 feet in breadth ; saving to the same

21

merchants the *appenticia* [penthouses], as to other stranger
merchants. Provided that none of the aforesaid merchants, of
whatsoever condition he may be, through the medium of any
hiring or payment, shall presume to hire a booth or booths, stall
or stalls, for the use of any stranger, but only for his own use,
nor shall he sell alien goods in the said booths or stalls unless
for his own profit, or for the use of any Nottingham merchant.
And if it shall be found that any one of the aforesaid merchants
shall sell or hire, in any other way than as abovesaid, the warden
of the fair shall have power to remove the said stranger merchant
or merchants, with the goods found in the said booths, until they
shall satisfy him for the collusion. And if any one of the aforesaid merchants shall have necessity for more booths than one,
he shall have [them] at the before-named price, and in accordance with the measure aforesaid, giving the better price for the
better, and the smaller price for the smaller, in form aforesaid.
The said Prior and Convent grant that the aforesaid merchants
who may desire to hire stalls, and do not occupy land, shall give
henceforth for the stall 2d., as they have hitherto been used to
give. And if there are any who are poor, who in past times have
been used to give nothing for the stalls, they shall be henceforth
quit of such stallage. And all men of Nottingham buying and
selling hides tanned or with the hair on, or skins, of whatsoever
manner, as well dry as fresh, and all from Nottingham passing
through Lenton in fair time with carts, wagons and pack-horses,
shall be quit of toll and all custom. For this quittance the said
Mayor and Burgesses of Nottingham have granted to the said
Prior and Convent of Lenton, a building in the Saturday market
for ever, which Gilbert de Beeston lately held, and which his
ancestors in times past assigned, by a certain composition, to the
predecessors of the aforesaid Prior and Convent. Moreover each
man of Nottingham shall be quit of toll of all things pertaining
to his food and clothing, but of the traffic of horses, oxen, and
other animals and herds, he shall give a moiety of the toll of
animals bought in the fair of Lenton and led elsewhere to be
sold ; but he shall give nothing for animals there slain. And
the said Mayor and Burgesses have granted, for them and their
successors, that no market shall be held within the town of
Nottingham so long as the fair of Lenton lasts, that is to say,
for eight days, of any description of merchandize, except within
houses, and in doors and windows ; not selling bread and fish
and meat, and other victuals, and leather, except in houses, doors,
and windows. And if the said Prior and Convent, or their
bailiffs, shall find anything elsewhere for sale, they shall have
power to have their will thereof, without contradiction. And
the said Prior and Convent, and their successors, or their bailiffs,
shall receive toll in Nottingham so long as the fair lasts, to wit,
for eight days, of all things of which toll ought or is used to be
received according to the custom of the fair of Lenton, without

contradiction or impediment of the aforesaid Mayor and Burgesses, or their heirs, and this they grant as far as in them lies. For this receipt of toll within the borough of Nottingham, for so long as the said fair lasts, and for the acquittance of a dinner which the said Prior and Convent have been used to give to the said Mayor and Burgesses of Nottingham every year, they and their successors shall render to the said Mayor and Burgesses, and their heirs, 20s. sterling on the day of Saint Edmund, at Nottingham, for ever. And the aforesaid Mayor and Burgesses, and their heirs, shall cause the said fair of Lenton to be proclaimed in Nottingham, at the will and summons of the said Prior and Convent, or their bailiffs, without difficulty, that it shall begin on the before-named day, receiving from them nevertheless full security for the said 20s., by them, to be faithfully paid to them, or their heirs, at the before-named term. Moreover, the Mayor and Burgesses, for themselves and their heirs, have promised in good faith that they will inviolably observe, and cause to be observed, as far as is in their power, everything aforesaid. In order that this composition, as well on the part of the aforesaid Prior and Convent of Lenton, as on the part of the said Mayor and Burgesses, and their heirs, may obtain the strength of perpetual stability, the said Prior and Convent of Lenton have set their common seal to the part remaining in the possession of the often-named Mayor and Burgesses, and their heirs ; and the said Mayor and Burgesses of Nottingham have caused the seal of the Community of Nottingham to be affixed to the part remaining with the said Prior and Convent of Lenton. And be it known that all merchants of the town of Nottingham [who] may wish to hire stalls or booths in the aforesaid fair, shall stand the better class amongst the better, the middle class amongst the middle, the smaller amongst the smaller, each one according to his condition, as is contained as above in the case of cloth merchants, apothecaries, pilchers, and mercers."[1]

The four following documents relating to Lenton fair are derived from "The Records of the Borough of Nottingham." The first of these shows how the hireling left his master's sheep, and went to Lenton fair, with the result that the sheep were

---

(1) *Records of the Borough of Nottingham*, i. 61. There are two copies of this agreement, the original not being preserved. One was copied out of the Red Book of the Corporation in 1646 by William Flamsteed, then Town Clerk, and Arthur Rickards (whom Thoroton, p. 499, describes as "Councillor at Law"). It is signed at the bottom by them as follows :—"Vera Copia Compositionis prout intratur in libro Record. Villae Nott., et examinata, 1 Febr. 1646, per nos, Willm. Flamsteed, Arthur Rickards." The other copy is among Greaves' papers, p. 50, *et seq.* It is also referred to in Will. Gregory's "Noates of the Contentes of the Redd Book" (No. 4,771, fo. 6D.). He gives the date "in die Sancti Edwardi apud Nott.,"—that is, November 20—but he mentions no year, as he invariably does when one existed in his original.

lodged in the pinfold at Nottingham, to the damage of their owner. The second gives the particulars of an action brought by a glover of Nottingham against a workman for failing to cut and work, according to agreement, 22 dozens of gloves in time for sale at Lenton fair. The demand for gloves at this date must have been considerable. The third is an action for deceit in the quality of ale bought for sale at Lenton fair; whilst the fourth is an action for the theft of bows brought to Nottingham for sale at Lenton fair.

I.—November 15, 1385. " Roger Wilding, of Radford, makes plaint of Richard Jeffson Nanneson, of Radford, on a plea of trespass : pledge of prosecuting the plea—John de Breadsall : that whereas the said Richard was engaged to serve the afore-said Roger from the feast of Saint Martin in Winter, in the eighth year of the reign of the present King, until Sunday next after the feast of Saint Martin in Winter, in the ninth year of King Richard the Second, to take care of his sheep, the said Richard, on the eve of Saint Martin now last past, went to the fair of Lenton without the license of the said Roger, and left his sheep uncared for, so that through the default of the said Richard the aforesaid sheep were taken by Henry Hostiler, of Notting-ham, at Nottingham, and were placed in the Pinfold for two days, to the damage of the said Roger of 40 shillings, wherefore he enters suit, etc. And the said Richard comes, and acknow-ledged himself to be guilty ; and afterwards by license [of the Court] the parties aforesaid are agreed, and the said Richard is in ' misericordia.' "[1]

II.—November 29, 1396. " Thomas de Lenton, glover, makes plaint of Thomas del Peek on a plea of trespass and contempt against the Statute, that whereas the same Thomas del Peek, in the week next before the feast of the Nativity of Saint John, in the 20th year of the reign of the present King, made an agree-ment, here at Nottingham, with the aforesaid Thomas de Lenton to cut and work 22 dozens of gloves of the gloves of the afore-said Thomas de Lenton, so that the same Thomas de Lenton should have every week from the said Thomas del Peek two dozens of gloves, well and faithfully cut and worked, until the eve of Saint Martin then next following, no week being wanting of the aforesaid two dozens being wanting in work, so that he should have all the aforesaid 22 dozens between the feasts of Saint Martin and Michael, taking for the dozen 3d. until 5s. 6d. for leather bought from the said Thomas de Lenton should have been paid back, the same Thomas del Peek only cut 6 dozens and 4 pairs of gloves of the aforesaid 22 dozens, and left 16 dozens and 8 pairs unworked, which the same Thomas de Lenton should have sold at the Fair of Lenton and of the working of the aforesaid Thomas del Peek, and he has never had them, but was deceived in default of the aforesaid Thomas del Peek, and so he says that the same Thomas has broken the said agreement with him, whereby the same Thomas de Lenton is injured and has received damages to the value of 20s., wherefore he enters suit, etc. And the aforesaid Thomas del Peek comes in his own person, and defends the force and injury, etc., and says that he broke no agreement with him as he has above set forth against him, and as to this he places himself upon the country ; and the other likewise. Therefore the Bailiffs are commanded to cause 12 [jurors] to come between them against the next [Court], etc. Mainpernor of the aforesaid Thomas del Peek to await the inquest of the Court, or for damages, if they be adjudged : Thomas Bulker. And now the aforesaid parties come in their own persons, and the jurors between them being formally required do not come. Therefore the Bailiffs are commanded to distrain the aforesaid jurors against the next [Court], etc. " [1]

III.—May 16, 1397. Roger [de Strelley] makes plaint of William [de Brodbury, of Nottingham,] and Agnes [his wife] on a plea of agreement, that whereas the same Roger bought from the same Agnes, here at Nottingham, on a certain day, ale of the brewing of the aforesaid Agnes before the feast of Saint Martin, in the 20th year of the reign of King Richard the Second, (at the price of) 2d. for a flagon, which ale the aforesaid Agnes guaranteed to the aforesaid Roger to make as good ale as the said Roger had previously had brewed by them at the Fair of Lenton, the said Agnes at the aforesaid time sold her best ale at Nottingham, and sent the inferior ale which she had to the aforesaid Roger, contrary to the agreement made between them, and so he says that the same William and Agnes have broken the agreement with him, whereby the said Roger is injured and has received damages to the value of 20s., wherefore he enters suit, etc. And the aforesaid William and Agnes come, by their attorney, John Breadsall, and defend the force and injury and damages, etc., and say that they have broken no agreement with him, and they seek that this may be inquired ; and the other likewise. Therefore it is commanded, etc.

The same Roger makes plaint of the aforesaid William and Agnes on a plea of trespass, that the said Alice should have made and sent as good ale to the Fair of Lenton as the said Roger had from them at the aforesaid fair at the feast of Saint Martin in the year before written, she sent to the aforesaid Roger bad ale which was not good, but she sold her good ale at home for 3d. whereas the said Roger should have had it from

---

(1) *Records of Borough of Nottingham*, i 328.

her for 2d., whereby the said Roger was deceived of the sale of
ale to divers men in the aforesaid fair, whereby the said Roger
is injured to the damage of the aforesaid Roger of 20s., wherefore he enters suit, etc.  And the aforesaid William and Agnes
come, by their attorney John Breadsall, and defend the force
and injury, etc., and say that they are therein of nothing guilty,
and they seek that this may be inquired; and the other likewise.
Therefore it is commanded, etc."[1]

IV.—July 25, 1397.  William de Clifton was attached to
answer to Richard Northwell, of Lincoln, bowyer, on a plea of
trespass : pledge of prosecuting—Thomas de Arnold : and he
makes plaint that whereas the said Richard, at the feast of St.
Martin in Winter, in the 20th year of the reign of King Richard
the Second, as he came to the Fair of Lenton with his saleable
bows to sell, lodged at the house of Thomas de Arnold here at
Nottingham, the said William, within the said house where the
aforesaid bows stood, opened the packing-cloths of the same,
and took and carried away with him three bows of the aforesaid
bows, value of each bow 2s., whereby the said Richard is injured
and has received damages to the amount of half a mark, wherefore he enters suit, etc.  And the aforesaid William comes in his
own person, and defends the force and injury, etc., and says that
he therein is guilty of nothing, and as to this he places himself
upon the country ; and the other likewise.  Therefore it is commanded, etc—And now the said William comes in his own
person, and acknowledged that he was guilty towards the aforesaid (Richard) in everything, excepting in the damages : and
the damages are now taxed at 6d.  Therefore it is decided by
the Court that the said Richard shall recover from the said
William the aforesaid three bows of the value aforesaid, or the
aforesaid price, and 6d. for damages ; and the said William is in
"misericordia."[2]

When the Lord-mayor and aldermen of London, during the
reign of Henry VII., prohibited any of the citizens from
repairing with their goods to any market or fair out of the city,
so many places remonstrated, and so loud an outcry was raised,
that the obnoxious prohibition was repealed by parliament in
1487.  In the appeal that was made on this occasion, we learn
the principal places at which fairs were then held in England,
and the kind of business transacted, as well as the persons who
frequented them.  " There be many fairs," it said, " for the
common weal of your said liege people, as at Salisbury, Bristow,
Oxenforth, Cambridge, Nottingham, Ely, Coventry, and at many

---

(1) *Records of Borough of Nottingham*, i. 346.          (2) *Ibid.* i. 348.

other places ; where lords spiritual and temporal, abbots, priors, knights, squires, gentlemen, and your said commons of every country, hath their common resort to buy and purvey many things that be good and profitable, as ornaments of holy church, chalices,[1] books, vestments, and other ornaments for holy church aforesaid ;[2] and also for household, as victual for the time of Lent, and other stuff, as linen cloth, woollen cloth, brass, pewter, bedding, osmund, iron, flax, and wax, and many other necessary things, the which might not be forborne among your liege people."

We find that in the year 1500 it was part of the duty of the Mayor of Nottingham to give the common council " knowledge for to see the sports at the fishings, bear baitings, and bull baitings within the town, after the old customs and usages, and to make search the week before Lenton fair for white herrings and salt fish."

As a result of the development in power of municipal institutions, men claimed the right of trading free from ecclesiastical control, and long and fierce contentions frequently arose between municipal and conventual authorities. Such was the case in 1517, when the Mayor and Sheriffs of Nottingham again disputed the rights of the Prior of Lenton as to Lenton Fair. The Prior complained that the Mayor had usurped privileges, and exacted dues which belonged exclusively to Lenton Priory. The Prior and the Mayor continued at variance for a long period, and, in order to prevent further strife, King Henry VIII. recommended the mediation of Sir Thomas Lovell, Steward of the Priory, and Governor of Nottingham Castle, who, together with the Mayor and Sheriffs of Nottingham, met and agreed as a compromise that the Prior was to " have, hold, occupy, and enjoy, without let or distrust from the mayor," the said fair at Lenton for the space of eight days, and during that period no market or sale was to be held in Nottingham, except food

---

(1) Margaret Cokefield (widow of John Cokefield, of Nuthall, Esq.), by her will dated June 17, 1462, bequeathed to the church of Nuthall, " a chalice, bought at Lenton Fair." *Test. Ebor*, ii, 263.

(2) Richard Willoughby, Esq., of Wollaton, by his will dated Sep. 15, 1469, bequeathed to the church of Wollaton two embroidered cloths, lately bought at Lenton Fair, for the high Altar. *Test. Ebor*, iii, 171.

"within houses, doors, or windows," and that corn brought into Nottingham during the fair should not be sold on the pavement. No market-bell was to be rung in Nottingham during the fair, and the Prior was empowered to exact all "tolls, passages, and customs," as if the goods were sold within the liberty of Lenton. The Prior was to grant to the Mayor, Sheriffs, and burgesses of Nottingham, who should desire to have any shop, booth, or stall, or should have the same before any stranger if they applied before the feast of St. Michael, and should be abated twelve-pence of rent from the usual prices ; and that those tanners and bakers who, not having previously paid rent, should continue to be exempt, and that burgesses should be quit of all manner of toll, if they caused buyers to pay "counter toll" to the Prior. To this deed of compromise the Mayor and Sheriffs affixed the town seal, and the Prior the convent seal, August 6th, 1517.

At the dissolution of the Priory, the yearly profit derived from Lenton Fair was £12. The following are some of the rates of stallage at the fair.

|  | s. | d. |
|---|---|---|
| In the vestment row at the west end of the church, 10 foot ... ... ... | 3 | 0 |
| Toward the south, 11 foot each ... | 3 | 4 |
| Near the church yard gate ... ... | 2 | 0 |
| One stall at the end of Cross lane, 10 foot ... ... ... ... ... | 2 | 6 |
| One in Lenton lane, 30 foot ... ... | 13 | 4 |
| Two cockpits at the west end of the churchyard, one 6s. 8d., the other 5s. per annum ... ... .. ... | | |
| One bay of the beddars, 20 yds. each bay ... ... ... ... ... | 3 | 4 |
| Two other bays of the beddars, each bay ... ... ... ... ... | 4 | 0 |
| Five bays in the Lundelen row, four at 1s. 8d. each, the others 2s. ... ... | | |

In the commonplace book[1] of Roger Columbell, Esq., of

---

(1) *Brit. Mus.*, Add. MSS., No. 6702, f. 107.

Darley Hall, Derbyshire (who died in 1605), we find the following
list of spices bought at Lenton fair, with the prices affixed.

Spices bought at Lenton fayre in Anno dni, 1584.

| | |
|---|---|
| In p'i'is peas, iii*li*. ... ... ... ... | 8s. |
| Cinamō, 2*oz*. ... ... ... ... | 12d. |
| Ginger, di.*li*. ... ... ... ... | 14d. |
| Mace, 2*os*. ... ... ... ... ... | 18d. |
| cloves, 2*oz*. ... ... ... ... ... | 10d. |
| proynes, 6*li*. ... ... ... ... | 16d. |
| great Raysons 6*li*... ... ... ... | 16d. |
| Corans, 6*li*. ... ... ... ... | 2s. |
| Aniseede, di.*li*. ... ... ... ... | 4d. |
| licorise, 1*li*. ... ... ... ... | 4d. |
| dates, di.*li*. ... ... ... ... ... | 6d. |
| Caraways, j*li*. ... ... ... .. | 16d. |
| safron, *oz*. ... ... ... ... ... | 8d. |
| bayes, 1*li*. ... ... ... ... ... | 4d. |
| Sugar, 4*li*. ... ... ... . . ... 5s. | 4d. |
| Sanders ? ... ... .. ... ... | 4d. |
| Turnefall, 1*oz*. ... ... ... ... | [no price.] |

In 1603, the plague raging in some parts of the country, it
was ordered that the Mayor and Aldermen of Nottingham,
assisted by three other persons, should be constituted overseers
of the town, to foresee the dangers of the visitation. The
sheriffs to serve by turn, weekly. It being feared that infection
might be carried into the town by some of the great number
of strangers who frequented Lenton Fair, all the inhabitants
of Nottingham were "forbade going to Lenton fair, unless to
buy horses or beasts, on pain of imprisonment and disfranchise-
ment; and none to go there to buy London wares, or to deal
with such wares for two months." It was ordered further
" that a sufficient watch be set betwixt this town and Lenton,
viz. : at the Bridge-end, four persons ; Castle-gate, two ; the
Postern-bridge, near to the Park, one ; Chapel-bar, two ; Sheep-
lane end, one ; Cow-lane bar, one ; at the malt-kiln, one ; St.
John's, one ; and at the Tyle-house, one ; and that four honest

men be assigned to go to Lenton, to observe and see if any of the inhabitants have offended against this order." [1]

King James the First, in consideration of the good and acceptable services of Thomas Webber, gentleman, granted to him, his executors, and assigns, by royal letters patent, dated October 22, 1605, a yearly fair at Lenton, for thirty-one years, to be held on Tuesday, the fifth week in Lent, and the eight following days (Sunday excepted), together with all payments, tolls, dues, etc. [2] We are unable to find any record that this fair was exercised, but as it was granted for a limited term, and the old fair of Lenton being in great repute, the probability is that it may have been regarded as a convenience by the inhabitants of the neighbourhood, and held annually during the term for which it was granted.

In the year 1640, Richard Velley and others, freemen of the city of London, licensed to sell tobacco by retail, presented a petition to the Council for redress in the following grievance :— About six years before, the petitioners took out licenses at £10 each, upon the order of the Commissioners appointed to compound with retailers of tobacco, that they should retail tobacco at all fairs. But, the petitioners state, of late Samuel Wildy, having obtained a license for Lenton, near Nottingham, one of the oldest fairs, for which he paid only forty shillings a year, opposed the petitioners, and caused some of them to be attached, others to be summoned to the Tobacco Office, where they were fined twenty shillings each, but were respited till the cause was heard by the Council. The petitioners prayed the Council to hear the cause, and confirm the order ; and if it appeared that Wildy had causelessly molested the petitioners, that he might be ordered to pay them their costs in the business. [3]

Alderman William Gregory, of Nottingham, who purchased the manor of Lenton, with its fair and other privileges, filed a bill in equity, in the year 1646, to compel the Corporation of Nottingham to enforce on the town the charter of Henry II.,

---

(1) Bailey's " Annals," i. 518.

(2) Record Office, Pat. Roll, 1663. This fair is not noticed by previous local writers.

(3) *State Papers, Domestic*, 1640, p. 91.

which commanded that during Lenton fair "no man should buy
or sell in Nottingham," and which injunction, it appears, had
long been disregarded.  Mr. Gregory having threatened certain
of the burgesses with legal proceedings for the violation of his
chartered rights, they petitioned the Hall "that they would
defend them against actions, in case they kept market and
opened their shops during Lenton fair," on which the Corporation held a meeting, and resolved, that "if Alderman Gregory
trouble any burgesses for not going to, or for keeping open
their shops in Nottingham during, Lenton fair, they shall be
defended."  This resolution appears to have effectually silenced
Mr. Gregory's claim.

George Gregory, Esquire, grandson of Alderman William
Gregory, obtained from King Charles II. his royal letters
patent, dated November 9th, 1663, granting permission for
another fair to be held at Lenton, every year, on the Wednesday
next after the feast of Pentecost, and on the six several days
following.

Lenton Fairs retained much of their ancient repute down to
the last century, and were resorted to by all classes of society.
The neighbouring 'squires were not above participating in the
annual business and merry-making, as appears from the following entry in the Household Book[1] of the Hon. Anchitell Gray,
of Risley Hall, in Derbyshire :—

1681.  November 11.  Spent at Lenton faire ... 00 01 00

In the "Compleat Horseman," by the Sieur de Solleysell,
equerry to the King of France, translated by Sir William Hope,
deputy-lieutenant of Edinburgh Castle, in 1696, the following
remark occurs :—"Lenton Faire in Notts. is a great fair for
all sorts of Horses."

For several years past the fairs at Lenton have, like the fairs
at Nottingham, been declining in their importance, and have
only been held on the Wednesday in Whitsun week, and on St.
Martin's day.  They are still, however, somewhat largely frequented by farmers and horse-dealers, and enjoy a considerable
reputation for the sale of horses and cattle.  All other business
has long since been discontinued.

---

(1) *The Reliquary*, iii. 100.

# SECTION XII.

## THE INCLOSURES.

N the year 1637, a petition was presented to King Charles the First by Marmaduke Marshall,[1] Esquire, praying that the King would be pleased to grant to the petitioner certain common or waste lands lying within the parishes of Lenton and Radford, in fee farm at a certain rental. Attached to the petition is a schedule of the lands (containing about 488 acres) which the petitioner desired might be granted to him, the greater portion being included in the first Inclosure Award of 1768. Although the King received Marshall's petition with favour, we are unable to find that his request was complied with.

"To the King's most Excellent Ma^tie

"The most humble Peticon of Marmaduke Marshall Esq^re your Maties most Loyall subiect.

"In all humilitie showeth

"That your subiect hath discovered that divers parcells of ground lying w'thin the Lordshipps or Parishes of Lenton & Radford in your Maties countie of Nottingham, or in one of them

---

(1) Marmaduke Marshall, of Morton-upon-Swale, in the county of York, and afterwards of Cole Park, in Wiltshire, was the son of John Marshall, of the first-named place, and was born in or about the year 1593, and married Anne, sole daughter and heiress of Sir George Marshall, of Cole Park, Knight, Equerry to King James the First (who died in 1636). In 1639, Marmaduke Marshall held the office of Gentleman Sewer to the Duke of Lennox. He had at least seven daughters, but appears to have left no male issue.

lying common or waist ground and the greatest part thereof being heather or barren ground doe belong unto your Ma^tie and are unlawfullie w^thheld from your Matie by colour or pretence of l'res patents heretofore respectively made by your Matie and your Maties late ffather of ever blessed memorie (w'ch said parcells of ground are severallie and more particularlie named menconed and expressed in a schedule hereunto annexed).

"May your Matie therefore be pleased to grant the same unto your said subiect & his heires in fee-farm rendering unto your Matie & to your Maties heires and successors for ever the Rent of vi*l* xiii. iiijd. p annu. And your Maties said subiect will at his owne perill and att his owne proper costs & charges recover the same ground, wch otherwise is like to be still kept and unlawfullie detained from your Matie, so as your subiect may inclose and improve the premisses

"And hee shall ever pray it."

(Copy of Schedule referred to.)

" One p'cell of ground called by y^e name of the Holmes, or Cow-pasture, with the tithe thereof, conteyning by estimacon one hundred and ffiftie acres w'thin the confines of the fforest of Sherwood in the County of Notingham ; The River of Trent lying or being on the south part, Wilford Meadowe towards the East p'te, and the Trent wong toward the west p'te.

" And one othe pcell of ground there lying called the Lings, by estimacon three hundred acres, w'th the tithe thereof, Basford Lings lying toward the Northe pte, Notingham feild lying towards the south pte, the Churche feild of Radford towards the West pte, and Notingham lings towards ye East pte.

" And one pcell of ground there lying, called, or knowne by the name of the common under Radford, conteyning by estimacon six acres, wth the tithes thereof, Radford lying towards the East pte, and the Moore ffeild towards the west pte.

" And one pcell of ground called the Bull piece, conteyning by estimacon, two acres.

" And one pcell of ground called Snowden hole conteyning by estimacon three acres.

" And one other pcell of ground conteyning by estimacon one acre and an halfe.

" And one other pcell of ground conteyning by estimacon two acres.

" And one pcell of ground called the Gorse conteyning by estimacon three acres.

" And one other pcell of ground (lying ut supra) there called the Becksyde, conteyning by estimacon three acres.

" And one Plott of ground lying in the parrish of Radford, called by the name of the two grove meadowe, conteyning seaven

acres and an halfe, or thereabouts, abutting towards a certain
place called Bobbers Milne upon the East, and upon the tith-
barne of Radford on the West, and upon the River Leen upon
the south, & upon the redd ffeild of Radford on the North, in
the ocupacon of Radford men, together with the tithes thereof.

"And one other Little Close, called by the name of ye towne
close, lying in the pish of Radford, conteyning one acre and an
hafe or thereabouts, lying between Bobbers Milne on the West,
and a heath ground called the Lings on ye East, in the ocupa-
tion of Radford men, together wth the tithes thereof.

"And a certaine quantitie of arrable & pasture ground, conteyning fower acres or thereabouts, called Radford townes lands,
in the feilds of Radford and Lenton, or one of them, in the
ocupacon of Radford men, together wth the tithes thereof.

"And one other peice of ground called the horse commons,
lying in Radford and Lenton, or one of them, conteyning fower
acres or thereabouts.

"And one plott of meadow ground in Lenton Holmes, conteyning one acre or thereabouts, in the ocupacon of Radford
men."

Written under the petition :—

" I.—Reference to the Lord Treasurer, who, calling to his
assistance the Attorney-General, is to certify his opinion.
Hampton Court, 15th October, 1637.

"II.—The Lord Treasurer to the Attorney-General and
Surveyor-General.    To certify what they think fit to be done.
London House, 25th October, 1637.

" III.—Report of the Attorney-General and Surveyor-General
to the Lord Treasurer.   We find the number of acres to be as
they are set down in the schedule annexed.   If the Lord
Treasurer thinks the lands should be enclosed, they lying within
the Forest of Sherwood, then they may be improved to 13s. 4d.
or 10s. an acre.   As touching the grant to petitioner, we leave
the same to your wisdom.   25th June, 1638.

" IV.—Report of the Lord Treasurer to the King.   Finds the
lands desired by petitioner are part of the Forest of Sherwood,
and to be very improvable if you will sever the same, and
so will the whole forest, I doubt not.    But how fit your
Majesty knows best."[1]

The first Inclosure Act for the parishes of Lenton and Radford
was passed in the year 1767, and the Commissioners' award was
made in the following year.

The Act, which has been printed, is entitled " An Act for

---

(1) State Papers, 1637, vol. 369, No. 82.

Dividing and Inclosing the Open Fields, Meadows, Common Pastures, and Commonable Lands, lying South of the Turnpike Road leading from *Nottingham* to *Alfreton*, within the Liberties and Townships of *Lenton* and *Radford*, in the County of Nottingham." [1767.][1]

Amongst other things, it was enacted "That all the said Lands hereby intended to be divided and inclosed as aforesaid shall be surveyed and measured by the said Commissioners, or any Two of them, or by such Person or Persons as they, or any two of them, shall order and direct, and a Plan made of the whole ; which Plan and Admeasurements shall be reduced into Writing, ascertaining the Contents of the whole and the Contents of the Lands belonging to each and every Proprietor interested therein, and shall be laid before the said Commissioners, or any Two of them, at one of their Meetings to be held in pursuance of this Act, to be by them kept for the Purposes of this Act."

### LENTON AND RADFORD INCLOSURE AWARD, 1768.

The following extracts from this Award refer only to the parish of Lenton.

The AWARD commences, " To ALL to whom these presents shall come," and after reciting several things contained in the Act, proceeds, " Now know ye, that we the said Tristram Exley,[2] John Stone,[3] and Thomas Oldknow,[4] Commissioners named in the same Act, having taken upon us the execution of the powers vested in us, in and by the said in part recited Act, etc., etc., and having appointed a survey to be taken of the lands intended by the said Act to be inclosed, as in and by the said

---

(1) It will be observed that this Inclosure does not appear to have included any portion of the Priory demesne, the whole of which seems to have been of old inclosure.

(2) The Reverend Tristram Exley was rector of the Second Mediety of Trowell from 1753 to 1792. He died April the 19th, 1792, aged 68, and was buried in the chancel at Trowell, where there is a mural tablet to his memory.

(3) John Stone, gent., died at Quorndon, Jan., 19, 1783, and was buried there on the 22nd of the same month.

(4) Thomas Oldknow was Sheriff of Nottingham in 1746; he was made an alderman in 1772, and was Mayor in 1773, and again in 1778. He died at Calverton, where he had a small estate, March the 31st, 1787, aged 78, and was buried at Heanor, in Derbyshire. His name appears as commissioner in various Inclosure Acts in this and other counties.

Act is directed, and the same having been accordingly taken
and laid before us, etc, we the said Commissioners having finished
the division of the said lands, do, by this our award or instrument in writing under our hands and seals, set out, allot and
award to and for the said several and respective proprietors the
several and respective pieces, plots, and parcels of land hereinafter mentioned, with a description of the buttals and boundaries
of each respective allotment, in the describing of which buttals
and boundaries the Eastward boundaries to each respective
allotment are first mentioned, and so on to the South, West,
and North about as they respectively adjoin to each other, which
may be more fully and clearly discovered by a plan of the
allotments herein made, which plan we have to this our Award
annexed."[1]

. . . "To the VICAR OF LENTON and his successors, one
piece, plot or parcel of land in a pasture called Lenton pasture
containing 1a. 2r. 31p., or thereabouts, bounded by land allotted
to the said vicar in lieu of vicarial tythes, and by land allotted to
George De Ligne Gregory, Esq. and is so allotted to the said
Vicar in lieu of the glebe land and common right lying within
the liberties of Lenton, and being part of the lands intended by
the said Act to be inclosed. One other piece, plot, or parcel of
land, lying in the said pasture containing 22a. 1r. 5p. or thereabouts, bounded by the lordship of Wilford, by land allotted to
the said George De Ligne Gregory, by land allotted the said
James Thane, and by the last mentioned allotment in lieu of
glebe land, and which said piece plot or parcel of land is allotted
to the said Vicars of Lenton and their successors, is, in the
judgment of us the said Commissioners, worth twenty-four
pounds a year as directed to be set out by the said Act, to and

---

(1) The map, or plan, formerly attached to the award has been lost for many
years.   In the year 1794 we find the following entry in the churchwardens'
accounts :—
    " To our Trobill Drying the Writings that was damaged by the flood—5s. "
    These writings would consist of the Parish Registers, the Inclosure Award of 1768,
etc.   The Registers and Award bear evidence of considerable damage from water,
and the probability is that the map, which would be folded up, was so much damaged
(particularly if it had remained in the chest since the great flood of 1792) that the
churchwardens, being illiterate men, to save themselves further " trobill," detached it
from the award and destroyed it.   It is probable that the loss of this map caused the
following resolution to be passed at a vestry meeting held at Lenton, April 3rd, 1812 :
    " Resolved unanimously that Mr. Roughton be directed to apply to Mr. Green for
such map, or maps, as may be in his possession, in order that it, or they, may be deposited in the parish chest with the other parochial documents."
    In addition to the loss of the original map, there does not appear to be a copy of it
in existence.   We have made inquiries at the office of the Clerk of the Peace for the
county of Nottingham, at the Public Record Office, the office of the Land Commissioners for England, and other Public Departments in London, with the result in
each case that no such plan, or copy, is known to exist.
    The Lenton and Radford Inclosure Awards of 1768 and 1799, which were formerly
kept in a chest in the parish church of Lenton, are now in the possession of the
Corporation of Nottingham.

for the said Vicar of Lenton and his successors for the time being, and by him and them taken and accepted in full recompense and satisfaction for all Vicarial tythes of all the lands within the Liberties of Lenton intended by the said Act to be divided and inclosed, and for all Vicarial Tythes of all the yards, gardens, orchards, homesteads, and old inclosures within the Liberties of Lenton, and for all Vicarial Tythes of all the common lands in the Liberties of Lenton aforesaid, which lie on the North side of the said turnpike road from Nottingham to Alfreton and which by the said Act was not intended to be divided and inclosed, mortuaries, surplice fees, and Easter offerings only excepted, which are to be paid as usual heretofore."

. . . "To the said GEORGE DE LIGNE GREGORY, one piece, plot or parcel of land, part in the said pasture called Lenton pasture, and part in a meadow thereto adjoining, containing 73 acres, or thereabouts, bounded by the Lordship of Wilford, by the river Trent, by old inclosed lands in the said Lordship of Lenton, and by other lands in the said pasture and meadow allotted to the said George De Ligne Gregory as a proprietor of lands and which allottment so made to the said George De Ligne Gregory is in lieu of all the impropriate tythe of all the land lying within the liberties of Lenton intended by the said Act to be inclosed, and in lieu of all the impropriate tythe of all the yards, gardens, orchards, and homesteads within the said liberties of Lenton aforesaid. To the said GEORGE DE LIGNE GREGORY as a proprietor of land, one piece, plot or parcel of land in the said pasture and meadow containing 183a. 3r. 26p. or thereabouts, bounded by the said Lordship of Wilford, by land allotted to the said Vicar of Lenton and his successors, by land allotted to James Thane, by land allotted to him the said George De Ligne Gregory in lieu of Tythe, by old inclosures in the said Lordship of Lenton, by the Lordship of Beeston, and by land in the said meadow, allotted to Rebecca Garland and George Brentnall. One piece, plot, or parcel of land, in a field called Beck field, containing 54a. 3r. 5p. or thereabouts, bounded by the said River Leen, by old inclosed lands belonging to him the said George De Ligne Gregory, by other old inclosed lands called the Abbey Field, and by the Turnpike Road leading from Nottingham to Derby. One piece, plot, or parcel of land in the said Beckfield and Thackholm meadow containing 91a. 2r. 36p., or thereabouts, bounded by the said River Leen, by land in the said Beckfield and Thackholm meadow allotted to the said Rebecca Garland and George Brentnall, by the said Turnpike road leading from Nottingham to Derby, by land allotted to Joseph Stubbins and by the said Turnpike road leading from Nottingham through Wollaton. . . . One piece, plot, or parcel of land in a field called Allen Field, containing 42a. 1r. 14p., or thereabouts, bounded by Nottingham Park, by the said River Leen, by an old inclosure

22

or garden belonging to Timothy Pym, by land allotted to the
said Rebecca Garland and George Brentnall, and by the Turnpike road leading from Nottingham to Derby.   One other piece,
plot, or parcel of land in the said Allen Field, containing
21a. 3r. 5p., or thereabouts, bounded by land allotted to the said
Rebecca Garland and George Brentnall, by ancient homesteads
in the Town of Lenton, and by the said Turnpike road leading
from Nottingham to Derby.   One other piece, plot, or parcel of
land in the said Allen Field, being two Field closes containing
9a. 1r. 16p., or thereabouts, bounded by the allotment of the said
Rebecca Garland and George Brentnall, and by old inclosures of
him the said George De Ligne Gregory.   One other piece, plot,
or parcel of land in a field called Sand Field, containing
85a. 3r. 26p., or thereabout, bounded by land allotted to William
Elliott, by the said Turnpike road leading from Nottingham to
Derby, by old Inclosure adjoining to the town of Lenton, by the
said River Leen, by land in the said Sand Field allotted to the
said William Bingham, and by the said Turnpike road leading
from Nottingham through Wollaton.   .   .   .   One piece, plot,
or parcel of land in certain places called the Bull Close and Leen
Crofts, containing 4a. 2r. 14p., or thereabouts, bounded by old
inclosures in Lenton aforesaid, by land allotted to John Webb,
by the said River Leen, and the said Turnpike road leading
from Nottingham to Derby.   .   .   .   We allot, set out, and
award to the said George De Ligne Gregory certain lands lying
on both sides the Turnpike road leading from Nottingham to
Derby, directed by the said Act to be allotted for keeping Fairs
for Cattle and as a recompense and satisfaction for his the said
George De Ligne Gregory's interest in the said waste lands intended by the said Act to be inclosed, which said land exclusive
of the Turnpike road contains 5a. 1r. 8p , or thereabouts.   To
LORD MIDDLETON, one piece, plot, or parcel of land in the said
Beck Field, and a small old inclosure of the said Rebecca
Garland and George Brentnall consented and agreed to exchange
for Field Land of the same value, which consent the said
Rebecca Garland and George Brentnall have testified to us the
said Commissioners by writing under their own hands, containing 25a. 2r. 8p., or thereabouts, bounded by land allotted to
Joseph Stubbins, by the said Turnpike road leading from Nottingham to Derby, by the lordship of Wollaton, and by the
Turnpike road leading from Nottingham through Wollaton.
.   .   .   To the said REBECCA GARLAND AND GEORGE BRENT-
NALL, one piece, plot, or parcel of land part being old inclosure
of the said George De Ligne Gregory, consented to be exchanged for Field Land and part being in the said Allen Field,
containing 22a. 3r. 32p., or thereabouts, bounded by the allotment hereinbefore made to the said George De Ligne Gregory
adjoining to Nottingham Park, by an old inclosure or garden
of the said Timothy Pym, by the River Leen, by old inclosures

of him the said George De Ligne Gregory, and others, by other allotments of the said George De Ligne Gregory in the said Allen Field, and by the said Turnpike road leading from Nottingham to Derby. One other piece, plot, or parcel of land in the said Lenton Meadow, containing 12a. 2r. 38p., or thereabout, bounded by land in the said Meadow and Pasture allotted to the said George De Ligne Gregory, and by old inclosures in the said Lordship of Lenton. One other piece, plot, or parcel of land in the old Beck Field and Nether Thackholme meadow containing 5a. 1r. 5p., or thereabout, bounded by the River Leen, by old inclosed lands, by the Turnpike road, and by land allotted to the said George De Ligne Gregory, all which three last mentioned allotments, made to the said Rebecca Garland and George Brentnall contain together 40a. 3r. 35p., or thereabout, and are made to them the said Rebecca Garland and George Brentnall in full satisfaction for all the land and common right which they had dispersed in and over the lands intended by the said Act to be inclosed, and also in full satisfaction for a small piece of old inclosed land lying in the first-mentioned allotment of the said Lord Middleton. . . . To JAMES THANE, one piece, plot, or parcel of land in the said pasture called Lenton Pasture, containing 1a. 1r. 26p., or thereabout, bounded by land allotted to the Vicar of Lenton and by land allotted to the said George De Ligne Gregory, and is allotted to the said James Thane in lieu of and full satisfaction for common belonging to him the said James Thane, in, over, or upon, all or any part of the Lands intended by the said Act to be inclosed. . . . To JOHN WEBB, one piece, plot, or parcel of land, being part of a piece of land called Bull Close, containing 3r. 22p., or thereabout, bounded by old homesteads within the Town of Lenton, by the river Leen, and by other parts of the said Bull Close allotted to the said George De Ligne Gregory, and is allotted to the said John Webb in lieu of and full satisfaction for two cow commons and eight sheep commons, in, over, and upon the lands intended by the said Act to be inclosed. . . . All which pieces, plots, or parcels of land so allotted as aforesaid to and for the several and respective proprietors, contain together in the whole the said quantity of 1219a. 3r. 29p. first mentioned to be intended by the said Act to be inclosed, and also 2a. 3r. 33p., contained in the several old inclosures, belonging heretofore to the said George De Ligne Gregory and the said Rebecca Garland and George Brentnall exchanged as before mentioned for Field land equal in value to the said old Inclosure."

## PUBLIC ROADS OR WAYS.[1]

Concerning the public roads and ways, other than the turnpike roads [Derby Road and Alfreton Road], the course of which has not been altered, the Commissioners ordered and directed that there be the following public, horse, carriage, and drift roads or ways :—

" From the town of Lenton southward, over the allotments of the said George de Ligne Gregory, by the side of the fence by the westward parts of the allotments of the Vicar of Lenton and James Thane, and continued in nearly a direct line to the ford place in the River Trent, where a public horse, carriage, and drift way has usually heretofore been from the town of *Lenton to Wilford.*"

" From the northward end of the town of Lenton to the southward end of the town of Radford, over the respective allotments of the said George de Ligne Gregory and William Bingham, where a Public, Horse, Carriage, and drift way has usually heretofore been from *Lenton to Radford.*"

### PRIVATE ROADS OR WAYS.

" Also a private horse, carriage and drift road westward from the public road leading from *Lenton to Wilford*, near where that road adjoins to the ford way in the River Trent, near the bank of the River Trent, on the allotment of the said George de Ligne Gregory to an old Inclosure called Trent Wong. Also a private horse, carriage and drift road from the Town of Lenton on a Lane called Birch Lane and continued over the allotment of the said Rebecca Garland and George Brentnall, to an old inclosure or garden belonging to the said Timothy Pym for the use and conveniency of the owner and occupiers of that old inclosure or garden for the time being for ever."

### PUBLIC FOOTWAYS.

" From the Lordship of Wilford, over the allotment of the

---

(1) " All such publick Highways shall be set out and remain Sixty feet broad at the least between the Ditches or Fences (except Bridle Ways and Foot Ways)." *Inclosure Act*, 1767.

said Vicar of Lenton, in Lenton pasture, and the lands in Lenton pasture and Lenton meadow, alloted to the said George de Ligne Gregory, to an old inclosure in the Lordship of Lenton called Trent Wong, where a public footway had usually heretofore been."

" From the town of Lenton westward, over the allotment of John Webb, in Bull Close, to a foot bridge over the river Leen, and from thence over the allotment of the said George de Ligne Gregory, No. 11, to a place in the said Lordship of Lenton called Abbey field, where a footway has usually heretofore been from Lenton to Beeston."

" From the town of Lenton eastward, on a Lane called Birch Lane, and over the respective allotments of Rebecca Garland and George Brentnall, and an allotment of the said George de Ligne Gregory, to a foot stile in the fence belonging to Nottingham Park, where a footway has usually heretofore been from Lenton to Nottingham."

" From the town street in Lenton into the allotment of the said George de Ligne Gregory, near the *Pinfold*, and over that allotment and the allotment of William Bingham, by the *east* side of the public horse, carriage, and drift road from Lenton to Radford, where a public footway from Lenton to Radford has usually heretofore been."

And the Commissioners furthur ordered and directed that good and convenient foot stiles should be made, and for ever after repaired, upon all the foot roads herein before appointed over all the fences lying across such foot roads, by and at the expense of the several proprietors, owners, and occupiers of such allotments who are to make the fences where such foot roads are directed, and that good and convenient foot bridges be made over all or any drains, where such foot roads are directed, by and at the expense of the owner of such allotments as have any such drains across any such foot roads, except such foot bridges as go across the river Leen, which are to be made, repaired and amended for ever hereafter by the Overseers of the Highways for such respective townships where such bridges happen to be. ·    ·    ·    ·    · ' In Witness of this being our Award, which we have caused to be engrossed on fourteen skins of parchment, we have hereunto set our hands and seals this ninth day of January in the eighth year of the reign of our Soverign Lord George the Third, of Great Britain, France and Ireland, King, Defender of the Faith, and in the year of our Lord one thousand seven hundred and sixty eight."

## Schedule of Allotments.

| | | A. | R. | P. |
|---|---|---|---|---|
| Attenborrow, Robert and John ... ... | R. | 6 | 1 | 8 |
| Bingham, William... ... ... ... | R. | 36 | 0 | 13 |
| Brentnall, G., and Garland, R. ... ... | L. | 40 | 3 | 35 |
| Bradshaw, John ... ... ... ... | R. | 1 | 2 | 32 |
| Elliott, William ... ... ... ... | R. | 46 | 2 | 8 |
| Gregory, George de Ligne ... ... | L. | 572 | 2 | 30 |
| Do. ... ... | R. | 252 | 0 | 5 |
| Gregory, Mrs. ... ... ... ... | R. | 29 | 3 | 37 |
| Hall, William ... ... ... ... | R. | | 1 | 13 |
| Holmes, Elizabeth ... ... ... | R. | | | 19 |
| Hornbuckle, Walter ... ... ... | R. | 18 | 1 | 9 |
| Merriman, Edward ... ... ... | R. | | 2 | 16 |
| Middleton, Lord ... ... ... ... | L. | 25 | 2 | 8 |
| Do. ... ... ... ... | R. | 42 | 0 | 15 |
| Radford Town Land ... ... ... | R. | 5 | 1 | 29 |
| Roughton, Gervase ... ... ... | R. | | 2 | 15 |
| Roughton, John ... ... ... ... | R. | 3 | 2 | 26 |
| Sherwin, John ... ... ... ... | R. | 1 | 2 | 24 |
| Smith, Sir George... ... ... ... | R. | 3 | 1 | 27 |
| Smith, John ... ... ... ... | R. | 2 | 0 | 23 |
| Smith, Mary ... ... ... ... | R. | 1 | 1 | 33 |
| Stubbins, Joseph ... ... ... .. | R. | 34 | 2 | 39 |
| Strey, Michael ... ... ... ... | R. | 1 | 0 | 32 |
| Thane, James ... ... ... ... | L. | 1 | 1 | 26 |
| Thoroton, Thomas... ... ... ... | R. | 2 | 0 | 25 |
| Townsend, Thomas ... ... ... | R. | | | 19 |
| Wayte, George, Vicar of Lenton ... | L. | 23 | 3 | 36 |
| Do. , Vicar of Radford ... | R. | 53 | 1 | 38 |
| Webb, John ... ... ... ... | L. | | 3 | 2 |
| Willoughby, Edward ... ... ... | R. | 7 | 0 | 22 |
| Wyld, William ... ... ... ... | R. | 4 | 2 | 15 |

| | A. | R. | P. |
|---|---|---|---|
| In Lenton parish ... | 665 | 1 | 17 |
| In Radford parish... | 557 | 2 | 17 |
| Total... | 1222 | 3 | 34[1] |

(1) It should be noted that there is a difference of 12 perches between this total and the total quantity of land (1222a. 3r. 22p.) stated in the Commissioners' Award to have been alloted by them. This is possibly accounted for by the fact that in the Book of Quality the total of land to be alloted to the Vicar of Radford is entered as 53a. 1r. 26p., whereas the quantity actually awarded by the Commissioners was 53a. 1r. 38p.

A dispute having arisen in the year 1774, between the inhabitants of Lenton and the inhabitants of Radford as to the repair of the road known as Radford Marsh, the matter was settled in accordance with the terms of an agreement, made June 29th, 1774, between the parishioners of each parish. It was then agreed that the parishioners of Radford should forthwith pay the sum of five pounds to the parishioners of Lenton towards the cost of repairing the road, and also contribute twenty loads of stone for the same purpose. The parishioners of Radford also agreed to relinquish their rights to depasture cattle on the road, and every other parochial right thereto. The inhabitants of Lenton agreed to repair the road forthwith, and to keep it in good and sufficient repair in the future, such road thereafter to be considered as being in the parish of Lenton. The agreement was signed on behalf of the inhabitants of Lenton by George Wayte, Curate, John Chamberlain, John Bradshaw, and several others, and on behalf of the inhabitants of Radford by Edward Willoughby,[1] George Wayte, Vicar, William Bingham, and others.

In the year 1792, the state of the Crown lands, or the claims of the Government on the domains of royalty in various forests, parks, chases, manors, etc., of the country, having begun to attract public attention, a commission was appointed, by the authority of Parliament, to make strict enquiries into these matters, in order to ascertain what lands were still unalienated from the Crown, and the value of the same. According to a great survey made of the limits and bounds of the forest of Sherwood in 1609, it was found to contain over 95,000 acres of land. To all this immense tract of land the Crown formerly held undisputed right, but the Commission of Inquiry, which sat at Mansfield in 1792, in their report, say that " not the right of common only, but the soil itself, of every part of the Forest,

---

(1) Edward Willoughby, Esq., of Aspley Hall, in the parish of Radford, whose signature heads the list of those who signed on behalf of that parish, was the representative of a younger branch of the noble family of Willoughby, of Wollaton.  Being a Romanist, and thus incapacitated from holding any public office, his name seldom appears in connection with parochial or county affairs.  He died October 17th, 1792, aged 86, and a few years later the Aspley Hall estate was sold by his representatives to the then Lord Middleton.

was claimed by the neighbouring proprietors, and that the rights of the Crown had long been lost sight of." To show the principle upon which the commissioners proceeded, in order to recover for the Crown its just share in the unenclosed lands, over which it still held a right of domain, one case may be cited. This royalty extended over 200 acres in the parishes of Lenton and Radford, which land, in fee simple, the commissioners estimated might be worth 5s. per acre. The property of the Crown was rated at one-fortieth part of this valuation, which was not claimed in land, but estimated in money. Thus the share of the parishes of Lenton and Radford due to the Crown, had it been reserved in land, would have amounted to five acres ; this, however, was commuted for a money payment of twenty-five shillings.

The second Inclosure Act for Lenton and Radford was passed in 1796, and the Award was made in 1799. The lands comprised in the award formed the detached portions of the parishes of Lenton and Radford subsequently known as *Hyson Green.*

The Inclosure Act, which has been printed, is entitled " An Act for Dividing and Inclosing the Forest, Commons, and Waste Lands, within the Liberties or Townships of *Lenton* and *Radford,* in the County of *Nottingham."* [1796.]

The Commissioners appointed to put the Act into execution were John Renshaw,[1] of Owthorpe, in the county of Nottingham, gentleman, and Robert Padley,[2] of Burton Joyce, in the said county of Nottingham, gentleman.

---

(1). Mr. John Renshaw for many years occupied Owthorpe Hall, the former seat of the Hutchinson family, and, dying there August the 24th, 1802, aged 60, his remains were interred in Owthorpe Church.

(2) Mr. Robert Padley, of Burton Joyce, who was subsequently in the Commission of the Peace for the county of Nottingham, died June the 16th, 1833, aged 74, and was buried at Burton Joyce. He married Ann, daughter and eventual heiress of John Newton, Esq., of Bulwell Hall, and was grandfather of the Reverend Charles John Allen Newton Padley, B.A., who sold the Bulwell Hall estate to the late Samuel Thomas Cooper, Esq.

LENTON AND RADFORD INCLOSURE AWARD, 1799.

After reciting the Act of 36 George III. for inclosure, the award states that a survey had been made, that the lands contained 276a. 1r. 37p., and that after making deductions for public and private roads, and the allotment for getting materials, there remained 261a. 1r. 11p.

The Commissioners appointed the following public carriage, bridle, and drift-roads :—

(1). From Nottingham to Alfreton, so far as the same goes over or passes through the said land inclosed. This road was sixty feet wide, and in Radford parish.

(2). From a lane in the parish of Radford called Outgang Lane, in a north-eastward direction over the said lands to be inclosed, to The Forest, within the liberties of Nottingham, being the public road from Radford towards Mapperley. This road, forty feet wide, was also in Radford parish. It is now known as Bentinck Road.

(3). A road branching northwards out of the last-mentioned road, and extending in nearly a straight direction over the said lands intended to be inclosed, to a lane in the parish of Basford, near the Paper Mill, being the public road from the westward end of the Town of Nottingham to Basford. This road was forty feet wide, and in Lenton parish.

The Commissioners then set out and appointed one public footway, of the breadth of ten feet, from Nottingham Forest, near the Race Stand, in a northward direction, into and over the lands awarded to George De Ligne Gregory, to a footstile leading into the parish of Basford, being the public footway from Nottingham, by the Bowling Alley House, to the town of Basford ; and the Commissioners further ordered that the owners of the said lands should make, or cause to be made, good and convenient footstiles where the footway crosses any of the fences of such lands, and at all times thereafter to repair the same.

The Commissioners also ordered that the footway or path leading from the town of Nottingham to a certain place called

Bobber's Mill, in the county of Nottingham, through part of certain lands known by the name of Radford Old Inclosures, should be stopped up.

" And we do set out and appoint one Private carriage bridle and drift road of the breadth of thirty feet from the Turnpike road leading from Nottingham to Alfreton near the northward end of a lane in the Parish of Radford, called Church Field Lane in a north-eastward direction over the said lands intended to be inclosed to join the public carriage road herein before described, and set out from the west end of the Town of Nottingham to Basford, which is for the use of the owners and occupiers of lands in Lenton and Radford to pass and repass along the same."

The Commissioners declared this road to be in the parish of Lenton.

The Commissioners allotted a piece of land, No. 15 in the map, containing 1a. 2r. 20p., to the Surveyor of Highways for the parishes of Lenton and Radford, for getting materials for the repair of highways and other roads in the parishes. The herbage and produce of the said land was granted to George De Ligne Gregory.

The allotments were made as follows :—

| No. in Award Map. | Names of Proprietors. | Lenton or Radford parish. | Areas of Allotments. | | |
|---|---|---|---|---|---|
| | | | A. | R. | P. |
| 1. | George De Ligne Gregory, Esq. ... | R. | 0 | 1 | 28 |
| 2. | William Hornbuckle ... ... | R. | 0 | 1 | 9 |
| 3. | George De Ligne Gregory, Esq. ... | R. | 0 | 1 | 21 |
| 4. | W. E. Elliott and John Elliott, Esqs. | R. | 0 | 0 | 23 |
| 5. | George De Ligne Gregory, Esq. ... | R. | 1 | 3 | 17 |
| 6. | Do. ... | L. | 21 | 3 | 37 |
| 7. | Elizabeth Hall ... ... ... | R. | 1 | 2 | 21 |
| 8. | Thomas Bostock ... ... ... | R. | 1 | 2 | 21 |
| 9. | Gervas Roughton ... ... ... | R. | 1 | 2 | 15 |
| 10. | William Bingham ... ... ... | R. | 1 | 2 | 34 |
| 11. | Vicar of Lenton ... ... ... | L. | 1 | 2 | 34 |
| 12. | Vicar of Radford ... ... ... | R. | 1 | 2 | ·34 |
| 13. | William Hornbuckle ... ... | R. | 4 | 3 | 21 |
| 14. | George De Ligne Gregory, Esq., for Tithes in Lenton ... ... | L. | 15 | 3 | 28 |

| No. in Award Map. | Names of Proprietors. | Lenton or Radford parish. | Areas of Allotments. A. R. P. | | |
|---|---|---|---|---|---|
| 15. | Surveyor of the Highways... ... | | 1 | 2 | 20 |
| 16. | George De Ligne Gregory, Esq., for Tithes in Radford ... ... | R. | 6 | 1 | 16 |
| 17. | Do. as Lord of the Manor of Radford... ... ... | R. | 6 | 3 | 11 |
| 18. | Do. received in exchange of John Sherwin, Esq. ... | R. | 1 | 2 | 24 |
| 19. | Do. , as Lord of the Manor of Lenton ... ... ... | L. | 7 | 3 | 17 |
| 20. | George De Ligne Gregory, Esq. ... | R. | 19 | 1 | 10 |
| 21. | John Sherwin, Esq. ... ... ... | R. | 4 | 0 | 32 |
| 22. | William Elliott Elliott and John Elliott, Esqs. ... ... ... | R. | 3 | 0 | 17 |
| 23. | Do. do. | R. | 8 | 0 | 32 |
| 24. | Lord Middleton ... ... ... | R. | 4 | 0 | 14 |
| 25. | Do. ... ... ... | L. | 2 | 0 | 0 |
| 26. | Thomas Webb Edge, Esq. ... ... | L. | 1 | 0 | 11 |
| 27. | Thomas Brentnall ... ... ... | L. | 2 | 0 | 22 |
| 28. | James Killingley ... ... ... | L. | 2 | 0 | 22 |
| 29. | Oliver Buck ... ... ... ... | R. | 2 | 0 | 22 |
| 30. | William Walker ... ... ... | R. | 1 | 3 | 8 |
| 31. | James Smith... ... ... ... | R. | 1 | 2 | 24 |
| 32. | Nathaniel Stubbins ... ... ... | R. | 1 | 2 | 34 |
| 33. | George De Ligne Gregory, Esq. ... | L. | 116 | 3 | 30 |
| 34. | Earl of Chesterfield, in right of Chase ... ... ... ... | R. | 3 | 0 | 0 |
| 35. | Do. do. | L. | 7 | 0 | 0 |
| 36. | Robert Hill ... ... ... ... | R. | 1 | 3 | 4 |
| 37. | Paul Barrett ... ... ... ... | R. | 1 | 0 | 32 |
| 38. | William Gregory Williams... ... | R. | 0 | 3 | 20 |

The Award is dated April 10th, 1799.

The "Nottingham Corporation Act, 1883," after reciting in its preamble that, by an Act passed in the seventh year of the reign of King George the Third, intituled "An Act for dividing and enclosing the open fields, meadows, common pastures, and

commonable lands lying south of the turnpike road leading from
Nottingham to Alfreton, within the liberties and townships of
Lenton and Radford, in the county of Nottingham," and an
award made under that Act dated the 9th of January, 1768,
certain highways in the parishes of Lenton and Radford were
directed to be set out not less than sixty feet wide, and certain
lands adjoining the turnpike road from Nottingham to Derby,
on each side thereof, were allotted to George De Ligne Gregory,
and certain cattle fairs directed to be held thereon, but by encroachments and otherwise parts of the said highways are now,
and have been for many years past, of less width than that
prescribed, and the last mentioned allotted lands have long
ceased to be used for the purpose of cattle fairs, and are not now
required for that purpose,[1] and that by an award dated the 10th
day of April, 1799, made in pursuance of an Act passed in the
36th year of the reign of King George the Third, intituled " An
Act for dividing and enclosing the forest commons and waste
lands within the liberties and townships of Lenton and Radford,
in the county of Nottingham," a certain piece or parcel of land
was allotted to the Surveyors of Highways of the parishes of
Lenton and Radford, for getting materials for the repair of highways in the said parishes, which highways are now vested in
and repairable by the Corporation: and whereas the above-
mentioned provisions of the said Acts and Awards have proved
unnecessary, or inconvenient, and it is expedient that they be
altered, and other provisions made in that behalf, enacts that notwithstanding anything contained in the recited Act of 1767, or
in the Award of 1768, the Corporation may continue, or permit
to be continued, the public highways hereinafter mentioned of
a less width than sixty feet, on such terms and conditions with
respect to the width of the said highways, or any of them, and
with respect to the vesting free from any right of way of the soil
of any inclosed lands which ought, under the provisions of the said
Act and Award, to form part of any such highway, and otherwise as may be agreed between the Corporation and the owners
of the lands abutting on or adjoining such highways.

The highways above referred to are—

A highway leading from Lenton to Wilford, and known as
Trent Lane.

A highway leading from Lenton to Radford, and known as
Marsh Road.

Any other public highway required by the said Act of 1767
to be set out of a width not less than sixty feet, with respect to
which the Corporation may deem a less width sufficient.

Notwithstanding anything contained in the recited Act of

---

(1) The cattle fairs have been held for many years in a field on the north side of
the Derby Road, and bounded on the east side by the Butt Houses, and on the west
side by Lenton Railway Station.

1767, and the Award of 1768, the Corporation may at any time, after the passing of this Act by deed, extinguish all right, whether of the Corporation, or of any person or persons, to hold fairs for cattle on certain lands adjoining the turnpike road leading from Nottingham to Derby, on both sides thereof, and by the said Award allotted to George de Ligne Gregory, for the purpose of holding such fairs for cattle, and such deed may be made by the Corporation upon and subject to any terms and conditions that may be agreed with the devisees or trustees for the time being of the settled estates, whereof those lands form part, and from and after the execution of such deed, and subject to any such terms and conditions, all right of the Corporation and of any person or persons to hold fairs on such lands, shall by virtue of this Act cease and be extinguished. The Corporation may, with the consent of Catherine Sherwin Gregory, Robert Wilmot Bradshaw, and John Holden, or other the devisees or trustees for the time being of the settled estates of John Sherwin Gregory, deceased, sell, let, or otherwise dispose of, free from the right of getting materials for the repair of any highway or road, the piece of land containing one acre, two roods, and twenty perches, or thereabouts, numbered 15 on the map referred to in the recited Award of 1799, and by that Award allotted to the surveyors of the highways of Lenton and Radford for the getting of materials for the repair of the highways and other roads in Lenton and Radford, and shall carry the proceeds of sale, or other disposition under this section, to the credit of the Borough fund. The Corporation may from time to time enter into and carry into effect any agreement or agreements with Catherine Sherwin Gregory, Robert Wilmot Bradshaw, and John Holden, or other the devisees or trustees for the time being of the settled estates of John Sherwin Gregory, deceased, or with any other owner of lands allotted under the recited Act of 1767, and Award of 1768, and the recited Act of 1796, and Award of 1799, with respect to all or any of the matters in this part of this Act contained, and may accept as consideration, or part consideration in the case of any such agreement, any lands, or interest in lands, and may from time to time appropriate any lands so acquired by them for purposes of public recreation, or for any other purpose for the benefit of the inhabitants of the borough.

# SECTION XIII.

## LOCAL GOVERNMENT.

**P**ARISHES were constructed out of the ancient manors. The ecclesiastical district of a parish takes its commencement, as an area for rating for the relief of the poor, from the Act of 43 Eliz., cap. 2, which constituted the overseers of the poor. It directed "that the churchwardens of every parish, and four, three, or two substantial householders therein," should be nominated as overseers of the poor, to undertake the relief of the poor and to provide a poor rate for the maintenance of the poor. The "parish" there is the then ecclesiastical parish. For the most part the parishes were well defined; and generally the term "parish" applied to places which were under the ecclesiastical control of a "parson," which is the very word used in the statute itself.[1]

But in recent legislation the definition of "parish" for the purposes of the statutes has embraced an ecclesiastical parish, a township, a chapelry, a hamlet, and every other place that separately maintained its own poor, until the time when the union chargeability was created, and then it became necessary to alter the definition of the term "parish," for the purposes of the Poor Laws, to a place for which a separate poor rate can

---

(1) Select Committee on Boundaries of Parishes, etc., 1873; questions 3, 14, 313.

be levied or a separate overseer appointed.[1]    But it was not until the maintenance of the poor was made a legal charge upon the parishes that the parish boundaries assumed their fixity of position.[2]

---

The following lists of the various parish officers of Lenton are compiled from the parish vestry books, ⁓overseers' accounts, surveyors' accounts, parish indentures, and other sources, the names being spelt as they occur in the books. A careful examination of the overseers' accounts, from which we have abstracted some of the more important items, shows that the office of Overseer was one which required the devotion of a considerable amount of time and labour. The old overseers appear to have performed their duties in a creditable manner, but this was not the case at a later period, as the following extract from the overseers' account book, dated March, 1836, will show.

" It was represented to the meeting that the annual overseers of the poor have of late been exceedingly negligent in the discharge of their duties, particularly in their almost total non-attendance at the usual parish meetings, thereby imposing upon the assistant overseer a responsibility which he ought not exclusively to bear, and subjecting him to the censures and odium of those paupers from whom in the proper discharge of the duties of his office, he feels himself obliged to withhold relief entirely, or to afford it in a limited degree; it was therefore unanimously resolved that in future if the annual officers for the time being be negligent in their attendance at the usual meetings of the parish, or in the discharge of their other official duties, that the assistant overseer report the same to the Parish.    Resolved that the above Resolution be transcribed and sent to those persons who may be elected overseers of the poor for the present and succeeding years."

## OVERSEERS OF THE POOR.

1678.   Thomas Kelladine ; William Selby.
1704.   Samuel Colishaw ; Mordecai Hall.

---

(1) Select Committee on Boundaries of Parishes, etc., 1873 ; question 17.
(2) *Ibid.* 589.

1705.  Humphrey Hopkins; George Swinscow.
1709.  William Davis; Griffith Davies.
1715.  Mordecai Hall; George Fewks.
1718.  Thomas Lester.
1719.  Francis Roberts; John Garland.
1720.  John Garland; Joseph Thompson.
1721.  John Hopkins.
1722.  Thomas Newham; Stephen Western.
1723.  Stephen Western; Thomas Newham.
1724.  Arthur Beardsley; John Roberts.
1725.  Thomas Wood; Thomas Greasley.
1726.  Richard Pyatt; William Black.
1727.  John Chamberlain; John Holmes.
1728.  William Marshall; Richard Gilbourn.
1729.  William Shaw; William Marshall.
1730.  Thomas Roughton; Richard Flinders.
1731.  Richard Crampton; William Shelton.
1732.  William Dickinson; Samuel Keatley.
1733.  William Dickinson; Samuel Keatley.
1734.  James Feild; William Norris.[1]
1735.       Do.          do.
1736.  John Clarke; Benjamin Ault.
1737.       Do.          do.
1738.  Robert Castle; John Fish.
1739.  William Burton; Thomas Townshend.
1740.  James Thaine; Henry Brown, junr.
1741.  Humphrey Hopkins; William Pike.
1742.  Francis Roberts; William Black.
1743.  William Shipman; Robert Castle, junr.
1744.  Thomas Wood; Thomas Newham.
1745.  John Chamberlain; Thomas Townshend.
1746.  Thomas Roughton; Joseph Lacey.
1747.  John Chapman; James Lacey.
1748.  William Dickinson; Samuel Keatley.
1749.       Do.          do.
1750.  William Norris; James Feild.
1751.  Benjamin Ault; Edward Hollingworth.
1752.  John Clarke;           do.
1753.       Do.     ; John Bradshaw.
1754.  Humphrey Hopkin; do.
1755.  Humphrey Hopkin; Joseph Roberts.
1756.  John Chamberlin;       do.

(1) "Apr: 9: 1734 it is agreed by ye inhabitants of Lenton that Ja. Feild & Wm Norris, is to be overseers of ye Poor for two years next ensuing, being both willing to it, & Jno Clark & Ben. Ault ye two following, if living & still inhabitants, being as ye others both willing."—*Vestry Book.* This arrangement was actually carried out.

1757. John Chamberlin ; Matthew Welch.
1758. Thomas Roughton ;        do.
1759.        Do.        ; Ralph Porter.
1760. Samuel Keetley ;        do.
1761.        Do.        ; William Norris.
1762. Edward Hollingworth ; do.
1763.        Do.        ; Joseph Castle.
1764. Joseph Roberts ; John Kettleby.
1765. John Bradshaw ;        do.
1766.        Do.        ; William Hopkin.
1767. Thomas Roughton ;        do.
1768.        Do.        ; William Norris.
1769. John Chamberlin ;        do.
1770. John Hopkins ; Matthew Welch.
1771. John Chamberlin ;        do.
1772.        Do.        ; John Keetley.
1773. John Keetley ; William Shaw.
1774. William Shaw ; Edward Hollingworth.
1775. Edward Hollingworth ; Elias Roberts.
1776. John Bradshaw ; Thomas Roughton.
1777. Thomas Stevenson ; Thomas Roughton.
1778. Thomas Roughton ; William Wilkinson.
1779. William Wilkinson ; William Norris.
1780. Gervase Boot ; William Norris.
1781. Thomas Roughton ; John Hopkins.
1782. John Hopkins ; John Chamberlin.
1783. " John Hopkins for John Chamberlin."
1784. John Keetley ; Edward Hollingworth.
1785. John Keetley for John Bradshaw ; John Shaw.
1786. John Shaw ; William Hopkins.
1787. Gervas Boot ; Thomas Roughton.
1788. Gervas Boot ; John Hopkins.
1789. Humphrey Hopkins ; John Hopkins.
1790. John Hopkins ; Mr. Chamberlin.
1791. Mr. Chamberlin ; John Keetley.
1792. John Shaw ; William Keetley.
1793. William Keetley ; Thomas Roughton.
1794. Thomas Roughton ; Edward Hollingworth.
1795. Edward Hollingworth ; William Wigley.
1796. William Wigley ; Thomas Stevenson.
1797. Thomas Stevenson ; Gervas Boot.
1798. Mr. Boot ; Mr. Chamberlin.
1799. John Shaw ; Mr. Chamberlin.
1800. Richard Nutt ; T. Roughton.
1801. J. W. Killingley ; John Shaw.
1802. My. Needham ; R. Nutt.
1803. J. Green ; Thomas Newham.

23

1804. William Surplice ; Thomas Newham.
1805. Francis Evans ; Thomas Newham.
1806. William Stretton ; Thomas Newham.
1807. John Wilkinson ; Thomas Newham.
1808. John Wright, Esq. ; Thomas Roughton ; Thomas Newham.
1809. Thomas Roughton ; John Burton.
1810. John Burton ; Richard Chamberlin ; John Roughton.
1811. Richard Chamberlin ; John Roughton ; William Hopkins.
1812. William Hopkins ; John Roughton ; William Weston.
1813. William Weston ; John Roughton ; James Nutt.
1814. James Nutt ; John Roughton ; Joseph [Hurst] Lowe.
1815. J. H. Lowe, Esq. ; John Roughton ; Samuel Keetley.
1816. Samuel Keetley ; John Roughton ; T. B. Milnes.
1817. T. B. Milnes ; John Roughton ; Isaac Bailey.
1818. Isaac Bailey ; John Roughton ; John Burton.
1819. John Burton ; John Roughton ; Nathaniel Gee.
1820. John Wilkinson ; John Roughton ; Alex. Foxcroft, Esq.
1821. Alex. Foxcroft, Esq. ; John Roughton ; Samuel Goodacre.
1822. William Surplice ; Samuel Goodacre ; George Brown.
1823. William Surplice ; George Brown ; T. B. Milnes.
1824. T. B. Milnes ; Thomas Roughton ; Francis Stout.
1825. John Ray ; Thomas Roughton ; John Lammin.
1826. Alfred Lowe ; Lorenzo Christie ; John Challands.
1827. Richard Chamberlin ; John Maples ; John Needham.
1828. John Maples ; William Cliff ; Francis Cheetham.
1829. John Maples ; Thomas Kirk ; William Wilkinson.
1830. John Swain ; John Needham ; John Maples.
1831. John Needham ; Samuel Goodacre.
1832. John Wilmot ; Edward Wilson.
1833. George Bradley ; William Goodhead ; Samuel Atkins.
1834. William Goodhead ; James Nutt ; William Potter.
1835. Isaac Fisher ; Thomas Wood.
1836. Thomas Roe ; William Hopkins.
1837. John Wilkinson ; John Hill.
1838. John Hutchinson ; George Langford.
1839. Thomas Roe ; Thomas Pegg.
1840. Richard Grant Tucker ; John Hill.
1841. John Godfrey ; George Bradley Harvey.
1842. Joseph Bell ; Thomas Shephard.
1843. Joseph Smith ; John Sylvester.
1844. Thomas Bayley ; Peter Coxon.
1845. William Best ; John Oldknow ; Edward Wilson.
1846. William Knight ; James Smith.
1847. William Kirk ; George Stanton.[1]

(1) From this date, the books are imperfect or inaccessible.

## EXTRACTS FROM THE ACCOUNTS OF THE OVERSEERS OF THE POOR.

1782.   To Expences at Mr Pacey's when we went to detect Rebecca
  Lovatt keeping a Disorderly house  -  -  -  -  0  0  6
  To John Kirkham for a Wheel for Jackson's wife  -  -  -  4  6
This was probably a spinning-wheel.

1783.   To a Glaziers Bill for the Poors Houses  -  -  -  -  -  1  0  1½
  Bought a new Lock for hand cuffs  -  -  -  -  -  -  10
  To a Lock for Garlands House  -  -  -  -  -  -  3  6

Numerous entries refer to a wretched man named Robert Clayworth, who appears to have been a lunatic, and to have been much trouble to the parish officers. We extract a few of the items :—

  To Two Men with a Cart bringing Clayworth from Nottm.  -  5  0
  To my own Trouble  -  -  -  -  -  -  -  -  1  0
  To Two Men taking care of R Clayworth one night -  -  -  3  0
  To Bread and Cheese and Ale at the same time  -  -  -  1  0
  To the Expense of Ellis's Family going to Ireland  -  -  -  10  9  2½
  To my trouble going with them to Liverpool  -  -  -  -  1  5  0
1784.   To Joseph Elvage putting in Window Gar'ds [Garland's] House  8
  To making New Window Duplicate and 'livering it in at Stamp
  Office  -  -  -  -  -  -  -  -  -  -  -  1  0

The unpopular tax on windows was increased this year, which accounts for this last entry.

In the next year's accounts the unfortunate Clayworth again appears upon the scene, and the barbarous inhumanity with which poor maniacs were treated at that time is strikingly illustrated by the following extracts from the overseer's accounts :—

1785.   To 2 Men sitting up with R Clayworth and Expenses and
  bringing him down to Lenton  6  0
  To 2 Men tentingr Clayworth 2 Days and 2 Nights, supposing
  he would be better  -  -  -  -  -  -  -  10  0
  To Meat and Drink they had same time  -  -  -  -  5  0
  To 3 Men bringing him down to be Chained at Lenton  -  -  3  0
  To some Goods he broke  -  -  -  -  -  -  2  0
  To Joseph Elvidge for setting Post down To Chain Clayworth
  and Staple and Chains and my trouble  -  -  -  -  -  2  6
  To his Board when Confined at my House  -  -  -  8  0
  To pr of Stockings and Shoes and Shirt and Hat and Handker-
  chief he had when he went home, the other being torn to pieces  9  0
  To Clayworth when he went back to Nottingham as was
  thought well  -  -  -  -  -  -  -  -  5  0
  For Cleworth for some windows that he broke before he was put
  in house of Correction at Nottingham  -  -  -  -  -  2  0
1786.   To a man that was gathering for Loss by fire at Armerton in
  Derbyshire, which he had a paper granted and signed by
  Neighbours and Justices, to gather only on Constables, which
  I think was right ; most Parishes paid 7s. some 5s. I paid him  4  0

The following relate to a compulsory marriage, and the care which the parish officials took to prevent the unwilling bridegroom from running away from his fair and frail bride is sufficiently amusing.

---

(1) This is a local word, still in common use amongst the lower orders, signifying to tend, or guard.

To John Shaw going to Bilboroug to take Geo Everson, and the
going to M<sup>r</sup> Cope's with him - - - - - - 2 0
To expenses that day - - - - - - - 4 2
To a Licience to be married - - - - - - 1 13 0
To the Parson's and the Clarke's dues - - - - - 7 6
To M<sup>r</sup> Maddock coming down for his advice before they was
marred - - - - - - - - - 2 6
To 2 Men tenting him 4 days and 3 nights Before married at
2s. 6d. day and night - - - - - - - 17 0
To M<sup>r</sup> Hopkins for 3 Mens board wile tenting him and wedding
Dinner and ale - - - - - - - - 1 2 0
To my Self and Thomas Lacy taking account of the number of
windows - - - - - - - - - 2 0
1787. Paid for five Duberleygates [duplicates] - - - - - 7 6
Paid Gorge Wilkinson for takeing John Marsh and is wife down
to the salt watter - - - - - - - - 10 0
Paid Mr Pearson for bringing them back again - - - - 10 0

Whether John Marsh and his wife were taken down to the "salt watter" that
their health might be benefitted by the sea breezes does not appear.

1788. Paid four Salers with apass - - - - - - 8

In this year we again find more items relating to the poor maniac, Clayworth.

pade Jhoseph Jacson for Tenting Clawerth one night one day - 3 0
Ditto for my trobel Geting him to the hous of Krection and
Exspenses - - - - - - - - - 1 0
pade Mr Glover at the hous of Krection one night - - - 1 0
Ditto pade Jhoseph Jaction for fetching Clawerth homagane - 6
pade dol when Ill - - - - - - - - 1 0
pade Samwell Shaperd for bleeding Roberd Clawerth - - 3
pade pataddams when Ill - - - - - - - 6
pade for Clawerth Coming hom from Mansfeild - - - 10 0
pade for Shifting post to Cassels barn for Clawerth[1] - - 4

At length the unfortunate Clayworth died, and the overseer became disrespectful
in consequence.

pade for one blankit that Clawerth had - - - - 3 0
pade for Jarsey for Clawerth - - - - - - 6
pade for Laing Clawerth out - - - - - - 1 0
pade fore men to Care Clawerth to Chirch - - - - 2 0
pade for bred and dring for Clawerth Funeral - - - - 2 0
bought ould Clawerth one Sheet - - - - - 4 2
pade parson and Clark for bureing Clawerth - - - - 2 8
1790. paid for a Lock for Garlands Chamber - - - - 1 4
1791. A meetg to consider of proper places to remove the poor out of
houses intended to be pulled down - - - - 3 0
Paid Glazr for repairg Windows at Abbey Gate house - - 6 9
1792. Paid for a Warrant from Mr. Charlton requiring two Waggons
to remove the Soldiers Baggage - - - - - 2 0
1793. [A similar entry to the last.]
Paid to Admarel Greaves Sun & Wife & 4 Children Being a
Naterf of Filledlfey Havend a Auder fron Govermente for
Every Parish to Pay to him - - - - - - 1 0
1795. Paid for Four Jurey Men for Auqurey Over the Man that was
Found In Kings meadows[2] - - - - - 10 0

(1) This barn stood at the back of a number of small houses which, facing the west,
formerly stood on the site of the house on the footroad to Nottingham, now occupied
by Mr. Samuel Froggatt. The village stocks were fixed where the water tank recently stood, and opposite to these old cottages.

(2) See p. 283, *ante*, for an entry in the Parish Registers relating to a Stranger
found dead in the King's Meadow, in 1752.

1796. To A Cratch to Bat Cotten for Hannah Bayley - - -        2 0
Paid Francis Simpson for Catching Moles half a year - -    3 6 8
To James Chadbourn for going to Wollarton 2 days & Expences
on Account of 2 skellertons found there - - - -       4 6

These "skellertons" were presumably found in that part of Wollaton Park which was within the parish of Lenton.

|  |  |  |  |  |
|---|---|---|---|---|
| | Paid Mr. Tod and my Expences Surveying the Lean - - | 3 | | 0 |
| 1797. | Paid on Account of Sea Men - - - - - - | 34 | 12 | 1 |
| | To Extra Expences for 6 Substitutes for Militia - - | 16 | 2 | 6 |
| | Pd James Chadburn for taking A Vagrant to Sandiacre - - | | 2 | 6 |
| | To a Soldier with a Pass - - - - - | | | 4 |
| | To A Lock for Pin Fold Gate - - - - - | | 1 | 2 |
| | To a Ship-Racked Rusian Sailor with a Pass - - - | | 1 | 0 |
| 1798. | To the Infirmary - - - - - - - | | 2 | 0 |
| | To a Lock for Pin Fold Gate - - - - - - | | 1 | 10 |
| | Paid for Assistance &c to take Mathew Reed to Justice - | | 5 | 0 |
| 1799. | To Expence for a Militia Man - - - - - | 6 | 15 | 11 |
| | To Joseph Needham mending Leen banks - - - - | | 6 | 0 |
| 1800. | To Sparrows - - - - - - - - | 1 | 16 | 9½ |
| | Paid for Sparrows - - - - - - - - | 2 | 2 | 2½ |
| | Paid Mrs. Brown for Cloathing & putting out hir Son Wm's Boy | 3 | 13 | 0 |
| | Paid for Sparrows - - - - - - - | 1 | 5 | 9½ |
| | do - - - - - - - - | 3 | 18 | 5 |
| 1801. | Paid Mr. Falkenor for 8 Militia Orders - - - - | 22 | 14 | 0 |
| | To A Book for takeing the Popolation of the Parish- - | | | 7 |
| | To an Account of Popolation taking - - - - | | 10 | 0 |
| 1803. | Expenses of Militia substitutes - - - - - | 32 | 1 | 11 |
| | County rates and damages for riots - - - - - | 25 | 7 | 0 |
| | Loss on account of the Army of Reserve - - - - | 46 | 8 | 9 |
| 1805. | To Advertizing the Feast 1 - - - - - - | | 11 | 0 |
| 1806. | Sam Fletcher, Pining & Seizing R Woodhouses Asses - - | | 5 | 0 |
| | Coroners Fee & 4 Jurymen over Collyer who was suffocated in Mr Wrights well - - - - - - - | | 17 | 6 |
| 1811. | Sarah Hopkin for Jury for the Lord of the Manor - - - | 1 | 0 | 0 |
| | A Bonnett & 2 Pinbefores for Mary Millot - - - | | 7 | 11 |
| | Takeing the Population of the Parish - - - | 1 | 0 | 0 |
| 1812. | Mrs. Wombwell a Bill for Watch & Ward - - - | 1 | 19 | 9 |
| | Attending the Hall to receive the Arms - - - | | 5 | 0 |
| | By one Blunderbuss & 2 Soards - - - - | 3 | 7 | 6 |
| | Mr. Scullthorpe fur a Blunderbuss - - - - - | 2 | 2 | 6 |
| | attending the meeting for Do. - - - - | | 5 | 0 |
| | Mrs. Wombwell a Bill for Watch Room Coals, &c. 2 - - | 5 | 5 | 1 |
| | F. Wayte for 4 lbs of Candles for the Guardhouse - - - | | 3 | 10 |
| | paid Sarah Hopkins for the Huzars being there - - | | 18 | 0 |
| | Postage to Mr Ward for Letters from the war office - - - | | 6 | 2 |
| | Thos. Wade a Bill for Masonry for Guard house - - - | 1 | 1 | 7 |

These items all refer to what are known as the "Luddite" outrages, arising out of the discontent amongst the local framework-knitters owing to the reduction of wages, which they attributed to the establishment of machinery. Having broken out into open violence, under the leadership of one "Ned Ludd," they proceeded to destroy all the stocking-frames that they could lay hands upon, and accompanied with such excesses that at length parties of soldiers had to be quartered in all the country villages. The inhabitants of Lenton first tried to keep the peace with two blunderbusses and as many swords, but apparently without effect.

---

(1) See p. 264.

(2) Previous to the introduction of the police system, the watch-house and lock-up were at the Lenton Coffee House, now the White Hart Inn.

| 1814. | By trouble & Intrust of 250£ for Hosiery as pr. Acct. | - | - | 36 | 9 | 0 |
| 1815. | Poastage of a Letter from Nottingham | - | - | - | - | - | 3 |
| 1817. | By Expenditure in Manufacturing | - | - | - | - | 412 | 17 | 9 |
| | Expences attending the Hosiers and frame-work Knitters | - | 12 | 6 |
| 1819. | By an Act of Parliament passed July 2nd, '19 - | - | - | - | 5 |
| 1821. | Edwd. Sherrock a Bill for Population Book - | - | - | - | 6 | 6 |
| 1823. | Thos Wright for Catching Moles | - | - | - | - | - | 1 | 0 | 0 |
| 1828. | Hallam, Hyson Green | - | - | - | - | - | - | 1 | 0 | 0 |

This entry proves that the portion of Lenton parish known as Hyson Green was thus spelled in 1828.

| 1829. | A Stamp for Lord Middleton's Poor Rate | - | - | - | 1 | 0 |
| 1833. | The Treasurer of the County, for Messrs Lowe & Smith's | | | | | |
| | damages | - | - | - | - | - | - | - | - | 723 | 1 | 1 |
| | Chief Constables Bill for damages at Beeston, Turton's & others | 46 | 5 | 6½ |

This was consequent on the riots in October, 1832, when Nottingham Castle and other property was destroyed.

| 1834. | Mr. Godfrey, Clerk of the Peace, on the High Constables order 17 County rates under the Damages Compensation Act - | 153 | 14 | 2 |
| | The General Hospital Subscription | - | - | - | - | 4 | 4 | 0 |
| 1835. | Mr. Godfrey, Clerk of the Peace, 17 County Rates for damage to Nottingham Castle in 1831 | - | - | - | - | 153 | 14 | 2 |
| 1836. | To Mr. Godfrey, for the Broxtowe damages | - | - | - | 307 | 8 | 4 |
| | To expenses incurred at Easter 1836 at the parish Baronial Court of G. Gregory, Esqr. | - | - | - | - | 2 | 0 | 0 |
| 1837. | The Clerk of the Peace, seventeen County Rates on Account of the Broxtowe damages compensation Act | - | - | - | 153 | 14 | 2 |
| 1838. | Clerk of the Peace, damages in 1831 under the Broxtowe Damages compensation act | - | - | - | - | 137 | 19 | 9½ |
| | Clerk of the Peace, Hundred Rates for damages in the riots in 1831 | - | - | - | - | 137 | 19 | 9½ |
| 1839. | Paid the Clerk of the Peace for damages by Rioters in 1831 to Nottingham Castle | - | - | - | - | - | 137 | 19 | 9½ |
| | [The same sum was paid in 1840.] | | | | | | |
| 1840. | Paid Chief Constable, Broxtowe Damages | - | - | - | 159 | 4 | 4½ |
| 1842. | To Losses upon Light Gold, as per account | - | - | - | 10 | 6 |
| 1843. | Paid for Loss upon Light Gold | - | - | - | - | 2 | 10 |
| | Received from the High Constable on Account of overcharges in the Broxtowe Hundred Compensation Act, and now returned | 10 | 12 | 3½ |
| 1844. | Loss on Light Gold | - | - | - | - | - | - | - | 1 | 11 |

## CONSTABLES² AND OVERSEERS OF HIGHWAYS.

1718.  Thomas Allicock.

1719.  John Scattergood ; William Marshall.

1720.  John Western ; Joseph Thompson.

1721.  John Swinscow ; John Hopkins.

(1) The total amount paid by the Parish of Lenton as compensation for damages done during the riots in the neighbourhood of Nottingham in 1831 was £2,238 8s. 8½d.

(2) Referring to the multifarous duties performed in the seventeenth and eighteenth centuries by these officials, a local historian has recently remarked that "the office is one of great antiquity, and its full importance can scarcely be realized in these days. The Parish, or Petty Constable, united in his person most of the functions of a police force, public prosecutor, exciseman, custom-house officer, collector and assessor of taxes, sanitary and building inspector, overseer, and a fully armed nineteenth century local board."—*Leigh in the Eighteenth Century*, by J. Rose.

1722. Stephen Western; John Swinscow.
1723. John Swinscow; Richard Norris.
1724. John Swinscow; John Chamberlain.
1725. John Swinscow; Arthur Beardsley.
1726. Thomas Wood; Thomas Greasley.
1727. Richard Pyatt; William Black.
1728. John Hopkins; Humphrey Hopkins.
1729. John Bradshaw; John Chamberlain; Thos. Firth.
1730. William Shaw; John Mosley.
1731. Thomas Roughton; Thomas Wheatley.
1732. Thomas Newham; William Marshall.
1733. William Marshall; Joseph Lacey.
1734. Samuel Keatley; Benjamin Ault.
1735. William Norris; William Dickinson.
1736. Robert Castle; William Burton.
1737. John Clarke; William Burton.
1738. John Clarke; William Dickinson, junr.
1739. William Dickinson, junr.; William Spencer.
1740. Benjamin Ault; John Chamberlain.
1741. John Chamberlain; James Field.
1742. Thomas Wood; William Dickinson, senr.
1743. Humphrey Hopkin; William Norris.
1744. Thomas Roughton; Samuel Keatley.
1745. William Norris; Robert Castle.
1746. Robert Castle; John Clarke.
1747. John Clarke; John Chapman.
1748. John Chapman; William Dickinson.
1749. William Dickinson; John Chamberlaine.
1750. John Chamberlain; Benjamin Ault.
1751. Benjamin Ault; Samuel Keatley.
1752. Samuel Keatley; Edward Hollingworth.
1753. Edward Hollingworth; James Feild.
1754. Joseph Roberts; John Bradshaw.
1755. John Bradshaw; Humphrey Hopkin.
1756. Humphrey Hopkin; Thomas Roughton.
1757. Thomas Roughton; William Norris.
1758. William Norris; Ralph Porter.
1759. Ralph Porter; Matthew Welch.
1760. Matthew Welch; John Chamberlain.
1761. John Chamberlain; Samuel Keatley.
1762. Samuel Keatley; Edward Hollingworth.
1763. Edward Hollingworth; Joseph Roberts.
1764. Joseph Roberts; Joseph Castle.
1765. John Kettleby; John Bradshaw.
1766. John Bradshaw; William Hopkin.
1767. William Hopkin; Thomas Roughton.
1768. Thomas Roughton;

1769.
1770. John Hopkin ;
1771. Matthew Welch ; John Chamberlin.
1772. John Chamberlin ; John Keetley.[1]

## CONSTABLES.

| | | | |
|---|---|---|---|
| 1773. | John Keetley. | 1789. | Humphrey Hopkins. |
| 1774. | William Shaw. | 1790. | John Hopkins. |
| 1775. | Edward Hollingworth. | 1791. | Richard Chamberlin. |
| 1776. | John Bradshaw. | 1792. | Mr. John Shaw. |
| 1777. | Thomas Stephenson. | 1793. | William Keetley. |
| 1778. | Thomas Roughton. | 1794. | Thomas Roughton. |
| 1779. | William Wilkinson. | 1795. | Edward Hollingworth. |
| 1780. | Gervase Boot. | 1796. | Mr. William Wigley. |
| 1781. | Thomas Roughton. | 1797. | Thomas Stevenson. |
| 1782. | John Hopkins. | 1798. | Thomas Newham. |
| 1783. | John Keetley. | 1799. | Do. |
| 1784. | John Keetley. | 1800. | Do. |
| 1785. | John Shaw. | 1801. | George Wombwell. |
| 1786. | John Shaw. | 1802 to 1821. | Thomas Newham. |
| 1787. | Thomas Roughton. | 1837. | Richard Burton. |
| 1788. | Gervas Boot. | 1838. | Henry Sissons or Syson. |

## SURVEYORS.

| | | | |
|---|---|---|---|
| 1773. | Edward Hollingworth. | 1816. | Humphry Hopkins. |
| 1774. | Joseph Roberts. | 1817. | Do. |
| 1775. | Elias Roberts. | 1818. | Do. |
| 1786. | Thomas Roughton. | 1819. | Do. |
| 1801. | J. W. Killingley. | 1820. | Humphrey Hopkins and G. Brown. |
| 1802. | Matthew Needham. | | [1821—1837 wanting.] |
| 1803. | J. Green. | 1838. | John Froggatt ; Thomas Mawby. |
| 1804. | William Surplice. | | |
| 1805. | Francis Evans. | 1839. | Robert James ; John Croshaw. |
| 1806. | William Stretton. | 1840. | Robert James ; John Godfrey. |
| 1807. | John Wilkinson. | 1841. | John Shaw ; Thomas Roe. |
| 1808. | Do. | 1842. | Thomas Roe ; R. G. Tucker. |
| 1809. | Thomas Roughton. | 1843. | R. G. Tucker ; Samuel Roe. |
| 1810. | John Burton. | 1844. | Do. ; William Greaves. |
| 1811. | Humphrey Hopkins. | 1845. | James Nutt ; do. |
| 1812. | Do. | 1846. | William Hickling ; do. |
| 1813. | Do. | 1847. | Thomas Shepherd ; do. |
| 1814. | Do. | 1848. | Do. ; William Hickling. |
| 1815. | Do. | | |

(1) The total expenditure of the Surveyors of Highways for the year ending October, 1772, was £34 3s. 5d., and for the year ending October, 1779, the expenditure was £22 3s. 5d.

## BURLEYMEN.

Halliwell, in his "Dictionary of Provincial and Archaic Words," says that Burleymen were to assist the constable in a court leet. They appear to have usually been appointed at manorial courts, and their special duties were to act as referees as to the amount due for damages, trespass, encroachments, etc., and on this account persons having experience in agricultural matters were commonly chosen for the office.[1]

1718. John Garland ; Samuel Collishaw.
1719. Thomas Allicock ; George Dickinson.
1720. John Swinscow ;
1721. John Hopkins ;
1722. John Chamberlain ;
1723. John Swinscow ;
1724. Stephen Western ;
1725. John Swinscow ; Stephen Western.
1726. Arthur Beardsley ; John Western.
1727. Thomas Wood ; Thomas Greasley.
1728. Thomas Wood ; John Chamberlain.
1729. Thomas Newham ;
1730. Robert Castle ; John Clarke.
1731. John Clarke ; William Marshall.
1732. William Marshall ; Thomas Roughton.
1733. Humphrey Hopkin ;        do.
1734.        Do.    ; William Burton.
1735. John Chamberlain ;        do.
1736. John Chamberlaine ; William Norris.
1737. William Norris ; Benjamin Ault.
1738. Benjamin Ault ; William Marshall.
1739. William Dickinson, junr. ; Thomas Wood.
1740. Samuel Keatley ; Robert Castle.
1741. William Dickinson, junr. ; John Chamberlaine.
1742. Thomas Wood ; William Dickinson, senr.
1743. Thomas Wood ; Humphrey Hopkin.

(1) That duties of this nature were performed by the Burleymen of this parish, is shown from the following entry in one of the old parish-books : "July ye 21st, 1744. Be it remembered yt Mr Trueman, Steward to Esqre Plumtree paid one shilling on this day to Humphrey Hopkins ye Burliman of Lenton for an acknowledgement of a trespass by carrying the hay from ye Horsedoles [in the parish of Beeston] to Nottm through ye Meadows belonging to Lenton and Radford." The Burleymen of Lenton were, however, evidently appointed by the parish, at the annual vestry meeting, and not at the manorial court.

1744. Humphrey Hopkin;
1745. John Clarke; William Pike.
1746. John Chamberlain; Thomas Roughton.
1747. Thomas Roughton; William Norris.
1748. William Norris; John Chapman.
1749. John Chapman; Benjamin Ault.
1750. Benjamin Ault; William Dickinson.
1751.        Do.      ; Thomas Wood.
1752. Humphrey Hopkin;    do.
1753.        Do.      ; John Clarke.
1754. John Clarke; Edward Hollingworth.
1755. Edward Hollingworth; John Bradshaw.
1756. John Bradshaw; John Chamberlain.
1757. Thomas Roughton;    do.
1758.        Do.      ; William Norris.
1759. Ralph Porter;          do.
1760.        Do.      ; Matthew Welch.
1761. Samuel Keetley;     do.
1762.        Do.      ; Edward Hollingworth.
1763. John Bradshaw;      do.
1764.        Do.      ; John Chamberlin.
1765. Thomas Roughton;    do.
1766.        Do.      ; William Norris.
1767. William Norris; William Hopkin.

The *Pinder* was another parochial officer, and appears to have been subordinate to the constable. Previous to the year 1841 there was only one pinfold for the joint parishes of Lenton and Radford, the constable of the latter parish paying to the Constable of Lenton a proportion of the cost of repairing the pinfold. The following entry to this effect occurs in the Lenton parish books under date of June 6th, 1740. "Memorand$^m$ y$^t$ Ben: Ault y$^e$ pst Constable is to Rec[eive] of Radford Constable one shilling & fourpence for y$^e$ Repairs of y$^e$ Pinfold y$^e$ late year past." The rules and instructions to be observed by the Pinder tend to prove that the pinfold, although used by the parishes of Lenton and Radford jointly, was under the control of the former parish.[1]

The inhabitants of Lenton also appointed a *neat-herdsman* to look after their cattle grazing on the common lands in Lenton

---

[1] See also the Overseer's Accounts for 1797 and 1798 for payments by the parish of Lenton for locks for the pinfold gates.

and Radford Holmes.   The following agreement is derived from the parish books of Lenton.

### Feb. 13<sup>th</sup> 1744.

Be it Remembred y<sup>t</sup> We y<sup>e</sup> Inhabitants of Lenton doe Now unanimously Agree Consent & Covenant w<sup>th</sup> William Burton to be y<sup>e</sup> Neatherdsman in Lenton & Radford Holmes to Enter this p<sup>st</sup> Year & y<sup>t</sup> he Upon Agreem<sup>t</sup>. is to Look after & attend y<sup>e</sup> Beasts Horses & Sheep dureing their abode & Continuance Upon y<sup>e</sup> Comons thereunto belonging Every Sort of Cattell in their Season & y<sup>t</sup> he shall pay pinship for Every Sort of Cattell trespassing in y<sup>e</sup> daytime & y<sup>t</sup> he shall take Care to drive & attend Every Comoners Beast to y<sup>e</sup> forrest Every Year whilst he Continues in his place begining about y<sup>e</sup> tenth of March   If y<sup>e</sup> Weather be Seasonable & from thence to Continue so doing till y<sup>e</sup> Comon Pasture be broken & also y<sup>t</sup> he shall take care y<sup>t</sup> y<sup>e</sup> Quick sett be Weeded yearly whilst it needs y<sup>t</sup> is now Sett And y<sup>t</sup> he shall doe his whole business Upon y<sup>e</sup> same Salary y<sup>t</sup> Belongs to y<sup>e</sup> place   In Wittness whereof y<sup>e</sup> Partys above Named have hereunto Sett our hands.

John    Chamberlin.—John    Clarke.—Will.    Dickinson.—Tho. Wood.—Saml.   Keetley.—Tho.   Roughton.—Robt.   Cassells.— Willm Norris.—Hum : Hopkins.—Willm Burton his W marke.

### THE HIGHWAY BOARD.

The Board for the Repair of the Highways in the Parish of Lenton was constituted under the provisions of the Act of Parliament, 5th and 6th William the Fourth, ch. 50, entitled " An Act to consolidate and amend the laws relating to Highways in that part of Great Britain called England."   The total expenditure of the Board in 1865 was £504 4s. 5d.   The Board continued its operations until it was superseded in 1870 by the Lenton Local Board.

### THE BURIAL BOARD.

At a public vestry meeting of the parish of Lenton, held December 1st, 1856, " for the purpose of determining whether a new burial ground, or an extension of the present one, should be provided for the parish of Lenton, and, appointing a Burial Board under the provisions of the recent Acts of Parliament," it was decided to form a Burial Board forthwith, and the following gentlemen were accordingly elected:—Rev. George Browne, Vicar (chairman), Messrs. Thomas Adams, John Shaw, Samuel Morley, Thomas Bayley, W. F. Gibson, William Kirk, Richard Savage, and Joseph Thompson. Party feeling in Lenton ran very high. The Nonconformists demanded a burial ground disconnected from the Church. The Church people simply asked for an extension of the existing Churchyard, to be acquired by subscription of the principal parishioners. The latter course was ultimately carried out, the Nonconformists conceding their strong objections, and subscribing liberally to the fund. The following were the principal subscribers:—The Rt. Hon. Lord Middleton, Wollaton Hall, £100; Gregory, George, Esq., Harlaxton Hall, £100; Adams, Thomas, Esq., Lenton Firs, £100; owner and occupiers of Bestwood Park, £100; Wright, Francis, Esq., Osmaston Manor, £50; Wright, Misses, Lenton Lodge, £50; Smith, Henry, Esq., Wilford, £25; Morley, Samuel, Esq., Lenton Grove, £25; Bayley, Mr. Thomas, Park Side, £25; Walker, Mr. Benjamin, Park Side, £25; Midland Railway Company, £25; Browne, Rev. George, Vicar of Lenton, £10. An acre of land on the south side of the churchyard was purchased from George Gregory, Esq., for the sum of £786, and walled in as an addition to the same, the total cost amounting to £1,020. At a meeting of the Board held July 5th, 1861, the following resolution was adopted, "that, as the purchase money for the land required for an extension of the churchyard has been obtained by voluntary contributions, and all the liabilities of the Board are now discharged, it is, in the opinion of the Board, unnecessary to continue the operations of the Burial Acts in this parish, and that the Board be now dissolved."

## THE LOCAL BOARD.

The Local Government Act, 1848, was adopted by the parish of Lenton in the year 1870. On this, as on other occasions, public feeling ran very high, and "stormy meetings" were the order of the day. The Board consisted of twelve members,

each of whom was elected for three years. The Board adopted
as its official seal the arms of Lenton Priory, suspended by a
broad belt from an oak tree—symbolical of the former connection of the parish with Sherwood Forest, and surrounded by
the words LENTON _ LOCAL ˙BOARD. This seal was
designed for the Board by Captain (now Major) A. E. Lawson
Lowe, of Highfield. The Board was dissolved by the 7th
section of "The Nottingham Borough Extension Act, 1877."

## THE SCHOOL BOARD.

In February, 1871, an unsuccessful attempt was made to form
a School Board. Considerable animosity was exhibited on this
occasion, and for some time after, until the Education Department "resolved that it was expedient to cause a School Board
to be formed." A Board, consisting of seven members, was
accordingly elected August 9th, 1872. In pursuance of the 74th
section of "The Elementary Education Act, 1870," the Board
made certain bye-laws at a meeting held April 28th, 1874. These
were confirmed by an Order of Her Majesty in Council, dated
October 20th, 1874, and published in the *London Gazette* on
the 23rd October following. By the 38th section of "The
Nottingham Borough Extension Act, 1877," "All the jurisdiction, rights, powers, liabilities, and obligations of the School
Board for the district of Lenton, in respect of that part of the
same district which is by this Act included within the area of
the extended borough, shall, at the commencement af this Act,
cease and be transferred to the School Board for the extended
borough." The following are the names of the members of
the dissolved Board:—Henry Smith Wright, Esq. (chairman),
Rev. W. R. Cripps, Messrs. Joseph Billyeald, and William Dallison, Churchmen ; and Messrs. John Renals, John Benjamin
Walker, and Thomas Bayley, Nonconformists. The seal of the
Board was similar to that of the Local Board, but surrounded
by the words LENTON SCHOOL BOARD.

## THE SEWERAGE OF LENTON.

Up to the year 1853 the principal drainage of Old Lenton was conveyed in open ditches along the streets of the village, and thence along a field belonging to John Sherwin Gregory, Esquire, and after passing through such field, it was conveyed by a culvert under the river Leen, and thence along an open ditch into and through a wooden trunk under the Nottingham Canal into the Tinker's Leen, which discharges itself into the river Trent.

In or about the year 1853, the ditches in the village streets of Old Lenton were converted into brick culverts, and subsequently, about the year 1858, the Board for the Repair of the Highways in the parish of Lenton, acting as the local authority for the execution of the Nuisances Removal Act, 1855, constructed a bricked culvert in connection with the same, and in lieu of the open ditch through the field of Mr. Gregory. The culvert entered the field at the same point as the former open ditch, but instead of following the circuitous route of the ditch, it was made in a straight course across the field to the same point under the Leen where the original ditch emptied itself, and it was thence continued further in a straight line under the canal, and to the Tinker's Leen, which it entered at a point about ninety yards higher up, or more westward, than the former old wooden trunk entrance into the Tinker's Leen.

The authorities of the town of Nottingham denied the right of the authorities of the Parish of Lenton to use the Tinker's Leen for their sewage, or in any manner to interfere therewith, and contended that the watercourses to the Trent were their proper drainage, and they considered themselves under no obligation to keep the Tinker's Leen cleared out, and allowed it to remain neglected. The Board of Highways for Lenton had no power or authority over it beyond the limits of the parish, and within those limits it was always kept properly cleaned out by the Board.

In the year 1858 the Highway Board also constructed, at great expense, a new main road sewer in Willoughby Street, New Lenton, by which the refuse and drainage of New Lenton, which was much greater in quantity than that of old Lenton, was conveyed into the River Leen.

In July, 1870, the sewerage of Lenton had become so offensive to the inhabitants of Nottingham Meadows, that instructions were given for the sewage matter deposited in the ditches in the King's Meadows to be examined by two Nottingham medical practitioners. They reported that "ordinary town sewage, moving freely in good sewers, cannot be compared with the contents of this ditch, which in our opinion contains an enormously greater amount of putrid organic matter."

In 1872, "The Nottingham and Leen District Sewerage Act,"[1] was passed, the object of which was the purification of the River Leen and the River Trent, and their tributaries, and the prevention of their future pollution. The powers of this Act were vested in a Board known as "The Nottingham and Leen District Sewerage Board," the interests of Lenton being represented by two members of the Local Board, Messrs. John Froggatt and Thomas Shepperson. The functions of the Board, as to sewerage, were restricted to the execution and maintenance of such intercepting and outfall sewerage works, authorized by the Sewerage Utilization Acts to be made by a Sewer Authority, as in the opinion of the Board were from time to time necessary for the purpose of intercepting, storing, disinfecting, and distributing the sewage of the districts under the control of the Board, but did not extend to the internal sewerage of the several districts.

Soon after the passing of the Act, the Board commenced the construction of a sewer for the interception of all the sewage between Nottingham and Bulwell at that time polluting the River Leen.

The Sewage of New Lenton was turned into the intercepting sewer in 1875, and two years later the Local Board of Lenton connected the outfall of Old Lenton with the sewer, near the railway bridge in Lenton footpath. The Nottingham and Leen District Sewerage Board was dissolved by section 41 of "The Nottingham Borough Extension Act, 1877."

---

(1) 35 and 36 Vict., Ch. cv.

## THE NOTTINGHAM BOROUGH EXTENSION ACT, 1877.

By this Act,[1] which came into operation November 1st, 1877, the parish of Lenton was absorbed into the Borough of Nottingham. By the seventh section of this Act, the Lenton Local Board was dissolved. By the sixteenth section the boundaries of the Borough of Nottingham were extended to include the parish of Lenton, except Bestwood Park, which is excluded from the operations of the Act. Section twenty-nine transferred the Lenton Police Station to the Corporation Sections thirty-eight and thirty-nine abolished the Lenton School Board, special provision being made by section forty for the future School Board at Bestwood Park. The Nottingham and Leen District Sewerage Board was dissolved by section forty-one. The fifty-seventh section provides that no bathing place shall, under section 66 of the Nottingham Improvement Act, 1874, be established on the River Trent in the Parish of Lenton unless with the consent of the riparian owner for the time being, upon or opposite to whose land such bathing places are to be placed. By section fifty-nine it is enacted that the present lady, or any future lady or lord, of the manor of Lenton, shall at all times hereafter, hold and enjoy all rents, services, franchises, rights, royalties, courts, perquisites, and profits of courts, and all other royalties, privileges, and jurisdictions to the said manor belonging, as though the Act had not been passed.

The Parish of Lenton is situate partly in Castle Ward and partly in Meadows Ward, the greater and more populous portion of the parish, however, being included in Castle Ward.

The first election of three councillors to represent Castle Ward in the Nottingham Town Council took place November 1st, 1877. The contest was a keen one, and the greatest excitement prevailed. The Liberals returned their three candidates, and the ward has returned a Liberal councillor at each annual election since. The following is a list of councillors

---

(1) 40 Vict., Chap. xxxi.

for Castle Ward since the extension of the borough, the first-
named in each year being elected for three years, and the
last one going out of office on the first day of November
following :—

1877. Thomas Bayley; John Renals; John Benjamin Walker.
1878. John Benjamin Walker; Thomas Bayley; John Renals.
1879. John Froggatt; John Benjamin Walker; Thomas Bayley.
1880. Thomas Bayley; John Froggatt; John Benjamin Walker.
1881. John Benjamin Walker; Thomas Bayley; John Froggatt.
1882. John Froggatt; John Benjamin Walker; Thomas Bayley.
1883. Thomas Bayley; John Froggatt; John Benjamin Walker.

## THE LOW LEVEL ROAD.

The chief inducement offered by the Corporation of Nottingham to the parish of Lenton to consent to the annexation
of the parish to the borough, was the promise that a Low
Level Road should be at once made from Lenton to Nottingham along the side of the River Leen. The scheme was not
by any means a new one, for at a meeting of the lessees and
occupiers of Nottingham Park, held at the Castle Lodge,
October 14th, 1867, it was stated that when the Right
Honourable William Ewart Gladstone, one of the Trustees
of the Nottingham Park Estate, was in Nottingham in 1864,
he inspected the Leen, and the plans projected to cover it
over for the purpose of making a road from the Midland
Railway Station to Lenton. "He (Mr. Gladstone) was so
pleased with it that he and his coadjutor, Lord de Tabley,
agreed to contribute to the cost of making a sewer, and give
land in the King's Meadows for a road between Nottingham
and Lenton. It rested entirely with the Corporation, who
generally took the initiative in such matters, and with the
owners of the adjoining lands to carry out the scheme." In
the month of November, 1877, the Improvement Committee
of the Nottingham Town Council were requested to take into
their consideration the desirability of opening a new communication between the parish of St. Mary and the parish of Lenton,
by means of a low level road. On June 18th, 1880, the
24

Committee issued its report, in which it is stated "that the proposed new road is a necessary improvement, and should be carried out if it can be done at a reasonable expenditure." A Provisional Order of the Local Government Board, dated May 11th, 1881, empowered the Corporation of Nottingham to put in force the powers of the Lands Clauses Consolidation Acts, 1845, 1860, and 1869, with respect to the purchase and taking of lands required for making this new road, otherwise than by agreement. This Order was confirmed by "The Local Government Board's Provisional Orders Confirmation (Birmingham, Tame, and Rea, etc.,) Act, 1881."[1] The road, which is sixty feet wide, and known as the Lenton Boulevard, extends from Church Street, New Lenton, through the gardens and wharves in Nottingham Park, past the Castle Rock, to Canal Street, Nottingham.

---

(1) 44 and 45 Vict., ch. cii.

# SECTION XIV.

## MANUFACTURES.

REVIOUS to the commencement of the present century, the inhabitants of Lenton were engaged almost exclusively in agricultural pursuits. We find, however, indications of other industries in the parish registers of the last century, framework-knitters appearing as early as 1717, a basket-maker in 1733, a weaver in 1735, and a needle-maker in 1777.

The principal trade carried on in the earlier part of this century was framework-knitting, a row of one-storey buildings in the main road, and facing the church, being occupied by stocking frames. This trade appears, however, to have left the parish about the year 1823, when the lace trade rapidly developed in the adjoining town of Nottingham. In the year 1844, there were only 23 stocking frames in the parish, out of a total of 16,382 frames in the whole of the county.

Mr. Henry Dunington, of Lenton, made, on the warp loom, elastic woollen cloth for gloves, and for some time the best of its kind. This mechanician patented several improvements in warp hosiery machinery and fabrics. In 1849 he took out a patent for his still further improved method of making hat-bands and gloves. To this manufacturer the trade owes an important advance in the fabrication and use of warp articles, on which he bestowed much time and money.

In the manufacture of lace, in which the inhabitants are now principally engaged, Lenton has taken a conspicuous place, the following important improvements in lace machinery having been made by Lenton men :—

In 1841, Joseph Wragg, of Lenton, smith, assisted by Bertie, used the cylinder and cards, but instead of holes they put on knobs of wood of different heights to act on guide bars, forcing them to greater distances than by compound levers, and thus got gimp threads round the flowered patterns, which had before been put in by the needle. This was a great discovery, operating however to displace the labour of many lace embroiderers, and to overturn some important arrangements of the trade. The goods being nearly finished for the market on the machines, much labour, time, and capital, previously employed in giving them out all over the midland counties to be run or tamboured, were saved ; but the hands were gradually thrown out of employment. This was not an unmitigated evil, for the labour was unhealthy and of late years ill-paid for long hours and close application.[1]

In 1844, Mr. Gravener Henson gave a plan and drawings to Crofts and Cox, of Lenton, for putting one bobbin of the usual size at the bottom of a steeple-top carriage, and another of smaller size at the top of the same. The bobbins above the bars being of the same size as the bottom bobbins, a fixed thread passed round both bobbins which were placed more than two inches above the others, holding double the quantity of thread, and the bobbins pulled nearly alike, so that no yarn was wasted.[2]

In 1845, John Oldknow, of Lenton, made Lever machines 24 quarters, or 216 inches, in width. It was intended to make muslin laces extensively from them, but as the bobbin threads did not traverse, the article fell into disuse.[3]

---

(1) Felkin, *History of Machine Wrought Hosiery and Lace*, p. 385. Much of the information in this section is derived from this work.

(2) *Ibid.*, p. 387.     (3) *Ibid.*, p. 388.

An invention appeared in 1846, produced upon circular machinery, by Mr. John Livesey, a draughtsman, of Lenton, called from the looped formation of the meshes and the threads not traversing, "straight-down" net; and it is upon this arrangement that curtain nets and curtains are principally made. The tissue is not solid or fast, and will not bear too much stress in wear; nevertheless cloth work of single, double, and three-fold texture, can be introduced at pleasure; and intermixed with open works, form elegant designs in the net work, by the application of Jacquard apparatus at the ends of the machine to one class of threads, and a separate one acting at the back upon another part of the threads, so as to produce the effects of light and shade in floral or geometric patterns. These are much admired for their beauty when hung up so as to intercept the light. Livesey began by using only one tier of carriages and bobbins. Where more warp threads were wanted in some parts for the pattern than in others, he supplied them from additional warp beams. Instead of the bobbin threads twisting with the separate warp threads, as in common bobbin net, one bobbin thread on this plan acts upon two warp threads, turn and turn about, which causes that the meshes, united by one and the same bobbin thread, are produced in a vertical line. This plan was not at first thoroughly successful; but by the consecutive assistance of Elsey, Sisling, and Cope, the proposed result was eventually more than realised.

John Livesey, the originator of the curtain net machinery, was so well acquainted with the various classes into which the lace manufacture had become sub-divided, that he was enabled to take instruments from each for the purpose of effecting new combinations, and for these he obtained additional patents. In 1851 he patented a mode of making articles resembling velvet and Brussels carpet ground; piled and cut, piled and embossed velvets, tapestry, or Berlin needlework; and lace with velvet figures, and internal pearls, spots, and ornaments. Also, having two or more piles to each carriage thread, and with a back and front ground, from between which the pile thread is drawn. Also a mixed ground, partly looped and partly woven, on which Berlin work stitches are formed. Also embroidered grounds with raised piled surfaces; and, finally, patterns in or on piled or cut piled, and in introducing more colours than were before practicable. The productions here enumerated were of most diversified character and great beauty. The ingenuity displayed in the bobbin net machinery thus modified, was highly creditable to the mind which devised and executed it.

Livesey patented in 1852, No. 1139, for lace piled fabrics. In 1854, No. 1571 and No. 1748, the former for improvements in making laces, the latter in fringes from lace machinery. In 1855, No. 32 was for printing lace, and No. 182 for machinery. In 1857, No. 2997 was for further improvements in the machinery for making piled fabrics. His last patent was taken out in 1861, No. 2043, for methods of making lace embroidered articles, trimmings, etc.

This aptitude for, and versatility of inventions, evidence a great amount of mechanical power, but in Livesey it was more suggestive than practical; he indicated the way to important objects rather than pursued it, so as to secure the beneficial results. Of these he obtained little beyond the needful supply of his daily wants. His mind seems to have been discursive, full of plans, certain, as he averred, to bring large gains, but he lacked the energy and determination to work them fully out. Thus, the greater part of life having passed without Livesey realising any pecuniary harvest from his inventions by a friendly contribution he was assisted to emigrate to Australia.[1]

About 1848, Mr. Peter Coxon, of Lenton, made embossed muslin laces from the Lever's machine. The article was too expensive, and did not sell in consequence. His method was to throw the wheels and tackle out of gear, and thus letting the warp accumulate where necessary for producing emboss-ment.

---

(1) *History of Machine Wrought Hosiery and Lace*, pp. 381—384.

To Sir James Oldknow, Knight,[1] a native of Lenton, the lace trade is indebted for the invention of the *perforated steel bar*, which has been universally adopted in place of the old guide bars previously in use.

" James Oldknow had the distinguished merit of devising and carrying into successful operation the plan now universally adopted, of substituting for the guide bars, in use until 1849, steel perforated bars. Having patented this invention in France, it was, in 1849, patented in England, and under that protection licenses were granted to English machine owners for the use of these improved instruments. But when the idea was first introduced to the notice of a large meeting of the Nottingham fancy machine owners, convened for that purpose, it was very generally thought to be impracticable. Mr. Oldknow having taken the precaution of bringing with him workmen from France, who had practical knowledge with himself of its feasibility, they shut themselves up in a room with darkened windows and locked doors, and put the steel drilled bars into a Lever's machine, which was ready there for the purpose. When seen really at work, it was with some difficulty those present could understand how the bars were so accurately drilled as to work exactly with the corresponding parts of a Lever's machine, wherein the bars must act with entire exactitude in the minute space allotted to them. They had to be so drilled as to operate with the combs, each to the exact gauge. It was necessary, therefore, to place the holes, not absolutely equi-distant, but with allowed shades of increased space, according as the holes were more or less distant from the sides of the machine. The heat generated by the operation of drilling and consequent expansion of the metal, had to be got rid of by cooling the bars repeatedly during the process.

---

(1) Sir James Oldknow filled the important office of Mayor of Nottingham in 1869, and on the death, in June, 1878, of Alderman Ward, the then Mayor, Mr. Oldknow was elected in his place on the 24th of the same month. On the occasion of the opening of Nottingham Castle as an Art Museum, July 3rd, 1878, by the Prince and Princess of Wales, Mr. Oldknow, in his official capacity, entertained their Royal Highnesses, on behalf of the town. In commemoration of this event, Mr. Oldknow received the honour of knighthood at Osborne, August 14th, 1878. Sir James was re-elected Mayor in November, 1878, and again in November, 1879, having thus filled that office four times.

The only drawback to their use is said to be that they are liable to be affected by expansion and contraction through changes of weather."[1]

Messrs. Maillott and Oldknow were amongst the first to introduce into France the manufacture of lace looped curtains upon Livesey's system.

The bleach works at New Lenton, formerly in the occupation of Mr. Thomas Brown Milnes, and known as Lenton Works, are now carried on by Mr. Alfred Cleaver. Part of these premises were occupied, about the year 1850, by Messrs. Manlove, Alliott, & Seyrig, patentees of the centrifugal drying machine. In this machine, invented by Mr. John Gotlob Seyrig, "instead of being wrung or pressed, and hung up in a hot room to dry, as is the usual mode, the article is wrapped round in a kind of coil between two copper cylinders, the outer one of which is perforated with holes, the apparatus is made to rotate, perhaps a thousand times in a minute, so that by the centrifugal force thus obtained, the water is quickly driven out from the damp article inclosed, through the holes of the cylinder, and left nearly dry. This valuable invention is applied with very important results in manufactures greatly diversified the one from the other."[2] The manufacture of these machines is now continued by Messrs. Manlove, Alliott, & Co., at Bloomsgrove Works, Radford.

The manufactures and trades now carried on in the parish are—lace making, leather dressing, cotton doubling, bleaching, merino spinning, lace machine building, malting, and iron founding.

Messrs. Bayley & Company's leather dressing works in Leen Gate were first established upon a very small scale by the late Mr. Isaac Bayley, of Lenton. They have since been conducted successively by Messrs. Bayley & Shaw, and Messrs. T. J. & T. Bayley, the latter firm being turned into a Limited Liability Company in 1875, under the style of "Thomas Bayley & Company, Limited." This well-known business has largely

---

(1) Felkin, *Machine Wrought Hosiery and Lace*, p. 426.
(2) *Ibid.*, p. 307.

increased during the last thirty years, the buildings erected a few years ago covering more than two acres of land, while at the present time the firm employs between 450 and 500 work-people.

Messrs. E. Peat & Son's cotton doubling mill in Park Street, New Lenton, finds employment for about 200 persons.

# SECTION XV.

## BESTWOOD PARK.

ESTWOOD—anciently Beskwood, Boskwood, Boscwod, or Buscwod—Park, formerly an outlying
portion of the parish of Lenton, contains 3,711
acres, 3 roods, and 21 perches of land, environed
by a buck-leap of fourteen feet, and, being principally under
cultivation, now forms an oval of arable farms. Although
the Park is completely surrounded by parishes situated in
the northern division of the hundred of Broxtow, it is
considered, as a former part of the parish of Lenton, to
constitute part of the southern division of the hundred.
It is bounded on the north by the parish of Papplewick, on
the south by Basford, on the east by Arnold, and on the
west by Bulwell and Hucknall Torkard.

The boundaries of Bestwood are thus defined in an old manuscript book relating to Sherwood Forest, preserved in Bromley
House Library, Nottingham. " The m'ks and bowndes of the
haye or the p'ke of our lorde the kynge of Beskwoode, Beginnyng
att the heade of Coldalle and so the hay of beskwoode is
devyded by the wai that is callid walton-gaytte unto the heithe,
and so from the hethe unto leen furth, that is callid beskwoode

furthe, and so by the watt$^r$ of leene, unto more broke and so by the more broke unto the wai that goithe betwix arnall and papillwike, unto the sike in th'end of the long valey, and so by the sike in th'end of the longe valye, unto the yate in the red Rodde, and from the said yate unto the felde of arnall by the red Rode, and so by the hegge betwix the feld of arnall and beskwoode, unto colldale y$^r$ it began."

The derivation of the name Beskwood, or Bestwood, is probably from the Old Norse (Icelandic) *buskr*, a thicket, and the Anglo-Saxon *wudu*, a wood.

Bestwood formed part of Sherwood Forest, and in an inquisition held at Nottingham in the reign of Henry the Third, it was stated that the hay of Bestwood was included in the southern "keeping" of the forest. As a part of Sherwood Forest, it belonged to the Crown, and was frequently resorted to by the monarchs of England for the enjoyment of the sports of the chase. Until about the middle of the fourteenth century, Bestwood remained an open hay or unenclosed wood, but was eventually emparked by King Edward III., whose partiality to the place caused him to erect a hunting-lodge here. The custody of Bestwood was granted by the Crown from time to time (as will subsequently be shown) to various persons, who, after Beskwood had been emparked, were styled keepers, but who, in previous times, were designated foresters, or rangers. Amongst the various privileges appended to this office, at all events in later times, was the right to occupy the royal lodge at such times when it was not required for the use of the sovereign.

The connection between Bestwood Park and Lenton may be traced back to an early period, for it is recorded that Henry the First, during his stay at Nottingham Castle, granted to Lenton Priory the right of having two carts to fetch dead wood and heather out of the royal forest of Beskwood.[1] This grant is said to constitute the foundation of the parochial connection between Bestwood and Lenton. Henry the Third made a somewhat similar grant,[2] allowing the monks to have two carts, or three

---

(1) Thoroton, *Antiquities of Nottinghamshire*, p. 244.
(2) Rot. Lit. Claus. i. 452.

carretts, daily wandering in "the hay of Boscwod," to bring
therefrom as much dead wood as should be required for fuel
for the use of the monastery.

According to an Inquisition held before Geoffrey de Langley,
Justice of Sherwood Forest, on the 4th of July, 1250, at the
Hospital of St. John the Baptist, in Nottingham, Bestwood was
styled "a hay or park of our lord the King, wherein no man
commons."[1]

On December 30th, 1261, the king granted to the Grey Friars
of Nottingham, ten oaks from Beskwood Hay, towards the
erection of their dormitory and chapter-house,[2] the grant being
repeated on March 16th in the following year.[3]

It was found by a jury in an enquiry regarding the lands
of Nottingham Castle, in 1284, that the Hay of Besk' Wode was
usually agisted by the Constable of the Castle.[4]

About the year 1304, Philip de Wyllughby, Clerk, held one
toft and two bovates of land in Beskwood, and eighty acres in
Bulwell, for the service of being forester, or ranger, of Beskwood
Park.[5] In 1329, at the request of Roger de Mortimer, the custody
of the wood was granted to Richard Strelley[6] for life, he paying
an annual acknowledgment for the same; and, in the same year,
Richard Strelley had a grant of allowance within the Forest of
Sherwood.[7]  On Feb. 22, 1334, King Edward III. granted him
all the dry zuches, or stovenes, or stubbes within the hay of
Beskwood.[8]

In 1339, the custody of the wood was granted to Robert
Maule, of Linby,[9] who was ordered, in 1350, to fell timber in the
woods of Linby, and with the profits to enclose Beskwood.[10]  In
1351, Robert Maule had orders to make trenches, and cut down
oaks and other trees fit for making the paling, and to make into
charcoal and sell those that were not fit for that purpose.[11]  In
1357, the custody of the wood of Beskwood was granted to

---

(1) Thoroton, p. 258.

(2) Rot. Lit. Claus., 45 Henry III., m. 20.          (3) Ibid., m. 15.

(4) Inq. post Mortem, 7 Edw. I., No. 80.

(5) Thoroton, p. 258.      (6) Ab. Rot. Orig. ii, 20, 55.  Tho oton, p. 506.

(7) Inq. post. mort., ii. 29.              (8) Thoroton, p. 258.

(9) Ab Rot. Orig., ii. 130.      (10) Ibid., ii. 206.      (11) Ibid., ii. 218.

Richard de la Vache.[1] According to a survey of Sherwood
Forest taken about this year, we find that "the kyngs hai of
beskwoode is closid in wth a paille and it is in kepyng of
Ricr Delaywache Knyght, &c."[2] On the 1st of September, 1363,
Edward III., by his letters patent, dated at his park of Bestwood, pardoned the Prior and Monks of Newstead certain rents
owing to him out of Linby Hay and Bulwell Wood.[3] In the
same year the king ordered Robert de Morton and Richard de
Clifford to cut down and sell the underwood in that part of
Bestwood which lay between the road called Rasgate, and the
road leading to Calverton, and which was then called "The
Hasels." The proceeds of this sale was to be devoted towards
the repairs (or more probably the completion) of the fence surrounding the park. In 1373, the custody of the park and manor
of Bestwood was granted to Nicholas Dabrichecourt, Esquire,
who received for the same as wages all the money paid for
cutting out the balls of the dogs' feet, and the tolls paid for
passing through the forest with loaded horses or carts, and as
much firewood as he required for his own use.[4] In 1376, William
Elmely superintended the works at the King's Lodge.[5] Geoffrey
de Kniveton was appointed July 16th, 1444, *int. al.*, keeper of the
lodge of Beskwode for life.[6] King Henry the Sixth, by Writ of
Privy Seal, February 1st, 1445, granted to Ralph, last Lord Cromwell, of Tattershall, in the county of Lincoln, *inter alia*, the office
of Steward and Custodian of the park of Beskwode.[7] On the 22nd
September, 1485, Henry VII. granted to Sir Simon Digby, or
Coleshill, in the county of Warwick, Knight, for life, the office
of Lieutenant of the forests of Sherwood, Bestwood, and Clip-
stone;[8] and, at the same time, the profits of the pannage of
Bestwood Park were granted to John Byron, Esq., for life.[9] In
February, 1511, the reversion of the keepership of Beskwood
Park, then held by James Savage by grant of Henry VII., was

(1) Ab. Rot. Orig., ii. 247.

(2) MS., Bromley House Library.    (3) Thoroton, p. 258.

(4) Ab. Rot. Orig., ii. 322.    (5) Ibid., ii. 339.    (6) Thoroton, p. 435.

(7) Cal. Rot. Litt. Pat., p. 287.

(8) Materials for Hist. of Hen. VII., i. 35.    (9) Ibid., i. 37.

granted to Sir Thomas Boleyn, Knight of the Body.[1]    Thomas
Manners, thirteenth Lord Ros, was appointed, July 12th, 1524,
warden and chief justice itinerant of Sherwood Forest, and *inter
alia*, of the park of Beskewode.[2]

On the 23rd of November, 1524, a commission was issued to
the Abbot of Welbeck, the Abbot of Rufford, the Prior of Newstead, Sir Brian Stapleton, Sir Richard Basset, Sir John Vyllers,
and John Hercy, to survey and report into Chancery the
condition of Nottingham Castle, and *int. alia*, of the park of
Beskewood.[3]  A second commission was issued in February,
1531, to the Abbot of Welbeck, Sir Richard Sacheverell, Sir
Brian Stapulton, John Hercy, and Roger———, to visit and
survey, *int. alia*, the park of Beskewod, and to certify into
Chancery the state and number of the deer.[4]  The Commissioners accordingly reported that on January 12, 1532, Beskwood
Park contained 691 fallow deer, of which 151 were deer of antler,
and 114 red deer, of which 60 were deer of antler.[5]

In his description of Sherwood Forest, about this period,
Leland says, " I roode by a mighty great Park by the space
almost of a 3 Miles.  This Park is caullid *Beskewood*, and
longith to the Castelle and Lordship of Notingham."[6]

Queen Elizabeth, by letters patent, dated at St. Albans, May
20, 1567, granted to Thomas Markham, of Ollerton, Esquire,
standard bearer of the gentleman pensioners, the keepership
of Bestwood, void by the death of Sir John Byron, of Newstead,
Knight, with the herbage and pannage, the customary fees and
commodities, and wages of fourpence a day.  The reversion
of the office was granted at the same time to Sir Roger Aston,
Knight.[7]  A year later this same Thomas Markham, who was
likewise ranger of the forest of Sherwood and high steward
of Mansfield, had a grant of the office of keeper of the manor
of Clipston, with the site of the late castle there, and all the

---

(1) Domestic State Papers.          (2) Ibid.

(3) Pat. 16 Hen. VIII., p. 2, m. 22, d.    (4) Pat. 22 Hen. VIII., p. 2, m. 26, d.

(5) Domestic State Papers.          (6) Leland's *Itinerary*, vol. 1, fo. 110.

(7) Domestic State Papers.  This Sir Roger Aston, who was subsequently gentleman of the bedchamber to King James I., was an illegitimate son of Thomas Aston,
of Aston, in Cheshire.

customary dues and fees, as had formerly been held by the said Sir John Byron and William West.

In 1598 a commission was constituted on Her " Majesty's behalf concerning the spoile and spoiles of her highness woods in ye righte of her Crown in the County of Nott.," and " p'ticularly and especially to enquire how many trees or trees like to be timber and of what price, hath there been felled in the wood called Lyndehurst haye in the fforest of Sherwood " between July 11th, 1569, and the date of the present commission. The Commission sat at Mansfield, January 3rd, 1598, and adjourned until January 12th, when the business commenced. According to the verdict of the jury, it appears that by warrant from the Lord Treasurer dated June 20th, 1593, eighty-six trees from the above wood were supplied " for ye repaire of Beskwoode Lodge."

On June 9th, 1603, James I. granted, in reversion, to Roger, fifth Earl of Rutland, the office of keeper of the parks of Bestwood and Clipston for life. On May 27th, 1607, the same king granted, in reversion, to Francis Manners (younger brother and eventual heir of the last named nobleman), the keepership of Bestwood Park for life. On June 27, 1609, Roger, Earl of Rutland, wrote from Belvoir to — Salisbury, urging the repair of Beskwood pale, and enclosed a statement of the decay of the pale, and an estimate of the expenses of its repair, and the number of trees and deer there. The repair of the fence was at once ordered. At " a view taken by speciall comandment from his Ma'tie to the Lord Warden of his fforests and from him to the Verderers, of all the Red Deare in this forest, the fifth of March, 1616, and sertefied as followethe —[*inter alia*]—Beskwood Parke, 28, whereof male, 16.

On March 27th, 1627, a warrant, dated at Westminster, was issued for the payment of £79 17s. 4d. to John Deverell for repairs at Bestwood Lodge.[1] King Charles I., October 16, 1638, granted to William Willoughby and John Cary, Esquires, for their lives successively, the keepership of Bestwood Park

---

(1) State Papers, Domestic Series. This is the earliest instance in which the modern form of the name has been seen.

with the herbage and pannage, and a fee of four pence per diem, as then held by the Earl of Rutland.

In a petition of George, seventh Earl of Rutland, to the King, *about* the year 1639,[1] the petitioner states that whereas he having the custody, herbage, and pannage of Bestwood Park, during life, by a grant of James I., your Majesty (Charles I.) commanded "that the conies in the park should be destroyed, to make the ground more safe for you to hunt there, it is conceived that your grant under seal is requisite in that case. Though the conies be destroyed, their burrows are so numerous that the ground will remain dangerous unless it may be ploughed up and sown with some grain for five years, to begin at Michaelmas next, which will prove no prejudice, but rather a benefit to the deer, and make the ground much the better many years after." The Earl prays license to destroy the conies and plough up the ground for the term of five years.

From an Inquisition held the 5th of April, 1650, at Bestwood Hall, before George Flower, of Hucknall Torkard, Gentleman, and a jury, concerning Bestwood Park, which the Government of the day appears to have entertained some idea of disposing of, we learn, among other particulars, that there was at that time a Hall, built of wood, lime, and plaster, and covered with slate and tile, containing thirty-eight rooms, all in tolerably good repair, with several lodges, a farmhouse, barns, etc. The materials of the hall, if pulled down, it was estimated would be of the value of fifty pounds.

In answer to the fourth article of inquiry, the jury say—

"That the report is common, that the whole circumference of the said park is now inclosed about, and that the park is three thousand acres, or thereabouts ; and that there is, in their judgment, about an hundred acres in tillage, the rest in pasture ; and that there be some old trees, but no underwood. And the said jury say, that the ground tilled, whilst it is in tillage, will lie but for six years, and is worth three shillings and four pence per acre. That the said pasture ground and park is worth two shillings an acre ; and that the said park is in the occupation of William Willoughby, Esquire, saving some small quantity of

---

(1) Domestic State Papers, 1639-40, p. 196.

inclosed land allowed to the keepers, to the quantity of sixteen acres. And that the boundary of the said park, upon the west and south, is by the highway leading from Papplewick to Nottingham; and upon the east by the highway leading from Basford towards Arnold; and from the Red Hill, near Arnold, on the highway between Mansfield and Nottingham, to Papplewick boundary eastward; from thence, on the north-west, or Papplewick lordship, to the highway from Papplewick as before. And that the said park is in the Forest of Sherwood, and subject to the forest laws. And that the said jury say, that the wood within the said park is worth, in their judgment, £150, beside the expense of cutting down; and that the herbage of the park (the pannage being little worth) the jury think, is worth, to be let, £250 per annum. What profit hath been made, the jury know not, nor what number of beasts it will keep; and that the value of a beast-gate there is worth six shillings for the summer, and that the park may be put into many divisions."

To the fifth article of inquiry, the jury say—

" There be eight brace of red deer, whereof two brace of male deer, and five young fallow deer, the value whereof the jury know not; and the jury say the number of rabbits they know not, but they are worth, in the condition they now are in, per year, £40; and that there be four fishponds, the fish of which were destroyed in those times of war. And the jury say, that they consider there is no profit to be made of hawking or hunting in the park, and that the value of all the park and site between the 15th day of July and the 29th of September, in the articles named, they can get no certain knowledge, but that it was the worst time of year to raise profit, the agistment being almost past, and the warrens not yielding benefit; but the jury think those two months, odd days, might be made thirty pounds."

To the sixth article, the jury say—

" That they have seen a copy of a patent, examined and attested, dated the 20th of October, in the 14th year of the late King Charles, wherein it appeareth that the keepership of Bestwood park, and the herbage, and pannage of the said park, and the issues and profits thereof, and also fourpence per diem for exercising the said keepership, to be paid out of the issues, rents, and profits of the county of Nottingham, at the feast of St. Michael, and Easter, by the Sheriff of that county; and the hay of four acres of meadow, in the King's Meadow, at Nottingham, worth, per annum, £10, were granted to William Willoughby, Esquire, for the term of his life; and after, to John Harvey, Esquire, to which patent for more certainty they refer themselves, and the jury say that there hath anciently been three under-keepers, one warrener, and one ground keeper, and that each of

25

the keepers there had for fees and allowances, from their former masters, yearly, five pounds, grass for two horses, twelve beasts, six two-year-old beasts, six calves, and forty sheep, in the park, and dry wood for fire ; which allowance was worth, for each of them, fourteen pounds per annum ; and that there is paid to the vicar of Lenton, seven shillings and sixpence, as a rate-tythe, and other  .  .  .  they know not."

The document is signed by Geo. Flower, Richard Brough, Ra. Smyth, Tho. Daws, Henry Challand, Ri. Shaw, William Langley, John Fairbrother, Henry Fairbrother, Tho. Horsley, John Robinson, and others—twenty-two in all.[1]

In a valuation of Bestwood Park as " parcell of the possessions of Charles Stuart late Kinge of England grounded upon a survey taken by Abell Richardson, gent, and others, in the month of May last and is made forth examined and signed by order of the Contractors. Dated the xth of June 1650," the following passages occur :—

" Memorandum that the said parke and p'misses with their appurtenances are Tythefree without payeing any kinde of Tythe whatsoever theire haveing been a composicon made ancciently with y⁰ viccar of Lenton, whereby the Impropriator and successor of the said viccar of Lenton are debarred from claymeing any more in respect of all Tythes for the p'misses than the yearely some of vj.s. viij.d."  " Memorandum, it is also certified that the Inhabitants in the other Tenements within the said Parke are pore people and doe inioye their habitations and y⁰ grounds adiacent thereunto with severall Beast Gates alsoe ffreely at mr Willoughbyes curtesie.  And should they be putt out, they would bee destitute of mayntenance."

" All the Deere, being seaven brase of redd Deere and three brace of ffallow Deere in the said Parke are vallued worth at present to be sould, xviili."

" The premisses above mentoned are Contracted for and agree'd to bee sold unto John Grove of the Cittie of Westminster Esqr on the behalfe of him selfe and diverse other originall Creditors by whome hee is sufficienly authorized."

" By vertue of an Act of Parliament entituled an Act of the Comons in Parliam't assembled for Sale of the Honors Manors and Lands——belongeinge to the late Kinge, Queen, and Prince, I doe hereby certifie unto the Right worp'll sir John Wollaston Knight Thomas Andrewes John Dethick & ffrancis Allen, Alder-

---

(1) Bailey's *Annals of Nottinghamshire*, i. 799.  The original Report was formerly in the possession of the late Henry Gally Knight, Esq., of Firbeck Park.

men of the Cittie of London, appointed Trustees by the said Act,
that there is due by three hundred and fforty severall Bills or
Debentors herewth sent, all of them signed and sealed by two of
the Trustees in the said Act named, to Cap'tn John Grove and
other persons officers and souldiers originall creditors hereafter
nominated, whoe by their writeings under their hands and seales
have authorized the said Captaine John Grove their Attourney
the severall Sumes hereafter specified :

[Here follows a list of the 340 creditors.]

Amountinge in all to the ffull sume of 6652 - 14 - 02¾ which
with xiiijs & ¼ to bee paid in money is to bee allowed by way
of defalcacon for and in discharge of the Sume of 6953 - 08 - 03
being the whole purchase money payable for Beskwood Parke
als Bestwood Parke with thappurtenances in the County of
Nottingham Certified by the deputy Register, to be sould unto
the said John Grove of the Cittie of Westminster Esqr. on the
behalfe of him selfe and divers other Originall Credditors by
whome hee is sufficiently authorized the vi th of June 1650, And
at the desire and by and with the Consent of the said John
Grove is rated in ffee simple for the said John Grove, Wm
Evanson of Colchester in the County of Essex Esqr John Savage
of the County of Berkshr. Esqr. Edmund Chillenden of London
Esqr Daniell Dale of Susse. Joseph Sabbarton of London and
Joseph Chamberlen of the County of Susse, gent: and to be
paid for eyther in readie money or in Originall Debentors:
charged upon the creddit of the Act of Parliament in that
behalfe." (Unsigned)[1]

On the accession of King Charles II. to the throne, he
confirmed the appointment of William Willoughby, Esq.,
Keeper of Bestwood Park, as follows :—

" Whereas our trusty & well beloved Will. Willoughby Esq're
hath the keeping of o'r Parke called Bestwood Parke, w'thin our
fforest of Sherwood in the county of Nottingham w'th the
Herbage & Pawnage of the sayd parke by Graunt from the
King our late Royall ffather of blessed memory, Wee doe now
hereby declare that our pleasure is, that ye s'd Willia' Willoughby
doe continue his custodie of the sd parke, & doe hold and enioy
ye same according to his Graunt, & to the end the same may
bee fitted & prepared for a Game of Deere & for o'r Royall
disport, and ye Coneyes there may bee taken of & distroyed o'r
pleasure is, & Wee doe hereby Graunt free leave & Licence unto
the sayd Will Willoughby & his Assigns to plough up reduce &
convert into culture or tillage such parts and places of the sayd
Parke as hee shall iudge most convenient, & the same soe

reduced & converted into culture or tillage, to hold use & enioy
& to plough & sow the same w'th any manner of Corns or
graine, that wthout any impeachm't, presentm't, Damage, paine,
or penalty of any Lawes of forest, or other Law, Ordinance,
order or Statute to be incurred for or by Reason of the same.
And wee are further pleased & doe consent that the sayd Will.
Willoughby doe settle a breed of or Race of Horses in the sayd
parke, & keep such number of Breeding Mayres as hee shall
thinke fitt.  And hereof as well our Cheife Justice & Justice in
Eyre o'r fforesters Verderers, Officers & Ministers of o'r sayd
fforest of Sherwood & all other Officers and Ministers whatsoever
are to take notice, & herein in any manner not to troble, disquiet
or molest the s'd Will' Willoughby or his assignes contrary to
o'r Royal Will, leave & licence herein & hereby granted and
Declared : Given 5th of Septemb'r 1660." [1]

In the month of February, 1661-2, the King sent the following orders to William Willoughby, Esq., keeper of the Park,
to repair the fence, so that it might be used for the breeding
and keeping of horses for the King's use, and instructed him to
cut down sufficient timber in Sansom wood to repair such
fence :—[2]

CHARLES REX.

Whereas William Willoughby Esq[r] Keeper of our Parke
of Bestwood in our fforest of Sherwood hath received Comand
from us to repaire the pale and fence of our said Parke and
make divisions there whereby it may be so fitted for the
brooding and keepeing of horses for our own use and service.
And in order thereunto and in pursuance of our Comand the
said M[r]. Willoughby hath lately bought a large quantity of
timber trees and woods called Sansom woods in our said fforest
w[ch] he intends to imploy and dispose for the use aforesaid To
the end therefore that the said service soe much conducing both
to our Royal pleasure and profitt may be the more speedily and
effectually proceeded with wee have thought fitt hereby to
signify to you that it is our will and pleasure y[t] all orders
licenses warrants and directions w[ch] the said M[r]. Willoughby or
his Agents shall from time to time demand of you as L[d] Warden
of our said fforest of Sherwood for the felling cutting down
converting disposeing and carrying away and imploying of the
said Timber and woods soe by him bought and to be imployed
for our said service be by you granted to him or them in as
large and Beneficiall a manner as hath beene formerly to any
p'son whatsoever And that you also grant unto the said M[r.]

---

(1) Egerton MSS., 2542, f. 422.

(2) MSS. Bromley House Library.

Willoughby or his Agents desiring your Order License & Warrant from time to time for the incloseing and coppiceing of parte of the said Woods after he shall have felled the same whereby the rest in our said fforest will be increased. And for soe doeing this shalbe your sufficient warrant. Given at our Court at Whitehall the 26th day of ffebruary 1661.

By his Ma<sup>ties</sup> Comand<br/>EDW NICHOLAS.

To o<sup>r</sup> Right Trusty and Right well beloved
Cousin Willm Marquis of Newcastle
Justice in Eyre on the northside of Trent
and warden of our Forest of Sherwood.

We learn from a report by Attorney-General Palmer and Surveyor Sir Charles Harbord, dated March 27, 1662,[1] on the petition of Sir Richard Spencer, Sir Gervase Clifton, Sir William Walter, and Sir Thos. now Lord Fanshawe, creditors of the late King (Charles I.), that on July 4, 1643, the New Forest, co. Hants, Sherwood Forest and Bestwood Park, co. Notts, and Clarendon and Bowood Parks, co. Wilts, were assigned to them and others by letters patent as standing security for certain debts with leave to sell the said lands, unless the debts were paid with interest in two years. The report gives an account of the debts, the advances made by the respective creditors to meet them, and the expenses to which they have been put by lawsuits upon their bonds, etc. ; and adds that the King is at great disadvantage, owing to this great debt, but these worthy gentlemen have deserved well.

Relative to the order issued by King Charles II. to William Willoughby, Esq., for repairing the fence of Bestwood Park, we find that on the 4th September, 1662, Rowland Dande, of Mansfield Woodhouse, and William Wylde, of Nettleworth, certified that Sansom woods contained 30 acres, forest measure, and that there were "between 700 and 800 loads of wood fit for stoopes rails and some pales, but very little fit for pales but only for stoopes and rails." "And we have alsoe viewed the Parke pale of Beskod w<sup>ch</sup> we finde very much decayed and fenced soe y<sup>t</sup> very few either of the pales stoopes or rayles will growe againe."

---

(1) State Papers, Domestic Series.

On May 3, 1667, a warrant was issued for a grant in reversion to Sir Humphrey Brigges, of Houghton, in the county of Salop, Baronet, nominee of William, Lord Willoughby, of Parham, of Bestwood Park, then disparked, the keepership and herbage of which were granted by the late King to the said Lord, with a reversion to John Carey.[1]

Dr. Thoroton, writing in 1677,[2] describes Bestwood Park as follows :—" It hath a very fair lodge in it, and in respect of the pleasant situation of the place, and conveniency of hunting and pleasure, this park and lodge hath for these many years been the desire and achievement of great men ; three Earls of Rutland had it, Roger, Francis, and George ;[3] before that Thomas Markham, a great courtier and servant to Queen Elizabeth, had it, and before him little Sir John Byron, a great favourite to King Henry the Eighth. It is now on lease to Lord Willoughby, of Parham. Before the troubles it was well stocked with red deer. But it is parcelled into little closes on one side, and much of it hath been ploughed, so that there is scarce either wood or venison : which is too likely to be the fate of the whole forest of Sherwood."

Shortly after this Bestwood Park appears to have been held by the celebrated Nell Gwynne,[4] under a lease from

---

(1) State Papers, Domestic Series.

(2) " Antiquities of Nottinghamshire," p. 258.

(3) These three noblemen were brothers. Roger, 5th Earl of Rutland, died without issue in 1612 ; Francis, 6th Earl, died without male issue in 1632 ; and George, 7th Earl, died unmarried in 1641.

(4) Nell Gwynne was born, according to authors of known veracity, in Pipe Street, in the city of Hereford, about the year 1642. Her father is said to have been "Thomas Gwyn, a captain, of an ancient family in Wales," who must have died before Nelly's birth, or when she was very young. In early life she gained a livelihood by selling oranges in the theatres in London, and eventually became an actress in the King's playhouse in the year 1663, quitting the stage in 1672. Her life, from her *debût* at the playhouse to the date of her death, is well known. She became the King's mistress about the year 1668, and bore him two sons, Charles Beauclerk, afterwards Duke of St. Albans, born in Lincoln's Inn Fields, May 8th, 1670, and James Beauclerk, who was born in 1671, and died in Paris in 1680. Not only was Nell the favourite mistress of the King, but in a short time she became the favourite of the people. After the King's death she secluded herself at her house in Pall Mall, and maintained an unimpeached fidelity to the King's memory up to the time of her death, which occurred November 13th, 1687. Her funeral was conducted, with great solemnity, at the parish church of St. Martin's-in-the-Fields. Dr. Thomas Tenison, afterwards Archbishop of Canterbury, preached her funeral sermon. The Earl of Jersey, who wanted to prefer Dr. Scott, of St. Giles, brought forward this sermon on Nell Gwynne as an objection to Tenison's promotion, but Queen Mary defended him. " It was a sign," she said, " that she died penitent ; for, if I can read a man's

the Crown, for in the year 1681 she leased portions of the Park to neighbouring yeomen for agricultural purposes. From the three counterpart leases preserved in the British Museum we have abstracted the following details :—The first lease, dated August 1st, 1681, is made "between the Lady Elianor Gwynne of the parish of St Martyne in the Fieldes" in the county of Middlesex, of the one part, and Thomas Gibson, William Maltby, George Rossell, Joseph Wood, John Bradley, Jonathan Sturtivant, William Beardsley, and Richard Tole, all of Arnold, in the county of Nottingham, yeomen, of the other part. The lessee grants to the lessors "all that peice or p'cell of Bestwood parke in the parish of Lenton in the county of Nottingham conteyninge by estimacon Two hundred and ffive and ffifty acres two Roods and twenty one perches be the same more or lesse," then in the occupation of John Barber and others, from Lady day, 1681, for the term of nine years at the yearly rent of £34 - 1 - 8 to be paid at Lady day and Michaelmas day "att the Mansion house in Bestwood parke called Bestwood hall." The witnesses to the counterpart lease were "Geo. Gregory, Fra. Holles, Tho. Herricke."[1] The second lease is of the same date and terms as the first, and grants to Charles Warren, John Sturtivant, John Wilkinson and Robert Fillingham, all of Arnold, yeomen, "one hundred and ffowre score acres abutting upon the Roadway leading from redd hill to Mansfeild in the east part and upon diverse lande & grounde in Bestwood parke afore said in possession of the said Charles Warren." Annual rent, £24. Same witnesses.[2] The third lease, of the same date and terms as the other two, grants to John Sturtivant, of Calverton, Notts, gent, Edward Davyes, of the same place, clerk, Thomas Grammer, Samuel Wilkinson, Thomas Wilkinson, and William Motteram, all of Calverton, yeomen, 180 acres of Bestwood Park, bounded by

---

heart through his looks, had she not made a truly pious and Christian end, the doctor never could have been induced to speak well of her." By her will, dated July 9th, 1687, she bequeathed the whole of her property to her "dear natural son, his Grace the Duke of St. Albans." The arms ascribed to Mrs. Eleanor Gwynne are : Per pale, *arg.* and *or,* a lion [sometimes called a leopard] rampant, *azure ;* and these arms appear to have been used at her funeral.

(1) Add. Charter, 15,863.          (2) Add. Charter, 15,862.

Arnold brook on the east, Sherwood Forest on the north-east,
etc., and then in the tenure of the said lessees.    Annual
rent, £25.    Same witnesses.[1]

The possession of Bestwood Park was finally secured to Nell
Gwynne, and her elder son, then recently created Duke of
St. Albans, by the payment by the Crown, on October 18th,
1687, of the balance of a sum of £3,774 2s. 6d., which had
been advanced on mortgage by Sir John Musters, Knight.
The transaction is thus recorded in the Secret Service
Accounts of King Charles the Second :—[2]

> " To Sir Stephen Fox, for so much by him paid to Sir
> Rob$^t$ Clayton, in full of 3,774$^{li}$ 2$^s$ 6$^d$ for redeeming
> the mortgage of Bestwood Parke, made to S$^r$ John
> Musters,[3] to settle the same upon Mrs. Ellen
> Gwynne for life, and after her death upon the
> Duke of St. Albans and his issue male, with the
> reversion in the Crowne - - - - 1256 - 0 - 2 "

King Charles II. ennobled Charles Beauclerk, the elder of
his two illegitimate sons by his mistress, Eleanor Gwynne, by
creating him, December 27th, 1676, when but six years old,
Baron Hedington, in the county of Oxford, and Earl of Burford,
in the same county, with remainder to his younger brother,
James Beauclerk.    The young Earl appears to have been placed
in the care of Thomas Otway,[4] successively actor, soldier, and
dramatist.

On January 10th, 1683-4, the Earl was advanced to the Dukedom of St. Albans, and was appointed hereditary Grand Falconer of England, and hereditary Registrar of the Court of

---

(1) Add. Charter, 15,864.

(2) " Copy of a schedule of the Receipts and Payments for the Secret Services of
Charles II. and James II. from Lady day 1679 to Christmas 1688."—Camden
Soc., vol. 52, p. 167.

(3) This was Sir John Musters, of Colwick, the direct ancestor of the present John
Chaworth Musters, Esq. Sir John, who appears to have originally resided at
Hornsey, in Middlesex, was knighted at Whitehall on the 2nd of June, 1662. He
purchased the ancient seat of the Byrons at Colwick, which he made his place of
residence, and, dying July the 28th, 1689, was buried in the chancel of Colwick
Church.

(4) Harl. MSS., 7, 319, f. 135. The sad death on April 14th, 1685, of the poet, who
was one of Nell Gwynne's oldest friends, and tutor to her son, was greatly felt by
that kind-hearted woman.

Chancery.[1]  The Duke early embraced the profession of arms,
serving with special distinction
in the Imperial army, more particularly at the siege of Belgrade
in 1688.  On the abdication of
James II., the Duke joined cor-
dially in the new measures adopted
by William III., and continued
in the confidence of the King
up to the time of that monarch's
decease.    On the 12th of November, 1714, King George I.
appointed    his    Grace    Lord

Lieutenant and Custos Rotulorum of Berkshire, and in March,
1718, he was made a Knight of the Garter.   He died at Bath, May
9th,[2] 1726, aged 56 years, and was interred in Westminster Abbey.
By Diana, his wife, eldest daughter and eventual heiress of Aubrey
de Vere, twentieth and last Earl of Oxford (who survived him),
he left eight sons, all of whom attained distinction, and was
succeeded in his titles and estates by the eldest, who, during the
lifetime of his father, had been made a Knight of the Bath.

Charles, second Duke of St. Albans, was created a Knight of
the Garter after his accession to the dukedom, and was appointed
a Lord of the King's Bedchamber, Governor of Windsor Castle,
and Lord Warden of the Forests, and continued in the personal
service of his Sovereign during the whole of his lifetime.   He
died July the 27th, 1751, and was buried in Westminster Abbey,
leaving an only son.

George, third Duke of St. Albans, so seriously impaired his
fortune by his magnificent establishment and lavish hospitality,
as to be compelled to quit his native country, and to spend

---

(1) The portrait of the first Duke, when a child, is from a print engraved by A.
Blooteling.

(2) This is the date given in the newspapers of the day, but Colonel Chester
(Westminster Abbey Registers, p. 317) points out that the Funeral Book belonging to
the Abbey states that he died on the 10th of May, and some of the old peerages give
the 11th of that month as the date of his decease.   It is remarkable that his will, dated
July 19th, 1694, shortly after his marriage, in which he left all his estate to his wife,
was never added to or altered in any way.

a considerable portion of his life in comparative retirement upon the Continent. He died at Brussels, February the 1st, 1786, in his 55th year, and his remains, being brought to England, were interred on the 11th of the following month in Westminster Abbey. He left no lawful issue,[1] and was succeeded by the only son of his cousin, Colonel Charles Beauclerk.

George, fourth Duke of St. Albans, enjoyed the title little more than a year, dying unmarried February 16th, 1787, aged 29 years. Upon the decease of the last-mentioned nobleman, the title devolved upon his kinsman, Aubrey, second Lord Vere, only son of Lord Vere Beauclerk (third son of the first Duke of St. Albans), who, in recognition of his valiant services as a naval officer, had been raised to the peerage, May the 28th, 1750, as Baron Vere, of Hanworth, in the county of Middlesex.

Aubrey, fifth Duke of St. Albans, died February the 9th, 1802, and from him the dukedom has descended (as shown in the accompanying pedigree) to the present noble owner of Bestwood Park, William Amelius Aubrey de Vere, tenth Duke of St. Albans, Earl of Burford and Baron Hedington, and seventh Baron Vere, of Hanworth, hereditary Grand Falconer of England, and Registrar of the Court of Chancery.[2] His Grace, who was formerly Captain of the Yeomen of the Guard, is Lord Lieutenant and Custos Rotulorum of the county of Nottingham, Honorary Colonel of the 1st Nottinghamshire (Robin Hood) Rifle Volunteers, Provincial Grand Master of the Freemasons of Nottinghamshire,[3] and a Justice of the Peace for the county. He has recently been appointed an ex-officio Governor of the Nottingham High School. The present Duke may be said to be the first of his family who has been intimately connected with Nottinghamshire, for, although Bestwood Park has been in the possession of his ancestors for two hundred years,

---

(1) See a note of his will in the *Westminster Abbey Registers, edited and annotated by Colonel J. L. Chester,* p. 441.

(2) The carriage way between Birdcage Walk and Buckingham Gate, London, was, until 1828, open only to the Royal Family, and the hereditary Grand Falconer, the Duke of St. Albans.

(3) The ceremony of Installation was performed by the Rt. Hon. the Earl of Carnarvon, Pro Grand Master of England, at a Provincial Grand Lodge, held at Nottingham Castle, September 20th, 1878.

none of the family (with one exception[1]) have ever made it their place of residence, nor do they seem to have ever interested themselves in any way in local affairs.

Some small detached portions of Bestwood Park were under cultivation, and much of the timber was felled towards the close of the seventeenth century,[2] but a considerable portion of it remained as open forest ground until the year 1775, when the greater part of it was broken up, and applied to agricultural purposes by Mr. Barton, a Norfolk farmer, who, having in that year obtained a lease of the park from the then Duke of St. Albans for twenty-one years, brought a great number of labourers from Norfolk, to cultivate it after the custom of that county.[3] Barton lost £10,000 by his farming operations, and was ruined thereby, notwithstanding which, the then Duke of St. Albans commenced an action against his widow for dilapidations. Mr. William Ellis became tenant on a lease for 21 years, from Michaelmas, 1796, at the rent of £1,500, and acquired a handsome profit of about £3,000 a year.[4] According to the "Agriculture of Nottinghamshire," by Robert Lowe, Esq., of Oxton, the whole park was, in 1798, divided into eight farms, the principal one, attached to the old hall, being occupied by the representatives of Mr. Barton. In 1844, the park was divided into thirteen farms.

BESTWOOD LODGE, the seat of the Duke of St. Albans, was erected in 1864, in the domestic style of architecture of the fourteenth century, from the designs of the late Mr. S. S. Teulon. The Lodge (which occupies the site of the old hall) is built of brick, with red and white Mansfield stone dressings, and contains many artistic features. The entrance is on the north side, under a semi-circular tower, somewhat heavily flanked with flying buttresses. Above and under the circular window are picture panels, extremely well carved in stone, of Robin Hood and his men, with exquisite

---

(1) The old house at Bestwood was occasionally occupied by Admiral Lord Amelius Beauclerk, G.C.B., a younger son of the 5th Duke of St. Albans. He died in 1846.

(2) In 1729, Mr. James Thain was the Steward.

(3) In 1778, Mr. Barton was rated in the parish books of Lenton at £504, as the amount of his rent of Bestwood Park.

(4) *Stretton MSS.*, No. 29, f. 4.

medallions. The south, or dining-room front is decorated with
two large stone panels, one illustrating the old legend of the
origin of the spring at · Bulwell, and the other a portrait of
King Edward the Third on horseback, returning from hunting,
and at the south end of the office wing there is a large figure
of King Charles the First raising the Standard at Nottingham ;
all these, finely chiselled out of white Mansfield stone, stand
well out in contrast with the brick and red sandstone. On the
north front is this inscription :—"This house was commenced
A.D. 1862, by William Amelius Aubrey de Vere, 10th Duke
of St. Albans, on the site of a hunting lodge of King
Edward III., and was completed A.D. 1865. Samuel Saunders
Tuelon, Architect, James Burford, Clerk of the works." The
several rooms open from a square central hall with a gallery
above and lighted from a glass dome. The dining-room, 40 feet
by 20 feet, and 15 feet high, is in the south front, and the
drawing or reception-room, 50 feet by 20 feet, in the west, and
commands a fine view over an undulating country, with the Derbyshire hills in the distance. The billiard-room was added at a
later date, the foundation stone being laid by the Earl of Cadogan.
It contains a picture of H.M. Ship "Dryad" of 36 guns,
commanded by Lord Amelius Beauclerk, bringing to close
action the French frigate "Prosperine." In the dining-room
is a bust, by *Roubiliac*, of Wilks, the founder of the Beefsteak
Club. The drawing-room contains a number of family portraits,
amongst which are the following :—

Charles Beauclerk, first Duke of St. Albans.

The same, as a child, by *Gascar*.

King Charles the First, in armour, by *Jamesone*.

George, first Earl of Berkeley, died 1698.

Elizabeth [Noel], Countess of Berkeley, by *Sir Peter Lely*.

Edward de Vere, seventeenth Earl of Oxford.

Diana de Vere, Duchess of St. Albans, daughter and eventual
heiress of the last Earl of Oxford.

Barbara Villiers, only daughter and heiress of William,
Viscount Grandison, wife of Roger, Earl of Castlemaine,
mistress of King Charles II., and afterwards created Duchess
of Cleveland, by *Sir Peter Lely*.

Lord Aubrey Beauclerk, eight son of the first Duke of St. Albans, born 1711, killed at Carthagena, 1740.

Lord Amelius Beauclerk, third son of the fifth Duke, G.C.B., and G.C.H., Admiral of the White, born 1771, died 1846.

———

In 1874, Bestwood Park was constituted a separate ecclesiastical district, under the provisions of the Act of Parliament authorising the formation of new benefices. The present Duke of St. Albans, who had previously given the site for the church and contributed largely towards its erection, endowed the living with £100 per annum, to which the Ecclesiastical Commissioners added £50 per annum; the present annual value of the living being £150, exclusive of fees. The right of patronage is vested in the Duke of St. Albans, and the Reverend William Richard Cripps, B.A., is the first and present Vicar of Bestwood. The Vicar of Lenton having formally resigned all rights in this portion of his parish, the annual rent-charge, paid to the Vicars of Lenton in lieu of tithes, has been transferred to the Vicar of Bestwood, so that, in point of fact, this benefice, although it has never been duly gazetted as such, is actually a Rectory, in consequence of the incumbent holding the entire rectorial tithe, or rent-charge in lieu thereof.

EMMANUEL CHURCH, a small building in the earlier French Gothic style, was erected in 1870, from designs by Mr. S. S. Tuelon (the architect of Bestwood Lodge), at a cost of over £1,000, defrayed by the present Duke and his tenantry. An inscription, cut upon a stone near the south-western corner of the nave, thus records the commencement of the fabric :—

"The first stone of this Chapel,[1] erected by the Duke of St. Albans and the inhabitants of Bestwood for the service of God, was laid by Mrs. Challand, on behalf of Lady Louise Beauclerk, May 17, 1869, the Revd. George Browne being Vicar of the parish."

---

(1) Until June, 1874, this was a chapel-of-ease only, Lenton being the parish church. Being duly licensed by the Bishop, it was first used for Divine service on Sunday, June the 5th, 1870, and was consecrated July the 4th following, on the enclosure of the surrounding burial-ground.

The church merely comprises a nave having an apsidal recess at the eastern end to form a chancel, with a small organ-chamber and vestry. The single bell is in an open turret upon the western gable. The interior arrangements, although simple, are particularly tasteful, and the decoration of the eastern end of the church is most effective. ˙This little church is intimately associated with the memory of the late lamented Duchess, whose remains repose in the adjoining churchyard. The five beautifully painted little windows in the apse, the embroidered altar-cloth, and the cloth covering the kneeling step before the altar are all her Grace's handiwork. A fine medallion portrait of the Duchess, carved by her Royal Highness the Princess Louise, is affixed to the wall at the western end of the church. There are also two windows in the same part of the church, containing stained glass, representing the Nativity and the Ascension, both of which are memorials of the late Duchess. One of these was erected by the Dowager Duchess of St. Albans and Lady Diana Beauclerk, and the other by Mrs. Webb, of Newstead Abbey. Beneath the five windows in the apse, already mentioned, runs the following inscription :—

" These windows were executed by Sybil, Duchess of St. Albans, in fond memory of her beloved father, General the Hon<sup>ble.</sup> Charles Grey, who died March 31st, 1870."

On the outside of the church, at the western end, beneath a plain stone canopy, surmounted by a cross, is a very fine representation of the Resurrection, in mosaic work, and beneath it is the inscription :—

" Sacred to the memory of Sybil Mary, Duchess of St. Albans. ' Blessed are the pure in heart, for they shall see God.' "

Just below is a ledger tomb of grey and red granite, simply inscribed :—

" Sybil Mary,

Wife of William, 10th Duke of St. Albans,

Daughter of General Hon<sup>ble.</sup> Charles Grey.

Born 28th Nov., 1848. Died 7th Sept., 1871."

EMMANUEL CHURCH BESTWOOD

Bestwood is the scene of the operations of the "Bestwood Coal and Iron Company, Limited," formed in August, 1872. The company has effected a long lease of the entire estate underground, and commenced its operations by the sinking of a colliery in March, 1873. Though many doubtful opinions had been expressed in reference to the value of the minerals beneath the surface, the directors prosecuted their labours, and eventually found what is called the "top hard," at a depth of about 420 yards. This result was realised after two years' hard labour. To the satisfaction of all concerned, the coal was found in a thick seam and in a high state of perfection. Thus encouraged, the promoters went to work in effecting the completion of the colliery, the result being that two large shafts, fitted with the most powerful machinery, were sunk. The prosecution of the work of developing the mine gave evidence that the extent and quality of the coal would be quite equal to the most sanguine expectations of the promoters. The seam consists at the top of household coal, known as "brights;" next comes the hard coal, which is brought into requisition for steam purposes and iron smelting; and the next portion is the "cannel coal," distinguished for its special illuminating power when converted into gas. So successful have the works been that at the present time the colliery is capable of raising about 350,000 tons per year; and the ironworks were projected in November, 1880, and carried out with the view of consuming a portion of the hard coal of this seam. The works are in close proximity to the famous oolitic ironstones of Northamptonshire, North Leicestershire, and South Lincolnshire; in fact, they are the nearest works to these ironstone fields. As some evidence of the importance of the works, it may be said that for some time past the three railway companies—the Midland, Great Northern, and London and North Western—have been engaged in a sharp rivalry for the acquisition of railway approach, and at the present time all three have found their way thither. By this means communication is easily obtained with all the commercial centres of the land. The ironworks, which are regarded as of the best character in the country, have two large furnaces with patent stoves, together with a pair of powerful blowing engines of 100 ins. diameter blowing cylinders each. The first of these furnaces was put in blast in November, 1881, and the second during the following month. Complete as all the appliances are to the minutest detail, the entire works are so constructed that they are capable of great enlargement at any time when circumstances render it necessary. It is admitted by all who have seen it, that the colliery is fitted up with one of the most powerful ventilating fans that has been invented. The number of men employed is 720, 550 underground and 170 on the surface.

Bestwood Park was regularly perambulated by the inhabitants of Lenton, the perambulation of 1719 being thus recorded in the parish books :—"May y⁵ 5, 1719, ffor Memorandam that the Parishonors of Lenton Went the parambleation Round Bestwood parke And thay Went the bounds ffourteen fut out of the pales as is witnessed by vs whose Names Are here vnto subscribed    Will : Rudsby vic :" and sixty-seven others.

In the year 1808 the neighbouring landowners addressed the following protest to the Constable of Lenton previous to the perambulation of the Park by the parish officials :—

"Mʳ. Thomas Newham. We whose names are hereunto subscribed being respectively Owners or Occupiers of Lands and Buildings in the Parish of Arnold in the County of Nottingham or their Agents do hereby give you Notice that if you or any person acting by your order or under your authority shall or do on the twenty sixth day of May instant commonly called Holy Thursday or on any other day in any year intrude or come upon any Lands or grounds or into any House or Buildings belonging to or in the occupation of us or any of us or for the proprietors of which we or any of us are Agents beyond the boundary fence of Bestwood Park under a pretence of perambulating and ascertaining the boundaries of Bestwood Park or on any other pretence whatsoever or shall do or commit any other Act in regard to such Lands and Buildings as an assertion of the pretended right or claim of any Body Politic Corporate or Collegiate or any Trustee or other person whatsoever one or more action or actions of trespass and other proceedings will be commenced and prosecuted to the utmost rigour of the Law against you and every person acting under your order or authority who shall offend in the premises aforesaid. As wit-

ness our hands this nineteenth day of May One thousand eight
hundred and eight.   W. Sherbrooke, Henry Coape, Robt. Lowe,
Junr., Benj. Thompson, John Need, Wm. Rhodes, Thos. Holt,
Wm. Daft, Charles Bramley, John Blatherwick, Jno. Rawson,
Thos. Marsden, Benj. Churchell, Daniel Simkins."

When the parish of Lenton was absorbed into the borough
of Nottingham, on the passing of the "Nottingham Borough
Extension Act, 1877,"[1] Bestwood Park was, by section 16,
excluded from its operations.   Section 40 of the same Act
provides that "at such time after the commencement of this
Act [Nov. 1, 1877,] as the Education Department shall think
fit, that Department shall issue an order for the election of
five persons to serve as members for the School Board for
that portion of the district of Lenton known as Bestwood
Park, which is not by this Act included within the extended
borough, in the place of the persons who at the time of the
making of such order shall be members of the said School
Board for Lenton."

In March, 1878, Bestwood Park was constituted a separate
and independent parish for all purposes.

---

(1) 40 Victoria, ch. xxxi.

26

# SECTION XVI.

## THE PEVEREL COURT.

THE Honour of Peverel is supposed to have been created by William the Conqueror, and granted by him to William Peverel.

To this Honour[1] was attached a Court of some description, but there is now no way of ascertaining correctly what was its nature or jurisdiction. It seems, however, to have comprised both a Tourn and a View of Frankpledge. The former, which was a Court of Record, had jurisdiction to hear and determine all felonies (death of man excepted) and common nuisances. It was holden twice a year at Nottingham, and all tenants of the Honour were bound to appear there when it was holden. The latter, also a Court of Record, had jurisdiction over those matters which were exempt from the Tourn. It met once in every three weeks, and the tenants of the Honour who owed suit and service were bound to appear before it. Over the

---

(1) "The title *Honour* means a more noble sort of Lordship, on which other inferior estates depend by performance of certain service to the superior chief, whose seigniory is frequently termed an *honour*, not a *manor*, particularly if it has ever belonged to the king, or to an ancient feudal baron. To constitute an *honour*, however, it was essential that it should be holden of the king, for though the king might grant it to a subject, it could not be holden *of* a subject, if the king assigned it to another."—*Thomson on Magna Charta*, p. 236.

Tourn, after the Honour came into the King's hands, the Constable or Warden of Nottingham Castle presided (and not the Sheriff, whose jurisdiction was confined to the Tourn held for the county, of which he was the chief officer), it being alleged " the King William the First, with the consent of his Council, ordained that from time to time, and at all times thereafter, when and so often as any freeman of dignity and fealty to the Crown of England should in lawful manner hold or be proprietor of the inheritance of the site and castle of Nottingham, whether by gift, descent, or purchase, the same man and his heirs (so long as he should be qualified) should be Constable, Marshall, and Steward of the Castle of Nottingham and Honor of Nottingham, alias Peverel."[1]

When in the height of its power, the Honour, as the jurisdiction of the Court was named, comprised no less than 127 towns and villages in Nottinghamshire, and 120 in Derbyshire, a list of which is given in Deering's *Nottinghamia Vetus et Nova*, pp. 354-6, and Pilkington's *Derbyshire* ii. 15. On the flight of William Peverel, the grandson, in 1155, the king seized his possessions, and retained them in his own hands until he bestowed them, with some exceptions, on his son John, Earl of Morteign and Nottingham, in 1174. The Court was then *de facto* a princely one, and continued in the hands of John until his accession to the throne in 1199, when it became merged in the Crown.

Over the Frankpledge an officer in the nature of Bailiff presided, and from the time that the Honour came into the hands of the Crown until the 10th of the reign of Edward III., the office was granted or leased out at an annual rent.[2]

In 1173 (19 Henry II.) the Honour was in the custody of Robert Fitz-Ralph (Sheriff of Notts. and Derbyshire, 1166), and in 1185 (31 Henry II.) it was in the hands of the King. [3] According to the Great Roll of 1183 (29 Henry II.) Ralph Murdac, Sheriff of the counties of Nottingham and Derby,

---

(1) *Sixteenth Report of the Deputy Keeper of the Public Records*, p. 41.

(2) " So also an Honor might be lett to ferm, or put into custody, like as a Manour or other estate in land." Madox, *Baronia Anglica*, p. 89.

(3) Madox, *History of the Exchequer*, 2 ed. i. 297-8.

rendered an account of £219 8s. od., of the farm of the Honour of Peverel.   In 1196-7 (8 Richard I.), the Sheriff, William le Briwerre, gave account of the scutage of the Honour of Peverel of Nottingham, assessed the year before, being the second for the army in Normandy.[1]

In 1204 (5 John) the Honour was in the custody of Hugh Bardolf[2] (Madox i., 405), and in 1207 it was in the hands of the King.   Sir Ralph Fitz-Nicholas, Governor of Nottingham Castle, was appointed Keeper of the Honour, May 18, 1225. He died 1257.   Sir Robert le Vavasour, of Shipley, in Derbyshire, held the same office.   He was Sheriff of the counties of Notts. and Derby from 1235 to 1254.   He died in the last-named year.   In 1250 a survey of the Honour of Peverel, co. Notts., was made, a transcript of which is preserved in the British Museum, Add. MSS., 25,459, pp. 1-14.

" In the forty-fourth year of K. *Henry III.* (1260), in a Plea moved in the Court of Exchequer between *John de Luvetot*, Keeper of the Honour of *Peverell of Nottingham*, then in the King's hands, and *Simon de Asselacton*, Sherif of the counties of *Nottingham* and *Derby*, Search was made in the Rolls of the Exchequer.   By those Rolls it was acertained (that is manifestly proved) that *Roger de Luvetot*,[3] Keeper of that Honor, did answer to the King upon his Account rendred in the fortieth year of that King, for the profits of View of Frankpledg, as pertaining to his Ferme of that Honor.   Thereupon the Barons gave judgment for the said *John de Luvetot*."[4]

The Chapter of Southwell and the Prioress of Brewood were certified in the *Testa de Nevil* to hold three parts of the town of Calverton, of the Honour of Peverel.[5]

The next holder of the Honour was probably Hugh de Stapleford, to whom it was granted by Henry III. for life.   In the

---

(1) Thoroton's *Antiquities of Nottinghamshire*, 1677, p. 207b.

(2) He was probably the brother of Robert Bardolf, feudal lord of Codnor, in Derbyshire, and father of Isolda, wife of Sir Henry de Grey, who built Codnor Castle early in the 13th century.

(3) Roger de Luvetot, lord of Wysall, was Governor of Bolsover Castle, and thrice Sheriff of Notts. and Derbyshire.   Sir John de Luvetot, his younger brother, was appointed Justice of the Common Pleas in 1275, and died Nov. 5, 1294.

(4) Madox, *Baronia Anglica*, p. 89.       (5) Thoroton, 296a.

18th year of Edward I., when Sir Gervase de Clifton, of Clifton, was Sheriff, great complaint was made, and a jury of Broxtowe wapentake found, that William de Tytheby and Aunsell de Gameleston held the farm of the Bailiwick of Broxtowe for nine marks, by which they got a living, and that it was to the great damage of the county. They also found that the greatest part of Broxtowe wapentake formed part of the Honour of Peverel which was held by Hugh de Stapleford by charter of King Henry III. for the term of life, and that the farm of the Honour was also raised in the same manner as Broxtowe wapentake, to the great abuse of the county.[1]

In the reign of Edward I., this same Sir Gervase de Clifton married the daughter and heiress of Gervase de Rabacy, who, with John de Skerrington and others, held a moiety of a messuage and of three oxgangs of land in Glapton, by the service of finding an *under-bailiff* to make summons and distress in the Court of Peverel.

The Court was originally held in the Chapel dedicated to St. James, the site of which was lately occupied by the Independent Chapel in St. James's Street, Nottingham. The Court continued to be held here until 1316,[2] when Edward II. discharged it from that burden by his charter to the Carmelite Friars.[3] In 1321 the King kept Court at Nottingham Castle, and gave the Corporation a further benefit (that is, in addition to his charter granted March 16, 1313), by exempting the town from the jurisdiction of the Court of the Honour of Peverel. In this year (1321) the Honour was in the hands of the King.[4]

On the 26th September, 1336 (10 Edward III.), the King granted, among other tokens of his royal favour, to his " well-beloved " William Eland, and his heirs, for ever, for the yearly payment of fourteen marcs, the Bailiwick of the Honour of Peverel, in consideration of the great services he had rendered in the capture of Roger Mortimer, Earl of March, at the Castle at Nottingham (see page 146). His son, William, afterwards

---

(1) Thoroton, 205.
(2) Dickinson, "History of Southwell," says 9th year of Edward III., 1335.
(3) Deering, p. 127.     (4) Madox, *Exchequer*, i. 535.

(41 Edward III.) held this Bailiwick of the King in the counties of Nottingham and of Derby by the service of paying fourteen shillings yearly. On the grant being made to William Eland, the elder (1336), it would appear that the Court was removed from the County Hall, where it had been held since the year 1316, to the mansion occupied by William Eland, constable of Nottingham Castle, at the manor of Algarthorpe, in the parish of Basford.

"In or about the fourteenth year of *King Richard II.* (1390) it was found by an Escheatours enquest, that *John de Loudham*, Chivaler, held the manor of *Walton* in *Derbyshire* of the King *in capite*, as of the *Honor* of *Peverell* by the service of suit to Court, for all services. Afterwards in the eighteenth year of King *Richard II.* it was alleged in the Court of Exchequer, that *John de Loudham* held the manor of *Walton* in *Derbyshire* of the King *in capite*, as of the *Honor* of *Peverel*, by the service of one Knight's Fee."[1]

In the reign of Henry VIII., that monarch did "by a private Act of Parliament made in the 28th year of his reign, convey to and settle on Thomas Lord Cromwell and his heirs the inheritance and property of the Castle and Honor of Nottingham, alias Peverel." Lord Cromwell [2] being thus seised of the premises did, by his Lease and Release severally dated 23rd and 25th of February, 30th Henry VIII., demise and grant them to his son Gregory, Lord Cromwell. The Grant above mentioned and the Indenture thereupon made, seem to have been forfeited on the attainder of Lord Cromwell in 1540, and the Honour taken into the hands of the Crown, where it remained until the reign of James I., when the Stewardship of the Honour was leased to Sir George Goring and his brother, as will be hereafter mentioned.

---

(1) Madox, *Baronia*, 185.

(2) This Thomas, Lord Cromwell, was the son of a blacksmith at Putney, and being in the suite of Cardinal Wolsey, was taken into the service of the King on the downfall of that ambitious prelate. The active part which he took in the dissolution of religious houses, and in the establishment of the spiritual supremacy of his royal master, gained for him rapid elevation. He was raised to the peerage as Baron Cromwell in 1536, and further advanced as Earl of Essex in 1539, and was constituted the King's Vice-Regent in spirituals; he was also a Knight of the Garter and Lord High Chamberlain of England. In 1540, he was attainted of high treason, and was beheaded on the 24th of July, 1540.

The Bailiwick remained with the Eland family until the time of Henry VIII. Henry Eland, the last male heir of this family, died September the 8th, 1493, aged 67, his only son, Thomas, having died previously, leaving an only daughter, Mary, who thereupon became heiress to her grandfather. She married Roland Revell, and after his death without issue, she conveyed (23 Henry VIII., anno 1531) the manor of Algarthorpe, and all her lands elsewhere, together with the Bailiwick of the Honour of Peverel to Randall Revell " because he had holpen her in her great suits she had with Nicholas Strelley, Esq., concerning her said inheritance." Hugh Revell,[1] cousin and heir of Mary Eland, was the next holder of the Bailiwick.

In 1546, he obtained licence from King Henry VIII. to alienate the office of the Bailiwick of Peverel to Henry Willoughby, of Wollaton, Esquire, in fee, at the old rent due to the Crown ; and by Indenture (reciting King Edward III.'s Letters Patent to William Eland, and that the estate, title, and interest, of the said William Eland, in the said office, had come to the said Hugh Revell, as well by lawful conveyance as by descent of inheritance, as right heir of the said William Eland), in consideration of £80, covenanted, bargained, and sold the said Office or Bailiwick of the Honour of Peverel, with all profits, charges, and all Records, Evidences, Court Rolls, and Writings concerning and belonging to the said Office, to the said Henry Willoughby.

In the 2nd year of the reign of Edward VI., Henry Willoughby, Esq., died[2] seised of the said Bailiwick, leaving a son, Thomas, then between eight and nine years of age. This Thomas Willoughby died before attaining his majority, and was succeeded by his younger brother, Francis, who was subsequently knighted, and who "out of ostentation to show his riches," as Camden remarks, built the magnificent old Elizabethan mansion at Wollaton, which was completed about

---

(1) He was son of the above-named Randall Revell, who had married Joan, sister of Thomas Eland.

(2) This gentleman lost his life in 1548, whilst engaged in quelling the insurrection in Norfolk, commonly known as " Ket's rebellion." His remains were brought to Wollaton, and there interred. There is a fine mural monument to his memory within the family pew at the east end of the north aisle in Wollaton church.

1588. Sir Francis Willoughby died in London, November the 16th, 1596, and having no male issue, the greater portion of his estates, including the Bailiwick of the Honour of Peverel, passed to his eldest daughter and coheiress, who had married Sir Percival Willoughby, Knight, a descendant of the great Lincolnshire house of Willoughby D'Eresby.

The Bailiwick appears to have continued in the Willoughby family until about the year 1617, without interruption.  In that year, King James I., by Letters Patent of the 26th February, in the 15th year of his reign, granted to Sir George Goring and Sir Edward Goring, Knights, " the office of High Steward of the Honor of Peverel, and of the King's Manors, Lordships, and Hereditaments, in the counties of Nottingham and Derby, to the said Honor in any way appertaining, and the keeping of all Courts within the said Honor for the term of fifty years."

In consequence of this Lease from the Crown, Sir Percival Willoughby, in whom the estate of the Bailiwick of the Court of Peverel had become vested in right of Dame Bridget, his wife, disputed King James's Lease to the Gorings ; whereupon they exhibited a Bill in the Exchequer Chamber against him, and "demanded to have the Court Rolls, the profits of the Stewardship and waifs estray, felons goods, common fines, amerciaments, and perquisites of Court," etc.

The Court, having decided (upon what grounds does not appear) against Sir Percival Willoughby, decreed that the Gorings " should hold and enjoy unto them and their assigns (*inter alia*) the said Stewardship, felon's goods, common fines, perquisites of Court, mentioned in the King's Lease to them ; and that all Court Rolls, Books of Account, and Evidences concerning the Bailiwick of the said Manor, and the Stewardship then remaining in the hands of the said Defendant Willoughby or his under officer should be delivered up to the Plaintiffs (the Gorings), to be brought unto that Court, there to remain for His Majesty's use."

Exceptions were taken by the Defendant's counsel to this Decree, but it was ordered that the said Decree should continue and stand in force.

On the 31st May, 1639, Charles I. issued his Letters Patent, appointing George, Lord Goring[1] (the first-named of the lessees in King James's demise above-mentioned), to the office of High Steward of the Honour of Peverel for and during his lifetime. By these Letters Patent the King "ordains, establishes, and declares that the jurisdiction of the Honor of Peverel shall for the future extend itself as well in and through all those places which of old were within the jurisdiction of the said Honor, as in and through the whole Wapentakes or Hundreds of Broxtow and Thurgarton by Leigh, in the county of Nottingham (to wit) in all parts of those wapentakes which previously were not within the jurisdiction of the said Honor, and that all the towns, townships, hamlets, and places within the wapentakes aforesaid which before were not within such jurisdiction, shall henceforth be called the additional limits of the Honor of Peverel." These Letters Patent also contained some regulations respecting the deputy-steward and other officers, and the prison of the Honour.

Previous to Lord Goring's appointment, Mr. James Chadwick, of Nottingham, was the prime mover in getting the powers of the Court revived.

"Chadwick, a fellow of most pragmatical temper, was at first a boy that scraped trenchers in the house of one of the poorest justices in the county, but yet such a one as had a great deal of formality and understanding of the statute law, from whom this boy picked such ends of law that he became first the justice's, then a lawyer's clerk ; then, I know not how, got to be a parcel judge in Ireland, and came over to his own country swelled with the reputation of it, and set on foot a base, obsolete, arbitrary court,[2] which the Conqueror of old had given one Peverel, his bastard, which this man entitling my lord Goring unto, executed the office under him, to the great abuse of the country. At the beginning of the Parliament they had

---

(1) Sir George Goring had been created Baron Goring, April 14. 1628 ; he was further advanced as Earl of Norwich, Nov. 8, 1646.. Pepys relates how "my Lord of Northwich, at a public audience before the King of France, made the Duke of Anjou cry, by making ugly faces as he was stepping to the King, but undiscovered."

(2) On the revival of the Court, it was for a time held in some old malt rooms, which stood on the site of the chapel in St. James's Street, previously mentioned.

prosecuted him for it, but that my Lord Goring begged of Sir Thomas Hutchinson to spare him, and promised to lay it down for ever ; so from the beginning of Parliament he executed not that office, but having an insinuating wit and tongue, procured himself to be deputy Recorder of Nottingham, my lord of Clare[1] being chief. Never was a truer Judas since Iscariot's time than he, for he would kiss the man he had in his heart to kill ; he naturally delighted in mischief and treachery, and was so exquisite a villian, that he destroyed those designs he might have thriven by, with overlaying them with fresh knaveries."[2]

Bailey says : " A careful perusal of the new charter under which the Court of the Honour of Peverel was at this time re-established, leads us to the conviction that the abuse directed by Mrs. Hutchinson against Chadwick, on account of the revival of this Court (save upon the principle that all Courts for recovery of debts, where a power to imprison is conferred, are radically base and arbitrary), is extremely unjust and improper. If imprisonment for debt was a cruelty and injustice to the country, the Peverel Court, as revived under Lord Goring, only shared the guilt which the rest of the legal tribunals of the country incurred in the incarceration of the persons of poor or fraudulent debtors, whilst the charter of its re-enactment contained divers provisions against the abuse of power, which did not exist in many of them, and more especially is this one, as it stood in its original formation : so that instead of Mr. Chadwick being deserving of the severe censures bestowed upon him, in such unbecoming language, by Mrs. Hutchinson, for the revival of this Court, it would more probably appear to every impartial person, that he was deserving of the highest praise for the care with which he guarded from abuse the administration of the law, in the case of actions for debt or trespasses, in this court,

---

(1) The above named " Lord of Clare " was John Holles, second Earl of Clare, eldest son of John, first Earl, by Anne, daughter of Sir Thomas Stanhope. He succeeded his father in 1637, and was appointed Recorder of Nottingham in 1642, Mr. Chadwick acting as his deputy. The Earl died January 2nd, 1665, and was buried in the Chapel of Our Lady (south transept) in St. Mary's Church, Nottingham.

(2) " Memoirs of Colonel Hutchinson," by his Widow.

by the wholesome provisions he caused to be engrafted in its charter."[1]

Besides being for several years deputy-recorder of Nottingham, as well as the Steward of the Peverel Court, Mr. Chadwick, sometimes known as Colonel Chadwick, served twice in Parliament as member for the town of Nottingham, and appears to have enjoyed the esteem and confidence of his constituents. By his own perseverance, combined with considerable talent, he had risen from very humble beginnings in life to the possession of property and influence beyond that of most men around him.[2] He appears to have had an extensive and profitable practice as a barrister, regularly keeping chambers in one of the Inns of Court, London, besides being engaged professionally as one of the inferior judges in Ireland. It is not difficult to discover, by a careful perusal of the *Memoirs*, what were the true grounds for the hostility which Colonel and Mrs. Hutchinson bore towards Chadwick. He considered the Colonel to be an enthusiast,[3] and the town to be insecure whilst in his keeping. In these respects he might be erroneous in his judgment, but there is no just reason for supposing that his motives were corrupt. There does not appear to be the least doubt that the charges brought against Mr. Chadwick by Mrs. Hutchinson, were false and malicious. It is impossible that any man, in those days, with such a character, could have secured the good-will and confidence, and lived in the esteem of persons of all ranks of life, as Mr. Chadwick did.[4]

---

(1) "Annals of Notts.," i. 642.    (2) See foot note, p. 394, *ante*.

(3) Colonel John Hutchinson was the eldest surviving son of Sir Thomas Hutchinson, by his first wife, Margaret, daughter of Sir John Byron, of Newstead, and was born at Nottingham, September, 1615. He married (July 3, 1638) Lucy, daughter of Sir Allen Apsley, Bart., late Lieutenant of the Tower of London, and served as Colonel in the Parliamentarian Army, having the Castle and Town of Nottingham in his keeping. At the trial of Charles I. he sat as a member of the High Commission Court, and signed the death warrant. After the Restoration he was confined in Sandown Castle, Kent. He died after eleven months' imprisonment, September 11, 1664, and was buried at Owthorpe, Notts.

(4) The descendants of Mr. James Chadwick continued for several generations in this neighbourhood. In 1742, upon the death of Thomas Mansfield, Esq., the manor of West Leeke and other estates devolved upon his nephew, Evelyn Chadwick, Esq., who was directly descended from the above named gentleman. This Evelyn Chadwick was the father of Georgiana, Lady Middleton, wife of Thomas, fourth Lord Middleton, who was High Steward of the Peverel Court, as will be seen hereafter.

On the 8th of April, in the 15th year of King Charles the First, George, Lord Goring, mortgaged the premises to Sir Thomas Lawley, Knight (afterwards created a baronet), for a large sum of money, but continued in possession until 1646, when, being a delinquent, his whole estate was sequestered.

On the 19th August, 1640, Lewis Chadwick and John Chadwick, farmers of the profits and perquisites of the Court of the Honour of Peverel, petitioned the King respecting the profits of the Court. The petitioners stated that the King by his letters patent had restored the courts and jurisdiction of his ancient honour of Peverel, and by a special warrant commanded his steward and judge of the courts to put them in full execution, wherefore petitioners had been persuaded by his steward, their kinsman, on his promise to perform the King's commands, to farm the profits of the courts, and thereupon increased the King's revenue five fold *(sic)* from 50*l.* to 300*l.* per annum, and that it would be increased to much more. Yet the Steward had not put the courts in full execution, to the great damage of the petitioners and the King's rights. They prayed the King to refer their petition to some of the Council, that they might call the Steward before them to show cause why he had not put the courts in execution according to the King's warrant, and to bring the warrant with him, and that he might be ordered thenceforth to put them in full execution, or that the increase of the King's revenue might be abated from 300*l.* to 50*l.* again, unless good cause was shown to the contrary. Under the petition was written a reference to the Lord Treasurer and another, authorising them to call the petitioners and the Steward before them and learn the true state of the business, and to certify the King their opinion what was fit to be done therein.[1] The result of this enquiry has not transpired.

Shaw[2] states that in 1638, Lewis Chadwick, of Mavesyn Ridware, in the county of Stafford, and John Chadwick, of Healey Hall, in the county of Lancaster, Esquires, succeeded

---

(1) *State Papers*, 1640, p. 606.
(2) Shaw's *History of Staffordshire*, vol. i., p. 183.

their kinsman, James Chadwick, in the office of Steward to
the Peverel Court. John Chadwick, who had married
Katherine, only daughter and eventual heiress of the above-
named Lewis Chadwick, took up his residence in Nottingham,
and held the rank of Lieut.-Colonel in the Parliamentary army.
Lewis Chadwick, who never appears to have resided in this
neighbourhood, was at one time Governor of the Island of
St. Lucia, in the West Indies, which he acquired by purchase.
He died in London, in 1655. John Chadwick died in 1669,
and was buried in the chancel of Rochdale Church, in
Lancashire.

After the estates of George, Lord Goring, had been escheated
for his alleged "delinquency," it was ordered, on the petition
of the widow of Sir Thomas Lawley, Baronet, to whom the
Bailiwick had been mortgaged, that the Committee of
Sequestration should either pay £1,450, then due to the Lady
Lawley for the principal and interest, or suffer her to enjoy
the premises.

In the meantime, Sir Percival Willoughby,[1] the Defendant
in the suit in the Exchequer (in which the Gorings were
Plaintiffs), took steps before the Committee of Sequestration
to recover some of his rights in the Honour of Peverel, as
did also his son, Sir Francis Willoughby, but without effect.

In 1658, the so-called "Lord Whalley,"[1] having expressed
his wish to have the jurisdiction of the Court of the Honour
of Peverel restored to Nottingham, from which, as we have
seen, it was exempted in 1321, the Corporation caused a letter

---

(1) Sir Percival Willoughby, Knight, represented the county of Nottingham in
the first Parliament of James I., and dying about the commencement of the civil
war, was succeeded by his only son, Sir Francis Willoughby, Knight, who married
Lady Cassandra Ridgway, daughter of Thomas, Earl of Londonderry. Sir Francis
died in 1665 and was succeeded by his only son, Francis Willoughby, Esq., the
eminent philosopher, who left two sons, Francis, the elder of whom, was created a
baronet in 1677, with remainder to his younger brother, Thomas, who eventually
succeeded to the baronetcy, and who was raised to the peerage as Baron Middleton,
of Middleton, in the county of Warwick, in 1711.

(1) Edward Whalley, a Major-General in the Parliamentary army, and one of the
Regicides, was a younger son of Richard Whalley, Esq., of Kirketon Hall, in the
parish of Screveton, by Frances, daughter of Sir Henry Cromwell, of Hinchinbroke,
in Huntingdonshire, and was thus cousin of Oliver Cromwell. During the Usurpation
he was called to the "Upper House," as one of Oliver's so-called peers. He fled
to America, and died at Hadley, Massachusetts, in 1678.

to be written to him, expressive of their disapproval of such proposed arrangement, when the project was abandoned.

On December 22, 1662, a Royal Warrant was issued authorizing the removal of the Court to the Shire Hall, Nottingham.

" Whereas O'r Court of Record for O'r Honour of Peverell was anciently kept in Our Castle of Nottingham, w'ch was demolished in the late Warrs, since w'ch time the same hath been kept in Our Shire-Hall for the County of Nottingham w'thin Our s'd Hono'r, Our will & pleasure [is] that Our s'd Court shall for the time to come, be held & kept in our s'd Shire-hall of Our s'd Countie of Nottingha' soe as the same in noe manor hinder or be prejudiciall to Our service of ye sd Countie. And Wee require Our Sheriff of Our sd Countie & all other Our officers & ministers to bee conformable hereunto. dated ye 22th day of Decemb. 1662."[1]

On the death of the first Earl of Norwich [2] (to whom the Bailiwick had been granted for life), Sir Francis Willoughby possessed himself again of his hereditary Bailiwick of the Honour of Peverel, though he does not seem to have exercised any jurisdiction in the Court of the Honour, as remodelled by King Charles I., inasmuch as King Charles II., by his Letters Patent bearing date April 14th, in the 16th year of his reign, granted to Charles, second Earl of Norwich,[3] and Henry Goring, Esquire,[4] the office of High Steward of the Honour of Peverel, and the office of keeping all Courts, Leets, Liberties and Views

---

(1) State Papers, 1662 : Warrant Book, p. 201.

(2) This nobleman was the son of George Goring, of Hurstpierpoint and Ovingdean, in Sussex. He received the honour of knighthood at Greenwich in 1608, and two years later was Gentleman of the Privy Chamber in Ordinary to Prince Henry, and afterwards Vice-Chamberlain to the Queen. He was elevated to the peerage in 1632, as Baron Goring, of Hurstpierpoint, and subsequently obtained a grant of the offices of Secretary, and clerk of the signet, and clerk of the council within the principality of Wales. He warmly espoused the cause of his sovereign on the outbreak of the unhappy civil contentions, and was further advanced to the earldom of Norwich in 1644. He died at Brentford, whilst on his way from Hampton Court to London, January the 6th, 1662-3, being then about eighty years of age, and was buried on the 14th of that month in Westminster Abbey.

(3) Charles, second Earl of Norwich, only surviving son of the first Earl, died without issue in 1672, when the title became extinct.

(4) Henry Goring derived his descent from an elder branch of the family, his great grandfather, Sir Henry Goring, of Burton, in Sussex, being the elder brother of George Goring, father of the first Earl of Norwich. This Henry Goring, who succeeded to a baronetcy, on the death of Sir James Bowyer, of Leighthorne, in Suffolk, by virtue of a special limitation, was the direct ancestor of the present Sir Charles Goring, Bart., of Highden, in Sussex.

of Frankpledge in the said Honour, for and during their lives and the life of the longer liver of them.

On the death of the second Earl of Norwich, without issue, and the surrender of the office in question by Henry Goring, the other co-grantee, King Charles II., by his Letters Patent, dated January 23rd, in the 25th year of his reign (1674), nominated and appointed Henry, Marquess of Worcester,[1] Charles, Lord Herbert, his eldest son, and Arthur, Lord Somerset, his second son, to the office of High Steward of the Honour of Peverel, for their lives, and the life of the longer liver of them. In these last-mentioned Letters Patent, the limits of this Court were further extended to the Manor of Worksop, to Chesterfield and other places in Derbyshire, and to Sheffield, Rotherham, etc., in Yorkshire, and a Court of Record was appointed to be held every Tuesday, in such place as the Steward of the Court of the Honour should from time to time appoint, and in the said Court should be heard and determined, all and singular pleas of debt, detinue, covenant, and broken account, trespass, trespass on the case, caption and detention of cattle, goods and chattels, and all other personal pleas and actions whatsoever, arising within the Honour aforesaid, so that the debts, damages, etc., exceed not the sum of 50l., etc. The Letters Patent also directed that the deputy steward to be appointed by the High Steward should be an utter Barrister; it also regulated his office and empowered him to appoint a Prothonotary. Simon Degge, a barrister,[2] was appointed Steward for life, and then Thomas Eyre for life, under the regulation of the High Steward.

---

(1) Henry, third Marquess of Worcester, succeeded his father in 1667, and was created Duke of Beaufort, December 2nd, 1682. He refused to subscribe the oath of allegiance to William III., and spent the latter part of his life in retirement. He died January 21st, 1699. Charles, Lord Herbert, was his eldest son, who, after his father was created Duke of Beaufort, had himself the courtesy title of Marquess of Worcester. He died in his father's lifetime. Arthur, Lord Somerset, was his younger brother.

(2) Sir Simon Degge (descended from Hugh Degge, of Stramshall,) was the son of Thomas Degge, who died in 1628. He married, first, Jane, daughter of Thomas Orrell, by whom he had one son, and, secondly, Alice Oldfield, widow of James Trollop, by whom he had two sons. He is described in Dugdale's *Visitation of Derbyshire* as "Symon Degge of Derby Esq on of ye Judges of South Wales Circuit 1667."

On the death of the last survivor of the three grantees
mentioned in King Charles II.'s Letters Patent, the family of
Willoughby once more endeavoured to obtain possession of the
Bailiwick of the Honour of Peverel, and for the purpose of
preventing all disputes for the future, applied to the Crown
for a grant in perpetuity of the Stewardship of the Honour
and the casual profits thereof. Queen Anne thereupon by Her
Letters Patent, dated June 22nd, in the fifth year of her reign
(1706), reciting that the office of High Steward of the Honour
of Peverel being only honorary, and having been long enjoyed
by the family of Sir Thomas Willoughby, Baronet, the Queen,
in consideration of the good and acceptable services performed
unto her by the said Sir Thomas Willoughby, granted "the
office and place of High Steward of the Honour of Peverel
in the county of Nottingham and Derby, and of all and every
the manors, lordships, lands, and hereditaments to the said
Honour belonging or appertaining together, to Sir Thomas Willoughby, Baronet, to have, hold, exercise, and enjoy, to the only
proper use and behoof of the said Sir Thomas Willoughby, and
of his heirs and assigns, for ever, in free and common soccage,
by the yearly rent of one peppercorn at the Feast of St. Michael,
if the same shall be lawfully demanded."

Sir Thomas Willoughby was raised to the peerage, December
the 31st, 1711, as Baron Middleton, of Middleton, in the county
of Warwick. His descendants held the office of High Steward
until the abolition of the Court in 1849, the last High Steward
being Digby, seventh Lord Middleton, who died unmarried,
Nov. 5, 1856.

The three successive Deputy Stewards of the Court at Basford, previous to the year 1751, were Mr. William Thorpe, Mr.
John Farnsworth, attorneys, and Edward Wilmot, Esq.,[1]
barrister-at-law, Mr. Francis Evans acting as Prothonotary
during the latter part of the Stewardship of the latter.

---

(1) Deering, p. 127. This author mentions a tradition that whilst the Court was
held at Nottingham, "the mace, which is now carried before the Mayor, used to be
carried before the Steward of the Peverel Court," this was probably an acknowledgment of the superior powers of the Court, and a similar custom is still observed in
some towns, where the Mayor's mace is carried before the Judges at the time of the
assizes.

John Howard, the philanthropist (born Sept. 2, 1726; died Jan. 20, 1790), visited in 1776 and 1779 the Peverel Prison at Basford, which he thus describes, "This is his majesty's gaol or prison of the court of record of his honour of Peverel and additional limits of the same in the counties of Nottingham and Derby. Thomas, Lord Middleton, high steward. One room with three beds. The keeper said he had another little room for women-prisoners; but having none of that sex, he made use of it for his servants. The house is his freehold. Fees; 13s. 4d. by the court roll. The debts were from forty shillings to fifty pounds, but *now* are from ten pounds (see 19 George III. cap. lxx.) to fifty pounds.[1] 1776, Sept. 24, 3 prisoners; 1779, Sept. 20, 2 prisoners."

In the Records of the Manor Court of Lenton is the following entry referring to the Peverel Court :—

" 1788. 25 Mar, Deduct for Mr. Cooper's Fine it appearing that he was obliged to attend the Court of Tryals at Basford being subpœned to give Evidence in a Cause Tryed there—5s."

In 1789, John Balguy, Esq., of Swanwick, in Derbyshire, was the Deputy Steward.

Previous to the removal of the Court to Lenton at the close of the year 1790, the Gaoler, John Sands, liberated all the prisoners because he had no food allowed for their support, and because he was legally advised that if any of them died from want of food, he would be liable to take his trial as a murderer. On December 1st, 1790, the Court was held for the first time at the Coffee-house, Lenton.

Blackner, who visited the prison in 1796, thus writes :—" I went with a friend, one morning in February, to see what havoc stern winter had made in the coffee-house gardens at Lenton, which had been represented to me as a kind of paradise in the summer season; being unconscious, at that time, that one of the most wretched mansions of human misery stood within their precincts. Several robins were fluttering upon the keenly frozen snow, in quest of scattered crumbs; and a black-

---

(1) " The State of the Prisons in England and Wales," by John Howard, F.R.S., second edition, 1780, p. 284.

27

bird, all shivering with cold, was hopping from spray to spray. The wind whistled, and bleak, from the north east, the angry blast blew. While walking in pensive admiration, my ears were stricken with the sound of a human voice, the tremulous cadence of which bespoke the anguish of the bosom whence it came. These were the words which it uttered :—'God bless you, master, pray relieve a poor prisoner, famishing for want of food, and trembling with cold.' A clap of thunder would not have made so deep an impression on the memory —death alone can remove the impression from the heart. Hastily turning about, a man appeared, peeping through a hole in a door, with a beard of four weeks' growth upon his face, which was otherwise haggard and meager, his eyeballs glaring with anxiety, and his body sparingly clad in filthy rags. 'What! a prison in a pleasure garden!' was the first exclamation that presented itself—'and pray what is your offence, my poor man? and what your means of subsistence?' 'My offence,' replied the victim, 'is that of running twenty-five shillings in debt, when my family was nearly perishing with hunger, during last year's famine (1795), and which I have not been able to pay ; and my means of subsistence (while, with a look which was half sarcastic, and half expressive of his sufferings, he pointed towards a pump), my means of subsistence are all within that well, except a few scraps which the keeper pleases to give me, for cleaning his knives and his shoes.' What! is it to be borne, that, in what is called a land of liberty, a human being is to be incarcerated within four walls, without bread and without fire. '*That is all*,' replied the prisoner, still pointing towards the pump; 'and, as my wife and children are now supported by the parish, not one of them can come near me to cheer me with a smile.' Without calculating upon consequences, or reflecting that my strength was inadequate to the performance of what the wounded feelings of the heart suggested, I immediately set my shoulder to the door, with the hope of wresting it from its hateful hinges ; but the unhappy man stopt me by saying, 'You will only, by a vain attempt, bring yourself into trouble, and add much to mine ; for, if I should obtain the keeper's displeasure, he will not give me a morsel of bread to prolong my miserable existence, till the rules of this court will permit me to leave this abode of sorrow; in which case I must die of want here, and never see my disconsolate family more.' A flood of tears gave relief to the writer's half-bursting heart, he forced the small contents of his pockets into the hands of the wretched sufferer, and then fled from this disgraceful dreg of the feudal law."[1]

Some authorities state that when the Court was first removed to Lenton it was held in a room over the Priory gateway, and was afterwards removed thence to the White Hart Inn, which was erected in 1804 by Mr. Wombwell, who afterwards had charge of the prisoners, special apartments in the rear being set apart as a prison.[2]

In 1815 the High Steward's deputy was John Balguy, Esq., barrister-at-law, and Mr. S. Sanders, solicitor, was prothonotary. The Court was held before the prothonotary every Tuesday, and the writs issued were returnable the next Court day following that on which they were issued; and a general Court, called "The Court of Trials," at which the High Steward, in whose name the processes were witnessed, was supposed to preside, was held twice a year, but the Act preventing arrests for debts under £10 deprived it of much of its business. The inhabitants of the Honour only were liable to serve on its juries.

It appears to have been the custom of the overseers of Lenton to pay for the maintenance of poor prisoners in the Peverel gaol, and to recover the amounts from the parishes to which they belonged. The following entries are taken from the accounts of the overseers of Lenton:—

| | | | |
|---|---|---|---|
| 1792. | Paid to a Man's wife, who is in the Peveral Prison, having fitts ... ... ... ... | 1 | 0 |
| 1823. | W & J Readish in P'v'r'l ... ... ... | 7 | 0 |
| 1824. | Recd of Parish of Stapleford for Peverel ... | 6 15 | 0 |
| 1827. | Recd. on Order for removal from Peverel of Wheatley (Lincoln) ... ... ... ... | 4 4 | 6 |

---

(1) Blackner's *History of Nottingham*, 1816, p. 105.

(2) In the year 1842, the Court was held temporarily at the Plough Inn, Old Radford.

1830.  To Relief of Wm. Pegg in Peveral prison, not
recovered    ...     ...     ...     ...     ...     **3**  6
1835.  Wm. Hopewell in Peverall Prison    ...     ...     **3**  6
1836.  Recovered from the Parishes of Hucknall Torkard and Denby for examinations of Peveral
Prisoners    ...     ...     ...     ...     ...     3  4  0
1837.  To 65 days relief to Joseph White a pauper of
this parish in Peveral Prison for debt from
the 27th Jany to 30th March inclusive at 6d.
per diem    ...     ...     ...     ...     ...     1  12  6
1838.  Received from the Overseers of Hoveringham
for Relief of Thomas Broughton in Peveral
Prison ...     ...     ...     ...     ...     ...     3  4  6

Close by the prison was (and is) a bowling green, where the
players and company were waited upon by the prisoners,
from which (notwithstanding Blackner's pathetic story, probably
somewhat highly coloured) it is evident that their confine-
ment was not very rigorous.   The Court room contained
several old portraits, presumably of former Stewards, but they
have been dispersed during the last few years.   The prison
still remains.   It is a small brick building, 48 feet long and
15 feet wide, two stories in height, and contains three rooms
on each floor.   The windows are protected by massive iron
bars set in strong oak frames, and overlook a small courtyard,
about 30 feet long by 18 feet wide, surrounded by a high
brick wall.   This courtyard appears to have been enclosed
after Blackner's visit to the prison in 1796, when he says the
prison overlooked the adjoining pleasure garden.

According to a return, in accordance with an order of the
House of Commons, it appears that the number of summonses
issued by the Court during the year ending July 1, 1848,
amounted to 1,344, being an increase of more than 850 on
the average of the three previous years.   During the same
year the fees received amounted to £228, being upwards of
£150 more than the average.   This great increase was principally owing to the fact that the number of summonses
issued in the town of Sheffield in the year ending July, 1848,
amounted to 880, or 850 above the average of the preceding
three years.   The return also contains the plaintiffs' costs
incurred in two actions, in one of which, where the amount

of debt recovered amounted to £2 14s. 11d., the plaintiff's costs alone were £17 11s. od., and in another, where the amount recovered was £5 12s. 8d., the plaintiff's costs amounted to £40 16s. 4d., or when they were taxed, to £26 17s. 10d.

Some idea of the manner in which the business of the Court was conducted in its latter days may be obtained from the following extract from the *Nottingham Review*, March 24, 1848 :—

### PEVEREL COURT OF TRIALS.

A court for the trial of causes was held on Tuesday last [March 21, 1848,] at the White Hart Inn, Lenton, near this town. John Barker, Esq., barrister-at-law, the Judge and Deputy Steward of the Honour of Peverel, attended by Abraham Cann, Esq., prothonotary, Mr. William Johnson, the capital bailiff, and a number of professional gentlemen, took his seat at ten o'clock in the morning, and the following gentlemen were sworn in as the jury. [Here follows list of jury and particulars of thirteen cases tried.]   The business occupied the court until four o'clock, when the judge, jury, and professional gentlemen sat down to dinner, which was got up in the most recherché style by the landlord, and consisted of every delicacy.   After the cloth was drawn, Abraham Cann, Esq., took the chair, and Mr. Thomas Flower (foreman of the jury) the vice-chair; and harmony and conviviality were kept up for some time.

At the Court held June 5, 1849, three men from Ripley were each ordered to be imprisoned for 40 days in Derby County Gaol, for refusing to pay debts and costs.

The following is a copy of a blank form of "jury summons" in the possession of the author :—

Mr.

By virtue of a Venire Facías to me directed, I do hereby summon you to appear and serve on the Jury, at the next Court of Trials, to be held for the Honor of Peverel, and additional limits of the same, at the House of the Lenton Coffee House, situate at Lenton, in the County of Nottingham, on Tuesday the        Day of          18

      Dated this              Day of          18

                       Capital Bailiff of the said Court.

The seal used by the Peverel Court obviously dates from about the time when the additional limits were granted to the Court. An old seal, here engraved full size, bears within its inner circle, on a field *vaire*, the Imperial Crown, to denote the possession of the Court by the Sovereigns of England ; and in the outer circle, the legend, HONOR DE PEVERELL ET ADDICONAL LIMIT. The seal in use previous to the abolition

of the Court, also engraved full size, from an engraving made for the late Mr. William Stretton, varies somewhat from the above, the legend on this latter seal being, HONOR DE PEVEREL ET ADDIC LIMIT EIVS.

In 1849, a Bill was prepared and brought into the House of Commons by the Attorney-General and Mr. Cornewall Lewis "to amend the Act for the more easy recovery of small debts and demands in England, and to abolish certain inferior Courts of Record." This Bill received the Royal assent, August 1st, and became law as 12th and 13th Vict., cap. 101. Sections 13 and 14 abolished "the Court of the Marshalsea of Household of the Kings of England, and the Court of our Lady the Queen of the Palace of the Queen at Westminster, and her Majesty's Court of Record for the Honour of Peveril and additional limits of the same," the powers of which ceased on the 31st day of December, 1849, the actions or suits then pending therein being transferred to the Court of Common Pleas, or the County Court, as the case required. The records of the abolished courts were, by section 16, placed under the care of the Master of the Rolls. Section 17 provided compensation to the officers of the abolished courts, the amounts of which were determined by the Commissioners of her Majesty's Treasury.

The last sitting (Nov., 1849) of this ancient Court was held without a case being heard, and it was formally adjourned, never to sit again. Thus, shorn of its former dignity and power, passed away a relic of the feudal system, which, after strange vicissitudes, survived to the middle of the nineteenth century.

The Records of the Court were removed, by virtue of a warrant of the Master of the Rolls, dated 18th July, 1854, to the New Repository at the Public Record Office, where they are now deposited.

# SECTION XVII.

## GEOLOGY.[1]

### PHYSICAL FEATURES.

HE greater part of the parish of Lenton lies in the Trent Valley, which crosses the southern part of the parish, and consists of low flat meadow, drained by several brooks and numerous artificial watercourses. The Trent Valley—here more than a mile and a quarter wide—approaches Lenton from the south-west, but about the middle of the parish this course becomes deflected into a more easterly direction. Viewed from the high ground on either side, the Trent Valley is seen to be a broad expanse of meadow, picturesquely dotted with trees, and divided by a network of hedgerows. It is bounded on each side by low escarpments, which sometimes take the form of steep grassy slopes half hidden by clumps of dense wood, sometimes a low cliff for a short distance. In some parts, again (though scarcely so within this parish), the escarpments merge almost imperceptibly into the river plain, and it is not easy to tell where the

---

(1) Contributed by Mr. James Shipman, of Nottingham, author of papers on "The Alluvial and Drift Deposits of the Trent Valley, near Nottingham," "Triassic Rocks of Nottingham and Cheshire," "Alluvial and Drift Deposits of the Leen Valley," etc.

plain ends and the escarpment begins. The northern escarpment or boundary of the alluvial plain of the Trent winds through Highfield Park, just in front of Highfield House, forming the cliff of Bunter Sandstone that overlooks the lake there, and then on towards Spring Close. Between Highfield Park and Spring Close the line of escarpment takes a sudden bend to the north for three or four hundred yards, and sweeps round so as to form a small bay, ending at the back in a low cliff of the crimson Lower Mottled Sandstone, the bright red rock forming a charming contrast with the dark green foliage of the young trees that cluster round its brow. This hollow—now smoothly grass-grown, and with little to indicate how it got formed—was probably scooped out by a sharp bend in the course of the Trent at this spot, at a time when it flowed at a slightly higher level than now, or, in other words, before the river had eaten its way down to its present level, and when its course lay along this side of the valley. Between Spring Close and New Lenton the Trent escarpment is broken through by the broad shallow gap by which the Leen enters the Trent Valley, but it reappears in the form of a low cliff of Bunter Sandstone at the back of the bleach works on the Lenton Boulevard, near the end of Willoughby Street. The continuation of the escarpment to the east is marked by the line of low cliffs, now for the most part crowned with villas, that overlooks the old course of the Leen, and on by the "Rock Holes" in Nottingham Park, to the noble buttress of Bunter Sandstone on which the Castle stands.

Thus the more elevated ground of the parish is confined to the northern half. The most important physical feature of this part is of course the Leen Valley. The Leen Valley is a somewhat wide but shallow depression that enters the parish on the north, and with a north-and-southerly trend joins the Trent Valley, as already stated, between Spring Close on one side and New Lenton on the other. The Leen itself meanders through a level tract of meadow land, comparatively dry in some parts, but marshy in others, and of an average width of about 400 yards throughout this parish, though much narrower in places higher up the stream.

As we recede from the banks of the Leen to the east the ground rises very gently at first, then more rapidly till we reach the most elevated parts of the parish. The highest point is at Sion Hill, on the Derby road, which is the extreme eastern limit of the parish. This is 257 feet above the sea-level, or about 170 feet above the level of the river Leen near Lenton Station, and about 174 feet above the average level of the Trent Meadow at Lenton. On the west a gently swelling ridge, picturesquely wooded here and there with plantations or clumps of trees, stretches from the edge of the Trent escarpment in Highfield Park on the south, to Wollaton Hall, near the extreme north-west corner of the parish. The highest point on this ridge—near Lenton Hall—is about 200 feet above the sea-level, or about 117 feet above the level of the alluvial plain of the Trent. West of this ridge lies one of the most picturesque bits in the parish. It is an irregular shaped shallow valley, very prettily wooded, along the bottom of which the diminutive Tottle Brook skips merrily on towards the Trent, and forms the boundary of the parish for some distance on that side.

## General Description.

No similar area within the extended borough of Nottingham contains so great a variety of rocks as the parish of Lenton. Indeed, all the formations met with in other parts of the borough, except the Permian Magnesian Limestone and Marl, are brought together here almost side by side, within a comparatively very small space. And the description of the rocks of Lenton will apply almost equally well, as far as it goes, to the same rocks where they happen to occur in other parts of Nottingham. It may be wondered why there should be so many different kinds of rocks in this parish compared with other parts of the borough. The secret of the matter is, that the rocks over a large part of the north-west corner of the parish have been very much shattered and dislocated by "faults," by means of which large patches and strips of the ground have been in some cases lowered two or three hundred feet, and thus brought down to the same level as some of the underlying older rocks. These earth-move-

ments have produced such a transformation that the more
disturbed portion of the ground forms quite a mosaic, composed
of different kinds of rocks, red clay being brought down alongside
yellow sandrock, and one kind of sandrock thrown down side by
side with another and much older kind, and so on. The rocks
have not only been fractured, and the broken patches displaced,
but in some instances the strata have been tilted, and caused to
slope in directions quite contrary to what they would do if
they had remained unbroken. These lines of fracture cross the
parish for the most part in a west-north-westerly direction, but
there are doubtless cross-fractures that run at right angles to
these in some spots. Some parts of the area, again, have
yielded unequally to the strain, and have left strips of older rocks
wedged in between newer strata. All this ground is now, however, carved into smoothly-rounded slopes and hollows, and we
may walk across these dislocations from one formation on to
another without meeting with any sign at the surface to indicate
that any such physical movement of the rocks had ever taken place.
Much of the ground of this part is concealed by plantations and
ornamental gardens attached to the mansions of the neighbourhood.
The ground is still further obscured by superficial deposits of
sand and clay, so that it is almost impossible to trace out all the
details of this complex area on the map. Curiously enough, too,
the features on which the geologist has to depend so much for
his information—such as cliffs, and quarries, and other natural
or artificial exposures, by which he is enabled to infer the
structure of the ground in parts where no rock is visible, are
remarkable for their scarcity. Such exposures of the rocks as
do exist have therefore to be made the most of. Fortunately,
however, the borings for coal on the Clifton estate, on the south-
east side of the parish, and at Highfield Park, have revealed the
character and thickness of the rocks in areas where they are
completely out of the reach of observation at the surface—
namely, underneath the alluvial gravel of the Trent. These
borings, and the sinking of the Clifton Colliery shafts, also
afford valuable data as to the direction taken by the main
"faults" when they disappear under the alluvium of the Trent.

The following is a list of the formations represented within

and was brought by rapid currents coming from different
quarters, which caused the materials to be thrown down irregularly along the bottom, in the form of small sand-banks, or
shoals. This kind of deposition takes place mostly at the
mouths of rivers, or where rivers empty their waters into lakes.
Slabs of sandstone, finely laminated, and containing broad
ripples, were occasionally met with. The ripples must, of
course, have been impressed on the sediment while it was still
in a soft state, and could only have been produced where the
water was very shallow. The same process may be seen going
on on our sea-beaches at the present day, where the ripples
produced by the wind on the surface of the water along the
shore become registered on the soft sand of the beach. Many
of the blocks of sandstone, when broken open, were found to
contain the stems and sometimes the rootlets of the trees and
plants that flourished during the Carboniferous Period, and that
helped to form the coal. The plant remains most frequently
met with, perhaps, were those of *Stigmaria*, so called on
account of the pittings arranged in lozenge-shaped pattern all
round the stem. Each pit contains a small nipple, and to the
nipple there is attached a long ribbon-shaped black filament.
The whole thing has a very root-like look, the *Stigmaria* being
the larger branches of the root and the filaments the rootlets.
These fossil plants generally made their appearance as flattened
stems, with a row of filaments down each side, the whole
being quite black and carbonised. These fossil *Stigmaria* are
the roots of the trees that went to form coal, and are always
met with underneath seams of coal, in what is known as the
"underclay," which is in reality the soil on which the coal-
plants grew. The same phenomenon was observed to occur
at Wilford. *Stigmaria* was at one time thought to be a distinct
plant of itself, but many years ago it was found to be merely
the root of another plant that had long been known as
*Sigillaria*, or "seal-like stem." The stem of *Sigillaria* is
marked by a broad fluting, studded at intervals with seal-like
impressions, on account of which the tree was so named.
Fragments of the stem of this tree are sometimes met with in
coal, but few or no specimens of it were met with in the Coal

Measure rocks at Wilford, though it is frequently found in Derbyshire. Another remarkable tree that seems to have flourished in great abundance in Coal Measure times is called *Lepidodendron*, or "scaly-tree," on account of the lozenge-shaped markings of the stem, which bear some resemblance to the scales of a fish. These markings are not the scales themselves with which the bark was originally covered, however. In its young state, the bark of *Lepidodendron* had scale-like leaves, which shrivelled up and fell off as it grew older, leaving its stem marked with lozenge-shaped leaf-scars, as we now find it. Some of these trees are estimated to have attained a height of a hundred feet. Stems of *Lepidodendron* are frequently found in the Coal Measures of Nottinghamshire and Derbyshire, and are easily recognised by the diamond-shaped markings all over their bark. Occasionally stems and leaves of coal plants, sometimes beautifully preserved, and showing the most delicate venation, were found when the slabs of shale came to be split open, all matted together, as if they had been washed down into a lake, and so got buried. Several beautiful leaves of *Sphenopteris* were met with in this way. A plant frequently met with in the massive sandstone beds passed through in the shafts at Wilford was a jointed and fluted stem, tapering at one end into an obtuse point, like a cucumber. The joints or nodes were three or four inches apart, and gave it the appearance of a sugar-cane; while branching from each side were flattened rootlets, about six inches long. This was the *Calamite*, or "stone-reed." The nearest approach to the *Calamite* among the flora of the present day is the *equisetum*, or "horse-tail," which, like its ancient prototype, loves marshy spots. The *Calamite* may have been floated down the rivers of the period till it lodged on some sandbank and got buried, or it may possibly have grown on the spots where we now find it. Thus, the flora of the Coal Measures consisted of gigantic tree ferns, conifers, and club-mosses, and reed-like plants allied to the "horse-tails." These ferns attained the size of the largest trees of the present day, and altogether the Coal Measure flora has been compared to the present aspect of the vegetation of New Zealand.

With regard to the origin of coal, it is now an established fact that it was formed from plants which sprang up, grew, and died on the spot where coal is now found. " It is now very generally admitted that many English and other coals are little else but an aggregation of minute rounded bodies known as spores, that were shed by a tree called *Lepidodendron*." " Professor Huxley says that these spores are always present, and in the purest and best coal they make up nearly the whole mass." It seems however, that the portions of the plants which furnished the coal are not always the same. " The ground on which the trees grew was probably such as we could hardly call dry land, but was rather a spread of swamps and marshes like those of Central Africa, or that border the delta of the Mississippi. In some cases it may have been covered with water to a moderate depth, so that the roots and the lower part of the stems were submerged, while the larger part of the trunks and branches rose into the air. But whether the plants grew in marshes or on ground just submerged beneath water, coal may be looked upon as a product of what was practically land growth, and each seam of coal indicates the existence of a land surface at the time it was formed."

" Cannel coal," a thin seam of which occurs in the Coal Measures underneath Lenton, " was probably formed in a somewhat different manner to black or common coal. Cannel coal always occurs in dish-shaped patches, thinning away to nothing on all sides. It frequently merges insensibly into highly carbonaceous black shale, and contains occasionally the remains of fishes. The presence of fossil fishes in cannel coal shows that it must have been formed under water, and it probably consists of vegetable matter which was drifted down into ponds or lakes and lay soaking till it became reduced to a pulp. The deposit was, of course, limited in extent by the banks of the sheet of water in which it was formed, and hence the lenticular shape which beds of cannel exhibit. The maceration it has undergone has to a large extent effaced all traces of vegetable structure in cannel coal, but spores can now and then be still detected in it." [1]

Two seams of ironstone containing the supposed fresh-water bivalve—*Anthracosia*—were passed through in sinking the Clifton pits. In these seams the shells lay thickly packed together, so thick, indeed, as to almost compose the whole bed, with their valves united, just as they had lived, showing that they had not been washed down from some other part, but that the ironstone had quietly segregated round the shells in the lake or marsh which they had inhabited. Four or five of these shelly ironstone bands were met with in the Highfield Park boring, and were, no doubt, the continuation of the same beds as those found at Wilford. They have been met with similarly in the Coal Measures of Derbyshire. The occurrence of these seams of ironstone crowded with shells goes to confirm the impression derived from other evidence, that the Coal Measure strata were mostly formed in shallow wide-spreading inland lakes and marshes, which soon became silted up sufficiently to give root to the moisture-loving plants of the period, and which a slight depression or sinking of the bottom after a time again converted into open lakes. That the sandstones, shales, and clays of the Coal Measures were deposited close to land is proved by the stems and leaves of plants which they contain, for these could not have been floated far without being destroyed altogether. Some of the laminæ or layers which go to make up the shales are so thin that a large number may be counted in the thickness of an inch. Only one of these layers could have been deposited at once, and there is reason to believe that an interval of time—how long or how short we cannot tell—elapsed between the formation of each thin leaf of sediment. It is therefore clear that an enormous amount of time must have been required to bring about the various physical changes by which the seams of coal came to be overlaid with considerable thicknesses of various kinds of strata piled layer upon layer.

---

(1) The passages above quoted, besides many of the notes about the coal plants, are extracted from "Coal: Its History and Uses," by Professors Green, Miall, etc., of the Yorkshire College of Science, in which will be found much valuable and interesting matter bearing further on this subject.

28

Returning now to the work of tracing what becomes of the Coal Measures when they pass out of sight underneath the Lower Mottled Sandstone north of Wollaton Park, the Government Geological Survey map of this district (71 N.E.) represents the Coal Measures as rising to the surface over a large area on the north side of Wollaton Park. This is a mistake, however, for a thickness of something like thirty feet of Lower Mottled Sandstone was met with where, according to the Government Geological Survey Map, there ought to have been Coal Measure rocks, during the excavations for a new gas-holder at Old Radford Gas-works. As a matter of fact, the Lower Mottled Sandstone stretches, in the form of a thin sheet of soft red sand, nearly as far north as the Radford Canal, or about a quarter of a mile north of the Ilkeston road. What probably led to the mistake in the mapping of this part, by which the Coal Measures were represented as forming the surface rock over a large space that is really occupied by the Lower Mottled Sandstone, was the dark stiff Drift clay which overspreads the surface of the ground over the north-east corner of Wollaton Park, and which was evidently derived from the Coal Measures, as we shall have occasion to notice at a later stage of these notes. Then, again, the Lower Mottled Sandstone being very thin, the Coal Measures actually do peep out in one spot along a slight depression in the ground at the foot of the north slope of the low ridge on which Wollaton Hall stands, but beyond the boundary of this parish. Grey shales and yellow clay belonging to the Coal Measures again make their appearance below the Lower Mottled Sandstone in the ditch by the east side of the pond in Wollaton Park. Coal Measure clays are also traceable in the plantation at the outflow of the pond on the west, where they are brought up by small dislocations alongside the Lower Mottled.

The continuation southward of the Coal Measures so close to the surface is, however, suddenly interrupted along a line drawn from the south side of the pond in Wollaton Park to Lenton Hall, and thence onward in a south-easterly direction. Along this line a "fault," or dislocation, throws down all the rocks on the south side ninety-five yards. The effect of this is that the whole of the Triassic rocks of the district—from the Lower Mottled Sandstone to the Upper Keuper Marl—have to be penetrated in order to reach the Coal Measures, which, north of this line of fissure, as we have seen, lie almost at the surface. Before the Clifton Colliery was opened out indeed, it was doubted by some whether workable Coal Measures would be found so far south, and underneath the newer rocks of the Trias. It was feared that the Coal Measures, the outcrop of which is seen, west of Wollaton, steadily veering round from a north-and-southerly to an east-and-westerly direction, would, for the most part, have cropped out north of the Trent, and that any attempt to reach coal farther south would be fruitless. This impression was not founded on any very scientific reasoning, or on a close acquaintance with the facts presented by the geological map of the district, and was certainly not warranted by the results of the borings on the Clifton estate. Nevertheless, the results of the boring operations were looked forward to with a good deal of curiosity, partly as clearing up a point of great local interest, partly on account of the effect the discovery of coal so close to Nottingham might be expected to have on the commercial aspect of the question.

The first attempt to solve the problem of the continuation of the Coal Measures on the south side of the great "fault" was made near Clifton Hall, on the south bank of the Trent, many years ago. No record of what was met with in this bore-hole, however, was preserved, and when, in the year 1867. boring operations were resumed on this estate, the work had to be begun *de novo*.

In a boring made in the Brickyard Spinney, at the entrance to Clifton Grove, on the south side of the Trent, in 1867, however, the Coal Measures were reached at a depth of 171 yards from the surface, which is here composed of Upper Keuper Marl; and at a depth of 186 yards a seam of coal, 6ft. 3in. thick, believed to be the "Top Hard," was passed through. Later in the same year another bore-hole was made on the north bank of the Trent, and only a few yards to the

south-west of the site of the present Clifton Colliery shafts.[1]
Here the Coal Measures were reached at a depth of 153 yards,
but the Top Hard coal was not recognised, on account of the
bore-hole passing through the great "fault" which traverses
the rocks at this spot, by which the strata were much broken
and confused, and great difficulty was experienced in obtaining
proper samples.    Below this, however, the strata became
stronger, and at 188 yards a seam of coal, 3ft. 2in. thick,
which afterwards proved to be the Dunsil, was passed through.
Large feeders of water were met with from 70 to 140 yards
deep, and the water rose forcibly over the top of the bore-hole,
increasing the difficulty of keeping the hole open below the
broken strata, and of obtaining samples.[2]    .

In sinking the shafts for the Clifton Colliery the Coal
Measures were reached at a depth of 52 yards, as against
153 yards at the adjacent bore-hole.    A heading was afterwards made from the Deep Hard workings through the "fault"
into the strata on the down-throw side in the vicinity of the
bore-hole, and a "staple pit" was sunk for a few yards.    The
Top Hard coal was then found at a depth of 165 yards from
the surface.    It was then proved by actual levellings that this
"fault" had a down-throw to the south-west of 95 yards.

A comparative section of the strata passed through in the
two boreholes at Wilford and in the shaft, shows some interesting facts :—

|  | Spinney Borehole. | Borehole north of the Trent. | Shaft. |
|---|---|---|---|
|  | Yards. | Yards. | Yards. |
| Thickness of Keuper | 93 | 64 | No Keuper. |
| Thickness of Bunter | 78 | 82 | 44 |
| Depth to Coal Measures | 171 | 153 | 52 |
| Depth to "Top Hard" | 186 | 166 | 70 |

At the Highfield Park borehole, which was made close by
the north side of the Midland line, south-east of the house,
and near the rising suburb of Dunkirk, the Coal Measures

---

(1) It may be here mentioned that the Clifton Colliery is situated just outside the
south-east boundary of the parish.

(2) "Description of some Borings on the Clifton Estate," etc., by J. Brown,
F.G.S., p. 3.

were reached below 22 feet of alluvium of the Trent, and
230 feet of Lower Mottled Sandstone and Bunter, no record
having been kept apparently of the thickness of these formations individually. Thus the Coal Measures were here found
to lie at a total depth beneath the meadow of 252 feet. The
first beds of Coal Measure strata passed through at this
spot consisted of gray sandstone with clay partings, below
which came ironstone and shale, blue bind, and so on. At
a total depth of 299 feet, a seam of coal, 2 feet 4½ inches thick,
was pierced, and in less than 20 feet below this another coal
seam, 2 feet thick, was found. The third coal proved to be a
seam of cannel, 2 feet in thickness, which was found at a depth
of 319 feet. A similar seam of cannel was also met with in
the Clifton Colliery shafts, but it was there only 9½ inches
thick, showing that Highfield Park lies nearer the centre of
the basin-shaped hollow, in which there is reason to suppose
it was formed. The fourth seam of coal, 1 ft. thick, was met
with at 354 feet. At a depth of 429 feet, the boring rod passed
through a band of shell ironstone (*Anthracosia*), and at 433 feet
more fossils were noticed. At 435 feet, there was a seam of
coal 7½ inches thick, which would, of course, be too thin to
work; and at a depth of 467 feet a bed of conglomerate was
passed through, though what its precise character was is not
recorded. A conglomerate was also met with at a similar
horizon in the Clifton shafts, where it is described as " cank,"
or impure coal, and may therefore be taken to indicate the
breaking up over a large area of a coal seam by the agents
of denudation, as we know did sometimes happen during the
formation of the Coal Measure strata. Ironstone bind, with
layers of plant impressions, was observed at a depth of 514
feet, and at 560 feet the " Deep Soft " coal, 4 feet thick, was
reached. Boring operations were discontinued at a total depth
of 610 feet from the surface, when the " Deep Hard " coal was
pierced, with a thickness of 6 feet 3 inches.

The following table shows the thickness and depth below
the surface of the seams of coal proved in the Clifton shafts
compared with the corresponding coals met with at Highfield
Park. The particulars relating to the coal seams met with at

the Clifton Colliery are taken from Mr. Brown's paper, already quoted ; the figures relating to the Highfield boring are from information courteously given me some years ago by Mr. E. J. Lowe, F.R.S.

| | | HIGHFIELD PARK. | | | CLIFTON COLLIERY. | |
|---|---|---|---|---|---|---|
| | | Thickness. Ft. In. | Depth. Ft. | | Thickness. Ft. In. | Depth. Ft. |
| 1. | Comb Coal ⎫ | | ... | | 2  8 | 180 |
| 2. | Top Hard ⎪ | Absent at | ... | | 6  0 | 210 |
| 3. | Dunsil ⎬ | Highfield | ... | | 3  0 | 282 |
| 4. | Waterloo ⎭ | | ... | | 3  3 | 309 |
| 5. | Coal | 2  4 | 299 | | 2  4 | 462 |
| 6. | Coal | 2  0 | 316 | | 1  11 | 482 |
| 7. | Cannel Coal | 2  0 | 319 | | 0  9½ | 486 |
| 8. | Coal | 1  0 | 354 | | 1  8[1] | 528 |
| 9. | Coal | ... | ... | | 0  11 | 608 |
| 10. | Coal | ... | ... | | 2  10 | 694 |
| 11. | Deep Soft | 4  0 | 560 | | 5  0 | 718 |
| 12. | Deep Hard | 6  3 | 610 | | 5  7 | 761 |
| 13. | Piper Coal[2] | ... | ... | | 3  4 | 801 |

From this table it will be seen that the Coal Measure strata met with at Highfield begin some distance down the Clifton section. As a matter of fact, the highest beds of the Coal Measures met with at Highfield come 267 feet below the top of the Coal Measures at Wilford ; in other words, 267 feet of strata have been removed from the top of the Coal Measures at Highfield Park, compared with their thickness at Clifton Colliery. The Highfield section, in fact, commences between the fourth and fifth coals of the Clifton section, and all the seams above this, including the " Waterloo," the " Dunsil," the " Top Hard," and the " Comb Coal," have cropped out in the intermediate ground. The measures below the " Waterloo," however, are tolerably well represented, showing that the attenuation of the Coal Measures going west is due to the rapid rise and consequent cropping out of the strata in that

(1) This coal, in reality, consists of two seams, each ten inches thick, parted by two inches of bass.

(2) Boring at Highfield was discontinued before reaching this coal.

direction, and not to any original diminution in thickness in that quarter.

A boring made in the Trent Valley at Chilwell, in 1875, about a mile-and-a-half south-west of the Highfield bore-hole, showed that the Coal Measure strata crop out still more rapidly in that direction.  Here the thickness of strata that has cropped out, or been removed, appears to be so great that it was found impossible to correlate the results met with in the two bore-holes, and it was believed that the Chilwell section commenced below the Highfield measures altogether.  The Chilwell boring was begun in the Trent alluvium, which was found to be 16 feet 6 inches thick.  Below the alluvium the boring rod entered the Upper Keuper Marl, and below this again, the Bunter and Lower Mottled Sandstone, but no record was kept apparently of the thickness of these subdivisions of the Trias, the various alternations of the strata being described as "brown rock," "red clay and white bands," "sand rock and thin bands," "rock band and clunch," and so on, according to their respective lithological characters, without any attempt being made to assign them to the particular formation to which they belonged. And even this was done in so crude a way, that it is impossible now for anyone to tell where one formation ends and another begins.  All we can do is to infer that in the 459 feet of strata passed through before reaching undoubted Coal Measures, all the sub-divisions of the Trias, which we know are well developed in the neighbourhood, are represented there.  The Coal Measures were penetrated to a depth of 549 feet, or a total depth from the surface of 1,008 feet, when· the boring operations were abandoned on account of some dispute between the manager and the proprietor of the estate. Only a few thin coals were met with, though many ironstone bands are mentioned.  The first seam of coal was pierced at a depth of 514 feet, and was found to be 6½in. thick.  Another seam was found at 560 feet, which was 1ft. 5½in. thick.  A third coal was met with at a depth of 614 feet, and was found to be 1ft. 1in. thick.  At 734 feet a seam of coal nine inches thick was reached, and a bed of shaly coal, or bat, was passed through at a depth of 834 feet, and this represents the total

thickness of coal met with.[1]  Although the results of the boring
were not so profitable as could have been wished, they afford
valuable data as to the extension towards the south-west of
workable seams of coal.  It is evident from this boring that all
the thick coals met with at Wilford and Highfield crop out
within a distance of about a mile to the south-west of the
Highfield bore-hole, though the fact that the "Top Hard" was
found in the "Spinney" bore-hole, south of the Trent, shows
that the higher strata of the Coal Measures are repeated by a
pre-Triassic "fault" somewhere south of Highfield Park, for
the "Top Hard," it will be remembered, does not occur in
the bore-hole there.  Thus, there is probably more coal under
the Trent Valley, immediately south of Highfield Park, than
was revealed by the boring at that spot.

A very interesting section, showing how the Coal Measure
strata regularly dip to the east or north-east, in the neighbourhood of this parish, was opened out during the excavations
for the Radford and Trowell Railway, about ten years ago.
Between Radford and Wollaton the line passes through a
rather deep cutting, unfortunately now grass-grown, however,
in the sides of which the various alternations of hard sandstone,
bright yellow and variegated clays and shales, with three
or four seams of coal, could be well seen rising gently one from
underneath the other going westward.  At the end nearest
Nottingham the angle of inclination was very small—probably
not more than 3°—but as the line travelled westward the
dip steadily increased till it was 5°, or more.

In the gasometer excavations at Old Radford, the Coal
Measures, consisting of light green and variegated shales and
clays, were found to slope at an angle of about 2° to the east.
At the Highfield Park boring the mean dip of the Coal
Measures was estimated to be 1 in 17, or an angle of $3\frac{1}{2}°$,
but the direction could not, of course, be ascertained.  At the
Clifton Colliery, however, as we might expect, the strata dip
gently towards the north.  Thus, all the evidence afforded by

---

(1) For these particulars I am indebted to Mr. E. J. Lowe, F.R.S., who kindly
favoured me with a glimpse of the MS. section.

borings and other excavations into the Coal Measures in this neighbourhood tends to confirm what has long been the impression, that these rocks slope inwards, or towards the north-east, and so form part of a gigantic basin-shaped area, many miles in diameter, and that the parish of Lenton is situated on the southern rim of this basin. The true basin-shaped character of the coal strata of this part, however, is concealed in a great measure by the thick mass of Triassic rocks, which, as we have seen, overlap the Coal Measures along their southern margin. .

## LOWER MOTTLED SANDSTONE.

The Lower Mottled Sandstone is the lowest subdivision of the Trias, or New Red Sandstone, and in Wollaton Park, as we have seen, rests directly on the Coal Measures, the Permian Magnesian Limestone and Marl, which intervene between the Coal Measures and the Lower Mottled at Bulwell, being here absent. The Permian Magnesian Limestone, indeed, may be traced thinning out on the north side of the railway at Radford Woodhouse, about one-third of a mile north of the Ilkeston Road, and is not again met with farther south. Along its southern edge the Permian Limestone becomes rather conglomeratic and brecciated, the pebbles, however, being exceedingly small and bean-shaped. At Bobbers Mill, about three-quarters of a mile north of the northern boundary of the parish, Mr. E. Wilson, F.G.S., noticed, during the progress of the Leen Valley Sewage Works, the Magnesian "Limestone gradually pass, in the last 200 yards of its range, from an ordinary crystalline yellow dolomite into a grit, and from this into a coarsely brecciated rock, an evident marginal deposit."[1] This clearly indicates that we are here in the neighbourhood of the ancient beach of this formation, and therefore that this is the approximate original southern boundary of the sea in which the Magnesian Limestone and Marl were deposited, an impression which is

---

(1) " The Permian Formation of the North-east of England."—*Mid. Nat.*, Vol. iv. p. 190.

borne out by the rapid attenuation of the Permian formation when traced south from North Notts.

The Lower Mottled Sandstone is a fine-grained, bright red, soft sandstone, seldom containing any pebbles, and often prettily mottled with streaks and patches of yellow. It is so soft as to have yielded more readily than any other rock in the neighbourhood to the disintegrating action of the weather, and the wearing away agency of running water. Hence, except where this rock is protected by a capping of harder rock, it mostly forms low ground or gentle slopes, and is easily traceable at the surface by its bright crimson colour, for it is a favourite haunt of rabbits. It forms the low ground in Wollaton Park between the pond and the low ridge on which Wollaton Hall stands, and is again seen on the east side of this ridge between Lenton Firs and Spring Close, where it breaks out into low cliffs, the bright crimson colour of which forms a pretty contrast with the dark green vegetation around. Along a tolerably straight line drawn from the south side of the pond in Wollaton Park, through Lenton Hall to the Trent alluvium, the Lower Mottled Sandstone is cut off in its extension southwards at the surface by a great fault, which throws the rocks down nearly 300 feet on the south, and lets in a broad wedge of Keuper Marl alongside. Of course, the Lower Mottled Sandstone continues on underneath these Keuper rocks in its natural position, except that it lies something like 270 feet lower on the south side of the line of fault. Between Spring Close and Ilkeston Road, along the low ground that forms the west bank of the Leen, this rock is much hidden by gravel and clay belonging to the Drift and river deposits, as we shall have occasion to notice by-and-by. The Lower Mottled Sandstone forms the lower slopes of the east side of the Leen Valley as far east as Radford Boulevard, where it passes out of sight beneath the Bunter Pebble Beds. The rock is much hidden on this side of the valley, where it borders the Leen, by a thick deposit of gravel, and sand, and brickearth (or silt), which completely covers it, and the rock itself is only exposed during excavations for the foundations of buildings.

The best exposure of this formation in the neighbourhood is in the sand-pit at Spring Close.  Here there is a section of about 20 feet of it, capped with a thick deposit of ancient river gravel, which will be described at a later stage.  The rock is of the usual bright red colour, streaked and blotched with greenish-yellow. It is horizontally bedded, and very fine grained, and soft enough to be easily crumbled between the fingers.  It is the same rock, in fact, as is found at Mansfield to be so peculiarly well adapted for iron moulding, and is quarried at Lenton for the same purpose.

Another good exposure of this rock occurs in a field north of Cut Through Lane, between Spring Close and Lenton Hall. A small cliff of this rock was formerly exposed in Cut Through Lane itself, and was a curious example of the striped and mottled colouring of this formation, but it has now been spoilt by the building of a boundary wall in front of it.

A considerable thickness of Lower Mottled Sandstone was passed through in an excavation for a large gasholder, at Old Radford Gasworks, in 1879-80.  Below nine feet of alluvium of the Leen, which itself occupies a ravine worn out of the Lower Mottled, there was 24 feet of this rock, below which came eight feet of brecciated conglomerate belonging to this formation, and forming its base, the brecciated conglomerate resting on a planed off and even surface of Coal Measures.  Thus, below the surface of the meadow at this spot, there was a total thickness of Lower Mottled Sandstone down to the Coal Measures of 41 feet.  The upper beds of the Lower Mottled consisted of the usual soft sandrock, but the lowest 14 feet was composed of a hard, compact and purplish variety of this rock, similar to that seen at the base of this formation in the Great Northern Line to Kimberley, just west of Bagnall.  The brecciated conglomerate varied in thickness from about two feet on the west side of the excavation (which was about 180 feet in diameter) to eight feet on the east side,[1] and was mainly composed of fragments of the underlying greenish and mottled Coal Measure shales, along with

(1) This thickness must be regarded as exceptional, for at the Clifton Colliery only eleven inches of conglomerate was met with at the base of the Lower Mottled, while at the Highfield Park boring only two inches of conglomerate parted the Lower Mottled from the Coal Measures.

rolled quartzite pebbles, and an abundance of sub-angular fragments of felspathic, granitic, and other igneous rocks, most of
them being too much decomposed for examination under the
microscope. The arrangement of the pebbles and the inclination
of the bedding clearly showed that the materials were trans-
ported from a westerly direction. Faint impressions of broad
ripple-marks were also met with in the Lower Mottled Sandstone
here. A slab of rock showing these ripple marks was presented
by the writer to the Natural History Museum at University
College, Nottingham, being the only traces of ripples yet
observed in this formation in the neighbourhood of Nottingham.

Although the Lower Mottled Sandstone is so well developed
at the Gas Works at Old Radford, it thins out against the
Coal Measures, which rise from underneath it about 500 yards
to the north. Less than that distance further on in the same
direction the Coal Measures are capped by the Permian Magnesian Limestone. Both these formations now form slightly higher
ground than the Lower Mottled Sandstone, just as they
did when the Lower Mottled was originally deposited around
the foot of the gentle slopes formed by these older rocks.
When the Magnesian Limestone was deposited, its extension
southwards was probably limited by a low ridge of Coal
Measure rocks which then stretched from east to west across the
ground now occupied by Radford Woodhouse and Wollaton.
But before the Triassic deposits began to be laid down, this
high ground had all been swept away by denudation, leaving
the Permian Limestone to form a sort of low plateau, overlooking
gently sloping ground towards the south and east, composed of
Coal Measure rocks. From this we may expect to find the
Triassic rocks steadily thickening, going south and east from
Old Radford. The same process of thinning out against the
westerly rise of the surface of the Coal Measures is observable
in Wollaton Park, where, north of the pond, the Coal Measures
make their appearance at the surface from underneath the
Lower Mottled, which is evidently very thin, for every slight
depression in the surface of the ground there reveals the existence of the Coal Measures close beneath.

It is difficult to draw the line exactly between the Lower

Mottled Sandstone and the overlying Bunter Pebble Beds, as
the one formation passes up into the other, and the change in
colour and texture is nowhere very sudden and well-marked.
Any estimate of its thickness, therefore, must be taken as
approximate. Yet there is a very broad difference between
the two formations on the whole, and a line of separation *can*
be drawn. About 79 feet of Lower Mottled Sandstone appears
to have been passed through in the Clifton Colliery shafts, and
this is probably its maximum thickness underneath Lenton.

## BUNTER PEBBLE BEDS.

If we now trace the Lower Mottled Sandstone up from the
low ground at Spring Close to the ridge on which Lenton Hall
is situated, we observe that the soft red sandstone of this formation passes steadily up into a rather harder sandrock of a
yellowish colour, that is coarser and contains well-rounded quartz
and quartzite pebbles. This is the Bunter—or Bunter Pebble
Beds, as it is called. Another feature more common in this
formation than in the Lower Mottled Sandstone, is the
abundance of oblique lamination, or "false bedding," which
characterises this rock almost wherever it is exposed. The
same sort of passage upwards from soft crimson sandstone
to harder yellowish pebbly sandrock, is traceable on the east
side of the Leen Valley in the roads leading into Nottingham ;
but, as the ground is being rapidly covered with buildings,
this feature will soon have to be looked for farther up the Leen
Valley, where the same transition is observable in several spots.

Next to the Lower Mottled Sandstone, the Bunter Pebble
Beds cover the largest area at the surface of all the rocks in
the parish. The ridge from Lenton Hall to Wollaton Hall is
capped with them. A narrow strip of these beds is traceable
on the footpath of the Derby road near Lenton Abbey, where
they form a wedge dovetailed in by "faults" between Keuper
rocks on either side. The Bunter also reveals its presence along
the Trent escarpment in Highfield Park in several small
detached bosses, as if the rock here was shattered by a series

of small dislocations that run in a north-west and south-easterly direction.

In the field just outside the north-west corner of Wollaton Park there is a small sand-pit, where the Bunter is also nicely opened out. The Bunter at this spot is very irregularly bedded, and contains many lenticular flakes of fine red clay, one of which was found to measure 19 inches in length by four inches in thickness in the middle. This quarry is also remarkable as having furnished an unusually large pebble, or boulder, which was described at the time in a short note in the *Midland Naturalist.*[1] The boulder consisted of hard fine-grained white sandstone, finely but unevenly laminated, and very fissile. It measured 7 in. by 3 in. by $3\frac{1}{2}$ in., and weighed over 9 lbs. It was quite angular, being only very slightly worn along the edges, and had, therefore, not been much rolled about by the action of currents. In texture, it resembled Caradoc sandstone[2] more than anything else, and was quite unlike the Coal Measure sandstone of the adjacent coalfield. These Bunter pebbles are chiefly interesting, it may be remarked, on account of the evidence they furnish of the source whence the sandy material of the Bunter itself was derived. But the pebble above described could hardly, one would suppose, have travelled many miles.

There are only two or three spots where anything like a good section of the Bunter is to be seen within the parish of Lenton. These are (1) in the Trent escarpment, by the side of the pond in Highfield Park, at (2) the back of the Bleachworks, in Lenton Boulevard, and (3) at Lenton Sands. The section in Highfield Park is about eighteen feet high, and shows the usual oblique bedding, with an abundance of well-rounded quartz and quartzite pebbles scattered through the mass. The Bunter also rises to the surface by the east side of the Tottle Brook at Lenton Grove; but whether it crops out from under the Lower Keuper in the ordinary course, or whether the marl close by is faulted down against it, is not clear. The ground is obscured by brickearth and other deposits left there by the Tottle Brook.

---

(1) Vol. vi. (1883), p. 264.

(2) The Caradoc sandstone, it may be mentioned, is one of the subdivisions of the Lower Silurian system, and is largely developed in North Wales.

The Bunter Pebble Beds, being much harder, are not so easily disintegrated and worn away by the insidious agents of denudation as the Lower Mottled Sandstone is, and consequently assume a somewhat bolder feature in the landscape.  Thus the line of junction between the Lower Mottled and the overlying Bunter Pebble Beds, is roughly indicated by the steeper slope of the ground where the Bunter comes on.  This feature is well seen as we approach Lenton Firs from the Wollaton Park (Lenton) Lodge, on 'the one hand ; or as we walk up Lenton Sands towards the top of Derby Road, on the other.  We cross the boundary line between the two formations about two hundred yards below, or west of the end of Willoughby Street, Lenton.  A few yards above Willoughby Street, the road has been cut down into the Bunter to a depth of several feet, and the oblique lamination and pebbly character of the rock here are at once apparent.  The oblique bedding slopes from north-west to south-east, and this is the predominant direction in the neighbourhood of Nottingham.  This tells us that the materials which form the Bunter Beds were brought by powerful currents that came, for the most part, from a north-westerly direction, or from the direction of Liverpool.  And it is a curious fact that the Bunter thickens out in that direction, being estimated to attain a thickness of 600 feet in Cheshire, while at Bootle, near Liverpool, over 1,200 feet of this formation has been penetrated in a borehole there.[1]

The finest exposure of the Bunter Pebble Beds in this neighbourhood, or perhaps in the Midland Counties, however, is the noble buttress of rock on which Nottingham Castle stands.  Most of the peculiarities of structure and weathering of this formation may there, indeed, be seen to advantage. This majestic cliff shows more than two-thirds of the total thickness of the Bunter formation in this neighbourhood, for it is 133 feet high, while the Bunter can hardly be more than 180 feet thick at Nottingham, and may not be so much—that is, according to the results of the borings on the Clifton estate, and in Highfield Park.

---

(1) " Geology of the Country around Chester," by Aubrey Strahan, M.A., p. 3.

About Nottingham, the Bunter sandstone has been largely excavated for caves and cellars and rock-houses. The most remarkable examples of this kind in or near Lenton are the " Hermitage " and the Columbarium, or " Doctor's Shop," in the cliff at the Rock Holes in Nottingham Park. Mortimer's Hole, at the Castle, is a secret passage that winds through the Castle rock from summit to base, and formed an outlet into the meadows below for the garrison. Mr. W. T. Aveline, F.G.S., of H.M. Geological Survey, aptly describes the facility with which the Bunter can be excavated, as observed while surveying this district twenty-six years ago. He says: " The rock is not so hard but that it can be easily worked, but such is its massive consolidation, and so few are the lines of bedding or joints, that it can be hollowed into large square-chambered caverns without requiring any artificial support for the roof. Advantage has been taken of this peculiar structure, and of the dryness of the rock, for along the faces of the cliffs chambers of various sizes have been hollowed, and when the front is built up with brick or stone, they are used for dwellings, stables, storehouses, etc." " In this rock many cellars in the town of Nottingham are formed, which vary but very little in temperature throughout the year." [1]

" Geologists have for years been puzzling themselves as to where all this Bunter sand and these pebbles could have been derived from ; for it is one of the fundamental principles of geology that all rocks that were accumulated as this appears to have been—in the form of sediment at the bottom of a large inland sea or lake—must have been built up of the ruins of some still older rocks that formed the dry land at that time. There has been so much of this wearing away of the dry land and the spreading out of the materials at the bottom of other seas and lakes since then, that the rest of this old land from which the Bunter sand and its pebbles were derived was probably long since either washed away altogether or else has been buried beneath accumulations of newer sediments and rocks. Nevertheless, a great deal of attention has been paid

---

(1) " Geology of the Country around Nottingham," Sec. Ed., p. 25.

to the subject of late years, and as the result, though geologists
are not yet able to point out exactly where the land lay, they
can tell what was the character of that land, or, rather, of the
rocks that composed it, and from which the pebbles were
derived. Professor Bonney, F.R.S., has identified some of these
pebbles as being precisely like certain rocks in the north-west
of Scotland, and, therefore, as having probably come from
there. Another geologist who has devoted a good deal of
attention to the subject, Mr. W. J. Harrison, F.G.S., of
Birmingham, has brought forward a mass of evidence to prove
that they were derived from a central ridge of very old rocks
that stretched from Charnwood Forest on the east to the
borders of Wales on the west, but which is now in great part
covered by newer rocks. That such a ridge of high land
striking from east to west across the South Midlands existed
during Bunter times there is abundant evidence to prove, but
it is doubtful whether it had much to do with the origin of
the pebbles in the Bunter. Most of these pebbles in the
Bunter are well rounded, and have had whatever sharp edges
they may once have possessed all smoothed away. On the
other hand, a few of them are angular, and still retain their
sharp edges and corners, as if they had just been broken off
a cliff somewhere. Some of the smoothed and rounded pebbles
consist of granite, felstone-porphyry, or of some kinds of
volcanic rocks, but the great majority are composed of the
mineral quartz, which generally takes a milky white colour,
and of quartzite—so called because they are composed of
almost pure quartz, in the form of grains of sand that have
been welded together by the action of heat, moisture, and
pressure when they formed part of some great rock-mass
buried deep down in the earth's crust. The other and more
angular class of pebbles consist of different kinds of sandstone,
slate, and indurated clay, all very ancient, and very much older
than the Bunter period. Some of these pebbles are made of
the same kinds of rock as now form a large part of the
mountains of Wales ; others are found to contain fossils that
prove that they were chipped off rocks of the same age and
character as those that form the hills of Devon. Whether
29

any of these pebbles actually came from Wales or from
Devon is not clear."[1]    The whole subject, indeed, seems surrounded with great difficulties, and a good deal of research
still requires to be done before the origin and source of the
Bunter and its pebbles can be determined.

### KEUPER BASEMENT BEDS.

Resting on the Bunter in some spots, and occasionally found
sandwiched between that formation and the overlying Keuper
"Waterstones" on the east side of Nottingham, certain white
or greyish grits, sometimes containing thin bands of conglomerate, have lately been discovered.    The grit is coarser
and "sharper" than the sand of either the Bunter or the
"Waterstones;" it is micaceous, and contains rounded quartzite
pebbles like those in the Bunter, along with occasional sub-
angular fragments of Permian Magnesian Limestone.    It rests
on a clearly eroded surface of the Bunter, and varies much
in thickness in different spots, as if it had itself suffered considerable denudation before the deposition of the "Waterstones."    The conglomerate bands which occur in it are
usually firmly cemented by calcareous and dolomitic matter,
and sometimes the deposit is represented by this conglomerate
alone, which then forms a very hard pebbly rib of rock, vary-
ing from two or three inches to about two feet in thickness,
and separating the Bunter from the Keuper sandstone and
marl.[2]    These are the Keuper Basement Beds.    The deposit
is not continuous, but occurs in isolated patches, and is frequently absent altogether.    Yet at Bramcote and Stapleford
Hills it must attain a thickness of about 120 ft., for it forms
the whole of Stapleford Hill and very nearly the full height
of Bramcote Hill.    It is well seen in the Hemlock Stone,
which is entirely carved out of this rock.    In Cheshire this

---

(1) From a paper on "A Bunter Pebble," read by the writer before the Nottingham Naturalists' Society, Oct., 1883.

(2) "Geology of the Country around Nottingham," W. Talbot Aveline, F.G.S.
Also, "On the Occurrence of Keuper Basement Beds in the Neighbourhood of
Nottingham," E. Wilson, F.G.S., and J. Shipman.  *Geol. Mag.*, 1879, p. 532.

formation attains a thickness of 250 ft.   At Bramcote Hill and
Stapleford Hill the rock varies from greyish white to crimson
or brownish red, while at Nottingham it is white.   The same
sort of irregular changes in colour are met with in Cheshire.
The fact that at Nottingham it is found resting on an eroded
surface of the Bunter, of course indicates that a considerable
amount of denudation took place in this area in the interval
between the formation of the Bunter and the dawn of the
Keuper period.   That a vast interval of time elapsed between
the two periods we know from the fact that the Upper
Mottled Sandstone, which in Cheshire is 600 feet thick, was
deposited in the interim.   The Upper Mottled Sandstone
is nowhere met with in this neighbourhood.   Hence it is
inferred that our Bunter Sandstone formed dry land
for a long period before the Keuper rocks were laid down
over it.

Traces, but only traces, of these Keuper Basement Beds have
hitherto been met with at Lenton.   On the north-east side
of the Bunter cliff in Highfield Park, overlooking the lake
there, thin alternations of white and greenish-grey compact
grit, with one or two seams of hard cemented quartzose conglomerate, were observed resting in a cavity worn out of the
underlying Bunter.   Only one side of this hollow, however,
is at all traceable, the continuation of the section being obscured
by a talus of earth deposited there, apparently, to give root
to a plantation of young trees.   There is a thickness of about
six feet of these beds here, but the spot is inaccessible, and
too much overgrown to make anything of it.

At the top of the bank of Bunter, in the end of which a
sand-pit has been opened out at the south-west corner of
Wollaton Park wall, there are one or two very small bosses
or blocks of highly calcareous quartzose conglomerate, with a
matrix composed of coarse grey grit, that belong to the Keuper
Basement Beds, and appear to be in their natural position.
A larger mass of similar conglomerate stands on the narrow
strip of Bunter, in the plantation on the south side of the
park, opposite Lenton Abbey Lodge, but it is uncertain whether
it is *in place*.

It is certainly a remarkable feature about this formation that it should be so fully developed a mile-and-a-half further west, and yet so scantily represented here. It seems highly probable that this rapid thinning out and disappearance within short distances is due to subsequent erosion, as well as to irregular deposition in the first instance, and would therefore point to a considerable lapse of time having occurred between the deposition of these beds and those of the "Waterstones" above them.

## LOWER KEUPER "WATERSTONES."

Next, in ascending order, comes the so-called Lower Keuper "Waterstones." This formation usually consists of alternations of greyish or brownish soft micaceous fine-grained sandstone and red marl. Although scarcely at all seen exposed at the surface of the ground on account of the absence of sections, and by reason of the Drift sand and clay which mantles the west side of the parish, the Keuper "Waterstones" appear to cover a comparatively large area of the low ground in the valley of the Tottle Brook.

The only exposure of these beds is at the south-west corner of Wollaton Park wall, where a few feet of them, consisting of red marl containing one or two thick beds of brown sandstone dipping gently towards the north-east, appear to have been wedged in alongside the Bunter by the "faults" that cross this spot. Hard brown Lower Keuper Sandstone is again traceable along the south edge of the park, close by the lake, and red and green marls belonging to this formation were at one time visible in the road side, a few yards west of the Beeston Lodge.

The sloping ground of Highfield Park, west of the house, is composed of Lower Keuper Sandstone, of a drab or brownish colour, which becomes coarser as you descend the slope, as was proved by a series of small holes which Mr. E. J. Lowe, F.R.S., had made at my suggestion, in order to determine the character

of the underlying rock there.[1]  This subdivision of the Trias is
about eighty feet thick on the east side of Nottingham, and
most likely attains a similar thickness here in those spots where
it is overlain by the Upper Keuper, and therefore retains its
full development.

Many of the beds of sandstone of this formation show the
impressions of the ripples produced in the sand when it formed
the margin of the ancient lake in which the sediment was
deposited.    The ripples run in wavy parallel lines across the
slabs of stone, and are best seen when the surface of the bed
of rock or the slab has been exposed to the weather for a
time.    These ripple-marks in the Keuper are not so broad
as those in the Coal Measures, already described, but, like
them, were formed by the action of the wind producing ripples
on the surface of the shallow water, the ripples becoming
registered in the soft sand of the beach, just as ripple-marks
are formed in the soft sediment along some parts of our sea-
shores at the present day.

## UPPER KEUPER MARL.

If we could see the Lower Keuper "Waterstones" passing
underneath the Upper Keuper Marl, where a continuous section
showed the transition from one formation into the other, as
we can do in some spots on the east side of Nottingham,
we should observe that the Lower Keuper "Waterstones"
graduate upwards into the Upper Keuper Marl so imperceptibly that it would be hard to say where the line ought
to be drawn between them.    Both formations consist of layers
of sandstone interbedded with more or less thick strata of red
clay or shale, and perhaps the most important difference between the two formations is that the lower one usually contains
more sandstone than clay, while the Upper Keuper undoubtedly

---

(1) For the courtesy and kindness received from E. J. Lowe, Esq., during the
many pleasant hours spent in working out and mapping the ground about Highfield
Park and the neighbourhood, and for the assistance which he was always ready to
lend in order to clear up any doubtful point, the writer of these notes here respect-
fully tenders his grateful acknowledgments.

contains more clay than sandstone. Hence it is the Upper Keuper that is chiefly used for brickmaking, though many of the old brickyards of Nottingham were opened out in the Lower Keuper, probably because that formation lay nearest the town and the main roads. Another point of difference is that the "Waterstones" consist of brownish or greenish-yellow soft sandstone, often in thick beds, while the Upper Keuper Sandstone beds are always thin, very compact, hard, and fine-grained, and of a pale bluish or cream colour. The clay of the "Waterstones," again, is of a duller red, and contains thin seams of greenish clay, sometimes purplish towards the top of the series ; while the Upper Keuper clay is of a much brighter red, contains no greenish-yellow clay, but sometimes bands of white clay, and occasionally gypsum. And these form perhaps the readiest tests of all. The lower beds of the Upper Keuper Marl are occasionally found to consist of shaly clay that breaks up into small squares or tesseræ, and about a quarter-of-an-inch thick. This character is observable in the Upper Keuper Marl exposed in Cut Through Lane. The Upper Keuper almost invariably forms a rather bold physical feature when it is present, and where it comes on above the Lower Keuper along a sloping hill-side gives rise to a steeper slope and a bolder swelling aspect of the ground.

The Upper Keuper Marl in the area under notice forms a patch about 400 yards wide, that stretches from the escarpment in front of Highfield House to near Beeston Lane, and is dovetailed into this position by dislocations which have the effect of bringing it down to the same level as the Bunter Pebble Beds and the Lower Mottled Sandstone. It forms the Trent escarpment for a stretch of 500 yards east of the Bunter Cliff by the lake in Highfield Park, and the fields along the slope of the escarpment here show the usual hummocks that often mark the spots where clay has been worked in former times. It is not unlikely, indeed, as some suppose, that an ancient pottery once existed here. How far to the north-west the Upper Keuper extends is not quite certain, but it probably ends along the sloping ground that overlooks Beeston Lane.

A small patch of this marl appears in the road side at the

south-west corner of Wollaton Park wall, and between there and the Tottle Brook.

It is probable that Upper Keuper Marl underlies the alluvium of the Trent over all the area south of a line drawn from the middle of Beeston to the Clifton Colliery.   The evidence for this supposition is as follows :—In excavating for the foundation of the large malt-house near Beeston station, Upper Keuper Marl was found below the Trent alluvium.   Keuper Marl was also found to underlie the superficial deposit of gravel at the bottom of Bramcote Lane, in the heart of Beeston, though Bunter is exposed at the surface two or three hundred yards to the north-east.   At the Highfield Park boring, as we have seen, the Keuper was absent altogether, but, at the bore-hole close by the Clifton Colliery, sixty-four yards of Keuper was passed through before reaching the Bunter.   Again, from Stapleford to Beeston, the Upper Keuper Marl is brought down alongside the Bunter by a considerable "fault."   This fault probably continues on through Beeston in the same south-easterly direction as hitherto, and may be expected to be met with passing underneath Dunkirk plantation, about a quarter of a mile south of the railway line there, from whence it may be expected to continue on to Clifton Colliery, where it most likely joins the other main "fault."   North of this line of "fault," Bunter appears to form the chief surface rock, while south of it Keuper may be expected to be found all the way.

The boundary wall of Highfield Park in Cut Through Lane is almost entirely composed of the hard thin-bedded light-grey and bluish-white stone drawn from this formation.

With regard to the physical conditions under which these rocks were formed, the ripple marks, which frequently occur in the beds of sandstone in this formation as well as in the Lower Keuper, and the sun-cracks observable in the clays, show that these two formations were accumulated in shallow water where the bottom occasionally became dry, and was thus exposed to the parching heat of the sun for a time.   Footprints of gigantic reptiles have been found in these rocks in other parts of England, the impressions being eight to ten inches in length ; besides the remains of fishes, a few plants, one or two small bivalve shells, and teeth of a small marsupial, the oldest mammalian fossil animal known. These facts, along with the presence of iron oxide, as a thin coating round each grain of the rock, the abundance of gypsum, and the frequent occurrence of pseudomorphous crystals of rock-salt in the Upper Keuper Marl, have led Professor Ramsay to infer that both these deposits were accumulated in a vast inland salt lake, or lakes, somewhat resembling the Dead Sea, or the Great Salt Lake of Utah, at the present day.[1] This great inland lake must have extended over the greater part of what is now the middle of England.

## "Faults," or Dislocations.

As if to render the geological structure of the rocks of this area more complex, the strata have been considerably displaced vertically out of their natural position and relation by means of several important "faults," or dislocations, which strike across the parish in a general east-and-westerly direction. The effect of these "faults" is to bring down rocks from a higher horizon alongside those belonging to a lower. [See Geological Section, No. 1.] By this means the Upper Keuper Marl, which, as we have seen, forms a broad strip of the high ground on which Highfield House and Lenton Hall are situated, has been dove-tailed in as it were between Lower Mottled Sandstone capped by Bunter Pebble Beds on the north, and Lower Keuper "Waterstones" on the south. And we can walk across the lines of fissure without being in the least aware that on one side of the fissure the rocks have been thrown down at some period in the past several hundred feet, and the cliff which must have been left has all been swept away and the ground levelled. The more northerly line of "fault," which brings the Upper Keuper down level with the lowest beds of the Bunter at Lenton Hall, is doubtless the same fault as is met with in the workings of the Clifton Colliery at Wilford. This fault

---

(1) "Physical Geology and Geography of Great Britain," Prof. A. C. Ramsay, F.R.S., p. 155.

was there found to throw down the rocks on the south side about 95 yards, and the shafts were sunk under the impression that they were on the down-throw side of the fault. The sinking, however, soon showed that the fault passed between the colliery shafts and the site of the trial boring, 270 yards to the south-west. The exact course of the fault in the Trent Valley is of course hidden by the alluvial gravel and silt of the Trent, but appears to bear in a west-north-westerly direction, and is first seen at the surface in Cut Through Lane. It was formerly much better exposed there, but a wedge of Bunter Sandstone, shattered and tilted, may still be seen dovetailed between Upper Keuper on the south-west side and Lower Mottled Sandstone on the north-east. The fault appears to pass underneath the back part of Lenton Hall, for in a well sunk there 114 feet of Keuper marl and sandstone was passed through before the underlying Bunter was reached, while the house itself stands on the Bunter formation. This fault was exposed lately during the laying down of pipes in Beeston Lane, and was found to cross this lane about 145 yards from the north end, opposite the Beeston Lodge of Wollaton Park. From hence to the outflow of the pond in Wollaton Park it brings Lower Keuper "Waterstones" down level with the bottom beds of the Lower Mottled Sandstone, but there is no clear exposure of it. The amount of displacement of the rocks on the two sides of the fault here can hardly be less than 270 feet.

Another powerful dislocation, though one less seen even than that just described, appears to run parallel with the Lenton Hall fault. Its exact course has not yet been ascertained, but it is certain that it runs close by the west side of Highfield House, and throws down the Upper Keuper Marl alongside Lower Keuper "Waterstones," the Upper Keuper Beds being evidently high up in that series. At a spot about 300 yards to the north-east of the Bunter cliff in Highfield Park, there is a small quarry showing about 15 feet of Upper Keuper Marl, dipping westerly at an angle of 35°. The high angle of inclination of the beds clearly indicates the proximity of some disturbing agency, and in all probability the neighbourhood of a fault. It was a favourite theory of Mr. E. J. Lowe, F.R.S., that this quarry marked one point in the course of a fault which trended westerly, by the front of his house, and through the middle of the grove of trees that runs from Highfield House down by the side of Cut Through Lane to the entrance lodge. What seemed to strengthen this impression to his mind was the curious fact that below a certain point in the plantation (the spot where he supposed the fault crossed) the trees did not grow to the same height as those higher up the slope and nearer the house. In order to decide the matter, therefore, he had holes dug at intervals all the way down the plantation, with the result that the fault was found to pass within a few yards of the house, and the rest of the ground of the plantation was found to be composed of Lower Keuper Sandstone. This fault must have a down-throw to the north-east of at least eighty or a hundred feet, and there are likewise indications that the Keuper is much shattered between these two main faults.

There is reason to believe, from the results of the borings for coal on the Clifton estate, that other faults, running nearly parallel with these, strike across the Trent Valley from Beeston towards Wilford, but their existence is as yet only vaguely indicated. There is evidently a fault of some magnitude south of the site of the Highfield boring, and between that spot and Clifton Grove, for no Keuper rock was met with in the High- field boring, yet, at the Spinney bore-hole, at Wilford, a mile and three furlongs to the south-south-east, ninety-three yards of Keuper was passed through. Then, again, at the Clifton Colliery bore-hole, north of the Trent, but still south of the main fault, 64 yards of Keuper was passed through. The existence of so much Keuper in this area can hardly be accounted for by the natural dip of the strata to the south-east.

In the underground workings of the Clifton Colliery, two other "faults," subordinate to the main dislocation above de- scribed, have been met with, which, although outside the parish boundaries, must have an important bearing on any future underground operations carried on in the adjacent parts of the parish itself. They both strike in a northerly direction—the

one on the west side of the pit, with a down-throw on that
side of 8 yards, bearing towards the Bleach-works in Lenton
Boulevard; the other, which lies east of Wilford Church, and
has a down-throw to the east of 11 yards, bearing towards
the Rock Holes in Nottingham Park. "Neither of these two
faults is known to affect the overlying Triassic rocks."[1]  Their
true direction is laid down on the second edition of the
Government Geological Survey Map of this district (71 N.E.)

The manner in which the Bunter Pebble Beds of the escarpment in Highfield Park stand out in disconnected bosses, seems
to indicate that the ground is much faulted hereabouts.  Indeed,
Mr. E. Wilson, F.G.S., mentioned to me, ten or twelve years ago,
that he had noticed, during the laying down of pipes in the
Beeston road on the east side of the Tottle Brook, that several
small dislocations broke through the rocks of this part. . The
numerous  fractures observable in the rocks at the south-west
corner of  Wollaton Park may be a continuation of the same
series.  Two of these faults unite to let in a narrow wedge of
Bunter there between Keuper rocks.  It would be a work of
great difficulty, however, to attempt to trace the extent of all
the dislocations of this part in detail.

### SUPERFICIAL DEPOSITS.

*Glacial Drift.*—The solid rocks of the more elevated ground
of the parish are hidden for a space in some parts by a mantle
of clay, or sand, or gravel, sometimes by a mixture of all three.
These deposits are not connected with the river gravels that
underlie the broad meadows of the Trent and the Leen, and
are, in fact, much older.  They do not attain any great thickness or importance within the area of the parish, yet they cover
a sufficient extent of ground to justify some mention here.  To
anyone unacquainted with geology, these loamy sheets of pebbly
sand or mottled clay might easily be mistaken for the ordinary
surface soil derived from the disintegration of the immediately

---

(1) "Geology of the Country around Nottingham," p. 43.

underlying rocks. Pebbly mottled clay of this kind is some-times found overlying the Lower Mottled Sandstone, which rarely contains any pebbles whatever, and certainly could not have furnished the clay. The character of the pebbles and the colour of the clay combine to show that the materials for its formation were derived from other rocks that rise to the surface farther north. These deposits must, therefore, belong to the Glacial period, or Great Ice Age, as it is called, during which the North of Europe, including nearly the whole of Britain and Ireland, endured a climate not unlike that of Greenland at the present day, and the high ground was shrouded in snow and ice, which crept seawards in the form of vast glaciers. This long period was marked by stages, during which the land at one time stood higher above the sea-level than now, and at another period the land that now forms the British Isles was submerged altogether beneath the waters for a time.

It was during the last of these periods of glaciation that the red loamy and pebbly sand seen along the foot of the south wall of Wollaton Park, and indeed the whole of the Drift of the parish, appears to have been deposited. It bears evidence of having been derived from the grinding down of the rocks by the passage of ice, as it descended from the Pennine Hills across the country in a south-easterly direction; for the chief ingredients of the deposit are invariably such as could only have come from the north or north-west, mixed up with materials derived from the grinding down of the rocks on which the deposits rest. Four or five miles farther west—in the neighbourhood of Stanton Gate, beyond the Erewash—Drift deposits of this age assume considerable importance, and betray all the usual signs of ice action, such as highly disturbed bedding, in which the strata have been crumpled and puckered, and the pebbles squeezed into a highly inclined or vertical position by the action of lateral pressure ; while in other spots the Drift consists of a heterogeneous mixture of pounded rock fragments torn up by the advancing ice-sheet, and crushed and kneaded into a stiff, lumpy clay.

At Cobden Park, the low ground there was covered with two or three feet of pebbly yellow sandy clay, containing an abun-

dance of pounded gritstone, evidently derived from the Lower
Coal Measures of Derbyshire. This deposit became thicker
towards the Leen. In some spots, the beds of clay and sand
could be seen twisted and crumpled, and the pebbles reared
on end in such a way as to clearly point to some powerful force
acting from the north-west, and crossing the Leen Valley
obliquely, ploughing up the gravel and older brick-earth along
the east bank of the river. Here and there the surface of the
soft Lower Mottled Sandstone had been kneaded into the
overlying gravel, so powerful was the disturbing force. This
deposit contained many large boulders of well-rounded Coal
Measure Sandstone, doubtless brought over from Derbyshire,
besides large pieces of Lower Mottled Sandstone.

Deposits of Drift age vary much in character in different
spots. Thus, along the south side of Wollaton Park, the Drift
consists of dull red loamy sand, containing some clay and a
few scattered pebbles. In the low ground attached to Lenton
Hall, on the east side of Beeston Lane, there is red loamy
sand without pebbles, while farther south it is a mixture of
clay and sand and pebbles. In the north-east corner of
Wollaton Park there is a dark, stiff, mottled clay ; while to
the south, the park slopes, as well as the top of the ridge on
which Wollaton Hall stands, are thickly covered with loose
pebbly sand that completely obscures the underlying sandrock.
A similar loamy covering, containing scattered pebbles, is traceable along the top of the low ridge from Spring Close westward.
Gravel, probably of Glacial age, covers the low ground along
the eastern side of Wollaton Park to the thickness of several
feet.

At the south end of Lincoln Street, Cobden Park, during
the progress of some excavations for buildings, a curious section
of Drift gravel was exposed. Below four feet of loam, there
was a foot-and-a-half of gravel resting on a level surface of
Lower Mottled Sandstone. At one part of the cutting, however,
a shallow cavity, about ten feet in width, and like the old course
of a small stream, had been scooped out of the sandrock, and
the hollow filled in with sand and pebbles slightly stratified,
the bedding coinciding with the shape of the cavity. It was

exposed in two sides of the excavation, and was probably of Glacial origin.

The whole of the eastern slope of the Leen Valley is, or was (for it will soon be completely covered with buildings), thickly covered with loamy sand and pebbles left there during Glacial times. This Drift gravel creeps down the sides of the valley and appears to blend with the more recent alluvial deposits, but excavations show that it really passes underneath the river deposits, except where it has been removed altogether, and the river gravel rests directly on the Lower Mottled Sandstone.

" Just at the angle formed by the Tottle Brook and the Trent escarpment in Highfield Park, the ground swells into a low rounded prominence at once suggestive to a geological eye of the presence of Drift beneath the grass which covers it. An excavation made in it showed that the surface was composed of dull brown sand and pebbles, below which there was about five feet of red and yellow sand arranged in thick bands, with a thin parting of drab clay now and then between. The sand rested on gravel, on the surface of which an *Ostrea*, very fragile, and a well-rounded pebble of coal were found. This deposit, like those high-level gravels which have just been described, was probably left there during the Glacial period ; and its stratified character and position seem to imply that it was laid down when the bed of the Tottle Brook had not been cut so deep as it is now, and when it was for a time still further choked up—perhaps by ice, perhaps by Drift accumulations." [1]

### ALLUVIAL DEPOSITS.

*Interglacial Alluvium.*—Before leaving the high ground and descending into the river valleys in order to examine the deposits of gravel, sand, and silt deposited by the rivers during the many thousands of years that must have elapsed since the Glacial Period, there is a deposit of sand and gravel that rests

---

(1) " Alluvial and Drift Deposits of the Trent Valley," by J. Shipman, p. 11.

high up on a ledge or terrace of the Lower Mottled Sandstone
at Spring Close that remains to be described, and that we
may now venture to examine. This terrace is about twenty-
five or thirty feet above the present level of the Leen, and the
gravel is ten or twelve feet thick in its deepest part, thinning
away to nothing as the hill slopes towards the Leen on the
east and towards the Trent on the south. This deposit is
composed of a mixture of red, grey, and yellow fine and
coarse sand, clay, and all sorts of quartz and quartzite pebbles
and flints, with other rocks that do not belong to this district
at all. The whole mass shows signs of stratification, but has
evidently been much kneaded and contorted, apparently by
the same force that crumpled the gravel and sand by the
Leen at Cobden Park, higher up the valley.

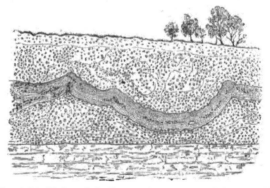

*Interglacial Alluvium of the Trent, resting on a terrace of Lower Mottled
Sandstone, Spring Close, Lenton (1879).*

Here, too, the level surface of red sand-rock on which the
gravel rests has been forced into puckers during the crumpling
process. The highly-contorted character of this deposit could
be seen better about sixteen years ago, and before so much of
it had been cut away. This curious deposit appears to be of
the same age as the thick mass of terrace-gravel on which
Beeston stands. That deposit was long thought to be of
Glacial origin, but recent joint researches by Mr. R. M. Deeley

and the writer have led to the conclusion that it is an ancient
deposit of the Trent, formed when the river flowed at a higher
level than now, or, in other words, before it had deepened its
valley to the present extent.  At Beeston the alluvial character
of this deposit is more clearly seen than it is here.

With regard to the geological age of this gravel, the presence
of Chalk flints in it implies that it was formed subsequently
to the Chalky Boulder Clay (the early part of the Glacial
Period), while its highly-contorted character proves that it
was overridden by ice before the close of Glacial times.  It
is therefore regarded as of interglacial age, and was formed
during the long interval that appears to have elapsed between
the formation of the Chalky Boulder Clay and the descent
of the last ice-sheet from the Pennine Hills, by which it
was crumpled, towards the close of the Great Ice Age.

*Alluvium of the Trent.*—The ground that lies within the
valley of the Trent is low flat meadow, elevated but a few
feet above the summer level of the Trent itself, and frequently
flooded after the heavy rains of autumn.  In some spots,
indeed, it is marshy all the year round.  The alluvial deposits
of the Trent consist of gravel, covered with a surface veneering
of silt and clay.  The gravel lies spread over the bottom of
the valley to a thickness of many feet, and completely hides
from view the solid rocks out of which the valley has been
hollowed.  These sheets of gravel and silt stretch across the
valley from side to side, ending abruptly at the foot of the
river escarpments where they form cliffs, but creeping up the
slopes where the high ground that bounds the valley descends
gradually into the river plain.  The valley bottom deepens,
and the thickness of the alluvial deposits of the Trent therefore increases slightly, as we approach the middle of the
valley, but not to such a marked extent as in the case of the
Leen alluvium.  Thus, at Clifton Colliery twenty-five feet of
alluvial gravel and soil was passed through before reaching
the solid rock beneath.  At Highfield Park boring, a few
yards north of the railway, the alluvium was found to be
twenty-two feet thick ; and at Chilwell boring, a mile and
a half north-west of that in Highfield Park, but rather nearer

to the side of the valley, only sixteen feet of alluvium was passed through.

The alluvial gravel of the Trent is composed for the most part of a great variety of well-rounded quartz and quartzite pebbles, along with sub-angular, or less rolled, pebbles of Carboniferous Limestone chert, Coal Measure sandstone, and Millstone Grit, Keuper sandstone, Lias, and flints, and a few other rocks that have probably travelled from the far north. Many of the quartz and quartzite pebbles were most likely derived from the wearing down of the Bunter, but a large proportion of the pebbles would seem to have been brought from the north and swept into the valley during the Glacial Period. The gravel is mixed with a coarse red sand that appears to have been largely derived from the Carboniferous grits of North Derbyshire, as it is coarser than the sandstone rocks around Nottingham.

Wherever this gravel is opened out by excavations, it is found to present a horizontally bedded arrangement, just as the deposits of gravel do which the Trent is forming at various points along its course at the present day. This, of course, proves that the gravel was deposited, or at least re-arranged, by the Trent, though perhaps many thousand years ago.

The gravel is covered at the surface in some parts by sand, silt, or tough clay (brick-earth). This superficial covering of clay varies rapidly in thickness and character, and occasionally is absent altogether, allowing the gravel to appear at the surface for a space. The clay is often dull red, or drab, but in some parts bluish, bright yellow, or mottled, and occasionally black and peaty. It mostly contains a few scattered pebbles, and is perhaps best seen in the sides of the brooks, especially of the Tottle Brook in its course through Highfield Park.

There are no gravel pits in the Trent Valley in or near Lenton. Hence, if we would observe the character of the alluvium of the Trent we must go farther up or down the valley. An interesting excavation was made, however, during one of my visits to Highfield Park, five or six years ago, at the instance of Mr. E. J. Lowe, F.R.S., in order to decide a

30

doubtful point as to the thickness of the brick-earth seen in the sides of the Tottle Brook. It was close by the spot where the Tottle Brook enters the Trent Valley, and just where the clay brought down by this brook might be expected to attain its maximum thickness. "About six feet of clay was passed through without reaching the gravel on which it probably rests, further progress being arrested by the influx of water. This thickness, however, must be regarded as exceptional on account of the close proximity of the channel by which the sediment was originally poured into the Trent Valley. The clay presented a faintly banded arrangement, consisting of broad alternations of, first, yellow mottled clay, with plenty of pebbles, then light blue clay, then white, then blue again, the pebbles becoming fewer as we went deeper, and being mostly large and split in two. Bits of fossil wood, in a bleached and pulpy state, were met with at a depth of about five feet. Dr. Carruthers, F.R.S., of the British Museum, to whom the specimens were submitted, found the wood to be exogenous, though its kind was undeterminable, and regarded the remains as of Glacial Age."[1]

A good section of these alluvial deposits of the Trent was exposed for a time in a large gravel pit, now converted into a lake, at Long Eaton Field, about five miles farther up the river. This section was the more interesting as it showed the whole thickness of the river gravel and clay down to the solid rock on which it rested. Although the upper beds of the section varied in thickness and character laterally every few yards, the lower deposit of gravel remained pretty much the same over the whole extent of the gravel pit, which was nearly a quarter of a mile long. The following was the succession of beds at one spot :—

|  |  | ft. | in. |
|---|---|---|---|
| c. | Reddish-brown argillaceous loamy sand, passing down into | 6 | 6 |
| b. | Dark-bluish and brownish stiff clay, resting on a level surface of | 1 | 6 |
| a. | Ferruginous sand and gravel | 12 | 0 |
|  |  | 20 | 0 |

(1) " Alluvial and Drift Deposits of the Trent Valley," p. 14.

A similar succession of these alluvial deposits of the Trent is said to have been met with while excavating a large well for a gasholder in Island Street, Nottingham, about thirty years ago. The spot is just on the margin of the alluvial plain, and the contractor had to go 24 feet down before reaching the solid rock. The first stratum of three feet was soil, the next ten feet was sand or silt, below which came eleven feet of gravel. Amongst other things found here were part of the skull of a deer, and an enormous tooth[1] (probably of the mammoth).

From these facts, and the thickness at different points already given, we can form some idea what must be the character and thickness of the deposits formed by the Trent that happen to come within the boundaries of the parish of Lenton. The river deposits of some parts of England are rich in the bones and teeth of extinct animals, but very few bones or teeth have been met with in this neighbourhood. Two teeth of the mammoth *(Elephas primigenius)* were found about six feet deep in the alluvial brick-earth or clay on the Clifton side of the valley some years ago. A few bones were also met with in sinking the shafts for the Clifton Colliery in 1869, but no scientific examination or record appears to have been made of them.[2] These remains were probably washed out of some older deposit that may have dated back to the dawn of the Great Ice Age, and before the rusty-coloured gravel that lines the bottom of the Trent Valley was deposited. The black peaty loam of course indicates the decay of vegetation that formerly flourished over certain parts of the valley. This peat is most likely due to the growth and decay of mosses, or of some of the lower orders of vegetation, for no evidence has yet been met with of the existence of a continuous bed of peat, or matted vegetation, such as would indicate that the Trent Valley had been the site of an ancient forest at any period of its history. With regard to evidence of physical changes that we know have taken place since the Glacial Period, the alluvial deposits of the Trent Valley seem to be peculiarly deficient, and the alluvium of the Leen,

---

(1) " White's Notts. Directory for 1864," p. 72.

(2) " Description of the Borings," etc., on the Clifton Estate, by John Brown, F.G.S., " Trans. Chesterfield and Derbyshire Mining Institution," p. 7.

which now remains to be described, is much more interesting in this respect.

ALLUVIUM OF THE LEEN.[1]

Small and unimportant a stream as this river is, the geological evidence furnished by its deposits invests it with an interest which it would not otherwise possess. Throughout the valley of the Leen, especially the lower half of its course, the ground is thickly covered with pebbles. There is scarcely a ploughed field or ditch-side that does not indicate the abundance of gravel all over the valley. But although this gravel lies eight or ten feet thick in some places, only occasional glimpses of its character can be obtained.

The pebbles most abundant in the gravels of the Leen Valley are quartzites of all sizes, many of them split, perhaps by intense frost, some perhaps by the pressure of glacier ice; but there are besides, quartz, Coal Measure sandstone, Millstone Grit, chert, flints, and, more rarely, pebbles composed of the harder rocks of the neighbourhood. .An examination of the rocks out of which the Leen Valley has been scooped shows that the pebbles in the valley gravels could not all have been derived from the rocks that bound the valley. The valley of the Leen has been worn for the most part out of the Lower Mottled Sandstone of the Trias, as may easily be seen by the little low cliffs of bright crimson sandstone which have been formed by the river here and there along its east bank. The Lower Mottled Sandstone, however, contains only a few small pebbles, so that they could hardly have been derived from the wearing away of this rock. In some parts of its course, indeed, the Leen has entirely swept away the thick mass of this Lower Mottled Sandstone that once stretched' across its bed and far away over the ground beyond, and has even eaten its way down into the Middle Marl of the Permian, and through that again into the underlying Permian Magnesian Limestone, which, along with a small strip of Coal Measures,

---

(1) The observations that follow are taken from the writer's paper on "The Alluvial and Drift Deposits of the Leen Valley," *Midland Naturalist*, vol. vi., p. 76, *et seq*.

form its western slopes. But there are very few pebbles to be
found that have been derived from these rocks. The majority
of the pebbles were no doubt derived from the wearing away
of the Bunter Sandstone, which forms so much of the country
to the north-east. Most of the others were in all likelihood
brought from North Derbyshire, while the flints must, of course,
have come out of the Chalk. Many of the pebbles now found
in the gravel of the Leen Valley, then, must have come a
very long way.

A large excavation, made in 1879-80, during the extension
of the Nottingham Corporation Gas Works at Old Radford
(now included in Lenton parish), opened out a very instructive
section. The evidence revealed by this section was found to
throw considerable light on what had hitherto been a blank
page in the geological history of the valley.

*Section of the Alluvium of the Leen at Old Radford.*

(*a*) Yellow, bluish, and dark gray clay.
(*b*) Peat, with upright stems of young trees.
(*c*) White and gray "sharp" sand and gravel.
(*d*) Brown gravel, with flakes of red hematite, and thin seams of red sand near
the bottom.
(*bbb*) Isolated small patches of peat.
(*e*) Lower Mottled Sandstone (Trias).

This excavation was made by the west side of the Leen at
Old Radford, and was for a well for a new gasholder, about
180 feet in diameter, and 40 feet deep. It passed through the
whole of the deposits of the Leen that form the alluvial flat,
and far down into the Lower Mottled Sandstone rock beneath.
The Leen now wanders through a level meadow, which varies
in width from a few yards to a quarter of a mile. The excava-

tion at Radford, however, revealed the fact that beneath the
middle of this flat meadow lay a ravine, not very broad—
probably not many yards—that is, supposing the part opened
out in this cutting to be only half the entire width, and nine or
ten feet deep, carved out of the solid rock. This cavity was
filled up by layers of gravel and sand, peat and clay, piled bed
upon bed, while the Leen itself now flowed over all. At the
bottom there was rusty brown gravel, stained crimson here
and there by bits and flakes of decomposing red earthy
hematite which it contained. The hematite could have been
derived from no other source in this district than the Coal
Measures, probably of Derbyshire. Above the coarse brown
gravel came a loose, sharp, coarse gray or white sand, in some
parts clayey and pebbly, but mostly free from pebbles. The
traces of oblique bedding in it indicated that this sand was
deposited by water flowing somewhat rapidly down the valley,
though not perhaps more rapidly than the Leen would flow
now, were the artificial dams and water-mills removed. Judging
from the horizontal extent and uniform thickness of this sand,
too, the stream must have been considerably wider than it is
now. Several stools of trees were found in this deposit in the
position in which they grew. Some of the fragments of these
trees were too much decomposed to make out what they were,
but one fragment of a stool, about ten inches in diameter, was
found by Dr. W. Carruthers, F.R.S., to be *Quercus robur* (Lin.)
"This fragment," says Dr. Carruthers, "belonged to a slow-
growing tree, as the annual rings are very small, and consequently the vessels very numerous and close together." Resting
upon this gray sand was a band of peat, from six to ten inches
thick, full of upright stems of young trees, along with leaves and
twigs, all in a confused and more or less decomposed or carbonised state. Another fragment of wood met with here is
believed by the same authority to belong to *Pinus sylvestris*,
and probably came out of the peat bed, which was covered by
about three feet of stiff clay, or silt, but which contained no
pebbles. This clay swelled out on the south side of the excavation to about five feet in thickness, as if it occupied an old
saucer-shaped hollow in that direction. Laterally, these alluvial

deposits rested against a mass of red sand and clay and pebbles, which appeared to partly line that side of the old river hollow, though it was not now easy to draw the line between the two. The red sand with pebbles was evidently all that remained of a mass of Glacial Drift that may once have entirely filled the ravine, and in which the Leen had eaten out a channel for itself.

No bones or other organic remains have been found in these ancient Glacial deposits of the Leen, though mammalian bones have been met with in other river valleys. The position of the Boulder Drift in the bottom of the Leen Valley shows that this valley, like most other river valleys in Britain, had been excavated to its present depth and deeper before the close of the Glacial Period.

Between this Glacial Drift and the much newer deposits of sand and gravel, peat and silt, met with at Old Radford—that is, intermediate in age—there was formed a mass of gravel, which occurs about two miles higher up the valley, but is absent at Radford. This gravel rested partly on the Boulder Drift and partly on a broad shelf of rock cut back out of the Bunter Sandstone that forms the east side of the valley at Basford, and was distinct from either the modern river deposits on the one hand, or the Drift on the other. It was about five feet thick, and passed up into five or six feet of loose pebbly sand that may have been washed down later. The deposit consisted of brown and yellow sand, obliquely laminated, surrounded and interbedded with pockets and beds of pebbles. From the tumultuous arrangement of this gravel, it was clear that it was accumulated when the Leen Valley was occupied by a broad sheet of water swiftly moving onward down towards the Trent. Some of the irregularities of the bedding may be due to the melting of lumps of ice or snow which may have got buried with the sediment. However this may be, the high angle of the bedding certainly indicated strong currents, interrupted, perhaps, by cross currents or some other obstacles. Its pebbles appeared to have mostly been derived from the destruction of Glacial Drift. There was evidently a long interval of time between the formation of the Drift at the bottom of the valley and the

*Section of the Alluvial and Drift deposits of the Leen at Basford, showing the position of the "Torrential Gravel."*

Scale—One inch = 66 feet horizontally, 35 feet vertically.

(*f*) Gray silt, or brick earth, and dark surface loam (2 feet—3 feet).

(*e*) Peat bed (1 foot—3 feet).

(*d*) Gray and yellowish laminated sand (2 feet).

(*c*) Ferruginous gravel, containing thin seams of bright red sand (2 feet).

(*b*) "Torrential Gravel" and sand (10 feet).

(*a*) Glacial Drift (2 feet—6 feet).

(*x*) Lower Mottled Sandstone (Trias).

accumulation of this torrential gravel, during which the ice-cap that had previously shrouded the land had melted away, and the climate had become less severe, while a large amount of gravelly material was probably swept away by the water of the stream. The torrential gravel would seem to belong to the beginning of post-Glacial times, when all the river valleys of Britain were occupied by torrential floods, probably caused by the melting of the winter's snow, or the heavy rains of this time. The floor of the terrace on which this gravel rested, was about three feet above the summer level of the Leen. It was now that the Leen appears once more to have begun to deepen its bed, and to form the "valley within a valley," which its later post-Glacial deposits, consisting of fine, soft gray sand, peat and silt, or brick-earth, were found to occupy.

The evidence furnished by these interesting sections of the Drift deposits of the Leen Valley goes back to the time when, as already pointed out, Arctic conditions prevailed in Britain, and immense glaciers descended slowly towards the coast, leaving patches and mounds of rocky *débris* in the more sheltered hollows, or at the spots where two or more ice-streams coalesced.

All the evidence afforded by the Drift deposits of the Leen Valley points to the conclusion that the ice which formed them crossed the valley more or less obliquely, and came from a north-north-westerly direction—or, in other words, from the southern extremity of the Pennine Hills. The Leen Valley then presented much the same general outline as it does now, except that the bottom of the valley was in some parts a ravine, in others a ⌣-shaped hollow, now filled with alluvial gravel and silt. There is abundant evidence that the British Isles stood higher out of the water then than they do now, and that England was united to the Continent. It seems probable that the Drift once lay much thicker in the Leen Valley than it does now, and may even have choked it up altogether for a time.

A long interval appears to have elapsed between the accumulation of the Drift and the deposition of the "tumultuous gravel," during which the ice melted away, and the climate became somewhat ameliorated, though perhaps still rigorous. The Leen then began to deepen its channel, and to carve out the hollow in the older deposits now occupied by the more recent gravel, sand, and silt. The climate soon became so far ameliorated that vegetation flourished down to the very bottom of the valley, and peat began to accumulate. The growth of plants at the bottom of the Leen Valley seems to suggest that the land had once more been raised after submergence. Only small fragmentary patches of this earlier growth of peat escaped the denudation that afterwards took place. How and when the red hematite was brought into the valley and came to be so mixed with the rusty-coloured gravel at the bottom of the alluvial deposits remains a mystery. Afterwards came the deposition of the gray sand in regular even layers, as if it had been quietly precipitated along the level bottom of a broad stream, many times broader than the Leen is now. Again, there appears to have been an elevation of the land, for we find the stools of oak trees with their rootlets embedded in the sand in such a way that deposition must have ceased for a time, and the area became dry ground. By-and-by the climate, which during the growth of the oak trees does not appear to have been very favourable, became more equable, and favoured the growth of pines and other plants which ultimately became choked with peat. Once more the ground was more or less continuously submerged, perhaps caused by increase in the rainfall, and the bottom of the valley became covered with the sheets of silt or clay which now mantle the alluvial plain, and which must themselves have taken many centuries to form.

# SECTION XVIII.

## MISCELLANEOUS.

THERE are various matters relating to the parish, which, not coming under the head of any of the previous sections, must form a kind of miscellaneous appendix, with which our history of Lenton may appropriately be brought to a close.

In the year 1487, the battle of Stoke-field, the most obstinately contested and sanguinary battle ever fought in this county, took place between the forces of Henry the Seventh and the partisans of Lambert Simnel. On the evening of Thursday, June 14th, the King's army lay encamped in the neighbourhood of Lenton, probably in the meadows to the south and south-west of Nottingham Park. "That nyght," according to the journal kept by a herald attached to the forces, "the King's hooste lay under the ende of al that hille towarde Notingham to Lenton warde, and his forwarde befor hym to Notingham Bruge warde; and the Erle of Derbyes host on the Kings lifte hand to the meadowes besides Lenton." Two days later, the King, "beside a village called Stook, a large myle out of Newarke, recountrede his enemies and rebells, wher he had the victorye."

In Stowe's Chronicles a terrific storm is recorded, which took place in the year 1558, and which seems to have been

specially violent here.  "On the 7th of July," writes the
chronicler, "within a mile of Nottingh\m, was a marvellous
tempest of thunder, which as it came through two towns, beat
down all the houses and churches, the bells were cast to the
outside of the church-yards, and some webs of lead 400 feet
into the Field, writhen like a pair of gloves.  The river Trent
running between the two towns, the water with the mud in
the bottom was carried a quarter of a mile and cast against
the trees, the trees were pulled up by the roots and cast
twelvescore foot off; also a child was taken forth of a man's
hands, two spears length high, and carried an hundred feet
and then let fall, wherewith his arm was broke and so died ;
five or six men thereabout were slain, and neither flesh nor
skin perished.  There fell some hailstones that were 15 inches
about"  The two towns have been identified by Deering and
other writers as Lenton and Wilford, but it is doubtful whether
these places are intended ; and, awful as the storm may have
been, it is evident that its effects are here greatly exaggerated.
That Wilford Church was not "beat down" in the time of
Queen Mary must be sufficiently obvious to everyone who
visits that interesting structure, nor is it likely that Lenton
Church was so greatly damaged.    At any rate, the parish
registers do not refer to the storm, either directly or indirectly.
The average burials at that period were only about three per
annum, and although Stowe says that five or six men, besides
the child, were killed in the storm, only four burials are recorded in that particular year.    A contemporary account of
this remarkable storm, which places the scene of devastation
on the other side of Nottingham, is to be found in a letter
of Gilbert Cousin[1] (Cognatus), written from Padua the same
year, which forms part of the narrative of his Italian journey,
published under the title of " Topographia Italicarum Aliquot
Civitatum."   It is included in the very scarce " Gilberti Cognati

---

(1) Gilbert Cousin was a canon of Nozeray, in Burgundy, and is best known as the
secretary of Erasmus.  He accompanied Claude de la Baume, the young Archbishop
of Besançon, to Padua in 1558, and spent some time there, whilst the Archbishop,
who, though he had occupied the See of Besançon for nearly fourteen years, was then
only twenty-eight years of age, was engaged in studying philosophy and law.   The
" Topographia " is in the form of letters addressed to Guillaume de Poupet, a kinsman of the Archbishop, and at that time a canon of Besançon.

Nozereni Opera (Basileae, 1562)," 3 vols. folio (vol. 1, pp. 380-393). The passage relating to the storm is from an undated letter, but written in August or September, 1558 (p. 388) · "Primo¹ die Julii incidit tempestas maxima in Anglia prope Nothingamiam quum rusticus quidam quatuor habens equos, cum puero suo intentus esset campis suis arandis, ventorum rabie, et grandinis magnitudine, ille cum tribus equis extinctus est puero cum quarto equo intacto manente. Alius dum currum suum in agris fæno onerasset, tantam videns imminere procellam, paululum secessit, et statim currus fæno onustus viventi sublatus evanuit. Pagus quidem nomine Snuentum fere totus destructus est, Plurimis disjectis ædificiis, templum totum corruit, sacro fonte intacto manente, et sum machori parte. Multas arbores radicitus evulsit, et Multas in Partes abrupit. Horreum Frumenti Plenum incendit fulmen. Grandinis Magnitudine Periere oves, anseres, gallinæ, et aviculæ infinitæ. Harum omnium reum. Oculatus est testis Duchessa Northumbriæ. Civis quoque Nothinghamiæ, a Joanne Beron equite Aurato, et nonnullis aliis nobilibus examinati, hujus rei Plenamfidem fecerunt." Snuentum is clearly Sneinton, where the church was blown down. Joannes Beron is Sir John Byron *(Little Sir John with the great beard)*, to whom the Priory of Newstead, in this county, was granted in 1540.

In 1736, a great flood occurred in the parish of Lenton, doing considerable damage to the hay crops on the low lands. The circumstance is thus recorded in one of the parish books :—
" Be it Remembered yᵗ on yᵉ 3ᵈ of July in the year 1736 there fell a great Rain wᶜʰ Caused a vast great flood wᶜʰ Washed away a great deal of Hay from yᵉ Meadows and other Grounds yᵉ Constable Swaths was all taken away Robert Cassell being Constable that same year."

John Townshend, a native of Lenton,² was executed at Nottingham, March 23rd, 1785, for having, in company with John Pendrill, robbed William Vinson, farmer, of Edwalton, on the highway near West Bridgeford, on the 1st of January

---

(1) Stowe says the 7th July.

(2) The following entry, under the year 1756, occurs in the parish register :—
" John son of Jonathan Townshend and Mary his wife, baptized Jan. 4."

in the same year. In passing sentence upon them, Mr. Justice Heath, whose severity as a judge was proverbial, remarked, "I will cause the laws to be executed with such severity as shall enable any gentleman to hang his watch by the highway-side, with the full confidence of finding it there on his return another day."

In 1789, the villagers testified their loyalty by joining heartily in the rejoicings which celebrated the recovery of King George the Third from the unhappy mental malady that had for a time overthrown his reason. On Monday, March 23rd, bonfires were made in different parts of the parish, at which three sheep were roasted whole, which, together with plenty of ale, were given to the populace. About seven o'clock a general illumination took place, a band of music paraded the village, playing "God Save the King," etc. A grand entertainment was provided at the Coffee House, at which sixty-eight persons supped. After supper, several toasts were drank, including "The King," "Queen," and "Royal Family," "Doctor Willis," (the King's physician), "the Lord Chancellor," and "Mr. Pitt."

Mr. John Keetley, an inhabitant of Lenton, died there, September 2nd, 1791. He was so extraordinarily corpulent, that at his burial, on the 4th of the same month, it was with difficulty that eleven men carried his remains to the grave. The coffin measured two feet ten inches across the shoulders, and was twenty inches in depth.

Amongst Mr. William Stretton's notes is the following :— " The last of the Shops in the Mart Yard at Lenton taken down and the present Tenements erected, 1792."[1]  This work was carried out by Mr. Stretton.

In 1793, the popular rage in Nottingham and its neighbourhood against the notorious Tom Paine and his work, "The Rights of Man," was at its culminating point—nothing being more common, on all public occasions, than to have the offender, with a pair of stays under his arm (it being alleged that Paine had once been a journeyman staymaker in Nottingham), burnt

---

(1) Stretton MSS., No. 32, f. 22.

in effigy.[1] The following extract from a local paper[2] records the feeling of the inhabitants of Lenton against this individual :—

"On Tuesday last (Feb. 12), the infamous THOMAS PAINE (one of the rag-a-muffin Convention of Paris), was apprehended and lodged in the Peverel Gaol at *Lenton*, near this town ; he was brought to Trial the same day, and after a fair and impartial examination (his crimes being as big with infamy, HE COULD NOT PLEAD !) he was found guilty of Treason against the KING who had formerly spared his Life, and against the Constitution of this country, in endeavouring, by his seditious writings, to overwhelm us in destruction, and our SOVEREIGN KING, whom all good Englishmen revere !—He was sentenced to be Hanged on the arm of a large tree, near the above Village, which was accordingly done, amidst a great concourse of people ; he was left hanging on the tree a considerable time, after which the Company retired to the Coffee House for refreshment ; soon after, they were informed that the Paineites had laid a plan to convey the remains of their Champion away from the Tree, which the LOYALISTS being aware of, fell on, routed, and put to flight the whole GANG of them.—In the evening, his body was cut down and burnt to ashes in a bonfire ; after which, the major part of them retired to the Coffee House, where the company gave repeated toasts to the Health and Long Life of GEORGE the Third, our Gracious KING, QUEEN CHARLOTTE, the ROYAL FAMILY, LORD MIDDLETON, and many other Gentlemen in the Neighbourhood."

One of the most remarkable floods in this neighbourhood commenced February 9th, 1795, owing to the breaking up of a frost which had continued without intermission from the 24th of December. The frost had been so intense as to freeze up the Trent as low as Gainsborough,

---

(1) Bailey's *Annals of Nottinghamshire*, iv. 150. Mr. Stretton, in his account of the church at Radcliffe-on-Trent, written in February, 1824, says : "Stephen Ratcliff. a prostrate figure, carved in Wood, used to lye under an arch in the south front of the Church—he was Lord of the Manor, and Patron of the living, he is supposed to have lain there for many Generations, untill the rejoicing took place on the Death of Tom Payne, when a number of Youths stole him away, and burned him in effigy, in lieu of Payne."—*Stretton MSS.*, No. 34.

(2) *The Nottingham Journal*, Feb. 16, 1793.

and was accompanied by immense and frequent descents of snow. When the thaw took place, it was so excessively rapid that there was not a valley in the counties of Stafford, Derby, and Nottingham that was not the channel of a river, the current of which carried along, with irresistible impetuosity, vast sheets of ice and half-melted snow, posts, rails, timber, sheep, etc., into the Trent. The river consequently swelled so inordinately, that its overflow entered the lower parts of Nottingham, and inflicted great damage. The canal banks were washed away in several places, many cattle, horses, and sheep perished, including 400 sheep at Wilford and Lenton ; and the scene the Trent itself presented, bearing down in its mighty stream horses and sheep, haystacks and trees, and farm produce of all kinds, was amply sufficient to show the extent of the calamity. When at its greatest altitude, the water was sixteen feet above the ordinary level of the Trent, and two feet ten inches higher than any previous flood on record. It is estimated to have been about fourteen inches higher than the flood of 1852, and ten inches higher than that of October, 1875.

In 1797, the " Amicable Society," which held its meetings at Old Lenton, was instituted on the 2nd of September. The object of the society, which existed until about the year 1842, was to provide assistance to its members in case of sickness. The officers consisted of a Father, a Deputy-Father, two Stewards, and Clerk. This appears to have been the first of these admirable associations formed within the parish, and it speaks well for the inhabitants of Lenton to have thus early recognised the principles of mutual self-help.

Several highway robberies were committed in the parish at the end of the last, and the commencement of the present, century. On March 31st, 1802, a young man named Ferdinando Davis, a native of Sawley, in Derbyshire, and a blacksmith by trade, was executed at Nottingham for robbing John Cockayne, a butcher's apprentice, of a silver watch and a sum of money on the Derby Road, in this parish. For many years previously the Derby Road seems to have had an unenviable notoriety from the numerous encounters with the so-called "gentlemen of the road," with whom it was a favourite resort.

Early in the present century, the fierce and systematised
hostility of Bonaparte to the commerce of this country, which,
instead of being allowed, through the return of peace, to flow
in its old channels, was actually more impeded in the countries
where the French held sway than it had been during the
war, combined with the continual departure of France from
the spirit, if not from the letter, of the treaty of Amiens,
while she pretended to bind England to the strict observance of every article in that treaty, which was against her,
finally terminated in a rupture, and the declaration of war
by England against France, in May, 1803. This action of
the English Government so enraged Napoleon, that on the
22nd of the same month he issued a decree that all the
English, of whatever condition, found on French territory,
should be detained as prisoners of war. About 10,000 British
subjects, of nearly every class and condition, thus fell into his
clutches. In the following July, a bill enabling the King to
raise a levy *en masse*, in case of invasion, passed both Houses
of Parliament. At the same time, the opposite coasts of France
and Belgium were lined with troops, and Napoleon was calculating how many days it would take him to reach London.
The excitement in the country was intense. The inhabitants
of Lenton, then few in number, showed great public spirit at
this crisis, and exhibited, in a very marked manner, their loyalty
and patriotism. The following account of their action is compiled from one of the parish books :—

At a numerous meeting of the inhabitants of Lenton
parish, held in the parish church on Thursday, August 11,
1803, assisted by the Right Honourable Lord Middleton,
present amongst others, the Reverend William Gill (Curate),
Messrs. Francis Evans, William Ellis, John Chamberlin,
James Green, Gervase Boot, Thomas Roughton, Humphrey
Hopkin, John Shaw, George Wombwell, and Matthew
Needham, the following resolutions were unanimously
agreed to :—First.—That from the present disposition and
preparations of the French Government for an invasion of
this country, and in order to guard against the calamitous
consequences which would attend the temporary success of such

31

an attempt, it is the duty of every British subject capable of
bearing arms, to qualify himself for their use, and to resist, by
every means in his power, the progress of an inveterate and
sanguinary foe. Second.—That it is extremely desirable for
the inhabitants of this parish to exhibit the same alacrity and
zeal which have been manifested in the neighbouring villages,
and that it be recommended to them, and in particular, to the
young and unmarried men, to enrol their names to serve as
volunteers in defence of their King and country. Third.—That
for accomplishing the above purposes, a subscription shall be
immediately opened, and that it be particularly recommended
to such of the inhabitants of this parish, who, from age or
infirmity, or from any other cause, are unable to appear in the
foremost ranks against the enemy, to contribute pecuniary aid.
Fourth.—That the subscription be applied to the purposes of
procuring arms and accoutrements, if necessary ; of affording
relief to the families of volunteers, and of rewarding merit and
heroism. Fifth.—That the subscriptions be called for by instal-
ments, and disposed of at the discretion of a committee of the
subscribers, any five of whom shall be competent to act. In
response to these resolutions the sum of £369 12s. 0d. was subscribed, augmented, in November, 1804, by the Government
allowance of £63, for clothing 63 men, making a total sum of
£432 12s. 0d. at the disposal of the committee. Lord Middleton, John Wright, Esq., Joseph Lowe, Esq , and Matthew Needham, Esq., were amongst the principal subscribers to the fund,
which was contributed to by a large majority of the parishioners
of all classes. The names of 148 persons were enrolled as
volunteers, from whom 63 were selected, as follows :—

> Humphrey Hopkins, Lieutenant,[1]
> John Hopkins, Ensign,
> Three permanent Sergeants,
> Three Sergeants,
> Three Corporals,
> A drummer, a fifer, and Fifty men.[2]

---

(1) The sword worn by Mr. Hopkins, when lieutenant of the Lenton Volunteers,
is now in the possession of the author.

(2) These formed part of the "Loyal Wollaton, Lenton, and Beeston Volunteer
Infantry," under the command of Lord Middleton, of Wollaton Hall.

In September, 1803, the following residents and occupiers of land in Lenton voluntarily agreed to furnish for the use of the army such hay, corn, forage, fuel, etc., as might be in their power, if they were required, the same to be paid for at prices to be ascertained by two magistrates, or deputy-lieutenants.   Offers of horses, carts, and waggons were also made, as stated against their respective names :—

Gervase Boot—2 waggons, 7 horses, 2 drivers.
John Wright—2 waggons, 6 horses, 2 drivers.
John Chamberlin—The same.
John Shaw—1 waggon, 3 horses, 1 driver.
John Hopkins—The same.
Mary Hopkins—The same.
Thomas Roughton—1 waggon, 1 cart, 5 horses, 2 drivers.
William Wigley—The same.
Edward Hollingworth—1 cart, 2 horses, 1 driver.
James Green—The same.
Francis Evans—1 tilted cart, 1 horse.
Matthew Needham—One horse for use of a guide.

James Weston offered to bake 120 or 240 loaves of bread (of 3½ or 4 pounds each) every 24 hours, and Daniel Hughes 60 or 120 loaves, as might be required.   Samuel Goodacre undertook to deliver at his mill every 24 hours, if required three sacks of flour of 240 pounds each, between Lady-day and Martinmas, and five sacks between Martinmas and Lady-day.   The wheat to be provided for him.   The bakers and millers were to be paid for their labour.   Thomas Millington and William Wigley offered their services as guides, and Richard Chamberlin and John Roughton undertook the office of conductors of waggons.   Mr. Matthew Needham was appointed superintendent of Lenton parish, excepting Bestwood Park.   John Gray, William Nuttall, Edward Edwards, John Bennet, Thomas Becket, and Joseph Hollis, inhabitants of Bestwood Park, each offered one waggon, four horses, and one driver.   John Challand offered one waggon, three horses, and a driver.   Edward Edwards was appointed guide, and Matthew Hollis conductor of waggons.   Mr. William Ellis, of Bestwood Hall, undertook to be superintendent of Bestwood Park.

In April, 1805, the Right Hon. Lord Middleton presented to the inhabitants of Lenton a "fine fat ox," weighing 107 stones, to be distributed amongst the volunteers and their families. In December, 1807, a similar gift was made by his lordship, under whose command the Lenton volunteers had been placed.

The following is a summary of the expenditure of the committee appointed for raising the volunteers in this parish:—

|  | £ | s. | d. |
|---|---|---|---|
| Clothing ... ... ... ... ... | 327 | 3 | 6 |
| Arms and accoutrements ... ... ... | 12 | 16 | 0 |
| Drummers and band... ... ... ... | 25 | 4 | 2 |
| Dinners ... ... ... ... ... | 34 | 0 | 8 |
| Instruction in military exercises ... ... | 9 | 19 | 6 |
| Payments on account of accident, travelling expenses, and printing ... ... ... | 7 | 6 | 0 |
| Balance in hand .. ... ... ... | 16 | 2 | 2 |
|  | £432 | 12 | 0 |

At a meeting of the subscribers, held in the parish vestry, June 6th, 1811, for the purpose of examining the accounts of Mr. Matthew Needham, the treasurer, and disposing of the balance, it was unanimously resolved "that Mr. Hopkins be requested to dispose of the balance of £16 : 2 : 2 amongst the late volunteers, or their families, in any way he thought proper."

In 1804, the Lenton Coffee House, now known as the "White Hart Inn," was rebuilt on the site of an older structure by Mr. Wombwell. Attached to the Coffee House were pleasure gardens and a bowling-green, which were then much frequented by the better class of the inhabitants of the neighbouring town of Nottingham, and which Blackner[1] describes as being "a kind of paradise in the summer season." Within the grounds also was the Peverel gaol, to which we have already referred. Previous to the introduction of railways, and for several years after, these gardens were the favourite resort of local pleasure-

---

(1) Blackner's *History of Nottingham*, p. 105.
(2) See p. 403.

seekers, while the bowling-green was patronised by the gentry and principal tradespeople in the neighbourhood.[1]

In the year 1809, on the Day of Jubilee, when King George the Third entered on the fiftieth year of his reign, the inhabitants of Lenton raised a subscription for the poor of the parish, by which eighty-three families were relieved ; 29 families with seven shillings each, 37 families with five shillings each, 12 families with four shillings each, and 5 families with smaller sums, besides bread and cheese and ale to all the children in the village attending the bonfires.[2]

The "Luddite" outrages in 1811 and 1812, have already been alluded to.[3] Parties of the Berkshire Militia were stationed in Lenton for some months, and cavalry patrolled the parish nightly.

The year 1831 will be memorable in the history of Nottingham in consequence of the Reform Bill riots and the burning of Nottingham Castle on the evening of October 10th. During the forenoon of the following day, a large mob collected in Nottingham Market Place. On leaving the town, the rioters called at the Greyhound Inn and the Durham Ox Inn, where they consumed all the food the houses contained, without payment. They then marched to Beeston, and set fire to the large silk mill belonging to Mr. William Lowe, of Nottingham. By three o'clock of the same day, the mill was reduced to a heap of ruins, and the 200 workpeople thrown out of employment, the loss of property being estimated at £7,790. On their return from Beeston, the rioters called at Lenton House,

---

(1) "Nearly every London racket-ground had its adjacent tavern ; but these taverns, it must be remembered, were the clubs for the middle classes of those days. In their parlours of an evening parochial matters and politics were amicably discussed, and here the notabilities of the district were wont to assemble for pleasant social intercourse when work was done. We venture to say that more courtesy and propriety were observed in the taverns that encouraged skill at rackets, or quoits, or the despised but excellent skittles, than are found in these modern days of constant nipping and fashionable refreshment bars. . . For what did one find at the old London taverns with attached recreation grounds, the places where, when work was done, the citizens congregated to amuse themselves in simple fashion? Not the tippling of modern times, not the drinking for drinking's sake, not the glitter and gaudiness of the modern bar, with the presiding Hebe bedecked with sixpenny bouquets, but a garden, or at any rate some semblance of it, a dozen or so of simple arbours, and certainly no more pipes and ale than are now seen and legitimately recognised on every known cricket-ground."

(2) *Stretton MSS.*, No. 27, f. 54.     (3) See p. 341.

the residence of Matthew Needham, Esq., where all the wine and eatables, and silver plate to the value of £40, were quickly appropriated. They also demanded food at Lenton Hall, the residence of John Wright, Esq., but went away on that gentleman giving them two sovereigns ; and also at Highfield House, the residence of Alfred Lowe, Esq.,[1] who appeared to have been mistaken by the rioters for Mr. William Lowe, the proprietor of the silk mill at Beeston, who, being a Tory and a somewhat ardent politician, had rendered himself specially unpopular with the mob. This fact was noticed at the time as showing that many of the rioters must have been comparative strangers to the neighbourhood. They next commenced an attack on the lodge to Wollaton Park, near the junction of the Derby and Birmingham roads, and speedily effected an entrance, but no sooner were they within the park than a charge was made upon them by a troop of yeomanry cavalry, which at once put them to flight. Sixteen of them were taken prisoners, and escorted by the yeomanry, with drawn swords, to the barracks, where they were handed over to a party of the 15th Hussars, by whom they were conveyed to the county gaol. Three of the rioters eventually suffered the extreme penalty of the law, being hung at Nottingham on the 1st of February, 1832.

A public dinner was given by the parishioners of Lenton, at the White Hart Inn, April 4th, 1853, to Captain James Anlaby Legard, R.N., J P. (who had for some years occupied Lenton Hall), previous to his leaving the neighbourhood, " as a mark of respect for the uniform kindness and courtesy shown by him to all parties during his residence in the parish."

In the last-named year the " Lenton and Radford Association for the prosecution of Felons " was established, the meetings of the association being held at the White Hart Inn, at Old Lenton.

A toll-gate was erected in the year 1854 on the Nottingham and Derby turnpike road, between New Lenton and the end of Barrack Lane, Nottingham Park, and there being already

---

(1) This gentleman was afterwards one of the Grand Jury for the county at the special Assizes held in Nottingham for the trial of the principal rioters in January, 1832.

another toll-bar within two miles on the same road, two full
tolls daily were demanded from, and paid by all persons who
used the road on the 1st day of January, 1855. The
parishioners of Lenton were evidently of the same opinion as
Lord Byron on the subjects of turnpike roads and toll-bars,[1] for
they held several public meetings and appointed deputations,
who had several interviews with the Trustees of the road,
but without getting any alteration of the toll. A memorial to
the Secretary of State for the Home Department, in opposition
to the application to Parliament by the Trustees for a renewal
of their Act, was prepared, and very numerously signed by
the parishioners of Lenton, and by many persons residing in
Nottingham. It was ultimately agreed that the parishioners
of Lenton should pay to the Trustees the sum of fifty pounds
and withdraw their opposition to the Trustees' bill, and that
the toll should be reduced to one-half toll daily. The £50
was raised by subscription, and paid to the Trustees in
December, 1855, and the toll reduced from January 1st, 1856.
The toll-house was removed in November, 1870.

The principal stock of a superior breed of prime shorthorn
cattle, bred by the late Mr. John Wilkinson, on his farm at
Old Lenton, was sold by Mr. Strafford, auctioneer, of London,
April 20th, 1854, the sale being attended by the most eminent
breeders in England, Ireland, and America. Fifty cows and
heifers, and fifteen bulls, were sold, the average price realised
by the former being £57 9s. od., and by the latter, exclusive
of one or two calves, £47. The aggregate of the sale exceeded
£2,900. Bull calves derived from this stock, shortly after the
sale, were sold for 150 guineas.

In the same year (1854), in consequence of the Crimean
War, a considerable sum was raised throughout the country by
voluntary subscription, in aid of the wives and families of the
killed and wounded. This "Patriotic Fund," as it was called,
received substantial support from the inhabitants of this parish,
and the sums paid over by Alfred Lowe, Esq., J.P., of Highfield,
who acted as chairman and treasurer to the fund (Mr. George

---

(1) *Don Juan*, Canto x., s. lxviii., lxix.

Bardsley being the honorary secretary), amounted in all to £238 13s. 3½d., the whole of which was collected within the parish.[1]

On Thursday evening, June 12th, 1856, a complimentary dinner was given to Mr. John Shaw, churchwarden of Lenton, at the White Hart Inn, by a committee of friends, as a token of their high esteem and appreciation of his efforts in procuring a peal of bells for Lenton Church.

The Lenton Rural Library was established December 21st, 1857, chiefly through the efforts of the late Rev. F. W. Naylor, of Upton, in this county. The Library prospered about six years, when the interest in it began, unfortunately, to decline, and it shortly afterwards ceased to exist.

At a meeting of the inhabitants of Lenton, held January 14th, 1861, after much enquiry and investigation into the state of the poor of the parish during the distress then prevailing, it was resolved to establish a Soup Kitchen to relieve the distress. A committee was appointed to carry out that important object, and to receive the subscriptions, which in two days amounted to over £100.

In 1873 the Mission Hall at New Lenton was erected, at a cost of £660, chiefly through the exertions of the late Rev. Francis Browne, M.A. (son of the present vicar), who at that time was curate of the parish.

The greatest flood in Lenton during the present century reached its height shortly before midnight, October 22nd, 1875. This flood, which did considerable damage in the parish, was 5¼ inches higher than that of 1852, 23½ inches higher than the floods of 1869 and July, 1875, 28 inches higher than the flood of January, 1877, 36 inches higher than the floods of 1857 and 1872, and 39 inches higher than that of 1864. The flood of 1795 is estimated to have been about 10 inches higher than the one under notice.

New Lenton was the scene of a murder, committed on the evening of December 11th, 1877, in one of the garden avenues leading out of Milne's Lane. Here a man named John Brooks took the life of his paramour, Caroline Woodhead, by cutting

---

(1) *Nottingham Journal*, December 29th, 1854.

her throat. Brooks soon afterwards surrendered to the police, and was executed in the Nottingham Borough Gaol on the 13th of February following.

The Annual Show of the Nottinghamshire Agricultural Society was held at Lenton in the years 1878, 1880, and 1883, when the total number of entries were—1878, 572 ; 1880, 732 ; 1883, 783.

The Lenton Liberal Club occupy a neat and convenient club-house near the Unsectarian Schools at New Lenton. This building was erected by the Lenton Liberal Club Company, Limited, and opened to the use of members, June 24th, 1881, the formal opening, by Cecil G. S. Foljambe, Esq., M.P. for North Nottinghamshire, taking place, January 26th, 1882, when a banquet was held in the club-house to celebrate the event. The cost of the site and club-house was £1,100, and there are at present 160 members. The Company was incorporated February 17th, 1881, with a capital of £1,500 in £1 shares.

On the occasion of the laying of the memorial stone for the restoration of the Old Church by Mrs. Sherwin-Gregory, Lady of the Manor, November 22nd, 1883, the following address, richly illuminated, was presented to that lady at the public luncheon which followed the ceremony :—

*To Mrs. Sherwin-Gregory.*

Madam,—We, the undersigned tenants and residents on your manor and estate of Lenton, beg to approach you on this occasion of your coming amongst us, and to assure you of our high appreciation of your kindness in taking the initial step in the noble and useful work of providing additional accommodation for public worship in the parish.

We feel sure that you will, with us, experience much gratitude and satisfaction in seeing a new and splendid edifice arise within the consecrated precincts of our ancient and venerable priory, hitherto so long abandoned to decay, as well as in knowing that the spiritual welfare of the inhabitants of the parish, under the direction of its devoted clergy, are and will be so well cared for.

Sincerely trusting that you, a lady so well known and prominent in all good works, may by Divine Providence long be spared in health and happiness,

We beg to remain, Madam,

Your faithful servants.

Lenton, 22nd November, 1883.

# INDEX.

## A.

Abbeville, Peter de, Prior of Lenton, 182
Ackworth, William, 158
Adams, Arms of, 203
—— John, 204
—— Lucy, 269
—— Thomas, 203, 265, 266, 268, 290, 348
Aiscough, John, 215
Alan, sub-Prior of Lenton, 71
Alan, sub-Prior of Lenton, seal of, 72, 232
Albemarle, William, Earl of, 180
Albini, W. de, 101
Aldelmus, 63, 87
Aldesworth, Adam de, 109
—— Robert de, 109
Alexander, Prior of Lenton, 179
Alestre, John, Warden of the Chapel in Nottingham Castle, 160
Alfer, of Basford, 87
Algarthorpe, Gerard de, 116
Allcock, Thomas, 287
Allen, Francis, 370
—— John, 287
Allicock, Thomas, 47, 342, 345
Allworthy, John, 283
Almeton, 101, 114
Alneo, Hugh de, 85
Amiens, Guy of, 20
Andegavansis, Robert, 110
Anglo-Normans, a building people, 54
Annesley, Gervase, 210
—— John, Prior of Lenton, 175, 190
Annis, Jester, 285
Antiquities, early, 11—17

Amyas, William de, 40
Andrewes, Thomas, 370
Anger, Robert, 240
Apsley, Sir Allen. Bart., 395
Arches, Thomas de, 96
Arden, Simon de, 122
Arksey Church (Yorks.), 170
Arksey Vicarage, 171
Arnale, Gervase de, 109
—— Sir Ralph de, 129
Arnesby (Leic.), 63, 84
Arnold, Thomas de, 310
Ashbourne (co. Derby), 63, 84
Ashby, Great, Manor of, 83
Ashford (co. Derby), 62, 68, 71, 77
Askewe, Thomas, 242, —— Reginald de, 111
Aspin, John, 260
Asply, 63, 85
—— Wood, herbage of, 215
Asselacton, Simon de, 388
Asson, William, 47
Aston, Gregory, 287
—— Sir Roger, Knt., 366
—— Thomas, 366
Astorgius, or Antorgius, Prior of Lenton, 182
Atherton, Miss, of Kersall, Lanc., 214
Atkins, Samuel, 338
Atkinson, John, 210
Attenborough, Church of, 88, 124
Attenborough, Edward, 47
Attenborrow, John, 326
—— Robert, 326
Athillewell, Augustin de, 39
—— Alice, widow of, 39

Ault, Benjamin, 287, 336, 343, 345, 346
Ault, Mercy, 284
Aveline, W. T., Geologist, 432
Avenel, Robert, 99
—— William de, 62, 63, 82, 83
Awsworth, 87
—— Mill at, 109
—— see Aldesworth
Ayscough, John, 41
Ayskough, Mary, 276
—— Roger, 276


## B.

Babington, Arms of, 38,
—— Sir Bernard, 36
—— Elizabeth, 160,
—— Sir John, 35, 160,
17c
Babington, Robert, buried at Lenton Priory, 159
Babington, Thomas, 170
—— Sir William, 35
—38, 159, 216
Babington, William, 160
Bacon, Thomas, 284
Bagshaw, John, 280
—— Mary, 280
Bailey, Isaac, 338
Bakepuz, Sir Geoffrey, 123
Bakewell (co. Derby), 62, 68, 70, 71, 72, 77
Bakewell Church of, 75
—— Matthew priest of, 83
Balguy, Charles George, 252
Balguy, John, 401, 403
Bardelby, R. de, 135
Bardolf, Hugh, 388
—— Robert, 388

Bardsley, George, 472
Barker, John, 405
Barn Houses, 8
Barneston, Gervase de, 95
———— Margaret, wife of
Gervase de, 95
Barneston, Richard de, 95
Barnwell Priory (Cambridge-
shire), 22
Barre, John, 126
—— Ralph, 88, 98
—— Richard, 126
Barrett, Paul, 331
Barri, Richard, lord of
Tollerton, 98
Barri, Beatrice, wife of, 98
Barry family, 98
—— see Barre, Barri
Barston, William, 158
Barton, Mr., of Bestwood,
379
Barton-in-Fabis, Church of,
88, 127, 136, 214
Barton-on-Trent, 128
Barwick, Peter, M.D., 194
Basford, 63, 84
—— Alluvial and drift
deposits at, 456
Basford, Lands of Safied,
83
Basford, Manor of, 40
Bassano, Francis, note on
Chelmorton Chapel, 77
Basset, Sir Richard, 366
—— Simon de, charter of,
83
Bate, Thomas, 177
Bath Hill, 14, 15, 17
Bath, Joceline, Bishop of,
121
Baume, Claude de la, Arch-
bishop of Besançon, 460
Bayley, Hannah, 341
—— Isaac, 360
—— & Co's. leather
dressing works, 8, 360
Bayley, Thomas, 209, 3 8,
348, 349, 353
Beacock, Thomasine, 278
Beardsley, Arthur, 287, 336,
343, 345
Beardsley, William, 375
Beauchamp, Richard de,
125
Beauclerk, Lord Amelius,
379, 380, 381
Beauclerk, Lord Aubrey,
381
Beauclerk, Charles, 274
———— Lady Diana, 382
———— James, 374, 376
———— Lady Louise, 381
———— Lord Vere, 378
Beaufort, Henry, first Duke
of, 399

Beaumes, Philip de, 114
Beaver, Ellen Maria, 258
Beaver, Herbert Napleton,
258
Becket, Thomas, 467
Beckley, Roman villa at, 14
Beckford, William de, Vicar
of Beeston, 150
Beesley, Richard, 287
Beeston, 125
—— Church, chantry of
St. Catherine, 150
Beeston, John de, 150
—— Gilbert de, 306
—— mill burnt, 469
—— Rectory of, appro-
piated to Lenton Priory,
145
Beeston, William de, 150
—— Vicars of, 145, 146
Beheleg, Warnet de, 116
Bell inscriptions, 248, 265,
293
Bell, Joseph, 251, 252, 290,
338
Bellew, William de, 97
Bellofago, Ralph de, bene-
faction of, 88
Bellofago, Thomas de, 89
———— William de, 89
Bellomont, Hugh de, 122
———— Robert de, 89,
90, 122
Bellomont, Roger de, lord
of Pont Andomar, 89
Belvoir, Roger Wendover,
Prior of, 61
Benested, J. de, 135
Bennet, John, 467
Benton, Catherine, 279
—— John, 279
Berene, Thomas, 248
Beresford, Elizabeth, 257,
266
Beresford, Francis, 257, 266
Berde, John de, 240
Berkeley, Elizabeth, Coun-
tess of, 380
Berkeley, George, first Earl
of, 380
Bernard, Henry, 46
Beskewod, Robert de, 236
Best, William, 338
Beston, William, 39
Bestwood Park, 5, 50, 117,
168, 362-385
area of, 44, 50
dead wood granted to
monks of Lenton, 117,
120, 121
held by Nell Gwynne,
374.
secured to her and first
Duke of St. Albans,
376

Bestwood Lodge, 379
Emanuel Church, 381
Colliery and Ironworks,
383
perambulations of, 48-52,
384
Beverston Castle, Gloucester-
shire, 193
Bigsby, Rev. Thomas, Vicar
of Beeston, 199
Billyeald, Joseph, 349
Bingham, Richard, 40
———— William, 326, 327,
330
Birche, Katherine, 274
———— Thomas, 221, 275,
287
Bishop, Ellen, 279
———— Henry, 278
———— John, 278, 279
———— William, Rector of
St. Nicholas, Nottingham,
87
Blacclivegate, Lenton, 39
Black, William, 336, 343
Blackcliff, mill of, 39, 66, 79,
85, 107, 116.
Blackwall, Oliver, 161, 162
Blackwell (co. Derby), 77
———— Nicholas, 145
Blakeman, John, 240
Blakeney, Rev. Richard Paul,
294.
———— Lieut. Richard, 293
Blakesley (Northants.), 63,
86
Blanchard, Ann, 254
———— George, 254
———— John, 254
Blatherwick, John, 385
Blisworth (Northants.), 62,
67
Bluet, Hugh, Prior of Len-
ton, 125, 181
Bluet, Robert, 125
Blundeville, Ralph, 27
Blundus, Serlo, 63, 85
Blyth, Robert Bubwith,
Prior of, 159
Blyth, Priory of, 110
———— William West, Prior
of, 159
Bobber's Mill, 109
Bochart, Jofrid, 99
Bohun, John, 28
Boleyn, Sir Thomas, 365
Bolles, William, 218, 219
Boney, Sir Geoffrey de, 234
———— Hugh de, 88
———— Odo de, 63, 88, 136
———— Ralph de, 88
Bonington, William, 276
Bonney, Professor, 433
Boot, Gervase, 288, 289,
337, 344, 465 467

Boroughbridge, battle of, 137
Bossu, Robert, Earl of Leicester, charter of, 90
Bostock, Thomas, 330
Bosworth (Leic.), 85
Botetourt family, 76
Botre, John, 157
Bowes, Walter, 160
Bowser, John, 247, 286
Bowyer, Sir James, Bart., 398
Boyer, Francis, 215
Bozun, Robert, 134
Bradforde, Andrew, 275
——— Thomas, 275
Bradley, George, 338
——— John, 375
——— John de, 95
Bradmere, Elias de, 131
——— Ralph de, 98
——— Sir Richard de, 98
Bradmore, 88, 98, 126, 136
——— see Bradmere
Bradshawe, John, 248, 288, 326, 327, 336, 337, 343, 344, 346
Bradwell (co. Derby), 62, 68, 77
Bramcote Chapel, 125
——— Herbert de, 109
Bramley, Charles, 385
Breadsall, John, 309, 310
Brentnall, George, 212, 282, 283, 322, 326
Brentnall, Lucy, 212, 282, 283
Brentnall, Thomas, 213, 331
Brereton, Francis, Lord, 173
——— Sir Henry, 171
——— Sir William, 172
——— William, Lord, 172
Brewer, William, 177
Brewood, Priory of, 112
Brigges, Sir Humphrey, Bart., 374
Brightman, Thomas, 237
Brikesard, Anketina de, 101
——— Nichola, wife of, 101
Brito, Helyus, 109
——— Roger, 63, 85
Briwerre, William, 109, 388
Broadband, Elizabeth, 277
——— William, 277
Broadbent, John, 211
Brock, Jeffery, 237
Broculstowe, Gilbert, son of Eustace de, 104
Brodbury, Agnes, 309, 310
——— William de, 309, 310
Broksop, Henry, 240
Brokestowe, Adam, 151
Brokilstowe, John de, 236
Brokstowe, John de, 157
Bromholm Priory, 54, 61

Bromley, William de, 104
Brooks, John, 472
Brough, George, 237
——— Richard, 370
Broughton, Anne, 282
——— Church of, 136
——— Peter, 282
——— Thomas, 404
Brouley, Elizabeth, 275
——— John, 275
Brown, Elizabeth, 282
——— George, 338, 344
——— Henry, 282, 336
——— John, 276
Browne, Right Hon. Denis, M.P., 244
Browne, Denis George, 268, 285
——— Edward, 268, 285
——— Elizabeth Ann, 267
Browne, Rev. Francis, 268, 472
Browne, Rev. George, 244, 251, 252, 265, 267, 285, 348, 381, 474
Browne, Henry, 287
——— James Peter, 268
——— Mary, 281
——— Thomas, 104
——— William John, 268
Brownlow, Hannah, 280
——— John, 280
——— Philip, 280
Broxtow, 1, 87, 104
——— See Broculstowe, Brokestowe, Brokilstowe, Brokstowe.
Broydeston, Richard de, 104
Brunnesley, Geoffrey de, 236
Brunt, George, 28
Brus, Robert de, 135
Bubwith, Nicholas, 145
Buck, Hannah, 281
——— Oliver, 331
Bugge, Ralph, 128
——— Richard, 128
Bulker, Thomas, 309
Bullington Priory, 108
Bunington, Elizabeth, 276
——— Ralph, 276
Bunny, 88, 98, 99, 136
——— see Boney
Burbage, Susanna, 210
Burdin, Elizabeth, 281
Burford, James, 280
Burgh, Hubert de, 109, 121
Burghley, William, Lord, 193
Burial Board, 346
Burleymen, list of, 345
Burr, Robert, 28
Burrow, Hugh, 28
Burton, Abbot of, 70, 71
——— John, 289, 338, 344
——— Mary, 280
——— Richard, 145, 344

Burton, Robert, 241
——— Robert de, 89
——— Roger de, 111
——— William, 287, 336, 343, 345, 346
Burun, arms of, 102
——— Hugo de, 63, 100, 101, 103, 136
Burun, Hugo, Albreda, wife of, 101
Burun, Hugo, Hugo Meschines, eldest son and heir of, Monk of Lenton, 100, 102
Burun, pedigree of, 102
——— Ralph de, 96
——— Robert de, 100
——— Roger de, 100, 101, 103
Burun, Roger de, Nichola, wife of, 101
Bury, Christopher, 161, 162
Busli, Hugo de, 100
Bussell, or Buisell, Albert, 91
Bussell, or Buisell, Richard, 92, 136
Bushell, Aloisia, 275, 276
——— William, 275, 276
Butterley Ironworks, 201
Buxton, 62, 68
Bylay, Bryan, 277
Byllay, Samuel, 275
Byngeley, John, 104
Byrom, of Kersall Cell, Lanc., arms of, 214
Byrom, Edward, 213, 214
——— Elizabeth, 213
——— John, F.R.S., 213, 214
Byrom, Joseph, 213
——— Ralph, 213
Byron, family, of Colwick, 376
Byron, Sir John, 108, 366, 367, 395, 461
Byron, John, Esquire, 365
Byron, Lord, poet, 102, 471
——— see Burun
Byshopp, John, 276


C.

Cadogan, Earl of, 380
Cadwallader, King of Wales, 108
Caisneta, Roger de, 112
Caketherngate, 39
Calais, Prior of Lenton raises money for defence of, 159
Callow (co. Derby), 62, 68
Calverley, Robert, bequest to Lenton Priory, 170

Cambridge, King's Hall, 118
—— Trinity College, 118
Camden's Britain quoted, 3
Campden, Viscount, 193
Canal, Nottingham and Cromford, 4
Cann, Abraham, 405
Cantelupe, Arms of, 131
—— Nicholas de, 130
—— William de, 130, 131
Canterbury, St. Augustine's Abbey, History of, 183
Canville, Richard de, 101
Capgrave, John, quoted, 146
Carlisle, Statute of, 135
Carmelite Friary at Lenton, 167
Carnebull, Thomas, 177
Carr, John, Architect, 204
Carruthers, Dr., 450, 454
Carver, Rev. David, 294
Cary, John, 367, 374
Cassells, Robert, 34, 346, 461
Castle, Joseph, 337, 343
—— Robert, 287, 336, 343, 345
Castleacre Priory, 54, 58, 61
Castleton, Derbyshire, Church of, 140
Catesby (Northants.), Manor of, 83
— — Nunnery of, 87
Cave, Mary, 276
—— Roger, 276
Cave, Sir Thomas, 276
Chadbourn, James, 341
Chadwick, Evelyn, 395
—— James, 33, 393, 394, 395, 397
Chadwick, John, 396, 397
—— Lewis, 396, 397
Chalens, Elizabeth, 274
Challand, Henry, 370
Challands, John, 338, 467
Chamberlain, or Chamberlin, Ann, 254, 283
Chamberlain, Elizabeth, 261, 274
Chamberlain, John, 239, 254, 261, 283, 284, 285, 287, 288, 327, 336, 337, 343, 344, 345, 346, 465, 467
Chamberlain, Joseph, 371
—— Martha, 254, 283
Chamberlain, Mary, 281
—— Richard, 289, 338, 344, 467
Chamberlain, William, 28, 274, 281

Chapel-en-le-Frith (Derby), 71, 73, 74, 75, 77, 124
Chapman, John, 287, 288, 336, 343, 346
Charley, Prior of, 75
Charlton, Lucy, 212
—— Nicholas, 212, 237
—— Tabitha, 212
—— Thomas, 212, 278
—— Thos. Broughton, 37
Charnocke, Anna, 275
—— James, 275
Chauz, Robert de, 63
Chaworth, Sir John, Knight, 215
Chaworth, Sir Thomas, 159
Cheetham, Francis, 338
—— James, 213
Chelmorton (co. Derby), 62, 68, 77, 78
Chelmorton Chapel, tomb of a Prior of Lenton at, 78
Cheney, Alexander de, 112, 114
Cheney, Hugh de, 114
—— Ralph de, 114
Chester, Adam de Stanford, Archdeacon of, 71, 72
Chester, Earl of, 25, 101, 107
Chester, Maud, Countess of, 25
Chester, Walter Durdent, Bishop of, 25
Chesterfield, Earl of, 331
—— Henry de, 39
Chilwell, 63, 85, 88, 136
Chilwell, coal, boring for, at, 423
Chilwell, fishery of, 105
Chilwell Hall, 37
Chillendon, Edmund, 371
Christie, Lorenzo, 338
Churchell, Benjamin, 385
Churches, The, 245-271
Church Goods, A.D. 1552, 246
Church, Old Church restored, 473, 474
Church rates, 286
Churchwardens' Accounts, extracts from, 285-286
Churchwardens, list of, 286-290
Clare, John Holles, second Earl of, 394
Clark, Milicent, 281
—— Peter, 281
—— William, 281
Clarke, Humphrey, 31
—— John, 216, 287, 288, 336, 343, 345, 346
Clarke, Margaret, 216
—— Richard, 216

Clay, Charles, 281
—— Mary, 281
Claydon, Little (Bucks.), 63, 85
Clayton family, 280
Clayton, Richard, 280
Clayworth, Robert, 339, 340
Cleaton, Richard, 280
—— Sarah, 280
Cleaver, Alfred, 360
Cliff, William, 338
Cliffe, Frances, 275
—— William, 275
Clifford, Richard de, 365
Clifton College, payment by Lenton Priory to, 177
Clifton Colliery, 411, 413, 420, 421, 422, 427, 439, 440, 442, 448, 451
Clifton, Sir Gervase, 31, 97, 159, 373, 389
Clifton, Gervase de, 102, 110
Clifton Hall, 419
Clifton, Robert, 159
Clifton water mill, 113
Clifton, William, 240, 310
Climate of Lenton, 475
Clinton and Saye, Edward, Lord, 215
Clugniac Monastery, arrangement of, 56-61
Clugny, Abbey of, 54
—— Pontius, Abbot of, 61, 64
Clugny, Raymund, Abbot of, 182
Coape, Henry, 385
Cobden Park, 11, 45
Cockayne, John, 464
Cockfield, see Cokefield
Codnor Castle, 97
Coins, discovery of, 15
Cokefield, Adam de, 114
—— Agatha de, 115
—— Agnes, 41
—— John, 40, 41, 311
—— Margaret, 40, 41, 311
Cokefield, Sir Robert, 115, 189
Collingwood, Roland, 178
Collishaw, Margaret, 281
—— Mary, 281
—— Samuel, 281, 335, 345
Colston Basset, 95
Columbell, Roger, 312
—— Thomas de, 156
Colwick, Sir Philip de, 126
Coningsby, Sir Henry, 194
Conksbery (co. Derby), 82
Constable, Alice de, 115
—— Geoffrey de, 115
Constables, list of parish, 342

Conyers, Richard, 216
Cookes, Sir Thomas, 195
Cooper, Samuel Thomas, 328
Cooper, Thomas, 210
Cope, Edward, 10, 204
Copley, Edward, 278
———— Joan, 278
Cortingstock, or Costock, Andrew de, 96
Cortingstock, Church of, 96, 97
Cortingstock, John de, 129
———————— Philip de, 96
———————— Robert de, 96, 100
Cortingstock, Roger de, 96
———————— William de, 96
Cossall, 87
Cost, Cecilia, 274
Costinton, Robert de, 128
Cotes (Leic.), 63, 85
Cotgrave, 96, 100, 128, 129, 136, 141, 144, 215
Cotgrave, Ralph, rector of, 96
Courteenhall (Northants.), 62, 66, 67, 116, 136, 216
Cousin, Gilbert, canon of Nozeray, 460
Coventry, 61
Coventry Lane, Beeston, 13, 14
Coventry and Lichfield, Bishops of—
    Cornhill, William, 68
    Muschamp, Geoffrey, 68
    Nonant, Hugo de, 68
    Stavenby, Alexander, 69, 71, 74
    Weseham, 70
Cowdale (co. Derby), 62, 68
Cowl, action to recover value of a, 158
Cowleyshaw, or Cowlishaw, Elizabeth, 279
Cowleyshaw, or Cowlishaw, Isaac, 179
Cowleyshaw, or Cowlishaw, Isabella, 279
Cowleyshaw, or Cowlishaw, John, 277
Cowleyshaw, or Cowlishaw, Mary, 276
Cowleyshaw, or Cowlishaw, Robert, 276, 279
Coxon, Peter, 338, 358
Crampton, Richard, 336
Creissi, Hugh de, 107
Crescy, William de, 40
Cresswell, Edward, 244
Cripps, Rev. William Richard, 349, 381
Croft, Hugh, 38

Cromford and Nottingham Canal, 6
Cromwell, Frances, 397
———————— Gregory, Lord, 390
Cromwell, Sir Henry, 397
———————— Oliver, 397
———————— Ralph, Lord, 37, 365
Cromwell, Thomas, Lord, 390
Crophill-Bishop, 89, 136
Croshaw, John, 344
Crossland, George, 28
Croweshaw, John de, 156
Croxall (co. Derby), 62, 68
Croxton, Abbot and Convent of, 93, 94
Croxton, Geoffrey, Abbot of, 94
Cuckney, Isabella de, 109
———————— Thomas de, 109
Cumin, John, justice itinerant, 95
Cumminge, Thomas, 237
Curci, R. de, 101
Curteys, Anthony, 28
" Cut-throat Lane," footroad from Lenton to Beeston, 8, 10, 16

D.

Dabrichecourt, Nicholas, 365
Daft, William, 385
Dalby, Walter the cook, of, 93
Dale, Daniel, 371
Dallison, William, 349
Dalmasius, Prior of Lenton, 181
Damascenus, Prior of Lenton, 94, 181
*Dan.* title applied to a monk, 178
Dand, Anne, 33
Dande, Rowland, 373
Daniel, Richard, 70, 71
———— Robert, 42
Darnall, 62, 68
*Darrien Presentment,* assize of, 81
Daubes, John, 42
Davidville, Robert de, 96
———————— William de, 114
Davies, Griffith, 336
Davis, Ferdinando, 464
———— William, 336
Davyes, Edward, 375
Daws, Thomas, 370
Dawson, Richard, 263
Dealtry, Jane, 260
Deeley, R. M., 447
Degge, Alice, 399

Degge, Hugh, 399
———— Jane, 399
———— Sir Simon, 399
———— Thomas, 399
Deincourt, family of, 37
Delves, John, 160
Denby Chapel (co. Derby), 160-162
Dene, Richard, Prior of Lenton, 160, 169, 189
Derbigate, 39
Derby, Earl of, 459
———— St. James' cell, payment to, 177
Derby, Thomas of, 151,
Deryngton, William de, 156
Desborough, Northants, 63, 68
Despencer, Geoffrey le, 84
———————— Hugh le, 135
Dethick, Sir Geoffrey de, 129
———————— John, 370
Deverell, John, 367
Dichfield, Edward, 31
Dickinson, George, 287, 345
———————— William, 34, 287, 336, 343, 345, 346
Digby, Sir Simon, Knt., 365
Digbye, Jane, 274
Dobb, Sarah, 282
Dolphin, Elizabeth, 274
———————— William, 275
Domesday survey quoted, 18, 35
Dowkyn, Richard, 78
Drewry, or Drury, Sarah, 280
Dryden, Sir Henry, Bart., 226
Dudley, John, 215
Dunham, Sir John, 179
Dunington, Henry, 355
Dunkirk, 8, 16
Dunningstede, 62, 68
Dunstanville, Robert de, 106
Dunston (co. Derby), manor of, 116, 136, 214
Duran, deacon at Flawford, 89
Durdent, Walter, 25
Duston, Northants., 62, 67, 68
Dyghton, John, monk of Lenton, 158

E.

Eastwood, Adam de Markham, rector of, 97
Eastwood, George, 283
———————— Mary, 283, see Esswayt, Estwait, Estwayt
Edge, of Strelley, family of, 43

Edge, Ralph, 43
—— Thomas Webb, 331
—— Walter, 43,
Edward I., at Lenton, 135
—— II., at Lenton, 135
—— charter to Lenton Priory, 136
Edwards, Edward, 467
Eland, Henry, 391
—— Joan, 391
—— Mary, 391
—— Thomas, 391
—— Sir William, 389, 391
Eldred, John, 211
Eller, Thomas, 287
Ellesley, Richard. 145
Elliott, John, 331
—— William, 326
—— William Elliott, 330
Ellis, William, 379, 465, 467
Ellys, Richard, 104
Elmham, John, Prior of Lenton, 158, 183, 189
Elmham, Thomas of, Prior of Lenton, 157, 158, 182—189
Elmely, William, 365
Elmore, Manor of, 35, 159
Elyngham, John, 151
Empingham, 63, 83, 84
—— Barbara, 277
Elsam, Elinora, 277
—— William, 277
Enfield, Eleanor Sara, 261
—— Henry, 261
Erchin, tenant of Sutton Passeys, 99
Ernis, Abbot of Rufford, 114
Emott, John, 145
Esswayt, Peter de, 128
Eston, Adam de, 73
Estwait, William, son of Godfrey de, 97
Estwayt, Walter de, 109
Etymology, 2
Evans, Anne Elizabeth, 203
—— Dorothy, 203
—— Francis, 198, 203, 262, 289, 338, 344, 400, 465, 467
Evans, Robert, 203
Evanson, William, 371
Everingham, Lancelot, 237
Exeter, arms of see of, 228
—— Bartholomew, bishop of, 107
Exley, Rev. Tristam, 319
Eyre, Rev. John, 249, 250, 251
Eyre. Thomas, 399
Eyton, John de, 148

32

F.

Fairs, Lenton, 3, 7, 141, 151, 303—315
Fair granted to Lenton Priory by Henry II., 106
Fairs, actions relating to, 307—310
Fairs, agreement between Prior of Lenton and Mayor of Nottingham as to Lenton Fair, 304—307
Fairs reduced four days in duration, 305
Fairs, spices bought at, 313
—— rates of stallage, 312
—— proclaimed in Nottingham, 307
Fairs, theft of bows brought to Nottingham for sale at, 310
Fairs, deceit in quality of ale brewed for, 309, 310
Fairs, manufacture of gloves for, 308
Fairs, Webber, Thomas, grant of fair to, 314
Fairs, Gregory, George, grant of fair to, 315
Fairs, tobacco, sale of, 314
—— decay of, 315
Faile, Anna, 275
Fairbrother, Henry, 370
—— John, 370
Fairfax, Guy, 158
Fairfield (co. Derby), 73, 74, 75, 77
Fanshawe, Sir Thomas, 373
Farmer, Henry, 8
Faukener, Henry le, 93
—— Honora, wife of, 93
Faukener, Ralph, 93
Farnworth, Henry, 279
—— Mary, 279
Farnsworth, John, 400
Feast, village, 264
Feild, Anne, 282
—— Elizabeth, 282
—— James, 260, 281, 282, 283, 284, 287, 288, 336, 343
Feild, Joseph, 260, 282
—— Mary, 282
—— Matthew, 283
—— Mercy, 283, 284
—— Sarah, 260, 281, 282, 283
Felley Priory, 97, 112, 125
Felmersham (Beds.), church of, 117, 118, 130
Fenton, Ann, 267
—— Helena, 276
—— Joseph, 267
—— Rev. Timothy, 281

Fernilee (co. Derby), 62, 68, 77
Ferrers, Margaret de, 82
—— Robert de, 73, 74, 73, 74, 81, 82, 136, 148
—— William de, 26, 27, 73, 74, 81, 82, 136, 148
Fewks, George, 336
Field names, 196—198
Fillingham, Robert, 375
Firth, Thomas, 287,
Fish, John, 336
Fisher, Emily 293
—— Isaac, 338
—— James, 293,
—— John, 242, 274
—— William, 215
Fitz-Aman, family of, 85
Fitz-Eustace, Richard, 105
Fitz-Herbert, Ralph, 88
Fitz-John, Eustace, of Castle Donington, 105
Fitz-John, William, 81 ·
Fitz-Nicholas, Sir Ralph, 388
Fitz-Nigel, William, Baron of Halton, and Constable of Chester, 105
Fitz-Pain, Robert, 63, 84
Fitz-Parnell, Robert, Earl of Leicester, 90
Fitz-Ralph, Hugh, 130
—— Ralph, 130
—— Robert, 387
—— William, 96
Fitz-Robert, Ralph, 151
Fitz-Simon, Simon, of Kyme, 108
Fitz-Thomas, William, 81
Fitz-William family, 278
—— Thomas, 179
Flammoynth, Walter, 63, 85,
Flanders, Matilda of, 21
Flawford, church of, 37
—— Duran, deacon of, 89
Fleet Prison, London, first warden of, 159
Fletcher, John, 281,
—— Mary, 279, 281
Flinders, Richard, 336
Flisco, Nicholin de, Cardinal of Genoa, at Lenton, 147
Flower, Elizabeth, 279, 281
—— George, 279, 368, 370
Flower, Hellina, 278
—— Henry, 279
—— Judith, 279
—— Thomas, 405
—— William, 278
Foljambe, Alice, 179
—— Cecil G. S., 473
—— family of, 40

Foljambe, George, 179
———— Helena, 179
— ——— Sir James, 179
———— James, 179
———— Roger, 179
———— Sir Thomas, 40
———— William, 40
Forster, Jane, 274
———— Sarah, 276
———— Thomas, 274
Foster, Bathshuah, 275
———— William, 275, 276
Foston, Leicestershire, church of, 62, 80, 216
Foxcroft, Alexander, 257, 338
Foxcroft, Herbert, 257
———— Sarah, 257
Frauncis, Robert, 97
Francis, Dorothy, 203
———— Rev. Henry, 203
———— John, 238. 243
Freeman, Grace, 284
Freschville, Ralph de, 131, 234
Fressenville, Britan de, 99
———— Willimina, 99
Frith, John, 239
———— Thomas, 343
Froggatt, John, senior, 223, 224, 271, 290, 344
Froggatt, John, junior, 50, 351, 353
Froggatt, Samuel, 50, 340
———— Sarah, 271
Fulwood, enclosed by Prior of Lenton, 97
Furneis, Ralph de, 105
Furneus, Alan de, justice intinerant, 95
Fyndern, William, 241

G.

Gadsby, Mary, 281
Gameleston, Aunsell de, 389
———— Henry, 157
Garendon Abbey, 75, 106, 126
Garforde, William, 146
Garland, arms of, 212
———— charity, 291
———— John, 212, 256, 280, 281, 336, 345
Garland, Lucy, 212, 280, 282
Garland, Mary, 281
———— pedigree of, 212
———— Rebecca, 34, 212, 270, 280, 283, 322, 326
Garland, residence of family of, 339
Gasworks, 11

Gatneby, Richard, 275
Gaunt, Gilbert de, 109
———— John of, 26
Gee, Anne, 281
——— Rev. John, 281
——— Nathaniel, 338
Geoffrey, Prior of Lenton, A.D. 1315, 182
Geoffrey, Prior of Lenton, A.D. 1327, 138, 182
Geography, 1
Geology, 408-458
Gerard, Archbishop of York, 63
Gernon, Sir John, 75
———— Matilda, Countess of Chester, 108
Gernon, Ralph, 27, 75
———— Ralph de, Earl of Chester, 107
Gervis, John, 236
Gibson, Thomas, 375
———— W. F., 348
Gilbert, chaplain of Nottingham Castle, 83
Gilbert, Baldwin, son of, 101
———— Joan, 41, 42
———— John, 41, 42
———— Humphrey, 275
——— Margery, 42
——— monk of Lenton, 158
Gilbourn, Richard, 336
Giles, John Thomas, 290
Gill, Francis, 259
——— Rev. W., 465
Gladwin, Herbert, son of, 99
Gladwyn, Lemuel, 282
———— Sarah, 282
Gladstone, Right Hon. W. E., 353
Glamorgan, Amabile de, 98, 99
Glamorgan, Philip de, 98, 99
———— Robert de, rector of Bunny, 98
Glanville, Ralph de, 107
Glossop (co. Derby), 77
Gloucester, Robert, Earl of, 108
Godfrey, a benefactor to Lenton Priory, 84
Godfrey, Catherine, 279
———— Jane, 271
———— John, 271, 280, 338, 344
Godfrey, Richard, 279, 280
———— Thomas, 49, 50, 51, 52
Godiva, Countess, 61
Gonalston, 63, 85, 111
Gonshill, Dame Matilda, 116
——— Sir Walter de, 116
Goodacre, Samuel, 338, 467
Goodhead, William, 338

Goodwin, Alice, 280
Gorges, Richard, Lord, 194
Goring, Sir Charles, 398
———— Sir Edward, 392
———— Sir George, 390, 392, 398
Goring, George, Lord, 393, 396, 397, 398
Goring, Sir Henry, 398, 399
Gonnyson, Thomas, 211
Graisley, Thomas, 275
———— William, 287
Grammer, Thomas, 375
Graneby, Adam de, 240
Gray, Hon. Anchitell, 315
——— John de, 117
——— John, 467
Greasley, Thomas, 336, 343, 345
Greatrakes (co. Derby), 69
Greaves, Admiral, 340
———— Gabriel, 28
———— Mary, 279
———— William, 344
Green, J., 337, 344
——— James, 285, 289, 465, 467
Green, Sarah, 285
——— Thomas, 209
Greendale, 100
Greene, John, 46
———— William, 226
Greenlow (co. Derby), 77
Gregory, Barbara, 34
———— Catherine Sherwin, 34, 43, 235, 253, 473
Gregory, Edward, 32
———— Elizabeth, 274
———— Francis, 32
———— George, 32, 33, 34, 47, 315, 348, 375
Gregory, George de Ligne, 34, 321, 326, 330, 331
Gregory, John, 32, 33
———— John Sherwin, 34
———— Margaret, 275
———— pedigree of, 34
———— Philip, 32
———— Susanna, 33
———— William, 31, 32, 210, 237, 274, 314, 315
Gregory, Winifred, 33
Grendon, Serlo de, 96
———— William de, 81
Gresley, Geoffrey de, 38
———— Robert de, 96
Grey, General the Hon. Charles, 382
Grey, Sir Edward, Viscount Lisle, 178
Grey, Sir Henry de, 97, 124, 388
Grey, Dame Isolda, 97, 388
——— John de, 125

INDEX.                    483

Grey, Sir Richard de, 97, 124, 125
Grey, Richard de, Vicar of Horsley, 104
Grey, Walter, Archbishop of York, 120, 123, 124
Grimsditch, Sarah, 212
——— Thomas, 212
Grove, John, 371
Grunquetel, 99
Grym, John de, 38
Gull, William, 160
Gunthorpe, ford, 89
——— mill at, 89
Guyllam, or Gillame, Thomas, Prior of Lenton, 190
Guyllam, or Gillame, Thomas, Abbot of Pipewell, 190
Gwyn, Thomas, 374
Gwynne, Nell, 51, 374, 375, 376
Gwynne, Nell, arms of, 375
Gylot, John, 104
Gynger, John, 145
Gyon, Robert, 129
——— William, 129

H.

Hacker, Dorothy, 203
——— family of, 203
——— John, 203
Hadden, Henry, 202, 203
Haddon (co. Derby), 62, 71, 76, 77, 82
Haddon, Reginald, chaplain of, 83
Haddon, Sir Simon de, 110
Hall, Catherine, 279
——— Elizabeth, 330
——— Mordecai, 335, 336
Hall, Thomas, 290
——— Truth, 283
——— William, 326
Hallam, Edward, 289
Halum, Henry de, 104
Haumer, Cicely, 277
——— Ellinor, 277
——— Grace, 277
——— Humphrey, 277
——— Mary, 277
——— Philip, 210, 277
——— Thomas, 210, 277
——— Sir William, 277
——— Winifred, 277
Harbord, Sir Charles, 373
Harleston (Northants.), 62
——— church of, 81, 215
——— Robert de, 109
Harpole (Northants.), 63, 85
Harrington, Dame Isabel, 193
——— Sir John, 193
——— John, 193

Harris, Benjamin, 216
Harrison, Anthony, 276
——— Mary, 301
——— W. J., 433
Hartill, Richard de, 116
Harvey, George Bradley, 338
Harvey, James, 290
——— John, 369
Hastings, William, Lord Chamberlain, 159
Hatfield Peverel, Priory of, 21
Hathersage, Cecilia de, 116
——— Matilda de, 116
——— Matthew de, 116, 136
Haversham (Bucks.), 63, 85
Hazelbeech (Northants.), 63, 85
Heanor, John de, 39, 236
Hearson, Isabel, 280
Heath, Mr. Justice, on highway robberies, 462
Heccredibire, William, 131
Helgot, 63, 85
Helion family, 76
Hemlock Stone, 434
Henry I., charter to Lenton Priory, 65
Henry II., charters granted to Lenton Priory, 106, 107
Henry V., Elmham's description of King, 187
Henson, Gravener, 356
Herbert, Knight of William Peverel, 63, 85
Herbert, Charles, Lord, 399
——— John, 290
Hercy, John, 366
Hereford, Humphrey de Bohun, Earl of, 135
Hereward, Margaret, 150
Heriz, Adelina de, 110, 111
——— Geoffrey de, 63, 86
——— Ivo de, 84, 85, 110, 112
Heriz, Sir John de, 112
——— Robert de, 63, 84, 86, 110, 111, 112
Heriz, William de, 84, 93, 110, 111, 112
Herricke, Thomas, 375
Heth, or Heythe, Nicholas, Prior of Lenton, 67, 190
Heth, or Heythe, Nicholas, letter from, 178
Heth, or Heythe, Nicholas, attainder of, 191
Hever, William, 218, 219
Heylowe, Richard, 28
Heyth, Nicholas, see Heth
Hickling, Adelina de, 89
——— Robert de, 89
——— William de, 89

Hickling, William, 344
Hicks, arms of, 247
——— Sir Baptist, 193
——— Elizabeth, wife of Sir Michael, 193
Hicks, Margaret, wife of Sir William, 194
Hicks, Marthagnes, wife of Sir William, 194
Hicks, Sir Michael, 193
——— Robert, 193
——— Sir William, 193, 194
High Peak of Derbyshire, 82
High Peak, tithe of lead ore, 76
Higham (Northants.), 24, 25
Highfield House, 5, 10, 11, 198—201, 409, 440, 475
Highfield Park, borings for coal at, 420, 421, 422, 424, 427, 439, 448
Highlord, John, 31
Highway Board, 346
Highways, Overseers of, list of, 342
Hill, John, 338
——— Robert, 331
——— William, 287
Hilston, or Ilkeston, John, Prior of Lenton, 189
Hinglesham, William de, 80
Hobson, Thomas, Prior of Lenton, 190
Holfin, Maud, 131
Holles, Francis, 375
Hollingworth, Edward, 248, 288, 336, 337, 343, 344, 346, 467
Hollis, Joseph, 467
——— Matthew, 467
Holme (co. Derby), manor of, 116, 136, 214
Holmes, Elizabeth, 326
——— John, 336
Holt, Thomas, 385
Hood, Dr., of London, 223
Hooley, Mary, 282
Hooton, Roger, 287
Hope (co. Derby), 70, 72, 73, 75, 77
Hope, church of, 73
——— Sir William, 315
Hopewell, William, 404
Hopkins, Humphrey, 34, 282, 287, 288, 336, 337, 343, 344, 345, 346, 465, 466, 468
Hopkins, John, 282, 288, 336, 337, 342, 343, 344, 345, 466, 467
Hopkins, Mary, 467
——— Sarah, 282, 341
——— William, 288, 337, 338, 346

Hopkins, Rev. Thomas, 49, 265, 270
Horiston Castle and Park (co. Derby), 100
Hornbuckle, Walter, 326
——— William, 330
Hornius, of Ruddington, 89
——— Margery, wife of, 89
Hornius, William, son of, 89
Horsley (co. Derby), church of, 100, 103, 130, 136
Horsley, Thomas, 370
——— list of Vicars of, 104
Hostiler, Henry, 308
Houghton (Northants.), 63, 85
Houghton, George, 28
Howard, John, 401
Howson, Charles, 177
Howtone, Roger, 210, 211
Hucklow (co. Derby), 62, 68, 77
Hucknall Torkard, 111, 114
Hugh, son of Richard, 63
——— Sheriff of Leicestershire, 63
Hugh, son of Simon, 89
Hughes, David, 467
Hulme (co. Derby), 62, 68, 77
Humet, Richard de, 107
Humfrey, Sarah, 279
Humphrey, Prior of Lenton, 92, 101, 179
Hundon, William de, 145
Hunsdon, Henry Carey, Lord, 173
Hunsworth (Yorks.), church of, 103
Hunt, Thomas, 47
Hurst, William, 42, 43
Husbands Bosworth (Leic.), 63
Hut, William, 148
Hutchinson, John, 28, 237, 338
Hutchinson, Colonel John, 395
Hutchinson, Lucy, 395
——— Dame Margaret, 395
Hutchinson, Mary, 281
——— Sir Thomas, 395
Huthwaite, Lucy, 259
——— William, 259
——— William Francis, 259
Huxley, Professor, 416
Hydes, Piers, 42
——— Roger, 42, 43
Hyson Green, 44, 45, 292
——— Chapel, 299
——— Church, 253, 292-294

Hyson Green, Schools, 297

I.

Ile, John del, 157
Ilkeston, or Hilston, John, Prior of Lenton, 189
Inclosures, 316-333
Inclosure Act, 1767, 318
——— 1796, 328
——— Award, 1768, 319-326
Inclosure Award, 1799, 329-331
Inclosure Map, 1768, 320
Ingram, Lawrence, 122
——— Robert, 122
Ingram's Mill, 9, 123
Innocent IV., Pope, 70
Insula, Brien de, 118
——— Ralph de, 88, 98
Irchester, (Northants.), 82
Ireton, Henry, 172, 173
Ironmonger, Thomas, 158

J.

James, Alderman John, 33
——— Prior of Thetford, 182
——— Robert, 344
Jerusalem, Patriarch of, 135
Jocelin, 85
John, King, charters granted to Lenton Priory by, 116-119
John, Prior of Lenton, 159
——— son of Thomas the Leech, 133
John XXII., Pope, 75
Johnson, Joan, 278
——— George, 278
——— Margaret, 283
——— Walter, 283
——— William, 405
Jora, Reginald de, Prior of Lenton, 131, 181
Jorz, Richard de, 129

K.

Katull, John, 145
Kaytsank, William, 39
Keetley, Ann, 283
——— Anne, 283
——— Elizabeth, 282, 283
——— George, 282
——— James, 282
——— Joanna. 282, 284
——— John, 282, 288, 337, 344, 462

Keetley, Joseph, 282
——— Matthew, 283
——— Samuel, 270, 282, 283, 287, 288, 289, 290, 293, 336-338, 343, 345, 346
Keetley, Thomas, 283
——— William, 282, 337, 344
Keighton, village of, 5, 8, 15, 16, 62, 152
Kelladine, Thomas, 287, 335
Kenilworth, Prior of, 70
Kenion, Ralph, 213
Kenrick, Rev. John, 261
Kent, Henry, 104, 160, 161
Kersall Cell, Lancashire, 107, 108, 117, 151, 213, 214
Kettleby, John, 288, 337, 343
Keyworth, 110, 122, 126
Kilborne, John, 210, 287
Kilburne, Albert, Knight of, 100
Killamarsh (co. Derby), 85
Killingley, Elizabeth, 259
——— James, 331
——— John Wright, 259, 285, 289, 337, 344
Kimberley, 116
Kinoulton, manor of, 136
Kirk, Joseph, 287
——— Thomas, 289
——— William, 271, 338, 348
Kirk Langley (co. Derby), 63, 87
Kirke, George, 211
Kirkton, see Keighton
Kivelix, Hugh, Earl of Chester, 27
Knaggs, John, 285, 287
Knight, William, 338
Kniveton, Geoffrey de, 365
Knolles, John, 171
Knowle (co. Derby), 63
Kyme, Simon de, 108
——— Rose, wife of, 109
——— Walter de, 109
Kynmerley, Robert de, 97, 124
Kyrkton, decay of, 152

L.

Lacey, James, 336
——— Joseph, 343
——— Robert, 285, 287
Laci, John de, Constable of Chester, 104, 105, 106
Laci, Robert de, lord of Pontefract, 105
Lacy, Henry de, Earl of Lincoln, 135

Lacy, Joseph, 287
Lambcote, Hugh de, 109
———— William de, 109
Lambert, William, 204
Lamin, John, 51, 338
Lancaster, Avicia de, 25
———— Duchy of, 26
———— Earl of, 137
———— John, Duke of, 75
Lancaster, William de, 25
Langar, 80, 119, 120, 158
———— church, 62
Langeton, Thomas de, 236
Langford, Cecilia de, 116
———— George, 290, 338
———— John, 237
———— Nigel de, 116
Langley (co. Derby), 63, 87
———— Geoffrey de, 364
———— William, 370
Langton, Alice de, 150
Langtree, —, 68
Lathom, Sir Robert de, 110
Latimer, Edward, Viscount, 165
Latimer, William de, 128
Launde, John de la, 145
———— Prior of, 70, 71
Lawley, Sir Thomas, Bart., 396, 397
Lecester, sometimes Leicester, Anne, 274, 276
Lecester, Edward, 276, 277
———— Henry, 275
———— Humphrey, 275
———— Isabella, 274
———— James, 274, 275, 276
Lecester, Jane, 274
———— Joan, 277
———— John, 247, 274, 276, 277
Lecester, Luke, 274
———— Margaret, 274
———— Mary, 276, 277
———— Richard, 274
———— Sarah, 277
———— Thomas, 278
———— William, 278
Ledwort, 214
Lee, Henry, 171
———— James Holwell, 203
———— Sarah, 202
———— William, 202
Leeds, Duke of, 214
Leek, Sir Francis, Knight, 214
Leek, Ralph, 36
———— see Leke
Leeminge, Elinora, 277
———— Frances, 275, 277
Leeminge, John, 275, 277
———— Mary, 276

Leen, River, 2—4, 61, 162, 169, 225
Lees, Ralph, 274
Legard, James Anlaby, 470
Leicester Abbey, 82
———— collegiate church of, founded, 89
Leicester, monks of, 91
———— Honour of, 91, 93
———— Richard, Abbot of, 99
Leicester, Robert de Bellomont, Earl of, 89
Leicester, Robert Fitz-Parnell, Earl of, 90
Leicester, St. Margaret's Church, 75
Leicester, St. Mary's Church, 71
Leicester, Walter, Warden of the Friars Minor at, 71, 72
Leicestershire, Hugh, Sheriff of, 63
Leke, Alan de, 125
———— John de, 109
———— Sampson de, 125
Leland's Itinerary quoted, 2, 366
Lennox and Richmond, James Stuart, Duke of, 32
Lenton "Abbey," 10, 209
———— aggravated assault at, 41
Lenton, Agricultural Shows at, 7, 473
Lenton, Amicable Society 464
Lenton, ancient keys found at, 230
Lenton, area of, 44
———— as a Roman Station, 12
Lenton, as a surname, 39
———— battle at, between Britons and Romans, 15
Lenton, Blacclivegate at, 39
———— Boulevard, 7, 8, 9, 354, 409, 430
Lenton, Carmelite Friary, 167
Lenton, celebration in honour of King George III. 1809, 469
Lenton church, see Churches
———— climate of, 475
———— Coffee House, 468
———— Domesday survey of, 18
Lenton, early history of, 38, 43
Lenton Eaves, 10
———— Everard de, 99
———— Fair, see Fairs
———— Fields, 202

Lenton Firs, 5, 9, 203, 204, 426, 431
Lenton floods, 461 463, 464, 472
Lenton, freeholders of, 46, 47
Lenton, Geoffrey de, 39
———— Gervase de, 99
———— Grove, 10, 203, 430
———— highway robberies at, 464
Lenton Hall, 5, 6, 10, 11, 201, 410, 418, 426, 427, 429, 440, 470
Lenton House, 5, 202, 469
———— itinerary of, 6—11
———— John de, 39
———— and Radford Association for the prosecution of felons, 470
Lenton Liberal Club, 473
———— Lodge, 7
———— Luddite outrages at, 341, 469
Lenton, Manor of, 18—34
———— Boundaries of 27, 31
Lenton Manor, Extracts from Court Roll, 34
Lenton, Mart Yard, Shops in, removed, 462
Lenton, Mary, 280
———— Mission Hall built, 472
Lenton, murder at, 1877, 472
Lenton, Paine, Tom, burnt in effigy, 463
Lenton parishioners prepare for invasion of England by Bonaparte, 465—468
Lenton parochial perambulations, 48, 52
Lenton "Patriotic Fund," 471
Lenton, pax found at, 226
———— physical features of, 45
Lenton Police Station, 11
———— Poplars, 8, 9
———— population of, 46
———— Prior and Convent of, passim
Lenton "Priory," 8, 204, 206, 209
Lenton Railway Station, 6
———— rain fall at, 474
———— rateable value of, 48
Lenton, rejoicings on recovery of King George III., 462
Lenton, riots at, 469, 470
———— Robert de, 39

Lenton, Roman antiquities found at, 15

Lenton, Roman Villa discovered at, 14

Lenton, Roger de, 39, 236
—— rural library, 472
—— sale of Shorthorn cattle, 471

Lenton Sands, 7
—— Simon d~, 39
—— Soup Kitchen, 472
—— terrific storm at, 1558, 459

Lenton, Thomas de, 39, 308, 309

Lenton, tiles found at, 226, 229

Lenton Toll Gate erected, 470

Lenton Vicarage, 7, 235—244
—— Volunteers, 466—468
—— White Hart Inn, 468
—— William de, 39

Lenton Priory, 53—234
—— accounts of Robert Bozun, 134

Lenton Priory, agreement between, and the Burgesses of Nottingham, regarding Lenton Fair, 305—307, 311

Lenton Priory, architecture of, 216, 217

Lenton Priory, arms of, 231
—— building in the Saturday Market, Nottingham, given to them by Gilbert de Beeston, 306

Lenton Priory cemetery, 223

Lenton Priory, corrody granted to Robert Penne, 173

Lenton Priory, demolition of, 217

Lenton Priory, descent of site of, 193, 213

Lenton Priory dissolved, 191
—— excavations at, 220, 223

Lenton Priory founded by William Peverel, 61

Lenton Priory gate house, 221, 340

Lenton Priory, lead from, 217

Lenton Priory made denizen, 148

Lenton Priory, possessions, grants of, 213—216

Lenton Priory, pleas regarding the repairing of a pyx belonging to, 148, 149, 150

Lenton, Prior of, summoned to Parliament, 127

Lenton Priory, remains of, 222

Lenton Priory, registers of, 232, 233

Lenton Priory, reports on, by visitors of Clugny Abbey. 126, 129, 130

Lenton Priory, seal of, 231, 232

Lenton Priory, seal of Alan, sub-Prior of, 232

Lenton Priory, *Valor Ecclesiasticus* relating to, 175—178

Leofric, Earl of Mercia, 61

Leominster, 61

Lester, Francis, 279
—— Hannah, 281
—— Thomas, 47, 281, 336

Leversage, Agnes, 170

Lewes Priory, 54, 55, 58, 61

Lewin, Ralph, son of, 99

Lewis, Cornewall, 406

Lexington, Henry de, 72, 179

Lexington, John de, Lord Keeper, 179

Lexington, Robert de, Prior of Lenton, and Justice Itinerant, 179—181

Lichfield, Dean and Chapter of, dispute with Lenton Priory as to the tithes in the Peak of Derbyshire, 68—77, 130

Lichfield, documents at, relating to Lenton Priory, 71—73

Lichelade, Huge de, 114

Linby Church, 62, 79, 80, 215

Linby, Michael de, 240

Lincoln, diocese of, 5
—— Christopher, Bishop of, 253

Lincoln, Henry de Lexington, Bishop of, 179

Lincoln, Hugh, Bishop of, 80, 90

Lincoln, Robert, Bishop of, 63

Lincoln, Henry de Lexington, Dean of. 72

Lincoln, Master of the Schools at, 70

Lindum, a Roman Station, 12

Lisle, Sir Edward Grey, Viscount, 178

Lister, Thomas, 46

Lisures Albreda de, 105

Livesey, John, 356, 357, 358

Loan, Contribution by Prior of Lenton to the, 1522, 175

Local Board, 348

Local Government, 334—354

Locke, Edmund, 28

Lollards, Elmham's antipathy to, 184

London, Corporation of City of, Lenton Manor granted to, 31

London, Gilbert, Bishop of, 106

London, Prior of the Black Preachers, 71

Londonderry, Thomas, Earl of, 397

Longebothem, 39

Long Eaton, alluvial deposits of Trent at, 450

Lord, Robert, 284

Loudham, John de, 390

Louise, H. R. H. The Princess, 382

Lovatt Rebecca 339

Lovelas, William, 275

Lovell, Sir Thomas, 311
—— Sir William, 37

Lovet, Ralph, 260

Lowdham, see Loudham and Ludham

Lowe, Alfred, 11, 199, 338, 470, 471

Lowe, Major A. E. Lawson, on tiles, 227

Lowe, Edward Joseph, 15, 16, 200, 201, 230, 422, 424, 436, 437, 442, 449

Lowe, John, 172
—— Joseph, Alderman, 172, 198, 466

Lowe, Joseph Hurst, 199, 338

Lowe, Lawrence, Recorder of Nottingham, 160, 161, 162

Lowe, Robert, of Newton Hall, 172, 173

Lowe, Robert, of Oxton, 379
—— Robert, jun, 385
—— William, 469, 470
—— William Drury, 280

Lucius III., Pope, 113

Luddite riots, 341

Ludham, Gervase de, 89

Lutterell, Geoffrey de, 110

Luvetot, Sir John de, 388
—— Roger de, 388

Lynham, Susanna, 206
—— William, 206

Lyndeby, Michael de, 240

M.

Malaherbe, Ralph, 63, 85
Malebisse, Matilda, 98
Malefield, John, 41, 42
Malet, Alan, 128
—— Thomas, 128
Malinere, William le, 104
Malmesbury, William of, 55
Malperteshal, Gilbert de, 118
Malquinci, Geoffrey de, 113
Maltby, William, 375
Manchester, John, 158
Mandeville, Geoffrey de, 105
Manistersons, Hugh, 150
Manlove, Alliott and Co., 360
Manners, Francis, 367
—— John, 28
—— Roger, 215
Mantell, Thurstin, 62, 67
Mansfield, Thomas, 395
Manufactures, 355
Maples, John, 285, 289, 290, 338
Mara, James de, 84
Marc, Anne, 122
—— Philip, 109, 119, 122
Marchall, Thomas, Vicar of Beeston, 145
Mareschall, Roger le, 39
Markham, Adam de, 97
—— Margaret, 178
—— Sir Robert, 178
—— Thomas, 366, 374
Markland, Elizabeth, 281
—— Matthew, 281
Marsden, Thomas, 385
Marsh, John, 340
Marshall, Sir George, 316
—— John, 316
—— Marmaduke, 316
—— William, 287, 336, 342, 343, 345
Martell, Alan, 121
—— family, 35, 89
—— Margaret, 37
—— Sir Peter, 37
Martyn, John, 237
Mason, Richard, 145
Matthew, Aloisia, 275
—— Anne, 274
—— Francis, 211, 279
—— Joan, 274
—— priest of Bakewell, 83
Matthew, Prior of Lenton, 181
Matthew, Richard, 237, 241
Maule, Robert, 364
Mauncestre, John de, 236
Mauntell, John, 173
—— Sir William, 173

Mawby, Thomas, 344
Mayburn, Robert, 241
Mayewe, John, 161, 241
Mayson, Thomas, 104
Meadow-place (co. Derby), 62, 69, 82
Meering, 112
—— Gilbert de, 112
Melton, A de, 135
Mellent, Hugh de Bellomont, Earl of, 89
Mellent, Robert, Earl of, 63, 89, 136
Mekesburgh, William de, 40
Meller, Thomas, 283
Mellers, Agnes, 174
—— Richard, bell-founder, 174
Meppershall (Beds.), church of, 117
Merriman, Edward, 326
Merynge, Francis, 191
Meyson, John, 145
Middleton, Thomas, first Lord, 397, 400, 401
Middleton, Francis, third Lord, 322, 326
Middleton, Thomas, fourth Lord, 395
Middleton, Henry, fifth Lord, 331
Middleton, Henry, sixth Lord, 9, 203, 465, 466, 468
Middleton, Digby, seventh Lord, 10, 202, 400
Middleton, Henry, eighth Lord, 202, 203, 209, 348
Middlewich Church, advowson of, 171
Middlewich church, purchased by Robert Lowe, 172
Middlewich Church, trial respecting, 173
Midland Railway line, 6
Mildmay, Thomas, 218, 219
Mill, Blaccliff, 79
—— Ingram's, 9, 123, 157
—— Prior's, 11
Millington, Thomas, 467
Mills, note on, 115
Milnes, Anne, 257
—— Elizabeth, 257
—— John, 241
—— Thomas Brown, 257, 289, 338, 360
Mirrian, or Merrian, Alice, 274
Mirrian, or Merrian, Christopher, 275
Mirrian, or Merrian, Elizabeth, 276, 279
Mirrian, or Merrian, Helen, 275

Mirrian, or Merrian, Isabella, 274
Mirrian, or Merrian, James, 279
Mirrian, or Merrian, Ralph, 275, 276, 279
Mirrian, or Merrian, William, 275
Miscellaneous, 459-475
Mollington (Northants.), 85
Molyneux, Darcy, 165
Monasteries, suppression of, 190-192
Monasteries, Thomas Carlyle on, 192
Monasteries, utility of, 192
Monboucher, Ralph, 40
Monk's Dale (co. Derby), 77
Montfautrel, Adeline de, 85
—— Norman de, 63, 85
Montford, Simon de, 127
Montgomeri, Roger de, 21, 25
Monyash (co. Derby), 62, 68, 77, 82
More, John, 177
—— Peter de la, 93
Moreton, Adam de, 93, 116
—— Eustachius de, 116
—— Robert de, 62, 87, 116
Morley, family of, 227
—— Samuel, 348
Mortaigne, John, Earl of, 26, 68, 69, 75, 83, 116, 179
Mortimer, Roger, 146, 364, 389
Morton, village of, 5, 16, 62
—— Domesday survey of, 35
Morton, Manor of, 35
—— Robert de, 365
Mosley, John, 287, 343
Mosse, Francis, 31
Mottram, William, 146, 375
Mundy, Francis, 277
—— John, 277
—— William, 277
Murdac, Ralph, 112, 114, 116, 387
Musters, Sir John, 376
—— John Chaworth, 376
Myddylburgh, John, Prior of Lenton, 189
Mylle, George, 215
—— John, 215

N.

Naile, Andrew, 277
—— Elizabeth, 277
Nanson, Richard Jeffson, 303

Naylor, Agnes Stella, 258
——— Rev. F. W., 472
——— Stella, 258
——— Thomas, 258, 284
Neat-herdsman, 346
Need, John, 385
Neede, Humphrey, 237
Needham, Caroline, 261
——— Francis, 281
——— George, 34
——— Isabel, 281
——— John, 338
——— Mary, 261
——— Matthew, 198,
  202, 261, 289, 337, 344,
  465, 466, 467, 468, 470
Needham, William, 202
Neep, Anne, 281
——— William, 281
Nether Broughton (Leic.),
  91, 92
Nether Broughton, church
  of, 93
Nether Broughton, John de
  Bradley, rector of, 94
Nevill, Hugh de, 109
——— John Benjamin, 290
——— Ralph de, 109
Neville, Alice, 159
——— George, Bishop of
  Exeter ; Lord Chancellor ;
  Archbishop of York, 228
Neville, Thomas, 159
Newbold (co. Derby), 62, 68
Newcastle, William, Marquis
  of, 373
Newham, Thomas, 287, 336,
  337, 338, 343, 344, 345,
  384
Newmarch, Adam de, 111
Newstead, Prior of, 38, 66,
  86, 365, 366
Newthorpe, 62, 66, 110, 124,
  136, 148, 214
Newthorpe, John de, 97
——— Ralph de, 148
——— Robert de, 97
Newton, Ann, 328
——— John, 328
——— Nathan, 237
——— Richard, 28
——— Thomas, 237
Nicholas IV., Bull of Pope,
  to Prior of Lenton, 131-
  133
Nix family, 123
— Leonard, 210, 211, 212
— Millicent, 212
— Robert, 212
— Sarah, 212
— Tabitha, 212
— William, 211, 212
Noble, Christopher, 279
——— Elizabeth, 279

Nonconforming Congrega-
  tions, 298-302
Norman, Roger, Prior of
  Lenton, 181
Normandy, William, Duke
  of, 19
Normanton, Roger de, Prior
  of Lenton, 94, 181
Normanton-on-Soar, Her-
  bert and family of, 96
Normanville, Thomas de,
  131
Norris, Elizabeth, 254
——— Richard, 47, 254, 342
——— William, 239, 254,
  284, 287, 288, 336, 337,
  343, 345, 346
North Wingfield church,
  chantry founded in, 170
Northampton, St. James's
  Priory, 20, 23, 67, 85
Northampton, Simon, Earl
  of, 63
Northwell, Richard, 310
Norton Abbey, 105
Norwich, George, first Earl
  of, 393, 398
Norwich, Charles, second
  Earl of, 398
Norwich, William, bishop of,
  106
Norwood, Agnes, 274
——— Richard, 274
Nottingham Barracks, 204,
  254
Nottingham Borough Exten-
  sion Act, 1877, 352
Nottingham Borough Gaol,
  204
Nottingham Canal, first boat
  on, 205
Nottingham Carmelite Friary
  79
Nottingham Coppice, Prior
  of Lenton has permission
  to dig for stone at, 125
Nottingham, Corporation of,
  7, 214
Nottingham, dinner given
  annually to the Burgesses
  of, by the Priory of Lenton,
  307
Nottingham exempt from
  jurisdiction of Honour of
  Peverel, 380
Nottingham, fairs at, 304
——— first slates used
  in, 205
Nottingham, fishery of, granted to Lenton Priory, 62
Nottingham Free School
  founded by Dame Agnes
  Mellers, 173, 174
Nottingham, Grey Friars of,
  364

Nottingham, Gubert de, 99
——— Guild of St.
George in St. Peter's
church, 173
Nottingham, Hethbeth
Bridge, chapel of St. Mary
on, 134
Nottingham, Hospital of St.
John the Baptist, 123
Nottingham, King's meadows
flooded, 128
Nottingham, land belonging
to Lenton Priory in Stoney
Street, 157
Nottingham Race Stand, 204
——— Reform Riots,
1831, 469, 470
——— St. James's
Church, 204
Nottingham, St. Leonard's
Hospital, 78
Nottingham, St. Mary's
church, 62, 78, 79, 123,
205, 222
Nottingham, St. Michael's
Chapel, 78
Nottingham, St. Nicholas's
Church, 62, 78, 79, 253
Nottingham, St. Peter's
Church, 62, 78, 79, 173,
205
Nottingham seven arch
bridge, 205
Nottingham Subscription
Library, 204
Nottingham, Thurland Hall,
203, 204
Nottingham, Thomas, Prior
of Lenton, 190
Nottingham, W. de Rother-
ham, Archdeacon of, 120
Nottingham, White Friars
of, 183
Nottingham Castle, 3, 364,
366, 389, 390, 431
Nottingham Castle burnt by
rioters, 342
Nottingham Castle, capture
of Mortimer at, 146
Nottingham Castle, action
against the Prior of Len-
ton for the rent of the tithes
of the Chapel in, 160
Nottingham Castle, Gilbert,
chaplain of, 83, 114
Nottingham Castle, lead from
Lenton Priory deposited
at, 218
Nottingham Castle, Mor-
timer's Hole, 432
Nottingham Castle, tithe of
mills of, 160
Nottingham Park, supposed
*sepulchrum commune* in,
164

Nottingham Park, 276
—————— chapel of St. Mary " le Roche " in, 61, 167, 169
Nottingham Park, Dovecote Close in, 164
Nottingham Park, rock holes in, 3, 4, 162-169, 409, 432
Nuthall, Agatha de, 114
—————— church of, 40, 86, 113
Nuthall, manor of, 40
—————— mill of, 115
Nutt, James, 289, 291, 293, 338, 344
Nutt, Richard, 289, 337
Nuttall, see Nuthall
—————— William, 467

O.

Ode, John, 158
Odo of Clugny, 54
—————— William, 241
Oldcastle, Sir John, 188
Oldfield, Alice, 399
Oldham, Thomas, 46
Oldknow, Sir James, Knt., 359, 360
Oldknow, John, 338, 356,
—————— Thomas, 319
Olive, William de, 98
Ollerenshawe, Frances, 277
—————— Robert, 238, 242, 275, 277
O'Reilly, Ann, 261
—————— Anthony Alexander, 261
Orrell, James, 399
—————— Thomas, 399
Orston, Elizabeth, 281
—————— Helen, 170
—————— Thomas, 170, 281
Osgoteby, A. de, 135
Osmaston, John, 202
—————— Manor, 202
Ossington church, 100, 136
—————— Geoffrey, parson of, 103
Ossington, Hugo de Burun's benefaction to Lenton Priory, 102
Otter, Isabel, 280
—————— Thomas, 280
Otway, Thomas, 376
Ouldfeeld, Mary, 276
Ousley, Richard, 216
Overseers of the Poor, extracts from the accounts of, 339-342
Overseers of the Poor, list of, 335-338
Owthorpe, manor of, 136

Oxcroft (co. Derby), 63, 84
Oxford, Edward, 17th Earl of, 380

P.

Padley, Ann, 328
—————— Rev. C. J. A. N., 328
—————— Robert, 328
Paget, Thomas, 195
—————— William, Lord, 194
—————— William, 202
—————— William Byerley, 202
Paine, Tom, 462, 463
Painel, William, 24
Palmer, Attorney General, 373
Palmer, Sir Edward, 216
—————— John le, 134
—————— Peter, 111
Papist Holes, Nottingham Park, 163
Papplewick, 62, 66, 116
Pares, Thomas, 195
Parish Constables, duties of, 342
Parish Register of Lenton, appointment of, 278
Parish Registers, 272-285
Parker, Dorothy, 243
Parker, Sir Henry, 195
—————— William, 242, 243
Parsons, William, 290
Pascayl, William, 97
Paskayle, Ralph, 97
Passeys, Alice, wife of Robert de, 99
Passeys, John de, 97, 129
—————— Robert de, 99, 216
—————— William de, 99, 100
Pattin, William, 260
Paveley, Robert de, 63, 85
Pavenham Chapel, 118
Pax found at Lenton, 226
Pearce, Michael, 194
Pearson, Francis, 275
—————— John, 275
Peat, Edward, 290
—————— Edward & Son, 361
Peckham, Archbishop, 78
Peek, Thomas del, 308, 309
Peeke, John, 240
Pegg, Thomas, 338
—————— William, 404
Pencriche, Hamlet, monk of Lenton, flight of, 178
Pendrill, John, 461
Penhill, Alexander, 241
Peninton, Thomas, 280
Penne, Robert, 173
Perche, Geoffrey de, 107
Perrin, Annie, 257, 267
—————— Richard, 257, 267

Peter, Prior of Lenton, 103, 109, 114, 119, 179
Peverel, Adelina, wife of Wm. Peverel, of Nottingham, 23, 178
Peverel, arms of, 22
—————— Hammo, 21
—————— Henry, son of William Peverel the younger, 23, 88
Peverel, Court of the Honour of, 81, 203, 221, 386-407
Peverel, Honour of, 80, 86, 386
Peverel, Margaret, 26
—————— of Nottingham, pedigree of, 22
Peverel, Odonna, wife of William, the younger, 88
Peverel of the Peak, 26
Peverel, Payne, 22
Peverel Prison, 8, 46, 401, 402, 404, 463, 468
Peverel, Ranulph, 19, 21, 22
Peverel, records of the Court of the Honour of, 407
Peverel, seals of the Court of the Honour of, 406
Peverel, William, of Dover, 22
Peverel, William, of Essex, 22
Peverel, William, of Nottingham, 3, 18, 19-27, 50, 63, 66, 67, 68, 69, 70, 71, 73, 75, 77, 78, 81, 82, 83, 84, 86, 87, 89, 101, 178, 386
Peverel, William, of Nottingham, Manor of Lenton granted to, 18
Peverel, William, of Nottingham, possessions of, 19
Peverel, William, of Nottingham, foundation charter of Lenton Priory, 63
Peverel, William, of Nottingham, death of, 23
Peverel, William, of Nottingham, anniversary celebrated by monks of Lenton, 178
Peverel, William, of Nottingham, the younger, 79, 88
Philip, Prior of Lenton, 67, 179
Philip, son of Safred, 84
Pickering, William, 244
Pierrepont, Henry, 216
—————— Sir Henry de, 97
Pigot, Gervase, 237
Pike, William, 336, 346
Pilgrimage of Grace, 190
Pilling, Jane, 275
Pinder, 346
Pinfold, 346
Pinkney, Ann, 259

Pinkney, Samuel, 259
Pinnebury, William de, Prior of Lenton, 182
Pipewell, Abbot of, 39
Place, Eliza, 262
—— John, 15
Place de Ambaston, Roger de la, 104
Plantagenet, Thomas, 135
Plumptre, Emma, wife of John de, 154
Plumptre, Henry de, 153
—— Huntingdon, 3, 33, 155
Plumptre Hospital, Nottingham, 153-155
Plumptre, John de, 153, 154, 155, 156
Poictiers, Guillaume de, 20
Poitou, Roger de, 25
Pole, Edmund de la, Earl of Suffolk, 171
Pont Andomar, Roger de Bellomont, lord of, 89
Pontius, Abbot of Clugny, 61
Porter, Henry, 47
—— Ralph, 288, 337, 343, 346
Potter, William, 338
Pottery, discovery of Roman, 17
Poucher, Herbert, 104
Pouger, Henry, 104
—— Herbert, 104
Pouget, Cardinal, 138
Poupet, Guillaume de, 460
Preston, Hellina, 278
—— M. I., 165
Preux, Abbey of, 89
Priories, alien, proceedings respecting, 156
Priors of Lenton, list of, 179-190
Priory, see Lenton Priory,
Pyatt, Richard, 336, 343
Pype, Richard, 215

Q.

Quatford (co. Derby), 62, 68
Quincy, Roger de, Earl of Winchester, 82, 90
Quincy, Saher de, Earl of Winchester, 90

R.

Rahacy, Gervace de, 389
Racket grounds, note on, 469
Radcliffe-on-Soar, church of, 138

Radcliffe-on-Trent, Tom Paine burnt in effigy at, 463
Radclive, Anselinus de, 99
Radford, alluvium of the Leen at, 453
Radford church, 62
—— land leased to Hugh Willoughby, 157
Radford, manor of, 216
—— Marsh, 11
—— Robert de, 240
—— Vicarage, 120
Ragg, Samuel, 293
Rahernt, Hugh de, justice itinerant, 95
Raley, Thomas, 127
Raunds (Northants.), church of, 24
Raynes, Robert, 237
Rawson, Francis George, 10
—— George, 50
—— John, 385
Ray, John, 338
Ray's *Catalogus Plantarum*, 7
Redinges, Hugh de, 110
—— Ralph de, 110
Reginald, of Chilwell, 88
—— Prior of Lenton, 182
Rempstone, church of, 96
—— manor of, 128
—— Robert de, 128
Renals, John, 349, 353
Renshaw, John, 328
Repton Priory (co. Derby), demolition of, 217
Repyngdon, Philip, 158
—— William, monk of Lenton, absconds, 155
Revell, Francis, 46
—— Hugh, 391
—— Randall, 391
—— Thomas, 170, 177
Revill, George, 277
Rhodes, Gerard de, 119
—— John, 211
—— Margaret, 211
—— Sir Ralph de, 119 120
Rhodes, Robert, 211
—— William, 211, 385
Richard I., 68
—— Prior of Lenton, 160
Richardson, John, 370
Richmond, John de Britannia, Earl of, 135
Richmond, Mary, 284
—— Thomas, 284
—— Thomas George, 284
Ridgway, Lady Cassandra, 397
Rivieres, Richard de, 23

Roades, Jeremiah, 263
Roberts, Elias, 288, 337, 344
Roberts, Francis, 287, 336
—— John, 287, 336
—— Joseph, 287, 288, 336, 337, 343, 344
Robinson, Agnes, 274
—— John, 370
Rocester, Abbot of, 70, 71
Rochero, Geoffrey de, Prior of Lenton, 123, 156, 182
Rochero, Geoffrey de, Prior of Thetford, 182
Rode (Northants.), property of Lenton Priory at, 173
Rode, Thomas, son of William de la, 97
Rodyngton, Robert de, 104
Roe, Samuel, 344
—— Thomas, 338, 344
Roger, Prior of Lenton, 98, 121, 124, 127, 130, 181
Roissalt, Richard de, 116
Rolleston, Thomas Neville, of, 159
Roman occupation, traces of, 13
Roman sword, discovery of, 116
Romans, King of the, Henry, son of, 74
Roper, Samuel, 232
Ros, Thomas Manners, Lord, 365
Rosell, Hugh, 101, 114
—— Ralph, 114
—— Robert de, 100
Rossell, George, 375
Rotherham Church, payment to Chantry priest in, 177
Rotour, Matilda, 150
Rotsey, Anthony, 215
Roughton, Gervase, 282, 326, 330
Roughton, John, 326, 338, 467
Roughton, Mary, 282
—— Thomas, 282, 287, 288, 289, 336, 337, 338, 343, 344, 345, 346, 465, 467
Rowland (co. Derby), 63, 86
Rowsley (co. Derby), mill at, 83
Ruddington, 89, 113
—— see Rodyngton and Rutington
Rudsby, Mary, 243
—— William, Vicar of Lenton, 46, 243, 273, 281, 384
Rufford, Abbot of, 366
Rufus, William, 109
Rushden, 62, 82, 215

Rutington, Fulco de, 113
——— Michael de, 113
——— Ralph de, 113
——— Richard de, 113
——— William de, 113
Rutland, Thomas, first Earl of, 28
Rutland, Henry, second Earl of, 218, 220
Rutland, Roger, fifth Earl of 367, 374
Rutland, Francis, sixth Earl of, 374
Rutland, George, seventh Earl of, 165, 368, 374
Ryale, Thomas, 216
Ryley, George, 210

S.

Sabbarton, Joseph, 371
Sacheverell, Millicent, 212
——— Sir Richard, 366
Sackville, Sir Richard, 218, 220
Safred, 62, 83, 87
Safred, Philip, son of, 84
St. Alban's, Abbey of, 85
——— Archdeacon of, 70, 71
St. Albans, Charles, first Duke of, 374, 376, 377, 380
St. Albans, Charles, second Duke of, 377
St. Albans, George, third Duke of, 377
St. Albans, George, fourth Duke of, 378
St. Albans, Aubrey, fifth Duke of, 378
St. Albans, William, tenth Duke of, 49, 50, 378, 380, 381
St. Albans, Diana de Vere, Duchess of, 380
St. Albans, Sybil Mary, Duchess of, 382
St. Andrew, Sir John de, 148
St. Anthony's Hospital, Lenton, 233, 234, 246, 248
St. Ebrulf, monks of, 91
St. John of Jerusalem, Hospitallers of, 102, 103
St. Patric, Sir Geoffrey de, 86, 112
St. Patric, Norman de, 63, 86, 112
St. Patric, William de, 112
St. Susanna, Cardinal of, 138
Salisbury, Richard, Bishop of, 121

Samon, Richard, 148
Sand Hill, 6
Sandiacre, Peter de, 99
Sands, John, 401
Saucei, or Salceto, Sir Robert de, 85
Savage, Arnold, 170
——— Edmond, 170
——— James, 365
——— Sir John, 170
——— John, of Berkshire, 371
Savage, John, of Hucknall, 170
Savage, Ralph, 169, 170
——— Richard, 348
Sewell, Robert, 28
Say, Sir John, 167, 169
——— Leonard, 167, 168, 169
Scales, Emma, 261
——— Lucy Abigail Rich, 261
Scales, William, 261
Scattergood, John, 342
——— Mary, 243
School Board, 349
Schools, 7, 295—297
Seagrave, Gilbert de, 119
——— Stephen de, 109
Searle, Henry, 145
Selby, Robert, 158
——— William, 49, 51, 335
Selone, miller of Rowsley, 83
Selston, William de, 236
Serlo, Robert, son of, 100
Sewell, John, 215
Sewerage, 350
Seyrig, John Gotlob, 360
Seywell, John, 211
——— Margaret, 211
Shalcross (co. Derby), 62, 68, 77
Shaldeford, William de, 136
Shaw, Adjutant, 284
——— John, 49, 50, 51, 265, 271, 288, 289, 337, 340, 344, 348, 465, 467, 472
Shaw, Margaret, 271, 284
——— Richard, 370
——— William, 288, 336, 337, 343
Sheffield, and Peverel Court, 404
Shelford Priory, 28
——— Remigius, Prior of, 89
Shelford, see Shaldeford
Shelton, Richard, 336
Shepherd, Thomas, 338, 344
Shepperson, Thomas, 351
Sherbrooke, W., 385
Sherwin, Joan, 278
——— John, 34, 326, 331
——— John Sherwin, 34

Sherwood Forest, 3, 5
Shipman, Alice, 279
——— James, 408
——— William, 287, 336
Shirebrook (co. Derby), 62, 68
Siddal, Richard, 213
Silan, Roger de, 116
Simkins, Daniel, 385
Simpson, Francis, 341
——— Henry, 201
——— Rev. Robert, 293
——— William, 287
Singlehurst, Francis, 279
——— John, 291
——— Sarah, 279
Sion Hill, 4, 6, 11, 410
Sissons, Henry, 344
Siviriaco, or Siriniaco, Peter de, Prior of Lenton, 131, 181
Sligo, first Marquess of, 244
Small, Francis, 210, 211
Smallet, Walter, 102
Smart, William, 282
Smedley, Thomas, 276
Smith, Edward, 278
——— Sir George, Bart., 326
Smith, George, 281
——— Henry, 348
——— Henry Abel, 43
——— James, 331, 338
——— John, 279, 326
——— Joseph, 338
——— Mary, 279, 281, 326
——— Rev. Percy E., 474
——— Sarah, 281
——— Thomas, 281
——— Thomasine, 278
——— William, 131
Smyth, R., 370
——— Thomas, 145, 237
Sneinton, St. Stephen's Church, 122
Somerset, Arthur, Lord, 399
——— Henry, 182
——— John, 183
Somerville Gervase de, 110, 233, 234
Somerville, Hugh de, 110
——— Richard de, 110
Southwell, Diocese of, 5
South Wingfield (co. Derby), 84, 86, 112
Southworth, Ann, 277
——— Edward, 215, 277
Southworth, Winifred, 277
Spaynynge, Ralph de, 140
Spelman, Clement, 237
——— P., 278
Spencer, Sir Richard, 373
——— William, 287, 343

Spring Close, 4, 11, 409, 426, 427, 447
Spybey, F. G., 230
Stacey, Thomas, 104
Staden (co. Derby), 62, 68
Stafford, Archdeacon of, 75
———— Richard, Prior of Lenton, 182
Stanhope, Edward, 28
———— Sir Michael, 28, 193
Stanlaw Abbey founded, 106
Stanley, Henry, 28
Stanton, George, 271, 338
———— Hannah, 271
Stapleford, 63, 86
———— Sir Brian, 366
———————— Sir Geoffrey de, 97
Stapleford, Hugh de, 129, 134, 389
Stapleford, Robert de, 134
Statham, Henry, 178
Stathum, John, 227
Staunton, Clemencia, 81
———— Hugh de, 81
———— Thomas, 81
———— William de, 81
Staynton, Agnes de, 81
Stephen, King, Charter of, to Lenton Priory, 88, 101
Stephen, Prior of Lenton, 182
Stephenson, William, 210
Sterndale (co. Derby), 62, 68
Stevens, Richard, 281
———— Sarah, 281
Stevenson, John, 283
———————— Thomas, 288, 289, 337, 344
Stockport, Margery, daughter of Robert de, 83
Stocks, Parish, 340
Stoke Field, battle of, 459
Stone, John, 319
Stone axe found in Wollaton Park, 11-12
Storer, Dr. John, 204
Stout, Francis, 338
Stoyle, Geoffrey, 110
Strelley, Sir Anthony, 30
———— Frideswide, 215
———— John de, 150
———— Richard, 364
———— Sir Robert de, 129
———— Robert, 215, 280
———— Roger de, 309, 310
———— Sampson de, 96, 105, 116
Stretton, Ann, 259, 283
———— arms of, 209
———— Elizabeth, 204, 254, 259, 283, 284
Stretton family, 204—209
———— George, 254, 259

Stretton, George Burbage, 254, 259
Stretton manuscripts, 205
———— Mary, 259, 283
———— Samuel, 204, 259, 283, 284
Stretton, Samuel Bilby, 259
———— Sarah, 283
———— Lieut.-Col. Sempronius, 206-208, 226, 258
Stretton, Severus, 258
———— Lieut.-Col. Severus William Lynham, 208-209
Stretton, Stella, 284
———— Susanna, 206, 257
———— William, 198, 204-206, 222, 225, 248, 250, 251, 256, 257, 269, 283, 284, 289, 338, 344, 406
Stretton, William, architectural works of, 204, 205
Stretton, William, museum of, 205
Stretton, William, obituary notice, 206
Strey, Michael, 326
———— Nicholas, 237
Stuart, James, Duke of Lennox and Richmond, 32
Stubbins, Joseph, 326
———— Nathaniel, 331
Sturtivant, John, 375
———— Jonathan, 375
Stuteville, Robert de, 107
Subterranean passage near Lenton, 17
Sulley, Sarah, 281
Sulney, Sir Alvery, 189
Surplice, William, 8, 9, 289, 338, 344
Sutborrow, Hannah, 280
———— Hannah Mariah, 280
Sutborrow, Rowland, 280
Sutton, Helric de, 99
———— Hugh de, 99
———— John de, rector of Lexington, 86
Sutton, Richard de, Canon of Southwell, 86
Sutton Passeys, 129
———————— disappearance of village, 99
Sutton Passeys, Robert, son of Ralph of, 99
Swaile, Cleasby, 243
———— John, 243
———— Mary, 243
Swain, John, 338
Swann, Kirke, 222, 224, 251
Swann, Rev. Kirke, 222
Swinburne family, 76
Swinecliff, 100
Swinscow, George, 336

Swinscow, John, 287, 342, 343, 345
Sylvester, John, 338
Syson, Henry, 344


T.

Tabley, Lord de, 353
Talbot, Robert, 12
Tannesley, Alice, 157
———— John, 157
Taylboys, John, 41
———— Margaret, 41
Taylor, Katherine, 274
———— Robert, 274
———— William, 145
Terwet, George, 278
———— Robert, 278
Teulon, Samuel Saunders, 294, 379, 380, 381
Thaine, or Thane, Christian, 282, 283
Thaine, or Thane, David, 282
Thaine, or Thane, Elizabeth, 282
Thaine, or Thane, Isabel, 282
Thaine, or Thane, James, 263, 282, 283, 284, 323, 326, 336, 379
Thaine, or Thane, Margaret, 283
Thaine, or Thane, Thomas, 282
Thaine, or Thane, William, 282
Thetford Priory, 54, 61
Thimelby, John, 145
Thomas, Prior of Lenton, 168, 169, 171
Thompson, Benjamin, 385
———— Joseph, 336, 342, 348
Thornes, William, 42
Thornton, Robert de, 240, 241
Thoroton, Thomas, 326
Thorp, William de, 151
Thorpe, William, 400
Thorpe-in-the-Glebe, 63, 85, 125
Throgmorton, Richard, 82
Thurgarton Priory, 80
Thurland, Alice, 159
———— Thomas, 159, 160
Tibshelf (co. Derby), 84, 86
Tibtot, Henry de, 129
———— Margaret, wife of Robert, 80
Tibtot, Pagan, 80
Tickhill Castle, chapel of, 167, 168, 169

Tickhill Castle, siege of, 137
Tideswell (co. Derby), 62, 68, 70, 72, 75, 77
Tideswell (co. Derby), seizure of wool and lambs by monks of Lenton, 69, 72
Tiles, manufactory of, at Nottingham, 229
Time, Joan, 277
Tirel, Gautier de, seigneur de Poix, 110
Tole, Richard, 375
Tollerton, 126
—— church, 98
—— see Torlavistune
Tompson, John, 46
Toone, Richard, 276
Torkard, Geoffrey, 114
—— Henry, 114
—— Maud, 114, 131
—— William, 129
Torlavistune, Adelina de, 98
—— Serlo de, 98
Toton, 63, 87
Tottle brook, a boundary of Lenton Parish, 10, 410
Toueton, Ralph de, 116
—— William de, 116
Towle, Catherine, 274, 276
—— Christiana, 277
—— Peter, 274, 276, 287
Towne, Anne, 282
—— Rev. John, 282
Townley, Sir Charles, 283
—— John, 283
—— Mary, 283
—— Sarah, 283
Townsend, Elizabeth, 283
—— George, 285
—— John, 461,
—— Jonathan, 239, 283
Townsend, Mary, 281, 282, 283, 461
Townsend, Rosomond, 279
—— Thomas, 239, 326
Townsend, Vicesimus, 279, 281, 282, 283, 284
Townshend, see Townsend
Trent, river, a boundary of Lenton parish, 1
Tresham, William, 36
Trestles, action to recover value of pair of, 158
Trollop, James, 399
Tucker, Richard Grant, 338, 344
Tumby, John de, 150
Tunstead (co. Derby), 69
Turner, Rev. Henry, 261, 262
Twistfeld, Christopher, 146
Twyford Arnald of, 119
—— Katherine, 119

Tyrell family, 76
Tytheby, William de, 389

V.

Vache, Richard de la, 365
Vale Royal, Abbot of, 140
Valor Ecclesiasticus, income of Priory as stated in, 175-178
Vavasour, Sir Robert le, 124, 388
Velley, Richard, 314
Vere, Roger de, 114
Vernon, Avicia, wife of Richard de, 83
Vernon, Dorothy, 28
—— Sir Henry, 76
—— Margery, wife of William de, 83
Vernon, Richard de, 83
—— William de, 83
Vicarage, 7, 235-244
Vicars of Lenton, see—
Anger, Robert; Askewe, Thomas; Berde, John de; Burton, Robert; Blakeman, John; Broksop, Henry; Browne, George; Clyfton, William; Creswell, Edward; Graneby, Adam de; Fisher, John; Fyndern, William; Lyndeby, Michael de; Mathew, Richard; Mayburn, Robert; Mayewe, John; Milnes, John; Odo, William; Ollerenshawe, Robert; Parker, William; Peeke, John; Penhill, Alexander; Pickering, William; Radeford, Robert de; Rudsby, William; Swaile, John; Thornton, Robert de; Wayte, George; Webster, John, West, Thomas; Wood, John.
Vilers, Sir John de, 126
Villiers, Barbara, Duchess of Cleveland, 380
Vinson, William, 461
Vycare, John, 104
Vyllers, Sir John, 366

W.

Wade, Thomas, 341
Walden Abbey, 105

Wales, Cadwallader, king of, 108
Walker, Avery, 247, 286
—— Benjamin, 10, 348
—— Elizabeth, 282
—— John Benjamin, 349, 353
Walker, Robert, 275
—— William, 282, 331
—— William Heape, 203
Walter, Sir William, 373
Walton (co. Derby), 63
Ward, Anna, 276
—— Isabella, 274
—— Robert, 274
—— Simon, 36
—— William, 248, 276
Warde, Anne, 274
—— Barbara, 277
—— Jo, 287
—— William, 274, 275, 277
Warde, William de, 236
Warner, named in Domesday Survey, 87
Warren, Charles, 375
Wartnaby, Barnaby, 280
—— Ellen, 280
—— Isabel, 280
Warton, Joan, 274
—— John, 274
Watch-house, 341
Watenhow, Henry de, 129
—— Robert de, 97, 110
Watenhow, Roger de, 110
Watson, Elizabeth, 256
—— Henry, 256
—— James, 257
—— Mary, 256
—— Thomas Wright, 198, 203, 256
—— see Watenhow
Wayte, George, 238, 239, 243, 244, 291, 326, 327
Weatherall, William, 271
Webb, John, 323, 326
—— Mrs., of Newstead, 382
Webber, Thomas, 314
Webster, Andrew, 287
—— Elizabeth, 279
—— John, 242
Welbeck, Abbey of, 111, 366
Welby (Leic.), 119
Welch, Matthew, 288, 337, 343, 344, 346
Welles, Hugh de, Bishop of Lincoln, 94
Wells, Simon, Archdeacon of, 117
Wenlock Abbey, 54, 61
Wentworth family, 76

West, Gilbert, 279
—— John, 279
—— Robert, 241, 279
—— Thomas, 241, 279
—— William, 279, 367
———————— monk of Lenton, appointed Prior of Blyth, 159
Western, John, 287, 342, 345, 345
———— Stephen, 336 343, 345
Westminster Abbey, 169
Weston, Anthony, 247
—— James, 467
—— Roger de, 105
—— William, 289, 338
Whalley Abbey, 106
———— Major Gen. Edward, 397
Whalley, Richard, 397
Whatton, Adelina de, 111
———— Beatrice de, 110, 111
Whatton, church of, 111
———— manor of, 111
———— Richard de, 111
———— Robert de, 110, 111
———— Walter de, 110, 111
———— William de, 110
Wheatley, Thomas, 287, 343
Wheeler, Anne, 282
———— Rev. William, 282
White, Agnes, 215
—— Joseph, 404
—— Thomas, 215
White Hart Inn, 8, 341, 403, 405, 468
Whitmore, William, 211
Whitwell (co. Derby), 214
Widmerpool, 111, 112
Wigley, William, 289, 337, 344, 467
Wigston (Leic.), church of, 89, 90, 91, 136
Wild, John, 301
—— Mary, 301
Wildbore, William, 171
Wilde, Sarah, 283
———— William, 283
Wilding, Roger, 308
Wilford church, 3, 460
———— Gervase de, 129
———— Richard, 156
Wilkins, Rev. George, 251
Wilkinson, George, 340
———— John, 289, 338, 344, 375, 471
Wilkinson, Samuel, 375
———— Thomas, 375
Wilkinson, William, 337, 338, 344
Willesthorpe, William de, 145
William, benefactor to Lenton Priory, 84

William, Prior of Lenton, 133, 181
Williams, William Gregory, 331
Willoughby, Alice, 158
———— Dame Anne, 178
Willoughby, Baldwin, 213, 279
Willoughby, Dame Bridget, 392
Willoughby, Bridgett, 276
———— Dame Cassandra, 397
Willoughby D'Eresby, house of, 392
Willoughby, Edward, 326, 327
Willoughby, Elizabeth, 276, 279
Willoughby, family of, 41, 43, 87, 279, 400
Willoughby, Sir Francis, 233, 391, 392, 397, 398
Willoughby, Francis, philosopher, 397
Willoughby, Gilbert, 43
———— Sir Henry, 171, 172, 178
Willoughby, Henry, 391
———— Sir Hugh, 158, 279
Willoughby, Hugh, 123, 157
———— Sir John, 178, 189
Willoughby, Dame Margaret, 178
Willoughby, Nicholas, 157
———— of Parham, William, Lord, 374
Willoughby, Sir Percival, 392, 397
Willoughby, Philip de, 364
Willoughby, Sir Richard de, 128
Willoughby, Richard, 41, 157, 159, 160, 210, 275, 276, 279, 311
Willoughby, Robert, 279
———— Sir Thomas, Bart, 397, 400
Willoughby, Alderman Thomas, 43
Willoughby, Thomas, 157, 391
Willoughby, William, 43, 367, 368, 369, 371, 372, 373
Willoughby Wood, 118
Willoughby-on-the-Wolds, 128
Wilmot, Edward, 195, 400
———— Elizabeth, 195
———— John, 338
———— Sir Thomas, 195

Wilson, E., 425, 443,
———— Edward, 338
———— Roger, 177
———— William, 301
Wiltshire, Earl of, 218, 220
Winchester, Roger de Quincy, Earl of, 82, 90
Winchester, Saher de Quincy, Earl of, 90
Windham, Sir John, attainder of, 170, 171
Windham, Sir Thomas, 171
Winford, Dame Beata, 195
———— Dame Elizabeth, 195
Winford, Henry, 195
———— Sir John, 195
———— Mercie, 195
———— Robert, 194
———— Sarah, 194
———— Sir Thomas, 194, 195
Winford, Sir Thomas Cookes, 195
Winford, William, 194
Winthorpe, William de, 39
Wissendon, mill at, 84
Wiverton, 95
———— Gervase de, 96
Wodishawe, Nicholas, 104
Wolf, Sir Adam, 127
———— Tortus, 127
Wolffe, James, 210
Wollaston, Sir John, 370
Wollaton, 87
———— Church, 311
———— Hall, 5, 391, 410, 429, 445
Wollaton, Henry de, 39
———— Hugh de, 39
———— John de, 40
———— Park, 9, 11, 44, 45, 48
Wollaton, Ralph de, 40
———— Skeletons found at, 341
Wollore, Thomas, Prior of Lenton, 189
Wolsey, Cardinal, 226, 390
Wombawl, William, 287
Wombwell, Elizabeth, 204, 284
Wombwell, George, 239, 344, 465
Wombwell, Mary, 281
Wood, Brigetta, 277
———— Cassandra, 274
———— Dorothy, 277, 279
———— Elizabeth, 276, 277, 279
Wood, Frances, 276
———— John, 213, 242, 271, 275, 276, 277, 279, 287, 290, 336, 338, 342, 343, 345, 346

Wood, Joseph, 375
Wood, Meriella, 275
—— Thomas, 276, 277
Woodhead, Caroline, 472
Worcester, Henry, third
  marquess of, 399
Wormhill (co. Derby), 62,
  68, 69
Worthington, William de,
  236
Wragg, Joseph, 356
Wrest, Christopher, 287
Wright, Alice, 279
—— Alice Josephine
  Smith, 271
Wright, Anna, 277
—— Caroline Henrietta
  Smith, 271
Wright, Elizabeth, 257, 266,
  284
Wright, Frances, 257

Wright, Francis, 202, 239,
  251, 252, 264, 265, 270,
  290, 295, 348
Wright, Frederick, 202, 290,
  474
Wright, Henry Smith, 202,
  290, 349
Wright, Ichabod, 201
—— John, 198, 201, 202,
  204, 213, 257, 266, 267,
  289, 338, 466, 467, 470
Wright, the Misses, 7, 295
—— pedigree of, 202
—— Rebecca, 284
—— Richard, 151
—— Thomas, 284
—— William, 277, 279
Wyld, William, 326, 373
Wylde, John, 28
—— Richard, 28
Wynkeburn, Henry de, 236

Wysow, John, parson of
  Hickling, 157

Y.

Yeomans, William, 289
York, diocese of, 5
—— Edmund, 278
—— Gerard, Archbishop
  of, 63
York, John Thoresby, Arch-
  bishop of, 150
York, Richard, Archbishop
  of, 154
York, Roger, Archbishop of,
  103, 106, 113
York, Walter Grey, Arch-
  bishop of, 120, 123, 124

# ADDITIONS AND CORRECTIONS.

Page 5, line 12, *for* Belviet *read* Belvoir.

P. 7, line 11, and p. 354, line 12. The Lenton Boulevard was opened for public use, September 18th, 1884.

P. 8, note 2, the initials upon the Barn-houses, now visible, are T. W.

P. 39, line 2 from bottom, *dele* [Chillewelle?]. In 1302, the Friars Minor of Nottingham had license given them to lead the watercourse of the spring in *Athilwelle* from thence to their house by a subterranean conduit.—*Records of the Borough of Nottingham*, i., 428.

P. 46, note 5, *add*—Some idea of the relative value of the parish of Lenton in those days may be formed from the sums then paid by other neighbouring parishes. Beeston paid £6 12s. od. ; Radford, £5 7s. od. ; yᵉ Brewhouses, 16s. ; Wollaton, £7 17s. od. ; Basford, £9 13s. od. ; Bilborough and Broxtow, £3 9s. od. ; Strelley, £5 16s. od. ; Trowell, £12 14s. od. ; Nuthall and Awsworth, £13 19s. od. ; Bramcote, £2 7s. od. ; Chilwell, £5 19s. od. ; and Toton and Attenborough, £4 15s. od.

P. 63, line 3, *for* Geoffrey *read* Godfrey. This error occurs in *Mon. Ang.* v. 108.

P. 85, line 2, *for* Geoffrey *read* Godfrey.

P. 99, last line of note 5, *for* this time *read* his time (*i.e.*, Thoroton's).

P. 114, note 6, line 3, *for* baronical *read* baronial.

P. 148, line 4—The statement, derived from Bailey's *Annals of Nottinghamshire*, i. 38, that Lenton Priory was "the only Monastery in the county of Nottingham subject to foreign jurisdiction" is incorrect. The Priory of Blyth, also in the county of Nottingham, was subject to the Abbey of St. Trinité, Rouen.

P. 161, note 1, line 3, *for* sergeant-at-law *read* serjeant-at-law.

P. 172, line 5 from bottom, *for* which is now vested *read* and these are now vested.

P. 173, line 7 from bottom. Fitzherbert, *Natura Brevium* (1581), fol. 231 h., prints an ancient roll in the Exchequer giving a list of the Abbeys and Priories in which the King had corrodies or pensions. This list was taken from the Red Book of the Exchequer : 'In prioratu de Lenton' i. pensio' occurs *fo.* 232 *dorso.*

P. 194, end of line 8, *dele* the comma.

P. 194, line 2 of note, *for* his father and grandfather *read* his father and son.

P. 195, line 12 from bottom, *for* Mary-le-bone *read* St. Mary-le-bone.

P. 206, line 11. Mr. William Lynam, of Eakring, who died August 16th, 1785, aged 67 years, married Ann, daughter of William and Anne Bielby, of Eakring, who died June 16th, 1790, aged 75 years. *Stretton MS. No.* 31, f. 19.

33

P. 208, line 15, *for* Viscount Castlemaine *read* Lord Castlemaine.

P. 209, line 4 from bottom, *for* Thomas Green, Esq., *read* James Green, Esq.

P. 216, line 3, *for* Courtenhall *read* Courteenhall.

P. 228, line 11, *for* seme *read* semée.

P. 232, line 10 from bottom, *for* 'SALANI SVB PRIOR' [DE LEN]TO' *read* S' : ALANI : SVBPRIOR' [DE LEN]TO'.

P. 234, lines 11 to 16, and p. 248, lines 2 to 7. The statements here made that the old parish-church was rebuilt of worked masonry from the Priory after the dissolution of the monastery requires modification, as several interesting discoveries have been made in restoring the chancel since these lines were written, proving that, at all events, that portion of the fabric dates from the pre-Reformation period. On removing the plastering from the wall below the three-light window on the south side, a piscina, with a quatrefoil basin (the projecting portion of which was broken off) and drain was discovered about a foot above the level of the floor. This piscina has been restored and built into the south wall, nearer the east end than where it was originally placed, at a height of 2 feet 8 inches above the new altar steps. The three-light Tudor window at the east end, as well as the large one on the south side (above mentioned), both of which have been recently removed, were found to be inserted in the place of older windows which were originally much larger and nearer the floor, the ancient openings having been partially filled up with masonry at the time when the more modern Tudor windows were inserted. On the north side a small priests' doorway, blocked with masonry, was disclosed. This doorway, which is 2 feet 9 inches wide, and 5 feet 2 inches from the level of the floor to the crown of the depressed arch, which forms the head, is just below the marble slab to the memory of Mr. George Stretton, and 2 feet 6 inches westward of the present vestry door. This latter doorway appears to have been partly formed out of an ancient window, 3 feet 4 inches wide and 6 feet high, the distance from the sill to the floor level being 2 feet 6 inches. Between this ancient window and the east wall, and above the aumbrey recently inserted (which does not, however, replace an older one), traces of black letter inscriptions and various ornamentations were found on removing the plaster. The prevailing colour in this ancient fresco work was a deep chocolate red. The floor level hitherto referred to was the level of the chancel floor previous to the recent restoration, when the pavement was raised 13 inches. But during this restoration the *ancient* floor was discovered at a depth of four feet below the recent, or 5 feet 1 inch below the present, floor level of the chancel. This remarkable difference in the floor levels will account for the position of the piscina in the south wall, and of the window on the opposite side of the chancel. On the ancient floor a Purbeck marble coffin lid, bearing a slightly raised cross of thirteenth century work, was found. The lid is 6 feet 3 inches long, 22 inches wide at the top, and 14 inches wide at the bottom. The two blocks of stone which form part of the new altar step were found at the same time. These stones appear to have originally formed one slab, 9 feet 6 inches long, and 6 inches thick, the original use of which is doubtful. The two blocks have now been fixed, so that the curious carving on the edge may be readily inspected. These features, as well as the important discovery of the foundations of walls about three feet within the north and south walls of the present nave, clearly indicate that some ancient chapel, within the precincts of the monastery, was enlarged, and adapted for the purposes of a parish church, by having the nave widened, and the walls partly rebuilt of old masonry from the Priory shortly after the dissolution of the monastery. The chancel seems, however, to have been preserved intact. We have already referred to the local tradition that the chapel of the Hospital of St. Anthony was converted into the parish church, and the facts brought to light during the recent restoration of the old church tend very strongly to confirm the popular belief.

P. 244, line 11. The Rev. Edward Creswell, who was at one time curate of Clarborough, near Retford, was the master of Wilford School previous to his institution to the vicarages of Lenton and Radford.—*Stretton MS. No.* 33.

P. 247, line 5, *for* Robert Gaybone *read* Robert ———, the name being difficult to decipher.

P. 300, line 1, *for* 1882 *read* 1832.

P. 307, line 4 from bottom. In addition to the four documents given, the *Records of the Borough of Nottingham* contain another document (vol. i. p. 75) relating to Lenton fair, which has been accidentally omitted from the foregoing pages. On March 23rd, 1312-3, Roger de Ancaster complained that John Bully had on a Sunday previously, at Lenton fair, brought a false suit against him for 40s., by which suit his goods and chattels, valued at ten pounds, were seized by the bailiff of the fair, and detained from Sunday until the following Tuesday, when "the said Roger came and waged his law against the said John." The latter thereupon "maliciously withdrew himself from the Court, and would not prosecute his suit," through which false suit "the said Roger lost his profits of the fair, to the value of 60s., to the damage of the said Roger of 40s., and of this he enters suit." The entry in the roll is damaged by damp, and incomplete.

P. 389, line 3, *dele* the comma after the word *found*.

P. 465, line 9 from bottom. The Rev. William Gill, curate of Lenton, at one time was master of Wilford School (*Stretton MS. No.* 33), and in 1808 was the chaplain of Nottingham Gaol.

BEMROSE & SONS, PRINTERS, DERBY; AND 23, OLD BAILEY, LONDON.

Lightning Source UK Ltd.
Milton Keynes UK
UKHW020800200223
417314UK00006B/364